# Europe
# Europa

| | Country | Code | Currency | SOS ☎ | 🛣 (motorway) | 🚗 (dual) | road | 🏘 (town) | MAUT/TOLL | ‰ |
|---|---|---|---|---|---|---|---|---|---|---|
| | Österreich / Austria | A | 1 Euro (EUR) = 100 Cent | 133 / 144 | 130 | 100 | 100 | 50 | 🛣 🚗 | 0,5 ‰ |
| | Shqipëria / Albania | AL | 1 Lek (ALL) = 100 Quindarka | 129 /126 | 120 | 100 | 80 | 40 | | 0,0 ‰ |
| | België/Belgique / Belgium | B | 1 Euro (EUR) = 100 Cent | 101 / 100 | 120 | 120 | 90 | 50 | | 0,5 ‰ |
| | Bŭlgarija / Bulgaria | BG | 1 Lew (BGN) = 100 Stótinki | 166 / 150 | 130 | 90 | 90 | 50 | 🛣 🚗 | 0,5 ‰ |
| | Bosna i Hercegovina / Bosnia and Herzegovina | BIH | Konvert. Marka (BAM) = 100 Fening | 92 / 94 | 120 | 100 | 80 | 60 | | 0,3 ‰ |
| | Schweiz/Suisse/Svizzera / Switzerland | CH | 1 Franken (CHF) = 100 Rappen | 117 / 144 | 120 | 100 | 80 | 50 | 🛣 | 0,5 ‰ |
| | Kypros/Kibris / Cyprus | CY | 1 Euro (EUR) = 100 Cent | 199 | 100 | 80 | 80 | 50 | | 0,5 ‰ |
| | Česká republika / Czech Republic | CZ | 1 Koruna (CZK) = 100 Haliru | 112 / 155 | 130 | 130 | 90 | 50 | 🛣 🚗 | 0,0 ‰ |
| | Deutschland / Germany | D | 1 Euro (EUR) = 100 Cent | 110 / 112 | ⊘ | ⊘ | 100 | 50 | | 0,5 ‰ |
| | Danmark / Denmark | DK | 1 Krone (DKK) = 100 Øre | 112 | 130 | 80 | 80 | 50 | | 0,5 ‰ |
| | España / Spain | E | 1 Euro (EUR) = 100 Cent | 112 | 110 | 100 | 90 | 50 | 🛣 | 0,5 ‰ |
| | Eesti / Estonia | EST | 1 Euro (EUR) = 100 Cent | 110 / 112 | 110 | 110 | 90 | 50 | | 0,0 ‰ |
| | France / France | F | 1 Euro (EUR) = 100 Cent | 112 | 130 | 110 | 90 | 50 | 🛣 | 0,5 ‰ |
| | Suomi/Finland / Finland | FIN | 1 Euro (EUR) = 100 Cent | 112 | 120 | 100 | 100 | 50 | | 0,5 ‰ |
| | United Kingdom / United Kingdom | GB | 1 Pound Sterling (GBP) = 100 Pence | 999 / 112 | 70 mph (112) | 70 mph (112) | 60 mph (96) | 30 mph (48) | | 0,8 ‰ |
| | Ellás (Hellás) / Greece | GR | 1 Euro (EUR) = 100 Cent | 100 / 166 | 120 | 110 | 90 | 50 | 🛣 🚗 | 0,5 ‰ |
| | Magyarország / Hungary | H | 1 Forint (HUF) = 100 Filler | 112 | 130 | 110 | 90 | 50 | 🛣 | 0,0 ‰ |
| | Hrvatska / Croatia | HR | 1 Kuna (HRK) = 100 Lipa | 112 / 94 | 130 | 110 | 90 | 50 | 🛣 | 0,5 ‰ |
| | Italia / Italy | I | 1 Euro (EUR) = 100 Cent | 112 / 118 | 130 | 110 | 90 | 50 | 🛣 | 0,5 ‰ |
| | Éire/Ireland / Ireland | IRL | 1 Euro (EUR) = 100 Cent | 999 / 112 | 120 | 100 | 60 / 100 | 50 | | 0,5 ‰ |
| | Ísland / Iceland | IS | 1 Krona (ISK) = 100 Aurar | 112 | | | 80 / 90 | 50 | | 0,0 ‰ |
| | Kosovo / Kosovo | RKS | 1 Euro (EUR) = 100 Cent | 112 / 92 | 130 | 110 | 80 | 50 | | 0,5 ‰ |
| | Luxembourg / Luxembourg | L | 1 Euro (EUR) = 100 Cent | 113 / 112 | 130 | 90 | 90 | 50 | | 0,5 ‰ |
| | Lietuva / Lithuania | LT | 1 Euro (EUR) = 100 Cent | 02 / 03 / 112 | 110 | 90 | 90 | 50 | | 0,4 ‰ |
| | Latvija / Latvia | LV | 1 Euro (EUR) = 100 Cent | 02 / 03 / 112 | 110 | 90 | 90 | 50 | | 0,5 ‰ |
| | Makedonija / Macedonia | MK | 1 Denar (MKD) = 100 Deni | 192 / 194 | 120 | 100 | 80 | 40 / 60 | 🛣 🚗 | 0,5 ‰ |
| | Norge / Norway | N | 1 Krone (NOK) = 100 Øre | 112 / 113 | 90 | 90 | 80 | 50 | 🛣 🚗 🏘 | 0,1 ‰ |
| | Nederland / Netherlands | NL | 1 Euro (EUR) = 100 Cent | 112 | 120 | 100 | 80 | 50 | | 0,5 ‰ |
| | Portugal / Portugal | P | 1 Euro (EUR) = 100 Cent | 112 | 120 | 100 | 90 | 50 | 🛣 | 0,5 ‰ |
| | Polska / Poland | PL | 1 Zloty (PLN) = 100 Groszy | 112 / 999 | 130 / 140 | 100 / 120 | 90 / 100 | 50 | 🛣 | 0,2 ‰ |
| | România / Romania | RO | 1 Leu (RON) = 100 Bani | 112 | 130 | 100 | 90 | 50 | 🛣 🚗 🏘 | 0,0 ‰ |
| | Rossija / Russia | RUS | 1 Rubel (RUB) = 100 Kopeek | 02 / 03 | 110 | 90 | 90 | 60 | | 0,0 ‰ |
| | Sverige / Sweden | S | 1 Krona (SEK) = 100 Öre | 112 | 110 | 110/90 | 70 / 90 | 50 | | 0,2 ‰ |
| | Srbija / Crna Gora / Serbia / Montenegro | SRB  MNE | 1 Dinar (CSM) = 100 Para ; Euro | 92 / 94 | 120 | 100 | 80 | 60 | 🛣 🚗 | 0,3 ‰ |
| | Slovenská republika / Slovakia | SK | 1 Euro (EUR) = 100 Cent | 112 / 155 | 130 | 90 | 90 | 60 | 🛣 🚗 | 0,0 ‰ |
| | Slovenija / Slovenia | SLO | 1 Euro (EUR) = 100 Cent | 113 / 112 | 130 | 100 | 90 | 50 | 🛣 | 0,5 ‰ |
| | Türkiye / Turkey | TR | 1 Lira (TRY) = 100 Kurus | 155 / 112 | 120 | 90 | 90 | 50 | 🛣 | 0,5 ‰ |
| | Ukrajina / Ukraine | UA | 1 Griwna (UAH) = 100 Kopijken | 02 / 03 | 130 | 110 | 90 | 60 | | 0,0 ‰ |

## 1:900 000

© Kunth Verlag GmbH & Co. KG 2015
Königinstraße 11, D-80539 München,
phone +49-89-458020-0, fax +49-89-458020-21
e-mail: info@kunth-verlag.de
www.kunth-verlag.de

Printed in Slovakia

© AA Media Limited 2015
Fanum House, Basing View,
Basingstoke, Hampshire RG21 4EA, UK
A05365

Reykjavík ● ⚲ 319.575
▢ 103.125 km²

IS

AL ⚲ 2.831.741
▢ 28.748 km²

MC ⚲ 35.881
▢ 1,6 km²

AND ⚲ 85.015
▢ 468 km²

MD ⚲ 3.560.000
▢ 33.800 km²

BIH ⚲ 4.621.598
▢ 51.129 km²

MK ⚲ 2.057.284
▢ 25.713 km²

FL ⚲ 36.476
▢ 160 km²

MNE ⚲ 625.266
▢ 13.812 km²

HR ⚲ 4.480.043
▢ 56.542 km²

RSM ⚲ 32.284
▢ 61 km²

RKS ⚲ 1.733.872
▢ 10.887 km²

SLO ⚲ 2.057.660
▢ 20.253 km²

L ⚲ 524.853
▢ 2.586 km²

V ⚲ 836
▢ 0,44 km²

M ⚲ 417.608
▢ 316 km²

North Se

IRL

⚲ 4.581.269 ● Dublin
▢ 70.182 km²

GB

⚲ 61.792.000
▢ 244.820 km²

⚲ 16.6
▢ 41.5

London ●   Amsterdam ●

Brussel/Bruxelles ●   B
⚲ 10.951.26
▢ 30.528 km

Paris ●   Luxemb●

F

⚲ 62.793.432
▢ 543.965 km²

ATLANTIC OCEAN

⚲ 10.602.000
▢ 92.212 km²

P

Andorra la Vella ● AND

Madrid ●

Lisboa ●

E

⚲ 47.212.990
▢ 504.645 km²

MC

Al Jaza'ir
(Alger) ●

Ar-Ribat
(Rabat) ●   MA   DZ

GIAN SEA

⚲ 5.404.956
□ 338.432 km²

**Helsinki**

Ⓕ 143.200.000
□ 17.075.400 km²

**Tallinn** Ⓔ
⚲ 1.340.021
□ 45.227 km²

**Moskva**

⚲ 2.074.605
□ 64.589 km²

**Riga** Ⓛ

Ⓡ
⚲ 4.985.900
□ 385.199 km²

⚲ 9.514.406
□ 450.295 km²

**Oslo**

**Stockholm**

Ⓓ
⚲ 5.475.791
□ 43.094 km²

*Baltic Sea*

⚲ 2.988.381
□ 65.301 km²

Ⓑ

**København**

Ⓡ
**Vilnius**

**Minsk**
⚲ 9.457.000
□ 207.595 km²

**Berlin**

Ⓟ **Warszawa**

⚲ 81.903.000
□ 357.121 km²

⚲ 38.501.000
□ 312.685 km²

**Kyjiv**

Ⓛ

Ⓓ Ⓒ **Praha**
⚲ 10.526.685
□ 78.866 km²

Ⓤ
⚲ 45.665.281
□ 603.700 km²

⚲ 5.404.322
□ 49.034 km²

Ⓢ

**Bratislava**

Ⓜ

**Chişinău**

Ⓒ **Bern** Ⓐ **Wien**

Ⓕ **Vaduz**

Ⓗ **Budapest**

Ⓡ

7.952.600
41.285 km²

⚲ 8.460.390
□ 83.878 km²

⚲ 10.005.000
□ 93.036 km²

⚲ 19.042.936
□ 238.391 km²

**Ljubljana** Ⓢ

**Zagreb**

**Beograd**

**Bucureşti**

*Black Sea*

Ⓡ
**San Marino**

Ⓗ

Ⓑ

**Sarajevo**

Ⓢ

⚲ 7.120.666
□ 77.474 km²

**Monaco**

Ⓘ

**Priština**

⚲ 7.364.570
□ 110.994 km²

Ⓥ **Roma**

Ⓜ

Ⓡ

**Sofija** Ⓑ

⚲ 60.626.442
□ 301.338 km²

**Podgorica**

**Skopje**

**Ankara**

Ⓜ

**Tiranë**

Ⓐ

Ⓣ

Ⓖ

⚲ 9.903.268
□ 131.957 km²

⚲ 74.724.269
□ 814.578 km²

**Athína**

*AN SEA*

**Tunis**

Ⓣ

⚲ 1.193.976
□ 9.251 km²

Ⓒ

| | | |
|---|---|---|
| Ⓐ | Österreich |
| Ⓐ | Shqipëria |
| ⒶⓃⒹ | Andorra |
| Ⓑ | België/Belgique |
| Ⓑ | Bâlgarija |
| Ⓑ | Bosna i Hercegovina |
| Ⓑ | Belarus' |
| Ⓜ | Crna Gora |
| Ⓒ | Schweiz/Suisse/Svizzera |
| Ⓒ | Kýpros |
| Ⓒ | Česká Republika |
| Ⓓ | Deutschland |
| Ⓓ | Danmark |
| Ⓔ | España |
| Ⓔ | Eesti |
| Ⓕ | France |
| Ⓕ | Finland |
| Ⓕ | Liechtenstein |
| Ⓖ | United Kingdom |
| Ⓖ | Elláda |
| Ⓗ | Magyarország |
| Ⓗ | Hrvatska |
| Ⓘ | Italia |
| Ⓘ | Éire/Ireland |
| Ⓘ | Ísland |
| Ⓡ | Kosovo |
| Ⓛ | Luxembourg |
| Ⓛ | Lietuva |
| Ⓛ | Latvija |
| Ⓜ | Malta |
| Ⓜ | Monaco |
| Ⓜ | Moldova |
| Ⓜ | Makedonija |
| Ⓝ | Norge |
| Ⓝ | Nederland |
| Ⓟ | Portugal |
| Ⓟ | Polska |
| Ⓡ | România |
| Ⓡ | San Marino |
| Ⓡ | Rossija |
| Ⓢ | Sverige |
| Ⓢ | Slovenská Republika |
| Ⓢ | Slovenija |
| Ⓢ | Srbija |
| Ⓣ | Türkiye |
| Ⓤ | Ukraijna |
| Ⓥ | Città del Vaticano |

| Legend | Zeichenerklärung | 1:900 000 | Légende | Legenda |
|---|---|---|---|---|
| Motorway (under construction) | Autobahn (im Bau) | | Autoroute (en construction) | Autosnelweg (in aanleg) |
| Toll motorway | Gebührenpflichtige Autobahn | | Autoroute à péage | Tolautosnelweg |
| Dual carriageway (under construction) | 4-oder mehrspurige Autobahn (im Bau) | | Double chaussée (en construction) | Hoofdroute, tweebaans (in aanleg) |
| Primary route (under construction) | Fernstraße (im Bau) | | Route principale (en construction) | Hoofdroute (in aanleg) |
| Main road (under construction) | Wichtige Hauptstraße (im Bau) | | Route principale importante (en construction) | Belangrijke verbindingsweg (in aanleg) |
| Main road | Hauptstraße | | Route départementale | Regionale verbindingsweg |
| Secondary road | Nebenstraße | | Route secondaire | Overige wegen |
| Railway | Eisenbahn | | Chemin de fer | Spoorweg |
| Restricted area | Sperrgebiet | | Zone interdite | Verboden gebied |
| National or nature park | National- und Naturpark | | Parc national, parc naturel | Nationaal park, natuurpark |
| Motorway number | Autobahnnummer | 4  2  A22 | Numéro autoroute | Nummering Autosnelwegen |
| Number of main European road | Europastraßennummer | E54 | Numéro des routes européennes | Nummering Europaroutes |
| Other road numbers | Andere Straßennummern | 34  28  N22  322 | Autre numéro de routes | Wegnummers |
| Motorway junction number | Autobahnanschlussnummer | 22 | Numéros d'échangeurs | Afrit met nummer |
| Motorway junction | Anschlussstelle | | Échangeur | Aansluiting |
| Not suitable / closed for caravans | Für Wohnwagen nicht geeignet / gesperrt | | Non recommandé aux caravans - interdite | Voor caravans niet aanbevelen - verboden |
| Filling station | Autobahntankstelle | | Station-service | Tankstation |
| Restaurant | Autobahnrasthaus | | Restaurant | Restaurant |
| Restaurant with motel | Autobahnrasthaus mit Motel | | Hôtel | Restaurant met motel |
| Major airport | Wichtiger Flughafen | | Aéroport important | Belangrijke luchthaven |
| Airport | Flughafen | | Aéroport | Luchthaven |
| Airfield | Flugplatz | | Aérodrome | Vliegveld |
| Ferry | Autofähre | | Ferry | Veerdienst |
| Border crossing | Grenzübergang | | Passage frontalier - douane | Grensovergang |
| Windmill | Windmühle | | Moulin | Windmolen |
| Lighthouse | Leuchtturm | | Phare | Vuurtoren |
| Place of interest | Sehenswerter Ort | COLMAR | Curiosités | Bezienswaardig |

GB | D | F | NL

## Significant points of interest · Herausragende Sehenswürdigkeiten · Curiosités remarquables · Opvallende bezienswaardigheden

| GB | D | F | NL | | GB | D | F | NL |
|---|---|---|---|---|---|---|---|---|
| Major tourist route | Autoroute | Autoroute | Autoroute | | Christian monastery | Christliches Kloster | Monastère chrétien | Christelijk klooster |
| Major tourist railway | Bahnstrecke | Ligne ferroviaire | Spoorwegtraject | | Cultural landscape | Kulturlandschaft | Paysage culturel | Cultuurlandschap |
| Highspeed train | Hochgeschwindig-keitszug | Train à Grande Vitesse | Hogesnelheidstrein | | Historical city scape | Historisches Stadtbild | Cité historique | Historisch stadsgezicht |
| Shipping route | Schiffsroute | Itinéraire en bateau | Scheepsroute | | Impressive skyline | Imposante Skyline | Gratte-ciel | Imposante skyline |
| | | | | | Castle/fortress/fort | Burg/Festung/Wehranlage | Château/forteresse/remparts | Burcht/vesting/verdedigingswerk |
| UNESCO World Natural Heritage | UNESCO-Weltnaturerbe | Patrimoine naturel de l'humanité de l'UNESCO | UNESCO-wereldnatuurerfgoed | | Castle ruin | Burgruine | Château ruine | Burcht ruine |
| Mountain landscape | Gebirgslandschaft | Paysage de montagne | Berglandschap | | Tower of interest | Sehenswerter Turm | Tour intéressante | Bezienswaardige toren |
| Rock landscape | Felslandschaft | Paysage rocheux | Rotslandschap | | Windmill | Windmühle | Moulin | Windmolen |
| Ravine/canyon | Schlucht/Canyon | Gorge/canyon | Kloof/canyon | | Palace | Palast/Schloss | Palais | Paleis |
| Glacier | Gletscher | Glacier | Gletsjer | | Technical/industrial monument | Techn./industrielles Monument | Monument technique/industriel | Technisch/industrieel monument |
| Active volcano | Vulkan, aktiv | Volcan actif | Actieve vulkaan | | Working mine | Bergwerk in Betrieb | Mine en activité | Mijn in bedrijf |
| Extinct volcano | Vulkan, erloschen | Volcan éteint | Dode vulkaan | | Disused mine | Bergwerk geschlossen | Mine fermée | Mijn buiten bedrijf |
| Geyser | Geysir | Geyser | Geiser | | Dam | Staumauer | Barrage | Stuwdam |
| Cave | Höhle | Grotte | Grotten | | Impressive lighthouse | Sehenswerter Leuchtturm | Très beau phare | Bezienswaardige vuurtoren |
| River landscape | Flusslandschaft | Paysage fluvial | Rivierlandschap | | Notable bridge | Herausragende Brücke | Pont remarquable | Opvallende brug |
| Waterfall/rapids | Wasserfall/Stromschnelle | Chute d'eau/rapide | Waterval/stroomversnelling | | Remarkable building | Herausragendes Gebäude | Bâtiment remarquable | Bijzonder gebouw |
| Lake country | Seenlandschaft | Paysage de lacs | Merenlandschap | | Tomb/grave | Grabmal | Tombeau | Grafmonument |
| Desert | Wüstenlandschaft | Désert | Woestijnlandschap | | Monument | Denkmal | Monument | Monument |
| Oasis | Oase | Oasis | Oase | | Memorial | Mahnmal | Mémorial | Gedenkteken |
| Depression | Depression | Bassin | Depressie | | Theater of war/battlefield | Kriegsschauplatz/Schlachtfeld | Champs de bataille | Strijdtoneel/slagvelden |
| Fossil site | Fossilienfundstätte | Site fossile | Fossielenplaats | | Space mission launch site | Weltraumbahnhof | Base spatiale | Ruimtestation |
| Nature park | Naturpark | Parc naturel | Natuurpark | | Space telescope | Weltraumteleskop | Télescope astronomique | Ruimtetelescoop |
| National park (landscape) | Nationalpark (Landschaft) | Parc national (paysage) | Nationaal park (landschap) | | Market | Markt | Marché | Markt |
| National park (flora) | Nationalpark (Flora) | Parc national (flore) | Nationaal park (flora) | | Festivals | Feste und Festivals | Fêtes et festivals | Feesten en festivals |
| National park (fauna) | Nationalpark (Fauna) | Parc national (faune) | Nationaal park (fauna) | | Museum | Museum | Musée | Museum |
| National park (culture) | Nationalpark (Kultur) | Parc national (site culturel) | Nationaal park (cultuur) | | State Historical Park | Freilichtmuseum | Musée de plein air | Openluchtmuseum |
| Botanic gardens | Botanischer Garten | Jardin botanique | Botanische tuin | | Theatre | Theater | Théâtre | Theater |
| Biosphere reserve | Biosphärenreservat | Réserve de biosphère | Biosfeerreservaat | | World exhibition/World Fair | Weltausstellung | Exposition universelle | Wereldtentoonstelling |
| Wildlife reserve | Wildreservat | Réserve animale | Wildreservaat | | | | | |
| Zoo/safari park | Zoo/Safaripark | Zoo/parc de safari | Dierentuin/safaripark | | | | | |
| Coastal landscape | Küstenlandschaft | Paysage côtier | Kustlandschap | | Arena/stadium | Arena/Stdion | Arène/stade | Arena/stadion |
| Beach | Strand | Plage | Strand | | Race track | Rennstrecke | Circuit automobile | Circuit |
| Island | Insel | Île | Eiland | | Golf | Golf | Golf | Golf |
| Underwater reserve | Unterwasserreservat | Réserve sous-marine | Onderwaterreservaat | | Horse racing | Pferdesport | Équitation | Paardensport |
| Spring | Quelle | Source | Bron | | Skiing | Skigebiet | Station de ski | Skigebied |
| | | | | | Sailing | Segeln | Voile | Zeilen |
| UNESCO World Cultural Heritage | UNESCO-Weltkulturerbe | Patrimoine culturel de l'humanité de l'UNESCO | UNESCO-wereldcultuurerfgoed | | Wind surfing | Windsurfen | Planche à voile | Surfen |
| Remarkable city | Außergewöhnliche Metropole | Métropole d'exception | Buitengewone metropolen | | Surfing | Wellenreiten | Surf | Surfriding |
| Pre-and early history | Vor- und Frühgeschichte | Préhistorie et protohistoire | Prehistorie en vroegste geschiedenis | | Diving | Tauchen | Plongée | Duiken |
| Prehistoric rockscape | Prähistorische Felsbilder/Naturvölker | Peintures rupestres préhistoriques | Prehistorische rotstekeningen | | Canoeing/rafting | Kanu/Rafting | Canoë/rafting | Kanoën/rafting |
| The Ancient Orient | Alter Orient | Ancien Orient | Oud-Oriënt | | Seaport | Seehafen | Port | Zeehaven |
| Minoan site | Minoische Kultur | Civilisation minoenne | Minoïsche cultuur | | Deep-sea fishing | Hochseeangeln | Pêche en mer | Zeevissen |
| Phoenecian site | Phönikische Kultur | Civilisation phénicienne | Fenicische cultuur | | Waterskiing | Wasserski | Ski nautique | Waterskiën |
| Etruscan site | Etruskische Kultur | Civilisation étrusque | Etruskische cultuur | | Beach resort | Badeort | Station balnéaire | Badplaats |
| Greek antiquity | Griechische Antike | Antiquité grecque | Griekse oudheden | | Leisure bath | Freizeitbad | Piscine découverte | Recreatiebad |
| Roman antiquity | Römische Antike | Antiquité romaine | Romeinse oudheden | | Mineral/thermal spa | Mineralbad/Therme | Station hydrothermale | Mineraalbad/thermen |
| Vikings | Wikinger | Vikings | Vikingen | | Leisure park | Freizeitpark | Parc de loisirs | Recreatiepark |
| Places of Jewish cultural interest | Jüdische Kulturstätte | Site juif | Joodse cultuurhist. plaatsen | | Casino | Spielcasino | Casino | Casino |
| Places of Islamic cultural interest | Islamische Kulturstätte | Site islamique | Islamitische cultuurhist. plaatsen | | Hill resort | Hill Resort | Station de montagne | Hill resort |
| Places of Christian cultural interest | Christliche Kulturstätte | Site chrétien | Christelijke cultuurhist. plaatsen | | Mountain refuge/alpine pasture | Berghütte/Alm | Refuge/pâturages | Berghut/alpenweide |
| Roman church | Romanische Kirche | Église romane | Romaanse kerk | | Rambling/rambling area | Wandern/Wandergebiet | Randonnées/zone de randonnées | Wandelen/wandelgebied |
| Gothic church | Gotische Kirche | Église gothique | Gotische kerk | | Viewpoint | Aussichtspunkt | Point de vue | Uitzichtpunt |
| Renaissance church | Renaissance-Kirche | Église renaissance | Renaissance kerk | | Mountain railway | Bergbahn | Chemin de fer de montagne | Kabelbaan |
| Baroque church | Barock-Kirche | Église baroque | Barok kerk | | Shipwreck | Schiffswrack | Épave de navire | Scheepswrak |

# Road Distances

Amsterdam
Athína
Barcelona
Belfast
Beograd
Berlin
Bern
Birmingham
Bordeaux
Bratislava
Bruxelles/Brussel
Bucureşti
Budapest
Calais
Dublin
Edinburgh
Frankfurt a.M.
Genova
Hamburg
Helsinki
Istanbul
København
Köln
Kyïv
Le Havre
Lisboa
Ljubljana
London
Luxembourg
Lyon
Madrid
Málaga
Marseille
Milano
Minsk
Moskva
München
Oslo
Paris
Praha
Riga
Roma
Rotterdam
Sankt-Peterburg
Sarajevo
Skopje
Sofija
Stockholm
Strasbourg
Tallinn
Tiranë
Vilnius
Warszawa
Wien
Zagreb

All distances in this chart are in kilometers and include any part of the route taken by ferry.

Scale 1:1 125 000

0  10  20  30 Kilometres
0      10      20 Miles

Aa | Ab | Ac | Ad | Ba | Bb

**G R E E N L A N D**

01

Vestfirðir
Hornbjarg
Straumnes
Kögur
Rytur
Aðalvík
Látravík
Hesteyri
Búrfell 498
Jökulfirðir
Hornstrandir

02
Deild
**Bolungarvík**
Suðureyri
Göltur
Sæbol
Sauðanes
Hnífsdalur
**Ísafjörður**
Flateyri
**Súðavík**
Reykjanes
Melgraseyri
Æðey
Vigur
Háafell 688
Ögur
Borganes
Laugaland
Skjaldfönn
Drangajökull
Drangafell 402
Eyvindarfjörður
Sælusker
Munaðarnes
**Siglufjörður**
Sauðanes
Skagatá
Vikur
Hvanndalir
Framnes
Straumnes
Barð
Neskot

03
Snæfell 793
Kaldalón
Kirkjuból
Heydalur
Gláma
Hrafnseyri
Dynjandisfoss (Fjallfoss)
**Bíldudalur**
Flókalundur
**Patreksfjörður**
**Tálknafjörður**
Breiðavík
Látrabjarg
Brjánslækur
Kross holt
Hagi
Steingrímsfjarðarheiði
**Hólmavík**
Drangsnes
Grímsey
Kollafjarðarnes
Óspaksstaðir
Broddanes
Stóra-Fjarðarhorn
Hindisvík
Þingeyrar
**Blönduós**
Vatnsdalur
**Sauðárkrókur**
Hólar
Hofsós
Skagaströnd
Skagafjörður
Tröllaskagi

04
Breiðafjörður
Reykhólar
Staðarhóll
Efri-Brúná
Prestbakki
Borðeyri
Brú
Staðarskáli
**Hvammstangi**
Laugarbakki
Kolufoss
Stórisandur

05
**Stykkishólmur**
Helgafell
Hellissandur
**Ólafsvík**
Grundarfjörður
Snæfellsjökull
Þjóðgarðurinn Snæfellsjökull
Tröllakirkja
Búðir
Hellnar
Arnarstapi
Skógarnes
Vegamót
Gerðuberg
Snorrastaðir
Búðardalur
Eiríksstaðir
Geldingafell
Breiðabólsstaðir
Hvammur Baula 934
Arnarvatnsheiði
Langjökull
**Kjölur**
Kjalfell 1000
Hveravellir
Kerlingarfjöll 1477

06
Barðagrunn
Akrar
**Myrar**
Hítarnes
Hólmakot
Hjörsey
Álftanes
Þormóðssker
**Borgarnes**
Hvanneyri
Varmaland
Reykholt
Hraunfossar
Húsafell
Lundur
Hæll
Tunga
Geitaberg
Norðtunga
Strútur 932
Surtshellir 1675
Eiríksjökull
Hrútfell 1398
Ok 1141
Þórisjökull 1350

07
Faxaflói
**AKRANES**
Hofsvík
Svið
Esja 914
Fellsendi
**Seltjarnarnes**
Garðskagi
**Garður**
**Sandgerður**
**REYKJAVÍK**
Álftanes
**KÓPAVOGUR**
**HAFNARFJÖRÐUR**
**GARÐABÆR**
**KEFLAVÍK**
Vogar
**Njarðvík**
Hafnir
**Mosfellsbær**
Þingvellir
Þjóðgarðurinn Þingvellir
Þingvallavatn
Laugarvatn
Nesjavellir
Geysir
Gullfoss
Bruarfoss
Skálholt
Flúðir
Strokkur
Gljúfurleitarfoss
Haifoss
Stöng

08
Hafnaberg
Blaa Lónið
Krýsuvík
Heiðin há
Kleifarvatn
**Grindavík**
Reykjanes
Strandarkirkja
**Hveragerði**
**Selfoss**
Skálafell 574
Kaldbakur
**Þorlákshöfn**
Eyrarbakki
Stokkseyri
Hella
Holt
**Hvolsvöllur**
Keldur
Hekla 1491
Landmannalaugar
Friðland að Fjallabaki
Torfajökull

09
Eyrarbakkabugur
Þridrangar
Faxasker
Ellirey
**Heimaey**
Bjarnarey
Smáey
**Vestmannaeyjar**
Álsey
Súðurey
Hellisey
Surtsey
Geldungur
Vestur-Landeyjar
Austur-Landeyjar
Kross
Bakki
Eyjafjallajökull 1666
Seljaland
Þórsmörk
**Mýrdalsjökull**
Skógafoss
Skógar
Pétursey
Dyrhólaey
Vík

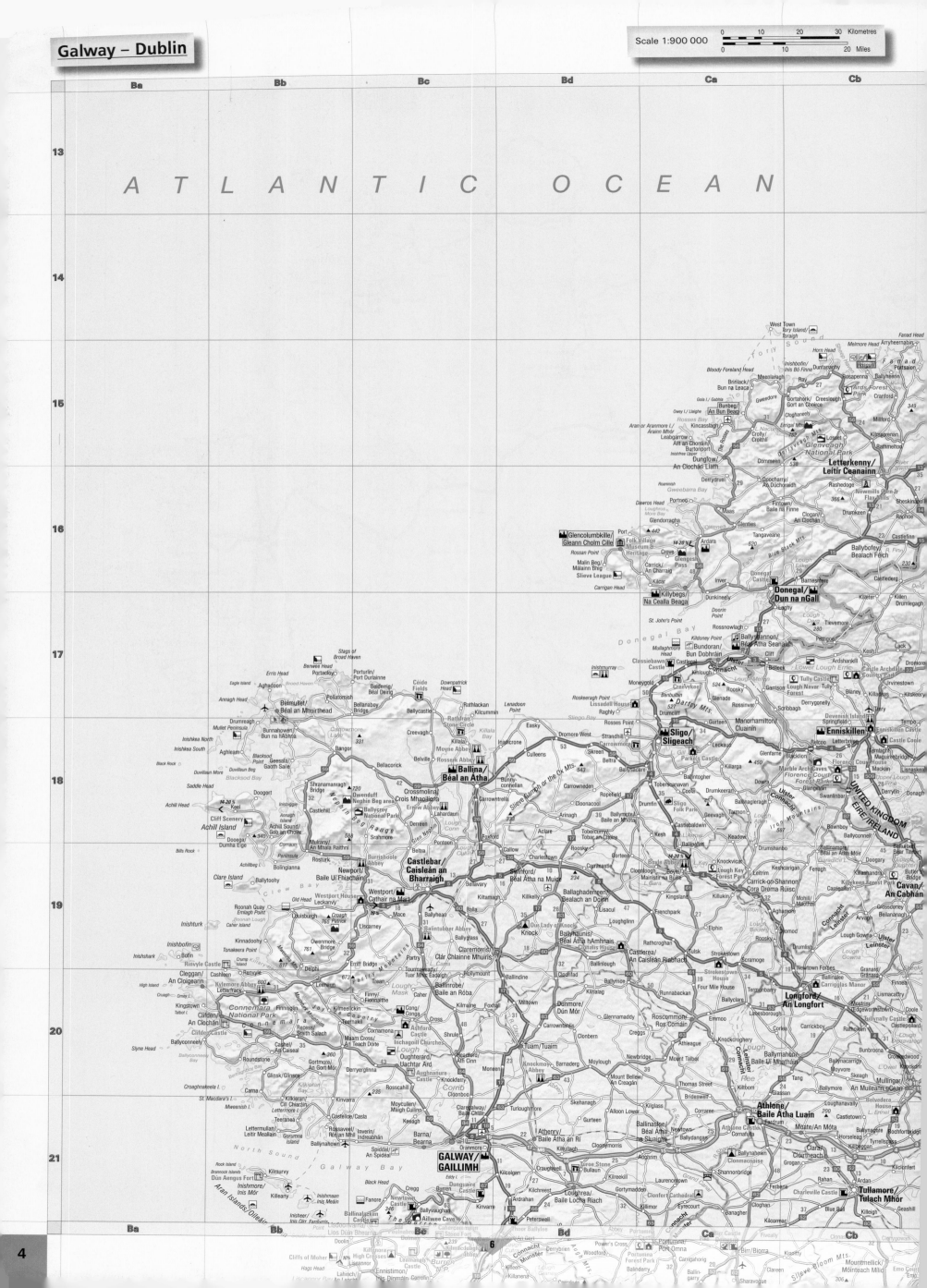

Scale 1:900 000

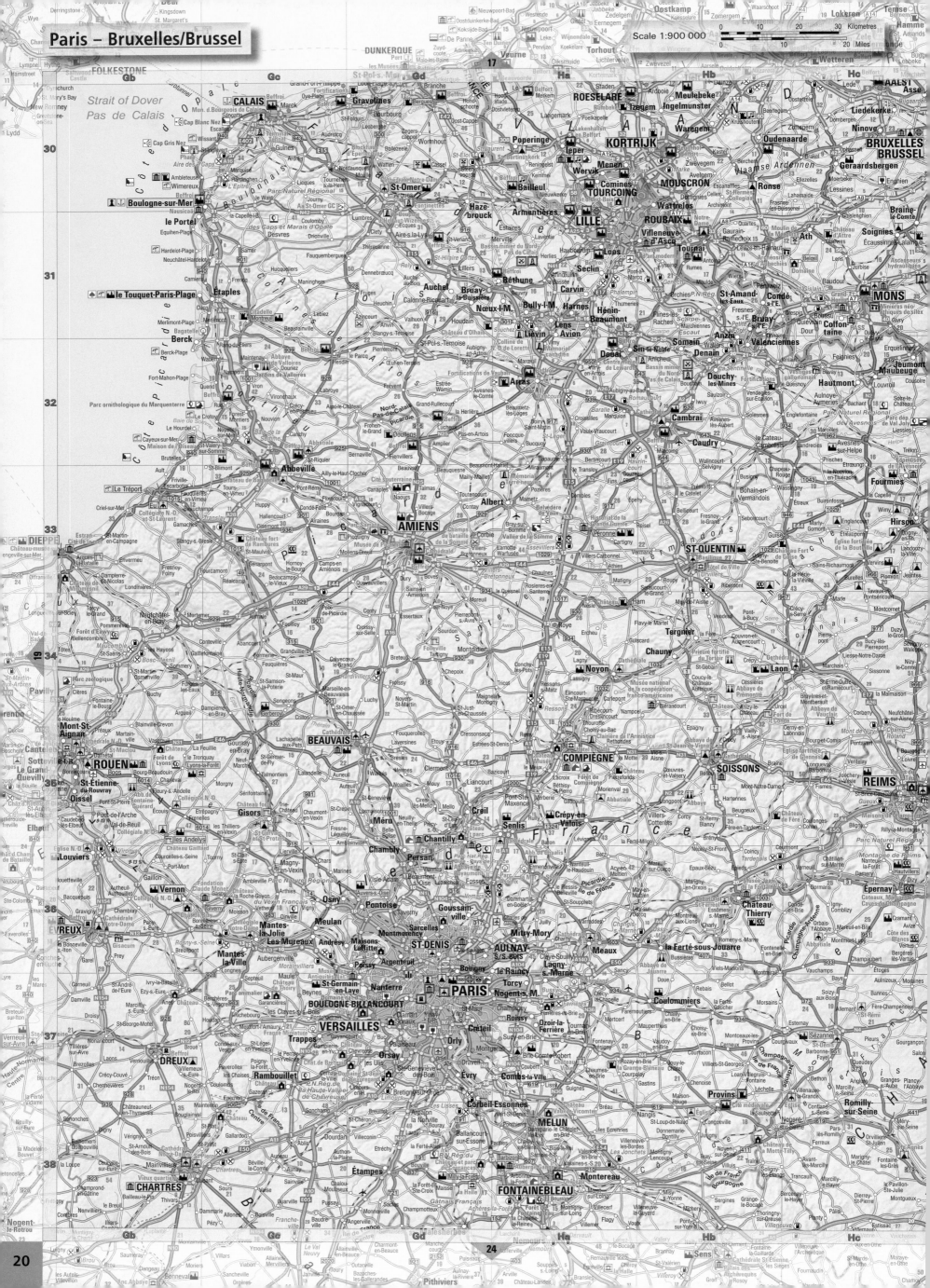

Scale 1:900 000

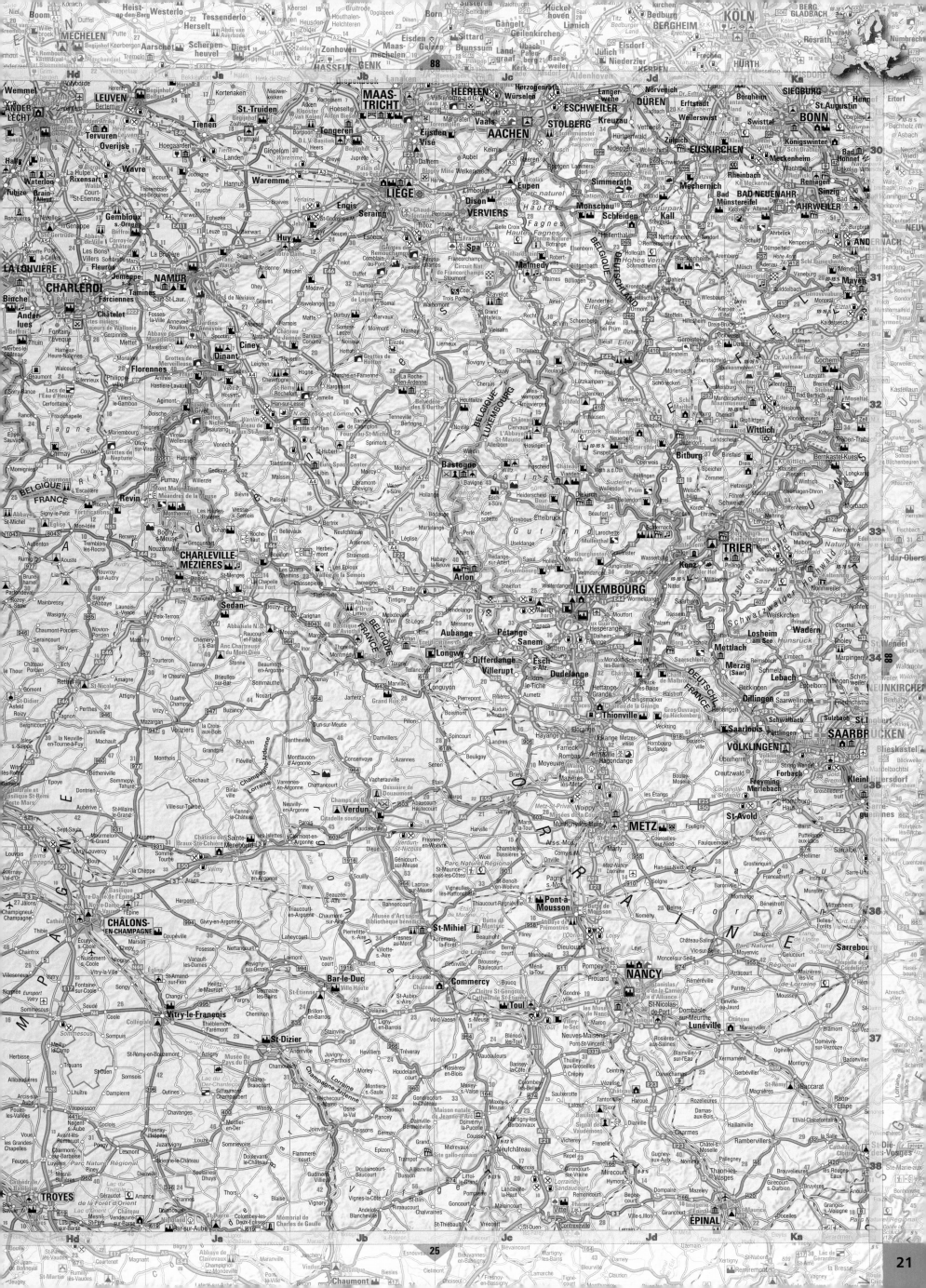

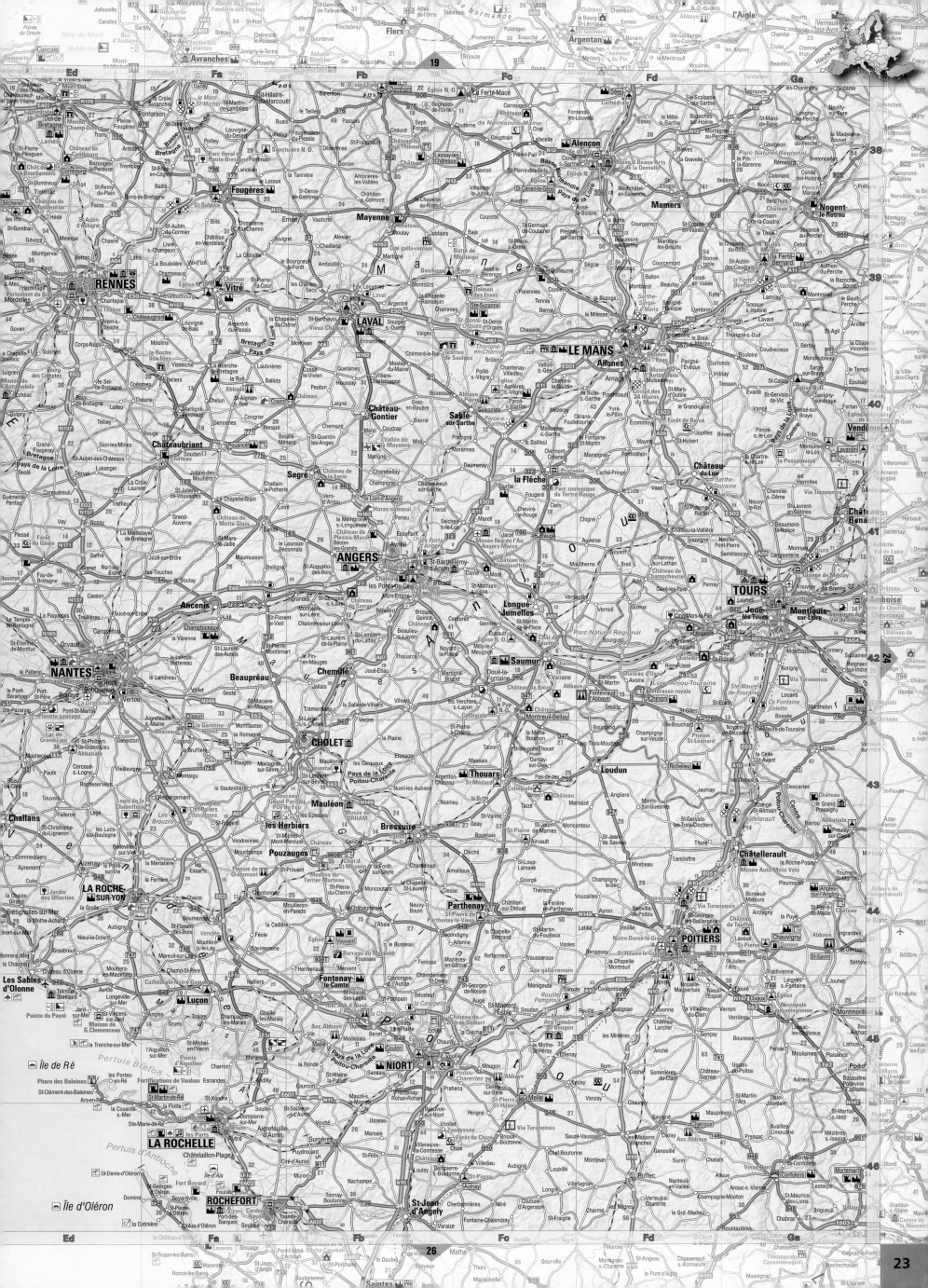

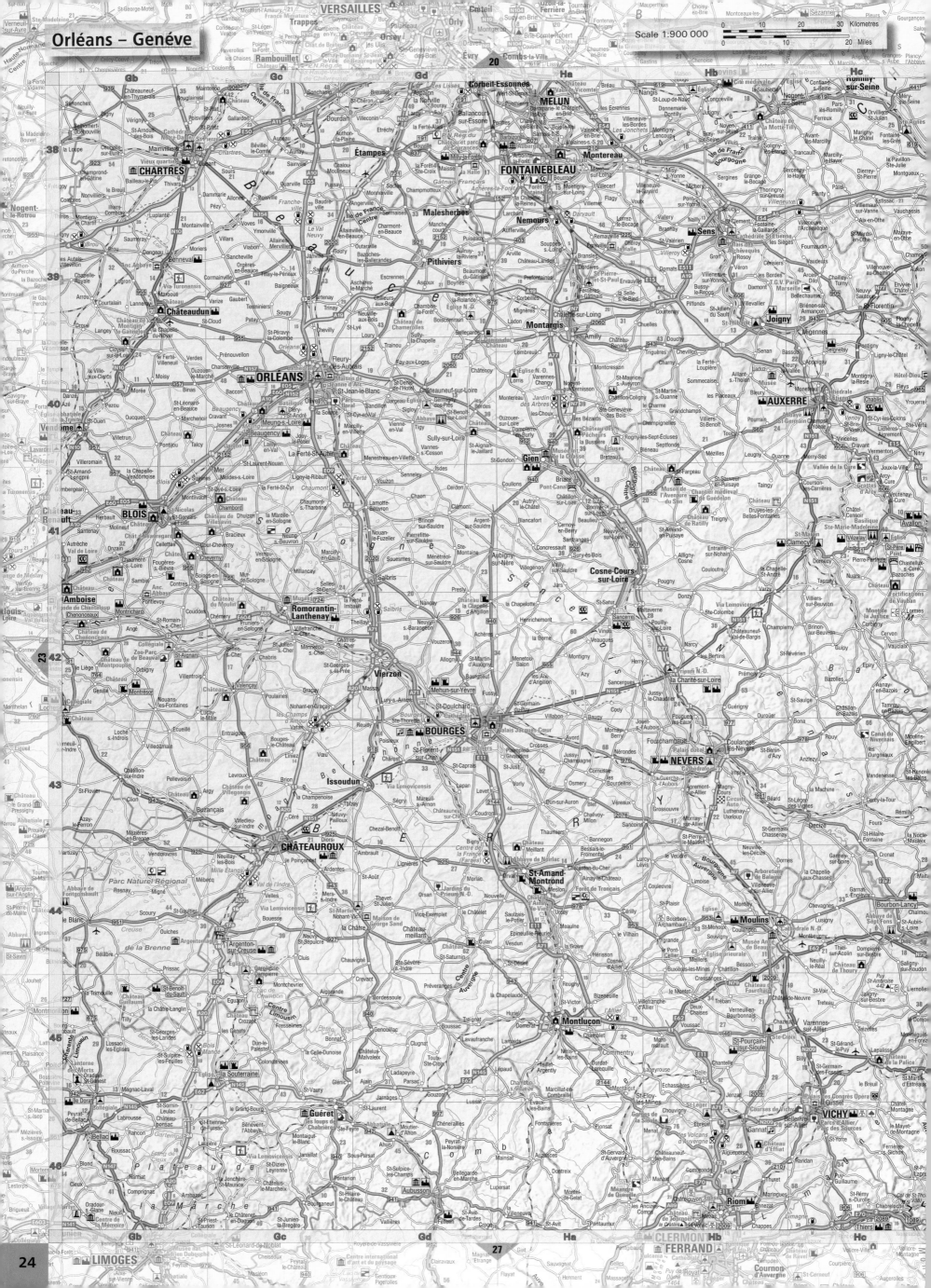

Scale 1:900 000

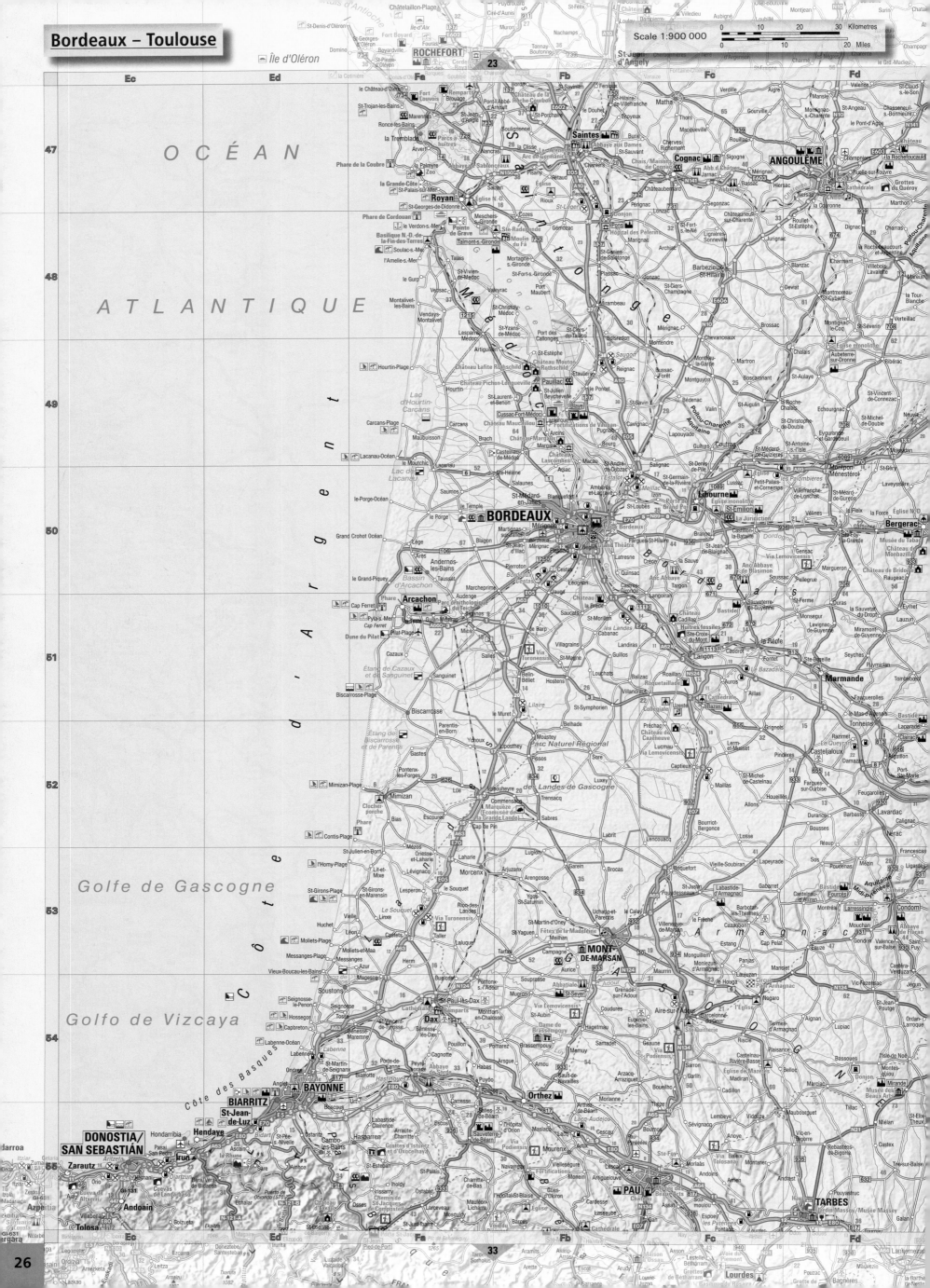

Scale 1:900 000

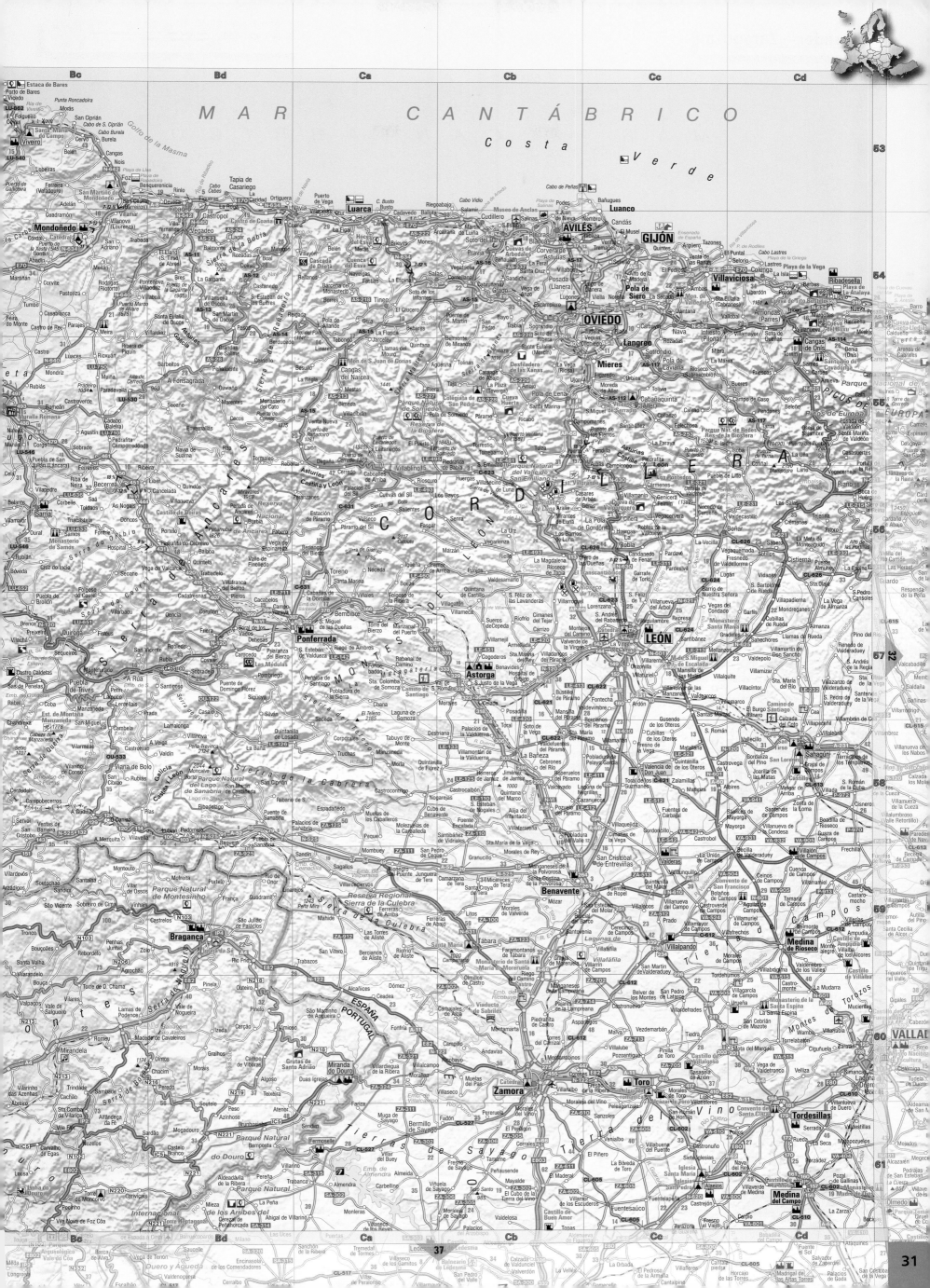

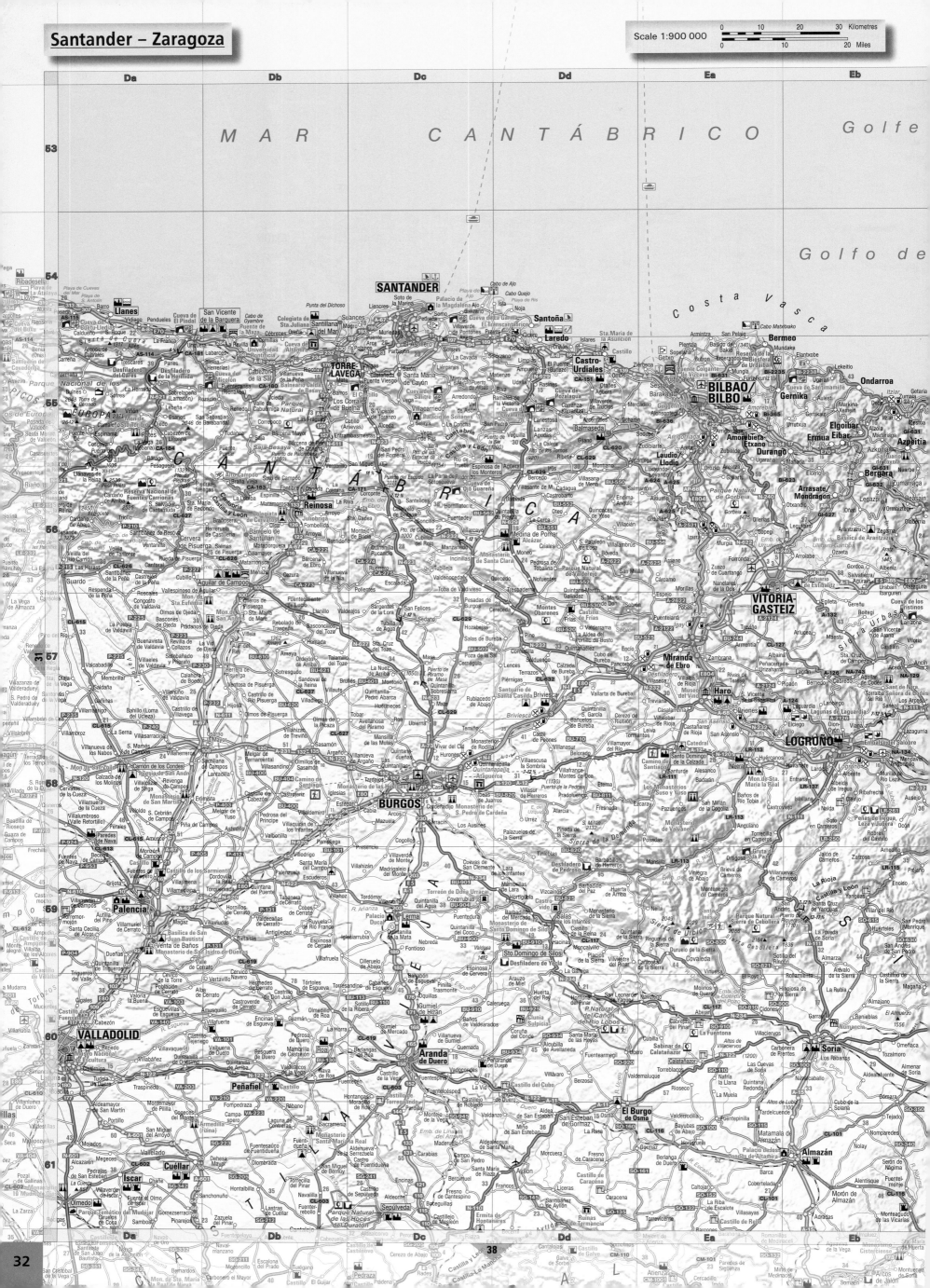

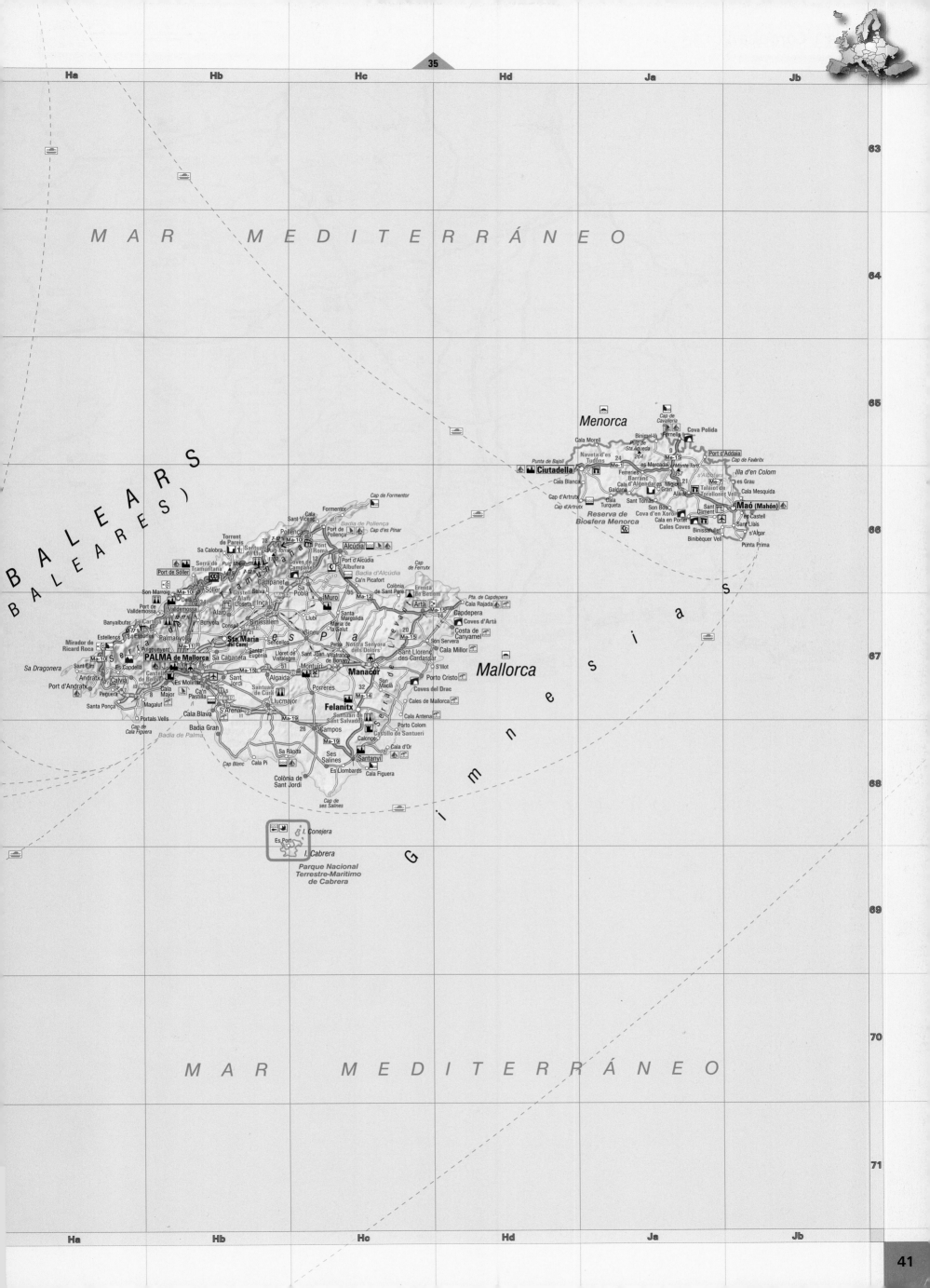

MAR MEDITERRÁNEO

BALEARS
(BALEARES)

Menorca

Cap de Cavalleria
Cova Polida
Binimel-là
Fornells
Port d'Addaia
Cala Morell
Puig de Sta. Agueda
Cap de Favàritx
Punta de Bajoli
Naveta d'es Tudons
24
es Mercadal
Me-15
 Me-1
Illa d'en Colom
Ciutadella
Ferreries
Monte Toro
s'Albufera
es Grau
Cala Blanca
Barranc
Cala d'Algendar
es Migjorn Gran
Talaiot de Trepellonet Vell
Cala Mesquida
Cap d'Artrutx
Galdana
Son Bou
Sant Climent
Maó (Mahón)
Cala Turqueta
Sant Tomàs
Cova d'en Xoroi
es Castell
Cap d'Artrutx
Reserva de Biosfera Menorca
Cala en Porter
Cales Coves
Binissafullet
s'Algar
Binibèquer Vell
Punta Prima

Cap de Formentor
Formentor
Sant Vicenç
Cala
Badia de Pollença
Cap d'es Pinar
Pollença
Port de Pollença
Torrent de Pareis
Sa Calobra
Santuari de Lluc
Puig Tomir
Ma-10
Coves de Campanet
Pont Roma
Alcúdia
Serra de Tramuntana
Port de Sóller
Puig Major
Albufera
Cap de Ferrutx
Son Marroig
Deià
Campanet
Ma-10
Badia d'Alcúdia
Sóller
Castell Selva
d'Alaró
Inca
sa Pobla
Can Picafort
Colònia de Sant Pere
Port de Valldemossa
Valldemossa
Ma-13
Muro
Ermita de Betlem
Pta. de Capdepera
Banyalbufar
la Cartuja
Bunyola
Llubí
Santa
Margalida
Ma-12
Artà
Cala Rajada
Estellencs
Alaró
Binissalem
Maria de
la Salut
Capdepera
Mirador de
Ricard Roca
Puigpunyent
Sta. Maria
del Camí
Sencelles
Sineu
Petra
Nostra Senyora
dels Dolors
Coves d'Artà
Costa de Canyamel
Sant Elm
Es Capdellà
Palmanyola
Ma-11
Santa
Eugènia
Llorenç
de Vistalegre
Sant Joan
Vilafranca
de Bonany
Son Servera
Cala Millor
Andratx
Calvià
Ma-10
Son
Macià
PALMA de Mallorca
Sa Cabaneta
Montuïri
Sant Llorenç
des Cardassar
Mallorca
Port d'Andratx
Castell
de Bellver
Son
Sant Jordi
Ma-15
Algaida
Manacor
S'Illot
Peguera
Es Molinar
Porreres
Cales de Mallorca
Porto Cristo
Magaluf
Ca'n Pastilla
Can Major
Coves del Drac
Santa Ponça
Llucmajor
Felanitx
Cala Antena
Portals Vells
S'Arenal
Santuari de
Sant Salvador
Porto Colom
Cap de
Cala Figuera
Cala Blava
Ma-19
Campos
Castillo de Santueri
Badia Gran
26
Calonge
Cala d'Or
Badia de Palma
Cap Blanc
Cala Pi
Ma-19
Ses
Salines
Santanyí
Sa Ràpita
Cala Figuera
Cala d'es Llombards
Colònia de
Sant Jordi
Cap de ses Salines

I. Conejera
Es Port
I. Cabrera
Parque Nacional
Terrestre-Marítimo
de Cabrera

MAR MEDITERRÁNEO

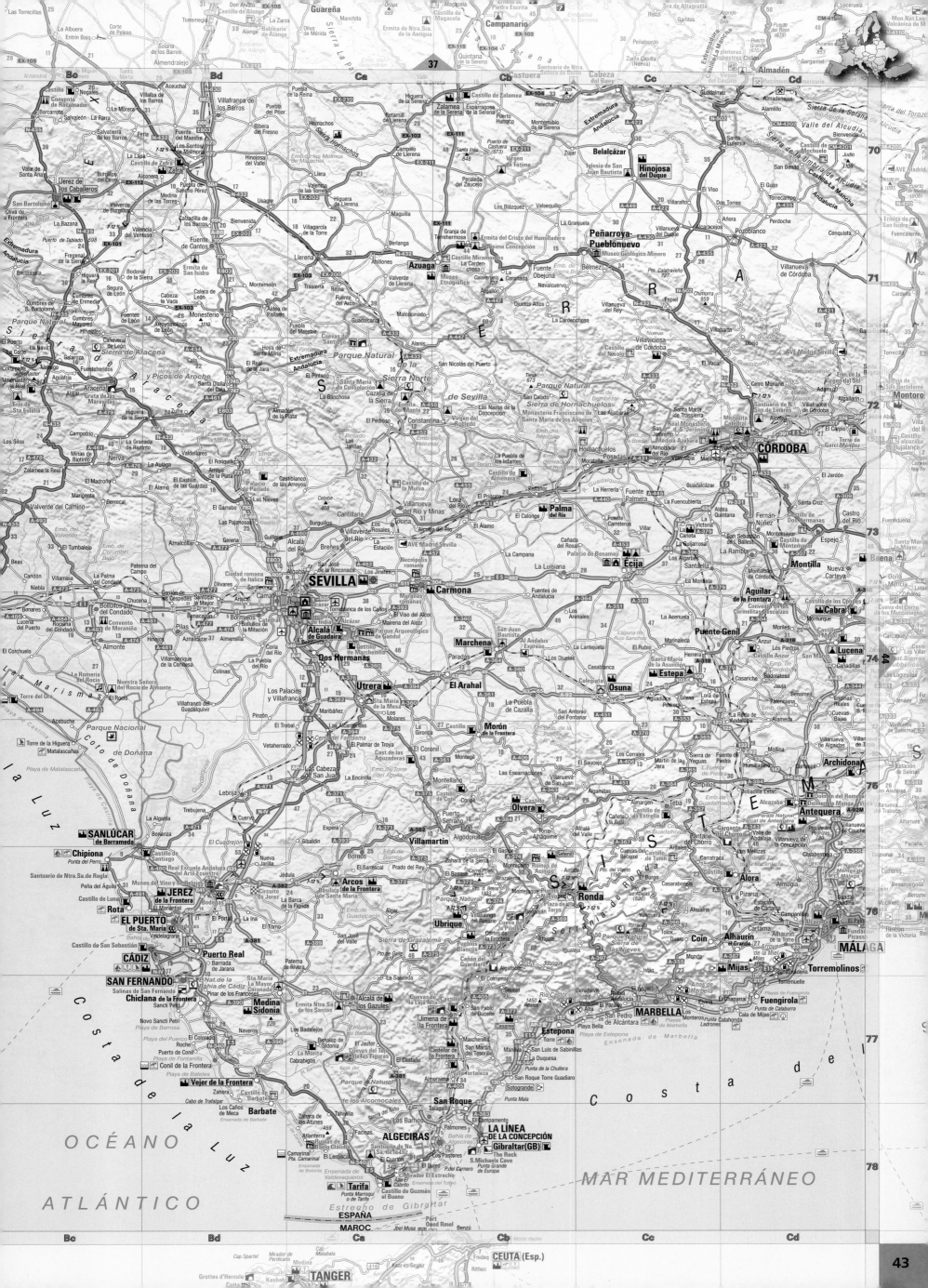

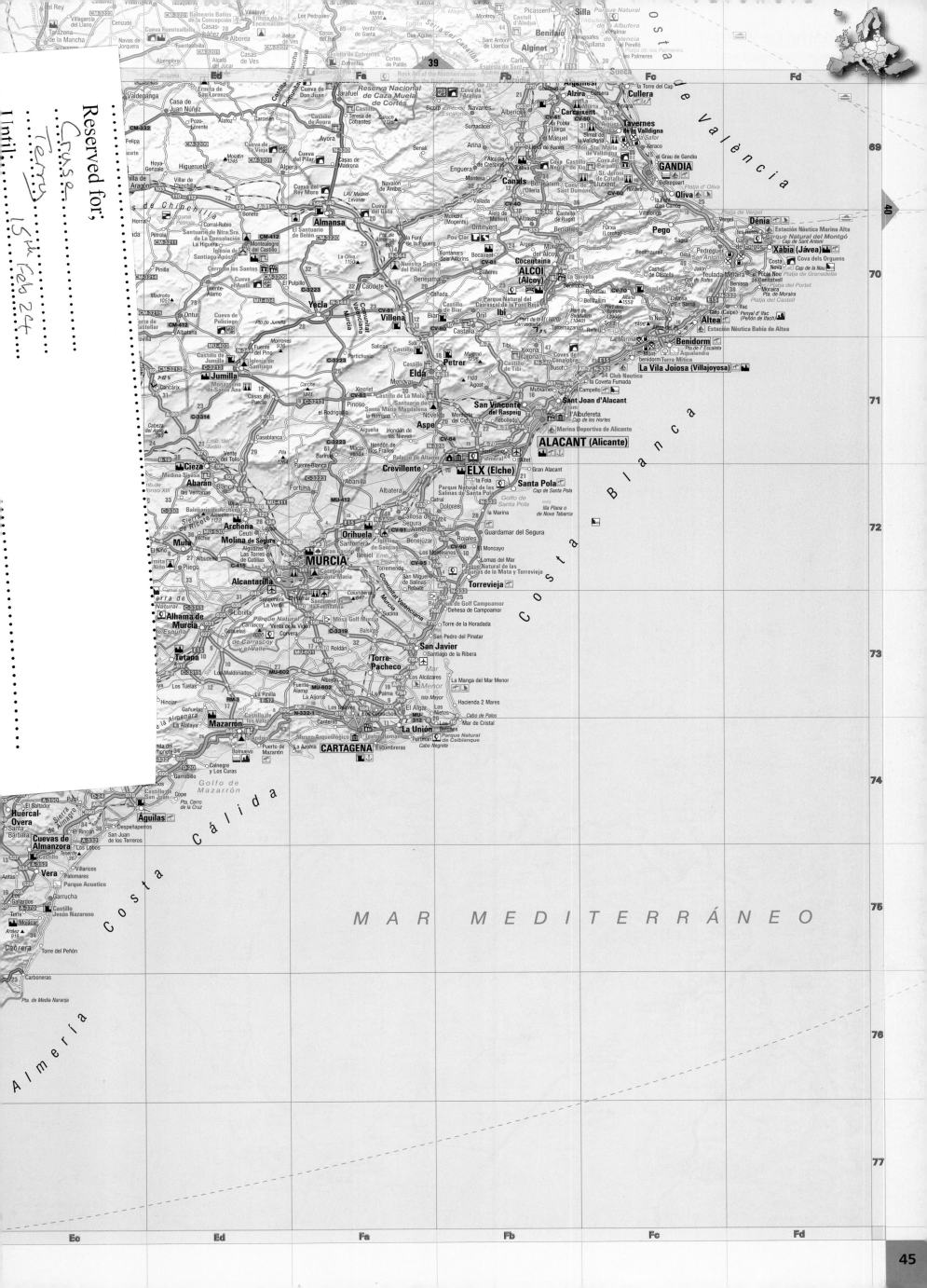

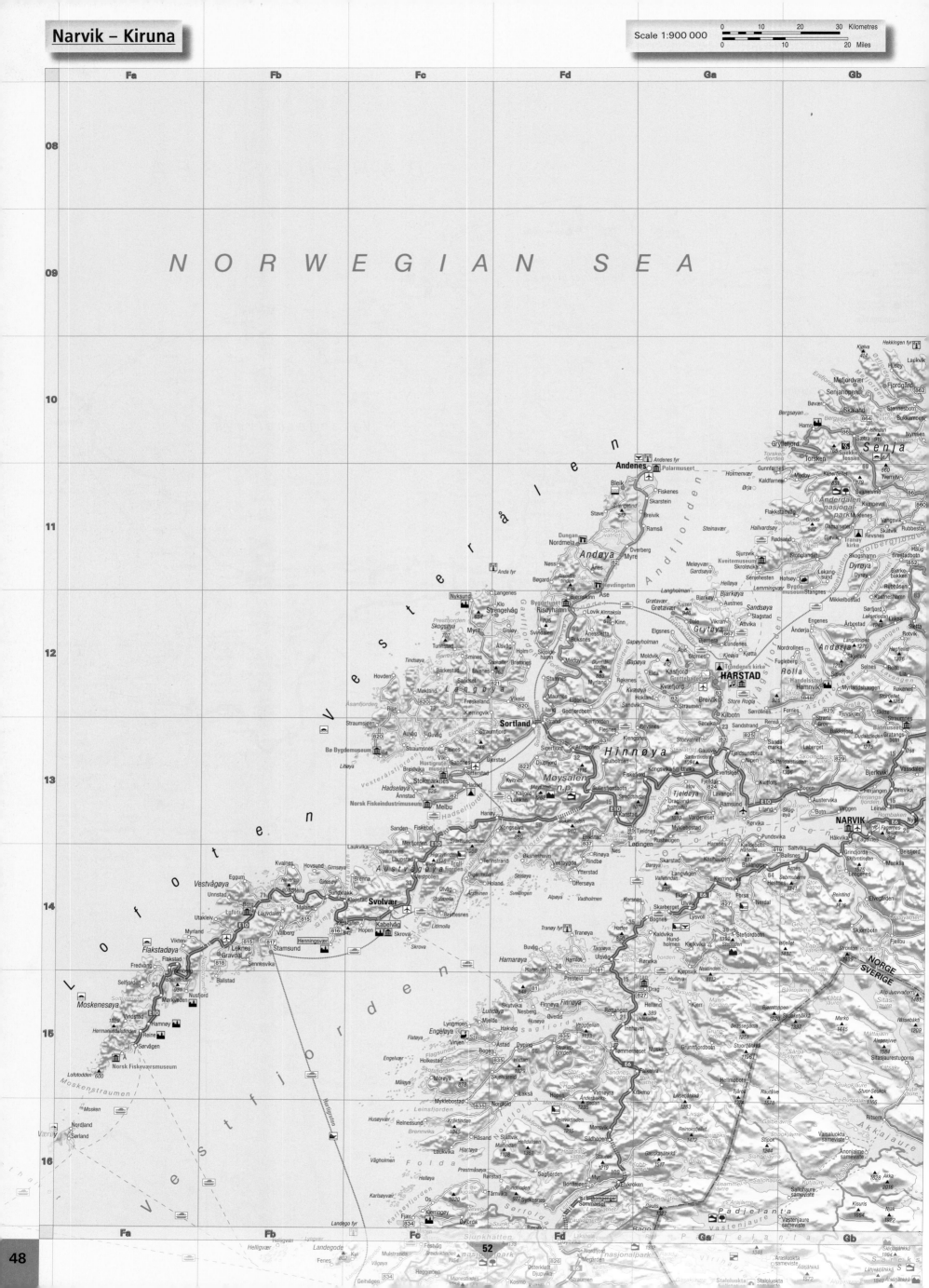

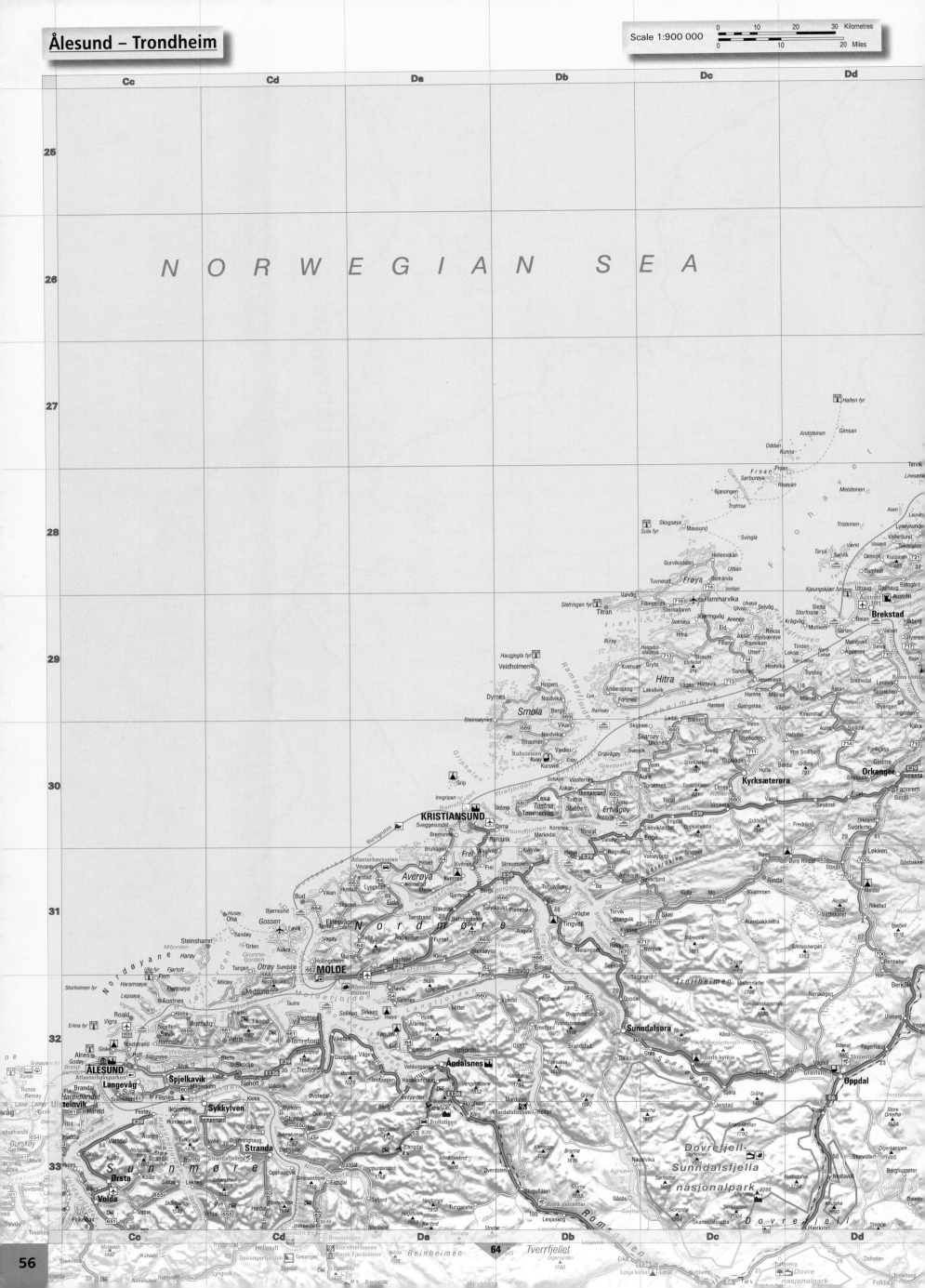

Scale 1:900 000

0    10    20    30 Kilometres

0         10         20 Miles

N O R W E G I A N   S E A

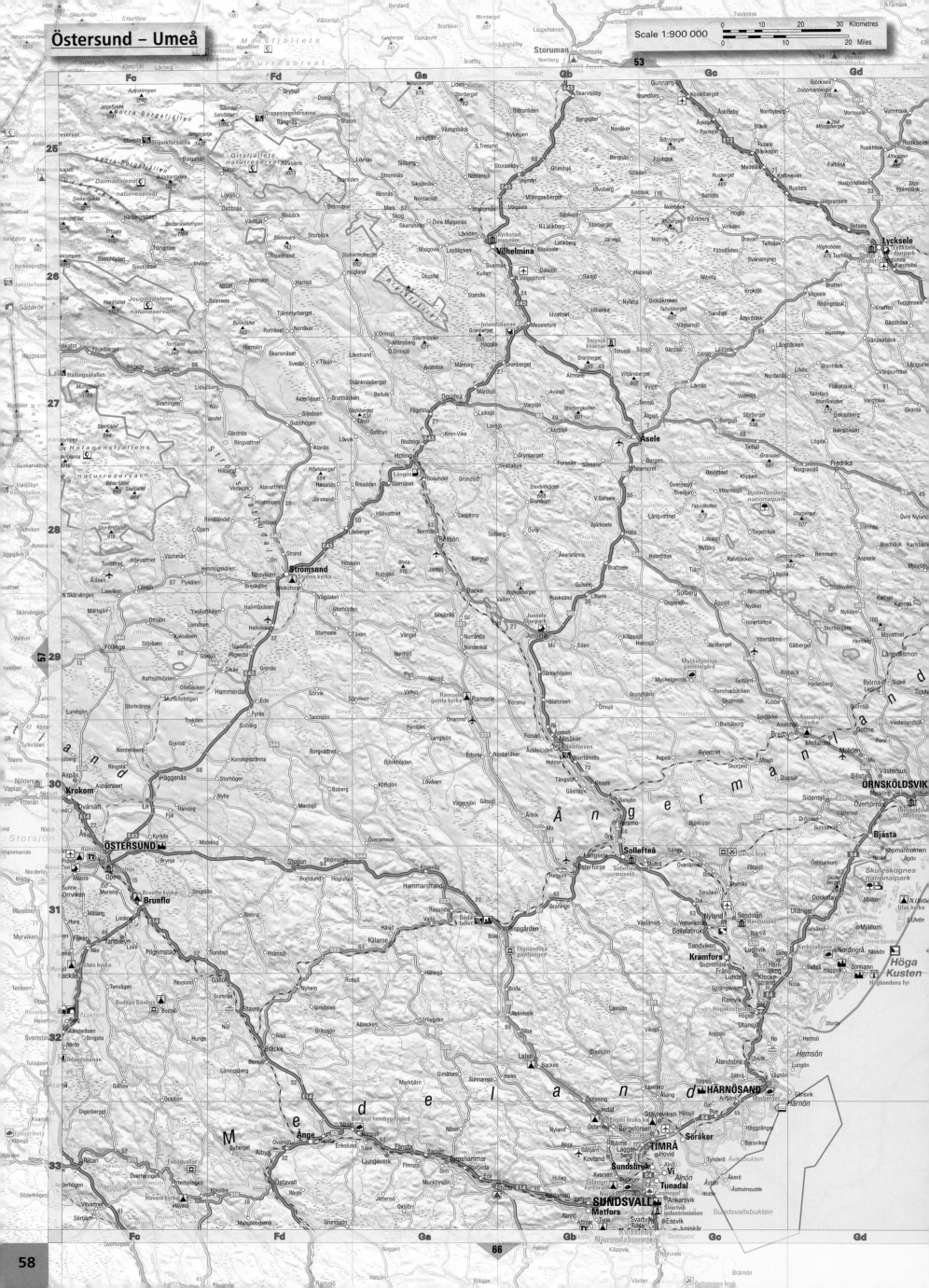

Scale 1:900 000

| 0 | 10 | 20 | 30 Kilometres |
| 0 | | 10 | 20 Miles |

Pohjanlahti

Jc  Jd  Ka  Kb  Kc  Kd

25

26

27

28

29

30

31

32

33

Raahe · Vanha Raahe · Ruukki · Oulainen · Haapavesi · Kajaani · Oulujärvi

Ylivieska · Nivala · Kärsämäki · Piippola · Vuolijoki

Kannus · Kälviä · Haapajärvi · Pyhäjärvi · Kiuruvesi · Iisalmi

Kokkola/Karleby · Toholampi · Reisjärvi · Pihtipudas · Lapinlahti

Vetel · Halsua · Kinnula · Viitasaari · Pielavesi · Maaninka

Evijärvi · Perho · Keitele · Vesanto

Alajärvi · Karstula · Saarijärvi · Äänekoski · Suolahti · Rautalampi · Suonenjoki

Lapua · Kauhava · Soini · Keuruu · Jyväskylä · Pieksämäki

Seinäjoki · Alavus · Ähtäri · Multia · Jyväskylän mlk

Virrat · Mänttä · Keuruu

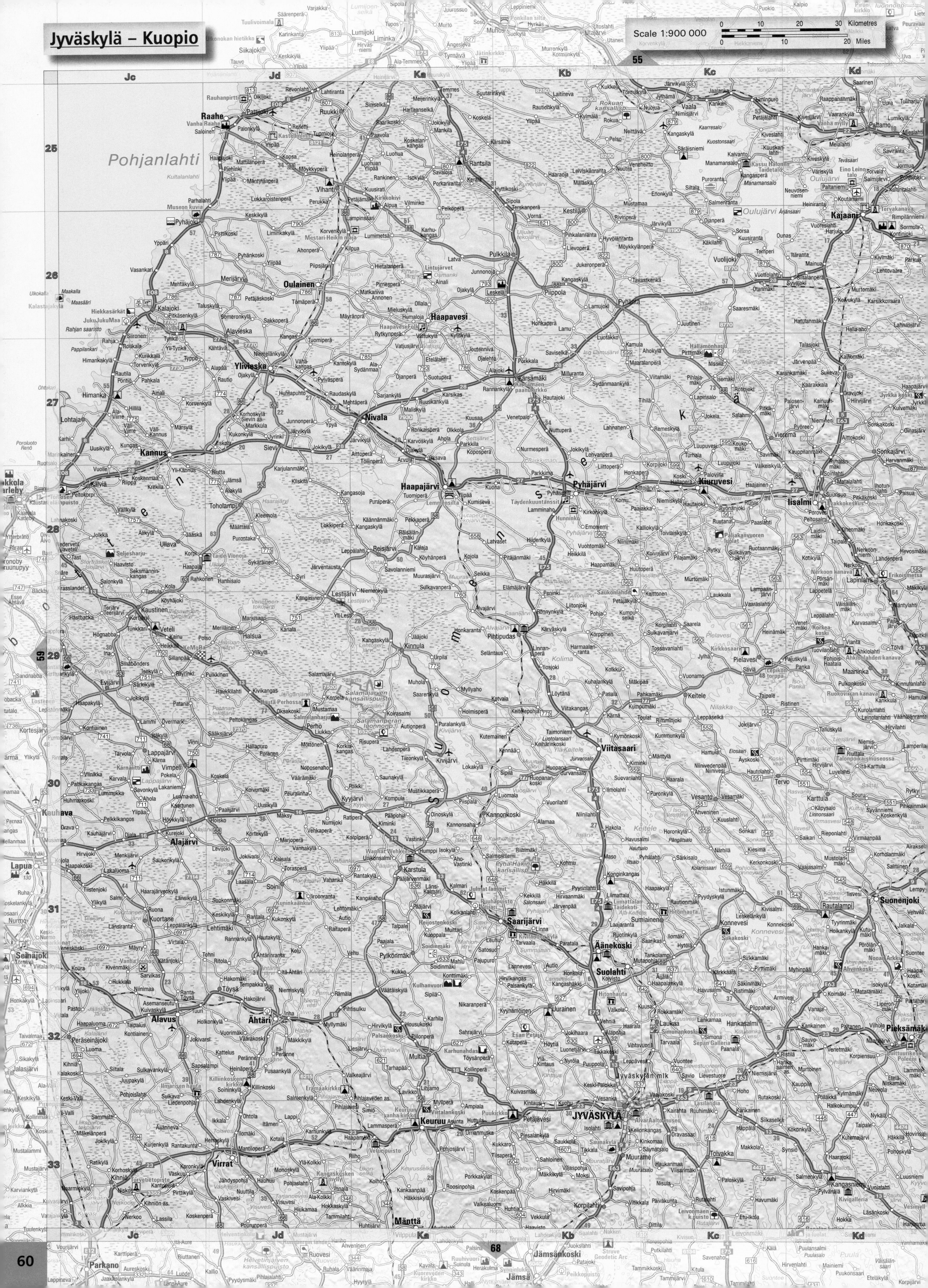

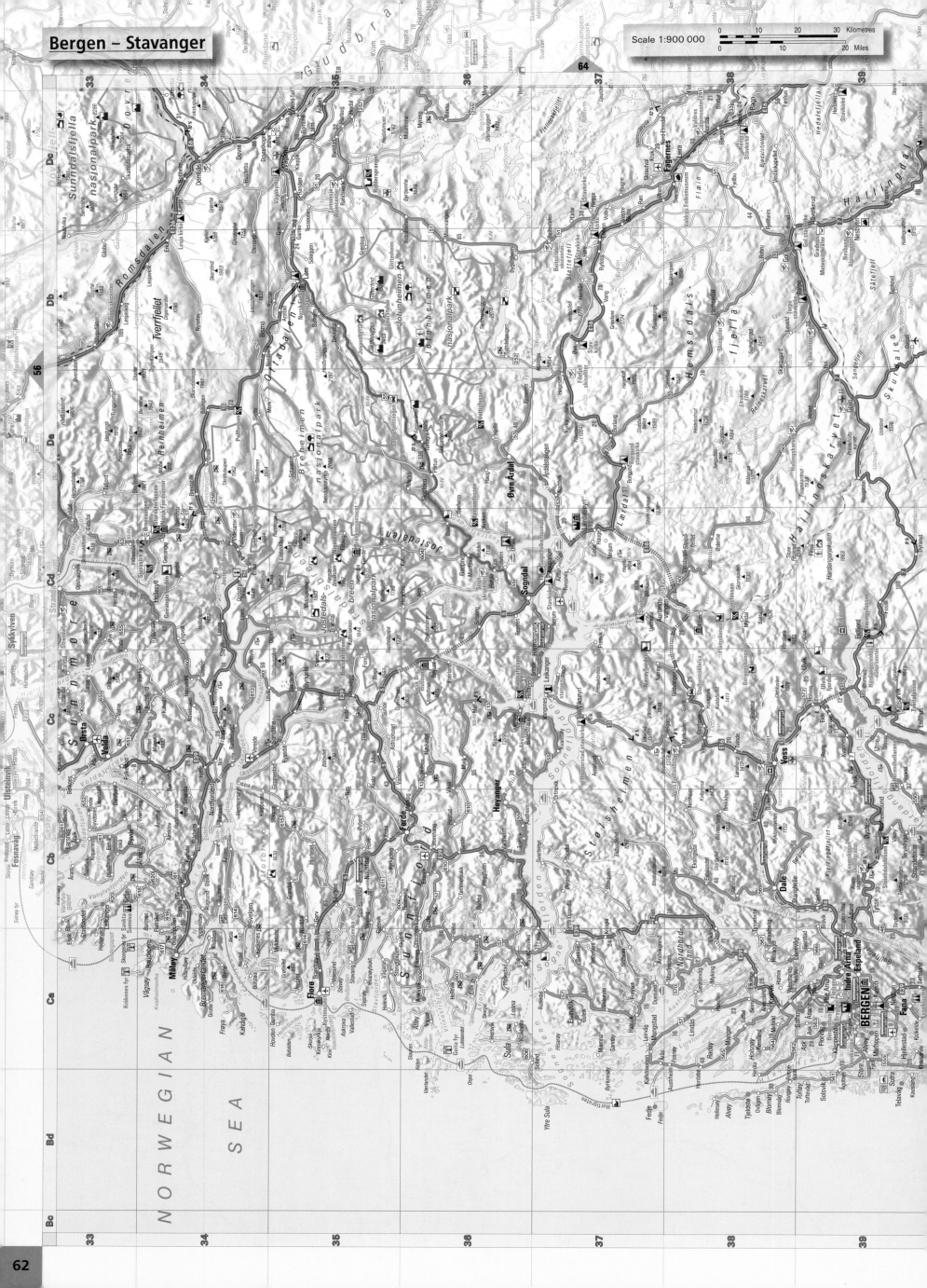

Scale 1:900 000

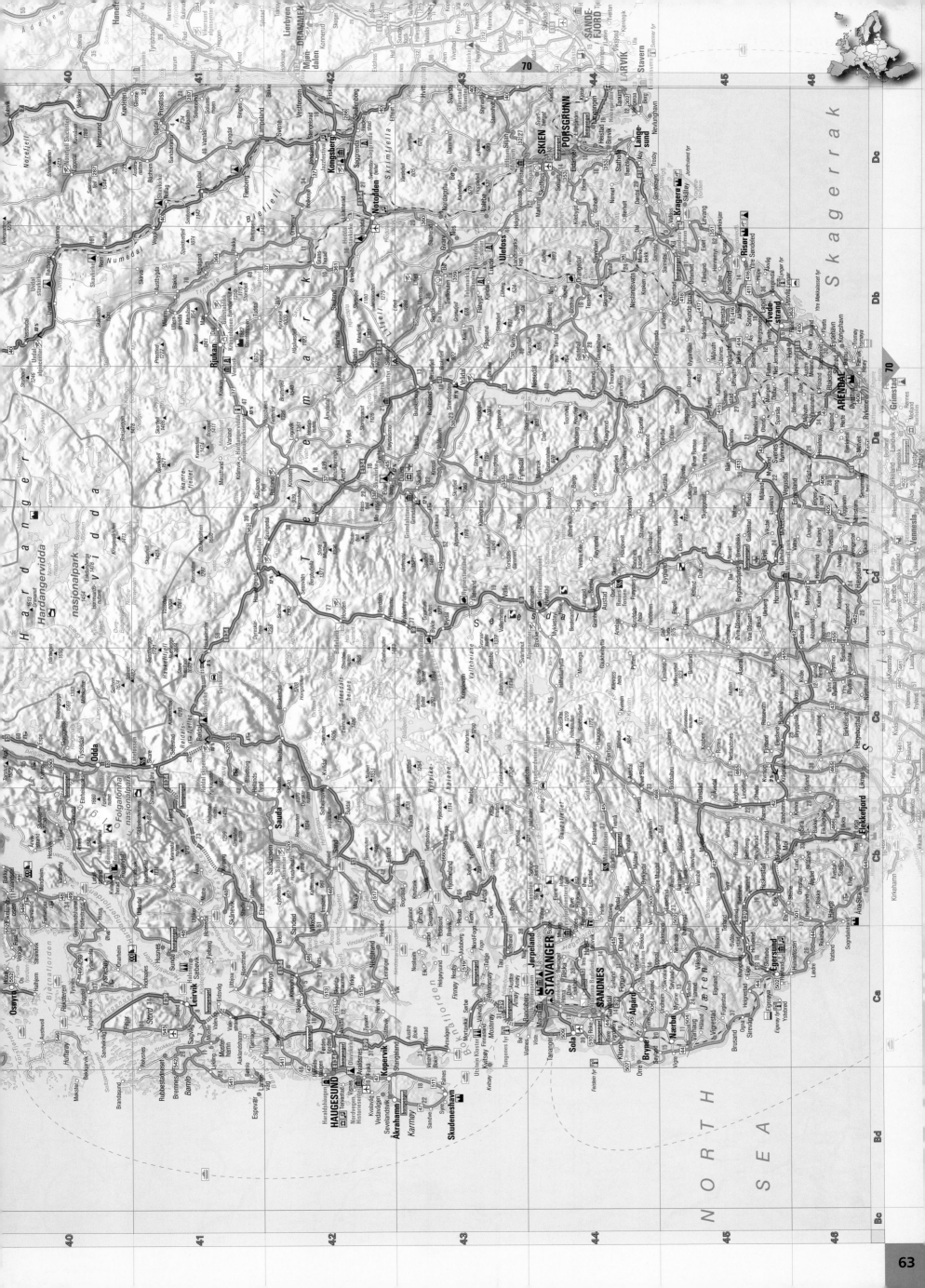

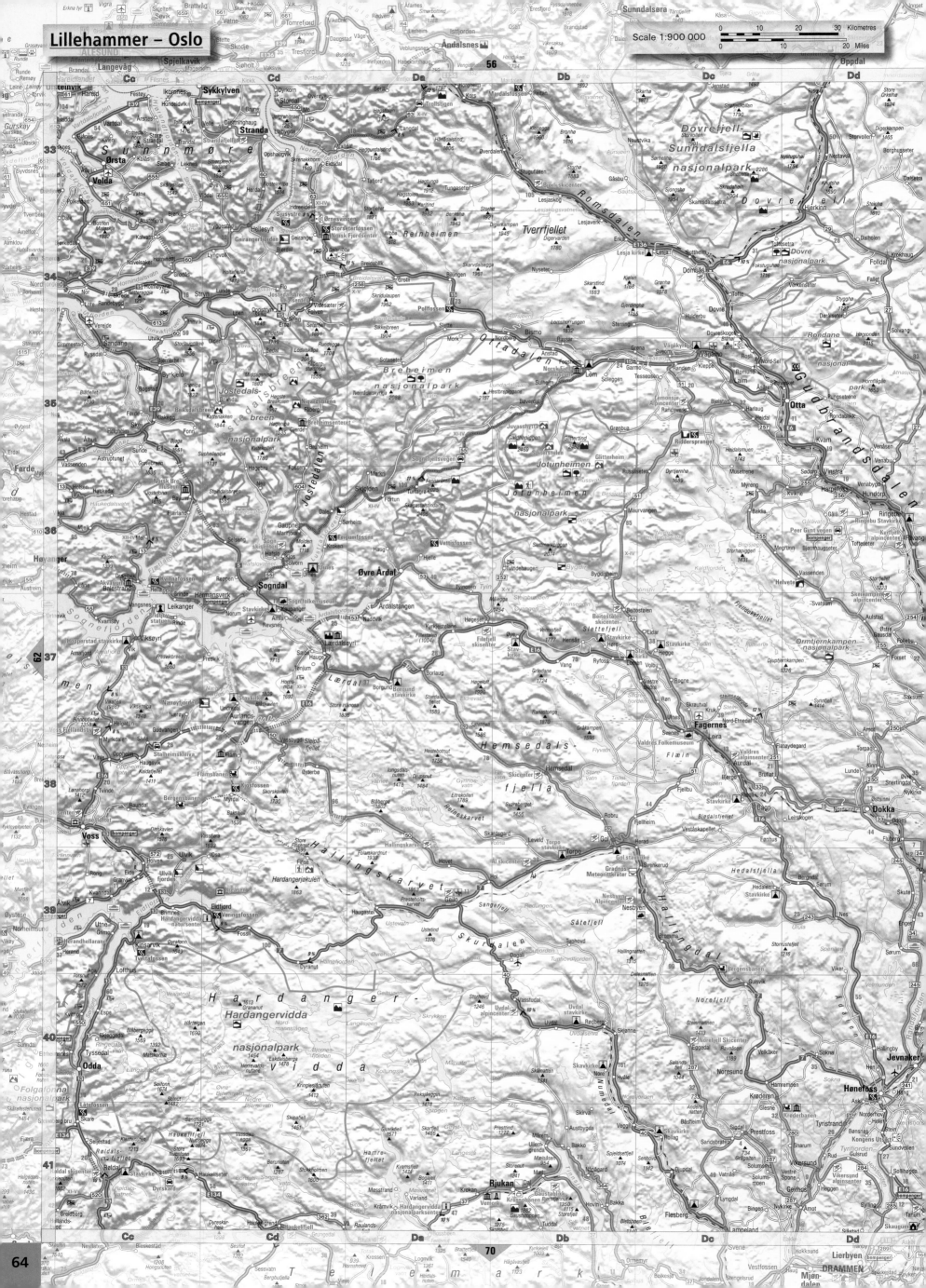

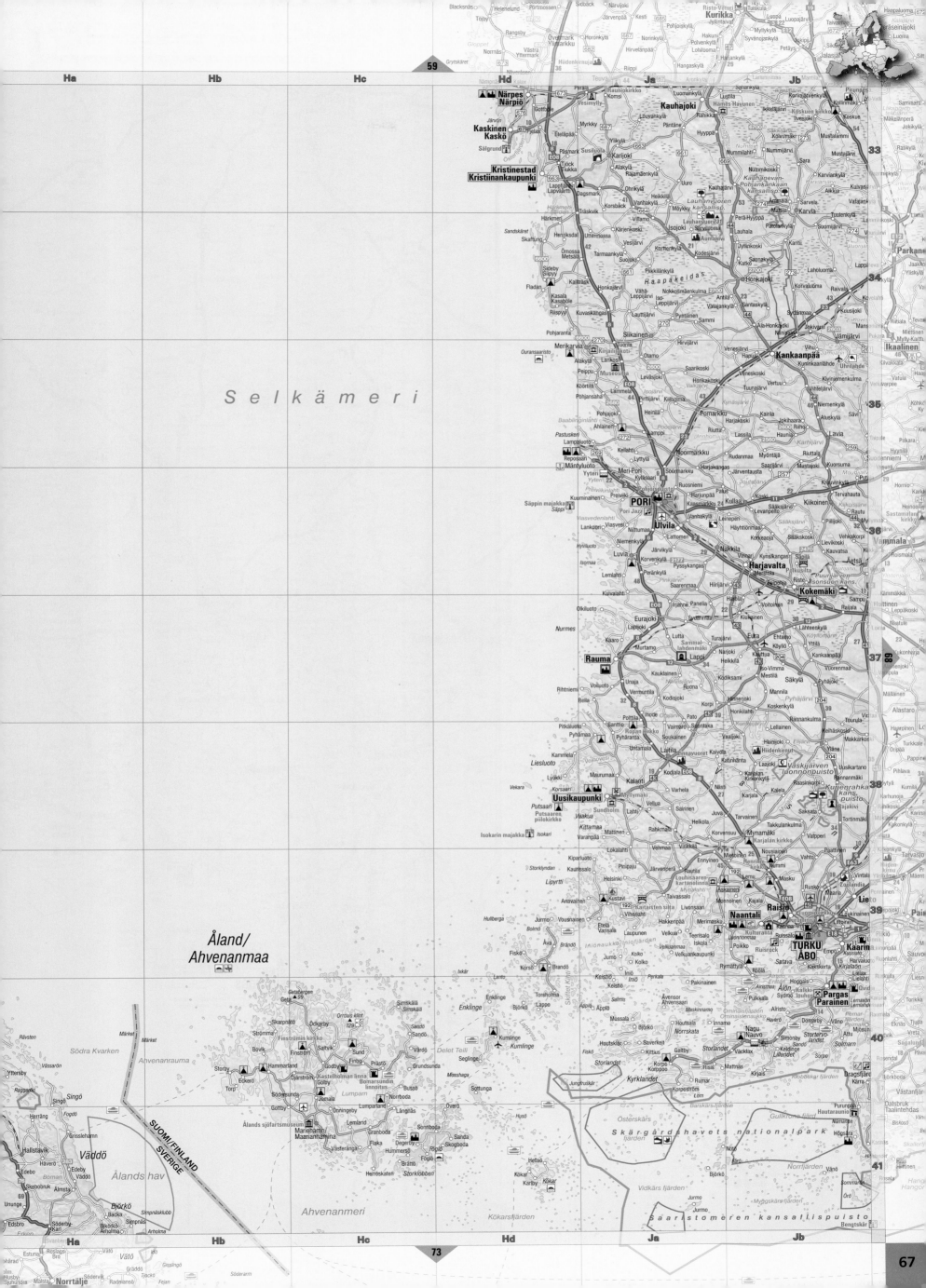

Scale 1:900 000

LAÄNEMERI

Soome

Hiiumaa

Saaremaa

Riia laht

EESTI
LATVIJA

Rigas juras licis

TALLINN

Haapsalu

Kuressaare

PÄRNU

Rapla

VENTSPILS

Talsi

RĪGA

Jūrmala

Sigulda

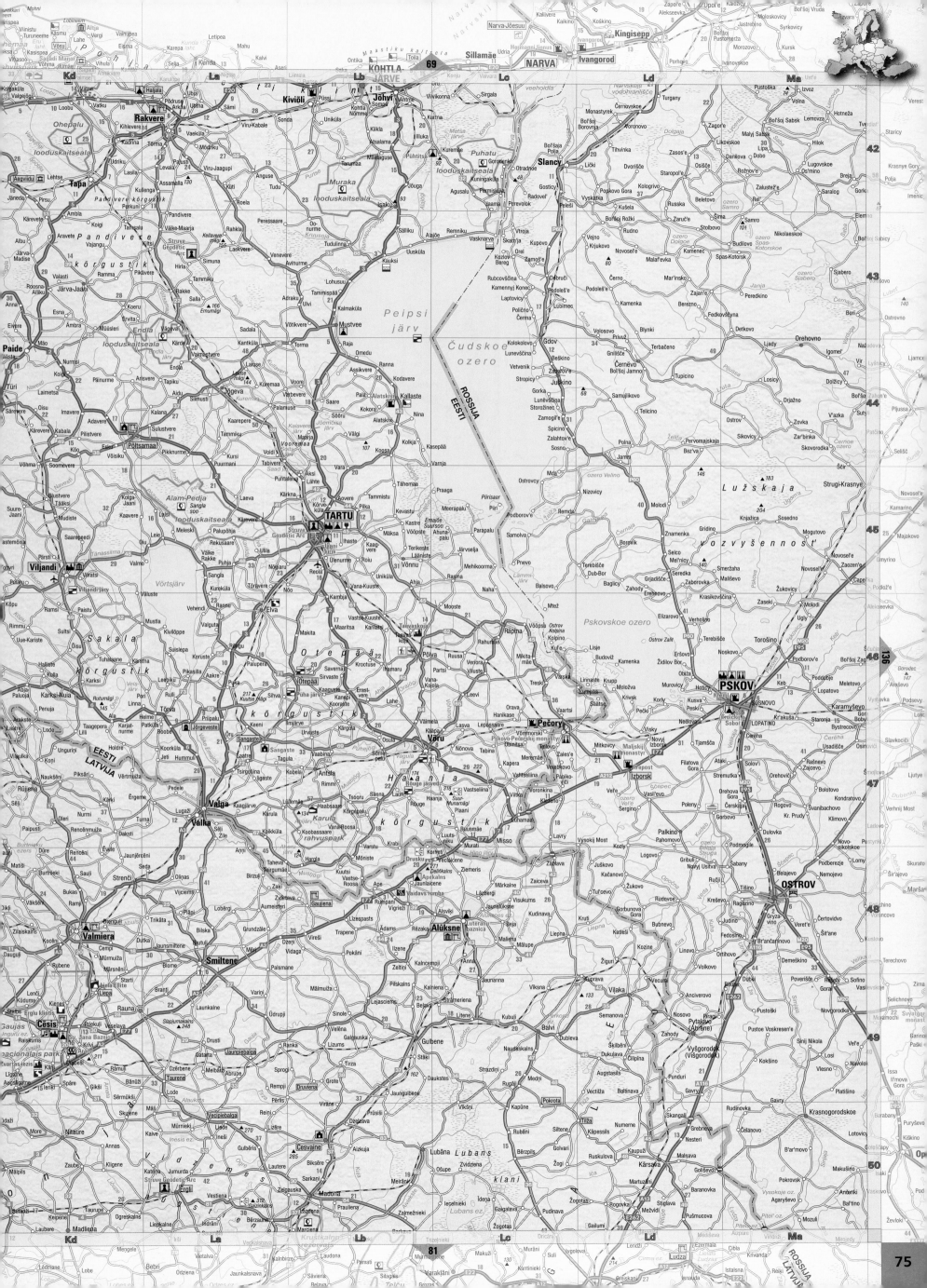

Scale 1:900 000

0    10    20    30 Kilometres
0         10         20 Miles

70 Hanstholm

Cb          Cc          Cd          Da          Db          Dc

51

Nationalpark Thy
Nordsøakvariet
Nørre Vorupør

Thy          Thisted
Nykøbing
Mors          Aars          AALBORG

N O R D -

52

Lemvig
Skive          Hobro

Struer

53

N O R D -          Holstebro          Viborg          RANDERS

S Ø E N          J Y L L A N D

Herning          Silkeborg

Ringkøbing          Ikast          AARHUS

54

Skjern          Skanderborg

Odder

Horsens

55

Grindsted          Legoland          Vejle

Varde

Juelsminde

Esbjerg          Vejen          Kolding          FYN

56          Fanø          Middelfart

Fredericia

ODENSE

Nationalpark
Vadehavet          Ribe          Haderslev

Rømø

57          Aabenraa          Nordborg

Sønderborg

Sylt          Tønder          Als

58          Nationalpark

FLENSBURG

Føhr

N O R D -          Nationalpark

59

S E E          Husum          Schleswig

Eckernförde

Cb          Cc          Cd          Da          Db          Dc

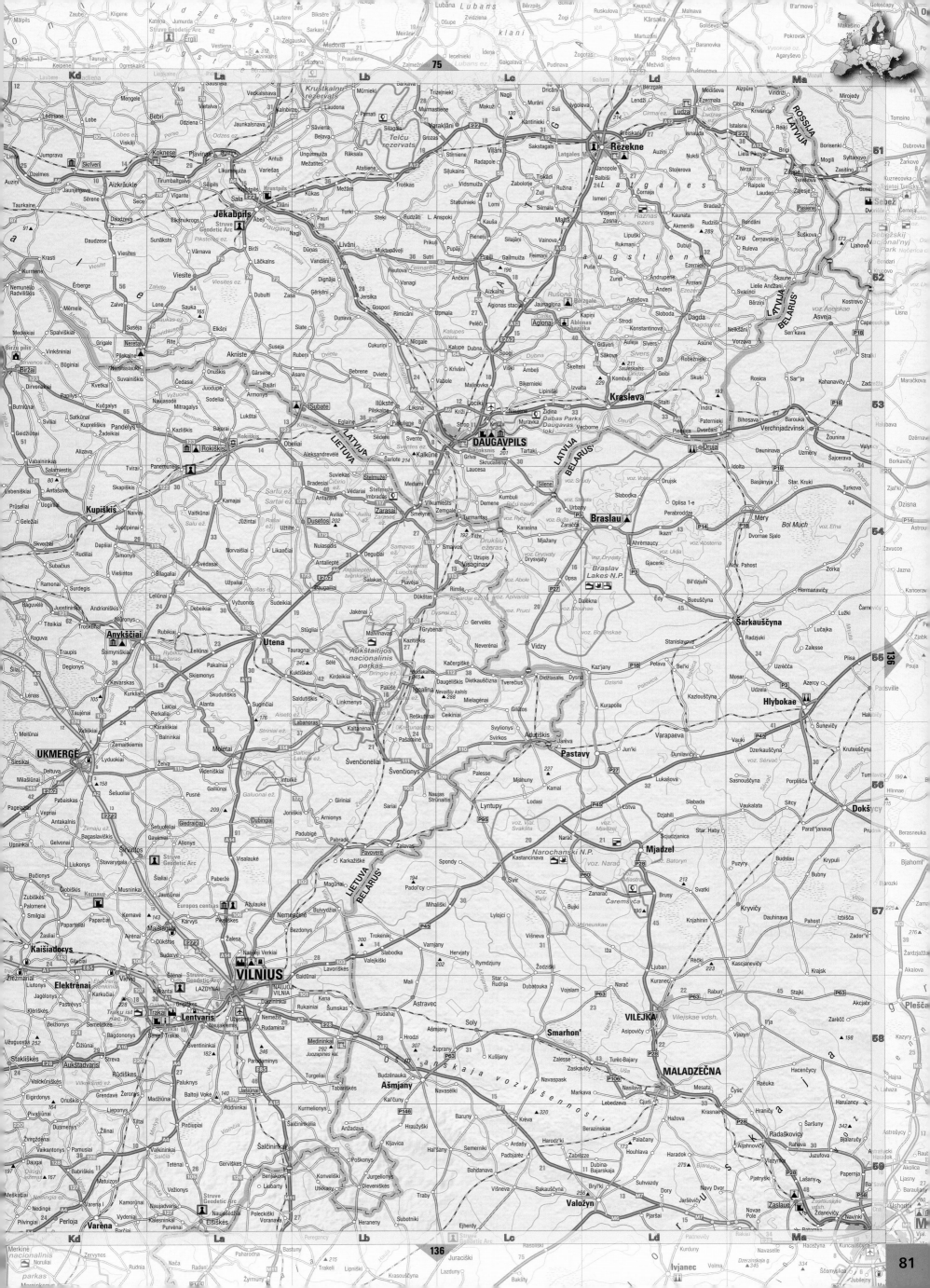

Scale 1:900 000

0   10   20   30 Kilometres
0        10       20 Miles

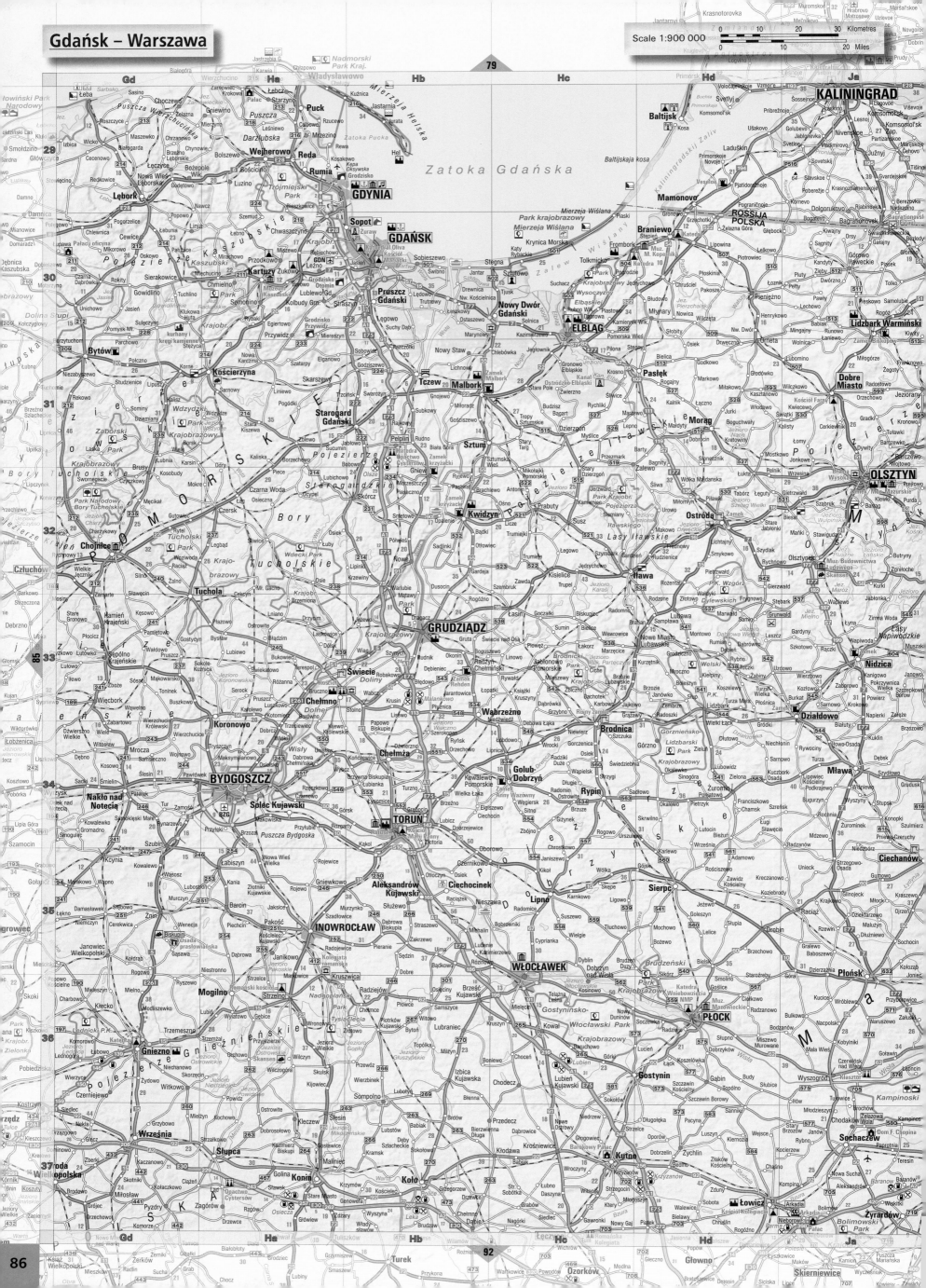

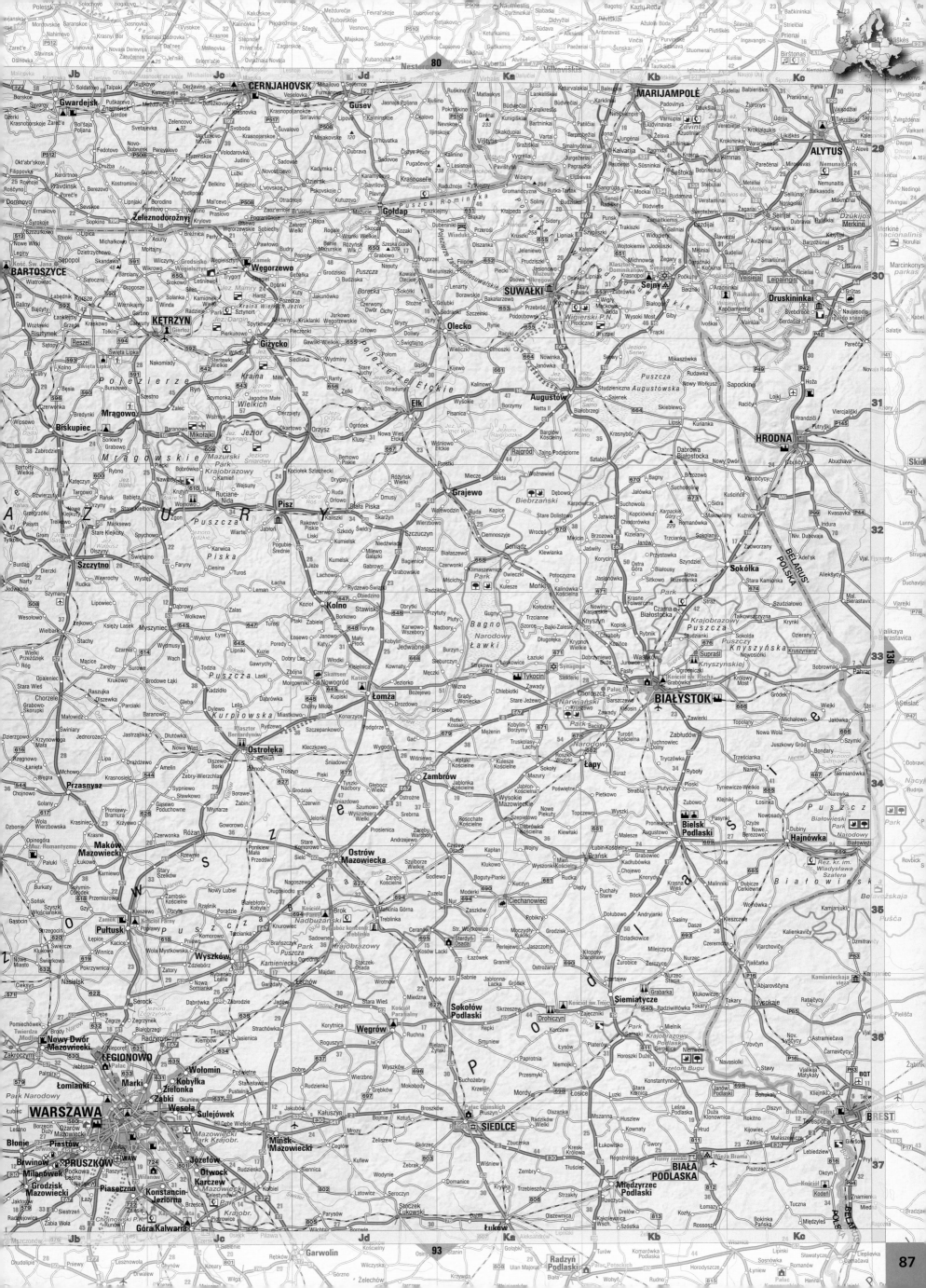

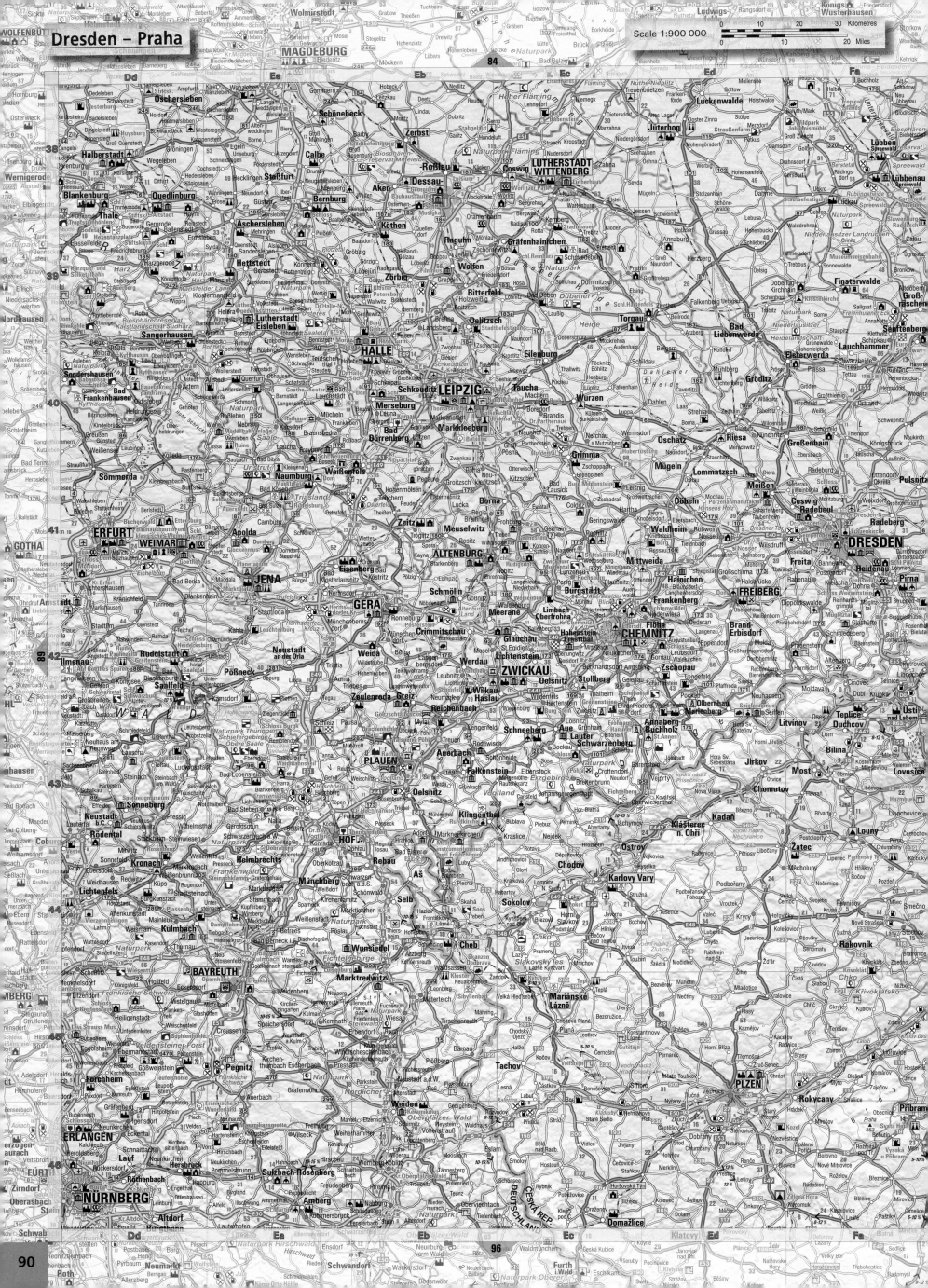

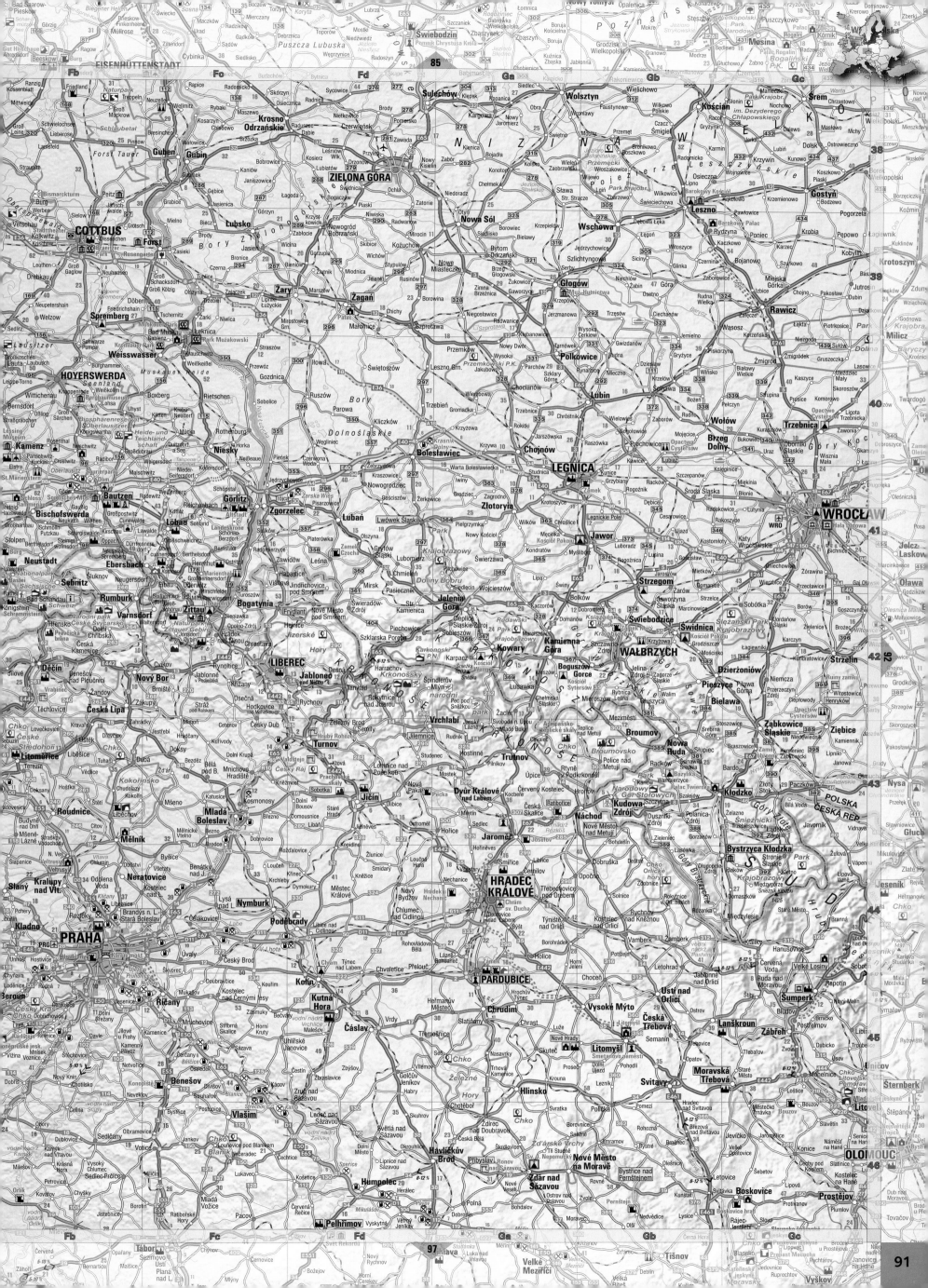

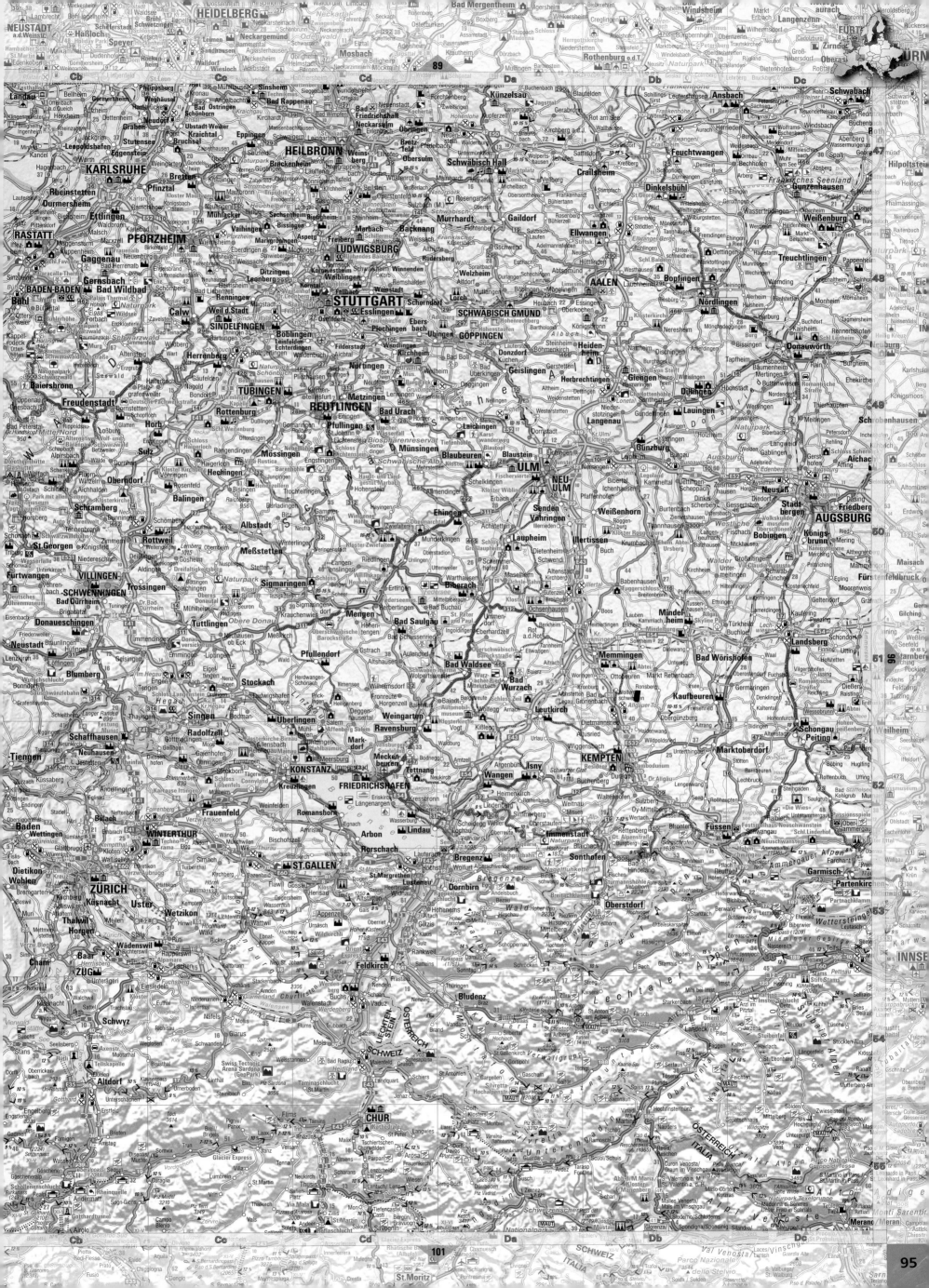

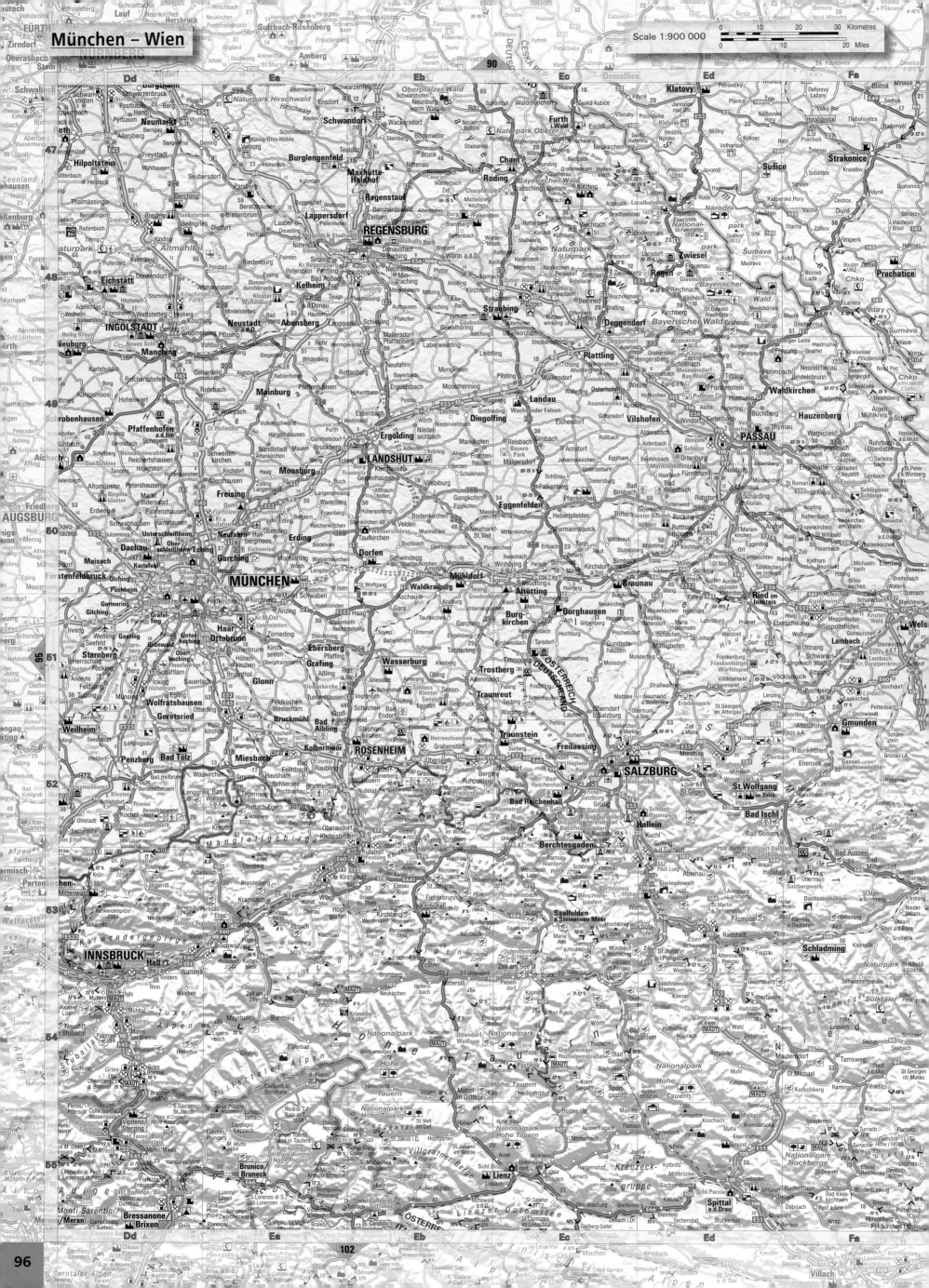

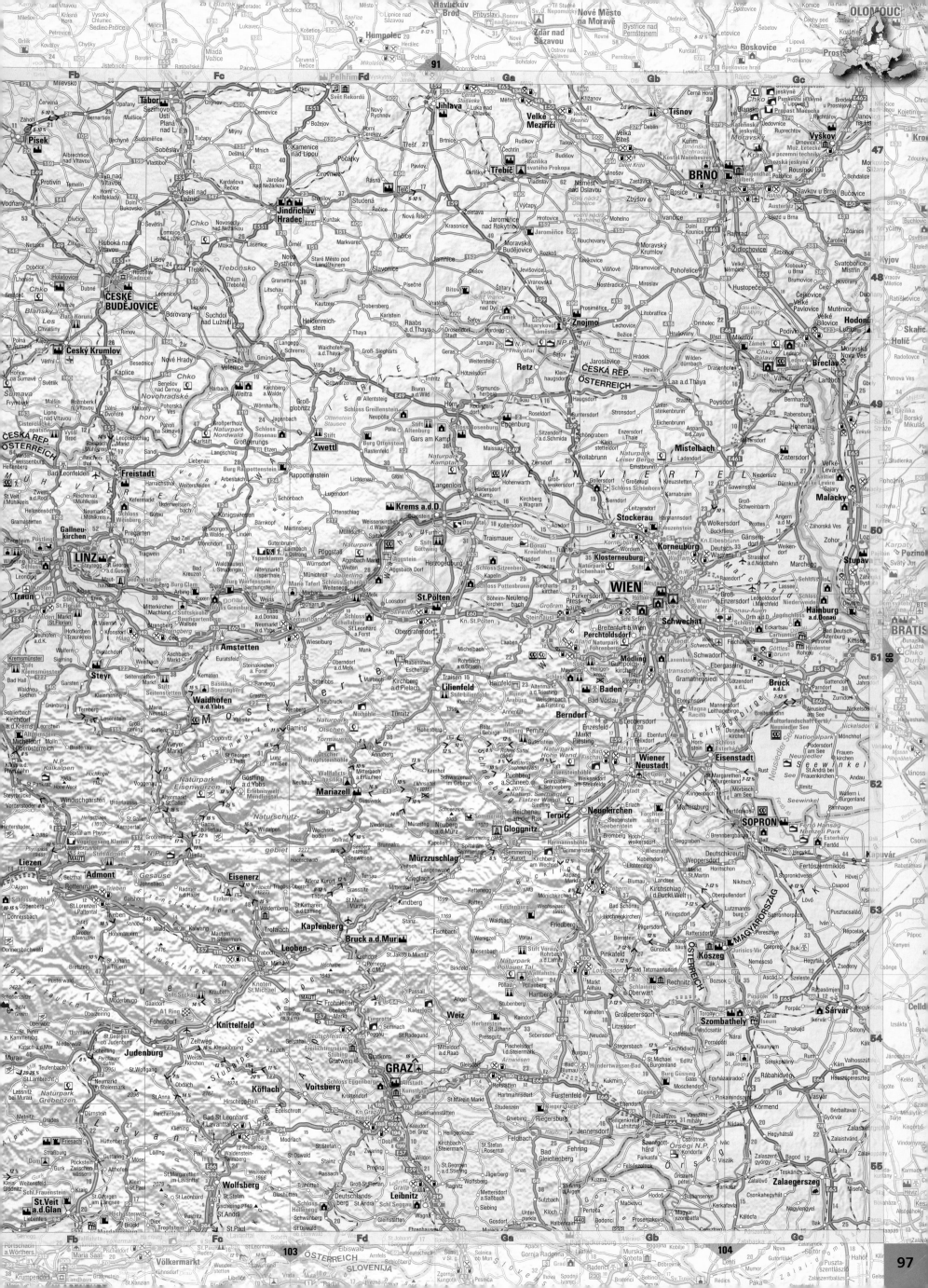

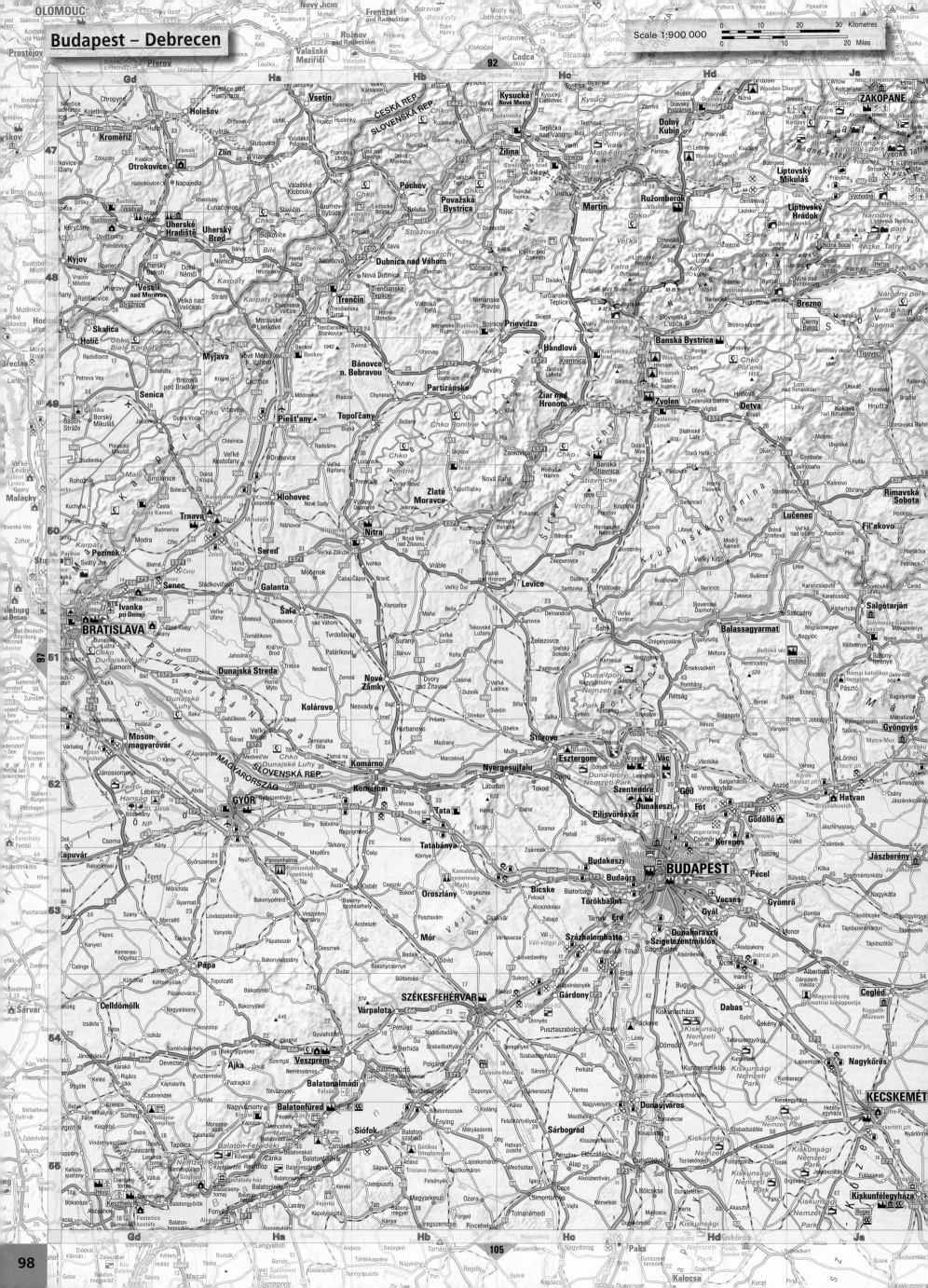

Scale 1:900 000

0 10 20 30 Kilometres
0 10 20 Miles

LAUSANNE
Lac Léman
GENÈVE
Annemasse
ANNECY
Aix-les-Bains
CHAMBÉRY
GRENOBLE
AOSTA
Valle d'Aosta
BIELLA
IVREA
VERCELLI
TORINO
MONCALIERI
Chieri
PINEROLO
Briançon
Gap
Embrun
CUNEO
Mondovì
ASTI
Alba
Acqui Terme
CASALE Monferrato
SAVONA
Finale Ligure
Albenga
Alassio
SANREMO
IMPERIA
Bordighera
Menton
MONACO
Monte-Carlo
NICE
ANTIBES
Riviera di Ponente

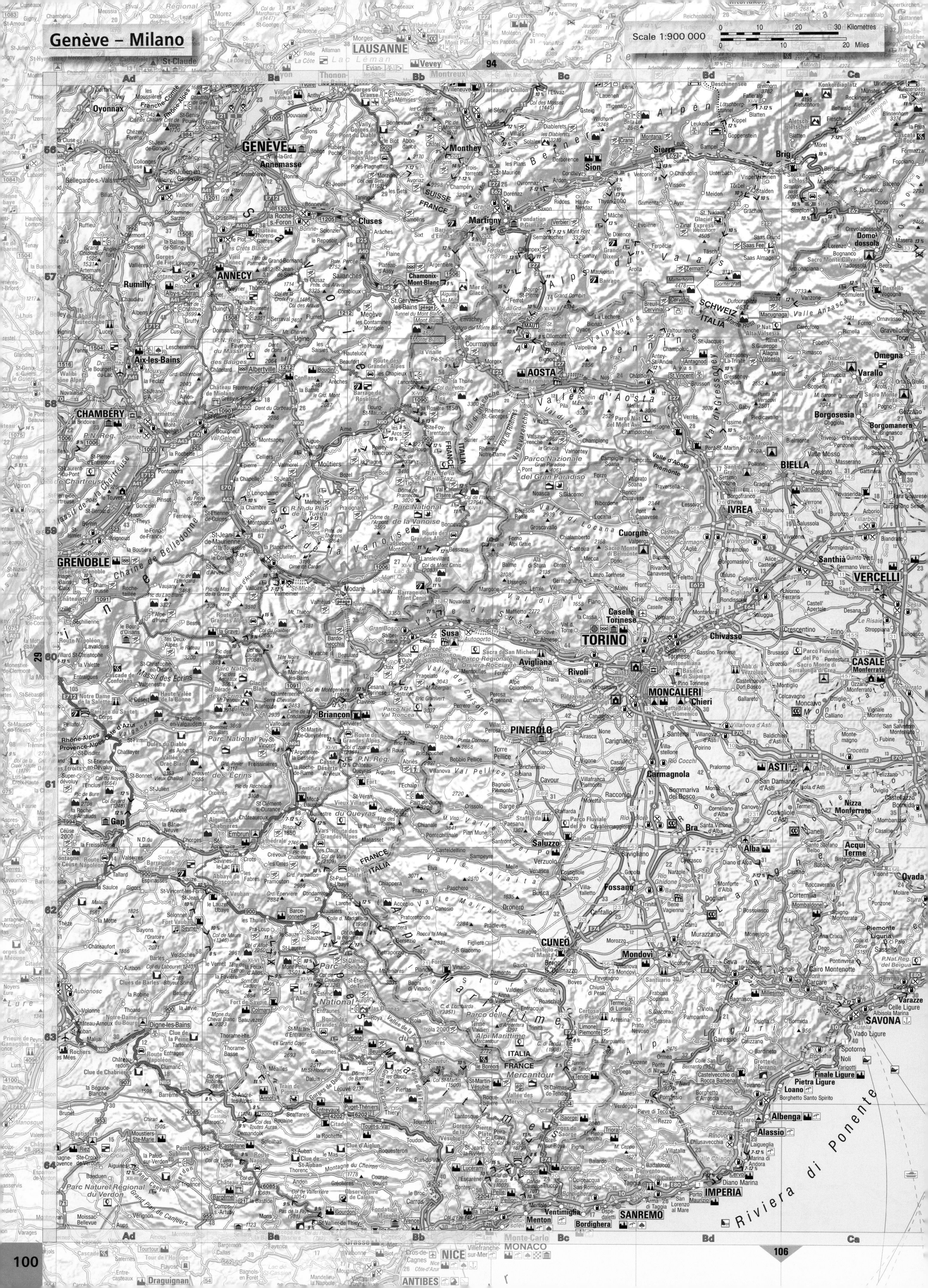

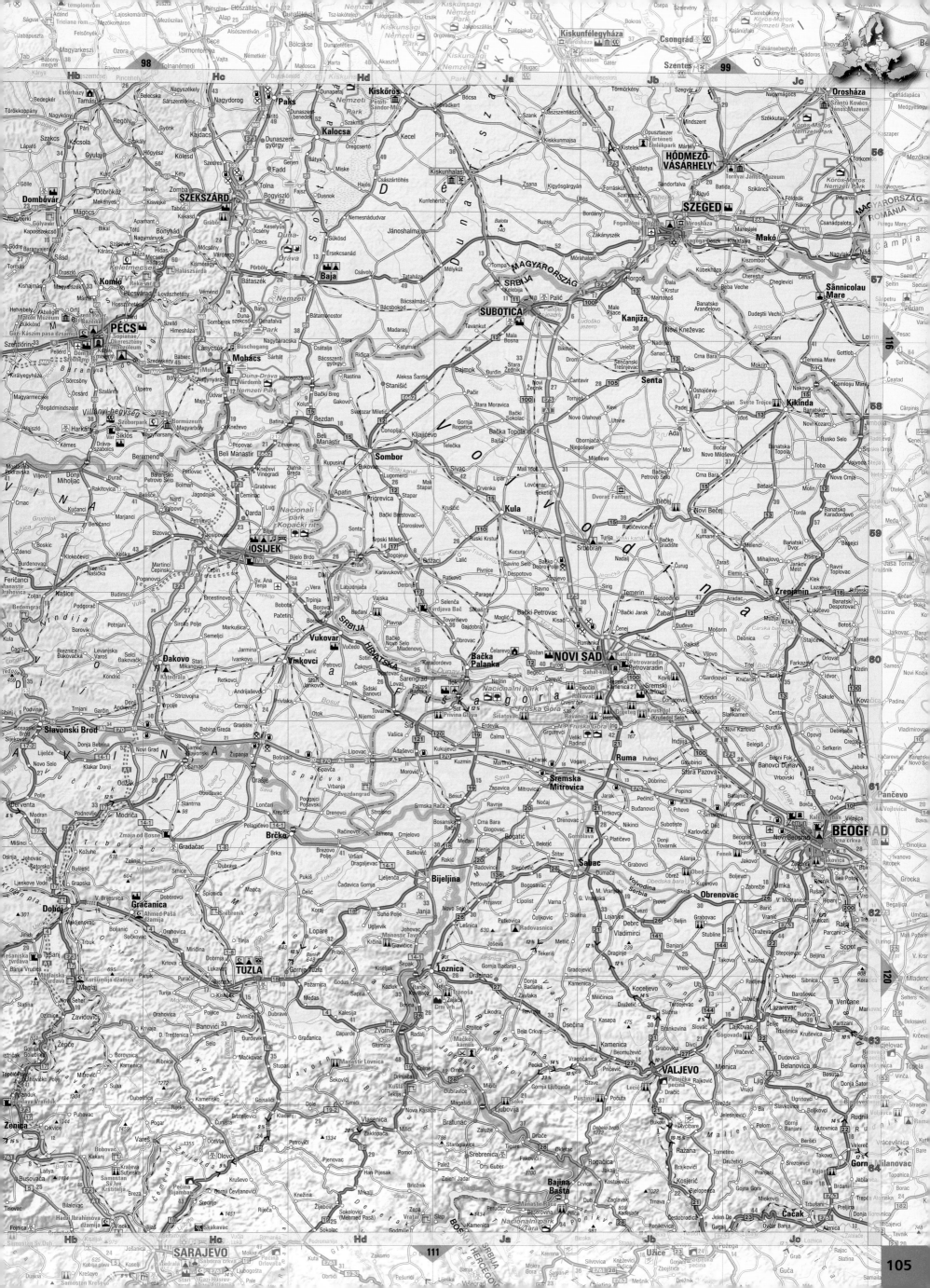

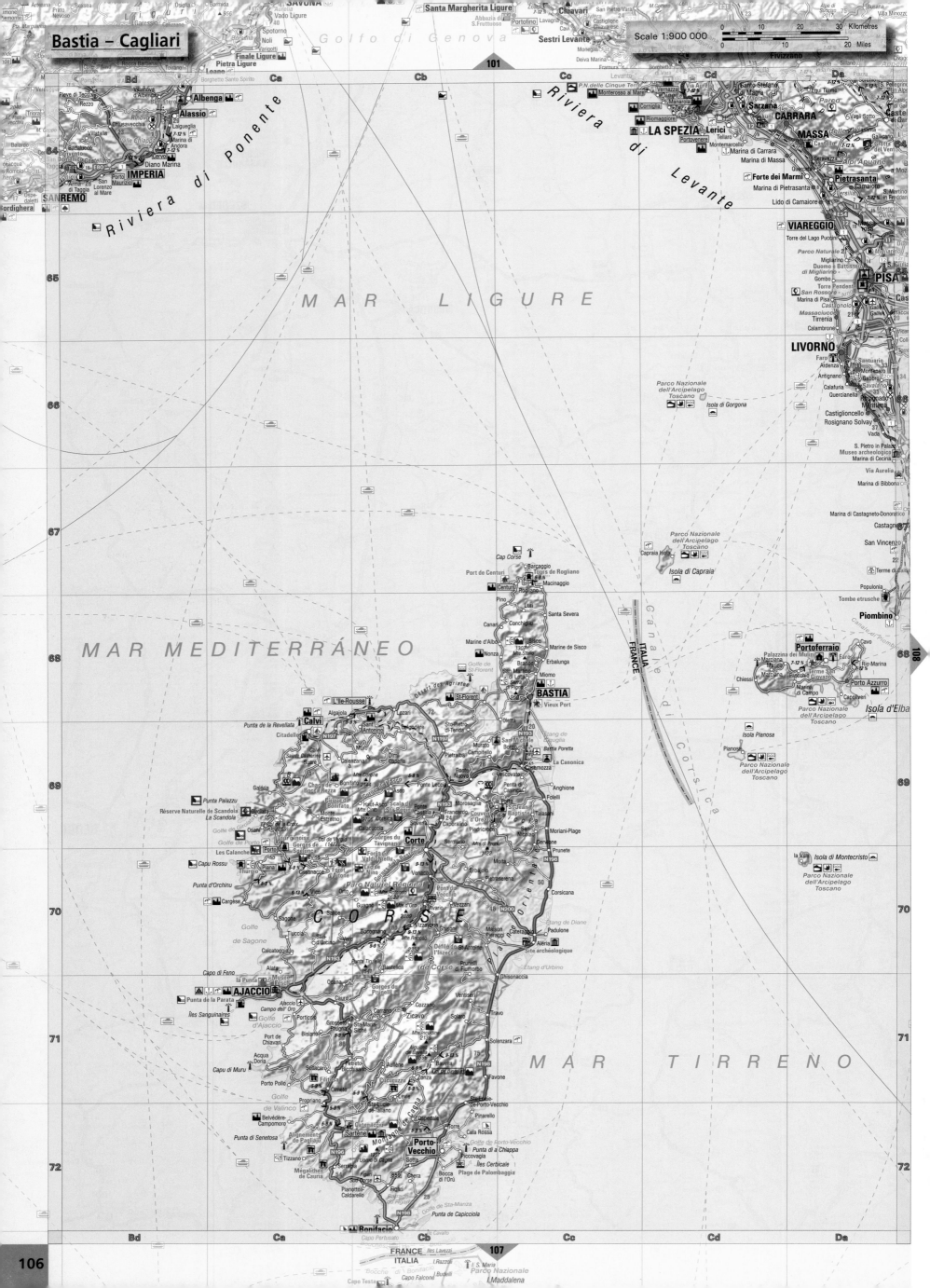

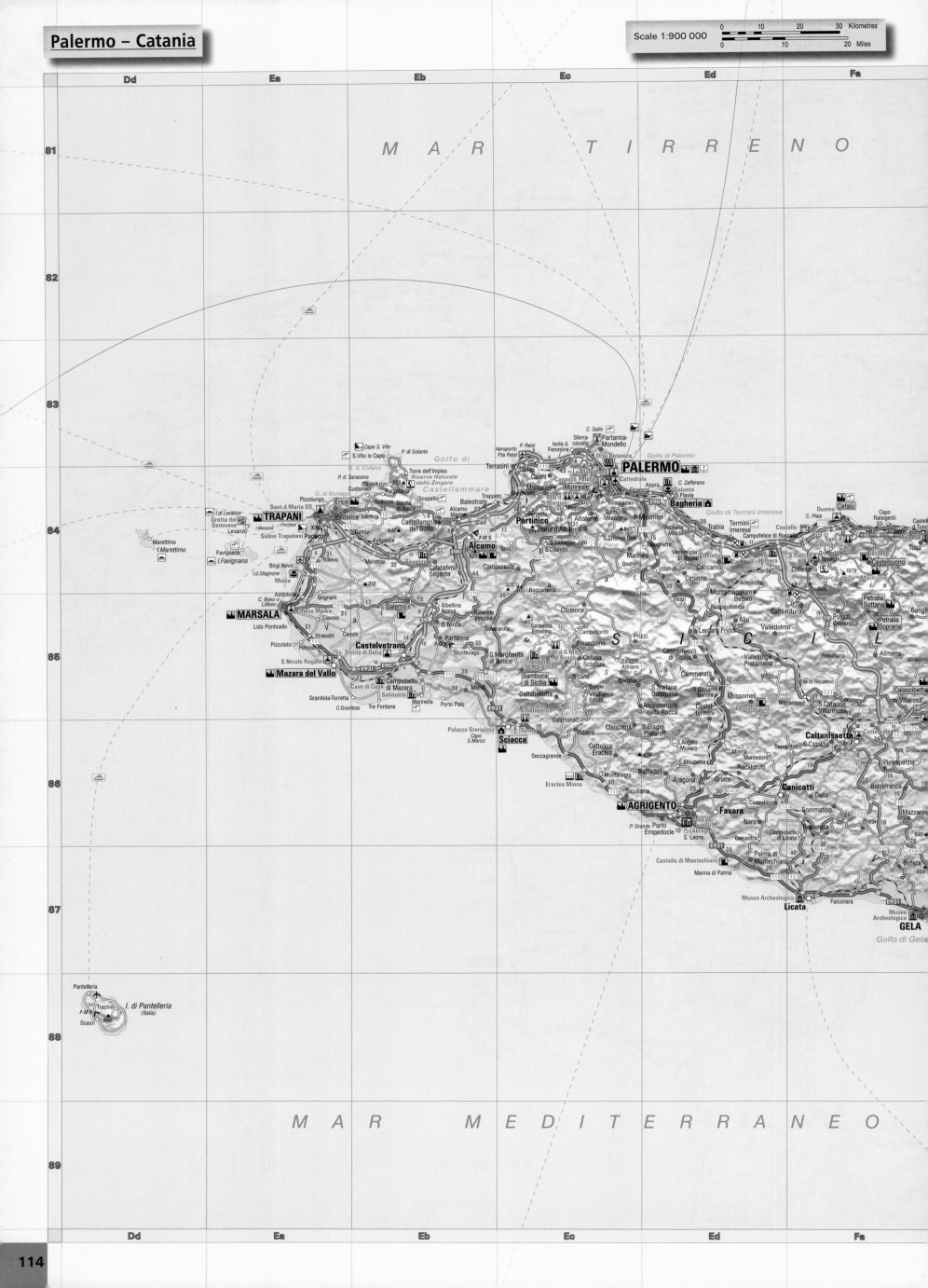

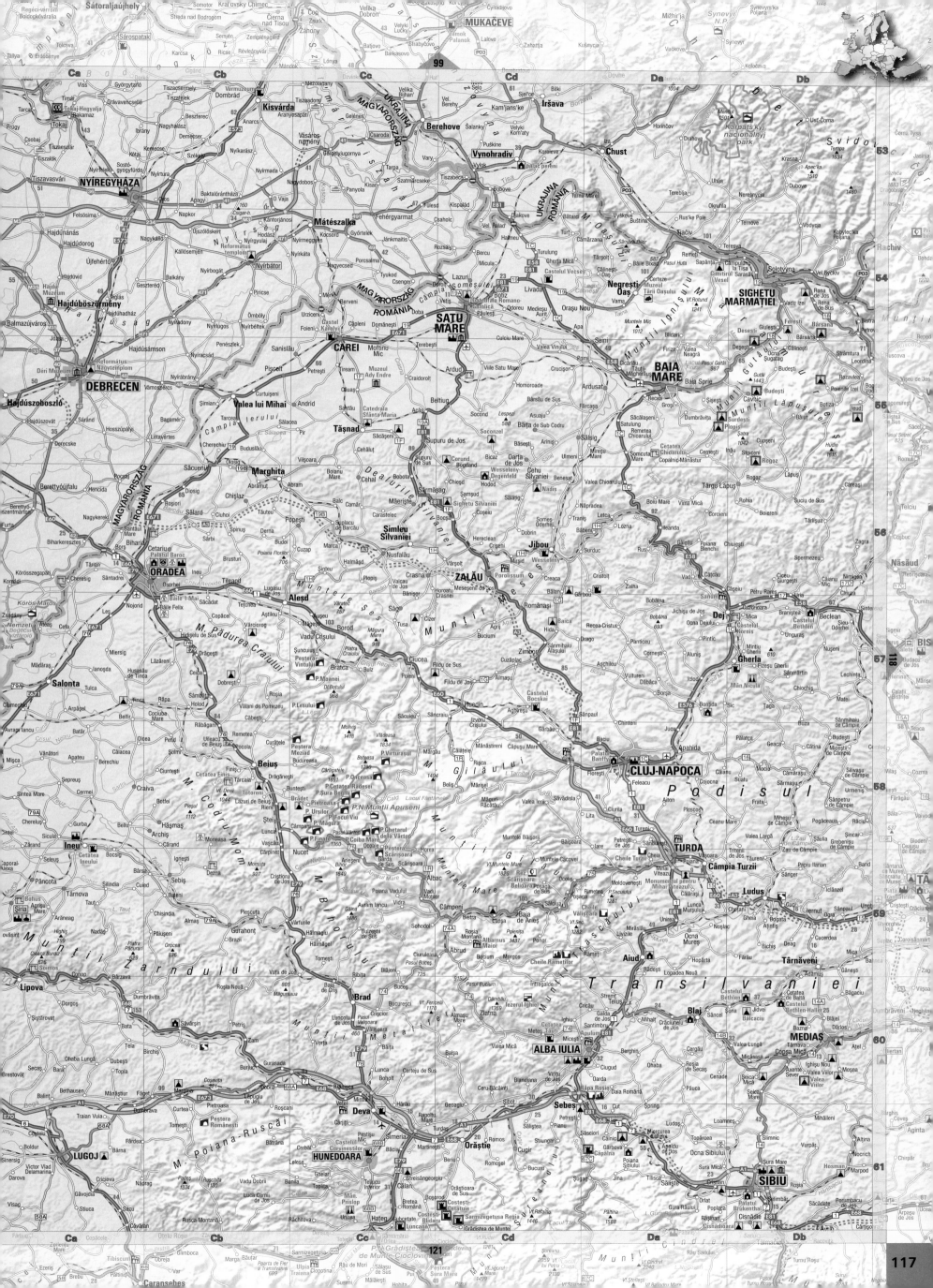

Scale 1:900 000

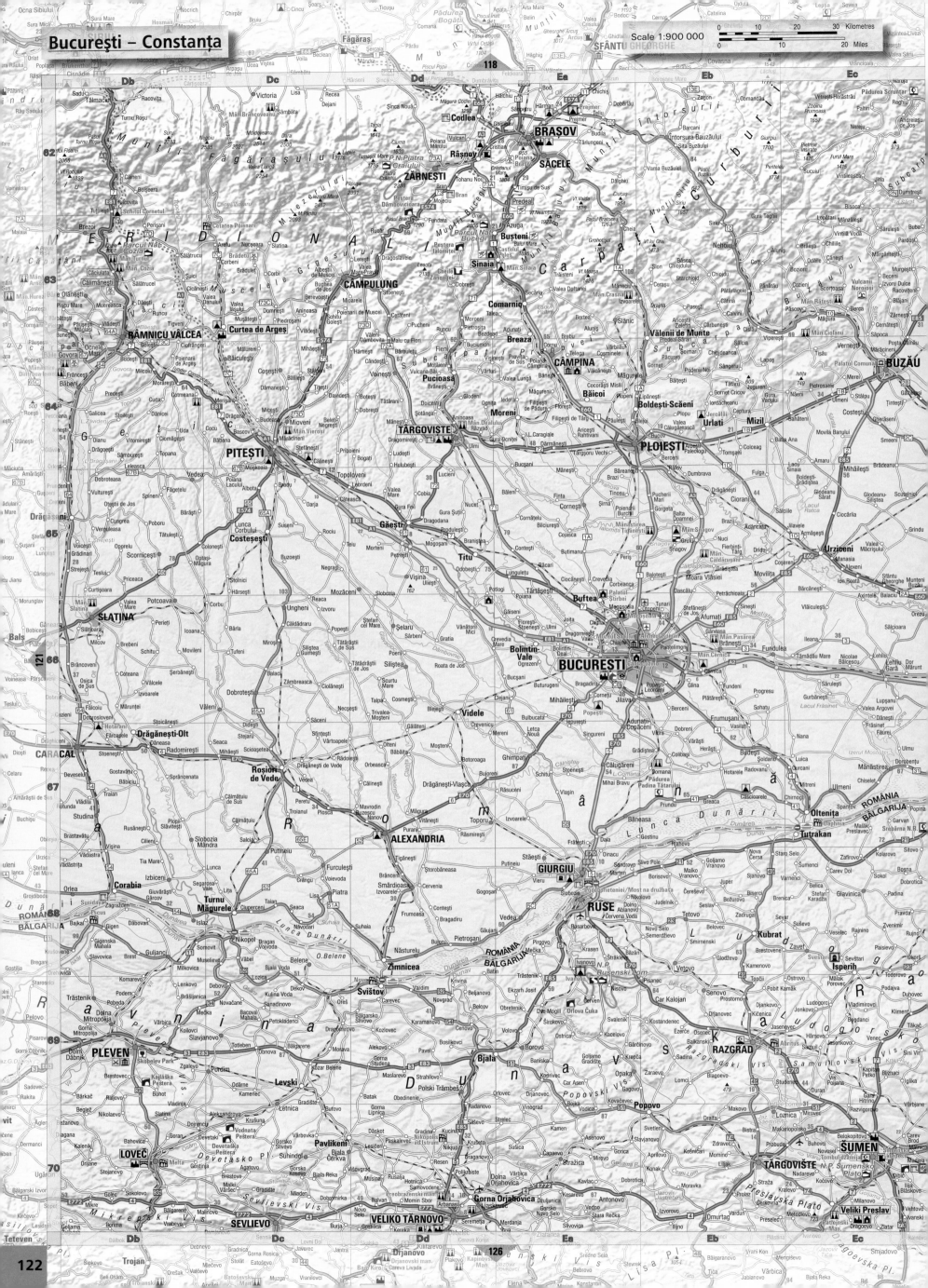

DETI ADRIATIC

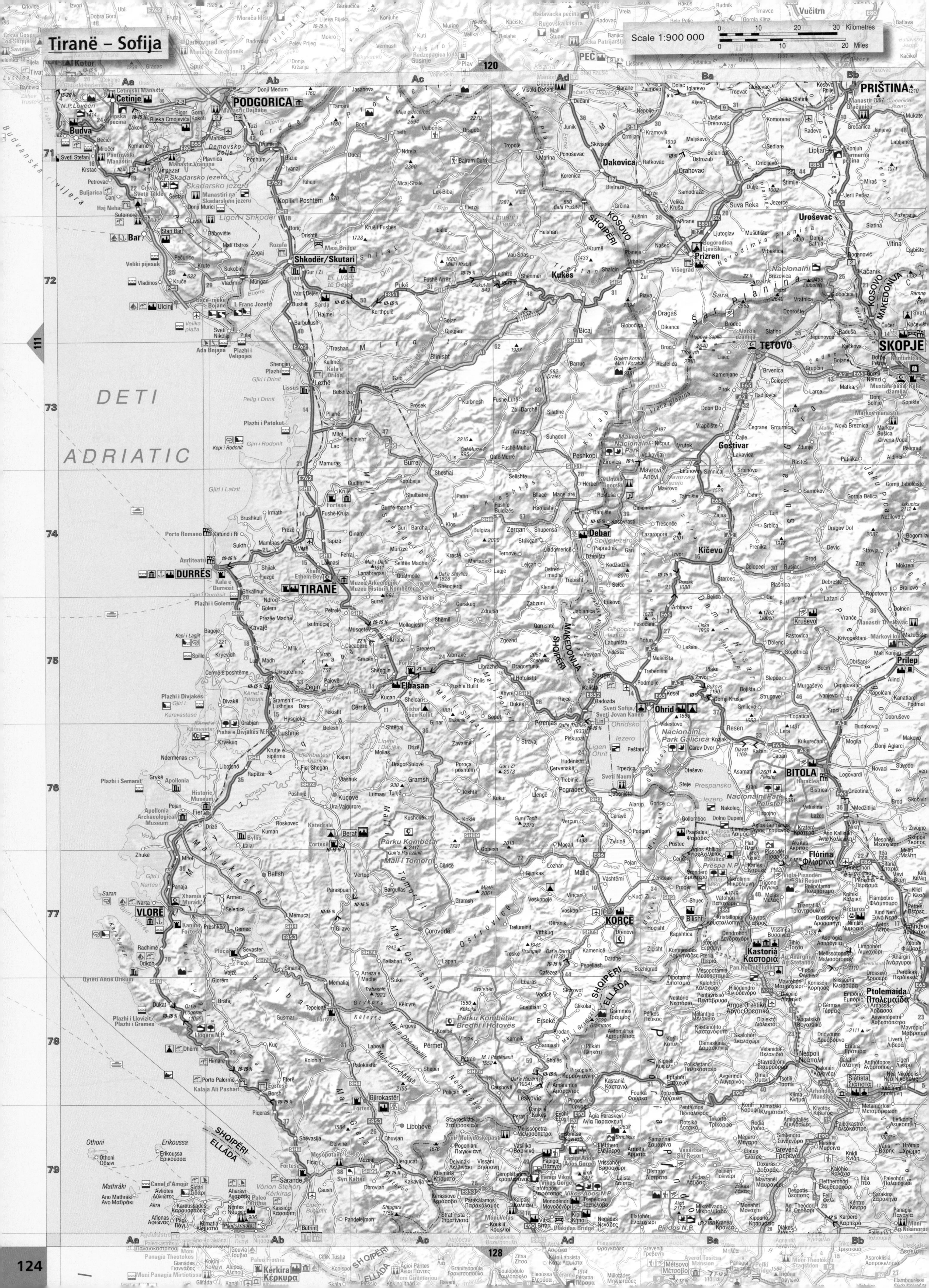

Budvanska civilijera

PRIŠTINA

PODGORICA

Kotor
Budva
Sveti Stefan
Cetinje
Bar
Ulcin

Shkodër/Skutari
Puké
Kukës

Dakovica
Prizren
Uroševac

TETOVO
SKOPJE
Gostivar
Debar
Kičevo

DURRËS
TIRANË
Elbasan
Ohrid
Struga

BITOLA

Prilep

Lushnjë
Fier
Berat
Korçë

Kastoría
Καστοριά

Flórina
Φλώρινα

Ptolemaída
Πτολεμαΐδα

VLORË

Gjirokastër
Sarandë

SHQIPËRI
ELLÁDA

Kérkira
Κέρκυρα

Scale 1:900 000

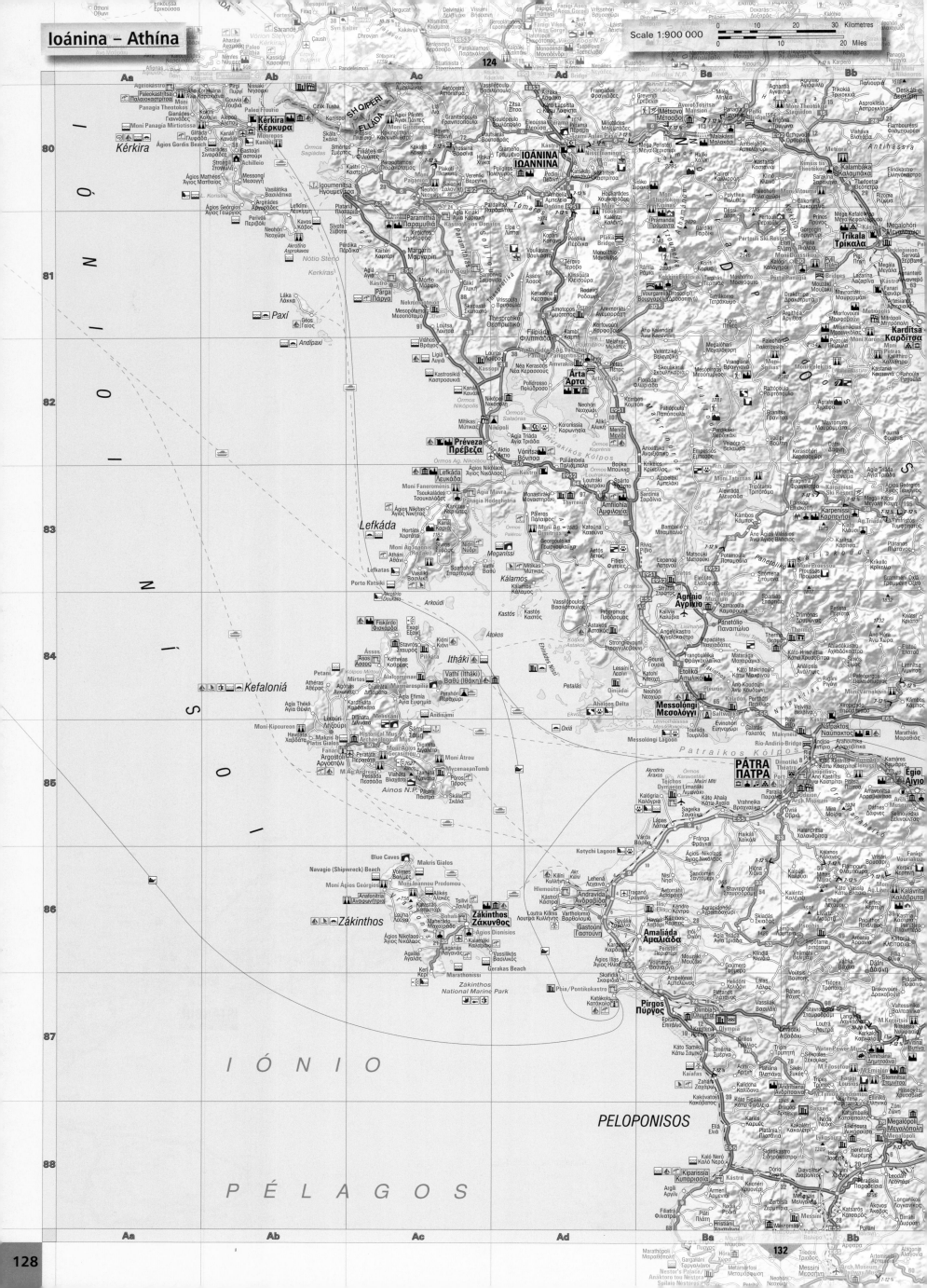

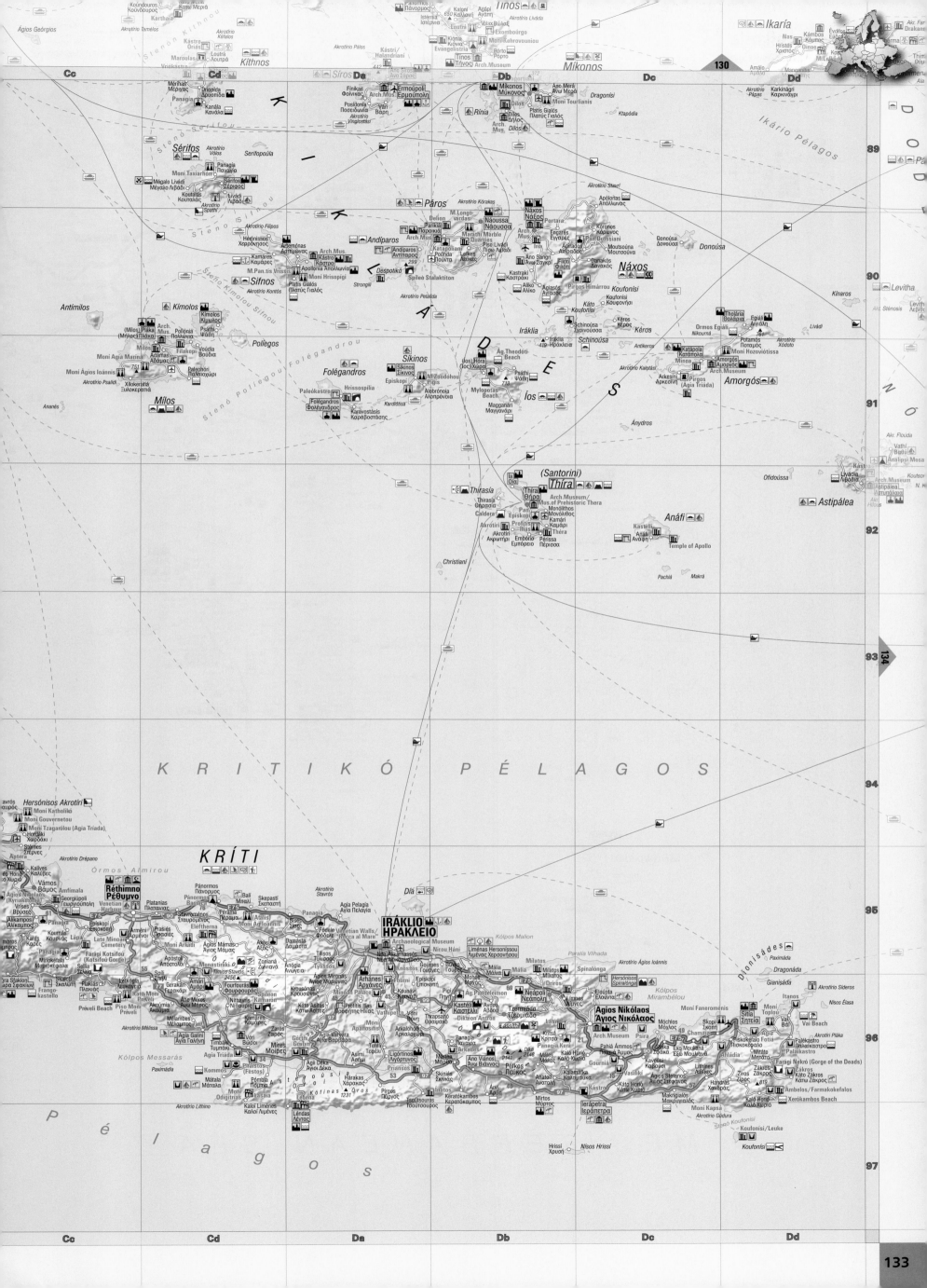

# Index Europe

138

Åsen – Bergama

Åsen N 64 Cc33
Åsen S 59 Hb26
Åsen S 65 Fb38
Asendorf D 83 Cd35
Asenovgrad BG 126 Db74
Asevelikylä FIN 59 Jb32
Asfordby GB 13 Fb24
Åsgårdstrand N 71 Dd43
Ash GB 16 Fd28
Ashbourne GB 13 Ed23
Ashbourne IRL 7 Cd21
Ashburton GB 14 Dd31
Ashbury GB 15 Ed28
Ashby-de-la-Zouch GB 13 Fa24
Ashdon GB 16 Fd26
Ashford GB 16 Ga29
Ashford IRL 7 Cd22
Ashford-in-the-Water GB 13 Ed22
Ashill GB 16 Ga24
Ashington GB 11 Fa16
Ashington GB 16 Fc30
Ashkirk GB 11 Ec14
Ashley GB 16 Fd26
Ashmore GB 15 Ec30
Ashperton GB 15 Ec26
Ashton-in-Makerfield GB 13 Ec21
Ashton Keynes GB 15 Ed27
Ashton-under-Lyne GB 13 Ed21
Ashwater GB 14 Dc30
Ashwell GB 13 Fb24
Ashwell GB 16 Fc26
Ashwellthorpe GB 16 Gb24
Asiago I 102 Dd58
Asikkala FIN 68 Kc36
Asipovičy BY 136 Eb13
Ask N 62 Ca39
Ask N 64 Dd40
Askainen FIN 67 Ja39
Askanmäki FIN 55 Kd23
Askeaton IRL 6 Bc23
Askern GB 13 Fa21
Askerswell GB 14 Eb30
Askesta S 66 Gb37
Askett GB 15 Fb27
Asklipío GR 134 Ed93
Askvoll N 62 Ca36
As Lamas E 30 Bb58
Asma E 30 Bb56
Ašmjany BY 136 Ea12
As Neves E 30 Ad58
Asnières-sur-Vègre F 23 Fc40
Asola I 101 Da60
Asolo I 102 Ea58
Asos GR 128 Ac84
Aspås S 58 Fc30
Aspatria GB 12 Eb17
Aspe E 45 Fb71
Aspeå S 59 Ha29
Asperen NL 82 Ba37
Asperg D 95 Cd48
Aspet F 34 Ga56
Aspliden S 53 Ha23
Aspö S 72 Gb43
As Pontes de García Rodríguez E 30 Bb54
Aspra I 114 Ed84
Aspremont F 29 Jd51
Asprováltа GR 125 Cc78
Assé-le-Boisne F 23 Fc38
Assen NL 82 Bd34
Assens DK 76 Dc57
Assérac F 22 Ec41
Assisi I 109 Eb67
Åsskard N 56 Db31
Aßlar D 89 Cc42
Aßling D 96 Ea51
Asson F 33 Fc56
Assoro I 115 Fb85
Astaffort F 27 Ga53
Astakós GR 128 Ad84
Astee IRL 6 Bb23
Asten NL 88 Bb39
Astfeld I 102 Dd56
Asti I 100 Ca61
Astipálea GR 134 Ea92
Aston GB 13 Fa22
Aston GB 15 Fa27
Astorga E 31 Cb57
Astradamovka RUS 137 Fd10
Ástros GR 129 Bd88
Astruptunet N 62 Cc35
Astryna BY 136 Dd13
Astudillo E 32 Db58
Asuni I 107 Ca77
Asuny PL 87 Jc30
Ászár H 98 Ha53
Aszófő H 98 Ha55
Atajate E 43 Cb76
Atalánti GR 129 Ca84
Atalaya del Cañavate E 38 Eb67
Atarte E 44 Db75
Ateca E 33 Ec61
Ateham GB 13 Ec24
Atella I 112 Ga75
Atena Lucana I 112 Ga76
Atessa I 109 Fb71
Atháni GR 128 Ac83
Athboy IRL 5 Cc20
Áth Cinn IRL 4 Bc20
Athea IRL 6 Bb23
Athée F 25 Jc42
Athen = Athína GR 129 Cb86
Athenry IRL 6 Bd21
Atherstone GB 13 Fa24
Athies F 20 Ha33
Athína GR 129 Cb86
Athleague IRL 4 Ca20
Athlone IRL 6 Ca21
Athy IRL 7 Cc22
Atienza E 38 Ea62
Atios E 30 Ba53
Atjaševo RUS 137 Fc10
Atlanterra E 43 Ca78
Atnmoen N 65 Ea35
Atrani I 112 Fb75
Åträsk S 54 Hc23
Atri I 109 Fa69
Atripalda I 112 Fc75
Attendorn D 89 Cb40
Attenkirchen D 96 Ea49
Attersee A 96 Ed52
Attiökylä FIN 55 Kb24
Attleborough GB 16 Ga25
Attlebridge GB 16 Gb24
Attmar S 66 Gb33
Attnang-Puchheim A 96 Fa51
Åtvidaberg S 72 Ga47
Atzara I 107 Ca77
Atzendorf D 90 Ea38
Aubagne F 29 Jd55
Aubenas F 28 Ja50
Aubenton F 21 Hd33
Aubergenville F 20 Gc36
Aubeterre-sur-Dronne F 26 Fd49
Aubiat F 24 Hb46
Aubiet F 27 Ga54
Aubigné F 23 Fc46
Aubigny F 23 Ed44
Aubigny-au-Bac F 20 Hb32
Aubigny-sur-Nère F 24 Gd41
Aubin F 27 Gd51
Aubonne CH 94 Ba55
Aubrac F 28 Hb51
Aubusson F 24 Gd46
Auby F 20 Ha31
Auch F 27 Ga54
Aucharnie GB 9 Ec08
Auchavan GB 11 Eb10
Auchel F 20 Gd31
Auchencairn GB 10 Ea17
Auchenmaig GB 10 Dc16
Auchentiber GB 10 Dd14
Auchronie GB 11 Ec10
Auchterarder GB 11 Ea12
Auchtermuchty GB 11 Eb12
Auchy-au-Bois F 20 Gd31
Auderville F 19 Ed34
Audierne F 22 Db39
Audincourt F 25 Ka41
Audlem GB 13 Ec23
Audun-le-Roman F 21 Jc34
Audun-le-Tiche F 21 Jc34
Aue D 90 Ec43
Auerbach D 90 Ea45
Auerbach D 90 Eb43
Auetal D 83 Da37
Aufhausen D 96 Eb48
Augé F 23 Fc45
Augerolles F 28 Hc47
Aughacasla IRL 6 Ba24
Augher GB 5 Cc17
Aughils IRL 6 Ba24
Aughnacloy GB 5 Cc18
Aughrim IRL 6 Ca21
Aughrim IRL 7 Cd23
Augsburg D 95 Dc50
Augusta I 115 Fd87
Augustdorf D 89 Cd38
Augustenborg DK 76 Db58
Augustów PL 87 Ka31
Augustów PL 93 Jc39
Augustusburg D 90 Ed42
Auklandshamn N 63 Ca41
Aukra N 56 Cd31
Aukrug D 83 Db31
Auktsjaur S 53 Ha22
Auleben D 90 Dd40
Aulendorf D 95 Cd51
Auletta I 112 Fd76
Aulla I 101 Cd63
Aulnay F 23 Fc46
Aulnay-la-Riviere F 24 Gd39
Aulnay-sous-Bois F 20 Gd36
Aulnizeux F 20 Hc37
Aulnoye-Aymeries F 20 Hc32
Aulstad N 64 Dd37
Ault F 20 Gb33
Aultbea GB 8 Dc06
Aulum DK 76 Da53
Aulus-les-Bains F 34 Gb57
Auma D 90 Ea42
Aumetz F 21 Jc34
Aumont F 25 Jc43
Aumühle D 83 Dc33
Aunay-sur-Odon F 19 Fb36
Aunet N 57 Ed25
Aunet N 57 Ed26
Aunet N 57 Eb27
Aunet N 57 Ea29
Aups F 29 Ka53
Aurach D 95 Db47
Auray F 22 Ea41
Aurdal N 64 Dc38
Aure N 56 Db30
Aureskoski FIN 68 Jc34
Aurice F 26 Fb53
Aurich D 83 Cb32
Aurillac F 27 Ha50
Auriol F 29 Jd54
Aurolzmünster A 96 Ed50
Auron F 29 Kc51
Aurons F 29 Jc53
Aurora RO 123 Fc68
Auschwitz = Oświęcim PL 92 Hd44
Auskarnes N 47 Ka05
Ausonia I 109 Ed73
Außervillgratten A 96 Eb55
Austefjord N 62 Cc34
Austervika N 48 Gb13
Austnes N 48 Ga12
Austnes N 56 Cc32
Austpollen N 48 Fd13
Auterive F 34 Gc55
Authon-la-Plaine F 24 Gc38
Autionperä FIN 60 Ka30
Autol E 33 Ec59
Autrans F 29 Jc48
Autrèche F 24 Gb41
Autrey F 25 Jc41
Autry-le-Châtel F 24 Ha41
Autun F 25 Hd43
Auvåg N 48 Fc13
Auverse F 23 Fd41
Auvillar F 27 Ga53
Auxerre F 24 Hc40
Auxon F 24 Hc39
Auxonne F 25 Jc42
Availles-Limouzine F 23 Ga46
Avaldsnes N 63 Bd42
Avallon F 24 Hc41
Avan S 54 Hd22
Avant-lès-Marcilly F 24 Hc38
Avasjö S 58 Gb27
Avaträsk S 58 Ga27
Avdijivka UA 137 Ed13
Ávdira GR 126 Db77
Avebury GB 15 Ed28
A Veiga E 31 Bc58
Aveiro P 36 Ac62
Avelengo I 102 Dc56
Avella I 112 Fb74
Avellanosa del Páramo E 32 Dc58
Avellino I 112 Fc75
Avenas F 25 Ja45
Avenches CH 94 Bc54
Avening GB 15 Ec27
Avereest NL 82 Bd35
Avernay-Val-d'Or F 21 Hd36
Aversa I 112 Fa74
Averton F 23 Fc38
Avesnes-le-Comte F 20 Gd32
Avesnes-sur-Helpe F 20 Hc32
Avesta S 66 Ga41
Avetrana I 113 Hb76
Avezzano I 109 Ed71
Aviano I 103 Eb58
Aviemore GB 9 Ea09
Avigliana I 100 Bc60
Avigliano I 112 Ga75
Avignon F 28 Jb53
Avignonet-Lauragais F 34 Gc55
Ávila E 37 Cd63
Avilés E 31 Cb54
Avilley F 25 Jd41
Avion F 20 Ha31
Avis P 36 Ad68
Avize F 20 Hc36
Avlémonas GR 132 Bd92
Avlonári GR 129 Cc85
Avô P 36 Ba64
Avoca IRL 7 Cd23
Avoch GB 9 Ea07
Avola I 115 Fd88
Avord F 24 Ha43
Avoriaz F 100 Bb56
Avoudrey F 25 Ka42
Avranches F 19 Fa37
Avrillé F 23 Fb41
Avvakajjo S 53 Ha17
Avvil FIN 51 Ka11
Axams A 96 Dd54
Axat F 35 Gd57
Axel NL 17 Hc29
Axford GB 15 Fa29
Ax-les-Thermes F 35 Gd57
Axminster GB 14 Eb30
Axós GR 133 Cd95
Axstedt D 83 Cd33
Ayamonte E 42 Ba74
Ayaz E 30 Bb56
Aydıncık TR 130 Dd80
Ayer CH 100 Bd56
Ayerbe E 33 Fb58
Aylesbury GB 15 Fb27
Aylesham GB 16 Gb29
Ayllón E 32 Dd61
Aylsham GB 16 Gb24
Aylton GB 15 Ec26
Aynac F 27 Gc50
Ayódar E 39 Fc66
Ayora E 39 Fa69
Ayr GB 10 Dd14
Aysgarth GB 13 Ed19
Äyskoski FIN 60 Kc30
Ayton GB 11 Ed13
Ayton GB 13 Fc19
Aytré F 23 Fa46
Ayvalık TR 130 Eb83
Azambuja P 36 Ab68
Azannes F 21 Jb35
Azaruja P 36 Ba69
Azaryčy BY 136 Eb13
Azay-le-Ferron F 24 Gb43
Azay-le-Rideau F 23 Fd42
Azé F 24 Gb40
Azinhal P 42 Ba74
Azinheira dos Barros P 42 Ac71
Aznalcázar E 43 Bd74
Aznalcóllar E 43 Bd73
Azoia P 36 Ab65
Azov RUS 137 Fc15
Azpeitia E 32 Eb55
Azuaga E 43 Cb71
Azuara E 39 Fa62
Azuel E 44 Da71
Azuqueca de Henares E 38 Dd64

## B

Baak NL 82 Bc37
Baal D 88 Bc40
Baar CH 95 Cb53
Baarland NL 17 Hc28
Baarle-Nassau B 88 Ad38
Baarlo NL 88 Bc39
Baarn NL 82 Bb36
Babaeski TR 127 Ec76
Babenhausen D 89 Cd44
Babenhausen D 95 Db50
Babensham D 96 Eb51
Babiak PL 86 Hb37
Babiak PL 86 Ja30
Babice PL 92 Hd44
Babilafuente E 37 Cc62
Babino Polje HR 110 Ha69
Babócsa H 104 Gd58
Babrujsk BY 136 Eb13
Bacares E 44 Ea75
Baccarat F 21 Ka37
Bach A 95 Db53
Bacharach D 88 Ca44
Bachmač UA 137 Ed14
Bachórz PL 93 Ka44
Bachórzec PL 93 Kb44
Bachotek PL 86 Hc33
Back GB 8 Db05
Backaland GB 9 Ec02
Bäckby FIN 59 Jb28
Backe S 58 Ga28
Bäckmark S 53 Gb23
Backnang D 95 Cd48
Bäcknäs S 53 Gd23
Backträsk S 54 Hc22
Bacoli I 112 Fa75
Bácsalmás H 105 Hd57
Bácsszentgyörgy H 105 Hd58
Bacton GB 16 Ga25
Bacup GB 13 Ed20
Bad Abbach D 96 Ea48
Badachro GB 8 Db07
Bad Aibling D 96 Ea52
Badajoz E 37 Bc69
Badalona E 35 Ha61
Bad Arolsen D 89 Cd40
Bad Aussee A 96 Fa53
Bad Bederkesa D 83 Cd32
Bad Bentheim D 82 Ca36
Badbergen D 83 Cc35
Bad Bergzabern D 94 Ca47
Bad Berka D 90 Dd41
Bad Berleburg D 89 Cc40
Bad Berneck im Fichtelgebirge D 90 Ea44
Bad Bertrich D 88 Bd43
Bad Bevensen D 83 Dc34
Bad Birnbach D 96 Ec50
Bad Blankenburg D 90 Dd42
Bad Bleiberg A 103 Fa56
Bad Bocklet D 89 Db43
Bad Bodenteich D 83 Dc35
Bad Boll D 95 Da49
Bad Bramstedt D 83 Db31
Bad Breisig D 88 Ca42
Bad Brückenau D 89 Da43
Bad Buchau D 95 Cd51
Badby GB 15 Fa25
Bad Camberg D 89 Cb43
Badcaul GB 8 Dc06
Bad Colberg-Heldburg D 89 Dc43
Bad Doberan D 84 Eb31
Bad Driburg D 89 Cd38
Bad Düben D 90 Ec39
Bad Dürkheim D 89 Cb46
Bad Dürrenberg D 90 Eb40
Bad Dürrheim D 95 Cb51
Badeborn D 90 Dd38
Bądecz PL 85 Gc34
Bad Eilsen D 83 Cd37
Badellou E 34 Ga60
Bad Elster D 90 Eb44
Bademli TR 130 Eb84
Bad Ems D 88 Ca43
Baden A 97 Gb51
Baden CH 95 Cb52
Baden-Baden D 95 Cb48
Bad Endbach D 89 Cc41
Badendiek D 84 Eb32
Bad Endorf D 96 Eb51
Badenscoth GB 9 Ec08
Badenweiler D 94 Bd51
Bad Essen D 83 Cc36
Bad Feilnbach D 96 Ea52
Bad Frankenhausen D 90 Dd40
Bad Freienwalde D 85 Fb35
Bad Friedrichshall D 95 Cd47
Bad Füssing D 96 Ed50
Bad Gandersheim D 89 Db38
Bad Gastein A 96 Ec54
Bad Gleichenberg A 97 Ga55
Bad Goisern A 96 Ed52
Bad Griesbach D 96 Ed50
Bad Grund D 89 Db38
Bad Hall A 97 Fb51
Bad Harzburg D 89 Dc38
Bad Heilbrunn D 96 Dd52
Bad Herrenalb D 95 Cb48
Bad Hersfeld D 89 Da41
Bad Hindelang D 95 Db53
Bad Hofgastein A 96 Ec54
Bad Homburg D 89 Cc43
Bad Honnef D 88 Bd42
Bad Hönningen D 88 Ca42
Badia Calavena I 102 Dc59
Badia Gran E 41 Hb68
Badia Polesine I 102 Dd61
Badia Prataglia I 108 Dd65
Bad Iburg D 83 Cb37
Bad Ischl A 96 Ed52
Badje-Sohppar S 49 Hc14
Bad Karlshafen D 89 Da39
Bad Kemmeriboden CH 94 Ca54
Bad Kissingen D 89 Db44
Bad Kleinen D 84 Ea32
Bad Kleinkirchheim A 96 Fa55
Bad Klosterlausnitz D 90 Ea41
Bad König D 89 Cd45
Bad Königshofen D 89 Dc43
Bad Kösen D 90 Ea41
Bad Köstritz D 90 Eb41
Bad Kreuznach D 88 Ca44
Bad Krozingen D 94 Bd51
Bad Laasphe D 89 Cc41
Bad Laer D 83 Cc37
Bad Langensalza D 89 Dc41
Bad Lauchstädt D 90 Ea40
Bad Lausick D 90 Ec41
Bad Lauterberg D 89 Dc39
Bad Leonfelden A 97 Fb50
Bad Liebenstein D 89 Db42
Bad Liebenwerda D 90 Ed40
Bad Lippspringe D 89 Cd38
Bad Lobenstein D 90 Ea43
Bad Marienberg D 89 Cb42
Bad Meinberg, Horn- D 89 Cd38
Bad Mergentheim D 89 Da46
Badminton GB 15 Ec28
Bad Mitterndorf A 96 Fa53
Bad Münder D 83 Da37
Bad Münster-Ebernburg D 88 Ca45
Bad Münstereifel D 88 Bd42
Bad Muskau D 91 Fc39
Bad Nauheim D 89 Cc43
Bad Neuenahr-Ahrweiler D 88 Bd42
Bad Neustadt D 89 Db43
Bad Oeynhausen D 83 Cd37
Badolato I 115 Gc82
Badolatosa E 43 Cd74
Bad Oldesloe D 83 Dc32
Bad Orb D 89 Cd43
Bad Peterstal-Griesbach D 95 Cb49
Bad Pyrmont D 89 Da38
Bad Radkersburg A 104 Ga56
Bad Ragaz CH 95 Cd54
Bad Rappenau D 95 Cd47
Bad Reichenhall D 96 Ec52
Bad Rodach D 89 Dc43
Bad Rothenfelde D 83 Cc37
Bad Saarow-Pieskow D 85 Fb37
Bad Sachsa D 89 Dc39
Bad Säckingen D 94 Ca52
Bad Salzdetfurth D 83 Db37
Bad Salzschlirf D 89 Da42
Bad Salzuflen D 83 Cd37
Bad Salzungen D 89 Db42
Bad Sankt Leonhard im Lavanttal A 97 Fc55
Bad Sassendorf D 89 Cc39
Bad Saulgau D 95 Cd51
Bad Schallerbach A 96 Fa50
Bad Schandau D 91 Fb42
Bad Schmiedeberg D 90 Ec39
Bad Schönau A 97 Gb53
Bad Schönborn D 95 Cc47
Bad Schussenried D 95 Cd51
Bad Schwalbach D 89 Cb43
Bad Schwartau D 84 Dd31
Bad Segeberg D 83 Dc31
Bad Sobernheim D 88 Ca45
Bad Soden D 89 Cc44
Bad Soden-Salmünster D 89 Cd43
Bad Sooden-Allendorf D 89 Db40
Bad Staffelstein D 90 Dd44
Bad Steben D 90 Ea43
Bad Suderode D 90 Dd39
Bad Sulza D 90 Ea41
Bad Sülze D 84 Ec31
Bad Tennstedt D 89 Dc41
Bad Tölz D 96 Dd52
Bad Überkingen D 95 Da49
Bad Urach D 95 Cd49
Bad Vilbel D 89 Cc43
Bad Vöslau A 97 Gb51
Bad Waldsee D 95 Da51
Bad Wiessee D 96 Ea52
Bad Wildbad D 95 Cb48
Bad Wildungen D 89 Cd40
Bad Wilsnack D 84 Eb35
Bad Wimpfen D 95 Cd47
Bad Windsheim D 89 Db46
Bad Wörishofen D 95 Db51
Bad Wurzach D 95 Da51
Bad Zell A 97 Fc50
Bad Zwesten D 89 Cd41
Bad Zwischenahn D 83 Cc33
Baena E 44 Da73
Baerenthal F 94 Bd47
Baesweiler D 88 Bc41
Baeza E 44 Dc72
Bagà E 35 Gd58
Bagamér H 99 Kb52
Bågede S 58 Fc27
Bâgé-le-Châtel F 25 Jb45
Bagenalstown IRL 7 Cc23
Bagenkop DK 77 Dd59
Bagheria I 114 Ed84
Baglad H 104 Gb56
Bagley GB 12 Eb23
Bagnac-sur-Célé F 27 Gd51
Bagnaia I 108 Ea70
Bagnasco I 100 Bd63
Bagnères de-Bigorre F 34 Fd56
Bagnères-de-Luchon F 34 Ga57
Bagni di Lucca I 102 Db64
Bagni di Mondragone I 112 Fa74
Bagni di Petriolo I 108 Dc67
Bagni San Cataldo I 112 Ga75
Bagno di Romagna I 108 Ea65
Bagnoli di Sopra I 102 Ea60
Bagnoli Irpino I 112 Fc75
Bagnolo Mella I 101 Da59
Bagnols F 27 Ha48
Bagnols-sur-Cèze F 28 Jb52
Bagnoregio I 108 Ea69
Bagod H 97 Gc55
Bagolino I 102 Db58
Báguena E 39 Ed62
Bagüés E 33 Fa58
Bahabón de Esgueval E 32 Dc60
Baia I 112 Fa75
Baia delle Zagare I 110 Gb72
Baiano I 112 Fb74
Baides E 38 Ea62
Baiersbronn D 95 Cb49
Baiersdorf D 90 Dd46
Baigneaux F 24 Gc39
Baile an Fheirtearaigh IRL 6 Ad24
Baile an Mhóta IRL 4 Bd18
Baile an Róba IRL 4 Bc20
Baile an Sceilg IRL 6 Ad25
Baile Átha IRL 7 Cc22
Baile Átha an Rí IRL 6 Bd21
Baile Átha Cliath IRL 7 Cd21
Baile Átha Fhirdhia IRL 5 Cd19
Baile Átha Luain IRL 6 Ca21
Baile Átha Troim IRL 5 Cc20
Baile Brigín IRL 5 Cd20
Baile Chláir IRL 6 Bc21
Băile Felix RO 117 Cb57
Băile Govora RO 121 Db64
Băile Herculane RO 121 Cb64
Baile Locha Riach IRL 6 Bd21
Baile Mhic Andáin IRL 7 Cb24
Baile Mhistéala IRL 6 Bd24
Baile Mór GB 10 Da11
Bailén E 44 Db72
Baile na Finne IRL 4 Ca16
Baile na Lorgan IRL 5 Cd19
Băile Tuşnad RO 118 Ea60
Baile Uí Fhiacháin IRL 4 Bc19
Baile Uí Mhatháin IRL 4 Cb20
Bailieborough IRL 5 Cc19
Baillé F 23 Fa38
Bailleul F 17 Ha30
Bailo E 33 Fb58
Bailyhaugh GB 10 Da10
Bailyhaugh GB 10 Da14
Baiñas E 30 Ac55
Bainbridge GB 13 Ed18
Baindt D 95 Da51
Bainton GB 13 Fc20
Baiona E 30 Ac58
Bairro P 36 Ac66
Baix F 28 Jb50
Baja H 105 Hd57
Bajáansenye H 97 Gb55
Bajki-Zalesie PL 87 Ka33
Bajram Curri AL 124 Ac71
Bakel NL 88 Bb38
Bakewell GB 13 Ed22
Bakkafjörður IS 3 Cc02
Bakkagerði IS 3 Cd03
Bakkeby N 49 Hb09
Bakken N 56 Dc29
Bakken N 57 Fb27
Bakketun N 52 Fb22
Bakkeveen NL 82 Bd33
Bakonycsernye H 98 Hb53
Bakonygyepes H 98 Ha54
Bakonypéterd H 98 Ha53
Baksan RUS 137 Ga17
Baksjöberg S 58 Gd27
Baktakék H 99 Jc50
Baktalórántháza H 99 Kb51
Bakum D 83 Cc35
Bala GB 12 Ea23
Balabanovo RUS 137 Ed11
Balaguer E 34 Ga60
Balahna RUS 137 Fb09
Balaklija UA 137 Fa14
Balakovo RUS 137 Ga11
Bălan RO 117 Cd56
Balanegra E 44 Dd76
Balašiha RUS 137 Fa10
Balašov RUS 137 Fc12
Balassagyarmat H 98 Hd51
Balata di Baida I 114 Eb84
Balatonalmádi H 98 Hb54
Balatonboglár H 98 Ha55
Balatonbozsok H 98 Hb55
Balatonfüred H 98 Ha55
Balatonfűzfő H 98 Hb54
Balatonmagyaród H 104 Gd56
Balatonszemes H 98 Ha55
Balatonújlak H 104 Gd56
Balazote E 38 Eb69
Balbeggie GB 11 Eb11
Balblair GB 9 Ea07
Balbriggan IRL 5 Cd20
Balčik BG 123 Fb70
Balcombe GB 16 Fc29
Baldichierid'Asti I 100 Bd61
Baldock GB 16 Fc26
Baleix F 33 Fc55
Balen B 88 Ba39
Băleşti RO 121 Cc63
Balestrand N 62 Cc36
Balestrate I 114 Eb84
Balf H 97 Gc52
Balfour GB 9 Ec03
Balfron GB 10 Dd12
Balge D 83 Da35
Balí GR 133 Cd95
Baligród PL 93 Kb46
Balıkesir TR 131 Fa82
Balinderry IRL 6 Ca22
Bälinge S 54 Hd22
Bälinge S 66 Gc41
Balingen D 95 Cc50
Balintore GB 9 Ea07
Balivanich GB 8 Cd07
Balizac F 26 Fb51
Balje D 83 Da31
Balk NL 82 Bb34
Balkbrug NL 82 Bd35
Balla IRL 4 Bc19
Ballabio Inferiore I 101 Cd58
Ballachullish GB 10 Dc10
Ballagh IRL 6 Bc24
Ballaghaderreen IRL 4 Bd19
Ballancourt-sur-Essone F 24 Gd38
Ballantrae GB 10 Dc16
Ballasalla GB 12 Dc19
Ballater GB 9 Ec09
Balle Bhuirne IRL 6 Bb25
Ballenstedt D 90 Dd39
Ballickmoyler IRL 7 Cc23
Ballina IRL 4 Bc18
Ballina IRL 6 Bd23
Ballinafad IRL 4 Ca19
Ballinagleragh IRL 4 Ca18
Ballinakill IRL 7 Cb23
Ballinalee IRL 4 Cb20
Ballinamore IRL 4 Cb19
Ballinascarty IRL 6 Bc26
Ballinasloe IRL 6 Ca21
Ballinclea IRL 7 Cd22
Ballincollig IRL 6 Bd26
Ballincurrig IRL 6 Bd25
Ballindine IRL 4 Bd20
Ballingarry IRL 6 Ca22
Ballingarry IRL 6 Bc24
Ballingarry IRL 7 Cb23
Ballingeary IRL 6 Bb26
Ballingurteen IRL 6 Bc26
Ballinhassig IRL 6 Bd26
Ballinlough IRL 4 Bd19
Ballino I 102 Db58
Ballinrobe IRL 4 Bc20
Ballinspittle IRL 6 Bc26
Ballintogher IRL 4 Ca18
Ballinunty IRL 6 Ca23
Ballinure IRL 6 Ca24
Ballivor IRL 5 Cc20
Balloch GB 10 Dd13
Balloch GB 10 Dd15
Ballon F 23 Fd39
Ballon IRL 7 Cc23
Balloo Cross Roads GB 5 Db18
Ballsnes N 48 Ga14
Ballvengland IRL 6 Bc23
Ballybay IRL 5 Cc18
Ballybofey IRL 4 Cb16
Ballyboghill IRL 7 Cd21
Ballybogy GB 5 Cd15
Ballybrittas IRL 7 Cc22
Ballybunnion IRL 6 Bb23
Ballycanew IRL 7 Cd24
Ballycastle GB 5 Da15
Ballycastle IRL 4 Bc17
Ballyclare GB 5 Da17
Ballyclare IRL 4 Ca20
Ballycolla IRL 7 Cb22
Ballyconneely IRL 4 Ba20
Ballyconnell IRL 4 Cb18
Ballycorick IRL 6 Bc23
Ballycotton IRL 6 Ca26
Ballydangan IRL 6 Ca21
Ballydehob IRL 6 Bb26
Ballydesmond IRL 6 Bb24
Ballyduff IRL 6 Bb23
Ballyduff IRL 6 Ca25
Ballyfad IRL 7 Cd23
Ballyfeard IRL 6 Bd26
Ballyferriter IRL 6 Ad24
Ballygalley GB 5 Da16
Ballygarrett IRL 7 Cd24
Ballygawley GB 5 Cc17
Ballyglass IRL 4 Bc19
Ballygowan GB 5 Da17
Ballygrant GB 10 Da13
Ballyhahill IRL 6 Bc23
Ballyhalbert GB 5 Db17
Ballyhaunis IRL 4 Bd19
Ballyhean IRL 4 Bc19
Ballyheerin IRL 4 Cb15
Ballyheige IRL 6 Ba24
Ballyhillin IRL 5 Cc14
Ballyhooly IRL 6 Bd25
Ballyhornan GB 5 Db18
Ballyjamesduff IRL 5 Cc19
Ballykeel GB 5 Da18
Ballylanders IRL 6 Bd24
Ballylongford IRL 6 Bb23
Ballylooby IRL 6 Ca24
Ballylynan IRL 7 Cc22
Ballymacarbry IRL 6 Ca25
Ballymack IRL 7 Cb24
Ballymacoda IRL 6 Ca26
Ballymacrevan GB 5 Da17
Ballymahon IRL 4 Cb20
Ballymena GB 5 Da16
Ballymoe IRL 4 Bd20
Ballymoney GB 5 Cd15
Ballymoney GB 5 Cc16
Ballymore IRL 4 Cb20
Ballymore Eustace IRL 7 Cd22
Ballymote IRL 4 Bd18
Ballymurphy IRL 7 Cc24
Ballynabola IRL 7 Cc24
Ballynacarrigy IRL 4 Cb20
Ballynacourty IRL 6 Ca25
Ballynagore IRL 7 Cb21
Ballynagree IRL 6 Bc25
Ballynahinch GB 5 Da18
Ballynahown IRL 6 Bb21
Ballynahown IRL 6 Ca21
Ballynakilla IRL 6 Ba26
Ballynakilly Upper IRL 6 Ba25
Ballynamona IRL 6 Bd25
Ballynamult IRL 6 Ca25
Ballynana IRL 6 Ad24
Ballynaskreena IRL 6 Bb23
Ballyneety IRL 6 Bd23
Ballynure GB 5 Da16
Ballypatrick IRL 7 Cb24
Ballyporeen IRL 6 Ca24
Ballyquin IRL 6 Ba24
Ballyragget IRL 7 Cb23
Ballyroebuck IRL 7 Cd23
Ballyroon IRL 6 Ba26
Ballysadare IRL 4 Ca18
Ballyshannon IRL 4 Ca17
Ballyshannon IRL 7 Cc22
Ballysteen IRL 6 Bc23
Ballytoohy IRL 4 Bb19
Ballyvaughan IRL 6 Bc21
Ballyvourney IRL 6 Bb25
Ballyvoy GB 5 Da15
Ballywater GB 5 Db17
Ballywilliam IRL 7 Cc24
Balmacara GB 8 Da05
Balmaseda E 32 Dd55
Balmazújváros H 99 Jd52
Balme I 100 Bc59
Balmedie GB 9 Ed09
Balmerino GB 11 Eb11
Balminnoch GB 10 Dc16
Balmonte E 31 Bd54
Balnafoich GB 9 Ea08
Balnahard GB 10 Da11
Balnapaling GB 9 Ea07
Balneario de Panticosa E 33 Fc57
Bálojotnjálbmi FIN 50 Ja13
Balquhidder GB 10 Dd11
Balrath IRL 5 Cd20
Balsa de Ves E 39 Fa68
Balsfjord N 49 Gd10
Balsham GB 16 Fd26
Balsicas E 45 Fa73
Balsjö S 59 Ha28
Balsorano Nuovo I 109 Ed72
Bålsta S 72 Gc43
Balsthal CH 94 Bd53
Balta UA 136 Ec16
Baltar E 30 Bb58
Baltasound GB 9 Fb03
Bălti MD 119 Fb55
Baltijsk RUS 136 Dc12
Baltimore IRL 6 Bb27
Baltinglass IRL 7 Cc22
Bałtów PL 93 Jd41
Balugães P 30 Ad59
Balve D 89 Cb39
Balya TR 131 Ed82
Bamberg D 89 Dc45
Bamburgh GB 11 Fa14
Bamford GB 13 Ed22
Bammental D 89 Cc46
Bampton GB 14 Ea29
Banagher IRL 6 Ca21
Banbridge GB 5 Da18
Banbury GB 15 Fa26
Bande E 30 Ba58
Bandeira E 30 Ba56
Bandenitz D 84 Ea33
Bandirma TR 131 Fa80
Bando I 102 Ea62
Bandol F 29 Jd55
Bandon IRL 6 Bc26
Bånes N 49 Hc08
Banff GB 9 Ec07
Bangor GB 5 Db17
Bangor GB 12 Dd22
Bangor IRL 4 Bb18
Bangor-is-y-coed GB 12 Eb23
Banie PL 85 Fc34
Banja Luka BIH 104 Gd62
Banjska KSV 120 Ba69
Bankeryd S 72 Fb48
Bannalec F 22 Dd40
Bannegon F 24 Ha43
Bannes F 20 Hc37
Bannewitz D 90 Fa41
Bannockburn GB 11 Ea12
Bannoncourt F 21 Jb36
Bannow IRL 7 Cc25
Banon F 29 Jd52
Bañón E 39 Fa63
Banos de Alicún de las Torres E 44 Dd74
Baños de Benasque E 34 Ga57
Baños de la Encina E 44 Db71
Baños de Río Tobia E 32 Ea58
Baños de Valdearados E 32 Dc60
Bánov SK 98 Hb51
Bánovce nad Bebravou SK 98 Hb49
Bánréve H 99 Jb50
Bansha IRL 6 Ca24
Bansin D 85 Fb31
Banská Bystrica SK 98 Hd49
Banská Stiavnica SK 98 Hc50
Bansko BG 125 Cc74
Banstead GB 16 Fc29
Banteer IRL 6 Bc25
Bantheville F 21 Ja35
Bantry IRL 6 Bb26
Bantzenheim F 94 Bd51
Bañugues E 31 Cc53
Banwell GB 14 Eb28
Banyoles E 35 Hb59
Bapaume F 20 Ha32
Bár H 105 Hc57
Bar MNE 111 Ja71
Bar UA 136 Eb15
Barajas E 38 Dc64
Barakaldo E 32 Ea55
Baranavičy BY 136 Ea13
Baranivka UA 136 Eb15
Baranów PL 86 Ja37
Baranowo PL 85 Gc36
Baranowo PL 87 Jc31
Baranów Sandomierski PL 93 Jd42
Baranyajenő H 105 Hb57
Baraque-Saint-Jean F 27 Ha52
Baraqueville F 27 Ha52
Barbacena P 36 Bb68
Barbadillo E 37 Cb62
Barbadillo de Herreros E 32 Dd59
Barbadillo del Pez E 32 Dd59
Barbalimpia E 38 Eb66
Barban HR 103 Fa61
Barbantes E 30 Ba57
Barbastro E 34 Fd59
Barbate E 43 Bd77
Barbâtre F 22 Ec43
Barbeitos E 31 Bd55
Barber Booth GB 13 Ed22
Barberino di Mugello I 102 Dc64
Barberino Val d'Elsa I 108 Dc66
Barbezieux-Saint-Hilaire F 26 Fc48
Barbing D 96 Eb48
Bárboles E 33 Fa60
Barbotan-les-Thermes F 26 Fc53
Barby D 90 Eb38
Barcaggio F 106 Cc67
Barcaldine GB 10 Dc11
Barcellona Pozzo di Gotto I 115 Fd84
Barcelona E 35 Ha61
Barcelonne-du-Gers F 26 Fc54
Barcelos P 30 Ad60
Bárcena del Monasterio E 31 Ca54
Barchem NL 82 Bd37
Barchín del Hoyo E 38 Eb67
Barcial del Barco E 31 Cb59
Barciany PL 87 Jb30
Barco P 36 Ba64
Barcus F 33 Fb55
Barczewo PL 86 Ja31
Bard I 100 Bd58
Bardejov SK 93 Jd46
Bardejovské Kúpele SK 93 Jd46
Bardi I 101 Cd62
Bardney GB 13 Fc22
Bardo PL 91 Gc43
Bardolino I 102 Db59
Bardonecchia I 100 Ba60
Bardowick D 83 Dc33
Bardsea GB 12 Eb19
Bardsey GB 13 Fa20
Bardujord N 49 Gc12
Barèges F 34 Fd56
Barendrecht NL 17 Hd26
Bärenstein D 90 Ed43
Barentin F 19 Ga34
Barford GB 16 Ga24
Barford Saint Martin GB 15 Ed29
Barga I 101 Da64
Bargas E 38 Db66
Barge I 100 Bc61
Bargeshagen D 84 Eb31
Bargfeld-Stegen D 83 Dc32
Bargłówka PL 92 Hb44
Bargoed GB 14 Ea27
Bargrennan GB 10 Dd16
Bargteheide D 83 Dc32
Bar Hill GB 16 Fd25
Bari I 113 Gd74
Barinas E 45 Fa71
Barisey-la-Côte F 21 Jc37
Barjac F 28 Hc51
Barjac F 28 Ja51
Bårjås S 53 Ha18
Bark D 83 Dc31
Barkelsby D 83 Db29
Barkestad N 48 Fc12
Barking GB 16 Fd28
Barkowo PL 85 Fd32
Barkston GB 13 Fb23
Barkway GB 16 Fd26
Bar-le-Duc F 21 Jb37
Barles F 29 Ka51
Barletta I 110 Gb73
Barlinek PL 85 Fd35
Barlow GB 13 Fa22
Barmouth GB 12 Dd24
Barmstedt D 83 Db32
Barna IRL 6 Bc21
Barnaderg IRL 4 Bd20
Barnard Castle GB 13 Ed18
Bärnau D 90 Eb45
Barnes GB 16 Fc28
Barnesmore IRL 4 Cb16
Barnetby le Wold GB 13 Fc21
Barneveld NL 82 Bb36
Barnewitz D 84 Ec36
Barney GB 16 Ga23
Barnim PL 85 Fc34
Barnoldswick GB 13 Ed20
Barnówko PL 85 Fc35
Barnsley GB 13 Fa21
Barnsley GB 15 Ed27
Barnstaple GB 14 Dd29
Barnstorf D 83 Cd35
Barntrup D 89 Cd38
Baron F 20 Ha36
Baronissi I 112 Fc75
Barqueiros P 30 Ac60
Barr F 94 Bd49
Barraduff IRL 6 Bb25
Barrafranca I 114 Fa86
Barral (Castrelo de Miño) E 30 Ba57
Barrax E 38 Eb69
Barreiro P 36 Aa69
Barrême F 29 Ka52
Barrhead GB 10 Dd13
Barrhill GB 10 Dc16
Barriada Las Canteras E 44 Eb75
Barrigone IRL 6 Bc23
Barri Mar E 39 Fc67
Barrio de Nuestra Señora E 31 Cc57
Barro E 32 Da54
Barrou F 23 Ga43
Barrowby GB 13 Fb23
Barrow-in-Furness GB 12 Eb19
Barrow-upon-Soar GB 13 Fa24
Barruelo de Santullán E 32 Db56
Barry GB 14 Ea28
Barsanges F 27 Gd48
Barsinghausen D 83 Da36
Barsinghausen D 83 Da37
Barßel D 83 Cb33
Barst F 21 Ka35
Bar-sur-Aube F 25 Ja38
Bar-sur-Seine F 25 Hd39
Bartenheim F 94 Bd52
Bartenstein D 89 Da46
Barth D 84 Ec30
Bartholomä D 95 Da48
Bartne PL 93 Jd45
Bartniki PL 92 Ja38
Barton GB 13 Ed24
Barton Mills GB 16 Fd25
Barton-upon-Humber GB 13 Fc21
Bartoszyce PL 87 Jb30
Barty PL 86 Hd31
Barun RUS 137 Ga14
Barvas GB 8 Da04
Barver D 83 Cd35
Bårvik N 46 Hc06
Barvinkove UA 137 Fb15
Barwice PL 85 Gb32
Baryš RUS 137 Fd10
Barysav BY 136 Eb12
Basauri E 32 Ea55
Basavžže N 47 Kb06
Baschi I 108 Ea69
Baschurch GB 12 Eb24
Basconcillos del Tozo E 32 Db57
Bascones de Ojeda E 32 Da57
Basdahl D 83 Da33
Basdorf D 84 Ed35
Basel CH 94 Bd52
Baselga di Piné I 102 Dc57
Basildon GB 16 Fd28
Basiliano I 103 Ec58
Basilique de Hennebont F 22 Ea40
Basingstoke GB 15 Fa29
Baška HR 103 Fc61
Båskas FIN 59 Ja30
Bäsksele S 58 Gb26
Baslow GB 13 Fa22
Bassano del Grappa I 102 Dd59
Bassenthwale GB 12 Eb17
Bassevuovdde N 50 Jc11
Bassignac-le-Haut F 27 Gd49
Bassilac F 27 Ga49
Bassingham GB 13 Fb22
Bassoues F 26 Fd54
Bassum D 83 Cd35
Båstad S 77 Ed53
Baštanka UA 137 Ed16
Bästdal S 66 Gc35
Bastelica F 106 Cb70
Bastia F 106 Cc68
Bastia Umbra I 109 Eb67
Bastogne B 21 Jc32
Baston GB 16 Fc24
Bastuträsk S 59 Hb25
Bastwick GB 16 Gb24
Baszków PL 92 Gd39
Batajsk RUS 137 Fc15
Batalha P 36 Ab66
Båtas S 58 Fd25
Batea E 34 Fd62
Bath GB 15 Ec28
Bathgate GB 11 Ea13
Bathmen NL 82 Bc36
Batley GB 13 Ed20
Batnfjordsøra N 56 Da31
Bátonyterenye H 98 Ja51
Båtsfjord N 47 Kc05
Batsí GR 130 Da87
Båtsjaur S 53 Gb21
Båtskärsnäs S 54 Jb21
Battaglia Terme I 102 Dd60
Battenberg D 89 Cc41
Bätterkinden CH 94 Bd53
Battipaglia I 112 Fc76
Battle GB 16 Fd30
Battonya H 116 Bc59
Båtvik S 54 Hc24
Batyk H 98 Gd55
Batyrevo RUS 137 Fd09
Baudreville F 24 Gc38
Bauduen F 29 Ka53
Baugy F 24 Ha42
Baulmes CH 94 Bb54
Bauma CH 95 Cc53
Baumbach, Ransbach- D 88 Ca42
Baumber GB 13 Fc22
Baume-les-Messieurs F 25 Jc43
Baunatal D 89 Da40
Bautzen D 91 Fb41
Bavanište SRB 120 Bb63
Bavigne L 21 Jc33
Bawdeswell GB 16 Ga24
Bawdsey GB 16 Gb26
Bawnboy IRL 4 Cb18
Bawtry GB 13 Fb21
Bayerisch Eisenstein D 96 Ed48
Bayeux F 19 Fb35
Bayonne F 26 Ed54
Bayons F 29 Ka51
Bayreuth D 90 Ea45
Bayubas de Abajo E 32 Ea61
Baza E 44 Ea74
Bazán E 44 Dc70
Bazarnye Mataki RUS 137 Ga09
Bazarnyi Karabulak RUS 137 Fd11
Bazas F 26 Fc51
Bazicourt F 20 Ha35
Bazna RO 117 Db60
Bazoches F 24 Hc41
Bazzano I 102 Dc63
Beaconsfield GB 15 Fb28
Beal IRL 6 Bb23
Bealach an Doirín IRL 4 Bd19
Bealach Conglais IRL 7 Cc22
Bealach Féich IRL 4 Cb16
Bealaha IRL 6 Bb23
Bealalaw Bridge IRL 6 Ba25
Béal an Átha IRL 4 Bc18
Béal an Átha Móir IRL 4 Cb19
Béal an Mhuirthead IRL 4 Bb17
Béal Atha an Ghaorthaidh IRL 6 Bb26
Béal Átha hAmhnais IRL 4 Bd19
Béal Átha na Muice IRL 4 Bd19
Béal Átha na Sluaighe IRL 6 Ca21
Béal Atha Seanaidh IRL 4 Ca17
Béal Deirig IRL 4 Bc17
Bealdovuobmi FIN 50 Jb13
Bealnablath IRL 6 Bc26
Beaminster GB 14 Eb30
Beanntrai IRL 6 Bb26
Béard F 24 Hb43
Beardsen GB 10 Dd13
Beare Green GB 16 Fc29
Bearna IRL 6 Bc21
Béar Tairbirt IRL 4 Cb18
Beasain E 32 Eb56
Beas de Segura E 44 Dd71
Beatenberg CH 94 Bd55
Beaucaire F 28 Jb53
Beaucamps-le-Vieux F 20 Gc33
Beauchamps F 19 Fa37
Beauchamps F 20 Gb33
Beaufort F 25 Ka46
Beaufort IRL 6 Bb25
Beaufort L 21 Jd33
Beaugency F 24 Gc40
Beaujeu F 25 Jc41
Beaujeu F 25 Ja45
Beaulieu F 19 Ga37
Beaulieu F 24 Ha41
Beaulieu GB 15 Fa30
Beaulieu-sur-Dordogne F 27 Gc50
Beauly GB 8 Dd08
Beaumaris GB 12 Dd22
Beaumetz-lès-Loges F 20 Ha32
Beaumont B 21 Hd32
Beaumont-de-Lomagne F 27 Gb53
Beaumont-le-Roger F 19 Ga36
Beaumont-sur-Oise F 20 Gd36
Beaumont-sur-Vingeanne F 25 Jb41
Beaune F 25 Ja42
Beaupréau F 23 Fa42
Beauquesne F 20 Gd33
Beaurainville F 20 Gc31
Beaurières F 29 Jc50
Beauvais F 20 Gd35
Beauvoir-sur-Mer F 22 Ec43
Beauvoir-sur-Niort F 23 Fb46
Beauzée-sur-Aire F 21 Jb36
Bebares E 31 Ca54
Bebington GB 12 Eb22
Bebra D 89 Da41
Beccles GB 16 Gb25
Beceite E 40 Fd63
Bečej SRB 116 Ba61
Béceleuf F 23 Fb45
Becerreá E 31 Bc56
Becerril E 32 Dd61
Becerril de Campos E 32 Da59
Bécherel F 23 Ed39
Becherov SK 93 Jd46
Bechhofen D 95 Dc47
Bečići MNE 111 Hd70
Beckenham GB 16 Fc28
Beckfoot GB 12 Eb17
Beckingen D 88 Bc46
Beckingen D 94 Bd47
Beckingham GB 13 Fb22
Beckinghausen D 88 Ca38
Beckington GB 15 Ec29
Beckov SK 98 Ha49
Beck Side GB 12 Eb19
Beckum D 89 Cb38
Bécon-les-Granits F 23 Fb41
Bečov nad Teplou CZ 90 Ec44
Bedale GB 13 Fa19
Bédarieux F 28 Hb54
Bédarrides F 28 Jb52
Bedburg D 88 Bc40
Bedburg-Hau D 88 Bc38
Beddau GB 14 Ea28
Beddgelert GB 12 Dd23
Beddingestrand S 77 Fa57
Beddwas GB 14 Ea27
Bédée F 23 Ed39
Bedford GB 16 Fc26
Bedlington GB 11 Fa16
Bedlno PL 86 Hd37
Bedonia I 101 Cd62
Bedum NL 82 Bd33
Bedworth GB 15 Fa25
Będzin PL 92 Hc43
Będzino PL 85 Ga31
Beedenbostel D 83 Dc36
Beeford GB 13 Fc20
Beek NL 88 Bb40
Beekbergen NL 82 Bc36
Beek en Donk NL 88 Bb38
Beelen D 89 Cc38
Beelitz D 84 Ed37
Beer GB 14 Eb30
Beerfelden D 89 Cd46
Beerse B 88 Ad39
Beerta NL 82 Ca33
Beesel NL 88 Bb39
Beesenstedt D 90 Ea39
Beeskow D 85 Fb37
Beeston GB 13 Fa23
Beeswing GB 11 Ea16
Beetsterzwaag NL 82 Bc33
Bégard F 18 Ea37
Begíjar E 44 Dc72
Beg-Meil F 22 Dc40
Begnecourt F 25 Jd38
Begonte E 30 Bb55
Behram TR 130 Ea82
Behren-Lübchin D 84 Ec31
Beian N 56 Dd29
Beiersdorf D 91 Fb41
Beilen NL 82 Bd34
Beilngries D 96 Dd48
Beilrode D 90 Ed39
Beilstein D 88 Bd43
Beilstein D 95 Cd47
Beirã P 36 Bb67
Beisfjord N 48 Gb14
Beith GB 10 Dd13
Beja P 42 Ad71
Béjar E 37 Cb64
Békés H 99 Jd55
Békéscsaba H 99 Jd55
Bekkarfjord N 47 Jd05
Bekken N 65 Ec36
Bekkevoort B 88 Ad40
Bekkjarvik N 63 Ca40
Belaazërsk BY 136 Ea13
Bel-Air F 22 Eb41
Belaja Kalitva RUS 137 Fc14
Belalcázar E 43 Cc70
Belá nad Cirochou SK 99 Ka47
Bélapátfalva H 99 Jb51
Bělá pod B. CZ 91 Fc43
Belarus BY 136 Ea12
Belascoáin E 33 Ec57
Belbroughton GB 15 Ed25
Belcastel F 27 Ha51
Belceğiz TR 135 Bc92
Bełchatów PL 92 Hd40
Belchite E 39 Fb62
Belcoo GB 4 Cb18
Belderrig IRL 4 Bc17
Beldibi TR 135 Cc92
Belec HR 104 Gb57
Belecska H 105 Hb56
Belek TR 135 Cd91
Belev RUS 137 Ed12
Belevi TR 131 Ed87
Belfast GB 5 Da17
Belford GB 11 Ed14
Belfort F 25 Ka40
Belgern D 90 Ed40
Belgorod RUS 137 Fa14
Belhomert-Guéhouville F 24 Gb38
Belianes E 34 Gb61
Belinchón E 38 Dd66
Bel'kovo RUS 136 Ec12
Bellac F 24 Gb46
Bellacorick IRL 4 Bc18
Bellagio I 101 Cc57
Bellanaboy Bridge IRL 4 Bc17
Bellanacargy IRL 5 Cc19
Bellananagh IRL 4 Cb19
Bellante I 109 Fa69
Bellarena GB 5 Cd15
Bellaria I 103 Eb64
Bellavary IRL 4 Bc19
Bellavista E 43 Ca74
Belle-Eglise F 20 Gd35
Belleek GB 4 Ca17
Bellegarde F 24 Gd39
Bellegarde F 28 Ja53
Bellegarde-sur-Valserine F 25 Jd45
Bellême F 23 Ga38
Bellerive-sur-Allier F 24 Hc46
Belleu F 20 Hb35
Bellevesvre F 25 Jc43
Belleville F 25 Ja45
Belley F 25 Jc46
Bellheim D 95 Cb47
Bellicourt F 20 Hb33
Belligné F 23 Fa41
Bellingham GB 11 Ed16
Bellingwolde NL 82 Ca33
Bellinzago Novarese I 101 Cb59
Bellinzona CH 101 Cc57
Bello E 39 Ed63
Belloc F 26 Fc54
Bellocq F 26 Fa54
Bellosguardo I 112 Fd76
Bellou F 19 Fd36
Bellpuig E 34 Gb61
Belluno I 102 Ea57
Bellvís E 34 Ga60
Belm D 83 Cc36
Belmont GB 9 Fb03
Belmont GB 13 Ec21
Belmonte E 38 Ea67
Belmonte de Miranda E 31 Cb54
Belmullet IRL 4 Bb17
Belœil B 20 Hc31
Belokopitovo BG 122 Ec70
Beloreèensk RUS 137 Fc17
Belotín CZ 92 Ha46
Belpasso I 115 Fc85
Belpech F 34 Gc55
Belper GB 13 Fa23
Belsay GB 11 Ed16
Belsk Duży PL 93 Jb38
Beltheim D 88 Ca43
Beltra IRL 4 Bd18
Beltra IRL 4 Bc19
Belturbet IRL 4 Cb18
Beluša SK 98 Hb48
Beluso E 30 Ac57
Belvédère-Campomoro F 106 Ca72
Belvedere Marittimo I 112 Ga79
Belvezet F 28 Hd51
Belville IRL 4 Bc18
Belvis de Monroy E 37 Cb66
Belvoir F 25 Ka41
Belvoir GB 13 Fb23
Belyj RUS 136 Ec11
Belz F 22 Ea40
Belzig D 84 Ec37
Bełżyce PL 93 Ka40
Bembridge GB 15 Fa31
Bemmel NL 82 Bb37
Bemposta P 36 Ad67
Benabarre E 34 Ga59
Benaguasil E 39 Fb67
Benajarafe E 44 Da76
Ben Alder Lodge GB 10 Dd10
Benalmádena E 43 Cd76
Benalmádena E 43 Cd77
Benalúa de Guadix E 44 Dd74
Benamargosa E 44 Da76
Benamaurel E 44 Ea73
Benaoján E 43 Cb76
Benasque E 34 Ga57
Benatae E 44 Ea71
Benátky nad Jizera CZ 91 Fc44
Benavente E 31 Cb59
Benavente E 36 Bb68
Bendestorf D 83 Db33
Bendorf D 88 Ca42
Beneden-Leeuwen NL 82 Bb37
Benefield GB 15 Fb25
Benejama E 45 Fb70
Benejúzar E 45 Fa72
Benešov CZ 91 Fc45
Beněšov nad Ploučnici CZ 91 Fb42
Bénesse-lès-Dax F 26 Fa54
Bénestroff F 21 Ka36
Beneuvre F 25 Jb40
Benevento I 112 Fc74
Benfeld F 94 Bd49
Beniarrés E 45 Fb70
Benicarló E 40 Fd64
Benicasim E 39 Fd66
Benicàssim E 39 Fd66
Benidorm E 45 Fc71
Benifaió E 39 Fb68
Benifallet E 40 Ga63
Benigànim E 39 Fb69
Benimaurell E 45 Fc70
Benington GB 16 Fd23
Benllech GB 12 Dd22
Benmore GB 10 Dd11
Benneckenstein D 89 Dc39
Bennettsbridge IRL 7 Cb24
Bennstedt D 90 Ea40
Bénodet F 22 Dc40
Bensbyn S 54 Hd22
Bensdorf D 84 Eb36
Bensheim D 89 Cc45
Bensjö S 58 Fd32
Benson GB 15 Fa27
Bentpath GB 11 Eb15
Benwick GB 16 Fc25
Beočin SRB 120 Ad62
Beograd SRB 120 Bb63
Beram HR 103 Fa60
Berane MNE 111 Jb68
Beranuy E 34 Ga58
Berastegi E 33 Ec56
Berat AL 124 Ab76
Beratzhausen D 96 Ea47
Berazino BY 136 Eb12
Berbes E 31 Cd54
Bercedo E 32 Dd56
Berching D 96 Dd47
Berchtesgaden D 96 Ec52
Bercianos de Aliste E 31 Ca59
Berck F 20 Gb32
Berck-Plage F 20 Gb32
Berdía E 30 Ad55
Berdjans'k UA 137 Fb16
Berdoias E 30 Ac54
Berducedo E 31 Bd55
Berdún E 33 Fa57
Berdyčiv UA 136 Eb15
Berehove UA 136 Dd16
Berekfürdő H 99 Jc53
Beremend H 105 Hc58
Bere Regis GB 15 Ec30
Berestečko UA 136 Ea15
Berettyóújfalu H 99 Ka53
Berezanka UA 136 Ec16
Berezanskaja RUS 137 Fc16
Berežany UA 136 Ea15
Berezna UA 136 Ec13
Berezne UA 136 Ea14
Bereznehuvate UA 137 Ed16
Berfay F 23 Ga40
Berg D 90 Ea43
Berg D 95 Cb47
Berg D 96 Dd51
Berga D 90 Eb42
Berga E 35 Gd59
Bergama TR 131 Ec84

Bergamo I 101 Cd58
Bergara E 32 Eb56
Bergdala S 78 Fd52
Berge D 83 Cb35
Berge D 84 Ec36
Bergeforsen S 66 Gc33
Bergen D 83 Db35
Bergen D 84 Fa30
Bergen D 96 Eb30
Bergen N 62 Ca39
Bergen NL 82 Ba34
Bergen aan Zee NL 82 Ad34
Bergen (Dumme) D 84 Dd35
Bergen = Mons B 20 Hc31
Bergen op Zoom NL 17 Hc28
Bergerac F 26 Fd50
Bergeres-lès-Vertus F 20 Hc36
Bergeyk NL 88 Ba39
Berggießhübel, Bad Gottleuba- D 90 Fa42
Bergheim D 88 Bd40
Berglisch Gladbach D 88 Bd40
Bergkamen D 89 Cb38
Bergkarlås S 66 Fc38
Berglia N 57 Fa27
Berglunda S 58 Gd26
Bergnäs S 53 Gb22
Bergnäset S 54 Hd22
Bergneset N 49 Gd11
Bergneustadt D 88 Ca40
Bergnicourt F 21 Hd34
Bergnicourt F 21 Hd35
Bergrheinfeld D 89 Db44
Bergsbyn S 59 Hc35
Bergsjö S 66 Gb35
Bergsläyen S 54 Hc23
Bergues F 17 Gd30
Bergviken S 53 Gd20
Bergwitz D 90 Ec36
Berhida H 98 Hb54
Berja E 44 Dd76
Berkåk N 56 Dd32
Berkatal D 89 Db40
Berkel NL 17 Hd26
Berkeley GB 15 Ec27
Berkenbrück D 84 Ed37
Berkheim D 95 Da55
Berkswell GB 15 Ed25
Berlanga E 43 Ca71
Berlanga de Duero E 32 Ea61
Berlanga del Bierzo E 31 Ca56
Berle N 62 Ca34
Berlevåg N 47 Kb04
Berlin D 84 Ed36
Bermeo E 32 Ea55
Bermés E 30 Ba56
Bermillo de Sayago E 31 Ca61
Bern CH 94 Bd54
Bernalda I 113 Gc76
Bernau D 84 Fa36
Bernau D 96 Ed52
Bernay F 19 Ga34
Bernay F 23 Fc39
Bernbeuren D 95 Dc52
Bernburg D 90 Ea38
Berndorf A 97 Gb51
Berne D 83 Cd32
Bernedo E 32 Eb57
Berngau D 96 Ea47
Bernhardswald D 96 Eb48
Bernhardthal A 97 Gc49
Bernin F 29 Jd48
Bernkastel-Kues D 88 Bd44
Bernon F 25 Hd39
Bernried D 96 Dd51
Bernsdorf D 91 Fb40
Bernstein A 97 Gb53
Beron CZ 91 Fb45
Berra I 102 Ea61
Berriedale GB 9 Eb05
Berrien F 22 Dd38
Berriew GB 12 Eb24
Berro E 44 Eb70
Berrocal de Salvatierra E 37 Cc66
Berrocalejo de Aragona E 38 Da43
Beršad' UA 136 Ec16
Bersenbrück D 83 Cb35
Berško I 100b Bb62
Bertamirans (Ames) E 30 Ad55
Berthelsdorf D 91 Fc41
Berville-sur-Mer F 19 Fd35
Berwick-upon-Tweed GB 11 Ed14
Berysław UA 137 Ed16
Berzé-la-Ville F 25 Ja45
Berzence H 104 Gd57
Berzocana E 37 Cb67
Besançon F 25 Jc42
Besankovičy BY 136 Eb11
Bescanó E 35 Hb58
Bescaran E 34 Gc58
Besednice CZ 97 Fd49
Besenyszög H 99 Jb53
Bęsia H 87 Jb31
Besigheim D 95 Cd47
Besoaker N 57 Ea27
Bessan F 35 Hc55
Bessans F 29 Kb48
Bessbrook GB 5 Cc18
Besse F 29 Ka49
Besse-et-Saint-Anastaise F 28 Hd48
Bessèges F 28 Hd52
Bessenay F 28 Ja47
Bessenbach D 89 Cd44
Bessé-sur-Braye F 23 Ga40
Best NL 88 Ba38
Bestensee D 84 Ed37
Bestwig D 89 Cc39
Betanzos E 30 Ba54
Bétera E 39 Fd67
Beteta E 39 Ec64
Bethelon D 83 Cb35
Béthéniville F 21 Hd35
Bethersden GB 16 Ga29
Betheny F 23 Ja44
Bethesda GB 12 Dd22
Béthines F 23 Ga44
Béthisy-Saint-Pierre F 20 Ha35
Bethon F 20 Hc35
Béthune F 17 Gd31
Betliar SK 99 Jb48
Bettembourg L 21 Jc34
Bettens CH 94 Bb54
Bettola I 101 Cd61
Bettona I 109 Eb68
Bettyhill GB 8 Ea04
Bettystown IRL 5 Cd19
Betws-y-Coed GB 12 Ea22
Betws E 39 Fc66
Betzdorf D 89 Cb41
Betzenstein D 90 Dd46
Betzweiler-Wälde D 95 Cb49

Bevagna I 109 Eb68
Bevensen D 83 Da36
Beverley GB 13 Fc20
Bevern D 89 Da33
Beverstedt D 83 Cd33
Beverungen D 89 Da39
Beverwijk NL 82 Ad35
Bewcastle GB 11 Ec16
Bexbach D 88 Bd46
Bexhill GB 16 Fd30
Beycik TR 135 Cc92
Beynac-et-Cazenac F 27 Gb50
Beynes F 20 Gd37
Bežanicy RUS 136 Eb10
Bézanaux-sur-Bine F 29 Jc50
Bezdėz CZ 91 Fc43
Bežeck RUS 137 Ed09
Bézenuck RUS 137 Ga10
Béziers F 35 Hc55
Biała PL 92 Gd43
Biała PL 90 Hd38
Biała Góra PL 86 Hb31
Biała Piska PL 87 Jd32
Biała Podlaska PL 87 Kb37
Biała Rawska PL 92 Ja38
Białobrzegi PL 87 Jb36
Białobrzegi PL 92 Ja46
Białobrzegi PL 93 Jb39
Białogard PL 85 Ga31
Białogóry PL 87 Kb30
Biały Bór PL 85 Gc32
Biały Dunajec PL 92 Ja46
Białystok PL 87 Kb33
Biancavilla I 115 Fc85
Bianco I 115 Gb84
Biar E 45 Fb70
Biarritz F 26 Ed54
Biasca CH 101 Cc56
Biatorbágy H 98 Hc53
Bibakvtad N 47 Jc07
Bibbiano I 101 Da62
Bibbiena I 108 Dd65
Bibbona I 108 Da67
Biberach D 89 Cc40
Biberach an der Riß D 95 Da50
Biberbach D 95 Dc49
Bibertal D 95 Db50
Bibione I 103 Ed59
Biblis D 89 Cc45
Bibury GB 15 Ed27
Bicaz RO 118 Ea58
Biccari I 110 Fd73
Bicester GB 15 Fa27
Bichl D 96 Dd52
Bichlbach A 95 Dc53
Bickendorf D 88 Bd43
Bicker GB 16 Fc23
Bickleigh GB 14 Ea30
Bickley Moss GB 13 Ec23
Bicorp E 39 Fb69
Bicske H 98 Hc53
Biddenden GB 16 Ga29
Biddestone GB 15 Ec28
Biddinghuizen NL 82 Bb35
Biddulph GB 13 Ed22
Bideford GB 14 Dd29
Bidegyan E 32 Eb56
Bidoni I 107 Ca77
Bidsteded D 89 Db45
Bieberehren D 89 Db46
Bieberggmünd D 89 Cd44
Biebersdorf D 90 Fa38
Biebertal D 89 Cc42
Biecz PL 91 Jd45
Biecz PL 93 Jd45
Bielawa PL 91 Gd41
Biedenkopf D 89 Cc41
Biederitz D 84 Eb37
Bidxter GB 9 Fa05
Bielawa PL 91 Gd41
Bielba (Herrerías) E 32 Db55
Biglanoml BY 136 Ea12
Białynicy BY 136 Eb12
Bielmonte I 100 Ca58
Bielsko-Biała PL 92 Hc45
Bielsk Podlaski PL 87 Kb34
Bienenbüttel D 83 Dc34
Bieniów PL 91 Ga40
Bienne CH 94 Bc53
Bienservida E 44 Ea71
Bienvenida E 43 Bd71
Bierawa PL 92 Hb44
Bière CH 94 Ba55
Bierge E 33 Fc64
Biertan RO 118 Da60
Bierun PL 92 Hc44
Biescas E 33 Fc67
Biesenthal D 84 Fa35
Biesles F 25 Jc42
Bietigheim D 95 Cb48
Bietigheim-Bissingen D 95 Cd48
Bieuzy-Lanvaux F 22 Ea40
Bieżuń PL 86 Hd34
Bigadiç TR 131 Fa83
Bigbury-on-Sea GB 14 Dd32
Biggar GB 11 Eb14
Biggleswade GB 16 Fc26
Bignan F 22 Eb40
Bignasco CH 101 Cb56
Bignor GB 15 Fb30
Bigüézal E 33 Fa57
Bihać BIH 104 Ga62
Biharia RO 117 Cb56
Biharkeresztes H 99 Ka53
Biharnagybajom H 99 Jd53
Bijeljina BIH 105 Hb62
Bíla Cerkva UA 136 Ec15
Bílá Voda CZ 91 Gc43
Bilbao E 32 Ea55
Bilbo = Bilbao E 32 Ea55
Bildudalur IS 2 Ab03
Bilgoraj PL 93 Kb42
Bilhorod-Dnistrovs'kyj UA 136 Ec17
Bilina CZ 90 Fa43
Bilisht AL 124 Ba77
Bilidal S 71 Fd49
Billerbeck D 82 Ca37
Billericay GB 16 Ga27
Billesdon GB 13 Fa24
Billigheim D 89 Cd46
Billingborough GB 12 Fc23
Billingham GB 13 Fa17
Billinghay GB 16 Fc23
Billingshurst GB 16 Fb30
Bilohir's'k UA 137 Fb14
Bilokurakyne UA 137 Fb14
Bilopillja UA 137 Fb13
Bilovec CZ 92 Ha45
Bilovods'k UA 137 Fb14
Bilzingsleben D 90 Ea40
Binarville F 21 Ja35
Binas F 24 Gd40
Binbrook GB 13 Fc21
Binche B 21 Hd31
Bingen D 89 Cb44
Bingen D 95 Db52
Bingham GB 13 Fb23
Bingley GB 13 Ed20
Bingsta S 58 Fd32
Binibeque Vell E 41 Ja66
Biniel-là-là E 41 Ja65
Binissalem E 41 Hb67
Binn CH 94 Ca56
Binn-Eadair IRL 7 Da21
Binsfeld D 88 Bd44
Binz D 84 Fa30
Biograd na moru HR 110 Fd65
Bionaz I 100 Bc57

Biorra IRL 6 Ca22
Biot F 29 Kc53
Birdhill IRL 6 Bd23
Birdlip GB 15 Ec27
Birdsmoor Gate GB 14 Eb30
Birgi TR 131 Fb85
Birgland D 90 Ea46
Biri N 65 Ea38
Biristrand N 65 Ea38
Birkenau D 89 Cc46
Birkenfeld D 88 Bd45
Birkenfeld D 89 Da45
Birkenfeld D 95 Cc48
Birkerod DK 77 Ec55
Birmingham GB 15 Ed25
Bírónico CH 101 Cc57
Birr IRL 6 Ca22
Birsay GB 9 Eb02
Birstein D 89 Cd44
Birštonas LT 80 Kc58
Bisceglie I 110 Gc73
Bischberg D 89 Dc45
Bischheim F 94 Ca48
Bischoffen D 89 Cc42
Bischofsheim D 89 Cb44
Bischofsheim D 89 Db43
Bischofshofen A 96 Ed53
Bischofsreut D 96 Fa48
Bischofswerda D 91 Fb41
Bischofswiesen D 96 Ed52
Bischofszell CH 95 Cd52
Bischwiller F 94 Ca48
Bisenti I 109 Fa69
Bishop Auckland GB 13 Fa17
Bishop's Castle GB 12 Eb24
Bishop's Lydeard GB 14 Eb29
Bishop's Stortford GB 16 Fd27
Bishop's Waltham GB 15 Fa30
Bisiano F 106 Ca71
Bisignano I 113 Gb79
Biskupiec PL 86 Hc33
Biskupiec PL 87 Jc31
Bisley GB 15 Ec27
Bismark D 84 Ea36
Bismervik N 46 Hd05
Bismo N 64 Db34
Bispgården S 58 Gb31
Bispingen D 83 Db34
Bissendorf D 83 Cc37
Bissendorf D 89 Db43
Bissingen D 95 Dc49
Bissone I 101 Cc58
Bissy-sur-Fley F 25 Ja44
Bistrita RO 118 Dc57
Bisztynek PL 87 Jb31
Bitburg D 88 Bd44
Bitche F 94 Bd47
Bitetto I 113 Gd74
Bitola MK 124 Bb76
Bitonto I 113 Gc74
Bitterfeld D 90 Eb40
Bitz D 95 Cc50
Biville F 19 Ed34
Bivio CH 101 Cd56
Bivona I 114 Eb85
Bixter GB 9 Fa05
Bizeneuille F 24 Ha44
Bizzarone I 101 Cb58
Bjahoml BY 136 Ea12
Bjalyničy BY 136 Eb12
Bjärnum S 59 Hb29
Bjärred S 79 Hd53
Bärby N 48 Ga12
Bjaroza BY 136 Ea13
Bjärred S 77 Ed56
Bjästa S 59 Hd33
Bjelovar HR 104 Gc58
Bjerangen N 52 Fb19
Bjerka N 52 Fb21
Bjerkvik N 48 Gb13
Bjerregård N 76 Cd54
Bjolstad N 64 Dc39
Bjordal N 62 Cd37
Bjørhaugslåtten N 58 Fd30
Björkås S 52 Fd23
Björkberg S 66 Fc36
Björkdal N 54 Hc24
Björkerud N 66 Fc41
Bjørkflåta N 63 Da40
Björklinden S 53 Hb24
Björksele S 54 Jb21
Björna S 58 Gd29
Bjørnevatn N 47 Kc07
Bjørnhaugseter N 64 Dd36
Björnlanda S 65 Ed34
Björnrike S 65 Fb33
Bjuråker S 66 Ga35
Bjurfors S 59 Hb29
Bjurholm S 59 Ha28
Bjursele S 54 Hc24
Bjurström S 59 Hb25
Bjurträsk S 59 Hc24
Bjurvatnet S 59 Hb26
Blaby GB 13 Fa24
Black Bull IRL 7 Cd21
Blackburn GB 13 Ec20
Blackburn GB 11 Eb13
Blackhall GB 8 Da07
Blackridge GB 11 Eb13
Blackrock IRL 4 Cc18
Blacklunans GB 11 Eb10
Blackmoor Gate GB 14 Dd29
Black Mount GB 10 Dd11
Black Notley GB 16 Ga27
Blackpool GB 12 Eb20
Blackridge GB 11 Ea13
Blackwater GB 15 Fa31
Blackwater IRL 7 Cd24
Blackwaterfoot GB 10 Db14
Blackwood GB 14 Eb27
Bladel NL 88 Ba39
Blaenau Ffestiniog GB 12 Dd23
Blaenavon GB 14 Eb27
Blagdon GB 14 Eb28
Blagnac F 34 Gb54
Blagodarnyj RUS 137 Ga15
Blagovgradd RUS 127 Cb73
Blagon F 26 Fa50
Blaibach D 96 Ec47
Blain F 23 Ed41
Blainville-Crevon F 20 Gd34
Blainville-sur-l'Eau F 21 Jd37
Blairgowrie GB 11 Eb11
Blaisy-Bas F 25 Jb42
Blaj RO 117 Da60
Blakeney GB 15 Ec27
Blakeney GB 13 Gb24
Blakstad N 63 Da44
Blâmont F 21 Jd37
Blanca E 45 Fb72
Blancey F 25 Ja42

Blancos E 30 Bb58
Blandford Forum GB 15 Ec30
Blangy-sur-Meuse F 21 Ja33
Blanes E 35 Hb60
Blangy GB 4 Ca17
Blankenberge B 17 Ha28
Blankenburg D 90 Dd38
Blankenhain D 90 Ea40
Blankenheim D 88 Bc42
Blankenheim D 90 Ea39
Blankenfelde-Mahlow D 84 Ed37
Blanquefort F 26 Fb50
Blansko CZ 97 Gb46
Blanzy F 25 Ja44
Blaron F 29 Kb52
Blåsmark S 54 Hc21
Blatné SK 98 Gd50
Blatnikse S 53 Gc23
Blaubeuren D 95 Da47
Blaufelden D 95 Da47
Blaustein D 95 Da49
Blåvik S 58 Gc25
Blavozy F 28 Hd49
Blaye F 26 Fb49
Błazowa PL 93 Ka44
Bleadon GB 14 Eb28
Bleckäsen S 57 Fb30
Bleckede D 84 Dd33
Bled SLO 100 Fa57
Błędów PL 92 Hd43
Bleialf D 88 Bc43
Bleichenrode D 90 Dd40
Bleik N 48 Fd11
Blekendorf D 84 Dc30
Blender D 83 Da34
Bléneau F 24 Ha41
Blénod-lès-Toul F 21 Jc37
Blesle F 28 Hc49
Blessington IRL 7 Cd22
Bletchingdon GB 15 Fa27
Bletsoe GB 16 Fc26
Bleury F 24 Ha36
Blévarincourt F 25 Jc39
Blévés F 23 Fd38
Blewbury GB 15 Fa28
Blieskastel D 88 Bd46
Bligny F 25 Ja39
Bliksvær N 52 Fb17
Blizanów PL 92 Ha41
Blockley GB 15 Ed26
Bloemendaal NL 17 Hd25
Blois F 24 Gd41
Blokhus DK 70 Dc50
Blokzijl NL 82 Bc34
Blomberg D 89 Cd38
Blönduós IS 2 Ba03
Błonie PL 87 Jb37
Błotnica PL 92 Hd43
Błotno PL 85 Fd32
Blovice CZ 90 Ed46
Błowatz D 84 Ea31
Bloxham GB 15 Fa26
Bludenz A 95 Da54
Bludov CZ 91 Gc45
Błudowo PL 86 Hd30
Blue Ball IRL 7 Cb21
Blueford GB 14 Eb24
Blumau I 102 Dd56
Blumberg D 84 Ec34
Blyberg S 65 Fc37
Blyth GB 11 Fa16
Blyth Bridge GB 11 Eb14
Bnin PL 85 Gc37
Bo GB 14 Dd31
Bo'Ness GB 11 Ea13
Boario Terme I 101 Da58
Boat of Garten GB 9 Ea08
Boa Vista P 36 Ac65
Bobadilla Estación E 43 Cd75
Bobbau D 90 Eb39
Bobbio I 101 Cc61
Bobenheim-Roxheim D 89 Cb45
Bobigny F 20 Gd36
Bobingen D 95 Dc50
Bobingen an der Rems D 95 Da48
Böblingen D 95 Cd48
Bobolice PL 85 Gb31
Bobowa PL 93 Jd45
Bobr BY 136 Eb12
Bobrov RUS 137 Fb13
Bobrovycja UA 136 Ec14
Bobrowko PL 85 Fd35
Bobrownik PL 86 Hc35
Bobrynec' UA 137 Ed16
Boc ŠK 99 Jb48
Boca de Huérgano E 31 Cc56
Bocairent E 45 Fb70
Bocca di l'Oru F 106 Cb72
Bocca di Piazza I 113 Gc80
Bochnia PL 93 Jd44
Bocholt B 88 Bb39
Bocholt D 88 Bc38
Bochov CZ 90 Ed43
Bochum D 88 Ca38
Bockau D 90 Ec43
Bockenem D 89 Db38
Bockhorn D 83 Cc32
Bockhorn D 83 Cc33
Böckwitz D 84 Ea36
Boda S 66 Ff38
Boda glasbruk S 78 Fd53
Bønnerup Strand DK 77 Dd53
Bonnétable F 23 Fd39
Bonneuil F 24 Gb39
Bonneval F 24 Gd38
Bonneval-sur-Arc F 29 Kb48
Bonneville F 29 Jd45
Bonneville-la-Louvet F 19 Fd35
Bönnigheim D 95 Cd47
Bönningstedt D 83 Db32
Bonny-sur-Loire F 24 Ha41
Bono E 34 Ga58
Bono I 107 Ca76
Bonorva I 107 Ca76
Bönov S 59 Ja28
Bonrepos F 27 Gc53

Brattbäcken S 58 Gd27
Bratfors S 72 Fb42
Brattholm N 48 Fd11
Bråtom N 56 Dc31
Bratsberg N 57 Ea30
Brattvåg N 56 Da30
Brauel D 83 Da33
Braunau a.Inn A 96 Ec50
Braunfels D 89 Cc42
Braunlage D 90 Dc39
Bräunlingen D 95 Cb51
Braunsbedra D 90 Ea40
Braunschweig D 83 Dc37
Braunton GB 14 Dd29
Bravuogn CH 101 Cd56
Bray IRL 7 Cd22
Bray Shop GB 14 Dc31
Bray-sur-Seine F 24 Hb38
Bray-sur-Somme F 20 Ha33
Brazatortas E 44 Cd70
Brčko BIH 105 Hc61
Brdów PL 86 Hb37
Bré IRL 7 Cd22
Brea de Aragón E 33 Ed61
Breakish GB 8 Db08
Bream GB 14 Eb27
Brean GB 14 Ea28
Breasclete GB 8 Da05
Brechfa GB 14 Dd26
Brechin GB 11 Ec12
Breckerfeld D 88 Ca40
Brecon GB 14 Ea26
Breda NL 17 Hd27
Bredbyn S 57 Fb29
Bredbyn S 58 Gb31
Breddorf D 83 Da33
Brede NL 17 Hd27
Bredebro DK 76 Da54
Bredelar D 89 Cd39
Bredene B 17 Ha29
Bredereiche D 84 Ed34
Bredgar GB 16 Ga29
Bredon GB 15 Ec26
Bredsjön S 57 Fc31
Bredsträsk S 58 Gd28
Bredviken S 54 Jb21
Bredwardine GB 14 Eb26
Bregana D 100 Ga59
Breganze I 102 Dd59
Bregenz A 95 Da53
Bréhal F 22 Ed37
Bréhan F 22 Ea40
Brehna D 90 Eb40
Breidablik IS 3 Ca06
Breidenbach D 89 Cc41
Bréil-sur-Roya F 29 Kd52
Breinton A 97 Fb52
Breisach D 94 Bd50
Breitenau A 97 Fb52
Breitenbrunn D 90 Ec43
Breitenbrunn D 90 Ec43
Breitenbrunn D 96 Ea48
Breitenfelde D 83 Dc32
Breitenweg D 89 Cc39
Breiwikbotn N 46 Hc05
Brejtovo RUS 137 Ed09
Brekken N 57 Ec29
Brekkøm N 57 Ea30
Brekstad N 56 Dd29
Breukelen NL 82 Bb35
Breuna D 89 Cd39
Brevik N 63 Db43
Brewood GB 15 Ec24
Březina CZ 91 Fd45
Breznik BG 124 Cd72
Brezno SK 99 Ja48
Brezová pod Bradlom SK 98 Gd49
Březovice CZ 91 Fc43
Brezziky PL 92 Ha41
Brg PL 92 Gd42
Briançon F 29 Kb49
Brianny F 25 Ja42
Briare F 24 Ha41
Briatexte F 34 Gd54
Briaucourt F 21 Jb38
Briceni MD 136 Ea16
Brickendon GB 16 Fc28
Briconmesnil F 20 Gb34
Bride GB 10 Dd18
Bridestowe GB 14 Dd30
Bridge GB 17 Gb29
Bridge of Allan GB 11 Ea12
Bridge of Balgie GB 11 Dd11
Bridge of Cally GB 11 Eb10
Bridge of Dye GB 9 Ec09
Bridge of Ericht GB 10 Dd11
Bridge of Orchy GB 10 Dd11
Bridgend GB 14 Ea28
Bridgetown IRL 7 Cc25
Bridge Trafford GB 13 Ec21
Bridgnorth GB 15 Ec24
Bridgwater GB 14 Eb29
Bridlington GB 13 Fc18
Bridport GB 14 Eb31
Brie F 23 Fa42
Brie-Comte-Robert F 20 Ha37
Briec F 22 Dc39
Brie-sous-Matha F 26 Fc46
Brienne-le-Château F 25 Ja38
Brienon-sur-Armançon F 24 Hc39
Brienz CH 94 Cb54
Brienza I 110 Ga77
Brieselang D 84 Ed36
Briesen D 84 Fb37
Brietlingen D 83 Dc33
Brieulles-sur-Bar F 21 Ja34
Brieva de Cameros E 32 Ea59
Briey F 21 Jc35
Brig CH 100 Ca56
Brigg GB 13 Fc21
Brighouse GB 13 Ed20
Brightling GB 16 Ga30
Brightlingsea GB 17 Gb27
Brighton GB 15 Fc30
Brihuega E 38 Ea63

Brignais F 28 Jb47
Brignogan-Plage F 22 Db37
Brignoud F 29 Jd48
Brig o'Turk GB 10 Dd12
Brihuega E 38 Eb28
Briksdal N 62 Cd39
Brimfield GB 15 Ec25
Brimnes N 62 Cc39
Brindisi I 113 Hb75
Brinlack IRL 4 Ca15
Brinon-sur-Beuvron F 24 Hc42
Brinon-sur-Sauldre F 24 Gd42
Brinzio I 101 Cb58
Brioneé F 24 Gd34
Brioude F 28 Hd49
Brioux-sur-Boutonne F 26 Fc46
Brisighella I 102 Dd64
Brissogne I 100 Bc57
Brisley GB 16 Ga24
Brissac-Quincé F 23 Fb42
Brissago CH 101 Cb57
Brive-la-Gaillarde F 27 Gc49
Brixen I 102 Dd56
Brixlegg A 96 Ea53
Brize Norton GB 15 Fa27
Brjanka RUS 137 Fb15
Brjanskt RUS 137 Ed12
Brnyan GB 9 Ec02
Bro S 72 Gc43
Broadchalke GB 15 Ed29
Broadford GB 8 Db08
Broadford IRL 6 Bd23
Broad Haven GB 14 Db27
Broad Hinton GB 15 Ed28
Broad Oak GB 16 Ga30
Broadstairs GB 16 Gb28
Broadwas GB 15 Ec25
Broadway GB 15 Ed26
Broadwell Ho GB 13 Ed17
Broadwindsor GB 14 Eb31
Broager DK 76 Db31
Broby S 78 Fd54
Brocas F 26 Fb52
Brochel GB 8 Db08
Bročów PL 86 Hd35
Brockel D 83 Da34
Bröckel D 83 Dc36
Brockenhurst GB 15 Ed30
Brockley GB 14 Eb28
Brodek u Prostějova CZ 97 Gc47
Brodek u Přerova CZ 92 Gd46
Brodick GB 10 Da14
Brodie Castle GB 9 Eb07
Brodnica PL 86 Hc34
Brodowe Łąki PL 87 Jb33
Brody PL 91 Fd39
Brøk PL 87 Jd35
Brokdorf D 83 Da31
Brokęcino PL 85 Gb33
Brokstedt D 83 Da31
Brolo I 115 Fc84
Bromberg = Bydgoszcz PL 86 Ha33
Bromé D 84 Dd36
Bromley GB 16 Fd28
Bromma S 78 Fd54
Bromölla S 78 Fc54
Brompton GB 15 Ed25
Bromsgrove GB 15 Ec25
Bromyard GB 15 Ec25
Bronice PL 91 Ga40
Bronkow D 91 Fb39
Brønnøysund N 52 Fa23
Bronte I 115 Fc85
Brook GB 15 Ed30
Brookhouse GB 13 Ec19
Brora GB 9 Ea06
Brösarp S 78 Fc55
Brørup DK 76 Da55
Brösby S 78 Fd53
Brostadbotn N 48 Ga12
Brotas P 36 Ad68
Brøttem N 57 Ea30
Brotterode D 89 Dc42
Brøttum N 65 Ea38
Brou F 24 Gc39
Brough GB 13 Ed18
Broughshane GB 5 Cd16
Broughton GB 11 Eb14
Broughton GB 13 Fb21
Broughton Astley GB 13 Fa24
Broughton-in-Furness GB 12 Eb18
Broughton Poggs GB 15 Ed27
Broumov CZ 91 Gb43
Broussey-Raulecourt F 21 Jc36
Brouwerswaven NL 17 Hc27
Brovary UA 136 Ec14
Brovst DK 70 Db50
Brown Candover GB 15 Fa29
Brownhills GB 13 Ed24
Brownston GB 14 Dd32
Broxton GB 13 Ec22
Brozas E 37 Bd66
Brozolo I 100 Bd60
Brozzo I 101 Da59
Bru N 63 Db43
Bruay-la-Buissière F 17 Gd31
Bruay-sur-l'Escaut F 20 Hb31
Bubakk N 57 Eb30
Bubenreuth D 90 Dd46
Bubwith GB 13 Fb20
Buc F 20 Gd37
Buča UA 136 Ec14
Bucarelli F 115 Fc87
Buccheri I 115 Fc87
Bucchianico I 109 Fa70
Buccino I 111 Ga76
Buces RO 117 Cd59
Buch D 95 Db50
Buch D 95 Db50
Buchboden A 95 Da54
Buchau, Bad D 95 Cd51
Buchau D 90 Dd41
Buchen D 89 Cd46
Büchen D 83 Dc32
Buchenberg D 95 Db52
Buchères F 25 Hd39
Buchholz (Westerwald) D 88 Ca42
Buchloe GB 95 Db51
Buchlovice CZ 98 Gd48
Buchs CH 95 Cd54
Buchs CH 95 Cd54
Buchy F 20 Gd34
Buckden GB 13 Ed19
Buckden GB 16 Fc26
Buckeburg D 83 Da37
Buckfastleigh GB 14 Dd31
Buckhaven GB 11 Eb13
Buckie GB 9 Ec07
Buckingham GB 15 Fb26
Buckley GB 13 Ec22
Bückeburg GB 83 Da36
Bucklev GB 13 Ec22
Buckminster GB 13 Fb24
Bucknell GB 14 Eb25
Bucków GB 15 Fb26
Bucks Green GB 15 Fb29
Bucy-lès-Pierrepont F 20 Hc34
Buczek PL 92 Hd40
Bud N 56 Da31
Budadörs H 98 Hc53
Budaörs H 98 Hc53
Budapest H 98 Hc53
Budča SK 98 Hc49
Buddusò I 107 Cb76
Bude GB 14 Dc30
Budel NL 88 Ba39
Budia E 38 Eb63
Budingen D 89 Cd43
Budišov nad Budišovkou CZ 92 Gd45
Budkoice SK 99 Ka49
Budleigh Salterton GB 14 Ea31
Budmerice SK 98 Gd50
Budřička Dužý PL 93 Kc43
Budoni I 107 Cc75
Budrio I 102 Dd63
Budva MNE 111 Hd70
Budynė nad Ohří CZ 90 Fb43
Budyně PL 86 Hc31
Buenache de Alarcón E 38 Eb67
Buggerru I 107 Bd79
Bugino S 72 Gc43
Buglose F 26 Fa54
Bugøyfjord N 47 Kb07
Bugøynes N 47 Kc07
Bugul'ma RUS 137 Ga09
Bühl D 89 Cc46
Bühl D 94 Ca49
Bühlertal D 94 Ca48
Bühlertann D 95 Da47
Bülach CH 95 Cc52
Bülkau D 83 Cd31
Bulken N 62 Cc38
Bullas E 45 Fa72
Bulle CH 100 Bc55
Bülkwitz GB 15 Fb24
Bünde D 83 Da37
Bullington GB 15 Fa29
Bully-les-Mines F 17 Gd31
Bülstringen D 84 Ea37
Bultei I 107 Ca76
Bunclody IRL 7 Cc23
Buncrana IRL 4 Ca15
Bunde D 83 Cb32
Bünde D 83 Da37
Bunessan GB 10 Cd11
Bungay GB 17 Gc25
Bunić HR 104 Fc62
Bunkris S 65 Fc37
Bunmahon IRL 7 Cb25
Bunnahowen IRL 4 Bc17
Bunnyconnellan IRL 4 Bc18
Buño E 30 Ad54
Buñol E 39 Fb68
Buñuel E 33 Ed59
Bunsbeek B 21 Hd30
Buntingford GB 16 Fc27
Buonabitacolo I 111 Ga77
Buonalbergo I 110 Fc73
Buoux F 29 Jd53
Burbáguena E 33 Ed62
Burbach D 89 Cc41
Burcei I 107 Cb79
Burdur TR 135 Cd90
Bures F 28 Jb47
Bureå S 59 Hc24
Büren D 89 Cd39
Büren an der Aare CH 94 Bc53
Burford GB 15 Ed27
Burg D 84 Eb37
Burg D 84 Fa32
Burg D 91 Fc38
Burg, Bad D 90 Ea41
Burgau A 97 Gb54
Burgau D 95 Db49
Burgau P 42 Ab74

Buitenpost NL 82 Bb33

Buitrago del Lozoya – Châteauroux


Buitrago del Lozoya E 38 Dc62
Bujalance E 44 Da72
Bujaraloz E 34 Fc61
Buje HR 103 Ed60
Buk H 97 Gc53
Buk PL 85 Gb37
Bukanovskaja RUS 137 Fc13
Bükkábrány H 99 Jc51
Bukowa PL 93 Kb42
Bukownica PL 92 Ha40
Buksnes N 48 Fd12
Buky UA 136 Ec15
Bülach CH 95 Cb52
Buldan TR 131 Fc87
Bulgar RUS 137 Fd09
Bulken N 62 Cb38
Bullas E 45 Ec72
Bullaun IRL 6 Bd21
Bulle CH 94 Bc55
Bullmark S 59 Hc27
Bully-les-Mines F 20 Ha31
Bultei I 107 Ca75
Bun an Phobail IRL 5 Cc15
Bunarkaig GB 8 Dc09
Bunbeg IRL 4 Ca15
Bunbrosna IRL 4 Cb20
Bunclody IRL 7 Cc23
Buncrana IRL 5 Cc15
Bun Cranncha IRL 5 Cc15
Bunde D 82 Ca33
Bünde D 83 Cd37
Bun Dobhráin IRL 4 Ca17
Bundoran IRL 4 Ca17
Bundorf D 89 Dc44
Bunessan GB 10 Da11
Bungay GB 16 Gb25
Bunkris S 65 Fa36
Bunmahon IRL 7 Cb25
Bun na hAbhna IRL 4 Bb18
Bunnahowen IRL 4 Bb18
Bun na Leaca IRL 4 Ca15
Bunnyconnellan IRL 4 Bd18
Buñol E 39 Fb68
Bunschoten NL 82 Bb36
Buntingford GB 16 Fc26
Buntowo PL 85 Gc34
Buñuel E 33 Ed59
Bunyola E 41 Hb67
Buochs CH 95 Cb54
Buoldavárre S 49 Hc16
Buonabitacolo I 112 Ga77
Buonconvento I 108 Dc67
Burbach D 89 Cb41
Burbia E 31 Bd56
Bureå S 59 Hc25
Bureåborg S 58 Gc30
Burela E 31 Bc53
Burelles F 20 Hc33
Büren D 89 Cc39
Buren NL 82 Ba37
Buren NL 82 Bc32
Bures GB 16 Ga26
Burfjord N 49 Hc08
Burford GB 15 Ed27
Burg D 83 Da31
Burg D 84 Eb37
Burg D 91 Fb38
Burgas BG 127 Ed73
Burgau D 95 Db49
Burgdorf CH 94 Bd54
Burgdorf D 83 Db36
Burgdorf D 83 Db37
Burgebrach D 89 Dc45
Burgess Hill GB 16 Fc30
Burghaun D 89 Da42
Burghausen D 90 Eb40
Burghausen D 96 Ec51
Burghead GB 9 Eb07
Burgheim D 95 Dc49
Burgh-Haamstede NL 17 Hb27
Burgh le Marsh GB 13 Fd22
Burgh Saint Peter GB 16 Gb25
Burgkirchen A 96 Ec51
Burgkirchen D 96 Ec51
Burgkunstadt D 90 Dd44
Burg Lauenstein D 90 Dd43
Burglauer D 89 Db43
Burglengenfeld D 96 Ea47
Burgo E 30 Bb55
Burgo P 36 Ad62
Burgoberbach D 95 Dc47
Burgohondo E 37 Cd64
Burgos E 32 Dc58
Burgos I 107 Ca76
Burgsinn D 89 Da44
Bürgstadt D 89 Cd45
Burgstädt D 90 Ec41
Burg Stargard D 84 Ed33
Burgsteinfurt D 82 Ca37
Burgthann D 96 Dd47
Burguete E 33 Ed56
Burguillos E 43 Ca73
Burgum NL 82 Bc33
Burgwald D 89 Cc41
Burgwedel D 83 Db36
Burhaniye TR 131 Ec82
Buriasco I 100 Bc61
Burie F 26 Fc47
Burjassot E 39 Fb67
Burkardroth D 89 Db43
Burkat PL 86 Ja33
Burkhardtsdorf D 90 Ec42
Burladingen D 95 Cc50
Burley in Wharfedale GB 13 Ed20
Burlo D 82 Bd37
Burlton GB 12 Eb23
Burness GB 9 Ed02
Burnham-on-Crouch GB 16 Ga27
Burnham-on-Sea GB 14 Eb29
Burnley GB 13 Ed20
Burntisland GB 11 Eb13
Buronzo I 100 Ca59
Burow D 84 Ed32
Burrafirth GB 9 Fb03
Burravoe GB 9 Fb04
Burren IRL 6 Bc21
Burringham GB 13 Fb21
Burry Port GB 14 Dd27
Bursa TR 131 Fd80
Burscheid D 88 Bd40
Burscough GB 12 Eb21
Bursiljum S 59 Hc26
Bürstadt D 89 Cc45
Burszewo PL 87 Jb31
Burtenbach D 95 Db50
Burton Agnes GB 13 Fc19
Burton Constable GB 13 Fc20
Burton-in-Kendal GB 13 Ec19
Burton Latimer GB 15 Fb25
Burtonport IRL 4 Ca15
Burton-upon-Stather GB 13 Fb21
Burton-upon-Trent GB 13 Fa23
Burträsk S 59 Hc26
Burwash GB 16 Fd30
Burwell GB 13 Fd22
Burwell GB 16 Fd25
Burwick GB 9 Ec04
Bury GB 13 Ec21
Bury Saint Edmunds GB 16 Ga25
Busalla I 101 Cb62
Busana I 101 Da63
Busca I 100 Bc62
Busdorf D 83 Db29
Buseck D 89 Cc42
Busendorf D 89 Dc44
Bushey GB 16 Fc27
Bushfield IRL 6 Bd23
Bushmills GB 5 Cd15
Busigny F 20 Hb33
Bus'k UA 136 Ea15
Busko-Zdrój PL 93 Jb43
Busot E 45 Fb71
Bussac-Forêt F 26 Fc49
Bussang F 25 Ka39
Busséol F 28 Hb47
Busseto I 101 Da61
Büßleben D 90 Dd41
Busson F 25 Jb38
Bussum NL 82 Ba36
Bussy-le-Repos F 24 Hb39
Bustadmon S 57 Fa30
Bustares E 38 Dd62
Bustidoño E 32 Db56
Bustillo de Páramo E 31 Cb57
Bustnes N 52 Fb20
Busto E 31 Ca53
Busto Arsizio I 101 Cb59
Büsum D 83 Da30
Butera I 114 Fa87
Butjadingen D 83 Cc32
Butler's Bridge IRL 4 Cb19
Butlerstown IRL 6 Bc26
Butley GB 16 Gb26
Butrint AL 124 Ab79
Butryny PL 86 Ja32
Büttelborn D 89 Cc44
Buttenwiesen D 95 Dc49
Buttevant IRL 6 Bd24
Buttington GB 12 Eb24
Buttlar D 89 Db42
Buttlerstown IRL 7 Cb25
Buttstädt D 90 Ea41
Büttstedt D 89 Db40
Buturlinovka RUS 137 Fb13
Butzbach D 89 Cc43
Bützow D 84 Eb32
Buurse NL 82 Bd37
Buvåg N 48 Fd14
Buvik N 56 Da32
Buvika N 52 Fa19
Buvika N 57 Ea30
Buxtehude D 83 Db33
Buxton GB 13 Ed22
Buxy F 25 Ja43
Büyükkarıştıran TR 127 Ed77
Buzançais F 24 Gb43
Buzancy F 21 Ja34
Buziaş RO 116 Bd61
Bweeng IRL 6 Bc25
Bwlch GB 14 Ea26
Bwlchllan GB 14 Dd25
Bwlch-y-ffridd GB 12 Ea24
Bwlch-y-Sarnau GB 14 Ea25
By N 57 Ea28
Byberget S 66 Fd33
Bychav BY 136 Eb12
Bychawa PL 93 Kb40
Bydalen S 57 Fb31
Bydgoszcz PL 86 Ha34
Byford GB 14 Eb26
Bygdeå S 59 Hc27
Bygdsiljum S 59 Hc26
Bykovo RUS 137 Fd13
Bylchau GB 12 Ea22
Byluft N 47 Kb07
Byrkjelo N 62 Cc35
Byrness GB 11 Ec15
Byrudstua N 65 Ea40
Byrum DK 71 Ea50
Byšice CZ 91 Fc44
Byske S 54 Hc24
Bystré CZ 91 Gb46
Bystřice CZ 91 Fc46
Bystřice CZ 92 Hc46
Bystřice nad Pernštejnem CZ 91 Gb46
Bystrzyca Kłodzka PL 91 Gc44
Byszyno PL 85 Ga31
Bytom PL 92 Hc43
Bytoń PL 86 Hb36
Bytów PL 86 Gd31
Bytyń PL 85 Gb36
Bzenec CZ 98 Gd48
Bzovík SK 98 Hd50


## C


Cabaj-Cápor SK 98 Ha50
Cabaleiros (Tordoia) E 30 Ad54
Cabañaquinta (Aller) E 31 Cc55
Cabanes E 40 Fd65
Cabanillas E 33 Ed59
Cabasse F 29 Ka54
Cabeça de Carneiro P 42 Ba70
Cabeça Gorda P 42 Ad71
Cabeço de Vide P 36 Ba68
Cabella Ligure I 101 Cc62
Cabezabellosa E 37 Ca65
Cabeza del Buey E 37 Cc69
Cabezamesada E 38 Dd66
Cabezas Rubias E 42 Bb72
Cabezón E 32 Da60
Cabezón de la Sal E 32 Db55
Cabezón de Liébana E 32 Da55
Cabourg F 19 Fc35
Cabra E 43 Cd74
Cabrach GB 9 Ec08
Cabragh GB 5 Cc17
Cabrahigos E 43 Ca77
Cabredo E 32 Eb57
Cabreiros E 30 Bb54
Cabrejas del Pinar E 32 Ea60
Cabrela P 36 Ac69
Cabrières F 28 Hc54
Cabruñana E 31 Cb54
Caccamo I 114 Ed84
Cacela Velha P 42 Ba74
Cáceres E 37 Bd67
Čačërsk BY 136 Ec13
Čačëvičy BY 136 Eb12
Cachtice SK 98 Ha49
Cacia P 36 Ac62
Cacin E 44 Db75
Cádabo (Baleira) E 31 Bc55
Cadafresnas E 31 Bd57
Cadagua E 32 Dd56
Cadaqués E 35 Hc58
Cadaval P 36 Ab67
Cadavedo E 31 Ca54
Čadca SK 92 Hc46
Cadenabbia I 101 Cc57
Cadenberge D 83 Da32
Cadillac F 26 Fc51
Cadis F 27 Gd54
Cádiz E 43 Bd76
Cadolzburg D 89 Dc46
Cadouin F 27 Ga50
Cadreita E 33 Ed59
Cadzand NL 17 Hb28
Caen F 19 Fc36
Caerleon GB 14 Eb27
Caernarfon GB 12 Dd22
Caerphilly GB 14 Eb28
Caersws GB 12 Ea24
Cagan Aman RUS 137 Ga14
Cagan-Nur RUS 137 Ga14
Cagli I 109 Eb66
Cagliari I 107 Ca80
Cagnano Varano I 110 Ga72
Cagnes-sur-Mer F 29 Kc53
Cagnotte F 26 Fa54
Caher IRL 4 Bc20
Cahir IRL 6 Ca24
Caherdaniel IRL 6 Ba26
Cahersiveen IRL 6 Ba25
Cahors F 27 Gc51
Cahul MD 119 Fb61
Cahuzac-sur-Vère F 27 Gd53
Caiazzo I 112 Fb74
Caín E 32 Da55
Cairnborrow GB 9 Ec08
Cairndow GB 10 Dc12
Cairnryan GB 10 Dc16
Cairo Montenotte I 100 Ca62
Caiseal IRL 6 Ca24
Caisleán an Bharraigh IRL 4 Bc19
Caisleán an Chomair IRL 7 Cb23
Caister-on-Sea GB 16 Gc24
Caistor GB 13 Fc21
Caivano I 112 Fb74
Cajarc F 27 Gc51
Cák H 97 Gb53
Čakino RUS 137 Fc12
Čakovec HR 104 Gb57
Çal TR 131 Fd87
Cala E 43 Bd72
Cala Antena E 41 Hc67
Calabernardo I 115 Fd88
Cala Blanca E 41 Ja66
Cala Blava E 41 Hb67
Cala de Mijas E 43 Cd77
Calaf E 34 Gc60
Calafell E 34 Gc62
Calafort Ros Láir IRL 7 Cd25
Cala Galdana E 41 Ja66
Cala Gonone I 107 Cc76
Calahorra E 33 Ec58
Calais F 16 Gc30
Cala Liberotto I 107 Cc76
Cala Llenya E 40 Gc69
Cala Major E 41 Hb67
Calambrone I 108 Da65
Cala Millor E 41 Hd67
Calamocha E 39 Ed63
Calamonaci I 114 Ec86
Cala Morell E 41 Ja65
Calanda E 39 Fc63
Cala Pi E 41 Hb68
Cala Rajada E 41 Hd67
Cala Rossa F 106 Cb72
Calascibetta I 114 Fa85
Calasetta I 107 Bc80
Calasparra E 45 Ec72
Calatafimi-Segesta I 114 Eb84
Calatañazor E 32 Ea60
Calatayud E 33 Ed61
Calatorao E 33 Ed61
Calau D 90 Fa39
Calbe D 90 Ea38
Calberlah D 83 Dc36
Calcinelli I 109 Ec65
Caldas da Rainha P 36 Ab66
Caldas de Reis E 30 Ad56
Caldas de Vizela P 30 Ad60
Caldbeck GB 12 Eb17
Caldelas P 30 Ad60
Calden D 89 Da39
Calderari I 115 Fb86
Calder Mains GB 9 Eb04
Calders E 35 Gd60
Caldes de Montbui E 35 Gd60
Caldirola I 101 Cc62
Caledon GB 5 Cd18
Calella E 35 Hb60
Calera y Chozas E 37 Cd66
Cales de Mallorca E 41 Hc67
Calestano I 101 Da62
Calfsound GB 9 Ec02
Calgary GB 10 Da10
Càlig E 40 Fd64
Calignac F 26 Fd52
Călimăneşti RO 121 Db63
Călineşti RO 122 Dc64
Calitri I 112 Fd75
Calizzano I 100 Bd63
Callainn IRL 7 Cb24
Callan IRL 7 Cb24
Callander GB 10 Dd12
Callanish GB 8 Da05
Callantsoog NL 82 Ba34
Callelongue F 29 Jc55
Calliano I 102 Dc58
Callington GB 14 Dc31
Callosa d'En Sarrià E 45 Fc70
Callosa de Segura E 45 Fa72
Callow IRL 4 Bd19
Callús E 35 Gd60
Calne GB 15 Ed28
Calnegre y Los Curas E 45 Ed74
Câlnic RO 117 Da61
Calolziocorte I 101 Cd58
Calonge E 41 Hc68
Calonne-Ricouart F 20 Gd31
Calp E 45 Fd70
Calpe E 45 Fd70
Caltabellotta I 114 Ec85
Caltagirone I 115 Fb87
Caltanissetta I 114 Fa86
Caltavuturo I 114 Fa85
Caluso I 100 Bd59
Calvão P 36 Ac63
Calver GB 13 Fa22
Calvering GB 16 Fd26
Calvi F 106 Ca69
Calvià E 41 Ha67
Calvi dell' Umbria I 109 Eb70
Calvine GB 11 Ea10
Calvinet F 27 Ha50
Calw D 95 Cc48
Calzada de Calatrava E 44 Db70
Calzada de los Molinos E 32 Da58
Calzadilla E 37 Bd65
Camaiore I 101 Da64
Camaldoli I 108 Dd65
Camarès F 28 Hb53
Camaret-sur-Mer F 22 Db38
Camarinal E 43 Ca78
Camariñas E 30 Ac54
Camarzana de Tera E 31 Cb59
Camas E 43 Bd74
Cambados E 30 Ad56
Cambela E 31 Bc58
Cambeo E 30 Bb57
Camber GB 16 Ga30
Cambil E 44 Dc73
Camblesforth GB 13 Fb20
Cambo GB 11 Ed16
Cambo-les-Bains F 33 Ed55
Camborne GB 14 Da32
Cambra P 36 Ad62
Cambrai F 20 Hb32
Cambre E 30 Ba54
Cambres P 30 Ba61
Cambridge GB 16 Fd26
Cambrils E 34 Gb62
Camburg D 90 Ea41
Camelford GB 14 Dc31
Camerano I 109 Ed66
Cameri I 101 Cb59
Camerino I 109 Ec67
Camerota I 112 Fd77
Caminha P 30 Ac58
Camineal E 39 Ed63
Çamlık TR 131 Ec88
Cammarata I 114 Ed85
Camogli I 101 Cc63
Camolin IRL 7 Cd24
Camp IRL 6 Ba24
Campagna I 112 Fd75
Campagnano di Roma I 108 Ea70
Campana I 113 Gd79
Campanario E 37 Cb69
Campanet E 41 Hb66
Campaspero E 32 Db61
Campbeltown GB 10 Db14
Campel F 22 Ec40
Camperduin NL 82 Ba34
Campi Bisenzio I 108 Dc65
Campiglia Marittima I 108 Da67
Campiglia Soana I 100 Bc59
Campigliatello Silano I 113 Gc80
Campillo de Altobuey E 39 Ec67
Câmpina RO 122 Ea64
Campi Salentina I 113 Hb76
Campitello F 106 Cb69
Campli I 109 Ed69
Campobasso I 109 Fc72
Campobello di Mazara I 114 Eb85
Campodarsego I 102 Ea59
Campo de Besteiros P 36 Ad63
Campo de Caso E 31 Cd55
Campo de Criptana E 38 Dd68
Campo de Viboras P 31 Bd60
Campo di Giove I 109 Fa71
Campodimele I 109 Ed73
Campo do Gerês P 30 Ba59
Campo Felice I 109 Ed70
Campofelice di Roccella I 114 Fa84
Campogalliano I 102 Db62
Campolattaro I 109 Fc73
Campoli Appennino I 109 Ed72
Campo Ligure I 101 Cb62
Campolongo E 30 Ba54
Campolongo Maggiore I 102 Ea60
Campo Lugar E 37 Cb68
Campo Maior P 36 Bb68
Campomarino I 113 Ha76
Camponaraya E 31 Bd57
Campo Real E 38 Dc65
Camporeale I 114 Ec84
Campo Redondo P 42 Ab72
Camporrells E 34 Ga59
Camporrobles E 39 Ed67
Campos E 41 Hc68
Camposampiero I 102 Ea59
Camposancos E 30 Ac58
Campo Staffi I 109 Ed71
Campotéjar E 44 Db74
Campotosto I 109 Ed69
Campo Vallemaggia CH 101 Cb56
Camps-en-Amiénois F 20 Gc33
Camptown GB 11 Ec15
Camrose GB 14 Db26
Camuñas E 38 Dc68
Camyuva TR 135 Cc92
Çan TR 131 Ec81
Caña SK 99 Jd49
Canabal E 30 Bb57
Cañada del Hoyo E 39 Ec66
Cañada Vellida E 39 Fa64
Çanakkale TR 130 Ea80
Canale I 100 Bd61
Canals E 39 Fb69
Canal San Bovo I 102 Dd57
Cañamares E 44 Ea70
Canaples F 20 Gd33
Canara E 45 Ec72
Canas de Senhorim P 36 Ba63
Cañaveras E 38 Eb65
Cancale F 19 Ed37
Cancelada E 31 Bd56
Cancello e Arnone I 112 Fa74
Candal P 36 Ad64
Candamil E 30 Bb54
Candanedo de Fenar E 31 Cc56
Çandarlı TR 130 Eb84
Candás E 31 Cc54
Candasnos E 34 Fd61
Candela I 112 Ga74
Candelario E 37 Cb64
Candeleda E 37 Cc65
Candelo I 100 Ca59
Candlesby GB 13 Fd22
Canelli I 100 Ca61
Canero E 31 Ca54
Canet F 28 Hc54
Canet F 35 Hb57
Canet de Mar E 35 Ha61
Cañete E 39 Ec66
Cañete de las Torres E 44 Da72
Canet lo Roig E 40 Fd64
Canet-Plage F 35 Hb57
Canewdon GB 16 Ga27
Canfranc E 33 Fb57
Canfranc-Estación E 33 Fb57
Cangas E 30 Ac57
Cangas E 31 Bc53
Cangas del Narcea E 31 Ca55
Cangas de Onís E 31 Cd54
Canha P 36 Ac69
Canhestros P 42 Ac71
Caniçada P 30 Ba59
Canicatti I 114 Ed86
Canicattini Bagni I 115 Fc87
Caniles E 44 Ea74
Canino I 108 Dd69
Cañizares E 38 Eb64
Canjáyar E 44 Ea75
Canna I 113 Gc77
Cannai I 107 Bc80
Cannes F 29 Kc54
Canneto sull'Oglio I 101 Da60
Cannich GB 8 Dd08
Canningstown IRL 5 Cc19
Cannington GB 14 Eb29
Cannobio I 101 Cb57
Cannock GB 13 Ed24
Cano P 36 Ba68
Canolo I 115 Gb83
Canonbie GB 11 Eb16
Canosa di Puglia I 113 Gb74
Canossa I 101 Da62
Ca'n Pastilla E 41 Hb67
Ca'n Picafort E 41 Hc66
Canstein D 89 Cd39
Cantalejo E 32 Db61
Canteleu F 19 Ga35
Canteras E 45 Fa74
Canterbury GB 16 Gb29
Cantillana E 43 Ca73
Cantoria E 44 Eb74
Cantù I 101 Cc58
Canvey Island GB 16 Ga28
Caoles GB 10 Cd10
Caorle I 103 Ec59
Caorso I 101 Cd61
Čapaevskij RUS 137 Ga10
Capalbio I 108 Dc69
Capbreton F 26 Ed54
Capdenac-Gare F 27 Gd51
Capel Curig GB 12 Dd22
Capel'ka RUS 136 Ea09
Capella E 34 Fd59
Capellades E 34 Gc61
Capelle aan de IJssel NL 17 Hd26
Capel Saint Mary GB 16 Ga26
Capestrano I 109 Fa70
Cap Ferret F 26 Fa51
Capidava RO 123 Fb66
Capistrello I 109 Ed71
Čaplygin RUS 137 Fb11
Čaplynka UA 137 Fa17
Capodimonte I 108 Dd69
Capo di Ponte I 101 Da57
Capo d'Orlando I 115 Fc84
Capo Raisigerbi I 114 Fa84
Capoterra I 107 Ca80
Cappagh GB 5 Cc17
Cappagh White IRL 6 Ca23
Cappeen IRL 6 Bc26
Cappeln D 83 Cc35
Cappercleuch GB 11 Eb14
Cappoquin IRL 6 Ca25
Capraria di Lecce I 113 Hc77
Caprese Michelangelo I 108 Ea66
Capri I 112 Fb76
Caprino CH 101 Cc57
Caprino Veronese I 102 Db59
Capua I 112 Fa74
Capurso I 113 Gd74
Caputh D 84 Ed37
Caputh GB 11 Eb11
Carabias E 32 Dc61
Caracena E 32 Dd61
Caramanico Terme I 109 Fa71
Carantec F 18 Dd37
Carasco I 101 Cc63
Carate Brianza I 101 Cc58
Caravaca de la Cruz E 45 Ec72
Caravaggio I 101 Cd59
Carbajo E 36 Bb66
Carballeda de Avia E 30 Ba57
Carballiño E 30 Ba57
Carballo E 30 Ad54
Carballo E 30 Bb55
Carballo (Verea) E 30 Ba58
Carbayín E 31 Cc54
Carbellino E 31 Ca61
Carbes E 31 Cd55
Carbis Bay GB 14 Da32
Carboneras E 45 Ec76
Carbonero el Mayor E 38 Db62
Carbonia I 107 Bd80
Carbonin I 102 Ea56
Carbonne F 34 Gb55
Carbost GB 8 Da07
Carcaboso E 37 Ca65
Carcaixent E 39 Fb69
Carcans F 26 Fa49
Carcans-Plage F 26 Fa49
Carção P 31 Bd60
Carcare I 100 Ca63
Carcassonne F 35 Ha55
Carcastillo E 33 Ed58
Carcelén E 39 Ed69
Carcès F 29 Ka54
Carcoforo I 100 Ca57
Cardedeu E 35 Ha60
Cardenete E 39 Ec67
Cardeñosa E 37 Cd63
Cardesse F 33 Fb55
Cardiff GB 14 Eb28
Cardigan GB 14 Dc26
Cardigos P 36 Ad66
Cardito I 109 Fa72
Cardross GB 10 Dd13
Carentan F 19 Fa35
Carew GB 14 Db27
Carhaix-Plouguer F 22 Dd38
Cariati I 113 Gd79
Carignan F 21 Jb34
Carignano I 100 Bc61
Cariñena E 33 Fa61
Carini I 114 Ec84
Carinish GB 8 Cd07
Cark GB 12 Eb19
Carland GB 5 Cd17
Carlanstown IRL 5 Cc20
Carlazzo I 101 Cc57
Carlentini I 115 Fc86
Carlet E 39 Fb68
Carlingford IRL 5 Da19
Carlisle GB 11 Eb16
Carlops GB 11 Eb13
Carlow D 84 Dd32
Carlow IRL 7 Cc23
Carloway GB 8 Da05
Carlton GB 13 Fa24
Carlton GB 15 Fb26
Carlton-on-Trent GB 13 Fb22
Carluke GB 11 Ea14
Carmagnola I 100 Bd61
Carmarthen GB 14 Dc26
Carmaux F 27 Gd53
Cármenes E 31 Cc56
Carmiano I 113 Hc76
Carmona E 43 Ca73
Carna IRL 4 Bb20
Carnac F 22 Ea41
Carnach GB 8 Dc08
Carn Domhnach IRL 5 Cc15
Carndonagh IRL 5 Cc15
Carnew IRL 7 Cd23
Carnforth GB 13 Ec19
Carnia Piani I 103 Ec57
Carnlough GB 5 Da16
Carno GB 12 Ea24
Carnoustie GB 11 Ec11
Carnwath GB 11 Ea14
Caromb F 29 Jc52
Caronia I 115 Fb84
Carosino I 113 Ha76
Carovigno I 113 Hb75
Carpaneto Piacentino I 101 Cd61
Carpenedolo I 102 Db60
Carpentras F 29 Jc52
Carpi I 102 Db62
Carpignano Salentino I 113 Hc77
Carpino I 110 Ga72
Carpinone I 109 Fb72
Carquefou F 23 Ed42
Carracastle IRL 4 Bd19
Carradale GB 10 Db14
Carragh IRL 7 Cc21
Carraig Mhachaire Rois IRL 5 Cd19
Carraig na Siúire IRL 7 Cb24
Carranque E 38 Db65
Carrara I 101 Da64
Carrascosa E 38 Eb64
Carrascosa de Haro E 38 Ea67
Carrascosa del Campo E 38 Ea66
Carrazeda de Ansiães P 31 Bc61
Carrbridge GB 9 Ea08
Carregado P 36 Ab68
Carregal do Sal P 36 Ba63
Carresse F 33 Fa55
Carrick GB 10 Dc12
Carrick IRL 4 Ca16
Carrickboy IRL 4 Cb20
Carrickfergus GB 5 Da17
Carrickmacross IRL 5 Cd19
Carrickmore GB 5 Cc17
Carrick-on-Shannon IRL 4 Ca19
Carrick-on-Suir IRL 7 Cb24
Carrig IRL 6 Bd25
Carrigadrohid IRL 6 Bc25
Carrigaholt IRL 6 Bb23
Carrigahorig IRL 6 Ca22
Carrigallen IRL 4 Cb19
Carriganimmy IRL 6 Bc25
Carrigkerry IRL 6 Bc23
Carrignavar IRL 6 Bd25
Carrigtohill IRL 6 Bd26
Carril E 30 Ad56
Carrión de Calatrava E 38 Db69
Carrión de los Condes E 32 Da58
Carrizo E 31 Cb57
Carrizosa E 38 Dd69
Carron Bridge GB 11 Ea13
Carros F 29 Kc53
Carrouge CH 94 Bb55
Carrowneden IRL 4 Bd18
Carrowntanlis IRL 4 Bd20
Carrowntrella IRL 4 Bc18
Carrù I 100 Bd62
Carryduff GB 5 Da17
Carsaig GB 10 Db11
Carsarsa della Delizia I 103 Ec58
Carsphairn GB 10 Dd15
Carstairs GB 11 Ea14
Cârța RO 118 Dc61
Cartagena E 45 Fa74
Cartama E 43 Cd76
Cartaxo P 36 Ab67
Cartaya E 42 Bb74
Carteret F 19 Ed35
Carterton GB 15 Ed27
Cartmel GB 12 Eb19
Carunchio I 109 Fb71
Carvalhal P 36 Ba62
Carvalho de Egas P 31 Bc61
Carvin F 20 Ha31
Carvoeiro P 42 Ab74
Casablanca E 45 Ed71
Casa Capitán E 38 Eb69
Casa de Benítez E 38 Eb68
Casa de Juan Núñez E 39 Ed69
Casalanguida I 109 Fb71
Casalarreina E 32 Ea57
Casalbore I 112 Fc74
Casalbuttano ed Uniti I 101 Cd60
Casal di Principe I 112 Fa74
Casale I 114 Ea85
Casalecchio di Reno I 102 Dc63
Casale Monferrato I 100 Ca60
Casalfiumanese I 102 Dd63
Casalgrasso I 100 Bc61
Casalmaggiore I 101 Da61
Casalpusterlengo I 101 Cd60
Casal Sabini I 113 Gc75
Casaluce I 112 Fa74
Casamassima I 113 Gd74
Casa Palacio E 45 Ec73
Casarano I 113 Hc77
Casar de Cáceres E 37 Bd67
Casares de Arbás E 31 Cb56
Casarrubios del Monte E 38 Db65
Casas de Don Pedro E 37 Cc68
Casas de los Pinos E 38 Eb68
Casas del Puerto de Tornavacas E 37 Cb64
Casas de Ves E 39 Ed68
Casas-Ibáñez E 39 Ed68
Casasimarro E 39 Ec68
Casas Novas P 36 Bb69
Casasola de Arión E 31 Cc60
Casatejada E 37 Cb66
Casbas de Huesca E 33 Fc59
Cascais P 36 Aa68
Cascante E 33 Ed59
Cascante del Río E 39 Fa65
Cascia I 109 Ec69
Casciana Terme I 108 Db66
Cascina I 108 Da65
Căscioarele RO 122 Eb67
Caseda E 33 Ed58
Casei Gerola I 101 Cb61
Casekow D 85 Fb34
Caselle Torinese I 100 Bc60
Casemurate I 102 Ea64
Caserta I 112 Fb74
Caserta Vecchia I 112 Fb74
Cashel IRL 4 Bb20
Cashel IRL 6 Ca24
Cashel IRL 7 Cb22
Cashleen IRL 4 Bb20
Cashlie GB 10 Dd11
Cashmore GB 15 Ed30
Casillas E 38 Da64
Casinos E 39 Fb67
Casla IRL 6 Bb21
Čáslav CZ 91 Fd45
Čašniki BY 136 Eb12
Casola in Lunigiana I 101 Da63
Casoli I 109 Fb71
Casorate Primo I 101 Cb60
Casoria I 112 Fb75
Caspe E 39 Fc62
Cassà de la Selva E 35 Hb60
Cassano allo Ionio I 113 Gb78
Cassano d'Adda I 101 Cd59
Cassano delle Murge I 113 Gc75
Cassano Spinola I 101 Cb61
Cassaro I 115 Fc87
Cassibile I 115 Fd87
Cassino I 109 Fa73
Cassis F 29 Jd55
Casson F 23 Ed42
Cassuejouls F 28 Hb50
Castagneto Carducci I 108 Da67
Castalla E 45 Fb70
Castañar de Ibor E 37 Cc67
Castañares de Rioja E 32 Ea57
Castañeda E 32 Dc55
Castanet-Tolosan F 27 Gc54
Castanheira de Pira P 36 Ad65
Castanheiro P 36 Ac64
Castano Primo I 101 Cb59
Castaromocho E 31 Cd59
Castayrols F 27 Gd53
Casteggio I 101 Cc61
Castejón de Sos E 34 Ga58
Castelbuono I 114 Fa84
Castelculier F 27 Ga52
Castel d' Ario I 102 Dc60
Casteldelci I 108 Ea65
Casteldelfino I 100 Bb62
Castel del Piano I 108 Dd68
Castel di Iudica I 115 Fb86
Castel di Sangro I 109 Fa72
Castel di Tora I 109 Ec70
Castelejo P 36 Bb64
Castelequin IRL 6 Ba25
Castelfidardo I 109 Ed66
Castelfiorentino I 108 Db66
Castelflorite E 33 Fc60
Castelfranco di Sopra I 108 Dd66
Castelfranco Emilia I 102 Dc62
Castelfranco in Miscano I 110 Fd73
Castelfranco Veneto I 102 Ea59
Castel Gandolfo I 109 Eb72
Castelgrande I 112 Fd75
Casteljaloux F 26 Fd52
Castellabate I 112 Fc77
Castellammare del Golfo I 114 Eb84
Castellammare di Stabia I 112 Fb75
Castellamonte I 100 Bd59
Castellana Grotte I 113 Gd75
Castellane F 29 Kb53
Castellaneta I 113 Gd75
Castellar de la Frontera E 43 Cb77
Castellar de la Ribera E 34 Gc59
Castellar del Vallès E 35 Gd61
Castell'Arquato I 101 Cd61
Castell'Azzara I 108 Dd68
Castellazzo Bormida I 100 Ca61
Castellbò E 34 Gc58
Castell de Cabres E 40 Fd64
Castelldefels E 35 Gd62
Castell de Ferro E 44 Dc76
Castellfollit de Riubregós E 34 Gc60
Castelli I 109 Ed69
Castellina Marittima I 108 Da66
Castelló de la Plana E 39 Fc66
Castello del Matese I 109 Fb73
Castelló d'Empúries E 35 Hb58
Castelluccio dei Sauri I 110 Fd73
Castelluccio Inferiore I 113 Gb78
Castell' Umberto I 115 Fc84
Castelluzzo I 114 Eb84
Castelmassa I 102 Dc61
Castelmoron-sur-Lot F 27 Ga51
Castelnaudary F 35 Gd55
Castelnau-le-Lez F 28 Hd54
Castelnau-Magnoac F 34 Ga55
Castelnau-Montratier F 27 Gb52
Castelnau-Rivière-Basse F 26 Fc54
Castelnou E 39 Fc62
Castelnou F 35 Ha57
Castelnovo ne' Monti I 101 Da63
Castelnuovo Berardenga I 108 Dd66
Castelnuovo di Garfagnana I 101 Da64
Castelnuovo Scrivia I 101 Cb61
Castelo Branco P 31 Bd61
Castelo Branco P 36 Bb65
Castelo de Vide P 36 Bb67
Castelo Melhor P 37 Bc62
Castelo Rodrigo P 37 Bc62
Castelraimondo I 109 Ec67
Castelrotto I 102 Dd56
Castel San Gimignano I 108 Db66
Castel San Giovanni I 101 Cc61
Castel San Lorenzo I 112 Fd76
Castel San Pietro Terme I 102 Dd63
Castelsardo I 107 Ca74
Castelsarrasin F 27 Gb53
Castelseprio I 101 Cb58
Castelserás E 39 Fc63
Casteltermini I 114 Ed86
Castelvecchio Subequo I 109 Ed71
Castelvetrano I 114 Eb85
Castel Volturno I 112 Fa74
Castenedolo I 101 Da59
Castets F 26 Fa53
Castex F 34 Fd55
Castiglioncello I 108 Da66
Castiglione dei Pepoli I 102 Dc64
Castiglione del Lago I 108 Ea67
Castiglione della Pescaia I 108 Db68
Castiglione delle Stiviere I 102 Db60
Castiglione di Garfagnana I 101 Da64
Castiglione di Sicilia I 115 Fd84
Castiglione d'Orcia I 108 Dd68
Castiglione Olona I 101 Cb58
Castiglion Fiorentino I 108 Dd66
Castilfabib E 39 Ed65
Castilléjar E 44 Ea73
Castillejo de Martín Viejo E 37 Bd63
Castillejo de Mesleón E 32 Dc61
Castillo de Locubín E 44 Db74
Castillon-du-Gard F 28 Ja53
Castillon-en-Couserans F 34 Gb56
Castillon-la-Bataille F 26 Fc50
Castillonnès F 27 Ga51
Castione della Presolana I 101 Da58
Castle Acre GB 16 Ga24
Castle Ashby GB 15 Fb25
Castlebaldwin IRL 4 Ca18
Castlebar IRL 4 Bc19
Castlebay GB 8 Cc09
Castlebellingham IRL 5 Cd19
Castleblayney IRL 5 Cd19
Castlebridge IRL 7 Cd24
Castle Bytham GB 16 Fc24
Castle Cary GB 15 Ec29
Castle Combe GB 15 Ec28
Castlecomer IRL 7 Cb23
Castlecove IRL 6 Ba26
Castlederg GB 4 Cb16
Castledermot IRL 7 Cc23
Castle Douglas GB 11 Ea16
Castleford GB 13 Fa20
Castlegal IRL 4 Ca17
Castlehill IRL 4 Bb18
Castleisland IRL 6 Bb24
Castlejordan IRL 7 Cc21
Castlemaine IRL 6 Bb24
Castlemartin GB 14 Db27
Castlemartyr IRL 6 Ca26
Castlepollard IRL 4 Cb20
Castlerea IRL 4 Bd19
Castleton GB 13 Ed22
Castleton GB 14 Eb28
Castletown GB 9 Eb04
Castletown GB 12 Dc19
Castletown IRL 6 Bc24
Castletown IRL 7 Cb21
Castletown IRL 7 Cd23
Castletownbere IRL 6 Ba26
Castletownshead IRL 6 Bb27
Castlewellan GB 5 Da18
Casto I 101 Da59
Castrejón de la Peña E 32 Da56
Castres F 27 Gd54
Castres-Gironde F 26 Fb51
Castricum NL 82 Ad35
Castries F 28 Hd54
Castrillo de Don Juan E 32 Db60
Castrillo de la Vega E 32 Dc60
Castrillo de Río Pisuerga E 32 Db57
Castrillo-Tejeriego E 32 Da60
Castro E 30 Ba53
Castro (Carballedo) E 30 Bb57
Castrocaro Terme I 102 Ea64
Castrocontrigo E 31 Ca58
Castro de Filabres E 44 Ea75
Castro del Río E 43 Cd73
Castro de Rei E 31 Bc54
Castrojeriz E 32 Db58
Castro Laboreiro P 30 Ba58
Castromonte E 31 Cd60
Castronuevo E 31 Cc60
Castronuovo di San Andrea I 113 Gb77
Castronuovo di Sicilia I 114 Ed85
Castropol E 31 Bd54
Castrop-Rauxel D 88 Ca39
Castro-Urdiales E 32 Dd55
Castrovega de Valmadrigal E 31 Cc58
Castroverde de Cerrato E 32 Db60
Castroviejo E 32 Ea58
Castrovillari I 113 Gb78
Castuera E 37 Cb69
Cataeggio I 101 Cd57
Çatalca TR 127 Fb77
Catania I 115 Fd86
Catanzaro I 113 Gc81
Catanzaro Marina I 113 Gc81
Catarroja E 39 Fb68
Cateraggio F 106 Cc70
Caterham GB 16 Fc29
Cathair na Mart IRL 4 Bc19
Cathair Saidhbhín IRL 6 Ba25
Catlowdy GB 11 Ec16
Catoira E 30 Ad56
Cattedrale di Anagni I 109 Ec72
Catterick Bridge GB 13 Fa18
Catterick Garrison GB 13 Ed18
Cattolica I 109 Eb65
Cattolica Eraclea I 114 Ec86
Caudebec-en-Caux F 19 Ga34
Caudecoste F 27 Ga52
Caudete E 45 Fa70
Caudete de las Fuentes E 39 Ed67
Caudiel E 39 Fb66
Caudiès-de-Fenouillèdes F 35 Ha57
Caudry F 20 Hb32
Caujac F 34 Gc55
Caulnes F 22 Ec39
Caunes-Minervois F 35 Ha55
Causeway IRL 6 Bb24
Caussade F 27 Gc52
Cava d'Aliga I 115 Fc88
Cava de' Tirreni I 112 Fc75
Cavagnac F 27 Gd51
Cavaillon F 29 Jc53
Cavaleiro P 42 Ab72
Cavalière F 29 Kb55
Cavallino I 103 Eb60
Cavan IRL 4 Cb19
Cavanagarvan IRL 5 Cc18
Cavarzere I 102 Ea61
Cavazzo Carnico I 103 Ec57
Caveirac F 28 Ja53
Cavour I 100 Bc61
Cavtat HR 111 Hc69
Čavusy BY 136 Ec12
Cawood GB 13 Fa20
Cawsand GB 14 Dc32
Cawston GB 16 Gb24
Caxton GB 16 Fc26
Cayeux-sur-Mer F 20 Gb32
Caylus F 27 Gc52
Caynham GB 15 Ec25
Caythorpe GB 13 Fb23
Cazalegas E 37 Cd65
Cazalla de la Sierra E 43 Ca72
Cazals F 27 Gb51
Cazanuecos E 31 Cb58
Cazères F 34 Gb55
Cazorla E 44 Dd72
Ceanannus Mór IRL 5 Cc20
Ceann Toirc IRL 6 Bc24
Ceapach Choinn IRL 6 Ca25
Ceatharlach IRL 7 Cc23
Ceaucé F 23 Fb38
Cebeceiras de Basto P 30 Ba60
Cebreros E 38 Da64
Cebrones del Río E 31 Cb58
Ceccano I 109 Ec72
Čečejovce SK 99 Jc49
Čečel'nyk UA 136 Ec16
Cecenowo PL 86 Gd29
Čechtín CZ 97 Ga47
Cecina I 108 Da66
Cedeira E 30 Bb53
Cedrillas E 39 Fa64
Cée E 30 Ac55
Cefalù I 114 Fa84
Ceggia I 103 Eb59
Cegléd H 98 Ja54
Ceglie Messapica I 113 Ha75
Cegłów PL 87 Jd37
Cehegín E 45 Ec72
Čehov RUS 137 Fa11
Ceilhes-et-Rocozels F 28 Hb53
Ceinos de Campos E 31 Cd59
Ceintrey F 21 Jd37
Ceira P 36 Ad64
Čejkovice CZ 97 Gc48
Cekcyn PL 86 Ha33
Ceków-Kolonia PL 92 Ha38
Cela E 31 Bc56
Čelakovice CZ 91 Fc44
Celano I 109 Ed71
Celanova E 30 Ba58
Čelarevo SRB 116 Ad61
Celbridge IRL 7 Cd21
Celestynów PL 87 Jc37
Celina RUS 137 Fd15
Celjachany BY 136 Ea13
Celje SLO 104 Fd57
Cella E 39 Ed64
Cellarhead GB 13 Ed23
Celldömölk H 98 Gd54
Celle D 83 Db36
Celle Ligure I 100 Ca63
Celles-sur-Belle F 23 Fc45
Cellettes F 24 Gb41
Celliers F 29 Ka47
Cellino San Marco I 113 Hb76
Cellole I 112 Fa74
Cel'ovce SK 99 Ka49
Celrà E 35 Hb59
Cembra I 102 Dc57
Cemmaes Road GB 12 Ea24
Cenajo E 45 Ec71
Cenarth GB 14 Dc26
Cenes de la Vega E 44 Dc75
Ceneselli I 102 Dc61
Cénevières F 27 Gc51
Cenicientos E 38 Da65
Censeau F 25 Jd43
Centallo I 100 Bc62
Cento I 102 Dc62
Centuripe I 115 Fc85
Cepagatti I 109 Fa70
Čepelare BG 126 Db75
Cépet F 27 Gc54
Ceppo I 109 Ed69
Ceprano I 109 Ed73
Cerachovka BY 136 Ec13
Cerano I 101 Cb59
Ceraso I 112 Fd77
Cerbaia I 108 Dc65
Cerbère F 35 Hc58
Cercal P 42 Ab72
Čerčany CZ 91 Fc45
Cercemaggiore I 109 Fc73
Cerchiara di Calabria I 113 Gc78
Cercs E 35 Gd59
Čerdakly RUS 137 Fd09
Cerdanyola E 35 Gd61
Céré F 24 Gc43
Cerea I 102 Dc60
Cereceda E 32 Dd57
Cerecinos de Campos E 31 Cc59
Cered H 98 Ja50
Cerekwica PL 86 Gd35
Cérences F 19 Fa37
Cereo E 30 Ad54
Céreste F 29 Jd53
Cerezo de Abajo E 38 Dc62
Cerezo de Riotirón E 32 Dd58
Cergnago I 101 Cb60
Ceriana I 100 Bc64
Cerignola I 110 Ga73
Cérilly F 24 Ha44
Cérilly F 25 Ja40
Cérisy-la-Forêt F 19 Fb36
Čerkasy UA 137 Ed15
Čerkessk RUS 137 Fd17
Cerknica SLO 103 Fb59
Cermenate I 101 Cc58
Cermone I 109 Ec70
Čern' RUS 137 Fa12
Cernache de Bonjardim P 36 Ad65
Černava RUS 137 Fa11
Černava RUS 137 Fa12
Cernay-la-Ville F 20 Gc37
Cerne Abbas GB 15 Ec30
Cerneux F 20 Hb37
Černihiv UA 136 Ec14
Černilov CZ 91 Ga44
Černivci UA 136 Ea16
Černjachiv UA 136 Eb14
Černjahovsk RUS 136 Dc12
Černjanka RUS 137 Fa13
Cernobbio I 101 Cc58
Černošín CZ 90 Ec45
Černovice CZ 97 Fc47
Cernoy-en-Berry F 24 Ha41
Cerny-en-Laonnois F 20 Hc35
Černyškovskij RUS 137 Fd14
Cerralbo E 37 Bd62
Cerredolo I 102 Db63
Cerreto Sannita I 109 Fb73
Cerrigydrudion GB 12 Ea23
Cerro Muriano E 43 Cd72
Certaldo I 108 Dc66
Čertižné SK 93 Ka46
Čertkovo RUS 137 Fc14
Čerusti RUS 137 Fa10
Cervaro I 109 Fa73
Cervatos de la Cueza E 32 Da58
Červen' BY 136 Eb12
Červená CZ 97 Fb47
Červená Voda CZ 91 Gc44
Červený Kostelec CZ 91 Ga43
Cervera E 34 Gb60
Cervera de Buitrago E 38 Dc63
Cervera del Maestrat E 40 Fd64
Cervera del Río Alhama E 33 Ec59
Cervera de Pisuerga E 32 Da56
Cervesina I 101 Cc60
Cerveteri I 108 Ea71
Cervia I 103 Eb64
Cervico Navero E 32 Db59
Cervignano di Friuli I 103 Ed59
Cervinara I 112 Fb74
Cervo I 100 Bd64
Cervon F 24 Hc42
Červonohrad UA 136 Dd15
Čërykav BY 136 Ec12
Cesarò I 115 Fc85
Cesarowice PL 91 Gb41
Cesena I 102 Ea64
Cesenatico I 103 Eb64
Cēsis LV 75 Kd49
Česká Bělá CZ 91 Ga46
Česká Kamenice CZ 91 Fb42
Česká Lípa CZ 91 Fb42
Česká Skalice CZ 91 Ga43
Česká Třebová CZ 91 Gb45
České Budějovice CZ 97 Fb48
České Velenice CZ 97 Fc49
Český Brod CZ 91 Fc44
Český Těšín CZ 92 Hb45
Çeşme TR 130 Ea86
Cesole I 102 Db61
Cespedosa de Tormes E 37 Cb63
Cessières F 20 Hb34
Cestas F 26 Fb50
Čestice CZ 96 Fa47
Cesvaine LV 75 Lb50
Cetina E 39 Ec62
Cetinje MNE 111 Hd70
Cetona I 108 Dd68
Cetraro I 113 Gb79
Céüse 2000 F 29 Jd51
Ceuti E 45 Ed72
Ceva I 100 Bd62
Cevico de la Torre E 32 Da59
Cevio CH 101 Cb56
Cewice PL 86 Gd30
Ceyzériat F 25 Jc45
Cézens F 28 Hb49
Cezura E 32 Db56
Chaam NL 88 Ad38
Chabanais F 27 Ga47
Chabielice PL 92 Hc40
Chablis F 24 Hc40
Chabreloche F 24 Hc46
Chaffayer F 29 Jd50
Chaffois F 25 Jd43
Chagny F 25 Ja43
Chailley-Turny F 24 Hc39
Chailly-en-Brie F 20 Hb37
Chailly-sur-Armançon F 25 Ja42
Chalais F 26 Fd49
Chalamera E 34 Fd60
Chale GB 15 Fa31
Châlette-sur-Loing F 24 Ha39
Chalindrey F 25 Jb40
Challacombe GB 14 Dd29
Challans F 23 Ed43
Challock GB 16 Ga29
Chalmazel F 28 Hd47
Chalonnes-sur-Loire F 23 Fb42
Châlons-en-Champagne F 21 Hd36
Chalon-sur-Saône F 25 Jb43
Chalou-Moulineux F 24 Gd38
Chałupy PL 86 Ha29
Cham CH 95 Cb53
Cham D 96 Ec47
Chambeire F 25 Jb42
Chambéria F 25 Jc44
Chambéry F 29 Jd47
Chambilly F 25 Hd45
Chamblet F 24 Ha45
Chambley-Bussières F 21 Jc36
Chambly F 20 Gd36
Chambord F 24 Gc41
Chambost-Allières F 25 Ja46
Chambray F 20 Gb36
Chamerau D 96 Ec47
Chammes F 23 Fc39
Chamonix-Mont-Blanc F 100 Bb57
Chamoy F 24 Hc39
Champagnac-le-Vieux F 28 Hc48
Champagné-les-Marais F 23 Fa45
Champagnole F 25 Jd43
Champdieu F 28 Hd47
Champeaux F 23 Fa39
Champéry CH 100 Bb56
Champigneul-Champagne F 21 Hd36
Champigny F 20 Ha37
Champigny-le-Sec F 23 Fd44
Champlemy F 24 Hb42
Champlitte F 25 Jc40
Champlong I 100 Bc58
Champvans F 25 Jc41
Chamrousse F 29 Jd49
Chanac F 28 Hc51
Chança P 36 Ba67
Chanceaux F 25 Ja41
Chancelade F 27 Ga49
Chancery GB 14 Dd25
Chancy CH 100 Ad56
Chandler's Ford GB 15 Fa30
Chandolin CH 100 Bd56
Chandrexa E 31 Bc58
Chañe E 32 Da61
Changé F 23 Fb39
Changy F 25 Hd45
Chantada E 30 Bb56
Chantelle F 24 Hb45
Chanteloup F 23 Fb44
Chantemerle F 29 Kb49
Chantilly F 20 Gd35
Chantonnay F 23 Fa44
Chão de Codes P 36 Ad66
Chaon F 24 Gd41
Chapel-en-le Frith GB 13 Ed22
Chapelle-Royale F 24 Gb39
Chapel Saint Leonards GB 13 Fd22
Charbonnat F 25 Hd43
Charcenne F 25 Jc41
Charchów Pański PL 92 Hc38
Chard GB 14 Eb30
Charenton-du-Cher F 24 Ha44
Charing GB 16 Ga29
Charkiv UA 137 Fa14
Charlbury GB 15 Fa27
Charleroi B 21 Hd31
Charles GB 14 Dd29
Charlestown GB 5 Cd17
Charlestown IRL 4 Bd19
Charleville-Mézières F 21 Ja33
Charlton Kings GB 15 Ed27
Charmant F 26 Fd48
Charmé F 23 Fd46
Charmes F 25 Jd38
Charmes-sur-Rhône F 28 Jb50
Charmoille F 25 Jd40
Charmont-en-Beauce F 24 Gd39
Charmont-sur-Barbuise F 25 Hd38
Charnay-lès-Mâcon F 25 Ja45
Charney Bassett GB 15 Fa27
Charolles F 25 Hd44
Charpey F 28 Jb49
Charquemont F 25 Ka41
Charras F 26 Fd48
Charritte-de-Bas F 33 Fa55
Charron F 23 Fa45
Charroux F 23 Fd46
Chartów PL 85 Fc36
Chartres F 24 Gb38
Chartridge GB 15 Fb27
Chasné F 23 Ed39
Chąśno PL 86 Hd37
Chasseneuil-sur-Bonnieure F 26 Fd47
Chassenon F 27 Ga47
Chasse-sur-Rhône F 28 Jb47
Chastanier F 28 Hd50
Chastleton GB 15 Ed26
Chatain F 23 Fd46
Château-Arnoux F 29 Ka52
Châteaubourg F 23 Fa39
Châteaubriant F 23 Fa40
Château-Chervix F 27 Gb47
Château-Chinon F 25 Hd42
Château-d'Oex CH 94 Bc55
Château d'Olonne F 23 Ed44
Château-du-Loir F 23 Fd41
Châteaudun F 24 Gb39
Châteaugiron F 23 Ed39
Château-Gontier F 23 Fb40
Château-Landon F 24 Ha39
Château-l'Evêque F 27 Ga49
Châteaulin F 22 Dc39
Châteaumeillant F 24 Gd44
Châteauneuf-du-Faou F 22 Dd39
Châteauneuf-du-Pape F 28 Jb52
Châteauneuf-la-Forêt F 27 Gc47
Châteauneuf-sur-Cher F 24 Gd43
Châteauneuf-sur-Loire F 24 Gd40
Châteauneuf-sur-Sarthe F 23 Fb41
Châteauponsac F 24 Gb46
Château-Porcien F 21 Hd34
Châteaurenard F 28 Jb53
Château-Renault F 23 Ga41
Châteauroux F 24 Gc43
Châteauroux F 29 Kb50

Château-Thierry – Desertmartin


Château-Thierry F 20 Hb36
Châteauvillain F 25 Ja39
Châtel F 100 Bb56
Châtelaillon-Plage F 23 Fa46
Châtel-de-Neuvre F 24 Hb45
Châtelguyon F 24 Hb46
Châtellerault F 23 Ga44
Châtel-Montagne F 24 Hc46
Châtelus-le-Marcheix F 24 Gc46
Châtenoy F 24 Gd40
Chatham GB 16 Fd28
Châtillon F 25 Jc44
Châtillon-Coligny F 24 Ha40
Châtillon-en-Diois F 29 Jc50
Châtillon-en-Vendelais F 23 Fa39
Châtillon-la-Palud F 25 Jc46
Châtillon-sur-Colmont F 23 Fb38
Châtillon-sur-Indre F 24 Gb43
Châtillon-sur-Loire F 24 Ha41
Châtillon-sur-Seine F 25 Ja40
Châtillon-sur-Thouet F 23 Fc44
Chatrans F 25 Jd42
Châtres-sur-Cher F 24 Gc42
Chatteris GB 16 Fd25
Chatton GB 11 Ed14
Chaudieu F 25 Jd46
Chaumont F 25 Jb39
Chaumont-en-Vexin F 20 Gc35
Chaumont-sur-Tharonne F 24 Gc41
Chauny F 20 Hb34
Chaussin F 25 Jc43
Chauvigny F 23 Ga44
Chavagnes-en-Paillers F 23 Fa43
Chavanges F 25 Ja38
Chaves P 30 Bb59
Chawleigh GB 14 Dd30
Chazelles-sur-Lyon F 28 Ja47
Cheadle GB 13 Ec22
Cheadle GB 13 Ed23
Cheb CZ 90 Eb44
Chechło PL 92 Hd43
Chęciny PL 93 Jb42
Checkendon GB 15 Fb28
Cheddar GB 14 Eb29
Cheddleton GB 13 Ed23
Chedworth GB 15 Ed27
Chef-du-Pont F 19 Fa35
Cheissoux F 27 Gc47
Cheles E 42 Bb70
Chelford GB 13 Ec22
Chełm PL 93 Kc40
Chełmek PL 92 Hd44
Chełmno PL 85 Gb36
Chełmno PL 86 Ha33
Chelmsford GB 16 Fd27
Chełmża PL 86 Hb34
Chełst PL 85 Ga35
Chelsworth GB 16 Ga26
Cheltenham GB 15 Ed27
Chelun F 23 Fa40
Chelva E 39 Fa67
Chémeré-le-Roi F 23 Fc40
Chémery F 24 Gc42
Chemillé F 23 Fb42
Chemillé-sur-Dême F 23 Ga41
Cheminon F 21 Ja37
Chemiré-le-Gaudin F 23 Fc40
Chemnitz D 90 Ec42
Chenay F 23 Fc45
Chénelette F 25 Ja45
Chénerailles F 24 Gd46
Chenies GB 16 Fc27
Chennebrun F 19 Ga37
Chennevières F 20 Gb37
Chenonceaux F 24 Gb42
Chenôve F 25 Jb42
Chepoix F 20 Gd34
Chepstow GB 14 Eb27
Chepy F 21 Hd36
Cherbourg-Octeville F 19 Ed34
Chérencé-le-Roussel F 19 Fa37
Cheresig RO 117 Ca56
Cheriton GB 15 Fa29
Cherson UA 137 Ed16
Chertsey GB 15 Fb28
Chesham GB 15 Fb27
Cheshunt GB 16 Fc27
Chesley F 25 Hd39
Chesney's Corner GB 5 Cd16
Cheste E 39 Fb67
Chester GB 12 Eb22
Chesterfield GB 13 Fa22
Chester-le-Street GB 13 Fa17
Chevagnes F 24 Hc44
Cheverny F 24 Gb41
Chevetogne B 21 Ja32
Chevillon F 24 Hb40
Chew Magna GB 15 Ec28
Chezal-Benoît F 24 Gd43
Chézery-Forens F 25 Jd45
Chialamberto I 100 Bc59
Chianale I 100 Bb61
Chianciano Terme I 108 Dd67
Chiaramonte Gulfi I 115 Fc87
Chiaramonti I 107 Ca74
Chiaravalle I 109 Ed66
Chiaravalle Centrale I 115 Gc82
Chiareggio I 101 Cd56
Chiari I 101 Cd59
Chiaromonte I 113 Gb77
Chiasso I 101 Cc58
Chiatona I 113 Gd76
Chiauci I 109 Fb72
Chiavari I 101 Cc63
Chiavenna I 101 Cd56
Chiché F 23 Fc44
Chicheley GB 15 Fb26
Chichester GB 15 Fb30
Chichilianne F 29 Jc50
Chiclana de la Frontera E 43 Bd77
Chiclana de Segura E 44 Dd71
Chiddingfold GB 15 Fb29
Chiddingstone GB 16 Fd29
Chieming D 96 Eb52
Chieri I 100 Bd60
Chiesa in Valmalenco I 101 Cd57
Chies d'Alpago I 103 Eb57
Chieti I 109 Fa70
Chieuti I 110 Fd72
Chigné F 23 Fd41
Chigwell GB 16 Fd28
Chilcompton GB 15 Ec29
Childrey GB 15 Fa28
Chilham GB 16 Ga29
Chillarón de Cuenca E 38 Eb65
Chilleurs-aux-Bois F 24 Gd39
Chilmark GB 15 Ed29
Chilsworthy GB 14 Dc30
Chimay B 21 Hd32
Chimeneas E 44 Db75
Chimparra E 30 Bb53
Chinchilla de Monte Aragón E 39 Ec69
Chinchón E 38 Dc65
Chingford GB 16 Fc27
Chinnor GB 15 Fb27
Chinon F 23 Fd42
Chioggia I 102 Ea60
Chipiona E 43 Bc76
Chippenham GB 15 Ec28
Chipping GB 13 Ec20
Chipping Campden GB 15 Ed26
Chipping Norton GB 15 Fa26
Chipping Ongar GB 16 Fd27
Chirbury GB 12 Eb24
Chirens F 29 Jc48
Chirnside GB 11 Ed13
Chişinău MD 119 Fd58
Chiusa I 102 Dd56
Chiusa Sclafani I 114 Ec85
Chiusavecchia I 100 Bd64
Chiusi della Verna I 108 Ea65
Chivasso I 100 Bd60
Chizé F 23 Fc46
Chlewnica PL 86 Gd30
Chlum CZ 96 Fa48
Chlumčany CZ 90 Fa44
Chlumec nad Cidlinou CZ 91 Fd44
Chmel'nyc'kyj UA 136 Eb15
Chmel'ov SK 99 Jd47
Chmieleń PL 91 Fd41
Chmielnik PL 93 Jb42
Chmielnik PL 93 Ka44
Chmielno PL 86 Ha30
Chmil'nyk UA 136 Eb15
Choceň CZ 91 Gb45
Choceń PL 86 Hc36
Chochołów PL 92 Ja46
Chocianów PL 91 Ga40
Chociw PL 92 Ja39
Chociwel PL 85 Fd33
Choczewo PL 86 Gd29
Chodaków PL 86 Ja37
Chodel PL 93 Ka40
Chodoriv UA 136 Ea15
Chodorówka PL 87 Kb32
Chodov CZ 90 Ec44
Chodský Újezd CZ 90 Ec45
Chodzież PL 85 Gc35
Choiny Młode PL 87 Jd33
Choiseul F 25 Jc39
Chojewo PL 87 Kb35
Chojna PL 85 Fb35
Chojnice PL 86 Gd32
Chojnik PL 92 Gd40
Chojniki BY 136 Eb13
Chojno PL 91 Gc39
Chojnow PL 91 Ga40
Cholderton GB 15 Ed29
Cholesbury GB 15 Fb27
Cholet F 23 Fb43
Chollerford GB 11 Ed16
Chomérac F 28 Jb50
Chomutov CZ 90 Ed43
Chorges F 29 Ka50
Chorley GB 13 Ec21
Chorol UA 137 Ed14
Choroszcz PL 87 Kb33
Chorupnik PL 93 Kb41
Chorzele PL 87 Jb33
Chorzów PL 92 Hc43
Choszczno PL 85 Fd34
Chotěboř CZ 91 Ga46
Chotilsko CZ 91 Fb45
Chouvigny F 24 Hb46
Chraboły PL 87 Kb33
Chr'aščevka RUS 137 Ga10
Chrast CZ 91 Ga45
Chrastava CZ 91 Fc42
Chrewt PL 93 Kb46
Chrisí Ammoudiá GR 126 Db78
Christchurch GB 15 Ed30
Christiansfeld DK 76 Db56
Chropyne CZ 98 Gd47
Chróścina PL 86 Ha35
Chrostkowo PL 86 Hc35
Chrudim CZ 91 Ga45
Chrystynivka UA 136 Ec15
Chrzanów PL 92 Hd44
Chrząstowo PL 91 Gc38
Chucena E 43 Bd74
Chulilla E 39 Fa67
Chulmleigh GB 14 Dd30
Chur CH 95 Cd55
Church Cross IRL 6 Bb26
Church Eaton GB 13 Ec24
Churchill GB 15 Fa26
Church Lench GB 15 Ed26
Church Stoke GB 12 Eb24
Churchstow GB 14 Dd32
Church Stretton GB 12 Eb24
Churchtown GB 12 Dd18
Churchtown IRL 7 Cd25
Chust UA 136 Dd16
Chustki PL 93 Jb40
Chvaleč CZ 91 Ga43
Chvaletice CZ 91 Fd45
Chvalšiny CZ 97 Fb48
Chwarstnica PL 85 Fc34
Chwaszczyno PL 86 Ha30
Chwiram PL 85 Gb34
Chyše CZ 90 Ed44
Chyšky CZ 91 Fb46
Ciacova RO 116 Bc61
Cianciana I 114 Ec86
Ciasna PL 92 Hb42
Cicero E 32 Dd54
Cichy PL 87 Jd30
Ciechanów PL 86 Ja35
Ciechanów PL 91 Gb39
Ciechanowiec PL 87 Ka35
Ciechocin PL 86 Hb34
Ciechocinek PL 86 Hb35
Cieksyn PL 87 Jb36
Ciemnik PL 85 Fd33
Ciemnoszyje PL 87 Ka32
Ciempozuelos E 38 Dc65
Ciepielów PL 93 Jd40
Čierna nad Tisou SK 99 Kb49
Čierny Balog SK 98 Ja48
Ciesina PL 87 Jc32
Cieszanów PL 93 Kc43
Cieszyn PL 92 Hb45
Cieza E 45 Ed72
Ciężkowice PL 92 Hd41
Çiftliköy TR 130 Ea86
Cigel'ka SK 93 Jc46
Cill Airne IRL 6 Bb25
Cill Chainnigh IRL 7 Cb23
Cill Chaoi IRL 6 Bb23
Cill Chiaráin IRL 4 Bb20
Cill Chiaráin IRL 6 Bb21
Cill Dalua IRL 6 Bd23
Cill Dara IRL 7 Cc22
Cilleruelo de Abajo E 32 Dc59
Cill Mhantáim IRL 7 Da22
Cill Mocheallog IRL 6 Bd24
Cill Orglan IRL 6 Ba25
Cill Rois IRL 6 Bb23
Cilmery GB 14 Ea26
Čil'na RUS 137 Fd09
Cimanes de la Vega E 31 Cc58
Čimelice CZ 90 Fa46
Číměř CZ 97 Fc48
Ciminna I 114 Ed84
Cimitile I 112 Fb74
Cimljansk RUS 137 Fd15
Cimolais I 103 Eb57
Cimoszki PL 87 Ka31
Çinarlı TR 127 Ed79
Cinco Casas E 38 Dd68
Cincu RO 118 Dc61
Cinderford GB 15 Ec27
Çine TR 131 Fa88
Cinfães P 30 Ba61
Cingoli I 109 Ec66
Cinisi I 114 Ec84
Cinovec CZ 90 Fa42
Cinquefrondi I 115 Gb83
Cintruénigo E 33 Ec59
Cionn tSáile IRL 6 Bd26
Cipérez E 37 Ca62
Ciral F 23 Fc38
Çıralı TR 135 Cc93
Cirat E 39 Fb66
Cirencester GB 15 Ed27
Cirey-sur-Vezouze F 21 Ka37
Ciriè I 100 Bc60
Cirò Marina I 113 Gd80
Ciruelos de Coca E 32 Da61
Cisano I 102 Db59
Cisnădie RO 117 Db61
Cisneros E 31 Cd58
Čistá CZ 90 Fa45
Cisterna di Latina I 109 Eb72
Cisternino I 113 Ha75
Cistierna E 31 Cd56
Citou F 35 Ha55
Cítov CZ 91 Fb43
Cittadella I 102 Dd59
Cittadella del Capo I 112 Ga79
Città della Pieve I 108 Ea68
Città del Vaticano V 108 Ea71
Città di Castello I 108 Ea66
Cittaducale I 109 Ec70
Ciudad Real E 38 Db69
Ciudad Rodrigo E 37 Bd63
Ciutadella E 41 Ja65
Civaux F 23 Ga45
Cividale del Friuli I 103 Ed58
Civita Castellana I 108 Ea70
Civitanova Marche I 109 Ed67
Civita Superiore I 109 Fb73
Civitavecchia I 108 Dd71
Civitella Casanova I 109 Fa70
Civitella Cesi I 108 Ea70
Civitella del Tronto I 109 Ed68
Civitella di Romagna I 102 Ea64
Civitella Marittima I 108 Dc68
Cizer RO 117 Cc57
Cjurupyns'k UA 137 Ed17
Čkalovsk RUS 137 Fb09
Clachan Mór GB 10 Cd10
Clacton-on-Sea GB 16 Gb27
Cladich GB 10 Dc11
Clady GB 5 Da17
Claigan GB 8 Da07
Clairac F 26 Fd52
Clairavaux F 27 Gd47
Clamart F 20 Gd37
Clamecy F 24 Hc41
Clamper Cross IRL 6 Bc24
Clanabogan GB 5 Cc17
Clane IRL 7 Cc21
Clanfield GB 15 Fa27
Claonaig GB 10 Db13
Clapham GB 13 Ec19
Clara IRL 7 Cb21
Clarborough GB 13 Fb22
Clár Chlainne Mhuiris IRL 4 Bd19
Clare GB 16 Ga26
Clarecastel IRL 6 Bc22
Clareen IRL 6 Ca22
Claregalway IRL 6 Bc21
Claremorris IRL 4 Bd19
Claro CH 101 Cc56
Clashmore IRL 6 Ca25
Claudon F 25 Jd39
Claudy GB 5 Cc16
Clausthal-Zellerfeld D 89 Dc38
Claverley GB 13 Ec24
Clavière I 100 Bb60
Clay Cross GB 13 Fa22
Claydon GB 16 Gb26
Claye-Souilly F 20 Ha36
Claypole GB 13 Fb23
Cleadale GB 8 Da09
Cleat GB 8 Cc09
Cleator Moor GB 12 Ea18
Cléder F 18 Dc37
Cleethorpes GB 13 Fd21
Clefmont F 25 Jc39
Clefs F 23 Fc41
Cleggan IRL 4 Ba20
Cleguérec F 22 Ea39
Clémont F 24 Gd41
Cleobury North GB 15 Ec25
Clephanton GB 9 Ea08
Cléré-les-Pins F 23 Fd41
Clères F 20 Gb34
Clérey F 25 Hd39
Clergoux F 27 Gd48
Clermont F 20 Gd35
Clermont F 25 Jd46
Clermont-Ferrand F 28 Hb47
Clermont-l'Hérault F 28 Hc54
Clermont-sur-Lauquet F 35 Ha56
Cléron F 25 Jd42
Clervaux L 21 Jc32
Cléry-Saint-André F 24 Gc40
Cles I 102 Dc56
Clevedon GB 14 Eb28
Cleveleys GB 12 Eb20
Clifden IRL 4 Bb20
Cliff IRL 4 Ca17
Cliffe GB 16 Fd28
Clifton Campville GB 13 Fa24
Clifton-upon-Teme GB 15 Ec25
Clisson F 23 Fa43
Clitheroe GB 13 Ec20
Clogan IRL 4 Cb16
Clogh IRL 7 Cd24
Cloghan IRL 6 Ca21
Clogheen IRL 6 Ca24
Clogher GB 5 Cc17
Clogherhead IRL 5 Cd20
Cloghjordan IRL 6 Ca22
Cloghroe IRL 6 Bc25
Cloghy GB 5 Db18
Clohernagh IRL 7 Cb25
Cloich na Coillte IRL 6 Bc26
Clóirtheach IRL 7 Cb21
Clonakenny IRL 6 Ca22
Clonakilty IRL 6 Bc26
Clonaslee IRL 7 Cb22
Clonbern IRL 4 Bd20
Cloncagh IRL 6 Bc24
Clondalkin IRL 7 Cd21
Clonea IRL 7 Cb25
Clones IRL 5 Cc18
Clonmany IRL 5 Cc15
Clonmel IRL 6 Ca24
Clonmellon IRL 5 Cc20
Clonoulty IRL 6 Ca23
Clonroche IRL 7 Cc24
Clontibret IRL 5 Cc18
Clonygowan IRL 7 Cb22
Cloonacool IRL 4 Bd18
Cloonbannin IRL 6 Bc25
Cloonboo IRL 4 Bc20
Cloonboo IRL 6 Bc21
Cloonfad IRL 4 Bd20
Cloonken IRL 6 Bb25
Cloonloogh IRL 4 Ca19
Cloonymorris IRL 6 Bd21
Cloppenburg D 83 Cc35
Clopton GB 16 Fc25
Closeburn GB 11 Ea15
Close Clark GB 12 Dc19
Clough GB 5 Da18
Cloughton GB 13 Fc18
Clova GB 11 Eb10
Clovelly GB 14 Dc29
Clowne GB 13 Fa22
Cluain Eois IRL 5 Cc18
Cluainín IRL 4 Ca18
Cluain Meala IRL 6 Ca24
Cluis F 24 Gc44
Cluj-Napoca RO 117 Da58
Clun GB 14 Eb25
Cluny F 25 Ja44
Cluses F 25 Ka45
Clusone I 101 Da58
Clynacantan IRL 6 Ad25
Clynnog-Fawr GB 12 Dd23
Clyro GB 14 Eb26
Clyst Hydon GB 14 Ea30
Ćmielów PL 93 Jd41
Coachford IRL 6 Bc25
Coad's Green GB 14 Dc31
Coalburn GB 11 Ea14
Coalisland GB 5 Cd17
Coalville GB 13 Fa24
Coaña E 31 Bd54
Coarraze F 33 Fc56
Coatbridge GB 11 Ea13
Cobatillas E 45 Ec71
Cóbdar E 44 Eb75
Cobertelada E 32 Eb61
Cobh IRL 6 Bd26
Cobos de Cerrato E 32 Db59
Cobres E 30 Ad57
Coburg D 90 Dd44
Coca E 38 Da62
Cocentaina E 45 Fb70
Cochem D 88 Bd43
Cochstedt D 90 Ea38
Cockerham GB 12 Eb20
Cockermouth GB 12 Eb17
Cockfield GB 16 Ga26
Cockington GB 14 Ea31
Cocksburnspath GB 11 Ed13
Coclois F 25 Hd38
Cocollos Vega E 44 Dc74
Codaval P 30 Bb60
Coddington GB 13 Fb23
Codeseda E 30 Ad56
Codicote GB 16 Fc27
Codigoro I 102 Ea62
Codlea RO 122 Dd62
Codogno I 101 Cd60
Codos E 39 Ed62
Codroipo I 103 Ec58
Coed Morgan GB 14 Eb27
Coedpoeth GB 12 Eb23
Coesfeld D 82 Ca37
Cœuvres-et-Valsery F 20 Hb35
Coevorden NL 82 Bd35
Coëx F 23 Ed44
Coggeshall GB 16 Ga27
Coggiola I 100 Ca58
Cognac F 26 Fc47
Cognac-la-Forêt F 27 Gb47
Cogne I 100 Bc58
Cognin-les-Gorges F 29 Jc48
Cogolin F 29 Kb55
Cogollos E 32 Dc58
Cogolludo E 38 Dd63
Cohiniac F 22 Eb38
Coignafearn GB 9 Ea09
Coill an Chollaigh IRL 5 Cc19
Coimbra P 36 Ad64
Coín E 43 Cc76
Coincy F 20 Hb36
Coirós E 30 Ba54
Coja P 36 Ba64
Colaboll GB 8 Dd06
Colbitz D 84 Ea37
Colbost GB 8 Da07
Colburn GB 13 Ed18
Colchester GB 16 Ga27
Colditz D 90 Ec41
Cold Norton GB 16 Ga27
Coldstream GB 11 Ed14
Coleford GB 15 Ec27
Colera E 35 Hc58
Coleraine GB 5 Cd15
Colinas E 43 Bd74
Colintraive GB 10 Dc13
Coll GB 8 Db05
Collado-Villalba E 38 Db63
Coll de Nargó E 34 Gb59
Colle di Val d'Elsa I 108 Dc66
Colleferro I 109 Ec72
Colle Isarco I 96 Dd55
Collepardo I 109 Ed72
Collepasso I 113 Hc77
Collesalvetti I 108 Da66
Colle Sannita I 109 Fc73
Collesano I 114 Fa84
Colli di Montebove I 109 Ec71
Collinas I 107 Ca78
Collinée F 22 Eb38
Collingbourne Ducis GB 15 Ed29
Collingham GB 13 Fa20
Collington GB 15 Ec25
Collinstown IRL 5 Cc20
Collio I 101 Da58
Collioure F 35 Hb57
Collon IRL 5 Cd20
Collonges F 25 Jd45
Collonges-la-Rouge F 27 Gc49
Colmar F 94 Bd50
Colmars F 29 Kb51
Colmenar del Arroyo E 38 Db64
Colmenar de Oreja E 38 Dc65
Colmenar Viejo E 38 Dc63
Colnabaichin GB 9 Eb09
Colne GB 13 Ed20
Coln Saint Aldwyns GB 15 Ed27
Colobraro I 113 Gc77
Cologna I 102 Ea61
Cologna Veneta I 102 Dd60
Colombier CH 94 Bb54
Colombier F 25 Jd40
Colombier F 25 Ka42
Colomera E 44 Db74
Colonard F 23 Ga38
Colondannes F 24 Gc45
Colònia de Sant Jordi E 41 Hc68
Colònia de Sant Pere E 41 Hc66
Colonnetta I 108 Ea68
Colorno I 101 Da61
Colsterworth GB 13 Fb24
Colston Bassett GB 13 Fb23
Coltishall GB 16 Gb24
Colunga E 31 Cd54
Colwyn Bay GB 12 Ea22
Colyford GB 14 Eb30
Comacchio I 102 Ea62
Comana RO 122 Eb67
Combe Martin GB 14 Dd29
Comber GB 5 Da17
Comblain-au-Pont B 21 Jb31
Combles F 20 Ha33
Combourg F 23 Ed38
Combres F 24 Gb38
Combs-la-Ville F 20 Ha37
Comeglians I 103 Ec56
Comelico Superiore I 103 Eb56
Comillas E 32 Db55
Comines F 17 Ha30
Comiso I 115 Fb87
Commarin F 25 Ja42
Commeen IRL 4 Ca15
Commentry F 24 Ha45
Commercy F 21 Jc37
Como I 101 Cc58
Comologno CH 101 Cb57
Cómpeta E 44 Da76
Compiègne F 20 Ha35
Comps-sur-Artuby F 29 Kb53
Comrie GB 11 Ea11
Comunanza I 109 Ed68
Concabella E 34 Gb60
Concarneau F 22 Dc40
Concas I 107 Cc75
Concèze F 27 Gb48
Conches-en-Ouche F 19 Ga36
Conchigliu F 106 Cc68
Conchra GB 10 Dc12
Conchy-les-Pots F 20 Ha34
Concordia Sagittaria I 103 Ec59
Concordia sul Secchia I 102 Dc61
Condamine-Châtelard, la F 29 Kb51
Condat F 27 Ha48
Condé-en-Brie F 20 Hc36
Condé-Folie F 20 Gc33
Condeixa a-Nova P 36 Ac64
Condé sur-Huisne F 23 Ga38
Condé-sur-les-Eaux F 20 Hb31
Condé-sur-Noireau F 19 Fb37
Condé-sur-Vesgre F 20 Gc37
Condofuri Marina I 115 Ga84
Condom F 26 Fd53
Condover GB 12 Eb24
Condrieu F 28 Jb48
Conegliano I 103 Eb58
Confolens F 23 Ga46
Confolent-Port-Dieu F 27 Ha48
Cong IRL 4 Bc20
Conga IRL 4 Bc20
Congleton GB 13 Ec22
Congresbury GB 14 Eb28
Coniale I 102 Dc64
Conil de la Frontera E 43 Bd77
Coningsby GB 16 Fc23
Conisbrough GB 13 Fa21
Conna IRL 6 Bd25
Connagh IRL 6 Bd22
Connah's Quay GB 12 Eb22
Connaux F 28 Ja52
Connel GB 10 Dc11
Connerré F 23 Fd39
Connonagh IRL 6 Bb26
Conques F 27 Ha51
Conselve I 102 Ea60
Consenvoye F 21 Jb35
Consett GB 13 Ed17
Consiston GB 12 Eb18
Constância P 36 Ad66
Constanța RO 123 Fc67
Constantine Bay GB 14 Db31
Constanzana E 37 Cd62
Consuegra E 38 Dc67
Contadero E 44 Db71
Contay F 20 Gd33
Contes F 29 Kd53
Contessa Entellina I 114 Ec85
Conthey CH 100 Bc56
Contin GB 8 Dd07
Contis-Plage F 26 Fa52
Contrada I 112 Fc75
Contrexéville F 25 Jc38
Controne I 112 Fd76
Contursi Terme I 112 Fd75
Contwig D 88 Bd46
Conty F 20 Gd34
Conversano I 113 Gd74
Conwy GB 12 Ea22
Coo B 21 Jc31
Cookham GB 15 Fb28
Cookstown GB 5 Cd17
Coola IRL 4 Ca18
Coole IRL 4 Cb20
Coolgrange IRL 7 Cb23
Coolham GB 16 Fc30
Coolkeeragh GB 5 Cc15
Coolroebeg IRL 7 Cb24
Coombe Bissett GB 15 Ed29
Coombe Hill GB 15 Ec26
Cooraclare IRL 6 Bb23
Coornagillagh IRL 6 Ba25
Cootehill IRL 5 Cc19
Copertino I 113 Hc77
Copons E 34 Gc60
Copparo I 102 Dd61
Coppenbrügge D 83 Da37
Copplestone GB 14 Dd30
Coppull GB 13 Ec21
Cora Droma Rúisc IRL 4 Ca19
Coral Bay CY 135 Bc96
Coralstown IRL 7 Cc21
Corato I 113 Gc74
Coray F 22 Dd39
Corbalán E 39 Fa65
Corbeil-Essonnes F 20 Gd37
Corbeilles F 24 Ha39
Corbelle E 31 Bc56
Corberon F 25 Jb42
Corbie F 20 Gd33
Corby GB 15 Fb25
Corby Glen GB 16 Fc24
Corcaigh IRL 6 Bd26
Corcelles-en-Beaujolais F 25 Ja45
Corcelles-Ferrières F 25 Jc42
Corchuela E 36 Bb69
Córcoles E 38 Ea64
Corcoué-sur-Logne F 23 Ed43
Corcubión E 30 Ac55
Corcy F 20 Hb35
Cordal E 31 Bc54
Cordesse F 25 Hd42
Cordes-sur-Ciel F 27 Gd53
Córdoba E 43 Cd72
Corella E 33 Ec59
Cores E 30 Ad54
Corfe GB 14 Eb30
Corhampton GB 15 Fa30
Cori I 109 Ec72
Coria E 37 Bd65
Coriano I 109 Eb65
Corigliano Calabro I 113 Gc79
Corinto E 39 Fc67
Corio I 100 Bc59
Cork IRL 6 Bd26
Corlay F 22 Ea38
Corlea IRL 4 Ca20
Corleone I 114 Ec85
Çorlu TR 127 Fa77
Cormeilles F 19 Fd35
Cormery F 23 Ga42
Cormons I 103 Ed58
Corna E 30 Ba56
Cornafulla IRL 6 Ca21
Cornago E 33 Ec59
Cornamona IRL 4 Bc20
Cornberg D 89 Db41
Corné F 23 Fc41
Corñeda E 30 Ba55
Cornellà de Llobregat E 35 Gd61
Cornhill GB 9 Ec07
Cornhill-on-Tweed GB 11 Ed14
Cornil F 27 Gc49
Cornimont F 25 Ka39
Čornobyl' UA 136 Ec14
Čornomors'ke UA 137 Ed17
Čornuchy UA 137 Ed14
Cornuda I 102 Ea58
Cornusse F 24 Ha43
Corny-sur-Moselle F 21 Jd36
Corpach GB 10 Dc10
Corporales E 31 Ca58
Corps-Nuds F 23 Ed40
Corpusty GB 16 Gb23
Corrakyle IRL 6 Bd22
Corral de Almaguer E 38 Dd66
Corral de Calatrava E 38 Db69
Corrales E 31 Cb61
Corrales E 42 Bb74
Corran GB 10 Dc10
Corrano F 106 Cb71
Corraree IRL 6 Ca21
Corre F 25 Jd39
Corredoiras E 30 Ba55
Correggio I 102 Db62
Correlha P 30 Ad59
Corrençon en-Vercors F 29 Jc49
Corridonia I 109 Ed67
Corrie GB 10 Dc14
Corris GB 12 Dd24
Corrofin IRL 6 Bc22
Corrubedo E 30 Ac56
Corseul F 22 Ec38
Corsham GB 15 Ec28
Corsica F 106 Cb69
Corsock GB 11 Ea16
Corston GB 15 Ec28
Corte F 106 Cb69
Corte de Peleas E 37 Bc69
Cortegada E 30 Ba57
Cortemaggiore I 101 Cd61
Cortemilia I 100 Ca62
Cortes E 33 Ed60
Cortés E 39 Fa67
Cortes de Arenoso E 39 Fb65
Cortes de Pallás E 39 Fa68
Corte Sines P 42 Ba72
Cortijos Nuevos del Campo E 44 Eb73
Cortina d'Ampezzo I 102 Ea56
Čortkiv UA 136 Ea16
Cortona I 108 Ea67
Coruche P 36 Ac68
Corullón E 31 Bd57
Coruña del Conde E 32 Dd60
Corvara in Badia I 102 Ea56
Corvera E 45 Fa73
Corwen GB 12 Ea23
Cosăuți MD 119 Fc54
Coscojuela de Sobrarbe E 34 Fd58
Cosenza I 113 Gb80
Cosgaya E 32 Da55
Cosham GB 15 Fa30
Cosne-Cours-sur-Loire F 24 Ha41
Cossato I 100 Ca59
Cossé-le-Vivien F 23 Fb40
Costa da Caparica P 36 Aa69
Costa de Canyamel E 41 Hd67
Costaros F 28 Hd50
Costa Valle Imagna I 101 Cd58
Costelloe IRL 6 Bb21
Costessey GB 16 Gb24
Costigliole d'Asti I 100 Ca61
Costinești RO 123 Fc68
Coswig D 90 Ec38
Coswig D 90 Fa41
Cotgrave GB 13 Fb23
Cotherstone GB 13 Ed18
Cotmeana RO 121 Db64
Cotnari RO 119 Ed57
Cotronei I 113 Gd80
Cottbus D 91 Fb39
Coublanc F 25 Jc40
Couches F 25 Ja43
Coucy-le-Château-Auffrique F 20 Hb34
Couddes F 24 Gb42
Coudekerque-Branche F 17 Gd30
Coudray F 23 Fb40
Coudrecieux F 23 Ga40
Coudures F 26 Fb54
Couhé F 23 Fd45
Couiza F 35 Ha56
Coulandon F 24 Hb44
Coulanges-lès-Nevers F 24 Hb43
Coulmier-le-Sec F 25 Ja40
Coulombiers F 23 Fd45
Coulommiers F 20 Hb37
Coulon F 23 Fb45
Couloutre F 24 Hb41
Coulport GB 10 Dc12
Coupar Anguse GB 11 Eb11
Coupray F 25 Ja39
Couptrain F 23 Fc38
Cour-Cheverny F 24 Gb41
Courcité F 23 Fc39
Courcon F 23 Fb45
Cour-et-Buis F 28 Jb48
Courgains F 23 Fd39
Courgivaux F 20 Hb37
Courmayeur I 100 Bb58
Courmont F 20 Hc36
Courniou F 27 Ha54
Cournon-d'Auvergne F 28 Hb47
Courpalay F 20 Ha37
Coursan F 35 Hb55
Cours-la Ville F 25 Ja46
Courson-les-Carrières F 24 Hc41
Courtacon F 20 Hb37
Courtalain F 24 Gb39
Courtown IRL 7 Cd24
Courville-sur-Eure F 24 Gb38
Cousolre F 20 Hc32
Coussac-Bonneval F 27 Gb48
Coussey F 25 Jc38
Coustouges F 35 Ha58
Coutances F 19 Fa36
Coutras F 26 Fc49
Couture-d'Argenson F 23 Fc46
Coutures F 23 Fc42
Couy F 24 Ha42
Covaleda E 32 Ea59
Covarrubias E 32 Dc59
Covas E 31 Bc53
Covas E 31 Bd57
Covas P 30 Ad58
Cove GB 8 Db06
Cove GB 14 Ea30
Covelo E 30 Ad57
Coventry GB 15 Fa25
Coverack GB 14 Db32
Covet E 34 Gb59
Covide P 30 Ba59
Covilhã P 36 Bb64
Cowbit GB 16 Fc24
Cowbridge GB 14 Ea28
Cowdenbeath GB 11 Eb12
Cowes GB 15 Fa30
Cowfold GB 16 Fc30
Cowshill GB 13 Ed17
Cox E 45 Fa72
Coxwold GB 13 Fa19
Coy E 45 Ec72
Coylton GB 10 Dd14
Cózar E 44 Dd70
Cozzano F 106 Cb71
Craigavon GB 5 Cd18
Craigellachie GB 9 Eb08
Craighouse GB 10 Da13
Craigmalloch GB 10 Dd15
Craignure GB 10 Db11
Craigton GB 11 Eb11
Craig-y-nos GB 14 Ea27
Craik GB 11 Eb15
Crail GB 11 Ec12
Crailsheim D 95 Db47
Craiova RO 121 Cd66
Cramant F 20 Hc36
Cramlington GB 11 Fa16
Cramme D 83 Dc37
Cranborne GB 15 Ed30
Cranbrook GB 16 Ga29
Crançot F 25 Jc43
Cranford IRL 4 Cb15
Cranleigh GB 16 Fc29
Cranny IRL 6 Bc23
Crans CH 100 Bc56
Cranwell GB 16 Fc23
Cranworth GB 16 Ga24
Cranzahl D 90 Ec43
Craon F 23 Fb40
Crask Inn GB 8 Dd05
Craster GB 11 Fa15
Crathie GB 9 Eb09
Cratloe IRL 6 Bd23
Craughwell IRL 6 Bd21
Cravant F 24 Gc40
Cravant F 24 Hc40
Craven Arms GB 14 Eb25
Crawfordjohn GB 11 Ea14
Crawinkel D 89 Dc42
Crawley GB 16 Fc29
Crayford GB 16 Fd28
Creagorry GB 8 Cd07
Creaguaineach Lodge GB 10 Dd10
Crécy-en-Ponthieu F 20 Gc32
Crécy-la-Chapelle F 20 Ha37
Credenhill GB 14 Eb26
Crediton GB 14 Ea30
Creegh IRL 6 Bb22
Creeslough IRL 4 Cb15
Creevagh IRL 4 Bc18
Creeves IRL 6 Bc23
Cregenzán E 34 Fd59
Cregg IRL 6 Bc21
Creggan GB 5 Cc17
Creggs IRL 4 Ca20
Creglingen D 89 Db46
Creil F 20 Gd35
Crema I 101 Cd60
Crémenes E 31 Cd56
Crémieu F 29 Jc47
Cremona I 101 Da60
Crépey F 21 Jc37
Crépy-en-Valois F 20 Ha35
Cres HR 103 Fb61
Crescentino I 100 Ca60
Crespos E 37 Cd63
Cressage GB 13 Ec24
Cressensac F 27 Gc49
Cresswell GB 11 Fa15
Crest F 28 Jb50
Créteil F 20 Gd37
Creully F 19 Fb35
Creussen D 90 Ea45
Creutzwald F 21 Ka35
Creuzburg D 89 Db41
Crevalcore I 102 Dc62
Crevant F 24 Gc45
Crevillente E 45 Fa72
Crevoladossola I 100 Ca57
Crévoux F 29 Kb50
Crewe GB 13 Ec22
Crewkerne GB 14 Eb30
Crianlarich GB 10 Dd11
Cribyn GB 14 Dd26
Criccieth GB 12 Dd23
Crick GB 15 Fa25
Crickhowell GB 14 Eb27
Cricklade GB 15 Ed27
Cricova MD 119 Fd57
Crieff GB 11 Ea11
Criel-sur-Mer F 20 Gb33
Criewen D 85 Fb35
Crikvenica HR 103 Fc61
Crillon F 20 Gc34
Crimmitschau D 90 Eb42
Crinan GB 10 Db12
Crinitz D 90 Fa39
Crispiano I 113 Ha76
Crissolo I 100 Bb61
Cristian RO 117 Da61
Cristian RO 122 Dd62
Cristinacce F 106 Ca70
Crivitz D 84 Ea33
Črni vrh SLO 103 Fa58
Črnomelj SLO 104 Fd59
Črnuče SLO 103 Fb58
Crockernwell GB 14 Dd30
Crocketford GB 11 Ea16
Crocq F 24 Gd46
Crodo I 100 Ca56
Croes-goch GB 14 Db26
Crofty GB 14 Dd27
Croggan GB 10 Db11
Croick GB 8 Dd06
Crois Mhaoilíona IRL 4 Bc18
Croissilles F 20 Ha32
Croithlí IRL 4 Ca15
Crolly IRL 4 Ca15
Cromarty GB 9 Ea07
Cromer GB 16 Gb23
Cromoge IRL 7 Cb22
Cronat F 24 Hc44
Crook GB 13 Ed17
Crookedwood IRL 4 Cb20
Crookhaven IRL 6 Ba27
Crook of Devon GB 11 Eb12
Crookstown IRL 7 Cc22
Croom IRL 6 Bd23
Cropalati I 113 Gc79
Cropani I 113 Gd81
Cropani Marina I 113 Gd81
Crosby GB 12 Dc19
Cros-de-Cagnes F 29 Kc53
Cross IRL 4 Bc20
Cross IRL 6 Bb23
Crossakeel IRL 5 Cc20
Crossbost GB 8 Da05
Crossdoney IRL 4 Cb19
Crossens GB 12 Eb21
Crosses F 24 Ha43
Crossgar GB 5 Da18
Crossgare GB 5 Cd15
Cross Hands GB 14 Dd27
Crosshavn IRL 6 Bd26
Cross Inn GB 14 Dd25
Cross Keys IRL 5 Cc20
Cross Keys IRL 7 Cd21
Crossmaglen GB 5 Cd19
Crossmolina IRL 4 Bc18
Croston GB 13 Ec21
Crostwitz D 91 Fb41
Crotone I 113 Gd81
Crove IRL 4 Ca16
Crowborough GB 16 Fd29
Crowcombe GB 14 Ea29
Crow Hill GB 15 Ec26
Crowland GB 16 Fc24
Crowle GB 13 Fb21
Crowthorne GB 15 Fb28
Croxton GB 16 Ga25
Croxton Kerrial GB 13 Fb23
Croy GB 9 Ea08
Croyde GB 14 Dc29
Croyden GB 16 Fc28
Crozon F 22 Db38
Črtil' RUS 137 Fb12
Cruden Bay GB 9 Ed08
Crudgington GB 13 Ec24
Crudwell GB 15 Ed27
Crug-y-bar GB 14 Dd26
Crulai F 19 Ga37
Crumlin GB 5 Da17
Crusheen IRL 6 Bc22
Cruz da Légua P 36 Ab66
Cruz de João Mendes P 42 Ab71
Cruzy F 35 Hb55
Crynant GB 14 Dd27
Csabrendek H 98 Gd54
Csanádpalota H 105 Jc57
Csép H 98 Hb53
Csepreg H 97 Gc53
Cserkeszőlő H 99 Jb55
Csernely H 99 Jb50
Csobaj H 99 Jd51
Csökmő H 99 Jd54
Csömör H 98 Hd52
Csongrád H 99 Jb55
Csonkahegyhát H 97 Gc55
Csorna H 98 Gd52
Csörnend H 104 Ha56
Csorvás H 99 Jd55
Csót H 98 Ha53
Csurgó H 104 Gd57
Cuacos de Yuste E 37 Cb65
Cualedro E 30 Bb58
Cuarte de Huerva E 33 Fa61
Cuba P 42 Ad71
Cubells E 34 Gb60
Cubillas de Rueda E 31 Cd57
Cubillejo del Sitio E 39 Ec63
Cubillo E 32 Da56
Cubo de la Solana E 32 Eb61
Cuckfield GB 16 Fc30
Čučkovo RUS 137 Fb11
Cucq F 20 Gc31
Cucuron F 29 Jc53
Cuddington GB 13 Ec22
Cudillero E 31 Cb54
Čudniv UA 136 Eb15
Čudovo RUS 136 Eb09
Cudworth GB 13 Fa21
Čudzin BY 136 Ea13
Cuéllar E 32 Da61
Cuenca E 38 Eb66
Cuers F 29 Ka55
Cuerva E 38 Da67
Cuevas Bajas E 43 Cd74
Cuevas de Almanzora E 45 Ec75
Cuevas de Cañart E 39 Fb63
Cuevas del Becerro E 43 Cc75
Cuevas del Campo E 44 Dd73
Cuevas del Sil E 31 Ca56
Cuevas de San Marcos E 43 Cd74
Cuevas Labradas E 39 Fa64
Cuges-les-Pins F 29 Jd55
Cuggiono I 101 Cb59
Cuglieri I 107 Bd76
Cugnaux F 27 Gb54
Čuhujiv UA 137 Fa14
Cuijk NL 88 Bb38
Cúil an tSúdaire IRL 7 Cc22
Cuillé F 23 Fa40
Cuiseaux F 25 Jc44
Cuisery F 25 Jb44
Culan F 24 Gd44
Culdaff IRL 5 Cc15
Culemborg NL 82 Ba37
Culkain GB 8 Dc05
Cullahill IRL 7 Cb23
Cúllar-Baza E 44 Ea74
Cullaville GB 5 Cd19
Culleens IRL 4 Bd18
Cullen GB 9 Ec07
Cullera E 39 Fc69
Cullompton GB 14 Ea30
Culmington GB 14 Eb25
Culmstock GB 14 Ea30
Culnacraig GB 8 Dc06
Culnaknock GB 8 Db07
Culross GB 11 Eb12
Culswick GB 9 Fa05
Cumalıkızık TR 131 Fd80
Cumbernauld GB 11 Ea13
Cumbres Mayores E 43 Bc71
Cuminestown GB 9 Ed08
Cumnock GB 10 Dd14
Cumnor GB 15 Fa27
Cuneo I 100 Bc62
Cunewalde D 91 Fb41
Cunha P 30 Ad58
Cunlhat F 28 Hc47
Cunningburn GB 5 Db17
Cuntis E 30 Ad56
Čunusavvon S 50 Hd16
Cuorgnè I 100 Bd59
Cupar GB 11 Eb12
Cupra Marittima I 109 Fa68
Curia P 36 Ad63
Curracloe IRL 7 Cd24
Curreeny IRL 6 Ca23
Curryglass IRL 6 Ba26
Curtea de Argeș RO 122 Dc63
Curticelle I 112 Fc75
Cushendall IRL 5 Da15
Cushendun GB 5 Da15
Cussac F 27 Ga47
Cussangy F 25 Hd39
Cusset F 24 Hc46
Cusy F 25 Jd46
Čuteevo RUS 137 Fd09
Cutnall Green GB 15 Ec25
Čutove UA 137 Fa14
Cutrofiano I 113 Hc77
Cuxhaven D 83 Cd31
Cvikov CZ 91 Fc42
Cwmafan GB 14 Dd27
Cwmbach GB 14 Dc26
Cwmbran GB 14 Eb27
Cwmcarn GB 14 Eb27
Cwmduad GB 14 Dc26
Cwmllynfell GB 14 Dd27
Cwmystwyth GB 14 Ea25
Cwrt-newydd GB 14 Dd26
Cybinka PL 85 Fc37
Cygany PL 93 Jd42
Čyhyryn UA 137 Ed15
Cymmer GB 14 Ea27
Cynghordy GB 14 Ea26
Cynwyd GB 12 Ea23
Czacz PL 91 Gb38
Czaplinek PL 85 Gb33
Czarna PL 93 Jc44
Czarna Białostocka PL 87 Kb33
Czarna Sędziszowska PL 93 Jd44
Czarnków PL 85 Gb35
Czarnocin PL 92 Hd39
Czarnowasy PL 92 Ha42
Czarnożyły PL 92 Hb40
Czarny Las PL 92 Gd39
Czchów PL 93 Jb45
Czechowice-Dziedzice PL 92 Hc45
Czechy PL 85 Gb32
Czekanów PL 92 Ha39
Czeladz PL 92 Hc43
Czemierniki PL 93 Kb38
Czeremcha PL 87 Kc35
Czermin PL 92 Gd38
Czermnica PL 85 Fc32
Czermno PL 92 Ja41
Czernica PL 92 Gd41
Czernichów PL 92 Hd44
Czerniejewo PL 86 Gd36
Czersk PL 86 Ha32
Czersk PL 93 Jc38
Czerwieńsk PL 91 Fd38
Czerwińsk nad Wisłą PL 86 Ja36
Czerwionka-Leszczyny PL 92 Hb44
Czerwonak PL 85 Gc36
Częstochowa PL 92 Hc42
Czeszów PL 92 Gd40
Człopa PL 85 Ga34
Człuchów PL 85 Gc32
Czorsztyn PL 93 Jb46
Czyczkowy PL 86 Gd32

## D

Daaden D 89 Cb41
Dabas H 98 Hd54
Dąbie PL 86 Hb37
Dąbie PL 87 Ka37
Dąbki PL 85 Gb30
Dabrowa Białostocka PL 87 Kb31
Dąbrowa Biskupia PL 86 Hb35
Dabrowa Chełmińska PL 86 Ha34
Dąbrowa Górnicza PL 92 Hc43
Dąbrowa Tarnowska PL 93 Jc44
Dąbrówka PL 86 Hc33
Dąbrówka PL 87 Jc36
Dabrówka PL 93 Jd41
Dąbrówka PL 93 Kb43
Dąbrówka-Kościelna PL 87 Ka34
Dabrówka Wielkopolska PL 85 Ga37
Dąbrówki PL 93 Ka43
Dąbrowy PL 87 Jc33
Dabryn' BY 136 Eb14
Dachau D 96 Dd50
Dačice CZ 97 Fd48
Dacón E 30 Ba57
Dädesjö S 78 Fc51
Dadiá GR 126 Ea77
Dafjord N 49 Gd08
Dagali N 64 Db39
Dagenham GB 16 Fd28
Daglingworth GB 15 Ed27
Dagomys RUS 137 Fd17
Dahlen D 90 Ed40
Dahlenburg D 84 Dd34
Dahme D 90 Ed38
Dahn D 94 Ca47
Dähre D 84 Dd35
Daikanberg S 53 Ga24
Dailly GB 10 Dc15
Daimiel E 38 Dc69
Dairsie GB 11 Ec12
Đakovo HR 105 Hc60
Dal S 58 Gc31
Dalaas A 95 Da54
Dalachów PL 92 Hb41
Dalavardo S 52 Fd21
Dalavich GB 10 Dc12
Dalbeattie GB 11 Ea16
Dalchalloch GB 11 Ea10
Dalchruin GB 11 Ea12
Dale GB 14 Db27
Dale N 62 Ca36
Dale N 62 Cb38
Dalen N 56 Db32
Dalen N 63 Da43
Dalen N 71 Eb42
Dalen NL 82 Bd35
Daleszyce PL 93 Jb41
Dalfsen NL 82 Bc35
Dalhavaig GB 9 Ea04
Dalheim L 21 Jd34
Dalheim N 52 Ed21
Dalías E 44 Dd76
Daliburgh GB 8 Cd08
Dalkarlså S 59 Hc27
Dalkeith GB 11 Eb13
Dallas GB 9 Eb07
Dalleagles GB 10 Dd15
Dallgow-Döberitz D 84 Ed36
Dallmin D 84 Eb34
Dállogilli S 54 Ja18
Dalmally GB 10 Dc11
Dalmellington GB 10 Dd15
Dalmine I 101 Cd59
Dalness GB 10 Dc10
Dalry GB 10 Dc14
Dalsøyra N 62 Ca37
Dalston GB 12 Eb17
Dalstuga S 66 Fd38
Dalton GB 11 Eb16
Dalton-in-Furness GB 12 Eb19
Daluis F 29 Kb52
Dalvík IS 3 Bc02
Dálvvadis S 53 Ha19
Dalyan TR 134 Bb91
Dalyanköy TR 130 Ea86
Damak H 99 Jc50
Damerham GB 15 Ed30
Dammarie-les-Lys F 24 Ha38
Dammartin-en-Goële F 20 Ha36
Damme B 17 Hb29
Damme D 83 Cc36
Dammet S 54 Ja21
Damnica PL 85 Gc30
Dampierre F 21 Hd37
Dampierre-en-Bray F 20 Gc34
Dampierre-en-Burly F 24 Ha40
Dampierre-en-Yvelines F 20 Gc37
Damsdorf D 84 Ec37
Damüls A 95 Da53
Damville F 20 Gb37
Damvillers F 21 Jb35
Damwoude NL 82 Bc33
Danasjö S 53 Ga23
Danbury GB 16 Ga27
Danby GB 13 Fb18
Danesfort IRL 7 Cb24
Dangy F 19 Fa36
Danilovka RUS 137 Fd13
Dänischenhagen D 83 Dc30
Dankov RUS 137 Fa12
Dannemarie F 94 Bc52
Dannenberg D 84 Dd34
Dannenwalde D 84 Ed34
Danzig = Gdańsk PL 86 Hb30
Daoulas F 22 Dc38
Darány H 104 Ha58
Darenth GB 16 Fd28
Darfo I 101 Da58
Dargosław PL 85 Fd31
Dargun D 84 Ec32
Darlaston GB 13 Ed24
Darlington GB 13 Fa18
Darłowo PL 85 Gb30
Darlton GB 13 Fb22
Darmstadt D 89 Cc44
Darnétal F 20 Gb35
Daroca E 39 Ed62
Darragh IRL 6 Bc22
Darro E 44 Dc74
Dartford GB 16 Fd28
Dartmouth GB 14 Ea32
Daruvar HR 104 Gd59
Darvel GB 10 Dd14
Darwen GB 13 Ec20
Dasing D 95 Dc50
Dassel D 89 Da38
Dassow D 84 Dd31
Daszyna PL 86 Hc37
Datça TR 134 Ed91
Datchworth GB 16 Fc27
Datteln D 88 Ca38
Daubach D 88 Ca44
Daugavpils LV 81 Lc53
Daun D 88 Bd43
Dautphetal D 89 Cc41
Dava GB 9 Eb08
Daventry GB 15 Fa25
Davidstow GB 14 Dc30
Davle CZ 91 Fb45
Dávlia GR 129 Bd84
Davos CH 95 Da55
Davyd-Haradok BY 136 Ea14
Dawley GB 13 Ec24
Dawlish GB 14 Ea31
Dax F 26 Fa54
Deal GB 16 Gb29
Deanich Lodge GB 8 Dd06
Deanshanger GB 15 Fb26
Deargget S 54 Hd17
Deauville F 19 Fd35
Debal'ceve UA 137 Fb15
Débanos E 33 Ec60
Debar MK 124 Ad74
Dębica PL 93 Jd44
Dębiec PL 92 Hb40
De Bilt NL 82 Ba36
De Blesse NL 82 Bc34
Dęblin PL 93 Jd39
Deblín CZ 97 Gb47
Dębnica Kaszubska PL 85 Gc30
Dębno PL 85 Fc35
Dębno PL 93 Jb44
Dębolęka PL 92 Hb39
Dębowa Łęka PL 91 Gb39
Dębowo PL 87 Ka32
Debrecen H 99 Ka52
Debrznica PL 85 Fc37
Debrzno PL 85 Gc33
Dębsk PL 86 Ja34
Decazeville F 27 Gd51
Decima I 102 Dc62
Decimoputzu I 107 Ca79
Děčín CZ 91 Fb42
Decize F 24 Hc43
De Cocksdorp NL 82 Ba33
Deddington GB 15 Fa26
Dedeleben D 90 Dd38
Dedems-vaart NL 82 Bd35
Dedenevo RUS 137 Ed10
Dedinky SK 99 Jb48
Dedoviči RUS 136 Eb10
Deelish IRL 6 Bb26
Deensen D 89 Da38
Deeping Saint Nicholas GB 16 Fc24
Deetz D 84 Ec36
Dég H 98 Hb55
Degerbäcken S 54 Hc21
Degerby FIN 67 Hc41
Degerfors S 59 Hc26
Degerfors S 72 Fb44
Degersheim CH 95 Cc53
Deggendorf D 96 Ec48
Deggenhausertal D 95 Cd51
Deggingen D 95 Da49
Dego I 100 Ca62
De Haan B 17 Ha29
Deidesheim D 89 Cb46
Deining D 96 Dd47
Deining D 96 Ea47
Deißlingen D 95 Cb50
Deiva Marina I 101 Cc63
Deje S 71 Fa43
Dekeleia CY 135 Cb96
De Koog NL 82 Ba33
De Kooy NL 82 Ba33
Delamere GB 13 Ec22
Delbrück D 89 Cc38
Delden NL 82 Bd36
Delecke D 89 Cb39
Deleitosa E 37 Cb66
Delémont CH 94 Bd53
Delfí GR 129 Bd84
Delft NL 17 Hd26
Delfzijl NL 82 Ca33
Delia I 114 Fa86
Deliceto I 112 Fd74
Delitzsch D 90 Eb39
Dellach im Drautal A 96 Ec55
Delligsen D 89 Db38
Delme F 21 Jd36
Delmenhorst D 83 Cd34
Delphi IRL 4 Bb19
Delsbo S 66 Gb35
Deltebre E 40 Ga63
Delvin IRL 5 Cc20
Demandice SK 98 Hc51
Demanová SK 98 Hd47
de Meca E 43 Bd77
Demecser H 99 Ka50
Demidov RUS 136 Ec11
Demjansk RUS 136 Eb09
Dem'jas RUS 137 Ga11
Demmin D 84 Ed32
Demre TR 135 Cb93
Dena E 30 Ac56
Denain F 20 Hb32
Denbigh GB 12 Ea22
Den Burg NL 82 Ba33
Denby Dale GB 13 Fa21
Dendermonde B 17 Hc29
Denekamp NL 82 Ca36
Den Haag NL 17 Hc26
Den Ham NL 82 Bd35
Den Helder NL 82 Ba33
Denholm GB 11 Ec15
den Hoorn NL 82 Bd32
Denia E 45 Fd70
Denkendorf D 96 Dd48
Dennebrœucq F 20 Gd31
Dennington GB 16 Gb25
Denny GB 11 Ea13
Denzlingen D 94 Ca50
De Panne B 17 Gd29
Derby GB 13 Fa23
Dergači RUS 137 Ga11
Derhači UA 137 Fa14
Dermbach D 89 Db42
Dernbach D 89 Cb42
Derreen IRL 4 Bc18
Derreendarragh IRL 6 Ba25
Derringstone GB 16 Gb29
Derry GB 5 Cc16
Derrybrien IRL 6 Bd22
Derrydruel IRL 4 Ca16
Derryerglinna IRL 4 Bc20
Derrygonelly GB 4 Cb17
Derrykeevan GB 5 Cd17
Derrylin GB 4 Cb18
Derrynawilt GB 5 Cc18
Dersingham GB 16 Fd23
Dervaig GB 10 Da10
Désaignes F 28 Ja49
Desana I 100 Ca60
Desborough GB 15 Fb25
Desenzano del Garda I 102 Db59
Desertmartin GB 5 Cd16

Desio – Facinas


Desio I 101 Cc59
Desna CZ 91 Fd42
Dešov CZ 97 Ga48
Dessau-Roßlau D 90 Eb38
Dessel B 88 Ba39
Desulo I 107 Cb77
Desvres F 20 Gc31
Deszk H 105 Jb57
Dětmarovice CZ 92 Hb45
Detmold D 89 Cd38
Dettelbach D 89 Db45
Dettenheim D 95 Cb47
Dettwiller F 94 Bd48
Detva SK 98 Hd49
Deuerling D 96 Ea48
Deuna D 89 Dc40
Deurne NL 88 Bb39
Deutsch Jahrndorf A 98 Gd51
Deutschkreuz A 97 Gc53
Deutschlandsberg A 97 Fd55
Deutsch-Wagram A 97 Gb50
Deva RO 117 Cc61
Devauden GB 14 Eb27
Dévaványa H 99 Jd54
Devecser H 98 Gd54
Deventer NL 82 Bc36
Deveso E 30 Bb53
Devil's Bridge GB 14 Dd25
Devizes GB 15 Ed28
De Wijk NL 82 Bc35
Dewsbury GB 13 Fa21
Dezna RO 117 Cb59
Dhërm AL 124 Aa78
Diafáni GR 134 Ec94
Diakoftó GR 129 Bc85
Diano Marina I 100 Bd64
Diarville F 25 Jd38
Didam NL 82 Bc37
Diddlebury GB 14 Eb25
Didim TR 134 Ec89
Die F 29 Jc50
Dieburg D 89 Cc44
Diedorf D 95 Dc50
Diego Álvaro E 37 Cc63
Diekholzen D 83 Db37
Diekirch L 21 Jc33
Diélette F 19 Ed34
Diemelstadt D 89 Cd39
Diemen NL 82 Ba35
Dienheim D 89 Cb45
Dienne F 27 Ha49
Dienstedt-Hettstedt D 90 Dd42
Diepenau D 83 Cd36
Diepenheim NL 82 Bd36
Diepenveen NL 82 Bc36
Diepholz D 83 Cc35
Dieppe F 20 Gb33
Dierdorf D 88 Ca42
Dieren NL 82 Bc37
Dierrey-Saint-Pierre F 24 Hc38
Diersbach A 96 Ed50
Dierzki PL 87 Jb32
Diespeck D 89 Dc46
Dießen D 95 Dc51
Diessenhofen CH 95 Cc52
Diest B 88 Ad40
Dietenheim D 95 Da50
Dietenhofen D 89 Dc46
Dietfurt D 96 Ea48
Dietikon CH 95 Cb53
Dietmannsried D 95 Db52
Dietramszell D 96 Dd52
Dietzenbach D 89 Cc44
Dietzhölztal D 89 Cc41
Dieulefit F 28 Jb51
Dieulouard F 21 Jd36
Dieupentale F 27 Gb53
Dieuze F 21 Ka36
Diever NL 82 Bd34
Diez D 89 Cb43
Differdange L 21 Jc34
Digne-les-Bains F 29 Ka52
Digoin F 25 Hd44
Dijon F 25 Jb41
Dikili TR 130 Eb84
Diksmuide B 17 Ha29
Diljatyn UA 136 Ea16
Dillenburg D 89 Cc41
Dillingen D 88 Bc46
Dillingen a.d.Donau D 95 Db49
Dílos GR 133 Db89
Dimitrovgrad RUS 137 Ga09
Dimitsána GR 128 Bb87
Dinami I 115 Gb82
Dinan F 22 Ec38
Dinant B 21 Ja32
Dinard F 18 Ec37
Dingé F 23 Ed38
Dingelstädt D 89 Dc40
Dingelstedt D 90 Dd38
Dingle IRL 6 Ba24
Dingolfing D 96 Eb49
Dingwall GB 8 Dd07
Dinkelsbühl D 95 Db47
Dinkelscherben D 95 Db50
Dinklage D 83 Cc35
Dinnington GB 13 Fa22
Dinnyés H 98 Hc54
Dinslaken D 88 Bd38
Dinteloord NL 17 Hd27
Dinxperlo NL 82 Bd37
Díon GR 125 Bd79
Diors F 24 Gc43
Dióskál H 104 Gd56
Dipkarpaz = Rizokarpaso CY 135 Cd94
Dippach L 21 Jc34
Dippen GB 10 Db14
Dipperz D 89 Da42
Dippoldiswalde D 90 Fa42
Dirksland NL 17 Hc27
Dischingen D 95 Db49
Disentis/ Mustér CH 95 Cb55
Diss GB 16 Gb25
Dissen D 83 Cc37
Dissenchen D 91 Fb39
Distington GB 12 Ea17
Dístos GR 129 Cc85
Ditchling GB 16 Fc30
Dittelbrunn D 89 Db44
Ditton Priors GB 13 Ec24
Ditzingen D 95 Cc48
Divčibare SRB 120 Ad65
Dives-sur-Mer F 19 Fc35
Dividal N 49 Gd12
Divnoe RUS 137 Ga15
Dixmont F 24 Hb39
Djäkneboda S 59 Hc28
Djat'kovo RUS 137 Ed12
Djuni BG 127 Fa73
Djupdal S 58 Ga26
Djupfjord N 48 Fd13
Djúpivogur IS 3 Cc06
Djupsjö S 57 Fa29
Djupslia N 65 Ea36
Djupvik N 49 Ha09
Djursdala S 72 Ga49
Długie PL 86 Hc34
Długołęka PL 87 Ka33
Długołeka PL 91 Gc41
Długopole-Zdrój PL 91 Gb44
Długosiodło PL 87 Jc35
Długoszyn PL 85 Fc36
Dłutówka PL 87 Jc34
Dmitrievka RUS 137 Fb12
Dmitriev-L'govskij RUS 137 Ed13
Dmitrov RUS 137 Ed10
Dmosin PL 92 Hd38
Dmusy PL 87 Jd32
Dmytrivka UA 137 Ed14
Dniprodzeržyns'k UA 137 Fa15
Dnipropetrovs'k UA 137 Fa15
Dniprorudne UA 137 Fa16
Dno RUS 136 Eb10
Doagh GB 5 Da17
Dobbertin D 84 Eb32
Dobčice CZ 97 Fb48
Dobczyce PL 92 Ja45
Dobel D 95 Cb48
Dobele LV 80 Ka52
Döbeln D 90 Ed41
Doberlug-Kirchhain D 90 Fa39
Döbern D 91 Fc39
Dobersberg A 97 Fd48
Dobiegniew PL 85 Ga35
Dobieszczyn PL 85 Fb33
Dobl A 97 Fd55
Doboj BIH 105 Hb62
Dobrá CZ 92 Hb46
Dobra PL 85 Fd33
Dobra PL 92 Hb38
Dobrá Niva SK 98 Hd49
Dobřany CZ 90 Ed46
Dobrá Voda SK 98 Gd49
Dobre Miasto PL 86 Ja31
Dobrești RO 117 Cb57
Döbriach A 96 Fa55
Dobrinka RUS 137 Fb12
Dobrjanka UA 136 Ec13
Dobrjatino RUS 137 Fb10
Dobrna SLO 104 Fd57
Dobromierz PL 91 Gb42
Dobromyl' UA 136 Dd15
Dobropillja UA 137 Fb15
Dobrosławice PL 92 Ha44
Dobrosołowo PL 86 Ha37
Dobrovice CZ 91 Fc43
Dobruš BY 136 Ec13
Dobruška CZ 91 Gb44
Dobry Las PL 87 Jd33
Dobrzany PL 85 Fd33
Dobrzelin PL 86 Hd37
Dobrzeń Wielki PL 92 Ha42
Dobrzyków PL 86 Hd36
Dobsza H 104 Ha58
Docelles F 25 Ka38
Docking GB 16 Ga23
Docksta S 58 Gd31
Dockweiler D 88 Bc43
Doddington GB 13 Fb22
Dodington GB 15 Ec28
Dodro E 30 Ad56
Doesburg NL 82 Bc37
Doetinchem NL 82 Bc37
Dogliani I 100 Bd62
Döhlau D 90 Ea44
Dohna D 90 Fa41
Dohren D 83 Cb35
Dokkum NL 82 Bc32
Doksy CZ 91 Fc43
Dokšycy BY 136 Ea12
Dokučajevs'k UA 137 Fb15
Dolancourt F 25 Ja38
Dolany CZ 90 Ed46
Dolbenmaen GB 12 Dd23
Dolcè I 102 Dc59
Dol-de-Bretagne F 23 Ed38
Dole F 25 Jc42
Dolenjske Toplice SLO 103 Fc59
Dolfor GB 14 Ea25
Dolgarrog GB 12 Ea22
Dolgellau GB 12 Dd24
Dołgie PL 85 Ga33
Dolianova I 107 Ca79
Doliwy PL 87 Jd30
Dolla IRL 6 Ca23
Dollar GB 11 Ea12
Döllnitz D 90 Eb40
Dollnstein D 96 Dd48
Dolná Krupa SK 98 Gd50
Dolná Mariková SK 98 Hb47
Dolní Benešov CZ 92 Ha45
Dolní Bousov CZ 91 Fd43
Dolní Břežany CZ 91 Fb45
Dolní Dvořiště CZ 97 Fb49
Dolní Kounice CZ 97 Gb48
Dolní Město CZ 91 Fd46
Dolný Kubín SK 98 Hd47
Dolo I 102 Ea60
Dolores E 45 Fb72
Dolsk PL 91 Gc38
Dolton GB 14 Dd30
Dołuje PL 85 Fb33
Dolus-d'Oléron F 23 Fa46
Dolyns'ka UA 137 Ed16
Dol. Žandov CZ 90 Ec44
Dolžanskaja RUS 137 Fb16
Domaniža SK 98 Hb48
Domanów PL 91 Ga42
Domaradz PL 85 Gc30
Domaradz PL 93 Ka45
Domaszków PL 91 Gc44
Domats F 24 Hb39
Domažlice CZ 90 Ec46
Domba N 62 Ca35
Dombaj RUS 137 Ga17
Dombås N 64 Dc34
Dombasle-sur-Meurthe F 21 Jd37
Dombóvár H 105 Hb56
Dombrád H 99 Ka50
Domburg NL 17 Hb28
Domerat F 24 Ha45
Domersleben D 84 Ea37
Domèvre-sur-Vezouze F 21 Ka37
Dómez E 31 Ca60
Dominowo PL 86 Gd37
Dömitz D 84 Ea34
Dommartin-les-Cuiseaux F 25 Jc44
Domme F 27 Gb50
Dommitzsch D 90 Ec39
Domodedovo RUS 137 Fa10
Domodossola I 100 Ca57
Domokós GR 129 Bc82
Dömös H 98 Hc52
Domoszló H 99 Jb51
Domousnice CZ 91 Fc43
Dompierre-sur-Mer F 23 Fa46
Dompierre-sur-Veyle F 25 Jb46
Dömsöd H 98 Hd54
Domsühl D 84 Eb33
Domusnovas I 107 Bd79
Domžale SLO 103 Fc57
Donabate IRL 7 Cd21
Donadea IRL 7 Cc21
Donagh GB 4 Cb18
Donaghadee GB 5 Db17
Donaghmore GB 5 Cd17
Don Álvaro E 37 Bd69
Doña Mencía E 44 Da73
Donaueschingen D 95 Cb51
Donaustauf D 96 Eb48
Donauwörth D 95 Dc49
Don Benito E 37 Ca69
Doncaster GB 13 Fa21
Donec'k UA 137 Fb15
Donegal IRL 4 Ca16
Dongen NL 88 Ba38
Donges F 22 Ec42
Dongo I 101 Cc57
Donji Kamengrad BIH 104 Gc62
Donji Murići MNE 111 Ja70
Donji Vakuf BIH 104 Ha64
Donkerbroek NL 82 Bd34
Donnalucata I 115 Fb88
Donnersbach A 97 Fb53
Donohill IRL 6 Ca24
Donop D 89 Cd38
Donostia E 33 Ec55
Donoughmore IRL 6 Bc25
Donskoe RUS 137 Fd16
Dontreix F 24 Ha46
Donyatt GB 14 Eb30
Donzdorf D 95 Da49
Donzère F 28 Jb51
Doocharry IRL 4 Ca16
Dooega IRL 4 Bb18
Doogary IRL 4 Cb19
Doogort IRL 4 Bb18
Doolin IRL 6 Bc22
Doon IRL 6 Bd23
Doorn NL 82 Bb37
Dørålseter N 64 Dd34
Dorchester GB 15 Fa27
Dorchester GB 15 Ec30
Dordives F 24 Ha39
Dordrecht NL 17 Hd27
Dore-l'Eglise F 28 Hc48
Dorénaz CH 100 Bc56
Dores GB 8 Dd08
Dorfchemnitz D 90 Ed42
Dorfgastein A 96 Ec54
Dörfles-Esbach D 90 Dd43
Dorf Mecklenburg D 84 Ea32
Dorgali I 107 Cc76
Doria I 101 Cb62
Dorking GB 16 Fc29
Dormagen D 88 Bd40
Dormánd H 99 Jb52
Dormans F 20 Hc36
Dormansland GB 16 Fd29
Dormitz D 90 Dd46
Dornas F 28 Ja50
Dornbirn A 95 Da53
Dornburg D 89 Cb42
Dornecy F 24 Hc41
Dornhan D 95 Cb49
Dornie GB 8 Dc08
Dornoch GB 9 Ea06
Dornstadt D 95 Da49
Dornstetten D 95 Cb49
Dornumersiel D 83 Cb32
Dorohoi RO 118 Ec54
Dorotea S 58 Ga27
Dörpen D 82 Ca34
Dorras N 49 Hc08
Dorrington GB 12 Eb24
Dorris S 58 Fd25
Dorsten D 88 Bd38
Dortan F 25 Jc45
Dortmund D 88 Ca39
Dörverden D 83 Da35
Dörzbach D 89 Da46
Dosbarrios E 38 Dc66
Dos Hermanas E 43 Ca74
Dossenheim D 89 Cc46
Dotkomyrene N 47 Kb06
Dötlingen D 83 Cc34
Douai F 20 Ha32
Douarnenez F 22 Dc39
Douchy F 24 Hb40
Douchy-les-Mines F 20 Hb32
Doucier F 25 Jd44
Doudeville F 19 Ga34
Doué-la-Fontaine F 23 Fc42
Douglas GB 12 Dd19
Doulaincourt-Saucourt F 25 Jb38
Doulevant-le-Château F 25 Ja38
Doullens F 20 Gd32
Dounby GB 9 Ec02
Doune GB 11 Ea12
Dourdan F 24 Gd38
Dourgne F 27 Gd54
Douriez F 20 Gc32
Douvaine F 25 Ka45
Douvres-la-Délivrande F 19 Fc35
Douzy F 21 Ja34
Dovadola I 102 Dd64
Dover GB 16 Gb29
Dovhe UA 136 Dd16
Dovre N 64 Dc34
Dovreskogen N 64 Dc34
Dovsk BY 136 Eb13
Downham GB 16 Fd25
Downhill GB 5 Cd15
Downpatrick GB 5 Da18
Dowra IRL 4 Ca18
Dowsby GB 16 Fc23
Drabiv UA 137 Ed14
Drača SRB 120 Bb66
Drachselsried D 96 Ec48
Drachten NL 82 Bc33
Drag N 48 Ga15
Drage D 83 Dc33
Dragoevo BG 122 Ec70
Dragomirești RO 118 Dc55
Dragør DK 77 Ec56
Dragsvik FIN 68 Jd40
Draguignan F 29 Kb54
Drahičyn BY 136 Ea14
Drahonice CZ 96 Fa47
Drakenburg D 83 Da35
Drammen N 71 Dd42
Drangan IRL 7 Cb24
Drangedal N 70 Db44
Drängsmark S 59 Hc25
Drangsnes IS 2 Ad03
Drangstedt D 83 Cd32
Dranske D 84 Ed29
Draveil F 20 Gd37
Dravograd SLO 103 Fc56
Drawno PL 85 Ga34
Drawsko Pomorskie PL 85 Ga33
Drążdżewo PL 87 Jb34
Draženov CZ 90 Ec46
Drebkau D 91 Fb39
Dreenagh IRL 6 Ba23
Drégelypalánk H 98 Hd51
Dreieich D 89 Cc44
Dreißigacker D 89 Db42
Drem GB 11 Ec13
Drenchia I 103 Ed57
Drenovë AL 124 Ad77
Drensteinfurt D 89 Cb38
Drëtun' BY 136 Eb11
Dreux F 20 Gb37
Drevvatn N 52 Fa21
Drewnica PL 86 Hb30
Drezdenko PL 85 Ga35
Driálos GR 132 Bc91
Driebergen-Rijsenburg NL 82 Ba36
Driedorf D 89 Cb42
Drienov SK 99 Jd48
Driesum NL 82 Bc33
Drietoma SK 98 Ha48
Driffield GB 13 Fc20
Drimnin GB 10 Db10
Drimoleague IRL 6 Bb26
Drimpton GB 14 Eb30
Drinagh IRL 7 Cd25
Drionville F 20 Gc31
Driopída GR 133 Cd89
Drøbak N 71 Ea42
Drobeta-Turnu Severin RO 121 Cb65
Drochtersen D 83 Da32
Drogheda IRL 5 Cd20
Drohiczyn PL 87 Ka36
Drohobyč UA 136 Dd16
Droichead Átha IRL 5 Cd20
Droichead na Bandan IRL 6 Bc26
Droisy F 20 Gb37
Droitwich GB 15 Ed25
Drolshagen D 89 Cb40
Drołtowice PL 92 Gd40
Droman GB 8 Dc04
Dromcolliher IRL 6 Bc24
Dromina IRL 6 Bc24
Drommahane IRL 6 Bc25
Dromod IRL 4 Ca19
Dromore GB 4 Cb17
Dromore GB 5 Da18
Dromore West IRL 4 Bd18
Dronero I 100 Bc62
Dronfield GB 13 Fa22
Dronninglund DK 71 Dd50
Dronten NL 82 Bb35
Drosbacken S 65 Ed35
Droskovo RUS 137 Fa12
Drosopigí = Vourgareli GR 128 Ba81
Drozdyn' UA 136 Ea14
Drożki PL 92 Ha41
Drübeck D 89 Dc38
Drugnia PL 93 Jb42
Drulingen F 94 Bd47
Drumbeg GB 8 Dc05
Drumcliff IRL 4 Ca17
Drumclog GB 10 Dd14
Drumcondra IRL 5 Cd19
Drumfin IRL 4 Ca18
Drumfree IRL 5 Cc15
Drumgoft IRL 7 Cd22
Drumkeen IRL 4 Cb16
Drumkeeran IRL 4 Ca18
Drumlegagh GB 4 Cb17
Drumlish IRL 4 Cb19
Drummannon GB 5 Cd17
Drummore GB 10 Dc17
Drumnadrochit GB 8 Dd08
Drumnakilly GB 5 Cc17
Drumreagh IRL 4 Bb18
Drumrunie GB 8 Dc06
Drumsallie GB 10 Dc10
Drumshanbo IRL 4 Ca19
Drunen NL 88 Ba38
Druskininkai LT 87 Kc30
Druten NL 82 Bb37
Druyes-les-Belles-Fontaine F 24 Hb41
Družba UA 137 Ed13
Drwalew PL 93 Jb38
Drybrook GB 15 Ec27
Drymen GB 10 Dd12
Drzązgowo PL 85 Gc37
Drzewce PL 86 Hb37
Drzewce PL 93 Ka39
Drzewica PL 93 Jb39
Drzonów PL 91 Fd38
Drzonowo PL 85 Fd31
Drzonowo PL 85 Gc32
Drzycim PL 86 Ha33
Duagh IRL 6 Bb24
Duas Igrejas P 31 Ca60
Dubá CZ 91 Fb43
Dubí CZ 90 Fa42
Dubicko CZ 91 Gc45
Dubiny PL 87 Kc34
Dublin IRL 7 Cd21
Dubna RUS 137 Ed10
Dubna RUS 137 Fa11
Dubňany CZ 97 Gc48
Dubnica nad Váhom SK 98 Hb48
Dubno UA 136 Ea15
Dubovka RUS 137 Fd13
Dubovskoje RUS 137 Fd15
Dubovyj Ovrag RUS 137 Fd14
Dubrivka UA 136 Eb15
Dubrovka RUS 137 Fc12
Dubrovnik HR 111 Hb69
Dubrovycja UA 136 Ea14
Duchally GB 8 Dd05
Duchcov CZ 90 Fa43
Duclair F 19 Ga35
Duddington GB 13 Fb24
Dudelange L 21 Jc34
Dudeldorf D 88 Bc44
Dudenhofen D 89 Cb46
Duderstadt D 89 Db39
Dudince SK 98 Hc50
Dudley GB 13 Ed24
Dueñas E 32 Da59
Dufftown GB 9 Eb08
Duffus GB 9 Eb07
Duhnen D 83 Cd31
Duhovnickoe RUS 137 Ga11
Duingen D 89 Da38
Duingt F 25 Ka46
Duinkerken = Dunkerque F 17 Gd29
Duino I 103 Ed59
Duirinish GB 8 Db08
Duisburg D 88 Bd39
Duiven NL 82 Bc37
Dukla PL 93 Jd45
Duleek IRL 5 Cd20
Dullingham GB 16 Fd26
Dülmen D 88 Ca38
Dulverton GB 14 Ea29
Dumbarton GB 10 Dd13
Dumbleton GB 15 Ed26
Dumfries GB 11 Ea16
Dumha Eige IRL 4 Bb18
Dummerstorf D 84 Eb31
Dümpelfeld D 88 Bd42
Duna N 57 Ec26
Dunafalva H 105 Hc57
Dunaff IRL 5 Cc15
Dunaharaszti H 98 Hd53
Dunajivci UA 136 Eb16
Dunajská Streda SK 98 Ha51
Dunakeszi H 98 Hd52
Dunakömlőd H 98 Hc55
Dunapataj H 105 Hd56
Dunaújváros H 98 Hc54
Dunavecse H 98 Hd55
Dunbar GB 11 Ec13
Dunblane GB 11 Ea12
Dunboyne IRL 7 Cd21
Dún Chaoin IRL 6 Ad24
Dunchurch GB 15 Fa25
Duncormick IRL 7 Cc25
Dundalk IRL 5 Cd19
Dun Dealgan IRL 5 Cd19
Dundee GB 11 Ec11
Dunderrow IRL 6 Bc26
Dundonald GB 5 Da17
Dundonnell GB 8 Dc06
Dundrenan GB 10 Ea17
Dundrum IRL 6 Ca23
Dunecht GB 9 Ed09
Dunes F 27 Ga53
Dunfanaghy IRL 4 Cb15
Dunfermline GB 11 Eb12
Dungannon GB 5 Cd17
Dún Garbhán IRL 6 Ca25
Dungarvan IRL 6 Ca25
Dungiven GB 5 Cd16
Dunglow IRL 4 Ca15
Dungourney IRL 6 Bd25
Dunholme GB 13 Fc22
Dunkeld GB 11 Eb11
Dunkerque F 17 Gd29
Dunkerrin IRL 6 Ca22
Dunkeswell GB 14 Ea30
Dunkineely IRL 4 Ca17
Dünkirchen = Dunkerque F 17 Gd29
Dunkirk GB 15 Ec28
Dun Laoghaire IRL 7 Cd21
Dunlavin IRL 7 Cc22
Dunleer IRL 5 Cd20
Dunlop GB 10 Dd14
Dún Manmhaí IRL 6 Bc26
Dunmanus IRL 6 Ba26
Dunmanway IRL 6 Bc26
Dún Mór IRL 4 Bd20
Dunmore GB 5 Da19
Dunmore IRL 4 Bd20
Dunmore East IRL 7 Cc25
Dunnamanagh GB 5 Cc16
Dunnamore GB 5 Cc17
Dun na nGall IRL 4 Ca16
Dunnet GB 9 Eb04
Dunningen D 95 Cb50
Dunoon GB 10 Dc13
Dunquin IRL 6 Ad24
Duns GB 11 Ed14
Dunscore GB 11 Ea16
Dünsen D 83 Cd34
Dunsford GB 14 Dd30
Dunshaughlin IRL 7 Cd21
Dunstable GB 15 Fb27
Dunster GB 14 Ea29
Dun-sur-Meuse F 21 Jb34
Dunte LV 74 Kc49
Duntish GB 15 Ec30
Dunure GB 10 Dc15
Dunvegan GB 8 Da07
Durach D 95 Db52
Durango E 32 Eb55
Duras F 26 Fd51
Durbach D 94 Ca49
Durban-Corbières F 35 Hb56
Durbuy B 21 Jb31
Düren D 88 Bc41
Durham GB 13 Fa17
Durlangen D 95 Da48
Durlas IRL 6 Ca23
Durmersheim D 95 Cb47
Durness GB 8 Dd04
Durnholz I 96 Dd55
Dürnkrut A 97 Gc50
Dürnstein A 97 Fd50
Durrës AL 124 Ab74
Durrington GB 15 Ed29
Durrow IRL 7 Cb23
Durrus IRL 6 Bb26
Dürrwangen D 95 Db47
Durtal F 23 Fc41
Dusnok H 105 Hd56
Düsseldorf D 88 Bd40
Dussen NL 82 Ba37
Dußlingen D 95 Cc49
Duston GB 15 Fb25
Duszniki PL 85 Gb36
Duszniki-Zdrój PL 91 Gb43
Duthil GB 9 Ea08
Duvberg S 65 Fb34
Duved S 57 Ed30
Duża Klonownica PL 87 Kb37
Duzy-le-Gros F 20 Hc34
Dvärsätt S 58 Fc30
Dverberg N 48 Fd11
Dvoriki RUS 137 Fa10
Dvory nad Žitavou SK 98 Hb51
Dvůr Králové nad Labem CZ 91 Ga43
Dwingeloo NL 82 Bd34
Dwórzno PL 86 Ja30
Dyan GB 5 Cd18
Dybów PL 87 Jd36
Dyce GB 9 Ed09
Dyffryn Ardudwy GB 12 Dd23
Dykan'ka UA 137 Ed14
Dyke GB 14 Dc29
Dykehead GB 11 Ec10
Dykends GB 11 Eb10
Dylife GB 12 Ea24
Dymchurch GB 16 Ga29
Dymer UA 136 Ec14
Dymock GB 15 Ec26
Dynów PL 93 Ka44
Dyrham GB 15 Ec28
Dyrkorn N 64 Cd33
Dyrnes N 56 Db29
Dyrøy N 48 Gb11
Dysberg S 65 Fb37
Dysbodarna S 65 Fa38
Dywity PL 86 Ja31
Džankoj UA 137 Fa17
Džebel BG 126 Dc75
Dzeržinsk RUS 137 Fb09
Dziadkowice PL 87 Kb35
Działdowo PL 86 Ja33
Działoszyce PL 93 Jb43
Dziekanowice PL 92 Ja45
Dziektarzewo PL 86 Ja35
Dzierżążno Wielkie PL 85 Gb35
Dzierzgoń PL 86 Hc31
Dzierzgowo PL 87 Jb34
Dzierzkowice Rynek PL 93 Ka41
Dzierżoniow PL 91 Gb42
Dzieslaw PL 91 Gb40
Dzikowo PL 85 Fd35
Dzików Stary PL 93 Kc43
Dziwnów PL 85 Fc31
Dzjaržynsk BY 136 Ea12
Dzjatlava BY 136 Ea13
Džubga RUS 137 Fc17
Džuryn UA 136 Eb16
Dźwierszno Wielkie PL 86 Gd34


## E


Ea E 32 Eb55
Éadan Doire IRL 7 Cc21
Eaglesfield GB 11 Eb16
Eaní GR 125 Bc79
Eanodat FIN 50 Ja13
Earby GB 13 Ed20
Earls Barton GB 15 Fb25
Earls Colne GB 16 Ga26
Earlsferry GB 11 Ec12
Earlston GB 11 Ec14
Easdale GB 10 Db11
Easington GB 13 Fa17
Easington GB 13 Fd21
Easington GB 15 Fb27
Easingwold GB 13 Fa19
Easky IRL 4 Bd18
Eastbourne GB 16 Fd30
East Brent GB 14 Eb29
Eastchurch GB 16 Ga28
Eastcote GB 16 Fc28
East Cowes GB 15 Fa30
East Dereham GB 16 Ga24
Eastergate GB 15 Fb30
East Grafton GB 15 Ed28
East Grinstead GB 16 Fc29
East Haddon GB 15 Fb25
East Hanningfield GB 16 Ga27
East Horsley GB 16 Fc29
East Ilsley GB 15 Fa28
East Kilbride GB 10 Dd13
East Leake GB 13 Fa23
Eastleigh GB 15 Fa30
East Linton GB 11 Ec13
East Morden GB 15 Ec30
East Norton GB 13 Fb24
Eastoft GB 13 Fb21
Easton GB 15 Ec31
Easton GB 16 Gb24
Easton Grey GB 15 Ec27
East Poringland GB 16 Gb24
East Portlemouth GB 14 Dd32
East Ravendale GB 13 Fc21
East Rudham GB 16 Ga24
East Tisted GB 15 Fb29
Eastville GB 16 Fd23
East Winch GB 16 Fd24
Eastwood GB 13 Fa23
Eaux-Bonnes F 33 Fc56
Eauze F 26 Fd53
Ebbw Vale GB 14 Eb27
Ebchester GB 13 Ed17
Ebeleben D 89 Dc40
Ebeltoft DK 77 Dd54
Ebenfurt A 97 Gb52
Ebensee A 96 Fa52
Ebensfeld D 89 Dc44
Eberbach D 89 Cd46
Eberdingen D 95 Cc48
Eberhardzell D 95 Da51
Ebermannsdorf D 96 Ea47
Ebermannstadt D 90 Dd45
Ebern D 89 Dc44
Ebernburg D 88 Ca45
Ebersbach D 90 Ed41
Ebersbach D 91 Fc41
Ebersbach D 95 Cd48
Ebersberg D 96 Ea51
Ebersburg D 89 Da43
Eberschwang A 96 Ed51
Ebersdorf D 90 Dd44
Ebersdorf, Saalburg- D 90 Ea43
Eberswalde D 84 Fa35
Eboli I 112 Fc76
Ebrach D 89 Dc45
Ebreichsdorf A 97 Gb51
Ebsdorfergrund D 89 Cd42
Ebstorf D 83 Dc34
Écaussinnes-Lalaing B 20 Hc31
Eccles GB 11 Ec14
Eccleshall GB 13 Ec23
Echalar E 33 Ed55
Echallens CH 94 Bb55
Echassières F 24 Hb45
Eching D 96 Ea50
Echiré F 23 Fc45
Echt GB 9 Ed09
Echt NL 88 Bb40
Echteld NL 82 Bb37
Echterdingen, Leinfelden- D 95 Cd49
Echternach L 21 Jd33
Écija E 43 Cc73
Eckartsberga D 90 Ea41
Eckental D 90 Dd46
Eckernförde D 83 Db29
Eckerö FIN 67 Hb40
Eckersdorf D 90 Dd45
Eckington GB 13 Fa22
Eclaron-Braucourt F 21 Ja37
Écommoy F 23 Fd40
Ecouché F 19 Fc37
Ecouflant F 23 Fb41
Ecoyeux F 26 Fb47
Ecques F 20 Gd31
Ecseg H 98 Ja51
Edam NL 82 Ba35
Edderton GB 9 Ea07
Eddleston GB 11 Eb14
Ede NL 82 Bb37
Ede S 66 Ga33
Edelény H 99 Jc50
Edemissen D 83 Dc36
Edenbridge GB 16 Fd29
Edenderry IRL 7 Cc21
Edenkoben D 89 Cb46
Edertal D 89 Cd40
Edesbyn S 66 Fd37
Édessa GR 125 Bc77
Edewecht D 83 Cc34
Edgbaston GB 15 Ed25
Edgeworthstown = Mostrim IRL 4 Cb20
Edinburgh GB 11 Eb13
Edırne TR 126 Eb75
Edith Weston GB 13 Fb24
Edlingham GB 11 Ed15
Edlitz A 97 Gb54
Edmundbyers GB 13 Ed17
Ēdole LV 80 Jb51
Edremit TR 131 Ec82
Edsta S 66 Gb35
Edzell GB 11 Ec10
Eeklo B 17 Hb29
Eelde NL 82 Bd33
Eemshaven NL 82 Ca32
Eemsmond NL 82 Ca32
Eerbeek NL 82 Bc37
Eernegem B 17 Ha29
Eersel NL 88 Ba39
Eferding A 96 Fa50
Effelder D 90 Dd43
Eforie Nord RO 123 Fc68
Eforie Sud RO 123 Fc68
Efremov RUS 137 Fa12
Egeln D 90 Ea38
Eger H 99 Jb51
Egersund N 63 Ca45
Eggenburg A 97 Ga49
Eggenfelden D 96 Ec50
Eggenstein-Leopoldshafen D 95 Cb47
Eggersdorf, Fredersdorf- D 84 Fa36
Eggesin D 85 Fb32
Eggingen D 95 Cb52
Eggiwil CH 94 Bd54
Egglescliffe GB 13 Fa18
Egglham D 96 Ec49
Egglkofen D 96 Eb50
Eggolsheim D 90 Dd45
Egham GB 15 Fb28
Egiáli GR 133 Dd90
Egilsstaðir IS 3 Cc04
Égina GR 129 Cb87
Eging am See D 96 Ed49
Égio GR 128 Bb85
Egíra GR 129 Bc85
Egling D 95 Dc50
Egling D 96 Dd51
Eglingham GB 11 Ed15
Egloffstein D 90 Dd45
Eglwysfach GB 12 Dd24
Eglwyswrw GB 14 Dc26
Egmond aan Zee NL 82 Ad34
Egor'e RUS 137 Ed11
Egor'evsk RUS 137 Fa10
Egorlykskaja RUS 137 Fc16
Egremont GB 12 Ea18
Egton GB 13 Fb18
Eguisheim F 94 Bd50
Eguzon F 24 Gc45
Egyek H 99 Jc52
Egyptinkorpi FIN 61 Lc27
Ehekirchen D 95 Dc49
Ehingen am Ries D 95 Dc48
Ehingen (Donau) D 95 Da50
Ehningen D 95 Cc48
Ehra-Lessien D 84 Dd36
Ehrenburg D 83 Cd35
Ehrenfriedersdorf D 90 Ec42
Ehrenhain D 90 Ec41
Ehrenkirchen D 94 Ca51
Ehringshausen D 89 Cc42
Eibar E 32 Eb55
Eibau D 91 Fc41
Eibelstadt D 89 Db45
Eibenstock D 90 Ec43
Eibergen NL 82 Bd37
Eibiswald A 104 Fd56
Eichendorf D 96 Ec49
Eichenzell D 89 Da43
Eichstätt D 96 Dd48
Eichstetten D 94 Ca50
Eichwalde D 84 Fa37
Eicklingen D 83 Dc36
Eiðar IS 3 Cc04
Eide N 56 Da31
Eidem N 52 Ec23
Eidet N 47 Kd07
Eidet N 48 Ga14
Eidevik N 62 Cb36
Eidfjord N 62 Cd39
Eidkjosen N 49 Gc09
Eidsberg N 71 Eb43
Eidsnes N 50 Hd08
Eidsøra N 56 Db31
Eidsvåg N 56 Db32
Eigeltingen D 95 Cc51
Eijsden NL 88 Bb41
Eikange N 62 Ca38
Eikelandsosen N 63 Cb40
Eiknes N 63 Cb40
Eilenburg D 90 Ec40
Èilgar RUS 137 Ga15
Eilsleben D 84 Dd37
Eime D 83 Db37
Eimen D 89 Db38
Eimke D 83 Dc34
Einavoll N 65 Ea39
Einbeck D 89 Db38
Eindhoven NL 88 Bb39
Einhausen D 89 Cc45
Einola FIN 61 Lb28
Einsiedel D 90 Ec42
Einsiedeln CH 95 Cb54
Eisenach D 89 Db41
Eisenberg D 89 Cb45
Eisenberg D 90 Ea41
Eisenerz A 97 Fc53
Eisenhüttenstadt D 85 Fc37
Eisenkappel A 103 Fb56
Eisenstadt A 97 Gb52
Eisfeld D 89 Dc43
Eiterfeld D 89 Da42
Eitorf D 88 Ca41
Eitrheimsnes N 63 Cc40
Eivindvik N 62 Ca37
Eivissa E 40 Gc69
Eixo P 36 Ac62
Ejea de los Caballeros E 33 Fa59
Ejheden S 66 Fd37
Ejsk RUS 137 Fb16
Ejulve E 39 Fb63
Ekaterinovka RUS 137 Fa12
Ekaterinovka RUS 137 Fc12
Ekeby S 73 Ha49
Ekenäs FIN 68 Jd40
Ekerö S 73 Gd44
Eketånga S 77 Ed52
Ekfors S 54 Jb20
Ekimoviči RUS 136 Ec12
Ekkerøy N 47 Kc06
Ekorrsele S 59 Ha26
Eksjö S 72 Fc49
Elafónissos GR 132 Bd91
El Álamo E 38 Db65
El Álamo E 43 Bd73
El Algar E 45 Fa73
El Alquián E 44 Eb76
Elämäjärvi FIN 60 Kb28
Elan' RUS 137 Fd12
Elan'-Kolenovskij RUS 137 Fc13
El Arahal E 43 Cb74
Elassóna GR 129 Bc80
El Astillero E 32 Dc55
Elátia GR 129 Bd84
Elat'ma RUS 137 Fb10
El Ballestero E 44 Ea70
El Barco de Ávila E 37 Cb64
Elbasan AL 124 Ac75
Elbeuf F 19 Ga35
Elbing = Elbląg PL 86 Hc30
Elbląg PL 86 Hc30
El Bocal E 33 Ed59
El Bodón E 37 Bd64
El Bonillo E 38 Ea69
El'brus RUS 137 Ga17
Elburg NL 82 Bc35
El Burgo E 43 Cc76
El Burgo de Ebro E 33 Fb61
El Burgo de Osma E 32 Dd60
El Burgo Ranero E 31 Cd57
El Buste E 33 Ed60
El Cabo de Gata E 44 Eb76
El Campillo E 44 Dd71
El Campillo E 44 Ea71
El Campo de Peñaranda E 37 Cc62
El Carpio E 43 Cd72
El Carpio de Tajo E 38 Da66
El Casar de Escalona E 38 Da65
El Casar de Talamanca E 38 Dc63
El Castaño E 43 Ca77
El Castellar E 39 Fa65
Elche E 45 Fb71
Elche de la Sierra E 44 Eb71
Elchingen D 95 Da49
el Cogul E 34 Ga61
El Collado E 39 Fa66
El Corchuelo E 43 Bc74
El Coronil E 43 Ca75
El Cubo de la Tierra del Vino E 31 Cb61
El Cuervo E 43 Bd75
Elda E 45 Fa71
Elda N 48 Ga12
Elec RUS 137 Fa12
Elefsína GR 129 Cb86
El Ejido E 44 Dd76
Elek H 116 Bd58
Èlektostal' RUS 137 Fa10
Eleón GR 125 Cc76
El Escorial E 38 Db64
Elfershausen D 89 Db44
Elford GB 13 Ed24
El Frago E 33 Fa58
Elganowo PL 86 Ha31
El Gargantón E 38 Da69
El Gastor E 43 Cb76
Elgin GB 9 Eb07
Elgiszewo PL 86 Hb34
Elgoibar E 32 Eb55
Elgol GB 8 Db09
El Guijar E 38 Db62
Elham GB 16 Gb29
Elhovka RUS 137 Ga09
Elincourt-Sainte-Marguerite F 20 Ha34
Elionka RUS 136 Ec13
Èlista RUS 137 Ga15
Elizondo E 33 Ed56
El Jardín E 44 Eb70
Ełk PL 87 Jd31
Elkstone GB 15 Ed27
Ellastone GB 13 Ed23
Ellenberg D 95 Db48
Ellen's Green GB 16 Fc29
Ellerau D 83 Db32
Ellesmere GB 12 Eb23
Ellesmere Port GB 12 Eb22
Ellewoutsdijk NL 17 Hc28
Ellingen D 95 Dc47
Ellinikά GR 129 Cb83
Ellon GB 9 Ed08
Ellrich D 89 Dc39
Ellwangen/Jagst D 95 Db48
El Madroño E 43 Bc73
Elmalı TR 135 Ca91
el Masnou E 35 Ha61
Elmdon GB 16 Fd26
Elmen A 95 Db53
Elmley Castle GB 15 Ed26
El Molar E 38 Dc63
El Molar E 44 Dd72
Elmore GB 15 Ec27
Elmshorn D 83 Db32
El Musel E 31 Cc54
Elnesvågen N 56 Cd31
El'nja RUS 136 Ec11
Elorrio E 32 Eb56
Eloúnta GR 133 Dc96
Eloyes F 25 Ka39
el Palmar E 39 Fc68
El Palmar E 45 Fa72
El Palmar de Troya E 43 Ca75
El Parador de las Hortichuelas E 44 Ea76
El Paraíso E 43 Cc77
El Pardo E 38 Dc64
El Pedregal E 39 Ed63
El Pedroso E 43 Ca72
El Pedroso de la Armuña E 37 Cc62
el Perelló E 40 Ga63
Elphin GB 8 Dc06
Elphin IRL 4 Ca19
El Picazo E 38 Eb68
El Piñero E 31 Cc61
El Pobo de Dueñas E 39 Ed63
El Portal E 43 Bd76
el Port de Borriana E 39 Fc66
El Priorato E 43 Cb73
El Provencio E 38 Ea68
El Puente del Rio E 44 Dd76
El Puerto E 43 Bc71
El Puerto de Santa María E 43 Bd76
El Real de San Vicente E 37 Cd65
El Rincón E 45 Ec74
El Rocío E 43 Bc74
El Romeral E 38 Dc67
El Rubio E 43 Cc74
El Sabinar E 33 Fa59
El Sabinar E 44 Eb72
El Salobral E 39 Ec69
El Saltador E 45 Ec74
El Santiscal E 43 Ca76
els Arcs E 34 Fd61
El Saucejo E 43 Cc75
Elsdon GB 11 Ed15
Elsdorf D 88 Bc40
Elsdorf-Westermühlen D 83 Db30
Elsenfeld D 89 Cd45
Elsenham GB 16 Fd27
Elsfleth D 83 Cd33
Elsing GB 16 Ga24
el Soleràs E 34 Ga61
Elspeet NL 82 Bb36
Elsrickle GB 11 Eb14
Elst NL 82 Bb37
Elstad N 57 Ed26
Elstal D 84 Ed36
Elstead GB 15 Fb29
Elsterwerda D 90 Fa40
Elstow GB 16 Fc26
Elstra D 91 Fb41
Elterlein D 90 Ec43
Eltham GB 16 Fd28
El Tiemblo E 38 Da64
El Toboso E 38 Dd67
Elton IRL 6 Bd24
Èl'ton RUS 137 Ga13
El Torno E 43 Bd76
El Toro E 39 Fa66
El Tricheto E 38 Da68
El Tumbalejo E 43 Bc73
Eltvik N 62 Cb33
Eltville D 89 Cb44
Elva EST 75 La46
Elva I 100 Bb62
El Vacar E 43 Cc72
Elvanfoot GB 11 Ea15
Elvas P 36 Bb68
Elvåsen N 57 Ec25
Elvebakken N 50 Hd08
Elveden GB 16 Ga25
el Vendrell E 34 Gc62
Elverum N 49 Gc11
el Vilosell E 34 Gb61
Elviria E 43 Cc77
El Viso del Alcor E 43 Ca74
Elvkroken N 48 Fd16
Elwick GB 13 Fa17
Elworthy GB 14 Ea29
Elx E 45 Fb71
Ely GB 16 Fd25
Elzach D 94 Ca50
Elztal D 89 Cd46
Emagny F 25 Jc41
Embid E 39 Ec63
Emborió GR 134 Eb90
Emden D 82 Ca33
Emet TR 131 Fd83
Emlichheim D 82 Bd35
Emly IRL 6 Bd24
Emmaboda S 78 Fd53
Emmeloord NL 82 Bc34
Emmelshausen D 88 Ca43
Emmen NL 82 Ca34
Emmendingen D 94 Ca50
Emmer-Compascuum NL 82 Ca34
Emmerich D 82 Bc37
Emmerik = Emmerich D 82 Bc37
Emmerthal D 83 Da37
Emmerting D 96 Ec51
Emmingen-Liptingen D 95 Cc51
Emmoo IRL 4 Ca20
Emo IRL 7 Cb22
Empoli I 108 Db65
Empuriabrava E 35 Hc58
Emsbüren D 82 Ca36
Emsdetten D 83 Cb37
Emskirchen D 89 Dc46
Emstek D 83 Cc35
Emyvale IRL 5 Cc18
Ena E 33 Fb58
Enånger S 66 Gb36
Encinas E 32 Dc61
Encinasola de los Comendadores E 37 Bd62
Encs H 99 Jd50
Endach A 96 Eb53
Endingen CH 95 Cb52
Endingen D 94 Ca50
Endon GB 13 Ed23
Endrup DK 76 Da56
Enego I 102 Dd58
Enerhodar UA 137 Fa16
Enez TR 126 Ea78
Enge N 56 Dc30
Engelberg CH 95 Cb55
Engelhartszell A 96 Fa50
Engels RUS 137 Fd12
Engelsbrand D 95 Cc48
Engelskirchen D 88 Ca41
Engen D 95 Cc51
Enger D 83 Cc37
Enger N 64 Dd39
Engerdal N 65 Ec35
Engerneset N 65 Ec36
Enghien B 17 Hc30
Engi CH 95 Cc54
Englancourt F 20 Hc33
Englefontaine F 20 Hc32
Engstingen D 95 Cd49
Enguera E 39 Fb69
Enguídanos E 39 Ed67
Engvoll N 65 Ea34
Eningen D 95 Cd49
Enkenbach-Alsenborn D 88 Ca46
Enkhuizen NL 82 Bb34
Enköping S 72 Gb42
Enna I 114 Fa86
Ennepetal D 88 Ca39
Ennezat F 24 Hb46
Ennigerloh D 89 Cb38
Ennis IRL 6 Bc22
Enniscorthy IRL 7 Cc24
Enniskean IRL 6 Bc26
Enniskerry IRL 7 Cd22
Enniskillen GB 4 Cb18
Ennistimon IRL 6 Bc22
Enns A 97 Fb51
Eno FIN 61 Ld30
Enodden N 57 Ea31
Enonkoski FIN 61 Lc32
Enonkylä FIN 60 Kc25
Enonlahti FIN 61 La30
Enontekiö FIN 50 Ja13
Ens NL 82 Bc35
Enschede NL 82 Bd36
Ensdorf D 96 Ea47
Ensisheim F 94 Bd51
Enstone GB 15 Fa26
Enter NL 82 Bd36
Entrages F 29 Ka52
Entraigues F 29 Jd49
Entrechaux F 29 Jc52
Entrena E 32 Eb58
Entre-os-Rios P 30 Ad61
Entrín Bajo E 37 Bc69
Entroncamento P 36 Ac66
Entzheim F 94 Ca49
Envendos P 36 Ba66
Enville GB 15 Ec25
Enzesfeld A 97 Gb52
Enzinger Boden A 96 Eb54
Eochaill IRL 6 Ca26
Čohkkiras S 49 Hb15
Epagny F 25 Jb41
Epaignes F 19 Fd35
Epaux-Bézu F 20 Hb36
Epe NL 82 Bc36
Épernay F 20 Hc36
Epernon F 24 Gc38
Epfig F 94 Bd49
Épila E 33 Fa61
Épinal F 25 Jd38
Epiry F 24 Hc42
Epizon F 25 Jb38
Époisses F 25 Hd41
Epoye F 21 Hd35
Eppan I 102 Dc56
Eppendorf D 90 Ed42
Eppe-Sauvage F 21 Hd32
Epping GB 16 Fd27
Eppingen D 95 Cc47
Eppstein D 89 Cc44
Epsom GB 16 Fc28
Epuisay F 23 Ga40
Epworth GB 13 Fb21
Équeurdreville-Hainneville F 19 Ed34
Equihen-Plage F 20 Gb31
Equi Terme I 101 Da64
Eraclea I 103 Eb59
Erahtur RUS 137 Fb10
Eräjärvi FIN 68 Ka35
Eratiní GR 129 Bc85
Erba I 101 Cc58
Erbach D 89 Cd45
Erbach D 95 Da50
Erbalunga F 106 Cc68
Erbendorf D 90 Eb45
Erchie I 113 Hb76
Ercolano I 112 Fb75
Erd H 98 Hc53
Erdal N 46 Ja06
Erdal N 62 Cd34
Erdek TR 127 Fa79
Erding D 96 Ea50
Erdington GB 13 Ed24
Erdőbénye H 99 Jd50
Erdut HR 105 Hd59
Erdweg D 96 Dd50
Erétria GR 129 Cc85
Erezée B 21 Jb32
Erftstadt D 88 Bd41
Erfurt D 90 Dd41
Ergersheim D 89 Db46
Ergolding D 96 Eb49
Ergoldsbach D 96 Eb49
Eriboll GB 8 Dd04
Erice I 114 Ea84
Ericeira P 36 Aa68
Erikli TR 126 Eb78
Eriskirch D 95 Cd52
Eriswell GB 16 Fd25
Eriswil CH 94 Ca54
Erkelenz D 88 Bc40
Erkheim D 95 Db51
Erkner D 84 Fa36
Erla E 33 Fa59
Erlabrunn D 89 Da45
Erlach A 97 Gb52
Erlangen D 90 Dd46
Erle D 88 Bd38
Erlenbach D 89 Cd45
Erlenbach D 95 Cd47
Erligheim D 95 Cd47
Erm NL 82 Bd35
Ermakovo RUS 137 Ga09
Ermelo NL 82 Bb36
Ermenonville F 20 Ha36
Ermesinde P 30 Ad61
Ermióni GR 129 Ca88
Ermiš RUS 137 Fb10
Ermita de Carrión E 36 Bb68
Ermita del Ramonete E 45 Ed74
Ermoúpoli GR 133 Da89
Ermsleben D 90 Dd39
Ermua E 32 Eb55
Erndtebrück D 89 Cc41
Ernée F 23 Fb39
Ernsgaden D 96 Ea49
Ernstbrunn A 97 Gb49
Erôme F 28 Jb49
Erp NL 88 Bb38
Erpingham GB 16 Gb23
Erquy F 18 Eb37
Erriff Bridge IRL 4 Bb19
Erril IRL 7 Cb23
Errol GB 11 Eb11
Erschwil CH 94 Bd53
Érsekcsanád H 105 Hd57
Ersfjordbotn N 49 Gc09
Erši RUS 137 Ed11
Ersmark S 59 Hc25
Ersmark S 59 Hb28
Ersnäs S 54 Hd22
Erstein F 94 Ca49
Erstfeld CH 95 Cb55
Ertingen D 95 Cd50
Ervedal P 36 Ba68
Ervedosa do Douro P 30 Bb61
Ervik N 62 Ca33
Erwitte D 89 Cc39
Erwood GB 14 Ea26
Esanos E 32 Da55
Esbjerg DK 76 Cd56
Escairón (Saviñao) E 30 Bb56
Escalada E 32 Dc56
Escalona E 34 Fd58
Escalonilla E 38 Da66
Escalos de Baixo P 36 Bb65
Escalos de Cima P 36 Bb65
Escañuela E 44 Da72
es Castell E 41 Jb66
Escatalens F 27 Gb53
Escatrón E 39 Fc62
Eschau D 89 Cd45
Eschborn D 89 Cc44
Escheburg D 83 Dc33
Eschede D 83 Dc35
Eschenau A 97 Fd51
Eschenbach D 90 Ea45
Eschenburg D 89 Cc41
Eschenfelden D 90 Ea46
Eschershausen D 89 Da38
Eschlkam D 96 Ec47
Esch-sur-Alzette L 21 Jc34
Esch-sur-Sûre L 21 Jc33
Eschwege D 89 Db40
Eschweiler D 88 Bc41
Escot F 33 Fb56
Escouloubre F 35 Gd57
Escource F 26 Fa52
Esens D 83 Cb32
es Grau E 41 Jb66
Esher GB 16 Fc28
Esh Winning GB 13 Fa17
Eskdale Green GB 12 Eb18
Eskdalemuir GB 11 Eb15
Eskifjörður IS 3 Cd05
Eskilstuna S 72 Gb43
Eskragh GB 5 Cc17
Eslarn D 90 Eb46
Eslida E 39 Fc66
es Llombards E 41 Hc68
Eslohe D 89 Cb40
Eslöv S 77 Ed55
Esme TR 131 Fc86
es Molinar E 41 Hb67
Esmoriz P 30 Ac61
Esnouveaux F 25 Jb39
Espadañedo E 31 Ca58
Espås N 57 Ea30
Espejo E 32 Ea56
Espejo E 43 Cd73
Espel NL 82 Bb34
Espelkamp D 83 Cd36
Espenau D 89 Da40
Espéraza F 35 Gd56
Esperstedt D 90 Dd40
Espevær N 63 Bd41
Espezel F 35 Gd57
Espinasses F 29 Ka51
Espinho P 30 Ac61
Espinosa de los Monteros E 32 Dc56
Espírito Santo P 42 Ba73
Esplantas F 28 Hc50
Esplús E 34 Fd60
Espolla E 35 Hb58
Esporles E 41 Hb67
Esposende P 30 Ac59
Esrange S 49 Hb15
Esse FIN 59 Jb29
Essen D 83 Cb35
Essen D 88 Bd39
Essenbach D 96 Eb49
Essentuki RUS 137 Ga17
Essertenne F 25 Jc41
Essingen D 95 Da48
Esslingen D 95 Cd48
Essômes-sur-Marne F 20 Hb36
Essoyes F 25 Ja39
Essvik S 66 Gc33
Establet F 29 Jc51
Estación de Cártama E 43 Cd76
Estación de Páramo E 31 Ca56
Estación de Salinas E 44 Da75
Estaing F 27 Ha51
Estaires F 20 Ha31
Estang F 26 Fc53
Estarreja P 36 Ac62
Este I 102 Dd60
Estela P 30 Ac60
Estella E 33 Ec57
Estenfeld D 89 Db45
Estepa E 43 Cc74
Estépar E 32 Dc58
Estepona E 43 Cb77
Esternay F 20 Hc37
Esterwegen D 83 Cb34
Estissac F 24 Hc38
Estivella E 39 Fc67
Estorf D 83 Da32
Estoril P 36 Aa68
Estorninhos P 42 Ad74
Estremoz P 36 Ba69
Estry F 19 Fb37
Esztergom H 98 Hc52
Étain F 21 Jc35
Étampes F 24 Gd38
Étaples F 20 Gc31
Etauliers F 26 Fb49
Eteläkylä FIN 68 Kd34
Etelä-Niskamäki FIN 60 Kd32
Eteläpää FIN 67 Hd33
Eterna E 32 Dd58
Etevaux F 25 Jb41
Etival F 25 Jd44
Étoges F 20 Hc36
Etoile-Rhône F 28 Jb50
Etolikó GR 128 Ba84
Etouy F 20 Gd35
Étréaupont F 20 Hc33
Etrépagny F 20 Gc35
Étreux F 20 Hc33
Etropole BG 125 Cd71
Etroubles I 100 Bc58
Etsaut F 33 Fb56
Ettelbruck L 21 Jc33
Ettenheim D 94 Ca50
Etten-Leur NL 17 Hd27
Ettiswil CH 94 Ca53
Ettlingen D 95 Cb48
Ettrickbridge GB 11 Eb14
Etxano E 32 Ea55
Eu F 20 Gb33
Euerbach D 89 Db44
Eugénie-les-Bains F 26 Fc54
Eupen B 21 Jc30
Euratsfeld A 97 Fc51
Eursinge NL 82 Bd34
Euskirchen D 88 Bd42
Euston GB 16 Ga25
Eutin D 84 Dd31
Euzet F 28 Ja52
Evanger N 62 Cb38
Evanton GB 9 Ea07
Evaux-les-Bains F 24 Ha45
Évdilos GR 130 Dd88
Evelix GB 9 Ea06
Evenstad N 65 Eb36
Evercreech GB 15 Ec29
Everleigh GB 15 Ed29
Eversley GB 15 Fb28
Everswinkel D 89 Cb38
Evesham GB 15 Ed26
Évian-les-Bains F 25 Ka44
Evijärvi FIN 60 Jc29
Evillers F 25 Jd42
Evja N 52 Fc17
Evje N 63 Cd45
Evlanovo RUS 137 Fa12
Évora P 36 Ad69
Évora Monte P 36 Ba69
Evran F 22 Ec38
Evrecy F 19 Fb36
Évreux F 20 Gb36
Evriguet F 22 Ec39
Évron F 23 Fc39
Évry F 20 Gd37
Ewell GB 16 Fc28
Exbourne GB 14 Dd30
Excideul F 27 Gb48
Exeter GB 14 Ea30
Exford GB 14 Ea29
Exilles I 100 Bb60
Exloo NL 82 Ca34
Exmouth GB 14 Ea31
Exogí GR 128 Ac84
Éxo Nímfio GR 132 Bc91
Extertal D 83 Cd37
Eyam GB 13 Ed22
Eydelstedt D 83 Cd35
Eye GB 16 Fc24
Eye GB 16 Gb25
Eyeries IRL 6 Ba26
Eygalières F 28 Jb53
Eyguians F 29 Jd51
Eyguières F 28 Jb53
Eygurande F 27 Ha47
Eymet F 26 Fd51
Eyrarbakki IS 2 Ad08
Eyrecourt IRL 6 Ca21
Eystrup D 83 Da35
Èzaro E 30 Ac55


## F


Faaborg DK 76 Dc57
Faak am See A 103 Fa56
Fabara E 34 Fd62
Fabbrica Curone I 101 Cc61
Fåberg N 65 Ea37
Fábiánsebestyén H 99 Jc55
Fäboda FIN 59 Jb28
Fäbodliden S 58 Gc26
Fabrègues F 28 Hd54
Fabriano I 109 Ec67
Fabrica di Roma I 108 Ea70
Fabro Scalo I 108 Ea68
Facho P 36 Ab66
Facinas E 43 Ca78

Faedis I 103 Ed57
Faenza I 102 Dd63
Fafe P 30 Ba60
Făgăraş RO 118 Dc61
Fågelsjö G 66 Cc65
Fågelsta S 58 Ga27
Fagerhaug N 56 Gd10
Fagernes N 49 Gd10
Fagnano Castello I 113 Gb79
Fagurhólsmýri IS 3 Ca08
Fahan IRL 5 Cc15
Fahrenkrug D 83 Dc31
Fahrenzhausen D 96 Dd50
Fahrland D 84 Fa34
Faido CH 101 Cb56
Fain-lès-Montbard F 25 Hd41
Fairbourne GB 12 Dd24
Fairford GB 15 Ed27
Fairlight GB 16 Ga30
Fairy Cross GB 14 Dc29
Fajstawice PL 93 Kb40
Fakenham GB 16 Ga23
Fåker S 58 Fc31
Faksdal N 57 Eb26
Fakse DK 61 Fc57
Fakse Ladeplads DK 77 Eb57
Falaise F 19 Fc37
Falces E 33 Ec58
Falconara Marittima I 109 Ed66
Falerna I 113 Gb81
Falerna Marina I 113 Gb81
Falfield GB 15 Ec27
Faliráki GR 134 Ba93
Falkenberg D 84 Fa35
Falkenberg D 96 Ec51
Falkenberg S 77 Ec52
Falkenhagen D 85 Fb37
Falkensee D 84 Ed36
Falkenstein D 90 Eb48
Falkenthal D 84 Ed35
Falkirk GB 11 Ea13
Falköping S 71 Fa47
Falków PL 92 Ja40
Falleron F 23 Ed43
Fällfors S 54 Hc24
Fällöneden S 53 Gb28
Fallon F 25 Ka41
Falmouth GB 14 Db32
Falnes N 63 Bd43
Falset E 34 Sa62
Falsnes N 49 Ha10
Falsterbo S 77 Ed57
Falun S 66 Fd39
Famagusta = Ammochostos CY 135 Cc96
Fameck F 21 Jd35
Fana N 62 Sa04
Fanagmore GB 8 Dc04
Fanano I 102 Dd64
Fanari GR 128 Bb81
Fane I 102 Dc79
Fångåmon S 54 Fc17
Fanjeaux F 35 Gd55
Fanmrem N 56 Dd30
Fanore IRL 6 Bc21
Fansta S 66 Ga33
Fantoft N 62 Ca39
Fara in Sabina I 109 Eb70
Faramontanos de Tábara E 31 Cb59
Fårberget S 59 Ha27
Farchant D 95 Dd53
Fardrum IRL 6 Ca21
Fareham GB 15 Fa30
Färgelanda S 71 Ed46
Fargues-sur-Ourbise F 26 Fd52
Färila S 66 Fc38
Faringdon GB 15 Ed27
Farini d'Olmo I 101 Cd62
Fariza E 31 Ca61
Färjestaden S 78 Gb52
Farkasfa H 97 Gb55
Farlete E 33 Fb60
Farmborough GB 15 Ec28
Farmtown GB 9 Ec08
Farnanes Cross Roads IRL 6 Bc26
Färnäs S 66 Fc38
Farnborough GB 15 Fb29
Farnborough GB 16 Fc28
Farnese I 108 Dd69
Farnham GB 15 Fb29
Farnstädt D 90 Ea40
Farnworth GB 13 Ec21
Faro P 42 Ad74
Fårö S 73 Hb48
Farranfore IRL 6 Bb24
Farnwd N 70 Cb47
Farum DK 77 Fc55
Fasano I 113 Ha75
Fáskrúðsfjörður IS 3 Cb05
Fasnacloich GB 10 Db11
Faßberg D 83 Dc35
Fässjöbal S 66 Fd34
Fästad S 51 Jd48
Fatež RUS 137 Fa13
Fátima P 36 Ac66
Fättjaur S 52 Fd24
Faugères F 28 Hb54
Fauldhouse GB 11 Ea13
Faulquemont F 21 Ka35
Faure E 39 Fc67
Fauske N 52 Gd17
Faux F 27 Ga50
Fåvang N 64 Dd36
Favara I 112 Fd84
Favara I 114 Ed86
Faverges F 25 Ka46
Faverney F 25 Jd40
Faverolles F 19 Ga36
Faversham GB 16 Ga28
Favignana I 114 Ea84
Fawley GB 15 Fa30
Fay-aux-Loges F 24 Gd40
Fay-de-Bretagne F 23 Ed42
Fayl-Billot F 25 Jc40
Fay-sur-Lignon F 28 Ja49
Feakle IRL 6 Bd22
Fearnan GB 11 Ea11
Fearn Lodge GB 9 Ea06
Fécamp F 19 Fd34
Feces de Abaixo P 30 Bb59
Fedamore IRL 6 Bd23
Fedje N 62 Sa02
Fëdorovka RUS 137 Fb15
Fehérgyarmat H 99 Kc50
Fehmarn D 84 Ea30
Fehrbellin D 84 Eb35
Feignes F 20 Hc32
Felitz D 90 Ea33
Feira de Monte E 31 Bc54
Feistritz im Rosental A 103 Fb56
Felanitx E 41 Hd67
Feldating D 96 Dc52
Feld am See A 96 Fa55
Feldbach A 97 Ga55
Feldberg D 84 Ed33
Feldberger Seenlandschaft D 84 Ed33
Feldioara RO 118 Dc61
Feldkirch A 102 Cd54
Feldkirchen D 96 Dc52
Feldkirchen in Kärnten A 103 Fa56
Feldkirchen-Westerham D 96 Ea53
Felgueiras P 30 Ba60
Felindre GB 12 Ea25

Felindre GB 14 Dd27
Felinfach GB 14 Ea26
Felixstowe GB 16 Gb26
Fell A 96 Ed54
Fellabær IS 3 Cd04
Fellbach D 95 Cd48
Fellering D 20 Ha40
Fellsätra S 73 Gd43
Fiskå N 62 Cb33
Fiskárdo GR 128 Ac84
Fiskarheden S 65 Fd34
Fiskavaig GB 8 Da08
Fiskefjord N 48 Ga13
Fiskenes N 48 Ga11
Fiskrøs A 95 Dd54
Fisås A 95 Dd54
Feren D 102 Db64
Fermo I 109 Ed67
Fermoselle E 31 Ca61
Fermoy IRL 6 Bd25
Fernán-Núñez E 43 Cd73
Ferndown GB 15 Ed30
Ferness GB 9 Ea06
Ferney-Voltaire F 25 Jd45
Fernhurst GB 15 Fb29
Ferns IRL 7 Cd24
Ferrandina I 113 Gc76
Ferrara I 102 Dd62
Ferrara di Monte Baldo I 102 Db59
Ferreira do Alentejo P 42 Ad71
Ferreiros E 31 Bc55
Ferreries E 41 Ja66
Ferrette F 94 Bd52
Ferriere I 101 Cd62
Ferrières-en-Gâtinais F 24 Ha39
Ferté F 30 Ba53
Ferry Bridge IRL 6 Bc23
Ferryhill GB 13 Fa17
Fertilia I 107 Bd75
Fertőd N 97 Gc53
Fertőszentmiklós H 97 Gc53
Ferwerd NL 82 Bc32
Festøy N 64 Cc33
Festvåg N 52 Fc17
Fethard IRL 6 Ca24
Fethard IRL 7 Cd25
Fethiye TR 135 Bc92
Fettercairn GB 11 Ec10
Fettwell GB 16 Fc25
Feucht D 90 Dd46
Feuchtwangen D 95 Db47
Feudingen D 89 Cc41
Feugarolles F 26 Fd52
Flestining GB 12 Dd23
Ffostrasol GB 14 Dc26
Fiano I 100 Bd66
Ficarolo I 102 Dd61
Fichtenau D 95 Db47
Fichtenberg D 90 Ed40
Fichtenberg D 95 Da48
Fiddleton GB 11 Eb15
Fiddown IRL 7 Cb24
Fieberbrunn A 96 Eb53
Fiera di Primiero I 102 Ea57
Fiesch CH 100 Ca56
Fiesole I 108 Dc65
Figaredo E 31 Cc55
Figeac F 27 Gd51
Figlás GR 129 Cd86
Figline GB 14 Ea26
Figline Valdarno I 108 Dc65
Figueira da Foz P 36 Ab64
Figueira de Castelo Rodrigo P 37 Bc62
Figueres E 35 Hb60
Figueró-Granja de Castelo Rodrigo
Figueras E 31 Cb59
Figueroles E 39 Fc65
Fijnaart NL 17 Hd27
Fil'akovo SK 98 Ja50
Filderstadt D 95 Cd48
Fildu de Sus RO 117 Cd57
Filettino I 109 Ec71
Filey GB 13 Fc19
Filiates GR 128 Ab81
Filiatra GR 136 Ed09
Filicudi Porto I 115 Fb82
Filinskoe RUS 137 Fb10
Filipów PL 87 Ka30
Filippiáda GR 128 Ad82
Filipstad S 72 Fa42
Filisur CH 100 Cb55
Filizmoos A 96 Ed53
Finale Emilia I 102 Dd62
Finale Ligure I 100 Ca63
Fiñana E 44 Dd75
Finchingfield GB 16 Fd26
Finchley GB 16 Fc28
Findhorn GB 9 Eb07
Findochty GB 9 Ec07
Findon GB 16 Fc30
Findon Valley GB 16 Fc30
Finike TR 135 Cb93
Finikoúnda GR 132 Ba90
Finja S 77 Fa54
Fintona GB 5 Cc17
Fintown GB 4 Cb16
Finvoy GB 5 Cd16
Fiodh Ard IRL 6 Ca24
Fiolleda S 30 Ba56
Fionnphort GB 10 Da11
Fiorenzuola d'Arda I 101 Cd61
Firkeel IRL 6 Ba26
Firminy F 28 Ja48
Firoga PL 86 Ha36
Fischamend A 97 Gc51
Fischbach D 95 Dc50

Fischbach D 88 Bd45
Fischbachau D 96 Ea52
Fischering A 97 Fd55
Fishbourne GB 15 Fb30
Fishburn GB 13 Fa17
Fishguard GB 14 Db26
Fiskätra S 73 Gd43
Fitero E 33 Ec59
Fittleton GB 15 Ed29
Fiuggi I 109 Ec72
Fiumefreddo di Sicilia I 115 Fd85
Five Ashes GB 16 Fd29
Fivelanes GB 14 Dc31
Fivemiletown GB 5 Cc18
Five Oaks GB 16 Fc29
Fivizzano I 101 Da63
Fjäl S 58 Fc30
Fjälkinge S 78 Fb54
Fjällgården S 65 Fb33
Fjällnäs S 57 Ec32
Fjelbu N 64 Dd38
Fjellerad DK 77 Dd53
Fjellkjøsa N 56 Dd30
Fjellstad N 49 Gc12
Fjelie N 77 Ed56
Fjon N 62 Cc37
Fjordgård N 48 Gb10
Flaca E 35 Hb59
Fladbury GB 15 Ed26
Fladungen D 89 Db43
Flagy F 24 Ha38
Flakaberg S 54 Hd19
Flakk N 57 Ga20
Flakstad N 48 Fa14
Flåm N 63 Cc38
Flamatt CH 94 Bc54
Flamborough GB 13 Fc19
Flamstead GB 16 Fc27
Flechtingen D 84 Dd37
Fleet GB 15 Fb29
Fleetmark D 84 Ea35
Fleetwood GB 12 Eb20
Flekke N 62 Ca36
Flekkefjord N 70 Cb46
Flem N 56 Cc32
Flensburg D 76 Db58
Flers F 19 Fb37
Flesberg N 64 Dc41
Flessau D 84 Ea35
Fleurance F 27 Ga53
Fleurville F 25 Jd44
Fleury-les-Aubrais F 24 Gc40
Fleys F 24 Hc40
Flieden D 89 Da43
Flims CH 95 Cc55
Flimwell GB 16 Fd29
Flines-lès-Raches F 20 Hb31
Flint GB 12 Eb22
Flintbek D 83 Dc30
Flittwick GB 16 Fc26
Flix E 34 Ga62
Flixton GB 16 Gb26
Flize F 21 Ja34
Flo N 56 Cc32
Floda S 59 Hb26
Floda S 72 Ga44
Flodigarry GB 8 Da07
Flöha D 89 Dd41
Florange F 21 Jd35
Florence = Firenze I 108 Dc65
Floreffe NL 82 Bc34
Flores de Ávila E 37 Cd64
Floridia I 115 Fd87
Flornes N 57 Eb30
Florø N 62 Ca36
Flörsbachtal D 89 Cd44
Florstadt D 89 Cd43
Flostrand N 52 Fa20
Flöthe D 84 Dd38
Flötningen S 65 Ec35
Flums CH 95 Cd54
Fluorn-Winzeln D 95 Db50
Fluren S 59 Ha29
Flykälen S 53 Gb28
Flytåsen S 66 Fd37
Focene I 108 Dd71
Fochabers GB 9 Ec07
Fockbek D 83 Db30
Fódele GR 133 Da95
Foggia I 110 Ga73
Foglia GB 16 Fc30
Föhren D 88 Bc44
Foiano della Chiana I 108 Dd67
Foissiat F 25 Jb45
Foix F 34 Gc56
Fojnica BIH 105 Hb64
Fokino RUS 137 Ed12
Földeák H 105 Jc56
Foldereid N 57 Eb26
Foldfjorden N 56 Da29
Foleá GR 128 Ab82
Folelli F 106 Cc69
Folgarida I 102 Dc57
Folgoso de la Ribera E 31 Ca57
Folgueiro E 30 Bc53
Foligno I 109 Eb68

Fontan F 29 Kd52
Fontanar E 44 Dd73
Fontanarejo E 38 Da68
Fontanars dels Alforins E 45 Fb70
Fontane Bianche I 115 Ha77
Fontanelice I 102 Dd63
Fontanella I 108 Dc65
Fontanellato I 101 Da61
Fontanières F 24 Ha46
Fontanosas E 37 Cd68
Fontdepou E 34 Ga59
Fontenay-le-Comte F 23 Fd45
Fontenay-Trésigny F 20 Ha37
Fontevraud-l'Abbaye F 23 Fd42
Fontibre E 32 Db56
Font-Romeu F 35 Gd58
Fontstown IRL 7 Cc22
Fonyód H 98 Ha55
Fonzaso I 102 Ea58
Foppolo I 101 Cd57
Forbach D 95 Cd48
Forbach F 21 Ka35
Forcalqueiret F 29 Ka54
Forcalquier F 29 Jd52
Forcarei E 30 Ba56
Forchheim D 90 Dd45
Ford GB 10 Db12
Ford GB 11 Ed14
Ford GB 15 Ed26
Ferde N 62 Cc35
Ferde N 62 Cc36
Ferde N 63 Ca41
Fordham GB 16 Fd25
Fordingbridge GB 15 Ed30
Fordoun GB 11 Ed10
Fordstown IRL 5 Cc20
Forenza I 112 Ga75
Forest Green GB 16 Fc29
Forest Row GB 16 Fd29
Forfar GB 11 Ec11
Foria I 112 Fd77
Forio I 112 Fa75
Forlimpopoli I 102 Ea64
Formby GB 12 Eb21
Formia I 109 Ed73
Formiche Alte E 39 Fb35
Formicola I 112 Fb74
Formigine I 102 Dd62
Formignana I 102 Ea62
Fornaci di Barga I 108 Db64
Fornalutx E 41 Hb66
Fornelli I 112 Fb74
Fornelos P 30 Ad59
Fornes N 48 Gb12
Forni Avoltri I 103 Ec56
Forni di Sopra I 103 Eb56
Forni di Sotto I 103 Eb57
Forno I 100 Bc60
Fornoli I 102 Db64
Fornovo di Taro I 101 Da62
Foros da Fonte de Pau P 36 Ac68
Foraya N 52 Fa19
Forres GB 9 Eb07
Forronda E 32 Ea56
Fors S 58 Gd30
Forsby FIN 68 Kd14
Forshaga S 71 Fa43
Forsholm S 54 Ha25
Fort Augustus GB 8 Dd09
Forte dei Marmi I 101 Da64
Forth GB 11 Ea13
Forton GB 13 Ec24
Fortrose GB 9 Ea07
Fortuna E 45 Fa72
Fortuneswell GB 15 Ec31
Fort William GB 10 Dc10
Forvika N 52 Fa20
Fosnavåg N 62 Cb33
Fossacesia I 109 Fb70
Fossacesia Marina I 109 Fb70
Fossano I 100 Bd62
Fossbakken N 49 Ha12
Fossbu N 49 Ha12
Fosses F 20 Gd36
Fossombrone I 109 Eb65
Fos-sur-Mer F 28 Jb53
Fót H 98 Hd52
Fotheringhay GB 16 Fc24
Fouesnant F 22 Db40
Fougères F 23 Fa38
Fougerolles F 25 Jd39
Fougerolles-du-Plessis F 23 Fb38
Fouly CH 100 Bd57
Foulain F 25 Jb39
Foulaynronnes F 27 Ga52
Foulsham GB 16 Ga24
Fountain Cross IRL 6 Bc22
Fountainhall GB 11 Ec14
Fouquerolles F 20 Gd35
Fourchambault F 24 Ha43
Four Crosses GB 12 Eb24
Fourfourás GR 133 Cd96
Fourmies F 20 Hc33
Four Mile House IRL 4 Ca20
Fournaudin F 24 Hc39
Fowey GB 14 Dc31
Fownhope GB 15 Ec26
Foxdale GB 12 Dc19
Foxup GB 13 Ed19
Foynes IRL 6 Bb23
Foz E 31 Bd53
Foz do Arelho P 36 Ab66
Foz do Odeleite P 42 Ba73
Frącki PL 87 Kb30
Fraddon GB 14 Db31
Fraga E 34 Ga61
Fraire B 21 Hc34
Fraize F 94 Bb53
Frammersbach D 89 Da44
Frampol PL 93 Kb42
Framura I 101 Cd63
França P 31 Bd59
Francavilla al Mare I 109 Fb70
Francavilla di Sicilia I 115 Hd37

Fontan F 29 Kd52
Francavilla Fontana I 113 Ha76
Franciszkowo PL 86 Hd34
Francofonte I 115 Fc87
Francova Lhota CZ 98 Ha47
Frankenberg D 89 Cb39
Frankenberg D 90 Ed42
Frankenberg D 90 Ed42
Frankenförde D 90 Ed42
Frankenhardt D 95 Da47
Frankenstein D 90 Eb49
Frankenthal D 89 Cb46
Frankfurt am Main D 89 Cc44
Frankfurt (Oder) D 85 Fb37
Frankrijk RUS 137 Fa16
Frankstowe IRL 7 Cc24
Fränő S 58 Gc31
Františkovy Lázně CZ 90 Eb44
Franzburg D 84 Ed31
Frascati I 109 Eb72
Frasdorf D 96 Eb52
Fraserburgh GB 9 Ed07
Frasne F 25 Jd43
Frassene I 102 Dd63
Frassinoro I 102 Db63
Frasso Telesino I 112 Fb74
Fratel P 36 Ba66
Frattamaggiore I 112 Fb74
Fratta Polesine I 102 Dd61
Frauenau D 96 Ed48
Frauenfeld CH 95 Cc52
Frauenkirchen A 97 Gc52
Frauenstein D 90 Fd42
Frauenwald D 89 Dc42
Fraunberg D 96 Ea50
Frayssinet-le-Gélat F 27 Ga51
Frechen D 88 Bd41
Frechilla E 31 Cd58
Freckleben D 90 Ea39
Freckleton GB 12 Eb20
Freden D 89 Db38
Fredenbeck D 83 Da32
Fredensborg DK 77 Ec56
Fredericia DK 76 Db56
Frederikshavn DK 71 Dd50
Frederikssund DK 77 Ec56
Frederiksværk DK 77 Ec55
Fredersdorf-Eggersdorf D 84 Fa36
Fredrika S 53 Gc28
Fredrikstad N 71 Ea44
Fredropol PL 93 Kb45
Freeland GB 15 Fa27
Freemount IRL 6 Bc24
Freethorpe GB 16 Gb24
Fregene I 108 Dd71
Freiamt D 94 Ca50
Freiberg D 90 Ed42
Freiberg (Neckar) D 95 Cd48
Freiburg D 94 Ca51
Freienstein D 89 Da43
Freiensteinau D 89 Da43
Freigericht D 89 Cd44
Freihung D 90 Eb46
Freilassing D 96 Ec52
Freising D 96 Ea51
Freissinières F 29 Kb50
Freistadt A 97 Fb50
Freiston GB 16 Fd23
Freital D 90 Ed41
Freixedas P 37 Bc63
Freixo F 31 Bc57
Freixo de Espada à Cinta P 31 Bd61
Fréjus F 29 Kb54
Frenchpark IRL 4 Ca19
Frensdorf D 89 Dc45
Frensham GB 15 Fb29
Frenštát pod Radhoštěm CZ 92 Hd46
Freren D 83 Ca36
Freshford IRL 7 Cb23
Freshwater GB 15 Ea31
Fresnay-sur-Sarthe F 23 Fd39
Fresnedillas E 38 Da64
Fresnes-au-Mont F 21 Jb36
Fresnes-sur-Apance F 25 Jc39
Fresnes-sur-les-Eaux F 20 Hb31
Fresno de Cantespino E 32 Dc61
Fresno de Sayago E 31 Cb61
Fresno el Viejo E 31 Cc61
Fresnoy-en-Bassigny F 25 Jc39
Fresnoy-Folny F 20 Gb33
Fresselines F 24 Gc45
Fressingfield GB 16 Gb25
Freswick GB 9 Ec04
Fretigney-et-Velloreille F 25 Jc41
Fretzdorf D 84 Ec34
Freudenberg D 89 Cb41
Freudenberg D 89 Cd45
Freudenstadt D 95 Cb49
Freudental D 95 Cc47
Freudenheim D 89 Da43
Freuding F 95 Da50
Freux B 21 Jb33
Freyburg D 90 Ea40
Freyming-Merlebach F 21 Ka35
Freystadt D 96 Dd47
Freyung D 96 Fa49
Frias E 32 Dd58
Frickenhausen D 89 Db45
Frickhofen D 89 Cb42
Frickingen D 95 Cc51
Fridaythorpe GB 13 Fb19
Fridingen D 95 Cb51
Fridolfing D 96 Ec52
Friedberg A 97 Ga54
Friedberg D 89 Cc43
Friedberg D 96 Dc50
Friedeburg D 82 Cb32
Friedeburg D 90 Ea39
Friedenfels D 90 Eb45
Friedersdorf D 89 Db39
Friedland D 84 Fa32
Friedland D 89 Db38
Friedrichroda D 89 Dc42
Friedrichsdorf D 89 Cc43
Friedrichshafen D 95 Cd52
Friedrichskoog D 76 Da55
Friedrichsthal D 88 Bd42
Friedrichsthal D 90 Fa41
Friedrichswalde D 84 Ed35
Friesack D 84 Ec36
Friesenheim D 94 Ca49
Friesoythe D 83 Cb34
Friggesund S 66 Fd34
Frigiliana E 43 Da76
Frigole I 115 Hc77
Frihetsli N 49 Ha12
Frillesås S 77 Ec52
Frilford GB 15 Fa27
Frimley GB 15 Fb29
Frinton-on-Sea GB 16 Gb27
Friockheim GB 11 Ec11
Frisange L 21 Jd34
Fritsla S 77 Ed50
Fritzlar D 89 Cd40
Friville-Escarbotin F 20 Gb33
Frjanovo RUS 137 Fa10
Froan N 56 Db28

Frohburg D 90 Ec41
Frohen-le-Grand F 20 Gd32
Frohnleiten A 97 Fd54
Froissy F 20 Gd34
Frolovo RUS 137 Ga13
Frombork PL 86 Hc30
Frome GB 15 Ec29
Fromental F 19 Fc37
Fromentel F 22 Ec43
Fröndenberg D 89 Cc39
Fronhausen D 89 Cc42
Fronreute D 95 Cd51
Frontenard F 25 Jb43
Frontenex F 29 Ka47
Frontenhausen D 96 Eb49
Frontignan F 28 Hd54
Frosinone I 109 Ed72
Frösö S 58 Fc30
Fróssa F 22 Ec42
Frostkåge S 59 Hc25
Frouard F 21 Jd36
Froxfield GB 15 Ed28
Frula E 33 Fb60
Fruniz E 32 Ea56
Frunzivka UA 136 Ec16
Frutigen CH 94 Bd55
Frýdek-Místek CZ 92 Hb45
Frýdlant CZ 91 Fd42
Frygnowo PL 86 Hd33
Fryksås S 66 Fc36
Fubine I 100 Ca61
Fucecchio I 108 Dc65
Fuchsstadt D 89 Da44
Fuencaliente E 33 Fd60
Fuendetodos E 33 Fa61
Fuengirola E 43 Cd77
Fuenlabrada E 38 Db65
Fuensalida E 38 Da65
Fuente-Álamo E 45 Ed70
Fuentecén E 32 Dc60
Fuente de Cantos E 43 Bd71
Fuente del Arco E 43 Ca71
Fuente el Fresno E 38 Db68
Fuente Obejuna E 43 Cb71
Fuente Palmera E 50 Hd08
Fuentepelayo E 38 Db62
Fuenterrobles E 39 Ed67
Fuentesaúco E 31 Cc61
Fuentes de Andalucía E 43 Cb73
Fuentes de Ebro E 33 Fb61
Fuentes de Oñoro E 37 Bc63
Fuentes de Ropel E 31 Cc59
Fuentespalda E 40 Fd63
Fuentidueña de Tajo E 38 Dd65
Fuestrup D 82 Cb37
Fuglstad S 52 Ed24
Fühlen D 82 Cb36
Fulda D 89 Da43
Fülesd H 99 Kc50
Fullerton GB 15 Fa29
Fulnetby GB 13 Fc22
Fülöpjakab H 98 Ja55
Fulunäs S 65 Ed37
Fumay F 21 Ja33
Fumel F 27 Ga51
Funäsdalen S 65 Ed33
Fundão P 36 Ba64
Fundres I 96 Ea55
Funes I 33 Ec58
Funzie GB 9 Fb03
Furci I 32 Ea55
Furiz E 32 Ea55
Furmanov RUS 137 Fa09
Furore I 112 Fb76
Furset N 56 Da31
Fürstenau D 83 Cb36
Fürstenberg D 84 Fa33
Fürstenfeld A 97 Ga54
Fürstenfeldbruck D 96 Dd50
Fürstenstein D 96 Ed49
Fürstenwalde D 85 Fb37
Fürstenwerder D 84 Fa33
Fürstenzell D 96 Fa50
Furtei I 107 Ca78
Fürth D 89 Cc46
Fürth D 89 Dc45
Fürth im Wald D 90 Ec47
Furtwangen D 95 Cb50
Furuflaten N 49 Ha10
Furuly N 51 Kd08
Furugrund S 54 Hc24
Fusa N 62 Ca39
Fuscaldo I 113 Gb79
Fuschl am See A 96 Ed52
Füssen D 95 Dc53
Füstianova E 33 Ec59
Fuurtti FIN 68 Kd35
Fuzine HR 103 Fc60
Fuźeyrarbymt W 50 Ja08
Fyfield GB 16 Fd27
Fyllinge S 77 Ec52
Fyrås S 58 Fd28
Fyvie GB 9 Ed08

## G

Gaanderen NL 82 Bc37
Gaas A 97 Gb54
Gabarret F 26 Fc53
Gabčíkovo SK 98 Ha51
Gabello D 84 Ea37
Gabicce Mare I 109 Eb65
Gabino PL 85 Gc29
Gablenz D 91 Fb40
Gablingen D 95 Dc49
Gabrova BG 126 Dc77
Gabrowo PL 87 Jd32
Frick CH 94 Ca52
Gaël PL 93 Kb44
Gac PL 93 Kb44
Gacé F 19 Fd37
Gacko BIH 105 Hb67
Gäddede S 57 Fb26
Gaddesby GB 13 Fb24
Gadebusch D 84 Dd32
Gadkowice PL 91 Gd40
Gador E 44 Dd76
Gæðdnovuoppe N 50 Ja10
Gäel F 23 Ed39
Gærum DK 71 Dd50
Gaeta I 112 Fa74
Gaeta E 32 Db55
Gæidar N 48 Ja11
Gäfete P 36 Ba66
Gaflenz A 97 Fd52
Gaganica BG 125 Cd75
Gaggenau D 95 Cb48
Gaibanella I 102 Dd62
Gaick Lodge GB 9 Ea09
Gaildorf D 95 Cd48
Gaillac F 27 Gc53
Gailingen D 95 Cb52
Gaillac F 27 Ga53
Gaillefontaine F 20 Gc34
Gaillon F 20 Gb36
Gaimersheim D 96 Dc49
Gainsborough GB 13 Fb21
Gairloch GB 8 Db07
Gairlochy GB 8 Dc09
Gairo I 107 Cb78
Gaishorn A 97 Fd53
Gaitsgill GB 12 Ed17
Gajewo PL 85 Ga35
Gała N 64 Dd40
Galambok H 98 Gd55
Gałąska SK 98 Hd49
Galan F 34 Ga55
Galanta SK 98 Ha51
Galaroza E 43 Bc72
Galashiels GB 11 Ec14
Gálata CY 135 Bd96
Galatás GR 129 Cb88
Galati I 115 Ga84
Galati RO 119 Eb63
Galatina I 113 Hc77
Galatone I 113 Hc77
Galaxidi GR 129 Bc85
Galbally IRL 6 Bd24
Galberget S 59 Ga28
Galera E 44 Ea73
Galera E 33 Ec59
Galgate GB 13 Ec19
Galgenen CH 95 Cc53
Galičnik MK 124 Ad74
Galiny PL 87 Jb30
Galisteo E 37 Ca65
Galizano E 32 Dc54
Gallarate I 101 Cb58
Gallardon F 24 Gc38
Gallareto I 100 Bd60
Gallegos de Argañán E 37 Bd63
Gallegos de Solmirón E 37 Cc64
Galliate I 101 Cb59
Gallio I 102 Dd61
Gallipoli I 113 Hb77
Gällivare S 53 Hb17
Gállneukirchen A 97 Fb50
Gällö S 58 Fd31
Gallspach A 96 Fa51
Galluzzo I 108 Dc65
Galston GB 10 Dd14
Galtelli I 107 Cb77
Gáltjärn S 66 Gc34
Galtström S 66 Gc34
Galugnano I 113 Hc77
Galway IRL 6 Bc21
Galízgjano Terme I 102 Dd60
Gamalseter N 48 Gb11
Gamas F 20 Gc37
Gambassi Terme I 108 Dc66
Gambettola I 102 Ea64
Gambia A 97 Fc52
Gamlingay GB 16 Fc26
Gammalstorp S 78 Fc57
Gammelgården S 54 Ja21
Gammelheim N 50 Hd08
Gammelsdorf D 96 Ea49
Gammelstaden S 54 Hd22
Gammertingen D 95 Cc50
Gamonal E 37 Cd66
Gamonero E 37 Cd66
Gamvik N 47 Ka04
Ganderkesee D 83 Cd34
Gandesa E 34 Fd62
Gandia E 33 Fd69
Gandino I 101 Da58
Gandrup DK 71 Dd51
Ganges F 28 Hd53
Gangi I 114 Fa85
Gangkofen D 96 Eb50
Gañinas E 32 Da57
Gannat F 24 Hb46
Gannay-sur-Loire F 24 Hc44
Gänserndorf A 97 Gc50
Gänsvik S 58 Gd32
Ganthorpe GB 13 Fb19
Gaoth Saile IRL 4 Bb18
Gap F 29 Ka50
Gara H 105 Hd58
Garaballa E 39 Ed66
Garaguso I 113 Gc76
Garancières F 20 Gc37
Garbatka-Letnisko PL 93 Jd39
Garbów PL 93 Jd39
Gárbova RO 117 Da61
Garbsen D 83 Db36
Garching D 96 Ea50
Garching an der Alz D 96 Eb51
Garcihernández E 37 Cc63
Garcigalindo E 37 Cd63
Garcihernández E 37 Cc63
Garcilaso E 37 Cc64
Gárciligaliego D 96 Eb49
Gara RO 117 Da61
Gardanne F 28 Jd54
Gárdány S 3 Ao07
Gárdeja PL 86 Hc32
Gardelegen D 84 Ea36
Gardermoen N 64 Eb41
Garderen NL 82 Bb36
Garding D 83 Cd30
Gardna Wielka PL 85 Gd29
Gardone Riviera I 101 Da59
Gardonne F 26 Fd51
Gárdony H 98 Hd53
Gardonne Val Trompia I 101 Da59
Gardsjönäs S 53 Gb23
Gárdslösa S 78 Gb52
Gárdsätra S 58 Gd27
Gárdskár S 66 Gb38
Gárdsjö S 58 Gd27
Garein F 26 Fc52
Garelochhead GB 10 Dc12
Garessio I 100 Bd63
Garforth GB 13 Fa20
Gargaliáni GR 132 Ba90
Gargantiel E 37 Cd69
Gargilesse-Dampierre F 24 Gc45
Gargnäs S 53 Gd23
Gargrave GB 13 Ed20
Garitz D 90 Eb38
Garlasco I 101 Cc60
Garlieston GB 10 Dc17
Garlin F 26 Fc54
Garlitos E 37 Cc70
Garlstorf D 83 Dc33
Garmisch-Partenkirchen D 95 Dc53
Garnat-sur-Engièvre F 24 Hc45
Gârnic PL 85 Gb34
Garpenberg S 66 Ga39
Garphyttan S 72 Fc42
Garrafe de Torío E 31 Cc56
Garrafe de Torío E 31 Cc56
Garray E 33 Eb60
Garrel D 83 Cc34
Garriguella E 35 Hb59
Garrison GB 4 Ca17
Garristown IRL 7 Cd21
Garrovillas de Alconétar E 37 Ca65
Garrucha E 45 Ec75
Gars am Inn D 96 Eb51
Gars am Kamp A 97 Ga50
Garsdale Head GB 13 Ec18
Garstang GB 13 Ec19
Garten N 56 Dd29
Gartow D 84 Ea34
Gadebusch D 84 Dc32
Gartz D 85 Fb33
Garvagh GB 5 Cd16
Garvaghy GB 5 Cc17
Garvald GB 11 Ec13
Garvao P 42 Ac72
Garve GB 8 Dd06
Gárvin E 37 Cc66
Garwolin PL 93 Jd38
Garz D 84 Ed31
Gasawa PL 86 Gd35
Gâschurn A 95 Da55
Gaschwitz D 90 Eb39
Gasen A 97 Ga54
Gaski PL 87 Jd31
Gaßbach D 95 Da54
Gasselte NL 82 Bd34
Gássino Torinese I 100 Bd60
Gassnò IS 2 Ao07
Gassville-Oisème F 20 Gb37
Gastellovo RUS 87 Kb30
Gastellovo RUS 137 Fd17
Gastes F 26 Fa52
Gatarina HR 103 Fc60
Gátér H 98 Ja55
Gata de Gorgos E 39 Fd70
Gateforth GB 13 Fb20
Gatehouse of Fleet GB 10 Dd17
Gateley GB 16 Ga24
Gaterslaben D 90 Ea38
Gateshead GB 13 Fa16
Gátova E 39 Fc67
Gattinara I 100 Ca59

Gau-Algesheim D 89 Cb44
Gaubert F 24 Gc39
Gaüfelden D 95 Cc49
Gaujiena LV 75 Lb48
Gaukönigshofen D 89 Db45
Gau-Odernheim D 89 Cb45
Gaupne N 62 Cd36
Gautefall N 70 Da44
Gauting D 96 Dd51
Gavá E 35 Gd62
Gavardo I 102 Db59
Gavarnie F 34 Fc57
Gävle S 66 Gb38
Gavorrano I 108 Db68
Gávres F 22 Ea40
Gavrilov-Jam RUS 137 Fa09
Gaweinstal A 97 Gc50
Gawronic PL 92 Ja41
Gawroniec PL 85 Ga32
Gawrychy PL 87 Jc33
Gawthorp GB 13 Ed19
Gawthwaite GB 12 Eb19
Gazimağusa = Ammochostos CY 135 Cc95
Gazzuolo I 102 Db61
Gdańsk PL 86 Ha29
Gdingen = Gdynia PL 86 Ha29
Gdov RUS 136 Ea09
Gdynia PL 86 Ha29
Geashill IRL 7 Cb21
Gebhardshain D 89 Cb41
Gebice PL 91 Fd38
Gedern D 89 Cd43
Gedesby DK 77 Fb59
Gedney Dove End GB 16 Fd23
Gedre F 34 Fc57
Geel B 82 Bb39
Geeste D 83 Ca36
Geesthacht D 83 Dc32
Geevagh IRL 4 Ca18
Gefell D 90 Ea43
Gefrees D 90 Ea44
Gehrden D 83 Da37
Gehrde D 83 Cc36
Gehren D 90 Fd39
Geilenkirchen D 88 Bb40
Geilo N 63 Cd40
Geinberg A 96 Fa51
Geiranger N 62 Cd34
Geisa D 89 Db42
Geiselhöring D 96 Eb48
Geisenfeld D 96 Dd49
Geisenhausen D 96 Eb49
Geisenheim D 89 Cb44
Geising D 91 Fa42
Geisingen D 95 Cb51
Geismar D 89 Db39
Geisnes N 57 Eb26
Geithain D 90 Ec41
Geithus N 64 Dd41
Gela I 114 Fb86
Geldermalsen NL 82 Bb37
Geldern D 88 Bc39
Geldrop NL 88 Bb39
Geleen NL 88 Bb40
Gelej H 99 Jc51
Gelenau D 90 Ec42
Gelendžik RUS 137 Fc17
Gelénes H 99 Kc50
Gelibolu TR 126 Ea79
Gellin F 25 Jd43
Gelnica SK 99 Jd48
Gelnhausen D 89 Cd44
Gelsa E 33 Fb61
Gelse H 104 Gd56
Gelsenkirchen D 88 Bd38
Geltendorf D 95 Dc51
Gelterkinden D 94 Ca52
Gelting D 76 Db30
Geltow D 84 Ed37
Gelucourt F 21 Ka36
Gelvárdo RUS 137 Ga16
Gelvárzano P 42 Ba73
Gembloux-sur-Orneau B 21 Hd31
Gemdersma-Panica SK 99 Jd49
Gemert NL 82 Bb38
Gemlik TR 127 Fd80
Gemmenich B 88 Bb40
Gemona del Friuli I 103 Fb56
Gemünd D 88 Bc41
Gemünden D 89 Cc42
Gemünden D 89 Da44
Gemünden D 89 Cd41
Genappe B 21 Hd31
Genarp S 77 Fa56
Génelard F 24 Hd44
Genemuiden NL 82 Bd35
Genenkirchen D 88 Bd38
Geneston F 23 Ed43
Genevad S 77 Ec53
Genève CH 100 Ba56
Gengenbach D 94 Ca49
Genicera E 31 Cc56
Génicourt-sur-Meuse F 21 Jb36
Genillé F 24 Gb42
Genk B 88 Bb40
Genlis F 25 Jb41
Gennádio GR 134 Ed94
Gennep NL 88 Bc38
Genner DK 76 Da57
Gennes F 23 Fc42
Genola I 100 Bd62
Genouillac F 24 Gd46
Genouillé F 23 Fb46
Gensac F 26 Fd51
Gensingen D 89 Cb44
Gent B 17 Hb29
Gentioux-Pigerolles F 24 Gd47
Genzano = Genova I 101 Cc63
Genzano di Lucania I 113 Gb75
Genzano di Roma I 109 Eb72
Georgenberg D 90 Eb46
Georgsmarienhütte D 83 Cc37
Georth GB 9 Ec02
Géos GR 128 Ab81
Gepatschhaus A 95 Db55
Geraardsbergen B 21 Hb31
Gerabronn D 89 Db47
Geraci Siculo I 114 Fa85
Gerahies IRL 6 Bb26
Gérardmer F 25 Ka38
Geras A 97 Ga50
Gerbéviller F 25 Ka37
Gerbstedt D 90 Ea39
Gerena E 43 Bd73
Gerenzago I 101 Cc60
Gerdau D 83 Dc35
Gérgeri GR 133 Cd96
Gerhardshofen D 89 Dc46
Geringswalde D 90 Ec41
Gerjen H 105 Hb56
Gerlev DK 77 Ec55
Gerlos A 96 Eb54
Germasogeia CY 135 Cb96
Germay F 25 Jc37
Germencik TR 135 Bd88
Germering D 96 Dd51
Germersheim D 89 Cc47
Gernika-Lumo E 32 Ea55
Gernrode D 90 Ea38
Gernsbach D 95 Cb48
Gernsheim D 89 Cb45

Gerolakkos GR 135 Cb96
Gerolsbach D 96 Dd49
Gerolstein D 88 Bc42
Gerolzhofen D 89 Db45
Gerona = Girona E 35 Hb59
Gersdorf D 90 Ec41
Gersdorf D 90 Ec42
Gersten D 83 Cb36
Gerstetten D 95 Da49
Gersthofen D 95 Dc50
Gerswick D 84 Ea37
Gescher D 82 Ca37
Geseke D 89 Cc39
Gessertshausen D 95 Dc50
Gesté F 23 Fa42
Gesualdo I 112 Fd74
Getafe E 38 Db65
Getxo E 32 Ea55
Gettorf D 83 Dc30
Getterón F 25 Jd40
Geversdorf D 83 Da31
Gevgelija MK 128 Bb75
Gévora del Caudillo E 37 Bd67
Gex F 25 Jd45
Geyer D 90 Ec42
Gföhl A 97 Fd50
Ghedi I 101 Da59
Gheorgheni RO 117 Db58
Gherla RO 117 Da57
Ghilarza I 107 Ca77
Ghimeş-Făget RO 117 Dc58
Ghisonaccia F 106 Cc70
Giardinelli I 114 Ed86
Giardini-Naxos I 115 Hd85
Giarratana I 115 Fc87
Giarre I 115 Hd85
Giat F 24 Ha47
Giaveno I 100 Bc60
Giba I 107 Bd79
Gibellina Nuova I 114 Ea85
Gibostad N 49 Gc10
Gibraltar GB 43 Cd78
Gic H 98 Ha53
Gidböle S 59 Ha30
Gideå S 59 Ha30
Gidea S 59 Ha30
Gieboldehausen D 89 Db39
Giekau D 83 Dc30
Gielas S 52 Fc23
Gielow D 84 Ec32
Gien F 24 Ha40
Giengen D 95 Db49
Giens F 29 Ka55
Gieraltowice PL 92 Hd44
Gierzwałd PL 86 Hd33
Giessen D 89 Cc42
Gießmanndorf D 90 Ec39
Gieten NL 82 Bd34
Giethoorn NL 82 Bd35
Gifford GB 11 Ec13
Gifhorn D 84 Dd36
Giganti RUS 137 Fd15
Gigean F 28 Hd54
Gignac F 28 Hd54
Gignese I 100 Ca58
Gigny F 25 Hd40
Gigors F 29 Ka51
Gijón E 31 Cc54
Gilău RO 117 Cd58
Gilberdyke GB 13 Fb20
Gilching D 96 Dd51
Gildeskål N 52 Fa18
Gilena E 43 Cb74
Gilford GB 5 Cd18
Gillamoos D 96 Ea49
Gilleleje DK 77 Ec55
Gillenfeld D 88 Bc42
Gillingham GB 15 Ec29
Gillingham GB 16 Ga28
Gilocourt F 20 Ha35
Gilserberg D 89 Cd41
Gilze NL 82 Bb38
Gim S 66 Ga33
Gimbsheim D 89 Cb45
Gimiat S 58 Gc29
Gimo S 66 Gc38
Gimont F 34 Ga54
Ginasservis F 29 Jd53
Ginestra degli Schiavoni I 109 Fc73
Ginosa I 113 Gc76
Ginostra I 115 Fd82
Ginsheim D 89 Cb44
Ginzling A 96 Ea54
Gioia dei Colle I 113 Gd75
Gioiosa Ionica I 115 Gc83
Gioia Tauro I 115 Gb83
Gioia Sannitica I 112 Fb74
Gioiosa Marea I 115 Fc83
Giovinazzo I 113 Gc74
Giralda GR 134 Ed94
Girancourt F 25 Jd38
Gironella E 35 Gd59
Girvan GB 10 Dc15
Gisburn GB 13 Ed20
Gislaved S 71 Fa50
Gislingham GB 16 Ga25
Gisors F 20 Gb35
Gissi I 109 Fb71
Gistad S 58 Ga27
Gistel B 21 Ha29
Giswil CH 94 Cb55
Githio GR 132 Bc90
Giugliano in Campania I 112 Fb74
Giulianova I 109 Fa69
Giurgiu RO 122 Ea68
Givenry F 20 Gc36
Givors F 28 Ja47
Givry F 25 Jb44
Givry-en-Argonne F 21 Ja36
Gizeux F 23 Fd42
Giżycko PL 87 Jd31
Gizzeria Lido I 113 Gb81
Gjelleråsen N 64 Eb41
Gjemnes N 56 Da31
Gjerde N 62 Cc37
Gjermundshamn N 62 Ca40
Gjern DK 76 Db54
Gjersjøen N 64 Eb41
Gjerstad N 48 Fd13
Gjerstad N 70 Db44
Gjesvær N 47 Ja02
Gjinkar AL 128 Ac74
Gjógv FR 50 Jb08
Gjólga N 56 Eb30
Gjøra N 56 Dc32
Gjøl DK 71 Dd50
Gjøvik N 64 Eb39
Gladbach D 88 Bc41
Gladbeck D 82 Ca38
Gladenbach D 89 Cb41
Gladstad N 51 Ed22
Glainant F 20 Hc33
Glamis GB 11 Ec11
Glamoč BIH 105 Gd64
Glamsbjerg DK 76 Dc57
Glandore IRL 6 Bb27
Glanegg A 103 Fb56
Glanshammar S 72 Fd42
Glanworth IRL 6 Bd25
Glarus CH 95 Cc54
Glasgow GB 10 Dd13
Glashütte D 90 Fa42
Glastonbury GB 15 Ec29
Glauchau D 90 Ec42

Glębock PL 86 Hd30
Glębokie PL 85 Fd36
Gleichen D 89 Db39
Gleinstätten A 97 Fd55
Gleisdorf A 97 Ga54
Glenade IRL 4 Ca17
Glenarif = Waterfoot GB 5 Da16
Glenarm GB 5 Da16
Glenbarr GB 10 Db14
Glenbeigh IRL 6 Ba25
Glenborrodale GB 10 Db10
Glenbrittle GB 8 Da08
Glencolumbkille IRL 4 Bd16
Glendalough IRL 7 Cd22
Glendorragha IRL 4 Ca16
Glenealy IRL 7 Cd22
Gleneely GB 5 Cc15
Glenegedale GB 10 Da13
Glenfeshie Lodge GB 9 Ea09
Glenfinnan GB 10 Dc10
Glengarriff or Waterford GB 5 Da16
Glengarnock GB 10 Dd14
Glenluce GB 10 Dc16
Glenmaye GB 12 Dc19
Glenmore IRL 6 Bd22
Glennamaddy IRL 4 Bd20
Glenridding GB 12 Eb18
Glentanner IRL 4 Ca16
Glenthorne GB 14 Dd29
Glen Trool Lodge GB 10 Dd16
Glería I 101 Cb62
Glinde D 83 Dc32
Glinojeck PL 86 Ja34
Glísson GR 129 Cb85
Glina HR 104 Gb60
Glinka D 84 Ea35
Glogovac SRB 124 Ba70
Gloggnitz A 97 Ga53
Głogoczów PL 92 Ja44
Głogów PL 91 Gb40
Glogów Małopolski PL 93 Jd43
Głogówek PL 92 Ha43
Głogów Matopolski PL 93 Jd43
Głomno PL 86 Ja32
Głomsk PL 85 Gc33
Glonn D 96 Ea51
Glonta S 92 Hc40
Glorenza I 101 Db57
Gloria do Ribatejo P 36 Ac68
Glossa GR 129 Cb83
Glössbo S 66 Gb37
Gloucester GB 15 Ec27
Gloup GB 9 Fb03
Głowienka GB 16 Fc29
Głowno PL 86 Ja37
Głubczyce PL 92 Ha43
Głuchołazy PL 92 Ha43
Głuchów PL 92 Ja40
Głuchowo PL 85 Gb37
Głuchowo PL 86 Gd37
Głuszyca PL 91 Gb42
Glückstadt D 83 Da32
Glušhov RUS 137 Ec13
Gluszyca PL 91 Gb42
Glyn Ceiriog GB 12 Eb23
Glyncorrwg GB 14 Ea27
Glyn-neath GB 14 Ea27
Gmünd A 96 Fa50
Gmünd A 103 Fa55
Gmund am Tegernsee D 96 Dd52
Gmunden A 96 Fa52
Gnarp S 66 Gb35
Gnarrenburg D 83 Da33
Gneevgullia IRL 6 Bb25
Gneisenaustadt Schildau D 90 Ec40
Gnesau A 96 Fa55
Gnesta S 72 Gc44
Gnieljno PL 92 Hd42
Gniew PL 86 Hc32
Gniewkowo PL 86 Hb35
Gniezno PL 86 Gd36
Gnoien D 84 Eb31
Gnojnik PL 92 Ja44
Gnojno PL 92 Jd43
Gnosall GB 13 Ec24
Gnosjö S 71 Fa51
Goathland GB 13 Fb18
Goat of Choire IRL 4 Bb18
Goce Delčev BG 128 Cc75
Goch D 88 Bc38
Gockenholz D 83 Dc35
Goczałkowice-Zdrój PL 92 Hc45
Göd H 98 Hd52
Godalming GB 15 Fb29
Godby FIN 62 Ha40
Goddfordbotn N 48 Fd12
Godelheim D 89 Cd39
Goderville F 19 Fd34
Godkowo PL 86 Hd31
Godmanchester GB 16 Fc25
Godøy N 62 Cb32
Godovič SLO 103 Fb58
Godów PL 92 Hd45
Godøynes N 52 Fd18
Godstone GB 16 Fc29
Godziszka PL 92 Hc45
Godziszewo PL 86 Hb31
Godziszów PL 93 Kb41
Goes NL 17 Hb28
Göhren D 84 Fa31
Gol N 63 Cd39
Goirle NL 82 Bb38
Góis P 36 Ad64
Goizueta E 33 Ec56
Gojsalici BIH 105 Hc63
Gójsk PL 86 Hd35
Gökçen TR 135 Bd90
Gökçeören TR 135 Ca91
Göktepe TR 135 Cb91
Gökköy RO 135 Cd94
Gol N 63 Cd39
Gola S 59 Hb25
Gołąb PL 93 Jd39
Golaj AL 124 Ad71
Golańcz PL 85 Gc35
Golbasi TR 127 Fd80
Golborne GB 13 Ec21
Golchen D 84 Ed32
Golczewo PL 85 Fd32
Goldach D 83 Cd35
Goldap PL 87 Jd30
Goldbach D 89 Da44
Goldbeck D 84 Ea35
Goldberg D 84 Ea33
Goldborg D 84 Ea33
Golden IRL 6 Ca24
Golden Cross GB 16 Fd30
Goldenstedt D 83 Cc35
Goldkronach D 90 Ea44
Goldsborough GB 13 Fb19
Gołdap PL 87 Jd30
Golfo Aranci I 107 Cc74
Gołębiewko PL 86 Ha31
Golema Rečica MK 128 Ba74
Golenice PL 85 Fc35
Golfe-Juan F 29 Kc54
Golfo Aranci I 107 Cc74

Gölhisar TR 135 Ca90
Golicyno RUS 137 Ed10
Gołkowice PL 93 Jb46
Gollin D 84 Fa34
Golling an der Salzach A 96 Ed52
Göllingen D 90 Dd40
Golpejas E 37 Ec43
Golspie GB 9 Ea06
Golub-Dobrzyń PL 86 Hc34
Golymin GR 37 Ka54
Gomadingen D 95 Cd49
Gomagoi I 102 Db56
Gómara E 32 Eb60
Gomaringen D 95 Cc49
Gombergean F 24 Gb41
Gommern D 90 Ea38
Gomont F 21 Hd34
Gomunice PL 92 Hd40
Gondomar E 30 Ad58
Gondomar P 30 Ad61
Gondorf D 88 Ca43
Gondrecourt-le-Château F 21 Jc37
Gönen TR 130 Ed80
Gonfaron F 29 Ka54
Gonfreville l'Orcher F 19 Fd35
Goni GR 129 Bd80
Goni I 107 Cb78
Goniądz PL 87 Ka32
Gonnosfanadiga I 107 Bd79
Gonsans F 25 Jd42
Gooderstone GB 16 Ga24
Goodwick GB 14 Db26
Goole GB 13 Fb21
Goor NL 82 Bd36
Gopegi E 32 Ea56
Goppenstein CH 100 Bd56
Göppingen D 95 Da49
Gor E 44 Dd74
Gorafe E 44 Dd74
Gorajec-Zagroble PL 93 Kb42
Góra Kalwaria PL 87 Jc37
Górczóny H 105 Hb58
Gorczenica PL 86 Hc34
Gördes TR 131 Fb84
Gordon GB 11 Ec14
Gordoncillo E 31 Cc58
Gorelki RUS 137 Fd16
Gorey GBJ 18 Ec36
Gorey IRL 7 Cd23
Gorgoglione I 113 Gb76
Gorgonzola I 101 Cc59
Gorgopotamos GR 129 Bc83
Goricy RUS 137 Ed09
Gorinchem NL 82 Ba38
Goring GB 15 Fa28
Gorizia I 103 Ed58
Gojačij Ključ RUS 137 Fc17
Gorjão P 36 Ad67
Górki PL 86 Hc36
Górki PL 93 Jc43
Gorlice PL 99 Jc46
Görlitz D 91 Fc41
Görmar D 89 Dc40
Gornjackij RUS 137 Fc14
Gornja Radgona SLO 104 Ga56
Gornji RUS 137 Fd09
Goroděic RUS 137 Fd11
Gorodišče RUS 137 Fd16
Górowo Iławeckie PL 86 Ja30
Gorran Heaven GB 14 Db32
Gorredijk NL 82 Bc34
Gorron F 23 Fb38
Goršečnoe RUS 137 Fa13
Gorseinon GB 14 Dd27
Górsk PL 86 Ha34
Gorssel NL 82 Bc36
Gort IRL 6 Bd22
Gortacéare GB 5 Cc17
Gortahork IRL 4 Cb55
Gort an Choirce IRL 4 Cb15
Gorteen IRL 4 Bd19
Gortin GB 5 Cc16
Gortmore IRL 4 Bb20
Gortnamaddeen IRL 6 Bd21
Gorv N 62 Cb35
Górwihl D 94 Ca52
Gorzanów PL 91 Gc43
Gorzków-Osada PL 93 Kc40
Górzna PL 85 Gc33
Gorzów PL 93 Jd38
Gorzów Wielkopolski PL 85 Fd36
Gorzupia PL 85 Fd39
Górzyca PL 85 Fd31
Gorżżam N 47 Jd07
Gosau A 96 Ed53
Gosberton GB 16 Fc23
Göschenen CH 95 Cb55
Gościcino PL 86 Ha29
Gościeradów Jordanowo PL 85 Fd37
Gościsław PL 91 Gb41
Gościszów PL 91 Ga41
Gosforth GB 12 Ea16
Gosheim D 95 Cb50
Goslar D 89 Dc38
Gösnitz GB 15 Fa30
Gossau CH 95 Cd25
Gossau D 90 Ea51
Gößweinstein D 90 Dd45
Gössting an der Ybbs A 97 Fc52
Gostyń PL 91 Gc38
Gostyń PL 86 Hd36
Goszcz PL 92 Ha38
Goszczanów PL 92 Hc38
Göteborg S 71 Eb49
Götene S 71 Ea46
Gotha D 89 Dc40
Gotham GB 15 Fa23
Gottfrieding D 96 Eb49
Göttingen D 89 Db39
Gottmadingen D 95 Cc52
Gottne S 58 Gc30
Gottskär E 71 Dd48
Götzendorf an der Leitha A 97 Gc51
Götzis A 95 Cd53
Gouda NL 17 Hd29
Goudhurst GB 16 Fd29
Goulven F 18 Dc37
Goumois F 25 Jd42
Goussainville F 19  Fc41
Gouveia m 36 Bb63
Gouves GR 130 Da04
Gouvia GR 128 Ab80
Gouzeaucourt F 20 Hb33
Gouzon F 24 Gd45
Gowidlino PL 86 Gd30
Gowran IRL 7 Cc23
Göynük TR 135 Cc92
Gozdnica PL 91 Fd40
Gozdowice PL 85 Fb35
Gozon = Luanco E 31 Cc54
Gozzano I 100 Ca58

Graal-Müritz D 84 Eb30
Graauw NL 17 Hc28
Grab PL 92 Gd38
Grabarka PL 87 Kb36
Gräben D 84 Ec37
Graben-Neudorf D 95 Cb47
Grabenstätt D 96 Eb52
Grabnik PL 87 Jd31
Grabovac D 84 Ba54
Grabow D 84 Ea37
Grabow D 84 Eb37
Grabów PL 87 Kb33
Grabów nad Prosną PL 92 Ha39
Grabownica Starzeńska PL 93 Ka45
Grabowo PL 87 Jd30
Gračanica BIH 105 Hb62
Gračevka RUS 137 Fd16
Gradačac BIH 105 Hc61
Graddis N 52 Fd19
Gradefes E 31 Cd57
Gradki PL 86 Ja31
Grado E 31 Cb54
Grado I 103 Ed59
Gräfelfing D 96 Dd51
Grafenau D 96 Ed48
Gräfenberg D 90 Dd46
Gräfenhainichen D 90 Ec39
Gräfenroda D 89 Dc42
Grafenschlag A 103 Fb56
Gräfenthal D 90 Dd42
Grafenwörd D 89 Dc41
Grafenwöhr D 90 Ea45
Gräfinau-Angstedt D 90 Dd42
Gräfing D 96 Ea51
Grafing D 96 Ec48
Grafrath D 96 Dd51
Greencastle GB 5 Ca19
Greencastle IRL 5 Cc15
Greenfield GB 12 Eb22
Greenhalgh D 91 Fb41
Grosshöhe D 83 Cb32
Großheim-Gerbe D 91 Fc41
Greenheubach D 89 Cd45
Groß Ippener D 83 Cd34
Großkarolinenfeld D 96 Ea51
Gußbar D 83 Bb54
Großkölzig D 91 Fc39
Großlangheim D 89 Db45
Großmugl A 97 Gb50
Groß Mühlingen D 90 Ea38
Großnaundorf D 91 Fc41
Großörner D 89 Cd44
Großossvore F 24 Hb43
Großpertholz A 97 Fc49
Groß Pösna D 90 Ec40
Großräschen D 91 Fc42
Großreifling A 97 Fc52
Großröhrsdorf D 91 Fc41
Großnhredorf D 90 Ea41
Großschirma D 90 Ed41
Großschönau D 91 Fc42
Groß Schwechten D 84 Ea36
Groß-Siegharts A 97 Fd49
Großök A 96 Fa53
Großumstadt D 89 Cc45
Großwallstadt D 89 Cc46
Großweitzschen D 90 Ed41
Grostenquin F 21 Kd38
Grosuplje SLO 103 Fc58
Grøtavær N 62 Da34
Groth N 62 Da34
Gråtnes N 46 Hd06
Grotniki PL 92 Hd38
Grotów PL 85 Ga35
Grottaglie I 113 Ha76
Grottaminarda I 112 Fc74
Grottammare I 109 Fa68
Grotte I 115 Gb83
Grottole I 113 Gc76
Grötvågen N 58 Dc30
Grou NL 82 Bc33
Grožnjan HR 103 Fa60
Grubbenvorst NL 88 Bc39
Gruibingen D 95 Da50
Grünberg D 89 Cc41
Grünburg A 97 Fb51
Grundarfjörður IS 2 Ab05
Grundfors S 58 Ga26
Grünstadt D 89 Cb45
Grüntal D 84 Fa35
Grünwald D 96 Dd51
Gruyères CH 94 Bc55
Gryb N 62 Cc39
Grybów PL 93 Jc45
Gryfice PL 85 Fb34
Gryfino PL 85 Fb34
Gryfów Śląski PL 91 Fd41
Gryllefjord N 48 Gb10
Grylsberg N 58 Ga34
Grytgöl S 58 Fc30
Grythyttan S 57 Fc30
Gryżyna PL 91 Gb38
Grząznica RUS 136 Dc12
Grzmiąca PL 91  Gd41
Grzybno PL 85 Fb34
Grzywna Biskupia PL 86 Hb34

Grönenbach D 95 Db51
Grönfjäll S 52 Fd24
Grong N 57 Ed26
Gröningen D 90 Dd38
Gröningen D 89 Da40
Gronov CH 101 Cc57
Grootegast NL 82 Bd33
Grosbous L 21 Jc33
Groscavallo I 100 Bc59
Grosebay GB 8 Da06
Grosio I 101 Da57
Grobaltingen D 95 Dc50
Großalmerode D 89 Db40
Großaitingen D 95 Dd49
Großbieberau D 89 Cc45
Großbodungen D 89 Dc39
Großburgwedel D 83 Db36
Großdubrau D 91 Fb40
Großefehn D 83 Cb33
Großelfingen D 95 Cc49
Großenbrode D 84 Ee54
Großenhain D 90 Fa40
Großenkneten D 83 Cc34
Großenlüder D 89 Da42
Großenwiehe D 83 Da29
Grossenzersdorf A 97 Gb54
Grosseto I 108 Dd68
Großgerau D 89 Cc45
Groß Gerungs A 97 Fb51
Groß Glienicke D 84 Ed36
Großglobnitz A 97 Fd49
Großgörschen D 90 Eb40
Groß Grönau D 84 Dd33
Großhabersdorf D 89 Dc46
Großhansdorf D 83 Dc32
Großheide D 83 Cb32
Großhennersdorf D 91 Fc41

Guben D 91 Fc38
Gubin PL 91 Fc38
Gubkin RUS 137 Fa13
Gudensberg D 89 Da40
Gudhjem DK 78 Fc57
Gronc CH 101 Cc57
Gudmont-Villiers F 25 Jb38
Gudmundrå S 58 Gc31
Gudow D 84 Dd33
Gudzasebay GB 14 Bc51
Guenrouet F 22 Ec40
Güérande F 22 Ec42
Guéret F 24 Gc46
Guérigny F 24 Hb42
Guernica = Gernika E 32 Ea55
Güesa E 33 Fa57
Gueugnon F 25 Hd44
Güglingen D 95 Cc47
Guglionesi I 109 Fc71
Gugney-aux-Aulx F 25 Jd38
Guhtás S 87 Ka33
Guichen F 16 Gc30
Guidizzolo I 102 Db60
Guidonia-Montecelio I 109 Eb71
Guignen F 23 Ed40
Guignes F 20 Ha37
Guijuelo E 37 Cb63
Guildford GB 15 Fb29
Guillena E 43 Bc73
Guillestre F 29 Kb50
Guillos F 26 Fb51
Guilsfield GB 12 Eb24
Guimaráes P 30 Ad60
Guînes F 16 Gc30
Guingamp F 22 Ec38
Guipavas F 22 Dc38
Guipry F 23 Ed40
Guisando E 37 Cc65
Guisborough GB 13 Fb18
Guiscriff F 22 Dd39
Guiseley GB 13 Fa20
Guitiriz E 30 Bb56
Gütting Power GB 15 Ed26
Guitres F 26 Fd49
Gukovo RUS 137 Fc15
Gulberg F 24 Gd57
Gul'kević RUS 137 Fc16
Gullane GB 11 Ec13
Gullber.by F 24 Gd57
Gullbrandsby S 59 Hd27
Gullringen S 71 Fd38
Gullspång S 59 Ed29
Gullträsk S 54 Hc20
Güllük TR 131 Ec04
Gülpınar TR 130 Dc80
Gulsele S 58 Gb28
Gušvik N 64 Dc40
Gumboda S 53 Hb24
Gummersbach D 88 Ca40
Gumowo PL 86 Ja35
Gumpersdorf D 96 Ec50
Gümptugelkirchen A 97 Fb51
Gumtow D 84 Eb35
Günzburg D 95 Db49
Gunzenhausen D 95 Dc46
Guovdageaidnu N 50 Hd11
Gurcy-le-Châtel F 20 Ha38
Guriezo E 32 Ea55
Gurk A 103 Fb55
Gurten GB 15 Ed27
Gurten IRL 6 Bd22
Gürün TR 127 Ga65
Gusev RUS 137 Jd11
Gusmar AL 110 Ha73
Gušow D 85 Fb36
Guspini I 107 Bd78
Güssefeld D 84 Ea35
Gustavsberg S 73 Gc43
Gustavsfors S 57 Ed31
Güstrow D 84 Eb32
Gusum S 59 Ga32
Gutach D 94 Cb50
Gutach D 95 Cb49
Gutcher GB 9 Fa01
Gutenstein A 97 Ga52
Gütersloh D 89 Cc39
Guttaring A 97 Fb54
Gützkow D 84 Fa31
Güvák N 48 Fc13
Guyhirn GB 16 Fd23
Gvarv N 64 Dd41
Gwda Wielka PL 85 Gb34
Gwittian GB 14 Da32
Gyál H 99 Jc54
Gyarmat H 98 Ja52
Gyergyószentmiklós RO 127 Ga65
Gyékényes H 98 Ja52
Györ H 98 Ja52
Gyöpárosfürdő H 99 Jd54
Gysinge S 57 Ga40

Grubben RUS 136 Dc12

**H**

Haag A 97 Fb51
Haaksbergen NL 83 Bd36
Haan D 88 Bd40
Haapajärvi FIN 60 Kb26
Haapajärvi FIN 61 La29
Haapakumpu FIN 51 Kc16
Haapala FIN 61 La29
Haapamäki FIN 60 Kb28

Grönenbach

Haapamäki FIN 68 Ka33
Haapaniemi FIN 61 Lb32
Haapasalmi FIN 61 Ld32
Haapavesi FIN 60 Ka26
Haapimaa FIN 82 Bd33
Haapsalu EST 74 Ka44
Haar D 96 Ea51
Haarajoki FIN 68 Kd30
Haaraia FIN 60 Kc30
Haaraoja FIN 60 Kb25
Haarbach D 96 Ed50
Haarbrück D 89 Da39
Haarlem NL 17 Hd25
Haaroinen FIN 68 Ka36
Haavisto FIN 68 Kb33
Habartice CZ 91 Fc41
Habichtswald D 89 Da40
Habo S 72 Fa48
Hachenburg D 89 Cb42
Hackethorn D 89 Cb42
Häckås S 58 Fc31
Hacksjö S 58 Ga30
Hadamar D 89 Cb42
Haddenham GB 15 Fb27
Haddenham GB 16 Fd25
Haddington GB 11 Ec13
Haderslev DK 76 Db57
Hadjač UA 137 Ed14
Hadleigh GB 16 Ga26
Hadle Szklarskie PL 93 Ka44
Hadmersleben D 90 Dd38
Hadsel N 48 Fc13
Hadsund DK 76 Dc52
Haelen NL 88 Bb39
Hafenlohr D 89 Da45
Hafnarfjörður IS 2 Ac07
Hafnir IS 2 Ab08
Haga S 73 Gc43
Hagby S 78 Ga53
Hage D 83 Cb32
Hagen D 83 Cd33
Hagen D 88 Ca40
Hagenbach D 95 Cb47
Hagenburg D 83 Da36
Hagfors S 57 Ed31
Häggenås S 58 Fc30
Häggvik S 58 Gd31
Hagondange F 21 Jd35
Hagshult S 72 Fb49
Haguenau F 94 Cd48
Hahausen D 89 Dc38
Hahnbach D 90 Ea46
Haibach D 90 Ed44
Haiger D 89 Cc42
Haigerloch D 95 Cc49
Haikkaanlahti FIN 69 Lb35
Hailanville F 25 Ka38
Hailsham GB 16 Fd30
Hailuoto FIN 54 Jd24
Haimausen D 96 Dd50
Haina D 89 Da41
Hainburg an der Donau A 97 Gc51
Hainfeld A 97 Ga52
Hainford D 96 Dd50
Hainichen D 90 Ed41
Hainneville, Équeurdreville-F 19 Ed34
Hainsfarth D 95 Dc48
Hainton GB 13 Fc22
Hajdúböszörmény H 99 Ka52
Hajdúdorog H 99 Ka51
Hajdúnánás H 99 Ka51
Hajdúszoboszló H 99 Ka52
Hajdúvid H 99 Ka51
Hajnówka PL 87 Kb31
Hajsyn UA 136 Ec15
Hakenstedt D 90 Dd38
Hakkas S 54 Hc21
Hakokylä FIN 55 Ka24
Hakonen FIN 82 Bd38
Haksyn UA 136 Ec15
Hal'ov UA 136 Ec15

Krześlin - Lescure-d'Albigeois


Krześlin PL 87 Ka36
Krzeszyce PL 85 Fc36
Krzymów PL 86 Hb37
Krzystkowice PL 91 Fd39
Krzyszkowice PL 92 Ja45
Krzywa PL 91 Ga40
Krzywcza PL 93 Kb44
Krzywe PL 87 Ka30
Krzyż PL 85 Ga35
Krzyżówka PL 93 Jc46
Kšenskij RUS 137 Fa13
Książ Mały PL 92 Ja43
Książ Wielkopolski PL 91 Gc38
Księżomierz PL 93 Ka41
Księżpol PL 93 Kb42
Kstovo RUS 137 Fb09
Ktery PL 86 Hc37
Ktová CZ 91 Fd43
Kuchen D 95 Da49
Kuchl A 96 Ed52
Küçükkuyu TR 130 Eb82
Kuczbork-Osada PL 86 Hd34
Kudowa-Zdrój PL 91 Gb43
Kufstein A 96 Eb53
Kugej RUS 137 Fc16
Kuha FIN 55 Kb20
Kühbach D 96 Dd49
Kühlungsborn D 84 Eb31
Kuhmalahti FIN 68 Ka35
Kuhmirn A 97 Gb54
Kuhmo FIN 61 Lb25
Kuhmoinen FIN 68 Kb35
Kühnsdorf A 103 Fc56
Kuhnusta FIN 61 Lc29
Kühren-Burkartshain D 90 Ec40
Kühsen D 84 Dd32
Kuhtur FIN 50 Jd12
Kuinre NL 82 Bc34
Kuivalahti FIN 67 Ja36
Kuivaniemi FIN 54 Jd22
Kuivanto FIN 68 Kc37
Kuivas järvi FIN 55 Ka23
Kuivaskylä FIN 60 Jc32
Kuivastu EST 74 Jd45
Kukasjärvi S 54 Jb20
Kukkaro FIN 68 Kb33
Kukko FIN 60 Ka32
Kukkola FIN 54 Jc21
Kukkola S 54 Jc21
Kukkolanvaara FIN 55 Lb20
Kukohijoki FIN 68 Ka36
Kukonharja FIN 68 Jc37
Kukonkylä FIN 60 Jd27
Kula TR 131 Fc86
Kuldīga LV 80 Jc51
Kulebaki RUS 137 Fb10
Kulen Vakuf BIH 104 Gb63
Kuleši RUS 137 Fa12
Kulesze PL 87 Ka32
Kulkwitz D 90 Eb40
Kullaa FIN 67 Jb36
Kullen S 58 Ga26
Kulmain D 90 Ea45
Kulmbach D 90 Dd44
Kuluntalahti FIN 60 Kd25
Kumhausen D 96 Eb50
Kumielsk PL 87 Jd32
Kumköy TR 127 Fd77
Kumla S 72 Fd44
Kumlinge FIN 67 Hd40
Kumluca TR 135 Cb93
Kümmersbruck D 90 Ea46
Kumpu FIN 69 Ld33
Kumpula FIN 60 Ka30
Kumpuranta FIN 61 Ld32
Kumpuselkä FIN 60 Kb29
Kumrovec HR 104 Ga58
Kumu FIN 68 Kc35
Kundl A 96 Ea53
Kunes N 47 Jd06
Kunfehértó H 105 Ja56
Kungälv S 71 Eb48
Kungsängen S 72 Gc43
Kungsbacka S 71 Ec50
Kungsör S 72 Ga43
Kun'je UA 137 Fb14
Kunow D 84 Eb35
Kunów PL 93 Jc41
Kunowice PL 85 Fc37
Kunpeszér H 98 Hd54
Kunrau D 84 Dd36
Kunszentmárton H 99 Jb55
Kunžak CZ 97 Fd48
Künzell D 89 Da42
Künzelsau D 95 Da47
Künzing D 96 Ec49
Kuomiokoski FIN 69 La35
Kuopio FIN 61 La30
Kuora FIN 61 Ld29
Kuormuvaara FIN 61 Lc29
Kuorpak sameviste S 53 Gd18
Kuortane FIN 60 Jc31
Kuosku FIN 51 Kc16
Kuparivaara FIN 55 La20
Kupferzell D 95 Da47
Kupiala FIN 61 Lb32
Kup'jans'k UA 137 Fb14
Kup'jans'k- Vuzlovyj UA 137 Fb14
Kuppenheim D 95 Cb48
Kupres BIH 104 Gd64
Küps D 90 Dd44
Kurdžinovo RUS 137 Fd17
Kurejoki FIN 60 Jc30
Kuremäe EST 75 Lc42
Kuressaare EST 74 Jc46
Kurganinsk RUS 137 Fd17
Kurhila FIN 68 Kb36
Kurianka PL 87 Kb31
Kurikka FIN 59 Jb32
Kuřim CZ 97 Gb47
Kurima SK 99 Jd47
Kurisjärvi FIN 68 Jd37
Kuřivody CZ 91 Fc43
Kurjala FIN 61 Lb31
Kurjenkylä FIN 68 Jc33
Kurkikylä FIN 55 Kd22
Kurkimäki FIN 61 La30
Kurkkio FIN 50 Jb14
Kurkkio S 50 Hd16
Kurlovskij RUS 137 Fa10
Kurolanlahti FIN 60 Kd29
Kurovskoe RUS 137 Fa10
Kurowo PL 85 Gb31
Kursk RUS 137 Fa13
Kürten D 88 Ca40
Kurtti FIN 55 Kd21
Kurtto FIN 55 Kd24
Kuru FIN 68 Jd34
Kuru FIN 68 Jd36
Kuru FIN 68 Kb38
Kurvinen FIN 55 Lb21
Kurzelów PL 92 Ja41
Kurzyna PL 93 Ka42
Kuşadası TR 131 Ec88
Kušalino RUS 137 Ed09
Kuščevskaja RUS 137 Fc16
Kuścińce PL 87 Kc32
Kusel D 88 Bd45
Kuslin PL 85 Gb37
Kusmark S 59 Hc25
Küsnacht CH 95 Cb53
Küssaberg D 95 Cb52
Küssnacht am Rigi CH 95 Cb54
Kustavi FIN 67 Ja39
Küsten D 84 Dd35
Kutajoki FIN 68 Kc36
Kutemainen FIN 60 Kb30
Kutemajärvi FIN 68 Kd33
Kutenholz D 83 Da33
Kutina HR 104 Gc60
Kutná Hora CZ 91 Fd45
Kutno PL 86 Hc37
Kuttainen S 50 Hd13
Kuttanen FIN 50 Hd13
Küttigen CH 94 Ca53
Kúty SK 97 Gc49
Kuuksenvaara FIN 61 Ma30
Kuumu FIN 55 Lb24
Kuusa FIN 60 Kc32
Kuusajoki FIN 50 Jc15
Kuusamo FIN 55 La20
Kuusiranta FIN 60 Kc26
Kuusivaara FIN 55 Kb18
Kuuslahti FIN 60 Kc30
Kuvala FIN 69 La34
Kuvšinovo RUS 136 Ec10
Kuzie PL 87 Jc33
Kuzmice SK 99 Jd49
Kuźmina PL 93 Kb45
Kuzneck RUS 137 Fd10
Kuznecovs'k UA 136 Ea14
Kuźnica Czarnkowska PL 85 Gb35
Kuźnica Zbąska PL 85 Ga37
Kvačany SK 98 Hd47
Kvæfjord N 48 Ga12
Kvæl N 52 Fd18
Kvalfjord N 46 Hd07
Kvalnes N 48 Fb14
Kvaløysletta N 49 Gd09
Kvalsund N 46 Ja06
Kvalsund N 62 Cb33
Kvalsvik N Cb32
Kvalvåg N 56 Db31
Kvam N 64 Dd35
Kvammen N 56 Dc31
Kvantorp S 59 Ha27
Kvarnriset S 59 Hc26
Kvarsätt S 66 Gb33
Kvasice CZ 98 Gd47
Kveina N 52 Ed24
Kvelia N 57 Fb26
Kvennland N 57 Eb27
Kvenvær N 56 Db29
Kvernes N 56 Da31
Kvernmo N 65 Ed37
Kvien N 64 Cc33
Kvikkjokk S 53 Gc18
Kvikstad N 52 Fc17
Kvinnherad N 63 Cb40
Kvissleby S 66 Gc34
Kviteberg N 49 Ha09
Kvitnes N 48 Fd13
Kvitno N 63 Cc40
Kwakowo PL 85 Gc30
Kwidzyn PL 86 Hb32
Kwiecewo PL 86 Ja31
Kyjiv UA 136 Ec14
Kyjov CZ 98 Gd48
Kylänpää FIN 59 Ja31
Kyläsaari FIN 67 Ja36
Kyle of Lochalsh GB 8 Db08
Kylerhea GB 8 Db08
Kylestrome GB 8 Dd05
Kylmälä FIN 60 Kb25
Kymi FIN 69 La38
Kyminlinna FIN 69 La38
Kynsikangas FIN 67 Jb36
Kynšperk nad Ohří CZ 90 Ec44
Kypäräjärvi FIN 61 Lb31
Kypasjärv S 54 Ja20
Kyre Park GB 15 Ec25
Kyritz D 84 Ec35
Kyrkås S 58 Fc30
Kyrksæterøra N 56 Dc30
Kyrkslätt FIN 68 Ka40
Kyrnyčky UA 136 Ec17
Kyrönlahti FIN 68 Jd35
Kyröskoski FIN 68 Jc35
Kyrospohja FIN 68 Jc35
Kysucké Nové Mesto SK 98 Hc47
Kytkylehto FIN 61 La25
Kytökylä FIN 60 Ka26
Kyyjärvi FIN 60 Jd30


## L


Laa an der Thaya A 97 Gb49
Laaber D 96 Ea48
La Adrada E 38 Da64
Laage D 84 Ec31
Laaja FIN 55 La23
Laakajärvi FIN 61 La27
Laakirchen A 96 Fa51
Lakajärvi
La Alberca E 37 Ca64
La Alberca de Záncara E 38 Ea67
La Albergueria de Argañán E 37 Bc64
La Aldea del Portillo de Busto E 32 Dd57
La Algaba E 43 Ca73
La Algaida E 43 Bd75
La Aliseda de Tormes E 37 Cc64
La Almarcha E 38 Eb67
Laamala FIN 69 Lc35
Laarne B 17 Hc29
Laas I 102 Db56
Laasala FIN 60 Jd31
Laatzen D 83 Db37
La Aulaga E 43 Bd73
La Bañeza E 31 Cb58
La Barrela E 30 Bb56
Labasheeda IRL 6 Bc23
la Bassée F 20 Ha31
la Bastide F 29 Kb53
Labastide-Beauvoir F 27 Gc54
Labastide-Clairence F 33 Fa55
la Bastide-des-Jourdans F 29 Jd53
Labastide-Murat F 27 Gc51
la Bastide-Puylaurent F 28 Hd51
Labastide-Rouairoux F 27 Ha54
Labastide-Saint-Pierre F 27 Gb53
Lábatlan H 98 Hc52
la Baule F 22 Ec42
la Bazoche-Gouet F 23 Ga39
l'Abbaye F 28 Hd52
Labby FIN 68 Kd38
Łabędnik PL 87 Jb30
Labège F 27 Gc54
la Bégude-Blanche F 29 Ka52
Labenz D 83 Dc32
la Bernerie-en-Retz F 22 Ec43
Laberweinting D 96 Eb49
l'Aber-Wrac'h F 18 Db37
Labin HR 103 Fa61
Labinsk RUS 137 Fd17
la Bisbal del Penedès E 34 Gc62
la Bisbal d'Empordà E 35 Hb59
La Bobadilla E 44 Da73
Lábod H 104 Gd57
Laboe D 83 Dc30
la Boissière F 19 Fd36
la Borne F 24 Ha42
La Bouëxière F 23 Fa39
la Bourboule F 27 Ha47
la Boutière F 29 Jd48
la Brède F 26 Fb51
la Bresse F 25 Ka39
Labrit F 26 Fb52
Labrousse F 24 Gb46
Labroye F 20 Gc32
Labruguière F 27 Gd54
l'Absie F 23 Fb44
la Caillère F 23 Fb44
La Calahorra E 44 Dd75
la Calmet F 28 Ja53
La Calzada de Oropesa E 37 Cc66
La Cañada de San Urbano E 44 Ea76
La Cañada de Verich E 39 Fc63
Lacanau-Océan F 26 Fa49
la Capelle F 20 Hc33
la Capelle F 28 Hc51
la Capelle-lès-Boulogne F 20 Gc31
Lacapelle-Marival F 27 Gd50
Lacapelle-Viescamp F 27 Gd50
La Carlota E 43 Cc73
La Carolina E 44 Db71
La Carrasca E 44 Db73
La Carrasca E 44 Da74
Lacaune F 27 Ha54
la Cavalerie F 28 Hb53
Lacave F 27 Gc50
Lacco Ameno I 112 Fa75
Lac de Tignes F 29 Kb47
Lacedonia I 112 Fd74
Lacelle F 27 Gc47
la Celle-en-Morvan F 25 Hd43
la Celle-Saint-Avant F 23 Ga43
La Cerca E 32 Dd56
la Chaize-Giraud F 23 Ed44
la Chambre F 29 Ka48
Lachamp Raphaël F 28 Ja50
La Chapelle F 21 Ja33
la-Chapelle-au-Riboul F 23 Fc38
la Chapelle-Bertrand F 23 Fc44
la Chapelle-d'Angillon F 24 Gd42
la Chapelle-du-Bois F 23 Ga39
la Chapelle-du-Noyer F 24 Gb39
la Chapelle-Montreuil F 23 Fd44
la Chapelle-Saint-Géraud F 27 Gd49
la Chapelle-Saint-Laurent F 23 Fb44
la Chapelle-Saint-Quillain F 25 Jc41
Lachapelle-sous-Rougemont F 94 Bc51
la Chapelle Verlain F 27 Ga48
la Chapelle-Vicomtesse F 24 Gb40
la Chapelle-Yvon F 19 Fd36
la Chapelotte F 24 Ha42
Láchar E 44 Db75
la Charce F 29 Jc51
la Charité-sur-Loire F 24 Hb42
la Chartre-sur-le-Loir F 23 Ga40
la Châtre F 24 Gd44
la Châtre-Langlin F 24 Gb45
la Chaume F 23 Ed44
La Chaux-de-Fonds CH 94 Bb53
Lachen CH 95 Cc53
Lachendorf D 83 Dc36
la Cheppe F 21 Hd36
la Ciotat F 29 Jd55
Lack GB 4 Cb17
la Clisse F 26 Fb47
la Clusaz F 25 Ka46
la Combe F 29 Jc47
La Concha E 32 Dc55
la Coquille F 27 Gb48
La Coruña E 30 Ba54
la Couronne F 26 Fd47
Lacourt F 34 Gb56
Lacq F 33 Fb55
la Croix-aux-Bois F 21 Ja35
la Croix-Avranchin F 23 Fa38
La Croixille F 23 Fa39
La Croix-Laurent F 23 Ed41
la Croix-Valmer F 29 Kb55
La Cumbre E 37 Ca67
Łączna PL 93 Jb41
Łącznik PL 92 Ha43
Łączno PL 86 Hd31
Lad H 104 Ha57
Ladbergen D 83 Cb37
Läde S 65 Fb38
Ladeburg D 84 Fa36
Lądek-Zdrój PL 91 Gc43
Ladelund D 76 Da58
Ladenburg D 89 Cc46
Ladignac F 27 Gb47
Ladispoli I 108 Ea71
La Duquesa E 43 Cb77
Laduškin RUS 136 Dc12
Laduz F 24 Hb40
Ladybank GB 11 Eb12
Ladyžyn UA 136 Ec16
La Encinilla E 43 Ca75
Laer D 82 Ca37
La Ermita E 44 Eb74
Laerru I 107 Ca74
La Espina E 31 Ca54
La Espina E 31 Cd56
La Estación E 43 Ca73
Lævvajokgiedde N 47 Jd07
la Faurie F 29 Jd50
la Favière F 29 Kb51
la Feclaz F 29 Jd47
La Felguera = Langreo E 31 Cc55
la Fère F 20 Hb34
la Ferière-en-Parthenay F 23 Fc44
la-Ferrière-sur-Risle F 19 Ga36
la Ferté F 25 Ja44
la Ferté-Alais F 24 Gd38
la Ferté-Bernard F 23 Ga39
la Ferté-Frênel F 19 Fd37
la Ferté-Gaucher F 20 Hb37
la Ferté-Loupière F 24 Hb40
La Ferté-Macé F 23 Fc38
la Ferté-Milon F 20 Hb36
La Ferté-Saint-Aubin F 24 Gc40
la Ferté-sous-Jouarre F 20 Hb36
Laferté-sur-Amance F 25 Jc40
la Ferté-Vidame F 23 Ga38
La Feuillie F 20 Gb35
La Figal E 31 Ca54
Navia E 31 Ca54
Lafka GR 129 Bc87
la Flèche F 23 Fc41
la Flotte F 23 Fa46
la Font de la Figuera E 45 Fa70
la Font d'en Carròs E 39 Fc69
la Forêt-Sainte-Croix F 24 Gd38
la Forie F 28 Hc47
Lafrançaise F 27 Gb52
la Freissinouse F 29 Jd50
la Frette F 29 Jc48
la Frua I 100 Ca56
La Fuencubierta E 43 Cc73
La Fuente de San Esteban E 37 Ca63
La Gacilly F 22 Ec40
Laganás GR 128 Ac86
la Garde F 29 Ka55
la Garde-Adhémar F 28 Jb51
la Garde-Guérin F 28 Hd51
La Garganta E 31 Bd54
La Garovilla E 37 Bd69
la Garriga E 35 Ha60
la Gaubretière F 23 Fa43
Lagavara GB 5 Da15
Lage D 83 Cd37
Lage Mierde NL 88 Ba39
Lägerdorf D 83 Db31
Lagg GB 10 Db13
Laggan GB 9 Ea09
Laggars FIN 59 Ja29
Laggerberg S 66 Gb33
Laghy IRL 4 Ca17
La Gironda E 43 Ca75
la Giustiniana I 108 Ea71
Laglio I 101 Cc58
Lagnieu F 25 Jc46
Lagny F 20 Ha34
Lagny-sur-Marne F 20 Ha37
Lago I 113 Gb80
Lagoa P 42 Ab74
Lagoa (Campo Lameiro) E 30 Ad56
la Godivelle F 28 Hb48
Lagonegro I 112 Ga77
Lágos GR 126 Dc77
Lagos P 42 Ab74
Lagrán E 32 Eb57
la Grand-Combe F 28 Hd52
La Granjuela E 43 Cb71
Lagrasse F 35 Ha56
la Grave F 24 Ha44
la Grave F 29 Ka49
la Gravelle F 23 Fd38
la Grolle F 23 Ed44
Laguardia E 32 Eb57
La Guardia E 38 Dc66
Laguarta E 33 Fc58
Laguépie F 27 Gd52
la Guerche-sur-l'Aubois F 24 Hb43
Laguiole F 28 Hb50
Laguna de Contreras E 32 Db61
Laguna de Duero E 32 Da60
Lagunilla E 37 Ca64
Lahardaun IRL 4 Bc18
la Haye-Pesnel F 19 Fa37
Lähden D 83 Cb35
Lahdentaus FIN 61 Ld32
la Hérie-la-Viéville F 20 Hc33
La Higuera E 45 Ed70
Lahinch IRL 6 Bc22
La Hinojosa E 38 Eb67
Lahišyn BY 136 Ea13
Lahnstein D 88 Ca43
Lahntal D 89 Cc41
Laholm S 77 Ed53
Laholuoma FIN 67 Jb34
La Hoya E 45 Ed73
Lahr D 94 Ca49
Lahstedt D 83 Dc37
Lahti FIN 68 Kc37
Laichingen D 95 Da49
Laide GB 8 Dc06
Laidinmäki FIN 60 Kd28
l'Aigle F 19 Ga37
La Iglesuela del Cid E 39 Fc64
Laigné F 23 Fb40
Laignes F 25 Hd40
l'Aiguillon-sur-Mer F 23 Fa45
Laihia FIN 59 Ja31
Laikko FIN 69 Ld34
Laiksjö S 58 Ga27
Lailly-en-Val F 24 Gc40
Laimbach am Ostrong A 97 Fd50
La Ina E 43 Bd76
Lainate I 101 Cc59
Lainejaur S 53 Gd24
Lair GB 8 Dc08
Laisbäck S 53 Gb24
Laissac F 28 Hb51
Laisvall S 53 Gb21
Laitamaa S 54 Hd17
Laitasaari FIN 55 Ka24
Laitse EST 74 Kb43
Laives I 102 Dd56
Laize-la-Ville F 19 Fc36
Lajoskomáron H 98 Hb55
Lajosmizse H 98 Ja54
Lakaniemi FIN 60 Jc30
Lakasjö S 58 Gc28
Lakenheath GB 16 Fd25
Łąkie PL 85 Gc33
Lakinsk RUS 137 Fa10
Lakkí GR 134 Eb90
Lakócsa H 104 Ha58
Lakolk DK 76 Cd57
Łakorz PL 86 Hc33
Laksåvik N 56 Dc29
Lakselv N 46 Jb07
Laktaši BIH 104 Gd61
Lakyle IRL 6 Bb23
Lalandelle F 20 Gc35
La Lapa E 43 Bd70
l'Albagés E 34 Ga61
l'Albaron F 28 Ja54
Lalbenque F 27 Gc52
l'Albufereta E 45 Fb71
l'Alcúdia E 39 Fb68
l'Alcúdia de Crespins E 39 Fb69
l'Alcúdia de Veo E 39 Fc66
Lalín E 30 Ba56
La Línea de la Concepción E 43 Cb78
la Llacuna E 34 Gc61
Lalleu F 23 Ed40
Lalm N 64 Dc35
l'Almadrava E 40 Ga63
Lalœuf F 21 Jd37
la Loupe F 24 Gb38
Lalouvesc F 28 Ja49
La Louvière B 21 Hd31
l'Alpe-d'Huez F 29 Ka49
La Luisiana E 43 Cb73
Lam D 96 Ec47
la Maçana AND 34 Gc57
la Machine F 24 Hc43
la Maddalena I 107 Cb73
La Madelaine F 19 Fa35
la Madeleine-Bouvet F 23 Ga38
la Main F 25 Ka42
la Malène F 28 Hc52
la Malmaison F 20 Hc34
Lamalonga E 31 Bd58
Lamandia I 113 Ha74
La Manga del Mar Menor E 45 Fb73
Lamarche F 25 Jc39
La Marea E 31 Cc55
la Marina E 45 Fb72
la Marolle-en-Sologne F 24 Gc41
Lamarque F 26 Fb49
la Martyre F 22 Dc38
Lamas de Podence P 31 Bc60
Lambach A 96 Fa51
Lamballe F 22 Eb38
Lamberhurst GB 16 Fd29
Lambley GB 11 Ec16
Lambourn GB 15 Fa28
Lambrecht D 89 Cb46
Lambrechten A 96 Ed50
Lambsheim D 89 Cb46
Lamego P 30 Ba61
La Meilleraye-de-Bretagne F 23 Fa41
La Melgosa E 38 Eb66
l'Amelie-sur-Mer F 26 Fa48
la Merlatière F 23 Fa44
l'Ametlla del Vallès E 35 Ha60
l'Ametlla de Mar E 40 Ga63
Lamía GR 129 Bd83
la Milesse F 23 Fd39
Lamington GB 11 Ea14
Lamlash GB 10 Dc14
Lamminkoski FIN 68 Jc34
Lamminkylä FIN 61 La25
Lamminkylä FIN 61 Ld31
Lamminperä FIN 55 Ka22
La Mojonera E 44 Ea76
la Môle F 29 Kb55
la Molina E 35 Gd58
la Mongie F 34 Fd56
La Morera E 43 Bc70
Lamosa E 30 Ad57
la Motte F 20 Ha35
la Motte-Bourbon F 23 Fc43
la Motte-Saint-Martin F 29 Jd49
Lampaluoto FIN 67 Ja35
Lampertheim D 89 Cc45
Lampertswalde D 90 Fa40
Lampeter GB 14 Dd26
Lamport GB 15 Fb25
Lamsfeld D 91 Fb38
Lamspringe D 89 Db38
Lamstedt D 83 Da32
Lamu FIN 60 Kb26
La Muela E 32 Ea60
La Muela E 33 Fa61
la Mure F 29 Jd49
Lamvik N 46 Hd07
Lana I 102 Dc56
Lanaja E 33 Fc60
Lanark GB 11 Ea14
La Nava de Ricomalillo E 37 Cd67
La Nava de Santiago E 37 Bd68
Lancaster GB 13 Ec19
Lanciano I 109 Fb70
Lancin F 29 Jc47
Lançon-Provence F 29 Jc54
Łańcucka PL 93 Kb43
Łańcut PL 93 Ka44
Landa S 71 Ec50
Landau a.d. Isar D 96 Ec49
Landau in der Pfalz D 95 Cb47
Landaul F 22 Ea40
Landaville-la-Haut F 25 Jc38
Landeck A 95 Db54
Landeleau F 22 Dd39
Landepereuse F 19 Ga36
Landerneau F 22 Dc38
Landerum NL 82 Bb32
Landesbergen D 83 Da36
Landford GB 15 Ed30
Landgraaf NL 88 Bb40
Landiras F 26 Fb51
Landivisiau F 22 Dc38
Landkey GB 14 Dd29
Landos F 28 Hd50
Landres F 21 Jc35
Landsberg D 90 Eb39
Landsberg = Gorzów Wielkopolski PL 85 Fd36
Landsberg a. Lech D 95 Dc51
Landshut D 96 Eb49
Landskrona S 77 Ed55
Landsmeer NL 82 Ba35
Landudec F 22 Dc39
Landze LV 74 Jb50
Lane End GB 15 Fb28
Lanesborough IRL 4 Ca20
Lanestosa E 32 Dd55
Langå DK 76 Dc53
Langa E 37 Cd62
Långbäcken S 58 Gc27
Långban S 72 Fb42
Långbo S 66 Ga36
Langdon Beck GB 13 Ed17
Langdorf D 96 Ed48
Langeais F 23 Fd42
Langedijk NL 82 Ba34
Langegg A 97 Fc49
Längelmäki FIN 68 Ka34
Langelsheim D 89 Dc38
Langemark B 17 Ha30
Langen D 83 Cb35
Langen D 83 Cd32
Langen D 89 Cc44
Langenaltheim D 95 Dc48
Langenargen D 95 Cd52
Langenau D 95 Db49
Langenbach D 96 Ea50
Langenberg/Westf. D 89 Cc38
Langenbernsdorf D 90 Eb42
Langenburg D 95 Da47
Langendernbach D 89 Cb42
Langeneichstädt D 90 Ea40
Langenenslingen D 95 Cd50
Langenes N 48 Fc12
Längenfeld A 95 Dc54
Langenfeld D 88 Bd40
Langenhagen D 83 Db36
Langenhoe GB 16 Ga27
Langenlois A 97 Ga50
Langennerie F 23 Ga41
Langen-Selbold D 89 Cd43
Langenthal CH 94 Bd53
Langenwang A 97 Ga53
Langenweddingen D 90 Ea38
Langenzenn D 89 Dc46
Langerringen D 95 Dc51
Langerwehe D 88 Bc41
Langesund N 70 Dc44
Langevåg N 56 Cc32
Langewiesen D 90 Dd42
Langfjordnes N 47 Ka05
Långforsselet S 54 Ja19
Langgöns D 89 Cc42
Langhagen D 84 Ec32
Långhed S 66 Ga37
Langhirano I 101 Da62
Langholm GB 11 Eb16
Langleeford GB 11 Ed14
Langli N 51 Kd08
Langnau im Emmental CH 94 Bd54
Langogne F 28 Hd50
Langoiran F 26 Fc51
Langon F 26 Fc51
Langosco I 100 Ca60
Langport GB 14 Eb29
Langquaid D 96 Ea48
Langreo E 31 Cc55
Langres F 25 Jb40
Langrick GB 16 Fc23
Långsel S 54 Hd20
Långsele S 58 Gd27
Långsele S 58 Gb31
Långselet S 59 Hb25
Långshyttan S 66 Ga40
Langslett N 49 Hb09
Langstrand N 46 Hd06
Langstrand N 47 Jc05
Langtoft GB 13 Fc19
Långträsk S 53 Hb23
Långträsk S 59 Ha26
Langvatn N 52 Fb20
Langviken S 59 Hc25
Långviksmon S 58 Gd29
Langwathby GB 13 Ec17
Langwedel D 83 Da34
Langweid D 95 Dc49
Langwies CH 95 Cd55
Langwyfan GB 12 Ea22
Lanhélin F 23 Ed38
Łanięta PL 87 Jb34
Lanilar GB 14 Dd25
Lanjarón E 44 Dc76
Lankamaa FIN 60 Kc32
Lankojärvi FIN 54 Jc18
Lanloup F 18 Ea37
Lannavaara S 49 Hc14
Lannéanou F 22 Dd38
Lannemezan F 34 Fd56
Lannevesi FIN 60 Kb31
Lannilis F 18 Db37
Lannion F 18 Ea37
la Nocle-Maulaix F 24 Hc43
Lans-en-Vercors F 29 Jc49
Länsi-Aure FIN 68 Jc34
Länsikylä FIN 60 Jc31
Länsi-Saamainen FIN 61 La31
Lanškroun CZ 91 Gb45
Lanslebourg-Mont-Cenis F 29 Kb48
Lantenay F 25 Ja41
Lantjärv S 54 Jb21
Lanuéjols F 28 Hc52
Lanusei I 107 Cb77
Lanuvio I 109 Eb72
Lanvéoc F 22 Db38
Lanvollon F 18 Ea37
Łany PL 92 Ha44
Lanza E 30 Ba55
Lanžhot CZ 97 Gc49
Lanzo Torinese I 100 Bc59
Lanzuela E 39 Fa62
Laon F 20 Hc34
Laons F 20 Gb37
La Paca E 45 Ec73
Lápafő H 105 Hb56
Lapalisse F 24 Hc45
la Palud-sur-Verdon F 29 Ka53
Łapanów PL 93 Jb45
La Paquelais F 23 Ed42
Laparade F 26 Fd52
La Pava E 44 Eb72
La Peral E 31 Cb54
La Peraleja E 38 Ea65
Laperdiguera E 33 Fc59
La Pescia I 110 Ga73
La Pesga E 37 Ca64
la Petite-Pierre F 94 Bd48
la Petrizia I 113 Gc81
La Peza E 44 Dc74
Lapford GB 14 Dd30
la Pierre-Percée F 24 Hb44
Lapinlahti FIN 60 Kd28
Lapiovaara FIN 61 Ma29
la Plagne F 29 Kb47
la Plaine F 23 Fb43
la Plaine-sur-Mer F 22 Ec42
Laplume F 27 Ga52
la Pobla de Cérvoles E 34 Gb61
la Pobla de Lillet E 35 Gd58
la Pobla de Massaluca E 34 Fd62
la Pobla de Montornès E 34 Gc62
la Pobla de Vallbona E 39 Fb67
La Pola de Gordón E 31 Cc56
la Porta F 106 Cc69
La Portera E 39 Fa68
La Póveda de Soria E 32 Eb59
Lappach I 96 Ea55
Lappajärvi FIN 60 Jc30
Läppäkoski FIN 68 Kb37
Lappea FIN 54 Jb17
Lappeenranta FIN 69 Lb36
Lappersdorf D 96 Eb48
Lappfjärd FIN 67 Hd33
Lappfors FIN 59 Jb29
Lappi FIN 55 La22
Lappi FIN 68 Jd33
Lappvattnet S 59 Hc26
la Praye F 25 Hd44
la Primaube F 27 Ha52
Läpsi FIN 61 Ld28
Lapua FIN 59 Jb31
La Puebla de Almoradiel E 38 Dd67
La Puebla de Cazalla E 43 Cb74
La Puebla de Híjar E 39 Fb62
La Puebla de Montalbán E 38 Da66
La Puebla de Valdavia E 32 Da57
la Puerta de Segura E 44 Ea71
Lapväärtti FIN 67 Hd33
Łapy PL 87 Kb34
L'Aquila I 109 Ed70
Laracha E 30 Ad54
Laragh IRL 7 Cd22
Laragne-Montéglin F 29 Jd51
La Rambla E 43 Cd73
La Rasa E 32 Dd61
Larbert GB 11 Ea13
Larche F 27 Gb49
Lardaro I 102 Db58
Larderello I 108 Db67
Laredo E 32 Dd54
La Redondela E 42 Ba74
La Regla E 31 Ca55
Laren NL 82 Ba36
Laren NL 82 Bc36
la Réole F 26 Fc51
Larer CH 95 Da55
La Revilla E 32 Db55
Larg GB 9 Ea06
l'Argentière-la Bessée F 29 Kb49
Largoward GB 11 Ec12
Largs GB 10 Dc13
La Riba de Escalote E 32 Ea61
Larino I 109 Fc72
Lárissa GR 129 Bd81
Larkhall GB 11 Ea14
Larkhill GB 15 Ed29
Larmor-Plage F 22 Ea40
Larnaka CY 135 Cb96
Larne GB 5 Da16
La Robla E 31 Cc56
la Roca del Vallès E 35 Ha61
la Rochebeaucourt-et-Argentine F 26 Fd48
la Roche-Chalais F 26 Fc49
La Roche-en-Ardenne B 21 Jb32
la Roche-Guyon F 20 Gc36
la Rochelle F 23 Fa46
Larochemillay F 25 Hd43
la Roche-Morey F 25 Jc40
la Roche-Posay F 23 Ga44
la Rochepot F 25 Ja43
la Roche-sur-Yon F 23 Ed44
la Rochette F 29 Ka47
Larochette L 21 Jd33
La Roda E 38 Eb68
La Roda de Andalucía E 43 Cd75
Laroles E 44 Dd75
la Romagne F 23 Fa43
la Romana E 45 Fa71
la Ronde F 23 Fb45
la Roque-d'Anthéron F 29 Jc53
Laroque-de-Fa F 35 Ha56
Laroque-d'Olmes F 35 Gd56
la Roque-Gageac F 27 Gb50
La Rösa CH 102 Da56
la Rosière 1850 F 29 Kb47
Larraga E 33 Ec57
Larraona E 32 Eb57
Larsmo FIN 59 Jb28
Larsnes N 62 Cb33
La Rubia E 32 Eb60
Laruns F 33 Fb56
Larvik N 71 Dd44
Las Aljabaras E 43 Cc72
la Salle-de-Vihiers F 23 Fb42
La Salzedella E 40 Fd64
La Sauceda E 43 Ca76
la-Saulsotte F 24 Hb38
Las Berlanas E 37 Cd63
Las Cabezas de San Juan E 43 Ca75
Las Casas de Xilxes E 39 Fc67
Las Cobatillas E 44 Eb73
La Seca E 31 Cd61
la Secuita E 34 Gb62
la Selle-sur-le-Bied F 24 Ha39
la Selva del Camp E 34 Gb62
la Sénia E 40 Fd64
La Serna E 32 Da58
la Serre F 27 Gd48
la Seu d'Urgell E 34 Gc58
la Seyne-sur-Mer F 29 Ka55
Lasham GB 15 Fa29
Łask PL 92 Hc39
Łaskarzew PL 93 Jd38
Laski PL 87 Jc33
Laško SLO 104 Fd57
Las Labores E 38 Dc68
Las Mesas E 38 Ea68
Las Navas de la Concepción E 43 Cb72
Las Navas del Marqués E 38 Da64
Las Nogueras E 39 Fa67
La Solana E 38 Dd69
La Solana E 44 Eb70
la Souterraine F 24 Gc45
Las Pedroñeras E 38 Ea68
Las Pedrosas E 33 Fa59
La Spezia I 101 Cd64
Las Rozas E 38 Db64
Lasseube F 33 Fb55
Lassigny F 20 Ha34
Lassila FIN 67 Jb35
Lassnitz bei Murau A 97 Fb54
Las Torres de Cotillas E 45 Ed72
Lastovo HR 110 Gd68
Lastra a Signa I 108 Dc65
Lastrup D 83 Cb35
Las Ventas de Retamosa E 38 Db65
Las Ventas de San Julián E 37 Cc65
la Tannière F 23 Fa38
la Terrasse-sur Dorlay F 28 Ja48
Laterza I 113 Gd76
la Teste F 26 Fa51
Lathen D 82 Ca34
Latheron GB 9 Eb05
Lathus F 23 Ga45
Latiano I 113 Hb76
Latina I 109 Eb73
Latisana I 103 Ec59
Látky SK 98 Ja49
la Torre de Cabdella E 34 Gb58
La Torre de Esteban Hambrán E 38 Da65
la Torre de l'Espanyol E 34 Ga62
la Torre dels Beltrans E 39 Fc65
Latoue F 34 Ga56
la Tour-Blanche F 26 Fd48
Latour-de-Carol F 35 Gd58
la Tour-du-Pin F 29 Jc47
la Toussuire F 29 Ka48
la Tranche-sur-Mer F 23 Ed45
la Tremblade F 26 Fa47
La Trinité-Porhoët F 22 Eb39
Latronico I 113 Gb77
Latsch I 102 Dc56
Latteluokta S 49 Ha14
Lattin IRL 6 Bd24
Lattrop NL 82 Ca36
Latva FIN 55 Kc21
Latva FIN 60 Ka26
Latvalampi FIN 61 Lc31
Latvaset FIN 60 Ka28
Laubach D 89 Cd42
Laubert F 28 Hc51
Laubrières F 23 Fa40
Laubusch D 91 Fb40
Lauchhammer D 90 Fa40
Lauchheim D 95 Db48
Lauda-Königshofen D 89 Da46
Laudenbach D 89 Cc45
Lauder GB 11 Ec14
Laudio E 32 Ea55
Laudun F 28 Jb52
Lauenau D 83 Da37
Lauenburg D 83 Dc33
Lauenförde D 89 Da39
Lauf D 90 Dd46
Laufach D 89 Cd44
Laufen CH 94 Bd52
Laufen D 96 Ec51
Laufenburg D 94 Ca52
Lauffen D 95 Cd47
Laugar IS 3 Bd03
Laugarás IS 2 Ba07
Laugarbakki IS 2 Ad04
Laugarvatn IS 2 Ba07
Laugharne GB 14 Dc27
Lauingen (Donau) D 95 Db49
Laujuzan F 26 Fc53
Laukaa FIN 60 Kc32
Laukka-aho FIN 61 Lb30
Laukkala FIN 69 Lb36
Lauksundskardet N 49 Ha08
Laukvik N 49 Gd08
Laukvika N 48 Fc14
La Uña E 31 Cd55
Launceston GB 14 Dc31
Laundos P 30 Ac60
La Unión E 45 Fa74
Launois-sur-Vence F 21 Hd34
Launonen FIN 68 Ka38
Laupen CH 94 Bc54
Laupheim D 95 Da50
Laura I 112 Fc76
Lauragh IRL 6 Ba26
Laureana di Borrello I 115 Gb82
Laurenan F 22 Eb39
Laurencekirk GB 11 Ec10
Laurencetown IRL 6 Ca21
Lauria I 112 Ga77
Laurière F 24 Gc46
Laurieston GB 10 Dd16
Lausanne CH 94 Bb55
Lauscha D 90 Dd43
Laussac F 27 Ha50
Lauta D 91 Fb40
Lautaporras FIN 68 Jd37
Lauteala FIN 69 Lb33
Lauter D 90 Ec43
Lauterach A 95 Cd53
Lauterbach D 89 Da42
Lauterbrunnen CH 94 Bd55
Lauterhofen D 96 Ea47
Lautertal D 89 Cc45
Lautertal D 90 Dd43
Lautiosaari FIN 54 Jc21
Lauttakylä FIN 55 Kd24
Lauttijärvi FIN 67 Ja34
Lauvsnes N 57 Eb26
Lauvuskylä FIN 61 Lc26
Lauwersoog NL 82 Bd32
Lauzerte F 27 Gb52
Lauzun F 26 Fd51
Lavachey I 100 Bb57
Lavagna I 101 Cc63
Laval F 23 Fb39
la Valette-du-Var F 29 Ka55
La Vall d'Alba E 39 Fc65
la Vall d'Uixó E 39 Fc66
La Valle Agordina I 102 Ea57
la Vallivana E 40 Fd64
Laval-Roquecézière F 27 Ha53
Lavangen N 48 Ga13
Lavangen N 49 Gc12
Lavardac F 26 Fd52
la Varenne F 23 Fa42
Lavarone I 102 Dc58
Lavaufranche F 24 Gd45
Lavaur F 27 Gc54
La Vega (Riosa) E 31 Cb55
Lavelanet F 35 Gd56
La Vellés E 37 Cb62
Lavello I 112 Ga74
Lavendon GB 15 Fb26
Lavenham GB 16 Ga26
la Venta del Poio E 39 Fb67
Laventie F 20 Ha31
la Verdière F 29 Ka53
la Verna I 108 Ea65
Lavertezzo CH 101 Cb56
Lavezzola I 102 Dd63
Lavia FIN 67 Jb35
La Victoria E 43 Cc73
La Vid E 32 Dc60
La Vid de Ojeda E 32 Db57
La Vila Joiosa E 45 Fc71
la Vilella Baixa E 34 Ga62
la Ville-aux-Clercs F 24 Gb40
la Villedieu F 23 Fc46
la Villedieu F 27 Gc47
Lavilledieu F 28 Ja51
la Villedieu-en-Fontenette F 25 Jd40
Lavinio-Lido di Enea I 109 Eb73
Lavis I 102 Dc57
Lavit-de-Lomagne F 27 Ga53
Lavoux F 23 Ga44
Lavre P 36 Ac69
Lavre S 53 Hb20
la Vrine F 25 Ka42
Lavrio GR 129 Cc87
la Wantzenau F 94 Ca48
Laxå S 72 Fc45
Laxe E 30 Ac54
Laxede S 54 Hc20
Laxey GB 12 Dd19
Laxfield GB 16 Gb25
Laxford Bridge GB 8 Dd05
Laxforsen S 49 Hb15
Laxnäs S 52 Fd22
Laxo GB 9 Fb04
Laxsjö S 58 Fc28
Laxsjön S 58 Gb32
Layer-de-la-Haye GB 16 Ga27
Layna E 38 Eb62
Layrac F 27 Ga52
Laytown IRL 5 Cd20
Laza E 30 Bb58
Lazarevskoe RUS 137 Fc17
Lazise I 102 Db59
Lazisko SK 98 Hd48
Łaziuki PL 87 Ka33
Lazkao E 33 Ec56
Lázně Bohdaneč CZ 91 Ga44
Łazówek PL 87 Ka35
Lazy CZ 90 Ec44
Łazy PL 85 Ga30
Łazy PL 87 Jb37
Lazzaro I 115 Ga84
Leabgarrow IRL 4 Ca15
Leadburn GB 11 Eb13
Leadenham GB 13 Fb23
Leaden Roding GB 16 Fd27
Lealt GB 10 Db12
Leányfalu H 98 Hd52
Leatherhead GB 16 Fc29
Łeba PL 86 Gd29
Lebach D 88 Bc46
le Barcarés F 35 Hb57
le Bastit F 27 Gc50
Łebcz PL 86 Ha29
Lebedjan RUS 137 Fa12
Lebedyn UA 137 Ed14
le Bégude-de Mazenc F 28 Jb51
Lebeña E 32 Da55
Lébény H 98 Gd52
Lebesby N 47 Jd05
le Bessat F 28 Ja48
Lebiez F 20 Gc31
le Biot F 25 Ka45
le Blanc F 24 Gb44
le Bleymard F 28 Hd51
le Bleymard-Mont-Lozère F 28 Hd51
le Bois F 29 Kb47
le Bois-d'Oingt F 25 Ja46
Leboreiro E 30 Bb55
le Boréon F 29 Kc52
Lębork PL 86 Gd29
le Boulay F 23 Fa41
le Boulou F 35 Hb57
le Bourg F 27 Gd50
le Bourg-d'Oisans F 29 Jd49
le Bourget-du-Lac F 29 Jd47
le Bourgneuf-la-Forêt F 23 Fb39
le Breil-sur-Mérize F 23 Fd40
le Breuil F 24 Gb38
Lebrija E 43 Bd75
le Broc F 29 Kc53
le Bugue F 27 Ga50
le Buisson-de-Cadouin F 27 Ga50
le Busseau F 23 Fb44
le Caloy F 26 Fc53
le Cap d'Agde F 35 Hc55
le Castellet F 29 Jd55
le Cateau-Cambrésis F 20 Hb32
le Catelet F 20 Hb33
le Caylar F 28 Hc53
Lecce I 113 Hc76
Lecco I 101 Cc58
Lécera E 39 Fb62
le Champ-Saint-Père F 23 Fa44
le Charme F 24 Hb40
le Château-d'Oléron F 26 Fa47
le Châtelet F 24 Gd44
le Châtelet-en-Brie F 24 Ha38
le Châtenet-en-Dognon F 24 Gc46
Lechlade GB 15 Ed27
Leck D 76 Da58
Leckanvy IRL 4 Bb19
Leckaun IRL 4 Ca18
le Conquet F 22 Db38
le Corbier F 29 Ka48
le Coteau F 25 Hd46
le Creusot F 25 Ja43
Le Crotoy F 20 Gc32
Lectoure F 27 Ga53
Lecumberri E 33 Ec56
Łęczna PL 93 Kb39
Łęczyca PL 92 Hc38
Łęczyce PL 86 Gd29
Ledaña E 39 Ec68
Ledbury GB 15 Ec26
Ledeč nad Sázavou CZ 91 Fd46
Ledesma E 37 Ca62
Lédignan F 28 Hd53
Ledmore GB 8 Dd06
le Douhet F 26 Fb47
Lędowo PL 86 Hb30
Ledrada E 37 Cb64
Lędziny PL 92 Hc44
Leeds GB 13 Fa20
Leedstown GB 14 Da32
Leek GB 13 Ed22
Leek NL 82 Bd33
Leek Wooton GB 15 Fa25
Leenaun IRL 4 Bb20
Leende NL 88 Bb39
Leer D 83 Cb33
Leerdam NL 82 Ba37
Leersum NL 82 Bb37
Leeuwarden NL 82 Bc33
Leffonds F 25 Jb39
Lefkáda GR 128 Ac83
Lefkógia GR 133 Cc96
Lefkoşa = Lefkosia CY 135 Ca95
Lefkosia CY 135 Ca95
le Fleix F 26 Fd50
le Folgoët F 18 Dc37
le Fossat F 34 Gc55
le Frasnois F 25 Jd44
Leganés E 38 Db65
Leganiel E 38 Dd65
le Gault-Perche F 23 Ga39
Legazpi E 32 Eb56
Legbąd PL 86 Ha32
Legden D 82 Ca37
Leginy PL 87 Jb30
Legionowo PL 87 Jb36
Legkovo RUS 137 Ed09
Legnago I 102 Dc60
Legnano I 101 Cb59
Legnaro I 102 Ea60
Legnica PL 91 Ga41
Legnickie Pole PL 91 Gb41
le Gouray F 22 Eb38
Łęgowo PL 86 Hb30
le Grand- Lucé F 23 Fd40
le Grand-Madieu F 23 Fd46
le Grand-Pressigny F 23 Ga43
Le Grand-Quevilly F 19 Ga35
le Grand-Serre F 28 Jb48
le Grau-du-Roi F 28 Ja54
Léguevin F 27 Gb54
le Gurp F 26 Fa48
Legutiano E 32 Eb56
Léh H 99 Jc50
Le Havre F 19 Fd35
Lehesten D 90 Ea43
Lehmikumpu FIN 54 Jd20
Lehmo FIN 61 Ld30
Lehnin D 84 Ec37
Lehnitz D 84 Ed35
Lehre D 83 Dc37
Lehrte D 83 Db36
Lehtimäki FIN 60 Jd31
Lehtiniemi FIN 55 Kc19
Lehtomäki FIN 60 Ka31
Lehtomäki FIN 61 La29
Lehtovaara FIN 60 Kd26
Lehtovaara FIN 61 Lb27
Leiblfing D 96 Eb49
Leibnitz A 97 Fd55
Leicester GB 13 Fa24
Leichlingen (Rheinland) D 88 Bd40
Leiden NL 17 Hd25
Leiderdorp NL 17 Hd25
Leiferde D 83 Dc36
Leifers I 102 Dd56
Leigh GB 13 Ec21
Leighinbridge IRL 7 Cc23
Leigh Sinton GB 15 Ec26
Leighton-Buzzard GB 15 Fb27
Leikanger N 62 Cb33
Leikanger N 62 Cc37
Leimbach D 89 Db42
Leimen D 89 Cc46
Leinach D 89 Da45
Leinburg D 90 Dd46
Leinefelde-Worbis D 89 Dc40
Leinfelden-Echterdingen D 95 Cd49
Leingarten D 95 Cd47
Leinolanlahti FIN 60 Kd30
Leinzell D 95 Da48
Leipämäki FIN 61 Lc32
Leipheim D 95 Db49
Leippe-Torno D 91 Fb40
Leira N 56 Db30
Leira N 64 Dc38
Leirbakken N 57 Fa26
Leirbotn N 46 Hd07
Leiria P 36 Ac65
Leirmoen N 52 Fc19
Leiro E 30 Ba57
Leirvåg N 62 Ca37
Leirvik N 46 Hc07
Leirvik N 48 Gb13
Leirvik N 63 Ca41
Leirvika N 52 Fa21
Leirviklandet N 56 Dc30
Leisnig D 90 Ec41
Leiston GB 16 Gb26
Leitír Ceanainn IRL 4 Cb16
Leitir Meallain IRL 6 Bb21
Leitrim IRL 4 Ca19
Leitzkau D 90 Eb38
Leiva E 32 Ea58
Leivonmäki FIN 68 Kc34
Leivset N 52 Fd17
Leixlip IRL 7 Cd21
Lejkowo PL 87 Jb33
Lekangsund N 48 Gb11
Łękawica PL 92 Hd45
Lekeitio E 32 Eb55
Łęki Dukielskie PL 93 Jd45
Łękińsko PL 92 Hd40
Lekkerkerk NL 17 Hd26
Leknes N 48 Fb14
Łęknica PL 91 Fc40
Łękno PL 86 Gd35
Leksa N 56 Dd29
Leksdalen N 57 Ec28
Leksvik N 57 Ea29
le Lac-d'Issarlès F 28 Hd50
Leland N 52 Fa21
le Lavandou F 29 Kb55
Lel'čycy BY 136 Eb14
Lelice PL 86 Hd35
le Lion-d'Angers F 23 Fb41
Lelkowo PL 86 Hd30
Le Locle CH 94 Bb53
le Logis-de-Nans F 29 Jd54
le Loroux F 23 Fa38
le Louroux-Béconnais F 23 Fb41
Lelów PL 92 Hd42
Lelystad NL 82 Bb35
Le Mans F 23 Fd40
le Mas-d'Agenais F 26 Fd51
le Massegros F 28 Hb52
Lembach F 94 Ca47
Lemberg F 94 Bd47
Lembeye F 33 Fc55
Lemele NL 82 Bd35
Lemelerveld NL 82 Bc35
le Mêle-sur-Sarthe F 23 Fd38
Lemešany SK 99 Jd48
Lemesos CY 135 Bd97
Lemförde D 83 Cc36
Lemgo D 83 Cd37
Lemi FIN 69 Lb36
Lemlahti FIN 67 Ja36
Lemmer NL 82 Bc34
le Monastier-sur-Gazeille F 28 Hd49
le Mont F 25 Jb40
le Mont-Dore F 27 Ha47
le Moutchic F 26 Fa49
Lempää FIN 68 Kc34
Lempäälä FIN 68 Jd36
Lempdes F 28 Hb47
Lempiälä FIN 69 Lc36
Lemreway GB 8 Da06
Lemu FIN 67 Jb39
Lemvig DK 76 Cd52
Lemwerder D 83 Cd34
Lemybrien IRL 7 Cb25
Lenart v. Slovenske gorice SLO 104 Ga56
Lencouacq F 26 Fc52
Lend A 96 Ec54
Lendak SK 99 Jb47
Léndas GR 133 Da97
Lendava SLO 104 Gb56
Lendinara I 102 Dd61
Lendínez E 44 Da73
Lengdorf D 96 Ea50
Lengede D 83 Dc37
Lengefeld D 90 Ed42
Lengenfeld D 90 Eb43
Lengerich D 83 Cb37
Lenggries D 96 Dd52
Lengronne F 19 Fa36
Lenham GB 16 Ga29
Lenina BY 136 Ec13
Lenine UA 137 Fb17
Leninogorsk RUS 137 Ga09
Leninsk RUS 137 Ga13
Leninskij RUS 137 Fa11
Lenkivci UA 136 Eb15
Lenne D 89 Da38
Lennestadt D 89 Cb40
Lenningen D 95 Cd49
Leno I 101 Da60
Lenola I 109 Ed73
Lenora CZ 96 Fa48
Lens F 20 Ha31
Lensahn D 84 Dd30
Lent F 25 Jb45
Lentate sul Seveso I 101 Cc58
Lentföhrden D 83 Db31
Lenti H 104 Gc56
Lentiai I 102 Ea58
Lentiira FIN 61 Lc25
Lentina I 114 Eb84
Lenting D 96 Dd48
Lentini I 115 Fc86
Lenzen D 84 Ea34
Lenzerheide CH 95 Cd55
Lenzkirch D 94 Ca51
Leoben A 97 Fc53
Leoberghe F 17 Gd30
Leobersdorf A 97 Gb52
Leofreni I 109 Ec70
Léognan F 26 Fb50
Leominster GB 14 Eb25
Léon F 26 Fa53
León E 31 Cc57
Leonberg D 95 Cc48
Leoncin PL 86 Ja36
Leonding A 97 Fb50
Leonessa I 109 Ec69
Leonforte I 115 Fb85
Leonídio GR 132 Bd89
Leonstein A 97 Fb52
Leopoldsburg B 88 Ba40
Leopoldshafen D 95 Cb47
Leopoldshagen D 84 Fa32
Leopoldshöhe D 83 Cd37
Léouvé F 29 Kc52
Leoz E 33 Ed57
Lepaa FIN 68 Ka37
le Pailly F 25 Jb40
le Palais F 22 Ea42
le Parcq F 20 Gd32
Lépaud F 24 Ha45
le Pavillon-Sainte-Julie F 24 Hc38
Lepe E 42 Bb74
le Péage-de-Roussillon F 28 Jb48
Lepel' BY 136 Eb12
le Perray-en-Yvelines F 20 Gc37
le Perthus F 35 Hb58
le Pertuis F 28 Hd49
Łepice PL 87 Jb35
l'Épine F 21 Hd36
Lepistö FIN 51 Kd16
le Poët F 29 Jd51
le Poinçonnet F 24 Gc44
Lepola FIN 55 Ka18
le Pont-de-Claix F 29 Jd49
le Porge F 26 Fa50
le Portel F 20 Gb31
le Pouldu F 22 Dd40
le Pouzin F 28 Jb50
Leppäkoski FIN 68 Ka35
Leppälahti FIN 60 Kd29
Leppävesi FIN 60 Kb32
Leppävirta FIN 61 La31
Leppiniemi FIN 55 Kb24
le Pradet F 29 Ka55
Leptokariá GR 125 Bd79
le Puy-en-Velay F 28 Hd49
le Puy-Notre-Dame F 23 Fc42
Lequile I 113 Hc76
Ler N 57 Ea30
le Raincy F 20 Ha36
Lercara Friddi I 114 Ed85
L'Eree GBG 18 Eb35
le Relecq-Kerhuon F 22 Dc38
le Reposoir F 25 Ka45
le Revest-les-Eaux F 29 Ka55
Lerici I 101 Cd64
le Rival F 29 Jc48
Lerma E 32 Dc59
Lerma I 101 Cb62
Lerm-et-Musset F 26 Fc52
Lermontovo RUS 137 Fc11
le Roc-Saint-André F 22 Eb40
le Rouget F 27 Gd50
le Rozier-Peyreleau F 28 Hb52
Lerum S 71 Ec49
Lerwick GB 9 Fb05
les 4 Routes F 28 Hb47
les Andelys F 20 Gb35
les Arcs F 29 Kb54
les Arques F 27 Gb51
les Aspres F 19 Ga37
le Sauze F 29 Ka51
le Sauze F 29 Kb51
les Avellanes E 34 Ga60
les Baux-de-Provence F 28 Jb53
les Bordes F 24 Hb39
les Borges Blanques E 34 Ga61
les Borges del Camp E 34 Gb62
les Bourdelins F 24 Ha43
Lesbury GB 11 Fa15
les Cabòries E 35 Gd61
l'Escala E 35 Hc59
les Cars F 27 Gb47
Lesce SLO 103 Fa57
les Chaises F 20 Gc37
Les-Champs-de-Losques F 19 Fa36
les Chênes-Secs F 23 Fb39
les-Choux F 24 Ha40
les Claux F 29 Kb50
les Clayes-sous-Bois F 20 Gc37
Lesconil F 22 Dc40
les Contamines-Montjoie F 100 Bb57
Lescun F 33 Fb56
Lescure-d'Albigeois F 27 Gd53

les Eaux-Chaudes – Malin Beg


les Eaux-Chaudes F 33 Fb56
les Écharmeaux F 25 Ja45
les Ecrennes F 24 Ha38
le Sel-de-Bretagne F 23 Ed40
le Sentier CH 94 Ba55
le Sépey CH 100 Bc56
les Estables F 28 Hd50
les Étangs F 21 Jd35
les Eyzies-de-Tayac F 27 Gb50
les Fabres F 29 Kb50
les Fins F 25 Ka42
les Genets F 24 Gc45
les Grandes-Chapelles F 25 Hd38
Les Hautes-Rivierès F 21 Ja33
les Herbiers F 23 Fa43
les Hermaux F 28 Hb51
les Iffs F 23 Ed39
les Islettes F 21 Ja35
les Issambres F 29 Kb54
Lesjaskog N 64 Db33
Lesjaverk N 64 Db34
Lesjötorp S 58 Ga28
Leskelä FIN 60 Kb26
Leskelänkylä FIN 60 Kc31
Lesko PL 93 Kb46
les Llosses E 35 Gd59
les Lucs-sur-Boulogne F 23 Ed43
les Mares F 19 Ga37
les Martys F 35 Ha55
les Mées F 29 Ka52
les Menuires F 29 Ka48
Lesmont F 25 Hd38
les Moulins CH 94 Bc55
les Moulins F 25 Hd46
les Moutiers F 22 Ec43
Les Mureaux F 20 Gc36
Lesná CZ 90 Ec45
Leśna PL 91 Fd41
Leśna Podlaska PL 87 Kb37
Lesneven F 18 Dc37
Lesní Albrechtice CZ 92 Ha45
Leśniewo PL 86 Ha29
Leśniewo PL 87 Jc30
Leśniowice PL 93 Kc40
Lesnoe RUS 136 Ec09
les Nonières F 29 Jd50
les Ollières-sur-Eyrieux F 28 Ja50
le Souquet F 26 Fa53
les Palmeres E 39 Fc68
l'Esperou F 28 Hc52
les Planches-en-Montagne F 25 Jd43
les Planes d'Hostoles E 35 Ha59
l'Espluga de Francolí E 34 Gb61
les Ponts-de-Cé F 23 Fb41
les-Ponts-de-Martel CH 94 Bb54
les Portes-en-Ré F 23 Ed45
les Pujols F 34 Gc56
les Rosaires F 22 Eb38
les Rotes E 45 Fd70
les Rousses F 25 Jd44
Les Sables-d'Olonne F 23 Ed44
les Scaffarels F 29 Kb52
les Sièges F 24 Hc39
Lessolo I 100 Bd59
Lestards F 27 Gc48
l'Estartit E 35 Hc59
les Ternes F 28 Hb49
Lesterps F 23 Ga46
les Thilliers-en-Vexin F 20 Gc35
les Thons-le-Grand F 25 Jc39
les Thuiles F 29 Kb51
Lestijärvi FIN 60 Jd29
l'Estréchure F 28 Hd52
les Trois-Moutiers F 23 Fd43
les Ulis F 20 Gd37
Leswalt GB 10 Dc16
Leszno PL 91 Gb38
Létavértes H 99 Ka53
Letchworth Garden City GB 16 Fc26
le Teil F 28 Jb51
le Temple F 23 Ga40
le Temple F 26 Fa50
Le Temple-de-Bretagne F 23 Ed42
Letham GB 11 Eb12
le Theil F 19 Fa34
le Theil F 23 Ga39
le Thillot F 25 Ka39
le Tholy F 25 Ka39
le Thor F 28 Jb53
le Thoronet F 29 Ka54
l'Etivaz CH 100 Bc56
Letkés H 98 Hc51
Letku FIN 68 Jd38
Letohrad CZ 91 Gb44
Letoianni I 115 Fd84
le Touquet-Paris-Plage F 20 Gb31
Le-Tour-du-Parc F 22 Eb41
le Touvet F 29 Jd48
Letovice CZ 91 Gb46
Le Trait F 19 Ga35
le Transloy F 20 Ha33
Le Tréport F 20 Gb33
le Trivalou F 27 Gd53
Letschin D 85 Fb36
Letterbreen GB 4 Cb18
Letterfrack IRL 4 Bb20
Letterkelly IRL 6 Bc22
Letterkenny IRL 4 Cb16
Lettermullan IRL 6 Bb21
Letur E 44 Eb71
Letyčiv UA 136 Eb15
Leubingen D 90 Dd40
Leubnitz D 90 Eb42
Leubsdorf D 90 Ed42
Leucate-Plage F 35 Hb56
Leuchars GB 11 Ec11
Leuglay F 25 Ja40
Leuk CH 100 Bd56
Leukerbad CH 100 Bd56
Leun D 89 Cc42
Leuna D 90 Eb40
Leupoldstein D 90 Dd45
Leutenbach D 95 Cd48
Leutershausen D 95 Db47
Leutkirch D 95 Da51
Leuven B 17 Hd30
le Val F 29 Ka54
le Val-André F 22 Eb38
le Val d'Ajol F 25 Ka39
Levänen FIN 69 Lb35
Levanger N 57 Eb29
Levanto FIN 68 Kc38
Levanto I 101 Cc63
Levanzo I 114 Ea84
Leväsjoki FIN 67 Ja35
le Vast F 19 Fa34
Leveld N 64 Db38
Leven GB 11 Ec12
Leven GB 13 Fc20
Levens GB 13 Ec19
Levenwick GB 9 Fb06
Leverano I 113 Hb76
Leverburgh GB 8 Cd06
Leverkusen D 88 Bd40
le Vernet F 29 Ka51
Levet F 24 Gd43
Levice SK 98 Hc50
Levico Terme I 102 Dc58
Levídi GR 129 Bc87
Levie F 106 Cb71
le Vigan F 28 Hc53
Lévignac F 27 Gb54
Lévignen F 20 Ha35
Levijoki FIN 60 Jd30
Levitha GR 134 Ea90
le Vivier-sur-Mer F 23 Ed38
Levoča SK 99 Jb47
Levroux F 24 Gc43
le Wast F 16 Gc30
Lewdown GB 14 Dc30
Lewes GB 16 Fd30
Lewice PL 85 Ga36
Leyburn GB 13 Ed18
Leyland GB 13 Ec20
Leysdown-on-Sea GB 16 Ga28
Leyton GB 16 Fc28
Leżajsk PL 93 Kb43
Lézan F 28 Hd52
Lézat-sur-Lezé F 34 Gb55
Lezay F 23 Fc45
Lézignan-Corbières F 35 Hb55
Lëzna BY 136 Eb11
Lezník CZ 91 Gb45
Leźno PL 86 Ha30
Lgiń PL 91 Gb38
Lgota PL 92 Hd44
L'gov RUS 137 Ed13
l'Haÿ-les-Roses F 20 Gd37
l'Herbaudière F 22 Ec43
l'Hermitage F 23 Ed39
l'Homy-Plage F 26 Ed53
l'Hôpital-Saint-Blaise F 33 Fb55
l'Hospitalet F 29 Jd52
l'Hospitalet F 35 Gd57
L'Hospitalet de Llobregat E 35 Ha61
Lia N 48 Gb12
Lia N 49 Gd10
Liancourt F 20 Gd35
Liart F 21 Hd33
Libardón E 31 Cd54
Libberton GB 11 Ea14
Libčeves CZ 90 Fa43
Liběchov CZ 91 Fb43
Liber E 31 Bd56
Liberec CZ 91 Fc42
Liběšice CZ 91 Fb43
Libhošť CZ 92 Ha46
Libiąż PL 92 Hd44
Libice nad Cidlinou CZ 91 Fd44
Libina CZ 91 Gc45
Liblar D 88 Bd41
Libočany CZ 90 Ed44
Libochovice CZ 90 Fa43
Libouchec CZ 90 Fa42
Libourne F 26 Fc50
Librilla E 45 Ed73
Libusza PL 93 Jc45
Licata I 114 Fa87
Liceras E 32 Dd61
Lich D 89 Cc42
Lichfield GB 13 Ed24
Lichnov CZ 92 Gd44
Lichtaart B 88 Ad39
Lichtajny PL 86 Hd32
Lichtenau D 89 Cd39
Lichtenau D 95 Dc47
Lichtenberg D 90 Ea43
Lichtenegg A 97 Gb53
Lichtenfels D 89 Cd40
Lichtenfels D 90 Dd44
Lichtensteig CH 95 Cc53
Lichtenstein D 90 Ec42
Lichtenstein D 95 Cd49
Lichtenvoorde NL 82 Bd37
Lichtervelde B 17 Ha29
Licodia Eubea I 115 Fc87
Licola Mare I 112 Fa75
Licze PL 86 Hc32
Lida BY 136 Ea12
Lidar N 64 Dc37
Liden S 58 Gb32
Lidingö S 73 Gd43
Lidköping S 71 Ed46
Lido I 103 Eb60
Lido Adriano I 102 Ea63
Lido Azzurro I 113 Gd76
Lido degli Scacchi I 102 Ea62
Lido delle Nazioni I 102 Ea62
Lido di Camaiore I 101 Da64
Lido di Classe I 102 Ea63
Lido di Fermo I 109 Fa67
Lido di Jesolo I 103 Eb59
Lido di Ostia I 108 Ea72
Lido di Portonuovo I 110 Gb72
Lido di Squillace I 115 Gc82
Lidón E 39 Fa63
Lidoríki GR 129 Bc84
Lido Sant'Angelo I 113 Gc79
Lido Specchiolla I 113 Hb75
Lidsjöberg S 58 Fd27
Lidzbark PL 86 Hd33
Lidzbark Warmiński PL 86 Ja30
Liebenau A 97 Fc50
Liebenau D 83 Da35
Liebenau D 89 Da39
Liebenburg D 89 Dc38
Liebenfels A 97 Fb55
Liebertwolkwitz D 90 Ec40
Liedakka S 49 Hc13
Liedakkala FIN 54 Jc21
Liedenpohja FIN 60 Jc32
Liège B 21 Jb30
Liegnitz = Legnica PL 91 Ga41
Lieksa FIN 61 Ld28
Lielstraupe LV 74 Kc49
Liencres E 32 Dc54
Lienen D 83 Cb37
Lienz A 96 Ec55
Liepāja LV 79 Ja52
Lier B 17 Hd29
Lierena E 43 Ca71
Liérganes E 32 Dc55
Liernais F 25 Hd42
Liernolles F 24 Hc45
Lieshout NL 88 Bb38
Liesjärvi FIN 60 Ka32
Lieskau D 90 Ea39
Liesse-Notre-Dame F 20 Hc34
Liessies F 20 Hc32
Liestal CH 94 Bd52
Lietavská Lúčka SK 98 Hc47
Liétor E 45 Ec71
Lietsa FIN 68 Ka38
Liettik S 49 Gd16
Lieurac F 34 Gc56
Lievikoski FIN 67 Jb36
Liévin F 20 Ha31
Lievisenmäki FIN 61 La27
Liezen A 97 Fb53
Liffol-le-Grand F 25 Jc38
Lifjell N 70 Db43
Lifton GB 14 Dc31
Ligiá GR 128 Ac82
Lignol-le-Château F 25 Ja39
Ligny-le-Ribault F 24 Gc41
Ligonchio I 101 Da63
Ligórtinos GR 133 Da96
Ligota PL 92 Gd39
Ligota Prószkowska PL 92 Ha43
Ligugé F 23 Fd45
Lihoslavl' RUS 137 Ed10
Lihovskoj RUS 137 Fc15
Liikavaara S 54 Hc17
Liittoperä FIN 60 Kb28
Liiva EST 74 Jd45
Likósoura GR 128 Bb88
Lilienfeld A 97 Ga51
Lilienthal D 83 Cd34
Liljendal FIN 68 Kd38
Lilla Moberget S 65 Ed37
Lillbo S 66 Ga35
Lille F 20 Ha31
Lillebekken N 51 Kc08
Lilledalen N 46 Jb06
Lillefjord N 46 Ja05
Lillehammer N 65 Ea37
Lille Molvik N 47 Ka05
Lillers F 20 Gd31
Lillesand N 70 Da47
Lillhärdal S 65 Fb35
Lillholmsjö S 57 Fb29
Lillholmträsk S 53 Ha24
Lillkågeträsk S 54 Hc24
Lillo E 38 Dd67
Lillpite S 54 Hc23
Lillsele S 58 Gb29
Limáni Litohórou GR 125 Bd79
Limanowa PL 93 Jb45
Limavady GB 5 Cd15
Limbach D 89 Cd46
Limbach-Oberfrohna D 90 Ec42
Limbaži LV 74 Kc48
Limbourg B 21 Jc30
Limburg D 89 Cb43
Limedsforsen S 65 Fa38
Limenária GR 126 Da78
Liménas Géraka GR 132 Bd90
Liménas Hersonissou GR 133 Db95
Limerick IRL 6 Bd23
Limingoån S 54 Ja18
Liminka FIN 55 Ka24
Liminkajärvi S 54 Ja18
Límni GR 129 Cb84
Límni Vouliagménis GR 129 Bd86
Limoges F 27 Gb47
Limone Piemonte I 100 Bc63
Limones E 44 Db74
Limone sul Garda I 102 Db58
Limours-en-Hurepoix F 20 Gd37
Limoux F 35 Gd56
Limpley Stoke GB 15 Ec28
Lina älv S 53 Hb17
Linarejos E 31 Ca59
Linares E 44 Db72
Linares de Mora E 39 Fb65
Linariá GR 130 Da84
Lincoln GB 13 Fc22
Linda D 90 Ea42
Lindale GB 12 Eb19
Lindau D 95 Cd52
Lindau, Katlenburg- D 89 Db39
Lindefallet S 66 Gb36
Linden D 89 Cc42
Lindenberg D 84 Fa36
Lindenberg D 95 Da52
Lindenfels D 89 Cc45
Lindern D 83 Cb34
Lindesberg S 72 Fd43
Lindhorst D 83 Da36
Lindkoski FIN 68 Kd38
Lindlar D 88 Ca40
Lindö S 72 Ga46
Lindome S 71 Ec49
Lindos GR 134 Ba93
Lindsdal S 78 Ga52
Lindwedel D 83 Db36
Líně CZ 90 Ed46
Linevo RUS 137 Fd12
Lingen D 82 Ca35
Lingen GB 14 Eb25
Lingenfeld D 89 Cb46
Lingfield GB 16 Fc29
Linghem S 72 Ga46
Linguaglossa I 115 Fd85
Linia PL 86 Gd30
Liniewo PL 86 Ha31
Liniez F 24 Gc43
Linköping S 72 Fd47
Linksness GB 9 Eb03
Linlithgow GB 11 Ea13
Linna FIN 60 Kb31
Linnich D 88 Bc40
Linowo PL 86 Hc33
Linsburg D 83 Da36
Linsengericht D 89 Cd44
Lintig D 83 Cd32
Linxe F 26 Fa53
Linyola E 34 Gb60
Linz A 97 Fb50
Linz D 88 Ca42
Lioni I 112 Fd75
Lios Dúin Bhearna IRL 6 Bc22
Lios Mor IRL 6 Ca25
Lios Tuathail IRL 6 Bb23
Lipany SK 99 Jc47
Lipari I 115 Fc83
Lipasvaara FIN 61 Lc29
Lipczynek PL 85 Gc32
Lipeck RUS 137 Fb12
Lipenec CZ 90 Fa44
Liperi FIN 61 Lc31
Liperinsalo FIN 61 Lc31
Liperonmäki FIN 60 Kd32
Liphook GB 15 Fb29
Lipiany PL 85 Fc35
Lipica SLO 103 Fa59
Lipicy-Zybino RUS 137 Fa12
Lipie PL 92 Hc41
Lipinlahti FIN 61 Lc27
Lipiny PL 92 Hd38
Lipka PL 85 Gc33
Lipki RUS 137 Fa11
Lipniak PL 87 Kb30
Lipnica Murowana PL 93 Jb45
Lipnica Wielka PL 92 Hd46
Lipnice CZ 97 Fc48
Lipnik PL 93 Jd42
Lipniki PL 91 Gc43
Lipniki Łużyckie PL 91 Fc39
Lipník nad Bečvou CZ 92 Gd46
Lipno PL 86 Hc35
Lipno PL 92 Hb40
Liposthey F 26 Fb52
Lipová CZ 91 Gc46
Lipoválázně CZ 91 Gc44
Lipovec CZ 97 Gc47
Lipowczyce PL 92 Hd41
Lipowiec Kościelny PL 86 Ja34
Lipówka PL 93 Kc38
Lippetal D 89 Cb38
Lippstadt D 89 Cc38
Lipsí GR 134 Eb89
Lipsko PL 93 Jd40
Lipsko PL 93 Kc41
Liptál CZ 98 Ha47
Liptingen, Emmingen- D 95 Cc51
Liptovské Revúce SK 98 Hd48
Liptovský Hrádok SK 98 Ja47
Liptovský Mikuláš SK 98 Hd47
Lipusz PL 86 Gd31
Liré F 23 Fa42
Lisacul IRL 4 Bd19
Lisboa P 36 Aa68
Lisburn GB 5 Da17
Liscannor IRL 6 Bc22
Liscarney IRL 4 Bc19
Liscarroll IRL 6 Bc24
Lisdoonvarna IRL 6 Bc22
Lisduff IRL 5 Cc20
Liseleje DK 77 Eb54
Lisia Góra PL 93 Jc44
Lisieux F 19 Fd36
Lisij Nos RUS 69 Mb39
Liskeard GB 14 Dc31
Liski RUS 137 Fb13
Lislea GB 5 Cd16
Lislea GB 5 Cd18
l'Isle-Adam F 20 Gd36
l'Isle-d'Abeau F 29 Jc47
l'Isle-en-Dodon F 34 Ga55
l'Isle-sur-la-Sorgue F 29 Jc53
Lisle-sur-Tarn F 27 Gc53
Lisma FIN 50 Jc13
Lismacaffry IRL 4 Cb20
Lismanaapa FIN 51 Ka16
Lismore IRL 6 Ca25
Lisnagry IRL 6 Bd23
Lisnaskea GB 4 Cb18
Lišov CZ 97 Fc48
Lisowo PL 85 Fd33
Lisronagh IRL 6 Ca24
Liss GB 15 Fb29
Lissamona IRL 6 Bb27
Lisse NL 17 Hd25
Lissett GB 13 Fc20
Lissycasey IRL 6 Bc23
List D 76 Cd57
Listellick IRL 6 Bb24
Listowel IRL 6 Bb23
Lisvane GB 14 Eb28
Liszkowo PL 85 Gc34
Lit S 58 Fc30
Litcham GB 16 Ga24
Lit-et-Mixe F 26 Fa53
Lith NL 82 Bb37
Litija SLO 103 Fc58
Litke H 98 Ja50
Litóhoro GR 125 Bd79
Litoměřice CZ 91 Fb43
Litomyšl CZ 91 Gb45
Litos E 31 Cb59
Litovel CZ 91 Gc46
Little Barningham GB 16 Gb23
Littleborough GB 13 Ed21
Little Brington GB 15 Fb25
Littleferry GB 9 Ea06
Little Glenshee GB 11 Ea11
Littlehampton GB 15 Fb30
Little Langdale GB 12 Eb18
Little Mill GB 14 Eb27
Littleport GB 16 Fd25
Littleton IRL 6 Ca23
Little Torrington GB 14 Dd30
Little Walsingham GB 16 Ga23
Little Weighton GB 13 Fc20
Little Weighton GB 13 Fc21
Little Wenlock GB 13 Ec24
Lituénigo E 33 Ec60
Litvínov CZ 90 Fa43
Litzendorf D 90 Dd45
Livádi GR 133 Cd89
Livadiá GR 129 Bd85
Livádia GR 133 Dd92
Livádia GR 134 Ec92
Livanátes GR 129 Ca84
Livarot F 19 Fd36
Liverpool GB 12 Eb21
Livingston GB 11 Eb13
Liviöjärvi S 54 Ja17
Livny RUS 137 Fa12
Livo FIN 55 Kb21
Livonniska FIN 55 Kc20
Livorno I 108 Da66
Livron-sur-Drôme F 28 Jb50
Lixnaw IRL 6 Bb24
Lizard GB 14 Da33
Lizarra E 33 Ec57
Lizy-sur-Ourcq F 20 Ha36
Lizzano I 113 Ha76
Lizzano in Belvedere I 102 Db64
Lizzola I 101 Da57
Ljachavičy BY 136 Ea13
Ljady RUS 136 Ea09
Ljaskovec BG 122 Dd70
Ljørdalen N 65 Ed37
Ljuban' BY 136 Eb13
Ljubaništa MK 124 Ad76
Ljubar UA 136 Eb15
Ljubešiv UA 136 Ea14
Ljubljana SLO 103 Fb58
Ljuboml' UA 136 Dd14
Ljubymivka UA 137 Fb15
Ljubytino RUS 136 Ec09
Ljudinovo RUS 137 Ed12
Ljungaverk S 66 Ga33
Ljungby S 78 Fb52
Ljungdalen S 57 Ed32
Ljunghusen S 77 Ed57
Ljungsbro S 72 Fd46
Ljusdal S 66 Ga35
Ljusnedal S 65 Ed33
Ljustorp S 58 Gc32
Ljusträsk S 53 Ha22
Ljusvattnet S 59 Hb26
Llamas del Mouro E 31 Ca55
Llanallgo GB 12 Dd22
Llanarmon Dyffryn Ceiriog GB 12 Eb23
Llanarthney GB 14 Dd26
Llanbadarn Fawr GB 14 Dd25
Llanberis GB 12 Dd22
Llanbister GB 14 Ea25
Llanboidy GB 14 Dc26
Llanddarog GB 14 Dd27
Llanddewi Ystradenni GB 14 Ea25
Llanddona GB 12 Dd22
Llandegla GB 12 Eb23
Llandeilo GB 14 Dd26
Llandenny GB 14 Eb27
Llandinam GB 12 Ea24
Llandissilio GB 14 Dc26
Llandovery GB 14 Dd26
Llandrillo GB 12 Ea23
Llandrindod-Wells GB 14 Ea25
Llandrinio GB 12 Eb24
Llandudno GB 12 Ea22
Llandyfaelog GB 14 Dc27
Llanelidan GB 12 Ea23
Llanelli GB 14 Dd27
Llanelltyd GB 12 Dd23
Llanerchymedd GB 12 Dd22
Llanerfyl GB 12 Ea24
Llanes E 32 Da54
Llanfaethlu GB 12 Dc21
Llanfaidr-Caereinion GB 12 Ea24
Llanfair-fechan GB 12 Dd22
Llanfair Talhaiarn GB 12 Ea22
Llanfair-yn-Neubwll GB 12 Dc22
Llanfihangel GB 14 Ea26
Llanfihangel-nant-Melan GB 14 Eb25
Llanfihangel-y-Creuddyn GB 14 Dd25
Llanfihangel-yng-Ngwynfa GB 12 Ea24
Llanfyllin GB 12 Eb24
Llanfynydd GB 14 Dd26
Llanfyrnach GB 14 Dc26
Llangadog GB 14 Dd26
Llangaffo GB 12 Dd22
Llangain GB 14 Dc27
Llangammarch Wells GB 14 Ea26
Llangedwyn GB 12 Eb23
Llangefni GB 12 Dd22
Llangeinor GB 14 Ea27
Llangeler GB 14 Dc26
Llangenith GB 14 Dc27
Llangernyw GB 12 Ea22
Llangollen GB 12 Eb23
Llangorse GB 14 Ea26
Llangrannog GB 14 Dc25
Llangurig GB 14 Ea25
Llangwm GB 12 Ea23
Llangwm GB 14 Db27
Llangwm GB 14 Eb27
Llangwnnadl GB 14 Dc25
Llangybi GB 14 Dd25
Llangybi GB 14 Eb27
Llangynidr GB 14 Ea27
Llangynog GB 12 Ea23
Llangywer GB 12 Ea23
Llanharan GB 14 Ea28
Llanhilleth GB 14 Eb27
Llanidloes GB 14 Ea25
Llanmadoc GB 14 Dd27
Llanon GB 14 Dd25
Llanrhaeadr-ym-Mochnant GB 12 Ea23
Llanrhystud GB 14 Dd25
Llanrug GB 12 Dd22
Llanrwst GB 12 Ea22
Llansilin GB 12 Eb23
Llansoy GB 14 Eb27
Llansteffan GB 14 Dc27
Llanthony GB 14 Eb26
Llantwit Major GB 14 Ea28
Llanuwchllyn GB 12 Ea23
Llanvetherine GB 14 Eb27
Llanwddyn GB 12 Ea24
Llanwrog GB 12 Dd22
Llanwrtyd Wells GB 14 Ea26
Llanybydder GB 14 Dd26
Llanynghenedl GB 12 Dc22
Llanystumdwy GB 12 Dd23
Llardecans E 34 Ga61
Llechryd GB 14 Dc26
Lleida E 34 Ga61
Llera E 43 Ca70
Llimiana E 34 Gb59
Llíria E 39 Fb67
Llithfaen GB 12 Dc23
L'Ile-Rousse F 106 Cb68
Llobera E 34 Gc59
Llodio E 32 Ea55
Lloggerheads GB 13 Ec23
Lloret de Mar E 35 Hb60
Llosa de Ranes E 39 Fb69
Llovio E 31 Cd54
Llubí E 41 Hc67
Lluçà E 35 Gd59
Llucmajor E 41 Hb67
Llutxent E 39 Fc69
Llwyngwril GB 12 Dd24
Llyswen GB 14 Ea26
Lniano PL 86 Ha33
Lo B 17 Ha30
Loanhead GB 11 Eb13
Loano I 100 Bd63
Löbau D 91 Fc41
Lobcovo RUS 137 Fa09
Löbejün D 90 Eb39
Lobera de Onsella E 33 Fa58
Löberitz D 90 Eb39
Łobez PL 85 Fd32
Lobinstown IRL 5 Cd20
Löbnitz D 90 Ec39
Lobonäs S 66 Fd36
Loburg D 84 Eb37
Locarno CH 101 Cb57
Loccum, Rehburg- D 83 Da36
Lochailort GB 10 Db10
Lochaline GB 10 Db11
Lochau A 95 Da52
Lochbuie GB 10 Db11
Lochcarron GB 8 Dc08
Lochdrum GB 8 Dd07
Lochearnhead GB 10 Dd11
Lochem NL 82 Bc36
Loches F 24 Gb42
Loché-sur-Indrois F 24 Gb43
Loch Garman IRL 7 Cd25
Löchgau D 95 Cd47
Lochgelly GB 11 Eb12
Lochgilphead GB 10 Db12
Lochinver GB 8 Dc05
Lochmaben GB 11 Eb16
Lochmaddy GB 8 Cd07
Lochore GB 11 Eb12
Łochów PL 87 Jd36
Lochranza GB 10 Dc13
Lochskipport GB 8 Cd08
Lochton GB 9 Ed09
Lochuisge GB 10 Db10
Lochvycja UA 137 Ed14
Lochwinnoch GB 10 Dd13
Lockerbie GB 11 Eb16
Löcknitz D 85 Fb33
Locmaria F 22 Ea42
Locmariaquer F 22 Ea41
Locminé F 22 Eb40
Locoal-Mendon F 22 Ea40
Locorotondo I 113 Ha75
Locquémeau F 18 Dd37
Locquirec F 18 Dd37
Locri I 115 Gb83
Locronan F 22 Dc39
Loctudy F 22 Dc40
Lødding N 57 Eb25
Loddon GB 16 Gb24
Lode GB 16 Fd25
Loděnice CZ 91 Fb45
Löderburg D 90 Ea38
Lodève F 28 Hc53
Lodi I 101 Cd60
Løding N 52 Fc17
Lødingen N 48 Fd13
Lodosa E 33 Ec58
Łódź PL 92 Hd38
Loeches E 38 Dc64
Loekton GB 13 Fb19
Loen N 62 Cd34
Loenen NL 82 Bc36
Lofer A 96 Ec53
Löffingen D 95 Cb51
Lofsdalen S 65 Fa34
Lofthouse GB 13 Ed19
Loftus GB 13 Fb18
Log RUS 137 Fd13
Logarska Dolina SLO 103 Fc57
Logatec SLO 103 Fb58
Lögdeå S 59 Ha29
Loghill IRL 6 Bc23
Logron F 24 Gb39
Logroño E 32 Eb58
Logrosán E 37 Cb67
Løgstør DK 76 Db51
Lohals DK 77 Dd57
Lohfelden D 89 Da40
Lohheide D 83 Db35
Lohikoski FIN 69 Lc34
Lohilahti FIN 69 Lc34
Lohiluoma FIN 59 Ja32
Lohiniva FIN 54 Jc17
Lohja FIN 68 Ka39
Lohm D 84 Eb35
Lohmar D 88 Ca41
Lohmen D 90 Fa41
Löhnberg D 89 Cb42
Lohne D 83 Cc35
Löhne D 83 Cd37
Lohnsburg A 96 Ed51
Lohr D 89 Da44
Lohra D 89 Cc42
Lohtaja FIN 60 Jc27
Loiano I 102 Dc63
Loima FIN 68 Jc37
Loimaa FIN 68 Jc38
Loisach A 96 Ec55
Loitz D 84 Ed31
Loivre F 20 Hc35
Loja E 44 Da75
Lojo FIN 68 Ka39
Lokalahti FIN 67 Ja38
Loke S 58 Fc31
Løkeng N 49 Hc08
Lokka FIN 51 Kb14
Løkken DK 70 Dc50
Løkken N 56 Dd31
Loknja RUS 136 Eb10
Lokot' RUS 137 Ed13
Lollar D 89 Cc42
Lom N 64 Db35
Lomåsen S 58 Fc29
Lombez F 34 Ga55
Lombreuil F 24 Ha40
Lombron F 23 Fd39
Lomello I 101 Cb60
Lomen N 64 Db37
Łomianki PL 87 Jb36
Lomma S 77 Ed56
Lommel B 88 Ba39
Łomnica PL 85 Gb34
Lomnice CZ 90 Ec44
Lomnice CZ 92 Gd45
Lomnice nad Lužnicí CZ 97 Fc48
Lomnice nad Popelkou CZ 91 Fd43
Lompolo FIN 50 Jc14
Lompolo FIN 50 Jb16
Lomträsk S 53 Ha22
Łomy PL 86 Ja31
Łomża PL 87 Jd33
Lonato I 102 Db59
Londa I 108 Dd65
London GB 16 Fc28
Londonderry = Derry GB 5 Cc16
Lonevåg N 62 Ca38
Longare I 102 Dd59
Longarone I 103 Eb57
Long Bennington GB 13 Fb23
Longbridge Deverill GB 15 Ec29
Long Crendon GB 15 Fb27
Long Eaton GB 13 Fa23
Longford GB 13 Ed23
Longford IRL 4 Cb20
Longformacus GB 11 Ec13
Longhorsley GB 11 Ed15
Longhoughton GB 11 Fa15
Longi I 115 Fc84
Longmanhill GB 9 Ed07
Long Melford GB 16 Ga26
Longno GB 12 Eb24
Longnor GB 13 Ed22
Longpont F 20 Hb35
Long Preston GB 13 Ed19
Longré F 23 Fc46
Longriddry GB 11 Ec13
Longride GB 13 Ec20
Longset N 52 Fa20
Long Stratton GB 16 Gb25
Long Sutton GB 14 Eb29
Long Sutton GB 16 Fd24
Longtown GB 11 Eb16
Longué-Jumelles F 23 Fc42
Longueville-sur-Scie F 20 Gb34
Longuich D 88 Bc44
Longuyon F 21 Jb34
Longwy F 21 Jc34
Lonigo I 102 Dd60
Löningen D 83 Cb35
Lønsdal N 52 Fd19
Lønset N 56 Dc32
Lons-le-Saunier F 25 Jc44
Lønstrup DK 70 Dc49
Lónya H 99 Kb49
Looe GB 14 Dc31
Loon op Zand NL 88 Ba38
Loon-Plage F 17 Gd30
Loos F 20 Ha31
Loosdorf A 97 Fd51
Loosdrecht NL 82 Ba36
Lopar HR 103 Fc62
Lopatino RUS 137 Fd11
Lopcombe Corner GB 15 Ed29
Loppersum NL 82 Ca33
Loppi FIN 68 Ka38
Łopuszna PL 92 Ja46
Loqueffret F 22 Dd38
Lora del Río E 43 Cb73
Loranca de Tajuña E 38 Dd64
Lorbé E 30 Ba54
Lorca E 45 Ec73
Lorch D 88 Ca44
Lorch D 95 Da48
Lorcha E 45 Fc70
Lordosa P 36 Ba62
Lorentzer F 94 Bd47
Loreo I 102 Ea61
Loreto I 109 Ed66
Lórév H 98 Hc54
Lorgues F 29 Kb54
Lorient F 22 Ea40
Lőrinci H 98 Ja52
Loriol-sur-Drôme F 28 Jb50
Lormaison F 20 Gd35
Loro Ciuffenna I 108 Dd66
Lörrach D 94 Bd52
Lorsch D 89 Cc45
Lorton GB 12 Eb17
Lorup D 83 Cb34
l'Orxa E 45 Fc70
Lörzweiler D 89 Cb44
Los S 66 Fd35
Los Alcázares E 45 Fa73
Los Algarbes E 43 Cc73
Los Ausines E 32 Dc58
Los Barrios E 43 Ca78
Los Barrios de Luna E 31 Cb56
Los Bayos E 31 Cb56
Los Belmontes E 44 Eb71
Los Blázquez E 43 Cb70
Los Caños E 43 Bd77
Los Castaños E 44 Eb75
Los Cerezos E 39 Fa66
Los Corrales de Buelna E 32 Db55
Los Cortijos de Arriba E 38 Db68
Loscos E 39 Fa62
Los Dolores E 45 Fa73
Los Escoriales E 44 Db71
Løsetdalen N 65 Ec36
Los Gallardos E 45 Ec75
Los Guiraos E 44 Eb74
Losheim am See D 88 Bc45
Los Hinojoso E 38 Ea67
Łosice PL 87 Kb36
Losilla E 39 Fa66
Loskeran IRL 6 Ca25
Los Lobos E 45 Ec74
Los Molinos E 38 Db63
Los Montesinos E 45 Fb72
Los Navalmorales E 37 Cd66
Los Nietos E 45 Fb73
Los Palacios y Villafranca E 43 Ca74
l'Ospedale F 106 Cb72
Los Pozuelos de Calatrava E 38 Da69
Los Ruices E 39 Ed67
Lossa D 90 Ea40
Loßburg D 95 Cb49
Losser NL 82 Ca36
Losset IRL 4 Cb15
Lossiemouth GB 9 Eb07
Los Silos E 43 Bc72
Lostallo CH 101 Cc56
Lostwithiel GB 14 Dc31
Los Villares E 44 Db73
Los Yébenes E 38 Db67
Löt S 78 Gb51
Lote N 62 Cc34
Løten N 65 Eb38
Lothmore GB 9 Eb06
Lotlax FIN 59 Ja30
Lotošino RUS 137 Ed10
Lotte D 83 Cb36
Lottefors S 66 Ga36
Lottum NL 88 Bc39
Louans F 23 Ga42
Louargat F 22 Ea38
Louchats F 26 Fb51
Loudéac F 22 Eb39
Loudun F 23 Fd43
Loué F 23 Fc40
Louejoki FIN 54 Jd19
Loughanavally IRL 4 Cb20
Loughborough GB 13 Fa24
Lougher IRL 6 Ba24
Loughglinn IRL 4 Bd19
Lough Gowna IRL 4 Cb19
Loughlinstown IRL 7 Cd22
Loughmoe IRL 6 Ca23
Loughrea IRL 6 Bd21
Loughton GB 16 Fd27
Lougratte F 27 Ga51
Louhans F 25 Jb44
Louhioja FIN 61 Ld29
Louisburgh IRL 4 Bb19
Loukunvaara FIN 61 Ma32
Loukusa FIN 55 Kd21
Loulé P 42 Ac74
Louny CZ 90 Fa43
Lourdes F 33 Fc56
Lourinhã P 36 Aa67
Lourmarin F 29 Jc53
Louro P 30 Ad60
Lousa P 31 Bc61
Lousada P 30 Ad60
Louth GB 13 Fd22
Louth IRL 5 Cd19
Loutrá GR 129 Cd88
Loutrá Edipsoú GR 129 Ca83
Loutrá Ipátis GR 129 Bc83
Loutráki GR 125 Bc76
Loutráki GR 129 Ca86
Loutra Kilínis GR 128 Ad86
Loutrá Thermopilón GR 129 Bd83
Loútsa GR 129 Cc87
Louvankylä FIN 67 Ja33
Louviers F 20 Gb36
Louvigné-du-Desert F 23 Fa38
Louvroil F 20 Hc32
Lovagny F 25 Jd46
Lövånger S 59 Hd26
Lovasberény H 98 Hc53
Lövberg S 52 Fc24
Lövberga S 58 Fd28
Loveč BG 121 Db70
Lovelhe P 30 Ad58
Lovere I 101 Da58
Loviisa FIN 68 Kd38
Lovik N 48 Fd12
Løvik N 56 Cd31
Lovikka S 50 Hd16
Lovisa FIN 68 Kd38
Lövnäs S 58 Ga25
Lövő H 97 Gc53
Lovoleto I 102 Dd62
Lovosice CZ 90 Fa43
Lovran HR 103 Fb60
Lövsjö S 58 Fd25
Łówcza PL 93 Kc43
Löwenberg D 84 Ed35
Löwenberger Land D 84 Ed35
Lower Beeding GB 16 Fc29
Lower Boddington GB 15 Fa26
Lower Cam GB 15 Ec27
Lower Diabaig GB 8 Db07
Lower Killeyan GB 10 Da14
Lowestoft GB 16 Gc25
Lowgill GB 13 Ec19
Łowicz PL 86 Hd37
Low Row GB 11 Ec16
Loxstedt D 83 Cd33
Loyers GB 8 Dd08
Löytänä FIN 60 Kb29
Löytökylä FIN 55 Kb23
Löytövaara FIN 55 Kd20
Löytty FIN 68 Kd37
Löyttymäki FIN 68 Kb37
Lozen B 88 Bb39
Łozina PL 91 Gc40
Łożnica PL 85 Fc32
Lozorno SK 97 Gc50
Lozova UA 137 Fa15
Lozoyuela E 38 Dc63
Luaces E 31 Bc55
Luanco (Gozon) E 31 Cc53
Luarca E 31 Ca54
Lubaczów PL 93 Kc43
Lubań PL 91 Fd41
Lübars D 84 Eb37
Lubartów PL 93 Kb39
Lubatowa PL 93 Ka45
Lübbecke D 83 Cd36
Lübben/Spreewald D 90 Fa38
Lübbenau/Spreewald D 90 Fa38
Lubcroy GB 8 Dd06
Lübeck D 84 Dd32
Lubián E 31 Bd58
Lubiatów PL 91 Fd38
Lubiatowo PL 85 Fc34
Lubicz PL 86 Hb34
Lubień PL 92 Ja45
Lubin PL 85 Fb32
Lubiń PL 86 Ha36
Lubin PL 91 Gb40
Łubin-Kościelny PL 87 Kb35
Lubiny PL 92 Ha38
Lubjaniki RUS 137 Fb10
Lublewo Gdańskie PL 86 Ha30
Lublin PL 93 Kb40
Lubliniec PL 92 Hb42
Łubniany PL 92 Ha42
Łubnice PL 93 Jc43
Lubno PL 85 Fc35
Lubno PL 85 Gb33
Lubny UA 137 Ed14
Lubochnia PL 92 Ja39
Lubomierz PL 91 Fd41
Luboń PL 85 Gc37
Luborzyca PL 92 Ja44
Lubostroń PL 86 Ha35
Lubosz PL 85 Ga36
L'ubotin SK 99 Jc47
Lubotyń PL 86 Hb36
Lubrza PL 85 Fd37
Lubrza PL 92 Gd43
Lubsko PL 91 Fc39
Lübtheen D 84 Dd33
Łuby PL 86 Ha32
Lübz D 84 Eb33
Lubzina PL 93 Jd44
Lucan IRL 7 Cd21
Lucca I 108 Da65
Lucena E 43 Cd74
Luc-en-Diois F 29 Jc50
Lučenec SK 98 Ja50
Luceni E 33 Fa60
Lucens CH 94 Bb55
Lucenza E 30 Bb58
Lucera I 110 Fd73
Lucéram F 29 Kd52
Lucey F 25 Jd46
Lucheux F 20 Gd32
Lüchow D 84 Dd35
Luchy F 20 Gd34
Lucień PL 86 Hd36
Lucito I 109 Fc72
Luc'k UA 136 Ea15
Lucka D 90 Eb41
Luckau D 90 Fa38
Luckenwalde D 90 Ed38
Lucker GB 11 Fa14
Lucksta S 66 Gb34
Lückstedt D 84 Ea35
Luco dei Marsi I 109 Ed71
Luçon F 23 Fa45
Ludborough GB 13 Fc21
Ludbreg HR 104 Gc57
Lüdelsen D 84 Dd35
Lüdenhausen D 83 Cd37
Lüdenscheid D 88 Ca40
Lüder D 83 Dc35
Lüderode, Weißenborn- D 89 Dc39
Ludford GB 13 Fc22
Ludgershall GB 15 Fb27
Ludgershall GB 15 Ed29
Ludgo S 72 Gc45
Ludiente E 39 Fc66
Lüdinghausen D 88 Ca38
Ludlow GB 14 Eb25
Ludwigsburg D 95 Cd48
Ludwigsfelde D 84 Ed37
Ludwigshafen D 95 Cc51
Ludwigshafen a. Rh. D 89 Cb46
Ludwigslust D 84 Ea33
Ludwigsstadt D 90 Dd43
Ludza LV 81 Ld51
Lüe F 26 Fa52
Luga RUS 136 Ea09
Lugagnano Val d'Arda I 101 Cd61
Lugano CH 101 Cc57
Lügde D 89 Da38
Lüge D 84 Ea35
Lugendorf A 97 Fd50
Luglon F 26 Fb53
Lugnvik S 58 Gc31
Lugo E 30 Bb55
Lugo I 102 Ea63
Lugoj RO 117 Ca61
Lugones E 31 Cb54
Lugton GB 10 Dd13
Luh RUS 137 Fb09
Luhanka FIN 68 Kc34
Luhans'k UA 137 Fb14
Lühmannsdorf D 84 Fa31
Luhovicy RUS 137 Fa10
Luhtapohja FIN 61 Ma30
Luib GB 8 Db08
Luigny F 24 Gb39
Luik = Liège B 21 Jb30
Luimneach IRL 6 Bd23
Luino I 101 Cb57
Luintra (Nogueira de Ramuín) E 30 Bb57
Luisenthal D 89 Dc42
Luka nad Jihlavou CZ 97 Ga47
Łukawiec PL 93 Kc43
Lukeswell IRL 7 Cb24
Lukojanov RUS 137 Fc10
Lukovnikovo RUS 136 Ec10
Łuków PL 87 Ka37
Łukowa PL 93 Jb42
Łukowo PL 85 Gc36
Lula I 107 Cb75
Luleå S 54 Hd22
Lüleburgaz TR 127 Ed76
Lullymore IRL 7 Cc21
Lumbarda HR 110 Gd68
Lumbrein CH 95 Cc55
Lumbres F 20 Gd31
Lumijoki FIN 55 Ka24
Lumio F 106 Ca69
Lummen B 88 Ba40
Lumparland FIN 67 Hc41
Lund N 57 Ec25
Lund S 77 Ed56
Lundamo N 57 Ea31
Lunde N 64 Dd38
Lunde S 58 Gc32
Lüneburg D 83 Dc34
Lunel F 28 Ja54
Lünen D 88 Ca38
Lunéville F 21 Jd37
Lungern CH 94 Ca55
Lungön S 58 Gd32
Luninec BY 136 Ea13
Lunino RUS 137 Fc10
Lünne D 82 Ca36
Lunning GB 9 Fb04
Lunow D 85 Fb35
Lunteren NL 82 Bb36
Lunzenau D 90 Ec41
Luode FIN 68 Jc34
Luoftjok N 47 Ka06
Luogosanto I 107 Cb74
Luohua FIN 60 Ka25
Luoma-aho FIN 60 Jc30
Luopa FIN 59 Jb32
Luopajärvi FIN 59 Jb32
Luopioinen FIN 68 Ka36
Luotakko FIN 60 Kb27
Luoto FIN 59 Jb28
Luotola FIN 69 Lb37
Łupawa PL 86 Gd30
Lupiac F 26 Fd54
Lupiñén E 33 Fb59
Luppa D 90 Ec40
Luppoperä FIN 55 Kc23
Lupșa RO 117 Cd59
Luque E 44 Da73
Luras I 107 Cb74
Lurcy-Lévis F 24 Hb44
Lure F 25 Ka40
Lurgan GB 5 Cd17
Lurøy N 52 Fa20
Lurs F 29 Jd52
Lusanger F 23 Ed41
Lusi FIN 68 Kc35
Lusignan F 23 Fd45
Lusina PL 91 Gb41
Lusk IRL 7 Cd21
Lus-la-Croix-Haute F 29 Jd50
Luso P 36 Ad63
Luson I 96 Ea55
Luspeholmen S 53 Gb24
Luss GB 10 Dd12
Lussac F 26 Fc50
Lussac-les-Châteaux F 23 Ga45
Lussac-les-Eglises F 24 Gb45
Lussan F 28 Ja52
Lussat F 24 Gd45
Lusta GB 8 Da07
Luszyn PL 86 Hd37
Lutago I 96 Ea55
Lütersheim D 89 Cd40
Luthenay-Uxeloup F 24 Hb43
Luthern-Bad CH 94 Ca54
Lutherstadt Eisleben D 90 Ea39
Lutherstadt Wittenberg D 90 Ec38
Lütjenburg D 84 Dd30
Lutocin PL 86 Hd34
Luton GB 16 Fc27
Lutówko PL 86 Gd33
Lutta FIN 67 Ja37
Lutter am Barenberge D 89 Dc38
Lutterworth GB 15 Fa25
Lüttich = Liège B 21 Jb30
Lutuhyne UA 137 Fb15
Lützelbach D 89 Cd45
Lützen D 90 Eb40
Lützow D 84 Dd32
Luujoki FIN 54 Jd21
Luumäki FIN 69 Lb36
Luupuvesi FIN 60 Kc27
Luusniemi FIN 68 Kd33
Luutalahti FIN 61 Ma31
Luvia FIN 67 Ja36
Luvos S 53 Gd19
Luxembourg L 21 Jd33
Luxemburg = Luxembourg L 21 Jd33
Luxeuil-les-Bains F 25 Jd40
Luynes F 23 Ga42
Luz P 42 Ba70
Luzaga E 38 Eb63
Luzaide-Valcarlos E 33 Ed56
Luže CZ 91 Ga45
Luzech F 27 Gb51
Luzern CH 94 Ca54
Lužice CZ 97 Gc48
Luzino PL 86 Ha29
Luz-Saint-Sauveur F 34 Fc57
Luzzi I 113 Gb79
L'viv UA 136 Dd15
Lwówek Śląski PL 91 Fd41
Lybster GB 9 Eb05
Lychen D 84 Ed34
Lycksaberg S 53 Gc24
Lycksele S 58 Gd26
Lydbury North GB 14 Eb25
Lydd GB 16 Ga30
Lydney GB 15 Ec27
Lygna N 65 Ea40
Lyly FIN 68 Ka34
Lylykylä FIN 55 Kd23
Lyman UA 137 Fa14
Lyme Regis GB 14 Eb30
Lyminge GB 16 Gb29
Lymington GB 15 Fa30
Lymm GB 13 Ec22
Lympne GB 16 Ga29
Lyndhurst GB 15 Ed30
Lyndlich GB 15 Ec30
Lyne GB 11 Eb14
Lyneham GB 15 Ed28
Lyness GB 9 Ec03
Lyngseidet N 49 Ha10
Lyngstad N 56 Da31
Lyngvoll N 62 Cd34
Lynmouth GB 14 Dd29
Lynton GB 14 Dd29
Lyon F 28 Jb47
Lyons-la-Forêt F 20 Gb35
Lypci UA 137 Fa14
Lypova Dolyna UA 137 Ed14
Łysaków PL 92 Ja42
Lysá nad Labem CZ 91 Fc44
Lysá pod Makytou SK 98 Hb47
Łysa Polana PL 98 Ja47
Łyse PL 87 Jc33
Lysekil S 71 Eb47
Lyski PL 92 Hb44
Lysnes N 49 Gc10
Lyss CH 94 Bc53
Lysthaugen N 57 Ec29
Lysvoll N 48 Ga14
Lysyčans'k UA 137 Fb14
Lysye Gory RUS 137 Fd12
Lytham GB 12 Eb20
Lytham Saint Anne's GB 12 Eb20
Lyttylä FIN 67 Ja35


## M


Maakeski FIN 68 Kb36
Maalahti FIN 59 Hd31
Maalismaa FIN 55 Ka23
Maam Cross IRL 4 Bb20
Maaninka FIN 60 Kd29
Maarheeze NL 88 Bb39
Maarianhamina FIN 67 Hc41
Maarianvaara FIN 61 Lb30
Maarn NL 82 Bb36
Maarssen NL 82 Ba36
Maas IRL 4 Ca16
Maasbracht NL 88 Bb40
Maasbree NL 88 Bc39
Maaseik B 88 Bb40
Maassluis NL 17 Hc26
Maastricht NL 88 Bb41
Määttälä FIN 60 Jd28
Määttälänvaara FIN 55 La19
Maavehmaa FIN 68 Kb37
Maavesi FIN 61 La32
Maavuskylä FIN 61 La32
Mablethorpe GB 13 Fd22
Macael E 44 Eb74
Maccagno I 101 Cb57
Macclesfield GB 13 Ed22
Macduff GB 9 Ed07
Mace IRL 4 Bc19
Macea RO 116 Bd58
Maceda E 30 Bb57
Macedo de Cavaleiros P 31 Bc60
Maceira E 30 Ad57
Macerata I 109 Ed67
Macerata Feltria I 109 Eb65
Mac Gregor's Corner GB 5 Da16
Machault F 21 Hd35
Mâche CH 100 Bc57
Machecoul F 23 Ed43
Machern D 90 Ec40
Machliny PL 85 Gb33
Machrihanish GB 10 Db14
Machynlleth GB 12 Dd24
Maciejów PL 92 Hb41
Mackan GB 4 Cb18
Macomer I 107 Ca76
Mâcon F 25 Jb45
Macroom IRL 6 Bc25
Macugnaga I 100 Bd57
Maczków PL 85 Fc37
Mád H 99 Jd50
Madara BG 122 Ec70
Maddaloni I 112 Fb74
Made NL 17 Hd27
Madekoski FIN 55 Ka24
Madeley GB 13 Ec23
Madesimo I 101 Cd56
Madiran F 26 Fc54
Madonna di Campiglio I 102 Dc57
Madonna di Senales I 95 Dc55
Madrid E 38 Dc64
Madridejos E 38 Dc67
Madrigal de las Altas Torres E 37 Cd62
Madrigalejo del Monte E 32 Dc59
Madrigueras E 39 Ec68
Madrona E 38 Db63
Madroñera E 37 Cb67
Madsøygrenda N 52 Ec24
Maël-Carhaix F 22 Ea38
Mælen N 57 Ea28
Maella E 34 Fd62
Maenclochog GB 14 Dc26
Maerdy GB 12 Ea23
Maesteg GB 14 Ea27
Mafra P 36 Aa68
Magallón E 33 Ed60
Maganey IRL 7 Cc23
Magaz E 32 Da59
Magdeburg D 84 Ea37
Magenta I 101 Cb59
Magerøystua N 46 Jb04
Magganári GR 133 Db91
Maghanlawaun IRL 6 Ba25
Maghera GB 5 Cd16
Magherabane IRL 5 Cc15
Magherafelt GB 5 Cd16
Magheralin GB 5 Da17
Magheramason GB 5 Cc16
Magheramorne GB 5 Da16
Maghull GB 12 Eb21
Magione I 108 Ea67
Maglaj BIH 105 Hb63
Maglehøj Strand DK 77 Ea59
Magliano de'Marsi I 109 Ed71
Magliano Sabina I 109 Eb70
Maglie I 113 Hc77
Magnac-Laval F 24 Gb45
Magnant F 25 Hd39
Magnières F 21 Ka37
Magnillseter N 65 Ea33
Magnuszew PL 93 Jc38
Magnuszowice PL 92 Gd42
Magny-en-Vexin F 20 Gc36
Magstadt D 95 Cc48
Maguelone F 28 Hd54
Maguiresbridge GB 4 Cb18
Magyarbóly H 105 Hc58
Magyarmecske H 105 Hb58
Magyarszentmiklós H 104 Gc56
Magyarszombatfa H 97 Gb55
Mahdalynivka UA 137 Fa15
Maherádo GR 128 Ac86
Mahide E 31 Ca59
Mahilëv BY 136 Eb12
Mahnala FIN 68 Jc35
Mahón E 41 Jb66
Mahon Bridge IRL 7 Cb25
Mahora E 39 Ec68
Mähring D 90 Eb45
Maia P 30 Ad61
Maiden Bradley GB 15 Ec29
Maidenhead GB 15 Fb28
Maiden Newton GB 14 Eb30
Maidstone GB 16 Fd29
Maienfeld CH 95 Cd54
Maiern I 96 Dd55
Maigh Chromtha IRL 6 Bc25
Maigh Cuilinn IRL 6 Bc21
Maigh Nuad IRL 7 Cd21
Maijanen FIN 54 Jc17
Maikammer D 89 Cb46
Mailand = Milano I 101 Cc59
Maillas F 26 Fc52
Mailly-le-Camp F 21 Hd37
Mailly-Maillet F 20 Gd33
Mainar E 39 Ed62
Mainbernheim D 89 Db45
Mainburg D 96 Ea49
Mainistir Fhear Maí IRL 6 Bd25
Mainistir Laoise IRL 7 Cb22
Mainistir na Búille IRL 4 Ca19
Mainistir na Corann IRL 6 Bd26
Mainleus D 90 Dd44
Mainsat F 24 Ha46
Mainstone GB 12 Eb24
Maintal D 89 Cc44
Mainvilliers F 24 Gb38
Mainz D 89 Cb44
Maiori I 112 Fb76
Mairago I 101 Cd60
Maisach D 96 Dd50
Maisey-le-Duc F 25 Ja40
Maison-Neuve F 28 Ja51
Maison Pieraggi F 106 Cb70
Maisons-Laffitte F 20 Gd36
Maissau A 97 Ga49
Máistir Gaoithe IRL 6 Ba25
Maitoinen FIN 68 Kb38
Maivala FIN 55 Lb19
Maizières-lès-Vic F 21 Ka36
Majadahonda E 38 Db64
Majak Oktjabrja RUS 137 Ga13
Majavaoja FIN 50 Jb14
Majdan RUS 137 Fd09
Majdan UA 136 Dd16
Majdan Królewski PL 93 Jd43
Majdan Nepryski PL 93 Kc42
Majdan Sieniawski PL 93 Kb43
Majdan Stary PL 93 Kb42
Majkop RUS 137 Fd17
Majorskij RUS 137 Fd15
Makarovo RUS 137 Fc12
Makarska HR 110 Gd67
Mäkiänen FIN 68 Jc38
Makijivka UA 137 Fb15
Mäkipää FIN 60 Kb29
Makkarkoski FIN 67 Jb38
Mäkkikylä FIN 68 Kb33
Makkola FIN 69 Lc33
Makkum NL 82 Bb33
Maklár H 99 Jb52
Makó H 105 Jc57
Mąkoszyce PL 92 Gd41
Maków PL 92 Ja38
Maków PL 92 Ja43
Maków Mazowiecki PL 87 Jb35
Makrakómi GR 129 Bc83
Mákri GR 126 Dd78
Makrigialós GR 133 Dc96
Makrinítsa GR 129 Ca82
Makriráhi GR 129 Ca82
Makrygialos GR 125 Ca78
Maksamaa FIN 59 Ja30
Maksatiha RUS 137 Ed09
Maksymilianowo PL 86 Ha34
Mala IRL 6 Bc25
Malå S 53 Gd24
Malá E 44 Db75
Malacky SK 97 Gc50
Maladzečna BY 136 Ea12
Málaga E 43 Cd76
Málaga del Fresno E 38 Dd63
Malagón E 38 Db68
Malahide IRL 7 Cd21
Málainn Bhig IRL 4 Bd16
Malaja Višera RUS 136 Eb09
Malakássi GR 128 Ba80
Malalbergo I 102 Dd62
Malanów PL 92 Hb38
Malarrif IS 2 Aa05
Malaryta BY 136 Dd14
Mäläskä FIN 60 Kb25
Małaszewicze PL 87 Kc37
Mala Vyska UA 137 Ed15
Mała Wieś PL 93 Jb38
Malax FIN 59 Hd31
Malbekkvatnet N 51 Kc08
Malbork PL 86 Hb31
Malbouzon F 28 Hb50
Malbuisson F 25 Ka43
Malchin D 84 Ec32
Malchow D 84 Ec33
Malčice SK 99 Ka49
Maldon GB 16 Ga27
Malechowo PL 85 Gb30
Máleme GR 132 Cb94
Malente D 84 Dd30
Malente D 84 Dd30
Malesherbes F 24 Gd38
Malesína GR 129 Ca84
Malešov CZ 91 Fd45
Malestroit F 22 Ec40
Malgersdorf D 96 Ec49
Malgovik S 58 Ga26
Malgrat de Mar E 35 Hb60
Malham GB 13 Ed19
Mália GR 133 Db96
Malicorne-sur-Sarthe F 23 Fc40
Malijai F 29 Ka52
Mali Lošinj HR 103 Fb63
Malin IRL 5 Cc15
Malin Beg IRL 4 Bd16

Málinec SK 98 Ja49
Malisensuo FIN 55 Kd22
Maliskylä FIN 60 Ka27
Mallaig GB 8 Db09
Mallemort F 29 Jc53
Mallén E 33 Ed60
Mallersdorf-Pfaffenberg D 96 Eb49
Mallow IRL 6 Bc25
Mallwyd GB 12 Ea24
Malm N 57 Eb28
Malmberget S 53 Hb19
Malmedy B 21 Jc31
Malmesbury GB 15 Ed28
Malmivaara S 53 Hb17
Malmköping S 72 Gb44
Malmö S 77 Ed56
Malnate I 101 Cb58
Malo I 102 Dd59
Maloarhangel'sk RUS 137 Fa12
Malogoszcz PL 92 Ja41
Maloja CH 101 Cd56
Malojaroslavec RUS 137 Ed11
Malo-les-Bains F 17 Gd29
Matomice PL 91 Fd39
Malowidz PL 87 Jb33
Måløy N 62 Ca34
Malpaas GB 12 Eb23
Malpaga I 101 Cd59
Malpartida de Plasencia E 37 Ca65
Malpica de Tajo E 38 Da66
Malsch D 95 Cb48
Malschwitz D 91 Fb41
Malsfeld D 89 Da41
Málšice CZ 96 Fb47
Maltat F 24 Hc44
Maltby GB 13 Fa21
Maltby le Marsh GB 13 Fd22
Malton GB 13 Fa19
Malveira P 36 Aa68
Malyn UA 136 Eb14
Malýševo RUS 137 Fb10
Mama RO 123 Fc67
Mambrilla de Castrejón E 32 Db60
Mamer L 21 Jc34
Mamers F 23 Fd38
Mametz F 23 Jd42
Mamirolle F 24 Jc42
Mammendorf D 96 Dd50
Mammola I 115 Gb83
Mamoiada I 107 Cb75
Mamonovo RUS 136 Dc12
Mamykovo RUS 137 Ga09
Mámyra N 57 Ea27
Mamuras AL 128 Ac71
Manamansalo FIN 60 Kc25
Manasterz PL 93 Kb44
Manchecourt F 24 Gd39
Manchester GB 13 Ec21
Manching D 96 Dd49
Manchita E 37 Bd66
Manciano I 108 Dc69
Manciet F 26 Fc53
Mandal N 70 Cc47
Mandanici I 115 Fd84
Mandas I 107 Ca78
Mandayona E 38 Ea63
Mandelieu-la Napoule F 29 Kc53
Mandello del Lario I 101 Cc58
Mandelsloh D 83 Da36
Mander NL 82 Bd09
Manderscheid D 88 Bc43
Mandeure F 25 Ka41
Mandra DK 76 Cd56
Mandra GR 129 Cc86
Mandráki GR 134 Eb92
Manduria I 113 Hb76
Mane F 34 Gb56
Manea GB 16 Fd25
Manerba del Garda I 102 Db59
Manerbio I 101 Da60
Maneset N 57 Ec27
Manevyci UA 136 Ea14
Mánfa H 105 Hb57
Manfredonia I 110 Ga72
Mangalia RO 123 Fc68
Manganeses de la Lampreana E 31 Cb60
Manganeses de la Polvorosa E 31 Cb59
Mangualde P 36 Ba63
Maniago I 103 Eb57
Manieczki PL 91 Gc36
Manilva E 41 Cc77
Manisa TR 131 Ed85
Manises E 39 Fb67
Manjärvträsk S 53 Hb23
Mank A 97 Fd51
Maňki PL 86 Ja32
Manlleu E 35 Ha59
Mannersdorf Leithagebirge A 97 Gc51
Mannheim D 89 Cc46
Manningtree GB 16 Ga26
Männistönpää FIN 54 Jb17
Manonville F 21 Jc36
Manorbier GB 14 Dc20
Manorhamilton IRL 4 Ca18
Manosque F 29 Jc53
Manresa E 35 Gd60
Mánsberg S 58 Ga27
Mansfeld D 90 Ea39
Mansfield GB 13 Fa22
Mansilla E 32 Ea59
Mansilla de la Mulas E 31 Cc57
Mansilla de las Mulas E 32 Dc58
Mansilla del Páramo E 31 Cb57
Mansle F 26 Fd47
Manso I 103 Bb58
Manteigas P 36 Bb63
Mantel D 90 Eb60
Mantes-la-Jolie F 20 Gc36
Mantes-la-Ville F 20 Gc36
Mantet F 35 Ha68
Mantiloperå FIN 68 Jd33
Mantova = Mantua I 102 Db60
Mäntsälä FIN 68 Ka38
Mänttä FIN 68 Ka33
Mantua = Mantova I 102 Db60
Mäntyharju FIN 68 Kd35
Mäntylä FIN 60 Kc30
Mäntyjärvi FIN 55 Kd21
Mäntyjärvi FIN 54 Jd19
Mäntyluoto FIN 67 Ja35
Mäntyvaara FIN 54 Jd19
Mäntyvaara FIN 61 Lc30
Manuden GB 16 Fd27
Manuel E 39 Fb69
Manzanares E 38 Dc69
Manzanares el Real E 38 Db63
Manzanedo E 32 Dc58
Manzano I 103 Ed58
Manzat F 28 Hb46
Maó E 45 Jd66
Maothail IRL 4 Cb19
Maqueda E 38 Db65
Mar P 30 Ac59
Mara I 107 Bd76
Marac F 25 Jd38
Maracena E 44 Db75
Marainviller F 21 Ka37
Maranchón E 38 Ea62
Maraneve I 115 Fc85
Marano di Napoli I 112 Fa75

Marano Lagunare I 103 Ec59
Marans F 23 Fa45
Maranville F 25 Ja39
Maratea I 112 Ga78
Marathókambos GR 130 Eb88
Marathónas GR 129 Cc86
Marazion GB 14 Da32
Marbach D 95 Cd48
Marbella E 43 Cc77
Marburg D 89 Cc41
Marby S 57 Fb31
Marcali H 104 Gd56
Marcaria I 102 Db60
Marceddí I 107 Bd78
Marcelová SK 98 Hb52
March D 94 Ca50
March GB 16 Fd24
Marchegg A 97 Gc50
Marcheprime F 26 Fb50
Marchiennes F 20 Hb31
Marchwiel GB 12 Eb23
Marciac F 26 Fd54
Marcianise I 112 Fb74
Marcigny F 25 Hd45
Marcillac-en-Combraille F 24 Ha46
Marcilliy-sur-Eure F 20 Gb37
Marcilly-en-Villette F 24 Gd40
Marcilly-le-Hayer F 24 Hc38
Marcilly-sur-Seine F 20 Hc37
Marcinkowice PL 93 Jb45
Marcinowice PL 91 Gb42
Marciszów PL 91 Ga42
Marck F 16 Gc30
Marckolsheim F 94 Bd50
Marco de Canaveses P 30 Ba61
Marden GB 16 Fd29
Mårdsele S 59 Ha26
Mårdsjö S 58 Ga27
Mårdsjö S 57 Fb30
Marebbe I 102 Ea56
Marennes F 26 Fa47
Marentes E 31 Bd55
Maresfield GB 16 Fd30
Mareuil-sur-Arnon F 24 Gd43
Mareuil-sur-Ourcq F 20 Hb36
Mar'evka RUS 137 Ga10
Mareuw RUS 136 Eb31
Margam GB 14 Dd27
Margaritovo RUS 137 Fc16
Margate GB 16 Gb28
Margaux F 26 Fb49
Margecany SK 99 Jc48
Margherita di Savoia I 110 Gb73
Margina RO 117 Cb60
Margon F 23 Ga38
Margone I 100 Bc60
Margraten NL 88 Bb41
Marhanec' UA 137 Fa16
María E 44 Eb73
Maria Elend A 103 Fa56
Marialva P 37 Bc62
Mariánské Lázné CZ 90 Ec45
Maria Saal A 103 Fb56
Maria Wörth A 103 Fb56
Mariazell A 97 Fd52
Maribo DK 77 Ea59
Maribor SLO 104 Ga56
Marieby S 58 Fc31
Mariefred F 72 Gc44
Mariehamn FIN 67 Hd41
Marielund S 53 Gd22
Marienberg D 90 Ec43
Mariënberg NL 82 Bd09
Marienfließ D 84 Eb33
Marienhagen D 83 Da37
Marienheide D 88 Ca40
Marienmünster D 89 Da38
Mariestad S 71 Fa46
Marifjøra N 62 Cc36
Marigenta E 43 Bc73
Marigliano I 112 Fb75
Marignac F 26 Fb48
Marignane F 29 Jc54
Marigny-en-Orxois F 20 Hb36
Marin E 30 Ad57
Marina HR 110 Gb66
Marina di Andora I 108 Bd64
Marina di Ascea I 112 Fd78
Marina di Bibbona I 108 Da67
Marina di Camerota I 112 Fd78
Marina di Caronia I 115 Fb84
Marina di Carrara I 101 Cd64
Marina di Caulonia I 115 Gc83
Marina di Chieti I 110 Fd71
Marina di Gioiosa Jonica I 115 Gc83
Marina di Leuca I 113 Hc78
Marina du la Imposti I 107 Cc54
Marina di Massa I 101 Da64
Marina di Minturno I 112 Fd74
Marina di Modica I 115 Fc88
Marina di Montenero I 109 Fc71
Marina di Pescia Romana I 108 Dc70
Marina di Pietrasanta I 101 Da64
Marina di Pisciotta I 112 Fd77
Marina di Ragusa I 115 Fc88
Marina di Ravenna I 102 Ea63
Marina di Sibari I 113 Gc77
Marina di Sorso I 107 Bd74
Marina di Torre Grande I 107 Bd77
Marineda E 43 Cc74
Marina Palmense I 109 Fa67
Marinella I 114 Eb85
Marines E 39 Fb67
Marines F 20 Gc36
Marineo I 114 Ec85
Marinha das Ondas P 36 Ac64
Marinha Grande P 36 Ab65
Marini I 113 Hc78
Marínkainen FIN 60 Jc27
Marinka RUS 137 Fb16
Mariupol' UA 137 Fb16
Marjaliza E 38 Db67
Marjokylä FIN 55 Lc23
Marjoperä FIN 60 Jd30
Marka E 31 Cc57
Marka N 52 Fd33
Mark Cross GB 16 Fd29
Markdorf D 95 Cd52

Markelo NL 82 Bd36
Market Bosworth GB 13 Fa24
Market Deeping GB 16 Fc24
Market Drayton GB 13 Ec23
Market Harborough GB 15 Fb25
Markethill GB 5 Cd18
Market Rasen GB 13 Fc22
Market Weighton GB 13 Fb20
Markfield GB 13 Fa24
Markgröningen D 95 Cd48
Marki PL 87 Jb36
Markitta S 54 Hc17
Markivka UA 137 Fb14
Markkleeberg D 90 Eb40
Marklkofen D 96 Eb49
Marklohe D 83 Da36
Marknesse NL 82 Bc34
Markneukirchen D 90 Eb43
Markop N 46 Ja06
Markowa PL 93 Ka44
Markranstädt D 90 Ea40
Markt Einersheim D 89 Dd45
Marktheidenfeld D 89 Da45
Markt Indersdorf D 96 Dd50
Marktl D 96 Ed51
Marktleugast D 90 Ea44
Marktleuthen D 90 Eb44
Marktoberdorf D 95 Db52
Marktoffingen D 95 Db48
Markt Piesting A 97 Gb52
Marktredwitz D 90 Eb45
Markt Rettenbach D 95 Db51
Marktrodach D 90 Ea44
Markt Schwaben D 96 Ea51
Marktsteft D 89 Dd45
Markušica HR 110 Gb66
Mark D 88 Ca38
Marlborough GB 15 Ed28
Marloes GB 14 Db27
Marlow F 24 Ha43
Marlow GB 15 Fb28
Marly F 21 Jd35
Marly-Gomont F 20 Hc33
Marmagne F 25 Ja43
Marmande F 26 Fd52
Marmári GR 129 Cd86
Marmári GR 134 Ba91
Marmaris TR 131 Ec87
Marmaw S 66 Gb37
Marmelete P 42 Ab73
Marmolejo E 44 Da72
Marmoutier F 21 Kb37
Marnach L 21 Jc34
Marnay F 24 Jb41
Marnheim D 89 Cb45
Maroúsi GR 129 Ec67
Maróstica I 102 Dd59
Marotta I 109 Ed65
Marple GB 13 Ec21
Marquartstein D 96 Eb52
Marquion F 20 Ha32
Marradi I 102 Dd64
Marsac-en-Livradois F 28 Hc46
Marsala I 114 Ea85
Marsberg D 89 Cd39
Marsciano I 108 Ea68
Marsden GB 13 Ec21
Marseillan-Plage F 35 Hc55
Marseille F 29 Jc55
Marseille-en-Beauvaisis F 20 Gc34
Marsh GB 14 Eb29
Marshfield GB 15 Ec28
Marsh Gibbon GB 15 Fb27
Marsia I 109 Ed68
Marsico Nuovo I 112 Ga76
Marsiliana I 108 Dc69
Marsjärv S 54 Hd19
Marske-by-the-Sea GB 13 Fb18
Mars-la-Tour F 21 Jc36
Marson F 21 Hd36
Marssac-sur-Tarn F 27 Gd53
Marssum NL 82 Bc33
Märsta S 73 Gd42
Marstal DK 77 Dd58
Marston GB 13 Fb22
Marston Magna GB 15 Ec30
Marstrand S 71 Eb44
Martano I 113 Hc77
Martelange B 21 Jb33
Martel F 27 Gc50
Martfeld D 83 Da37
Martfu H 106 Jb53
Martham GB 16 Gb24
Marthon F 26 Fd48
Martigné-Briand F 23 Fc42
Martigné-Ferchaud F 23 Fa40
Martigny CH 100 Bc56
Martigny-le-Comte F 25 Ja44
Martin SK 98 Hc47
Martín E 34 Gc58
Martina Franca I 113 Ha75
Martín del Río E 34 Fa63
Martín de Yeltes E 37 Ca63
Martin Drove End GB 15 Ed30
Martinniemi FIN 54 Jd23
Martinsicuro I 109 Fa68
Martinstown GB 5 Da16
Martos E 44 Da73
Martti FIN 55 Kd20
Marttila FIN 67 Jc39
Maruggio I 113 Hb76
Marum NL 82 Bd33
Maruševec HR 104 Gb56
Maruszów PL 93 Jd40
Marvejols F 28 Hc51
Marville F 21 Jb35
Marwald PL 86 Hd33
Marxzell D 95 Cb48
Mary GB 9 Dd06
Marybank GB 8 Dd07
Maryfield GB 9 Fb05
Marykirk GB 9 Ec07
Marypowy PL 86 Hb30
Maryport GB 9 Dd08
Mary Tavy GB 14 Dc31
Marzahna D 90 Eb37
Marzamemi I 115 Fd88
Marzán E 31 Cb56
Marzell D 94 Bd51
Marzocca I 109 Ed65
Marzó I 102 Db57
Masboquera E 44 Db73
Mas de las Matas E 34 Fc63
Masegoso de Tajuña E 38 Ea63

Masevaux F 94 Bc31
Mas-Grenier F 27 Gb53
Masham GB 13 Fa19
Mași Mäon N 50 Ja10
Maskjok N 47 Ka06
Masku FIN 67 Jb39
Maslacq F 33 Fb55
Maso Corto I 95 Db56
Masquefa E 35 Gd61
Massa I 101 Da64
Massa Fiscaglia I 102 Ea62
Massafra I 113 Gd76
Massagette F 27 Ha47
Massais F 23 Fc43
Massamagrell E 39 Fc67
Massa Marittima I 108 Db67
Massarosa I 108 Da65
Massbach D 89 Db44
Masseret F 27 Gc48
Masseria Airill I 110 Fd73
Masseria Anzani I 110 Ga73
Masseria Monaco Cappelli I 110 Ga72
Masseria Motta Panetteria I 110 Fd72
Masseria Stimpato I 115 Fc86
Massford GB 5 Da18
Massiac F 28 Hb48
Massignac F 23 Ga47
Massing D 96 Eb50
Mästäri GR 134 Eb91
Masty BY 136 Dd13
Masua I 107 Bd79
Måsvik N 49 Gd08
Maszewo PL 85 Fc33
Mata N 36 Ac66
Matabuena E 38 Dc62
Mata de Alcántara E 37 Bd65
Magara GR 129 Cc86
Måtala GR 133 Cd90
Matalascañas E 43 Bc75
Matamala de Almazán E 32 Ea61
Matamorosa E 32 Db56
Matara FIN 61 Ld28
Matarsey F 23 Fd37
Mataró E 35 Ha61
Matching Green GB 16 Fd27
Matelica I 109 Ec67
Matera I 113 Gc75
Mátészalka H 99 Kb51
Matfors S 66 Gb33
Matha F 26 Fc47
Mathieu F 19 Fc35
Matignon F 22 Ec38
Matilla de los Caños del Río E 37 Cb63
Matko HR 110 Gb66
Matlock GB 13 Fa22
Matour F 25 Ja45
Matrafüred H 98 Ja52
Matrei I A 96 Eb54
Matrei am Brenner A 96 Dd54
Matrei in Osttirol A 96 Eb55
Matsigny S 52 Fd23
Mattersburg A 97 Gb52
Mattilanmäki FIN 55 Kc17
Mattisudden S 53 Ha19
Mattmar S 57 Fb31
Måttsund S 54 Hd22
Matveev Kurgan RUS 137 Fc15
Mátyásdomb H 98 Hb55
Maubeuge F 20 Hc32
Mauborget CH 94 Bb54
Mauchline GB 10 Dd14
Mauerkirchen A 96 Ed51
Mauern D 96 Dd49
Maughold GB 10 Dc18
Mauguio F 28 Hd54
Maule F 20 Gc37
Mauléon F 23 Fb43
Mauléon-d'Armagnac F 26 Fc53
Mauléon-Licharre F 33 Fa55
Maumusson F 23 Fa41
Maunola FIN 69 Lb35
Maupertuir F 23 Ga46
Maura N 65 Ea40
Mauron F 23 Eb39
Maurs F 27 Gd50
Maury F 35 Ha57
Maussane-les-Alpilles F 29 Jb53
Mautern A 97 Fd51
Mauterndorf A 96 Fa54
Mautern in Steiermark A 103 Fc55
Mauvezin F 27 Gd54
Mauvezin F 34 Fd56
Mauzé-sur-le-Mignon F 23 Fb46
Mavagissey GB 14 Db32
Mavrommáti GR 128 Bd88
Mavrovoúni GR 132 Bc90
Maxey-sur-Meuse F 25 Jc38
Maxhütte-Haidhof D 96 Ea48
Maxieira P 36 Ad66
Maxmo FIN 59 Ja30
Mayalde E 31 Cb61
Maybole GB 10 Dc15
May-en-Multien F 20 Ha36
Mayet F 23 Ga40
Mayerling A 97 Gb51
Mayfield GB 13 Ec23
Mayfield GB 16 Fd30
Maynooth IRL 7 Cd21
Mayobridge GB 5 Da18
Mayorga E 31 Cc58
Mayres F 28 Hd50
Mayrhofen A 96 Dd54
Mäyry FIN 60 Jc31
Mazagón E 42 Ba74
Mazamet F 27 Gd54
Mazara del Vallo I 114 Ea85
Mazarambroz E 38 Db67
Mazarete E 38 Ea63
Mazaricos E 30 Ac55
Mazarrón E 45 Ed74
Maześów E 21 Hd35
Mazè I 100 Bd59
Mazéres F 27 Gc55
Mazéres-lès-Metz F 21 Jd35

Medbourne GB 13 Fb24
Medby N 48 Gb11
Meddo NL 82 Bd37
Meddon GB 14 Dc30
Mede I 101 Cb60
Medebach D 89 Cc40
Medelás S 53 Hb19
Medelim P 36 Bb65
Medellín E 37 Ca68
Medesano I 101 Da62
Medevi S 72 Fc45
Medgidia RO 123 Fc67
Medgyesegyháza H 116 Bc58
Medias RO 117 Db60
Médière F 25 Ka41
Medinaceli E 38 Ea62
Medina del Campo E 31 Cd61
Medina de Pomar E 32 Dc56
Medina de Rioseco E 31 Cd59
Medinasidonia E 43 Bd77
Medininkai LT 81 Lb58
Medle S 59 Ha25
Medovdær S 72 Ec39
Medstugan S 57 Ed29
Medvenka RUS 137 Fa13
Medynia Głogowska PL 93 Ka43
Medzilaborce SK 93 Ka46
Meeder D 89 Dc43
Meerane D 90 Eb41
Meerbusch D 88 Bd39
Meerhout B 88 Ba39
Meerkerk NL 82 Ba37
Meerssburg D 95 Cd52
Meeth GB 14 Dd30
Meeuwen-Gruitrode B 88 Ba40
Mefjordvær N 48 Gb10
Megálo Horio GR 134 Ec92
Megálo Livádi GR 133 Cd89
Megara GR 129 Cc86
Mégara E 52 Fd17
Méga Spileo GR 129 Bd86
Megeces E 32 Da61
Megève F 25 Jd46
Mégve F 25 Gb51
Meggenhofen A 96 Fa51
Megrunn N 64 Dc36
Mehlis, Zella– D 89 Dc42
Mehren D 88 Bd43
Mehternäpera H 99 Cd42
Mehün-sur-Yèvre F 24 Gd42
Meidrim GB 14 Dc26
Meifod GB 12 Eb23
Meigle GB 9 Ec07
Meilán E 31 Bc54
Meilen CH 95 Cb53
Meillant F 24 Ha44
Meina I 100 Cb58
Meine D 83 Dc36
Meinersen D 83 Dc36
Meinerzhagen D 88 Ca40
Meijen D 90 Fa42
Meisenheim D 89 Ca45
Meisingset N 56 Db31
Meissen D 90 Ed41
Meißner D 89 Da41
Meitingen D 95 Dc49
Meixide P 30 Bb58
Mejorada E 37 Cd65
Meka PL 92 Hb39
Mel I 102 Ea58
Melalahti FIN 61 La30
Meland N 62 Ca38
Melbourn GB 16 Fd26
Melbourne GB 13 Fa23
Melbu N 48 Fc13
Melč CZ 98 Ha46
Melchsee Frutt CH 94 Ca55
Meldal N 56 Da31
Meldola I 103 Dd64
Meldorf D 83 Da31
Melegnano I 101 Cc59
Melen N 57 Ec29
Melendugno I 113 Hc77
Melenki RUS 137 Fb10
Meleski PL 92 Hb40
Meleti E 38 Dc66
Melfi I 112 Gb74
Melfjorbotn N 52 Fd20
Melgaço P 30 Ad58
Melgar de Arriba E 31 Cc58
Melgar de Fernamental E 32 Db58
Melgar de Yuso E 32 Db58
Melhus N 57 Ea30
Melia E 44 Fb64
Melide CH 101 Cc57
Melide E 30 Ba55
Melilla E 43 Cc78
Mélisey F 25 Ka40
Melissa I 113 Gd80
Melito di Porto Salvo I 115 Gd84
Melk A 97 Fd51
Melkarlia N 52 Fd19
Melkkola FIN 69 Lb36
Melksham GB 15 Ec28
Mellakoski FIN 54 Jc19
Mellansel S 58 Gd30
Mellansjö S 59 Ha28
Mellanzs S 57 Ec29
Mellau A 95 Da53
Melle D 83 Cc37
Melle F 23 Fc46
Mellendorf D 83 Da36
Mellerud S 71 Ec44
Mellieha M 116 Cc79
Mellin D 83 Dc35
Mellionnec F 22 Ea38
Mellmen S 52 Fd17
Mellösa S 73 Ga44
Melnice RUS 137 Fb10
Mělník CZ 90 Fc44
Mel'nikovo RUS 137 Fb11
Melón E 30 Ba58
Melrose GB 11 Ec14
Mels CH 95 Cd54
Melsträsk S 53 Hb24
Melsungen D 89 Da40
Melswik N 50 Ja06
Meltaus FIN 54 Jd19
Meltham GB 13 Ed21
Melton Mowbray GB 13 Fb24
Meltosjärvi FIN 54 Jc19
Melun F 20 Ha38
Melvaig GB 8 Db06
Melvich GB 9 Ea03
Melýkút H 105 Ja77
Melzo I 101 Cc59
Memaliaj AL 128 Ac72
Membrio E 37 Bc66
Memer F 27 Gd52
Memmelsdorf D 89 Dc45
Memmingen D 95 Db51
Mena UA 136 Ec13
Menaggio I 101 Cc57
Menai Bridge GB 12 Dc22
Menaldum NL 82 Bc33
Menârguens E 34 Ga60
Menasalbas E 38 Da67
Menat F 24 Ha46
Mende F 28 Hc51
Menden D 89 Cb39
Mendenítsa GR 129 Cc84
Mendeš RUS 137 Fb10
Mendez TR 131 Ec86

Mendig D 88 Bd43
Mendola E 114 Eb84
Meneou GR 128 Bd91
Menen B 17 Ha30
Menči I 101 Cb60
Menetou-Salon F 24 Ha42
Ménétréol-sur-Sauldre F 24 Gd41
Menfi I 114 Eb85
Menga I 109 Fb67
Mengara I 109 Ea68
Mengen D 95 Cd51
Mengerskirchen D 89 Cb42
Mengíbar E 44 Db72
Mengkofen D 96 Eb49
Menidi GR 128 Ad82
Ménigoute F 23 Fc45
Menil-la-Tour F 21 Jc36
Menisjavi FIN 50 Jd11
Menkijärvi FIN 60 Jc30
Mennetou-sur-Cher F 24 Gd41
Mensignac F 26 Fd49
Menslage D 82 Cb35
Menston GB 13 Fa20
Mentana I 109 Bd71
Menton F 29 Kd53
Méntrida E 38 Da65
Meopham GB 16 Fd28
Mepal GB 16 Fd25
Meppel NL 82 Bc35
Meppen D 82 Ca35
Mequinenza E 34 Fd61
Mera I 101 Cc56
Meråker N 57 Ec30
Meran = Merano I 95 Dc55
Merano I 95 Dc55
Merás E 31 Ca54
Merasjärvi S 49 Hc16
Mercadillo E 32 Dc55
Mercatale I 108 Ea67
Mercatello sul Metauro I 109 Ea67
Mercatino Conca I 109 Ea66
Mercato San Severino I 112 Fc75
Mercues F 27 Gb51
Merdrignac F 22 Ec39
Mere GB 15 Ec29
Merefa UA 137 Fa14
Merelbeke B 17 Ha30
Méreville F 20 Gd38
Mérey-sous-Montrond F 24 Jb42
Mergozzo I 100 Cb57
Méribel F 25 Jd47
Méric F 26 Fc47
Mérida E 37 Ca69
Mérignac F 26 Fb50
Mérignac F 26 Fd47
Merijärvi FIN 60 Jc26
Merikarvia FIN 67 Ja35
Merrilänen FIN 60 Jd30
Merimasku FIN 67 Ja39
Mering D 95 Dc50
Meri-Pori FIN 67 Ja35
Mérk H 99 Kb51
Merklín CZ 90 Ed46
Merkevenez F 22 Ea40
Merне H 100 Bd56
Merone I 101 Cc58
Mersch L 21 Jc34
Mers-les-Bains F 20 Gb33
Merscheid D 88 Bd39
Merseburg D 90 Ea40
Mersevat H 98 Ha54
Mersin TR 128 Bd91
Mértola P 42 Ad72
Méru F 20 Gd35
Merville F 20 Ha31
Merzen D 82 Cb36
Merzenich D 88 Bc41
Merzig (Saar) D 88 Bc45
Mesagne I 113 Hb76
Mesão Frio P 30 Ba61
Meschede D 89 Cc40
Meschers-sur-Gironde F 26 Fa48
Meselefors S 58 Gb26
Mesenikólas GR 128 Bb81
Meshaw GB 14 Dd29
Mesic SRB 120 Bc69
Mesinge DK 77 Dd57
Mesklá GR 132 Cb95
Meslan F 22 Ea39
Meslay-du-Maine F 23 Fb40
Meslon F 24 Ha44
Mesnali N 65 Ea40
Mesnil-Saint-Père F 25 Jc38
Mesocco CH 101 Cc56
Mesola I 102 Ea62
Mesoraca I 113 Gd81
Mešovo RUS 137 Ed11
Mespotam GR 128 Ac82
Mesquer F 22 Ec42
Messac F 23 Ed40
Messanges F 33 Fa54
Messdorf D 83 Dc35
Messei F 23 Fb37
Messejana P 42 Ac72
Messina I 115 Ga84
Messingham GB 13 Fb21
Messini GR 128 Bb88
Messingen D 82 Ca36
Messlingen S 57 Fc32
Mesta I 112 Fb75
Mestas E 31 Ca55
Mestas de Con E 31 Cc55
Město Albrechtice CZ 92 Ha44
Město Libavá CZ 92 Gd45
Město Touškov CZ 90 Ed45
Mestre I 102 Ea60
Mesztegnyő H 104 Gd57
Metajna HR 110 Fd67
Metamórfosi GR 128 Bd84
Metelen D 82 Ca37
Methana GR 129 Cc87
Metheringham GB 13 Fc22
Methlick GB 9 Ed08
Methóni GR 128 Bb88
Methven GB 11 Eb11
Methwold GB 16 Fd24
Metlika SLO 104 Ga58
Metnitz A 96 Fb55
Metsäkansa FIN 68 Jd36
Metsäkylä FIN 69 La37
Metslawier NL 82 Bc32
Metsovo GR 128 Bb82
Mettendorf D 88 Bc44
Mettevoll N 49 Hb08
Mettingen D 82 Cb36
Mettlach D 88 Bc45
Mettmann D 88 Bd39
Mettmenstetten CH 95 Cb53
Metz F 21 Jd35
Metzervisse F 21 Jd35
Metzingen D 95 Cd49
Meucon F 22 Eb41
Meulan F 20 Gc36
Meung-sur-Loire F 24 Gc40
Meuselwitz D 90 Eb41
Mevagissey GB 14 Db32
Mévouillon F 29 Jc51
Mexborough GB 13 Fa21
Mey GB 9 Eb04

Meyrueis F 28 Hc52
Meysey Hampton GB 15 Ed27
Meyzieu F 28 Jb47
Mézapos GR 132 Bb91
Mèze F 28 Hc55
Mezek BG 126 Ea75
Mézel F 29 Jd45
Mézica SLO 103 Fb57
Mézières-en-Brenne F 24 Gb41
Mézín F 26 Fd53
Mézilhac F 28 Ja51
Mézières F 24 Hd40
Mézilles F 24 Hb40
Mezőberény H 99 Jd55
Mezőcsát H 99 Jd51
Mezőfalva H 98 Hc55
Mezőhegyes H 100 Jd56
Mezőkeresztes H 99 Jd51
Mezőkovácsháza H 116 Bc58
Mezőkövesd H 99 Jd51
Mezőörs H 98 Ha53
Mézos F 26 Fa52
Mezőtúr H 100 Jb54
Mezzana I 101 Db57
Mezzano I 102 Ea57
Mezzolombardo I 102 Dc57
Mgarr M 115 Bd80
Miajadas E 37 Ca68
Miały PL 85 Gb35
Miasteczko Krajeńskie PL 85 Gc34
Miasteczko Śląskie PL 92 Hc43
Miastko PL 85 Gc31
Miavaig GB 8 Cd05
Michaelchurch Escley GB 14 Eb26
Michalín PL 86 Hb35
Michalová SK 99 Ja48
Michałów PL 93 Jd43
Michałowo PL 87 Kc33
Michelau D 89 Dc45
Michelbach D 95 Da45
Michelbach an der Bilz D 95 Da47
Micheldorf in Oberösterreich A 97 Fd52
Michelfeld D 89 Cd45
Michelstadt D 89 Cd45
Michendorf D 89 Ed37
Michery F 24 Hb38
Michorzew PL 91 Ga37
Michów PL 92 Jc40
Mickelsträsk S 59 Hb27
Mickhausen D 95 Dc50
Mickleton GB 11 Ec17
Mickleton GB 15 Ec27
Micula RO 99 Kb51
Miculjci PL 92 Hd41
Mid Ardlaw GB 9 Ed07
Mid Yell GB 9 Fb03
Miechów PL 93 Ja43
Miechucino PL 85 Gd30
Miechowice Bielskie PL 91 Ga39
Mieciszów PL 91 Gb39
Miedes E 34 Fa62
Miedes de Atienza E 38 Ea62
Międzybrodzie Bialskie PL 92 Hc45
Miedzychowo PL 85 Gb35
Miedzychod PL 85 Gb35
Międzygórze PL 91 Gc44
Miedzyleś PL 91 Gc42
Międzyrzec Podlaski PL 87 Kc37
Międzyrzecz PL 85 Ga36
Międzyzdroje PL 85 Fb33
Miehikkälä FIN 69 Lb37
Miejska Górka PL 91 Gc40
Miejkowo PL 85 Fc33
Miękinia PL 91 Gc41
Mielag PL 85 Gc33
Mielan F 34 Fd55
Mielcin PL 87 Kb36
Mielec PL 93 Jd43
Mielenko Drawskie PL 85 Ga33
Mieleszyn PL 86 Gd36
Mielno PL 85 Ga31
Mielno PL 86 Hb30
Mielżyn PL 86 Hb36
Miemala FIN 68 Jd36
Mieming A 95 Dc53
Mieraslompolo FIN 50 Ka08
Miercurea Sibiului RO 117 Da61
Mieres E 31 Cb55
Mierasluobbal FIN 50 Ka08
Mierzeszyn PL 86 Hb32
Miesbach D 96 Dd52
Mieścisko PL 86 Gd35
Mieste D 83 Dc36
Mieszków PL 91 Gc38
Mieszkowice PL 84 Fc35
Mietków PL 91 Gb42
Mifol AL 128 Ab72
Migennes F 24 Hc40
Migné F 24 Gb44
Miglionico I 113 Gc76
Mignano Monte Lungo I 109 Fa73
Mihăilești RO 117 Db60
Mihail Kogălniceanu RO 123 Fc67
Mihajlov RUS 137 Fa11
Mihajlovgrad BG 125 Cc75
Mihalgazi TR 131 Ec86
Mihalyfa H 98 Ha54
Miháld H 104 Gd57
Mihla D 89 Dc41
Mijares E 38 Da65
Mijas E 43 Cd77
Mijdrecht NL 82 Ba36
Mijoska MNE 111 Ja69
Mike H 104 Gd57
Mikkeli FIN 68 Kd34
Mikkelvik N 48 Gd08
Mikleuš HR 110 Gc60
Miklavž na Dravskem polju SLO 104 Ga56
Mikniūnai LT 81 Kd54
Mikolaiv UA 137 Fa16
Mikoleiv UA 136 Eb15
Mikołajki PL 87 Jc32
Mikołajki Pomorskie PL 86 Hb31
Mikołów PL 92 Hc44
Mikre BG 125 Cd76
Mikró Dério GR 130 Ea84
Mikrókambos GR 128 Bc84
Mikstat PL 92 Ha40
Mikulčice CZ 98 Gd48
Mikulintsy UA 136 Ea15
Mikulov CZ 97 Gb49
Mikulovice CZ 92 Gd44

Míkonos GR 133 Db89
Mikorzyn PL 92 Ha40
Mikulov CZ 97 Gb49
Milano I 101 Cc59
Milano Marittima I 102 Ea63
Mílas TR 131 Ec87
Milatos GR 133 Db95
Milazzo I 115 Fd83
Milborne Saint Andrew GB 15 Ec30
Milcza PL 92 Ha40
Mildenhall GB 16 Fd25
Mildstedt D 83 Da29
Milehouse IRL 7 Cc24
Milejów-Wieś PL 93 Kb40
Milešti Mici MD 119 Fd58
Mileszewy PL 86 Hc33
Miletin CZ 91 Gb43
Milevsko CZ 91 Fb46
Milevsko Galazki PL 87 Jd32
Milford GB 15 Fb29
Milford Haven GB 14 Db27
Milíč PL 92 Ha44
Milicz PL 91 Gc40
Miliés GR 129 Cd82
Milín CZ 91 Fb46
Militello in Val di Catania I 115 Fc86
Miljana HR 104 Ga58
Millares E 39 Fb68
Millas F 35 Ha57
Millau F 28 Hb52
Millerovo RUS 137 Fc14
Millesimo I 108 Bd63
Millevaches F 27 Gd48
Millford IRL 4 Cb15
Mill Hill GB 16 Fc27
Millicent IRL 7 Cc21
Millíni GR 129 Cd86
Millisle GB 5 Db17
Millom GB 12 Eb19
Millport GB 10 Dc13
Millstatt A 96 Ed55
Millstreet IRL 6 Bc25
Milltown GB 11 Eb16
Milltown GB 5 Da18
Milltown IRL 6 Bb24
Milltown IRL 4 Bb21
Milltown Malbay IRL 6 Bb22
Milly-la-Forêt F 24 Gd38
Milly-le-Meugnon F 23 Fc42
Milmarcos E 34 Ed62
Milná I 110 Gc66
Milnthorpe GB 13 Ec19
Miločer MNE 111 Hd70
Milón E 32 Ea55
Milos I 133 Cd91
Milovaig GB 8 Da07
Milovice CZ 90 Fc44
Milow D 84 Eb36
Milówka PL 98 Hc46
Milton GB 8 Dd08
Milton Abbas GB 15 Ec30
Milton Abbot GB 14 Dc31
Milton Keynes GB 15 Fb26
Milton-on-Stour GB 15 Ec30
Milutinac SRB 120 Bd70
Milzyn PL 86 Hb35
Mimizan F 26 Fa52
Minard GB 10 Dc12
Minas de Riotinto E 43 Bd73
Minaya E 38 Eb68
Minchinhampton GB 15 Ec27
Mincsány PL 93 Jb39
Mindelheim D 95 Db51
Mindelstetten D 96 Ea48
Minden D 83 Cd36
Mindszent H 105 Jd56
Mineo I 115 Fc86
Mineral'nye Vody RUS 137 Ga16
Minerbe I 102 Dd61
Minerbio I 102 Dd62
Minervino Murge I 113 Gb74
Mingajny PL 86 Ja29
Minglanilla E 39 Ed67
Mingorria E 38 Da63
Minia LT 80 Jd56
Mining A 96 Ed50
Minkió FIN 68 Jd38
Minkowskie PL 92 Ha41
Miñovce SK 99 Jd47
Minsk BY 136 Ea13
Minsk Mazowiecki PL 87 Jd37
Minster GB 16 Ga28
Minster GB 16 Gb28
Minster Lovell GB 15 Fa27
Mintlaw GB 9 Ed08
Mintraching D 96 Eb48
Mión F 28 Jb47
Mios F 26 Fb51
Mira E 39 Ec67
Mira I 102 Ea60
Mira P 36 Ac63
Mirabel E 37 Ca66
Mirabeau F 29 Jc53
Mirabel F 28 Ja51
Mirabella Imbaccari I 115 Fc86
Miradoux F 34 Gb53
Miramar P 30 Ac61
Miramas F 29 Jc54
Miramont-de-Guyenne F 26 Fd51
Miranda de Arga E 33 Ec58
Miranda de Ebro E 32 Ea57
Miranda do Corvo P 36 Ac64
Miranda do Douro P 31 Ca60
Mirandela P 31 Bc61
Mirandilla E 37 Ca68
Mirandola I 102 Dc61
Mirandol Bourgnounac F 27 Gd52
Mirano I 102 Ea60
Miravet E 34 Ga62
Mirebeau F 23 Fd44
Mirebeau-sur-Bèze F 25 Jc41
Mireval F 28 Hd54
Mirina GR 130 Dd81
Mirna SLO 104 Fd58
Mirna Peč SLO 104 Fd58
Miroslav CZ 97 Gb48
Miroslavas LT 80 Kc59
Miroslov RUS 137 Fc16
Mirošov CZ 91 Fb45
Mirotice CZ 91 Fb46
Mirovice CZ 91 Fb46
Mirów PL 93 Jd41
Mirpol' UA 136 Ea15
Mirsk PL 91 Ga42
Mirto I 115 Gb80
Mirueña de los Infanzones E 38 Da63
Misano Adriatico I 102 Eb64

Misefa H 115 Gb55
Misi FIN 55 Kb18
Misilmeri I 114 Ec84
Miskolc H 99 Jd50
Miskolctapolca H 99 Jd51
Mislata E 39 Fb67
Misten N 52 Fc18
Mistelbach A 97 Gb50
Mistelgau D 90 Dd45
Misterbianco I 115 Fd85
Misterton GB 13 Fb21
Mistrás GR 132 Bc89
Mistretta I 115 Fb84
Misy-sur-Yonne F 24 Hb38
Miszewo PL 86 Ha30
Mitcham GB 16 Fc28
Mitchell GB 14 Db31
Mitchelstown IRL 6 Bd25
Mitra TR 134 Ec89
Mitilíni GR 130 Ea83
Mittelberg A 95 Da54
Mittelberg A 95 Db53
Mittenaar D 89 Cb42
Mittenwald D 96 Dd53
Mitterdorf im Mürztal A 97 Fd53
Mittersheim F 21 Ka36
Mittersill A 96 Eb54
Mitterteich D 90 Eb45
Mittweida D 90 Ec41
Mitwitz D 90 Ea44
Mizhhirja UA 136 Ea16
Mjadzel BY 136 Ea12
Mjälom S 58 Gd31
Mjell N 62 Cc36
Mjølby S 72 Fd47
Mjölkbacken S 52 Gb17
Mjønes N 56 Db30
Mladá Boleslav CZ 91 Fc43
Mladá Vožice CZ 91 Fc46
Mladenovac SRB 120 Bb67
Mladikovina BIH 110 Gd67
Mláka CZ 97 Fd48
Mława PL 87 Jb33
Mlini HR 111 Hd70
Mlynárovce SK 99 Jd47
Mlyniv UA 136 Ea15
Mlýny CZ 97 Fd47
Mníchovo Hradiště CZ 91 Fc43
Mnišek nad Hnilcom SK 99 Jc48
Mniszew PL 93 Jd40
Mniszków PL 92 Ja40
Mo N 52 Ed23
Mo N 64 Dd33
Mo S 58 Gb30
Mo S 66 Gb37
Mo S 57 Fb30
Mo S 71 Eb46
Moacşa RO 117 Ea61
Moaña E 30 Ad57
Moate IRL 7 Cc21
Mo i Rana N 52 Fd20
Mochy PL 91 Ga38
Močidlec CZ 90 Ed45
Möckern D 84 Ea37
Möckmühl D 95 Cd46
Mocsa H 98 Hb52
Moczydły PL 87 Kc35
Modane F 29 Kb48
Modave B 21 Jb33
Modbury GB 14 Dd32
Modena I 102 Dd62
Modica I 115 Fc88
Modigliana I 102 Dd64
Mödingen D 95 Db49
Modliborzyce PL 93 Ka42
Modliszewko PL 86 Gd36
Modra SK 98 Gc50
Modran BIH 110 Gd65
Modravy CZ 96 Fa48
Modriach A 103 Fc55
Modrany SK 98 Hb52
Modriča BIH 110 Gd65
Modrý Kameň SK 98 Hd49
Modugno I 113 Gc74
Moelfre GB 12 Dc22
Moelv N 65 Ea40
Moen N 48 Gb12
Moena I 102 Dd57
Moergestel NL 82 Bb38
Moers D 88 Bd39
Moffat GB 11 Eb15
Mofreita P 31 Bd60
Mogadouro P 31 Bd61
Mogán E 100 Bd60
Mogeltonder DK 76 Da31
Mogente E 45 Fa70
Móggio Udinese I 103 Ed56
Mögglingen D 95 Da48
Moglia I 102 Dc61
Mogliano I 109 Fa67
Mogliano Veneto I 102 Ea59
Mogón E 44 Dd72
Mogor E 30 Ac57
Mohács H 105 Hb58
Moheda S 62 Fb51
Mohedas de la Jara E 37 Cd66
Moheliv-Podil's'kyj UA 136 Ec16
Mohelnice CZ 91 Gb45
Mohill IRL 7 Cb23
Möhlin CH 94 Bd52
Mohon F 22 Ec39
Mohora H 98 Ja51
Mohrkirch D 83 Db29
Moià E 35 Gd60
Moie I 109 Ed66
Moikipää FIN 59 Hd31
Moimenta da Beira P 36 Bb62
Moincourt-lès-Provenchères F 25 Ka38
Moira GB 5 Da17
Moirans F 29 Jc48
Moirans-en-Montagne F 25 Jc44
Moirax F 26 Fd52
Moisdon-la-Rivière F 23 Ed41
Moisio FIN 68 Kd35
Moişei RO 117 Db58
Moisiovaara FIN 55 Lb24
Moissac F 27 Gb52
Moissey F 25 Jc42
Moisson F 20 Gc36
Moita P 36 Ac69
Moita dos Ferreiros P 36 Ab68
Moixent E 45 Fa70
Mojacar E 44 Ed75
Mojados E 32 Da61
Mojkovac MNE 111 Ja69
Mojstrana SLO 103 Fa57
Mokobody PL 87 Jd36
Mokra Gora SRB 120 Bb67
Mokro Polje HR 110 Gb65
Mokronog SLO 104 Fd58
Mokrous RUS 137 Ga11
Mokrzyska PL 93 Jd44
Mola di Bari I 113 Gd74
Moland N 64 Db42
Molare I 100 Ca62
Molaren S 52 Gb23
Molas F 34 Gb55
Molat HR 109 Fd65
Molbergen D 82 Ca34
Mold GB 12 Eb22
Molde N 56 Da32
Moldjord N 52 Gb18
Moldova-Sulița RO 118 Eb58
Moldova Nouă RO 120 Bd65
Moldovita RO 118 Ea58

Molompize F 28 Hb49
Moloy F 25 Jb41
Molpe FIN 59 Hd31
Molsheim F 94 Bd49
Moltajny PL 87 Jb30
Moltjorda N 52 Fc18
Moltrasio I 101 Cc58
Moltustranda N 62 Cb33
Molveno I 102 Dc57
Molvizar E 44 Db76
Molývos = Míthimna GR 130 Ea83
Mómán E 30 Bb54
Mömbris D 89 Da44
Mömlingen D 89 Cd45
Momuy F 26 Fc54
Monaghan IRL 5 Cc18
Monar Lodge GB 8 Dc08
Monasterevin IRL 7 Cc22
Monasterio de la Sierra E 32 Dd59
Monasteryščina RUS 136 Ea16
Monastyrys'ka UA 136 Ea16
Monbahus F 27 Ga51
Moncada E 39 Fc67
Moncalieri I 100 Bd60
Moncalvo E 37 Bd62
Moncarapacho P 42 Ad74
Moncel-sur-Seille F 21 Jd36
Mönchberg D 89 Cd45
Mönchdorf A 97 Ga50
Mönchengladbach D 88 Bc40
Mönchhof A 97 Gc52
Mönchweiler D 95 Cb51
Mönchsdeggingen D 95 Dc48
Monclar-de-Quercy F 27 Gc53
Moncofa E 39 Fc66
Moncontour F 22 Eb38
Moncoutant F 23 Fc44
Monda E 43 Cd77
Mondariz E 30 Ad58
Mondavio I 109 Ec66
Mondéjar E 38 Dd65
Mondello, Partanna– I 114 Eb83
Mondim de Basto P 30 Ba60
Mondoñedo E 31 Bc54
Mondorf-les-Bains L 21 Jd34
Mondoví I 100 Bd62
Mondragon F 28 Jb52
Mondragone I 112 Fa74
Mondsee A 96 Fa52
Moneasa RO 117 Cb58
Moneen IRL 6 Bd21
Monein F 33 Fb55
Monemvassía GR 132 Bd90
Monesi I 108 Bc63
Mónesiglio I 100 Bd62
Monesteiro E 43 Bd71
Monestiés F 27 Gd52
Moneteau F 24 Hc40
Moneygall IRL 6 Ca22
Moneyglass GB 5 Cd17
Moneymore GB 5 Cd16
Moneyneany GB 5 Cc16
Moneyslane GB 5 Da18
Monfalcone I 103 Ed59
Monfarracinos E 31 Cb60
Monforte P 37 Bb68
Monforte d'Alba I 100 Bd62
Monforte de Lemos E 30 Bb57
Mongiana I 115 Gc82
Monguelfo I 96 Eb55
Monheim D 95 Dc48
Monheim am Rhein D 88 Bd40
Moniaive GB 11 Ea15
Monikie GB 11 Ec11
Monimail GB 11 Eb12
Monistrol-d'Allier F 28 Hc49
Monistrol de Montserrat E 35 Gd60
Monistrol-sur-Loire F 28 Hd48
Mönkeberg D 83 Dc30
Monk Fryston GB 13 Fa20
Monki PL 87 Ka32
Monkton GB 10 Dd14
Monmouth GB 15 Ec27
Monnai F 19 Fd37
Monnerville F 24 Gd38
Mönni FIN 61 Ld30
Monnickendam NL 82 Ba35
Monódendri GR 128 Ad79
Monopoli I 113 Ha74
Monor H 98 Ja53
Monpazier F 27 Ga51
Monreal del Campo E 34 Fa63
Monreale I 114 Ec84
Monroy E 37 Ca66
Monroyo E 34 Fd63
Mons B 20 Hb32
Mønsås S 66 Gb33
Monschau D 88 Bc42
Monségur F 26 Fd51
Monsélice I 102 Dd60
Monsheim D 89 Cb45
Monster NL 17 Ad37
Monsummano Terme I 108 Db65
Monta I 100 Bd61
Montabaur D 89 Ca42
Montady F 35 Hb55
Montagnac F 28 Hc54
Montagnana I 102 Dd60
Montaigu F 23 Fa43
Montaigu-de-Quercy F 27 Gb52
Montaiguët-en-Forez F 24 Hd45
Montaigu-les-Bois F 19 Fa37
Montalbán E 34 Fb63
Montalbán de Córdoba E 43 Cc73
Montalbanejo E 38 Ea67
Montalbo E 38 Ea66
Montalcino I 108 Dc68
Montalegre P 30 Ba59
Montalieu-Vercieu F 29 Jc46
Montalivet-les-Bains F 26 Fa48
Montallegro I 114 Ec86
Montalto delle Marche I 109 Fa68
Montalto di Castro I 108 Dd70
Montalto Marina I 108 Dd70
Montalto Pavese I 101 Cc61
Montalto Uffugo I 113 Gb79
Montán E 39 Fb66
Montana BG 125 Cc75
Montánchez E 37 Ca67
Montanejos E 39 Fb66
Montargil P 36 Ad68
Montargis F 24 Ha40
Montargull E 34 Gb59
Montastruc-la-Conseillère F 27 Gc54
Montauban F 27 Gb53
Montazzoli I 109 Fc71
Montbard F 24 Hd41
Montbazens F 27 Gd51
Montbazon F 23 Ga42
Montbéliard F 25 Ka41
Montbenoît F 25 Ka42
Montbeugny F 24 Hc45
Montblanc E 34 Gb61

Montbovon – Nordhamna


**Montbovon CH** 94 Bc55
**Montbozon F** 25 Jd41
**Montbrison F** 28 Hd47
**Montbrun-les-Bains F** 29 Jc52
**Montceau-les-Mines F** 25 Ja44
**Montceaux-les-Provins F** 20 Hb37
**Montcenis F** 25 Ja43
**Montchanin F** 25 Ja43
**Montchevrier F** 24 Gc45
**Montcornet F** 20 Hc34
**Montcuq F** 27 Gb52
**Mont-Dauphin F** 29 Kb50
**Mont-de-Marsan F** 26 Fb53
**Montdidier F** 20 Gd34
**Monteagudo de las Salinas E** 39 Ec66
**Montealegre del Castillo E** 45 Ed70
**Montebello Vicentino I** 102 Dd59
**Montebelluna I** 102 Ea59
**Montebourg F** 19 Fa35
**Montebruno I** 101 Cc62
**Monte Buono I** 108 Ea67
**Montecalvo Irpino I** 112 Fc74
**Monte-Carlo MC** 29 Kd53
**Montecarotto I** 109 Ec66
**Montecastrilli I** 109 Eb69
**Montecatini Terme I** 108 Db65
**Montecchio Emilia I** 101 Da62
**Montecchio Maggiore I** 102 Dd59
**Montechiarugolo I** 101 Da62
**Monteciccardo I** 109 Eb65
**Montecorto E** 43 Cb76
**Montecorvino Rovella I** 112 Fc75
**Monte da Pedra P** 36 Ba67
**Monte das Flores P** 36 Ad69
**Monte de Goula P** 36 Ba65
**Montederramo E** 30 Bb57
**Montedor P** 30 Ac59
**Montedoro I** 114 Ed86
**Monte do Trigo P** 42 Ba70
**Monte Estremo F** 106 Ca69
**Montefalco I** 109 Eb68
**Montefalcone nel Sannio I** 109 Fc71
**Montefiascone I** 108 Ea69
**Monte Fidalgo P** 36 Ba66
**Montefiore Conca I** 109 Eb65
**Montefiorino I** 102 Db63
**Monteforte Cilento I** 112 Fd76
**Monteforte da Beira P** 36 Bb66
**Montefrío E** 44 Da74
**Montefurado E** 31 Bc57
**Montegiordano Marina I** 113 Gc77
**Montegiorgio I** 109 Ed67
**Monte Gordo P** 42 Ba74
**Montehermoso E** 37 Bd65
**Montejo de Bricia E** 32 Dc56
**Montejo de la Sierra E** 38 Dc62
**Montejo de la Vega E** 32 Dc61
**Montelanico I** 109 Ec72
**Montelepre I** 114 Ec84
**Montélimar F** 28 Jb51
**Montella I** 112 Fc75
**Montellano E** 43 Cb75
**Montelupo Fiorentino I** 108 Dc65
**Montemaggiore Belsito I** 114 Ed85
**Montemassi I** 108 Db68
**Montemayor E** 43 Cd73
**Montemayor del Río E** 37 Cb64
**Montemerano I** 108 Dc69
**Montemesola I** 113 Ha76
**Montemiletto I** 112 Fc74
**Montemolín E** 43 Bd71
**Montemonaco I** 109 Ed68
**Montemor-o-Novo P** 36 Ad69
**Montemurro I** 113 Gb77
**Montendre F** 26 Fc49
**Montenero I** 108 Da66
**Montenerodomo I** 109 Fb71
**Monteneuf F** 22 Ec40
**Monte Novo P** 42 Ab70
**Monte Petrosu I** 107 Cc74
**Montepiano I** 102 Dc64
**Montepulciano I** 108 Dd67
**Montereau F** 24 Ha38
**Montereau F** 24 Ha40
**Monte Redondo P** 36 Ac65
**Monteriggioni I** 108 Dc66
**Monterosso Calabro I** 115 Gb82
**Monterotondo I** 109 Eb71
**Monterroso E** 30 Bb56
**Monterrubío de la Sierra E** 37 Cb63
**Montesa E** 39 Fb69
**Monte San Giusto I** 109 Ed67
**Monte San Maria Tiberina I** 108 Ea66
**Montesano Salentino I** 113 Hc77
**Montesano sulla Marcellana I** 112 Ga77
**Monte San Savino I** 108 Dd67
**Monte Sant'Angelo I** 110 Gb72
**Montesarchio I** 112 Fb74
**Montesclaros E** 37 Cd65
**Montesilvano Marina I** 109 Fa69
**Montesquieu-Volvestre F** 34 Gb55
**Montesquieux F** 27 Gb52
**Montestruc-sur-Gers F** 27 Ga54
**Montevarchi I** 108 Dd66
**Montevecchio I** 107 Bd78
**Monteverde I** 112 Ga74
**Montfaucon F** 23 Fa43
**Montfaucon-d'Argonne F** 21 Jb35
**Montfaucon-en-Velay F** 28 Ja49
**Montfleur F** 25 Jc45
**Montfoort NL** 82 Ba36
**Montfort F** 27 Ga53
**Montfort NL** 88 Bb40
**Montfort-en-Chalosse F** 26 Fb54
**Montfort-sur-Meu F** 23 Ed39
**Montfort-sur-Risle F** 19 Ga35
**Montfranc F** 27 Ha53
**Montfront-le-Gesnois F** 23 Fd39
**Montgarri E** 34 Gb57
**Montgeron F** 20 Gd37
**Montgerval F** 23 Ed39
**Montgomery GB** 12 Eb24
**Montgueux F** 24 Hc38
**Montguyon F** 26 Fc49
**Monthermé F** 21 Ja33
**Monthey CH** 100 Bb56
**Montiano I** 108 Dc69
**Monticelli I** 113 Ha75
**Monticelli d'Ongina I** 101 Cd61
**Montichiari I** 101 Da60
**Montier-en-Der F** 25 Ja38
**Montiers-sur-Saulx F** 21 Jb37
**Montignac F** 27 Gb49
**Montigny F** 24 Ha42
**Montigny-le Chartif F** 24 Gb39
**Montigny-le-Roi = Val-de-Meuse F** 25 Jc39
**Montigny-lès-Metz F** 21 Jd35
**Montijo E** 37 Bc69
**Montijo P** 36 Ab69
**Montilla E** 43 Cd73
**Montilly F** 24 Hb44
**Montivilliers F** 19 Fd34
**Montjean F** 23 Fd46
**Montlivault F** 24 Gb41
**Mont-Louis F** 35 Gd58
**Montlouis-sur-Loire F** 23 Ga42
**Montluçon F** 24 Ha45
**Montluel F** 25 Jb46
**Montmajor E** 34 Gc59
**Montmarault F** 24 Hb45
**Montmaur F** 29 Jd50
**Montmédy F** 21 Jb34
**Montmelian F** 29 Jd47
**Montmerle-sur-Saône F** 25 Jb46
**Montmesa E** 33 Fb59
**Montmeyran F** 28 Jb50
**Montmirat F** 28 Hd53
**Montmoreau-Saint-Cybard F** 26 Fd48
**Montmorency F** 20 Gd36
**Montmorillon F** 23 Ga45
**Montmort-Lucy F** 20 Hc36
**Montmoyen F** 25 Ja40
**Montoir-de-Bretagne F** 22 Ec42
**Montone I** 108 Ea66
**Montorio E** 32 Dc57
**Montorio al Vomano I** 109 Ed69
**Montoro E** 44 Da72
**Montpellier F** 28 Hd54
**Montpezat-de-Quercy F** 27 Gc52
**Montpon-Ménestérol F** 26 Fd50
**Montpont-en-Bresse F** 25 Jb44
**Montréal F** 35 Gd55
**Montrésor F** 24 Gb42
**Montret F** 25 Jb44
**Montreuil F** 20 Gc31
**Montreuil-Bellay F** 23 Fc42
**Montreuil-l'Argillé F** 19 Fd36
**Montreux CH** 94 Bb55
**Montrevel-en-Bresse F** 25 Jb45
**Montrichard F** 24 Gb42
**Mont-roig del Camp E** 34 Gb62
**Montrose GB** 11 Ec10
**Monts F** 23 Ga42
**Mont-Saint-Michel F** 19 Ed37
**Montsalvy F** 27 Ha50
**Montségur F** 35 Gd56
**Monts-sur-Guesnes F** 23 Fd43
**Montsûrs F** 23 Fb39
**Montsurvent F** 19 Ed36
**Montuïri E** 41 Hc67
**Montvert F** 27 Gd49
**Monza I** 101 Cc59
**Monzón E** 34 Fd60
**Monzón de Campos E** 32 Da59
**Mooncoin IRL** 7 Cb24
**Moone IRL** 7 Cc22
**Moorenweis D** 95 Dc50
**Moormerland D** 83 Cb33
**Moorrege D** 83 Db32
**Moortown GB** 13 Fc21
**Moos D** 95 Cc52
**Moosburg a.d.Isar D** 96 Ea50
**Moosthenning D** 96 Eb49
**Mór H** 98 Hb53
**Mora E** 38 Db67
**Mora S** 66 Fc38
**Móra d'Ebre E** 34 Ga62
**Mora de Rubielos E** 39 Fb65
**Morąg PL** 86 Hd31
**Morais P** 31 Bd60
**Móra la Nova E** 34 Ga62
**Moral de Calatrava E** 38 Dc69
**Moraleja E** 37 Bd65
**Moraleja del Vino E** 31 Cb60
**Morales de Toro E** 31 Cc60
**Morancelle E** 30 Ac55
**Morar GB** 8 Db09
**Morás E** 31 Bc53
**Morata de Jalón E** 33 Ed61
**Morata de Jiloca E** 39 Ed62
**Moratalla E** 45 Ec72
**Moravec CZ** 91 Gb46
**Moravská Nova Ves CZ** 97 Gc49
**Moravská Třebová CZ** 91 Gc45
**Moravské Budějovice CZ** 97 Ga48
**Moravské Lieskové SK** 98 Ha48
**Moravský Beroun CZ** 92 Gd45
**Moravský Krumlov CZ** 97 Gb48
**Morbach D** 88 Bd44
**Morbegno I** 101 Cd57
**Morbier F** 25 Jd44
**Mörbisch am See A** 97 Gc52
**Morcenx F** 26 Fa53
**Morciano di Romagna I** 109 Eb65
**Morcillo E** 37 Bd65
**Morcone I** 109 Fc73
**Morcote CH** 101 Cb58
**Mordelles F** 23 Ed39
**Mordiford GB** 15 Ec26
**Mordoğan TR** 130 Eb85
**Mordovo RUS** 137 Fb12
**Mordy PL** 87 Ka36
**Morebattle GB** 11 Ec14
**Morecambe GB** 12 Eb19
**Morella E** 39 Fc64
**Mores I** 107 Ca75
**Morestel F** 29 Jc47
**Moretonhampstead GB** 14 Dd31
**Moreton-in-Marsh GB** 15 Ed26
**Moreton Say GB** 13 Ec23
**Morez F** 25 Jd44
**Mörfelden D** 89 Cc44
**Morfou CY** 135 Bd95
**Morfovoúni GR** 128 Bb81
**Morgan's Vale GB** 15 Ed30
**Morgat F** 22 Db39
**Morges CH** 94 Bb55
**Morgowniki PL** 87 Jd33
**Mori I** 102 Dc58
**Mória GR** 130 Ea83
**Moriani-Plage F** 106 Cc69
**Mórichida H** 98 Gd53
**Moricone I** 109 Eb71
**Morienval F** 20 Ha35
**Moriers F** 24 Gb39
**Morillas E** 32 Ea56
**Moringen D** 89 Db39
**Moritz D** 90 Eb38
**Moritzburg D** 90 Fa41
**Morjärv S** 54 Ja21
**Mork N** 62 Da34
**Mørkøv DK** 77 Ea56
**Morkovice-Slížany CZ** 98 Gd47
**Mörkret S** 65 Ed36
**Mørkri N** 62 Da36
**Mørkveden N** 48 Fa15
**Morl D** 90 Eb39
**Morlaix F** 18 Dd37
**Mörlenbach D** 89 Cc45
**Morley F** 21 Jb37
**Morley GB** 13 Fa20
**Mormanno I** 113 Gb78
**Mornay-Berry F** 24 Ha43
**Morón de Almazán E** 32 Eb61
**Morón de la Frontera E** 43 Cb75
**Moros E** 33 Ec61
**Morosaglia F** 106 Cb69
**Morottaja FIN** 55 Kd18
**Morøya N** 48 Fc15
**Morozovsk RUS** 137 Fc14
**Morpeth GB** 11 Fa16
**Morsains F** 20 Hb37
**Moršansk RUS** 137 Fb11
**Mörsbach D** 89 Cb41
**Morschen D** 89 Da41
**Mörsil S** 57 Fa30
**Mörskom FIN** 68 Kc38
**Morsleben D** 84 Dd37
**Morsovo RUS** 137 Fb11
**Mortagne-au-Perche F** 23 Ga38
**Mortain F** 19 Fb37
**Mortara I** 101 Cb60
**Mörtberg S** 54 Hc20
**Mortcerf F** 20 Ha37
**Morteau F** 25 Ka42
**Mortelle I** 115 Ga83
**Mortemer F** 20 Gb34
**Mortensnes N** 47 Kb06
**Morvich GB** 8 Dc08
**Morwenstow GB** 14 Dc30
**Moryń PL** 85 Fb35
**Morzeszczyn PL** 86 Hb32
**Morzyczyn PL** 85 Fc33
**Mosal'sk RUS** 137 Ed11
**Mosätt S** 65 Fb34
**Mosbach D** 89 Cd46
**Moščenice HR** 103 Fb60
**Moschendorf A** 97 Gb54
**Moscoso E** 30 Ad57
**Mosculdy F** 33 Fa55
**Mosėdis LT** 80 Jb53
**Mosel D** 90 Eb42
**Mosfellsbær IS** 2 Ad07
**Mosina PL** 85 Gc37
**Mosjö S** 58 Gc30
**Mosjøen N** 52 Fa22
**Moskog N** 62 Cb36
**Moskojärvi S** 49 Hc16
**Moskosel S** 53 Ha22
**Moskva RUS** 137 Ed10
**Mosles F** 19 Fb35
**Moșna RO** 117 Db60
**Mosonmagyaróvár H** 98 Gd52
**Mošovce SK** 98 Hc48
**Moss N** 71 Ea43
**Mossat GB** 9 Ec09
**Mossautal D** 89 Cc45
**Mosset F** 35 Ha57
**Mössingen D** 95 Cc49
**Mösslacher A** 103 Ed56
**Mosstodloch GB** 9 Eb07
**Most CZ** 90 Fa43
**Mostar BIH** 111 Hb67
**Mosteiro P** 36 Bb62
**Mostek CZ** 91 Ga43
**Mosti N** 52 Fc17
**Mostkowo PL** 86 Hd31
**Móstoles E** 38 Db65
**Mostovskoj RUS** 137 Fd17
**Mostowo PL** 85 Gb31
**Mostrim IRL** 4 Cb20
**Mosty u Jablunkova CZ** 92 Hc46
**Mota del Cuervo E** 38 Ea67
**Mota del Marqués E** 31 Cd60
**Motala S** 72 Fc46
**Motarzyno PL** 85 Gc30
**Motherwell GB** 11 Ea13
**Möthlow D** 84 Ec36
**Motilla del Palancar E** 39 Ec67
**Motilleja E** 39 Ec68
**Motkowice PL** 93 Jb42
**Motovun HR** 103 Fa60
**Motril E** 44 Dc76
**Motta di Livenza I** 103 Eb59
**Motteggiana I** 102 Db61
**Mottisfont GB** 15 Fa29
**Mottola I** 113 Gd75
**Motycz PL** 93 Ka40
**Mötzing D** 96 Eb48
**Mouchamps F** 23 Fa44
**Moúdros GR** 130 Dc81
**Mougins F** 29 Kc53
**Mouhijärvi FIN** 68 Jc35
**Moulay F** 23 Fb39
**Mouliherne F** 23 Fd41
**Moulins F** 24 Hb44
**Moulismes F** 23 Ga45
**Moulsoe GB** 15 Fb26
**Moult F** 19 Fc36
**Mountain Ash GB** 14 Ea27
**Mount Bellew IRL** 4 Bd20
**Mountbenger GB** 11 Eb14
**Mountcollins IRL** 6 Bc24
**Mountfield GB** 5 Cc17
**Mount Garret IRL** 7 Cc24
**Mount Hamilton GB** 5 Cc16
**Mountmellick IRL** 7 Cb22
**Mount Nuggent IRL** 5 Cc19
**Mountrath IRL** 7 Cb22
**Mount Talbot IRL** 4 Ca20
**Mount Uniacke IRL** 6 Ca25
**Moura P** 42 Ba71
**Moure P** 30 Ad59
**Mourentán E** 30 Ad58
**Mourenx F** 33 Fb55
**Mouriès F** 28 Jb53
**Mouriscas P** 36 Ad66
**Mousehole GB** 14 Da32
**Moustiers-Sainte-Marie F** 29 Ka53
**Moutfort L** 21 Jd34
**Mouthe F** 25 Jd43
**Mouthier-Haute-Pierre F** 25 Jd42
**Moutier CH** 94 Bd53
**Moutier-d'Ahun F** 24 Gd46
**Moûtiers F** 29 Ka47
**Moutiers-sur-le-Lay F** 23 Fa44
**Moux-en-Morvan F** 25 Hd42
**Mouzon F** 21 Ja34
**Moville IRL** 5 Cc15
**Moy GB** 5 Cd17
**Moyarget GB** 5 Da15
**Moyasta IRL** 6 Bb23
**Moycullen IRL** 6 Bc21
**Moyeuvre F** 21 Jc35
**Möykky FIN** 67 Ja33
**Moylgrove GB** 14 Dc26
**Moylough IRL** 4 Bd20
**Moymore IRL** 6 Bd22
**Moyne IRL** 7 Cd23
**Moyvalle IRL** 7 Cc21
**Moyvore IRL** 4 Cb20
**Možajsk RUS** 137 Ed10
**Mózar E** 31 Cb59
**Mozzecane I** 102 Db60
**Mrągowo PL** 87 Jb31
**Mrkonjić Grad BIH** 104 Gd63
**Mrkopalj HR** 103 Fc60
**Mrozy PL** 87 Jd37
**Mrzezino PL** 86 Ha29
**Mścichy PL** 87 Ka32
**Mscislav BY** 136 Ec12
**Mšec CZ** 90 Fa44
**Mšené Lázně CZ** 91 Fb43
**Mšeno CZ** 91 Fc43
**Mstyczów PL** 92 Ja42
**Mszana Dolna PL** 92 Ja45
**Mszanna PL** 87 Kb37
**Mszczonów PL** 93 Jb38
**Much D** 88 Ca41
**Muchalls GB** 9 Ed09
**Mücheln D** 90 Ea40
**Muchówka PL** 93 Jb45
**Much Wenlock GB** 13 Ec24
**Mucientes E** 31 Cd60
**Mücka D** 91 Fc40
**Muckamore GB** 5 Da17
**Mučkapskij RUS** 137 Fc12
**Mücke D** 89 Cd42
**Muckross IRL** 6 Bb25
**Mudanya TR** 131 Fc80
**Mudau D** 89 Cd46
**Muelas de los Caballeros E** 31 Ca58
**Muff IRL** 5 Cc15
**Muga de Sayago E** 31 Ca61
**Mugaire E** 33 Ed56
**Mugardos E** 30 Ba53
**Mügeln D** 90 Ed38
**Mügeln D** 90 Ed40
**Muggensturm D** 95 Cb48
**Muggia I** 103 Fa59
**Muğla TR** 134 Bb90
**Müglitztal D** 90 Fa42
**Mugnano del Cardinale I** 112 Fc75
**Mühlacker D** 95 Cc48
**Mühlberg D** 90 Ed40
**Mühldorf a.Inn D** 96 Eb50
**Mühlenbach am Hochkönig A** 96 Ec53
**Mühlhausen D** 89 Dc40
**Mühlhausen D** 89 Dc45
**Mühlhausen D** 96 Dd47
**Mühlhausen/Kraichgau D** 95 Cc47
**Mühlhausen = Mulhouse F** 94 Bd51
**Mühlheim D** 89 Cc44
**Mühlheim D** 95 Cc51
**Mühlhofen D** 95 Cd52
**Mühltal D** 89 Cc45
**Muhos FIN** 55 Kb24
**Muhr A** 96 Ed54
**Muhr am See D** 95 Dc47
**Muides-sur-Loire F** 24 Gc41
**Muikirk GB** 11 Ea14
**Muinchille IRL** 5 Cc19
**Muineachán IRL** 5 Cc18
**Muine Bheag IRL** 7 Cc23
**Muir of Ord GB** 8 Dd08
**Muittari FIN** 60 Ka31
**Mukačeve UA** 136 Dd16
**Mukkajärvi FIN** 54 Jd18
**Mukkala FIN** 51 Kb15
**Mula E** 45 Ed72
**Mularinperä FIN** 55 Kc20
**Mulbarton GB** 16 Gb24
**Mulben GB** 9 Ec08
**Mulda D** 90 Ed42
**Mulfingen D** 89 Da46
**Mülheim an der Ruhr D** 88 Bd39
**Mulhouse F** 94 Bd51
**Mullach Íde IRL** 7 Cd21
**Mullagh IRL** 7 Cd21
**Mullardoch House GB** 8 Dc08
**Müllheim D** 94 Bd51
**Mullinahone IRL** 7 Cb24
**Mullinavat IRL** 7 Cb24
**Mullingar IRL** 4 Cb20
**Mullion GB** 14 Da32
**Mullsjö S** 59 Hb29
**Mullsjö S** 71 Fa48
**Mulrany IRL** 4 Bb19
**Mulsanne F** 23 Fd40
**Multeddu I** 107 Ca74
**Multia FIN** 60 Ka32
**Multiperä FIN** 55 Lb20
**Mumby GB** 13 Fd22
**Münchberg D** 90 Ea44
**Müncheberg D** 85 Fb36
**München D** 96 Dd51
**Münchenbernsdorf D** 90 Ea42
**Münchhausen D** 89 Cc41
**Münchsmünster D** 96 Ea49
**Münchwilen CH** 95 Cc52
**Mundão P** 36 Ba62
**Mundesley GB** 16 Gb23
**Mundford GB** 16 Ga24
**Mundheim N** 63 Cb40
**Munera E** 38 Ea69
**Mungret IRL** 6 Bd23
**Muniesa E** 39 Fb62
**Munkbysjön S** 66 Ga33
**Munkedal S** 71 Eb46
**Munkflohögen S** 58 Fc29
**Münnerstadt D** 89 Db43
**Muñopedro E** 38 Da63
**Munsala FIN** 59 Ja29
**Münsing D** 96 Dd51
**Münsingen CH** 94 Bd54
**Münsingen D** 95 Cd49
**Münster D** 83 Cb37
**Munster D** 83 Db34
**Münster D** 89 Cc44
**Munster F** 21 Ka36
**Munster F** 94 Bc50
**Münster/Lech D** 95 Dc49
**Münstermaifeld D** 88 Ca43
**Münstertal D** 94 Ca51
**Münzenberg D** 89 Cc43
**Muonio FIN** 50 Ja14
**Muonionalusta S** 50 Ja14
**Muotathal CH** 95 Cb54
**Muotkavaara FIN** 50 Jb15
**Muratátka H** 104 Gc56
**Murato F** 106 Cb69
**Murat-sur-Vèbre F** 28 Hb54
**Murau A** 97 Fb54
**Murazzano I** 100 Bd62
**Murcia E** 45 Fa72
**Murczyn PL** 86 Gd35
**Mur-de-Sologne F** 24 Gc41
**Mureck A** 104 Ga56
**Mürefte TR** 127 Ec78
**Mures E** 44 Db74
**Muret F** 34 Gb55
**Murg D** 94 Ca52
**Murgenthal CH** 94 Ca53
**Murgia E** 32 Ea56
**Muri CH** 95 Cb53
**Muriedas E** 32 Dc54
**Murillo de Río Leza E** 32 Eb58
**Murillo el Fruto E** 33 Ed58
**Mürlenbach D** 88 Bc43
**Murley GB** 5 Cc17
**Murnau am Staffelsee D** 96 Dd52
**Muro E** 41 Hc67
**Muro del Alcoy E** 45 Fb70
**Muro Lucano I** 112 Fd75
**Murom RUS** 137 Fb10
**Muron F** 23 Fb46
**Muros E** 30 Ac55
**Murrhardt D** 95 Da48
**Murs F** 29 Jc53
**Mûrs-Erigné F** 23 Fb42
**Murska Sobota SLO** 104 Gb56
**Mursley GB** 15 Fb26
**Murter HR** 110 Ga65
**Murtomäki FIN** 60 Kd26
**Murtomäki FIN** 60 Kc28
**Murton GB** 13 Fa17
**Murtovaara FIN** Lc24
**Muruvik N** 57 Eb30
**Murviel-lès-Béziers F** 28 Hb54
**Mürzzuschlag A** 97 Ga53
**Müsch D** 88 Bd42
**Musetrene N** 64 Dc36
**Musken N** 48 Ga15
**Musorka RUS** 137 Ga10
**Musselburgh GB** 11 Eb13
**Musselkanaal NL** 82 Ca34
**Mussidan F** 26 Fd49
**Mussomeli I** 114 Ed85
**Mustafakemalpaşa TR** 131 Fb81
**Müstair CH** 102 Db56
**Mustajärvi FIN** 67 Jb33
**Mustajärvi FIN** 68 Jd34
**Mustasaari FIN** 59 Ja30
**Mustavaara FIN** 55 La22
**Mustikkaperä FIN** 60 Ka30
**Mustinlahti FIN** 61 Lb30
**Mustinsalo FIN** 61 Lb32
**Mustolanmäki FIN** 60 Kd31
**Mustvee EST** 75 Lb43
**Muszaki PL** 86 Ja33
**Muszyna PL** 93 Jc46
**Mutapohja FIN** 60 Kb31
**Mutěnice CZ** 97 Gc48
**Muthill GB** 11 Ea12
**Mutka FIN** 54 Jd20
**Mutlangen D** 95 Da48
**Mutterberg-Alm A** 95 Dc54
**Mutterstadt D** 89 Cb46
**Mützlitz D** 84 Ec36
**Muurame FIN** 68 Kb33
**Muurikkala FIN** 69 Lb37
**Muuruvesi FIN** 61 La29
**Muxía E** 30 Ac54
**Muzzana del Turgnano I** 103 Ec58
**Mybster GB** 9 Eb04
**Mychajlivka UA** 137 Fa16
**Mycielin PL** 92 Ha38
**Myckle S** 59 Hc25
**Myckling S** 58 Gd30
**Myddfai GB** 14 Dd26
**Mydroilyn GB** 14 Dd25
**Myjava SK** 98 Gd49
**Mykolajiv UA** 136 Dd15
**Mykolajiv UA** 137 Ed16
**Mykolajivka UA** 137 Fa17
**Mylau D** 90 Eb43
**Myllyaho FIN** 60 Ka29
**Mylly-Karttu FIN** 68 Jc34
**Myllykselä FIN** 68 Kb36
**Myllykylä FIN** 68 Ka35
**Myllymaa FIN** 68 Jc36
**Myllymäki FIN** 60 Jd32
**Mylopótamos GR** 132 Bd92
**Myran N** 57 Ea29
**Myre N** 48 Fd11
**Myre N** 48 Fc12
**Myrhorod UA** 137 Ed14
**Myrland N** 48 Fd12
**Myrland N** 48 Fa14
**Myrnes N** 46 Hc07
**Myronivka UA** 136 Ec15
**Myrorna S** 59 Hc28
**Myrviken S** 57 Fb31
**Myshall IRL** 7 Cc23
**Myślenice PL** 92 Ja45
**Myślibórz PL** 85 Fc35
**Myślibórz PL** 91 Ga41
**Myślina PL** 92 Hb42
**Mysłowice PL** 92 Hc44
**Myszków PL** 92 Hd42
**Myszyniec PL** 87 Jc33
**Mytišči RUS** 137 Ed10
**Mýto CZ** 90 Fa45
**Mýto pod Ďumbierom SK** 98 Ja48

## N

**Naaldwijk NL** 17 Hc26
**Naamanka FIN** 55 Kc21
**Naamijoki FIN** 54 Jb18
**Naantali FIN** 67 Jb39
**Naapurinvaara FIN** 61 La26
**Naarajärvi FIN** 60 Kd32
**Naarajoki FIN** 59 Ja31
**Naarden NL** 82 Ba36
**Naarminkylä FIN** 68 Jc33
**Naarva FIN** 61 Ma28
**Naas IRL** 7 Cc22
**Näätävaara FIN** 55 Lb23
**Naatule FIN** 68 Jc37
**Nabburg D** 90 Eb46
**Naburn GB** 13 Fb20
**Na Cealla Beaga IRL** 4 Ca16
**Nachamps F** 23 Fb46
**Náchod CZ** 91 Gb43
**Nachrodt-Wiblingwerde D** 88 Ca39
**Nacina Ves SK** 99 Ka48
**Näckådalen S** 65 Fb37
**Nackenheim D** 89 Cb44
**Na Clocha Liatha IRL** 7 Da22
**Nacpolsk PL** 86 Ja36
**Nad IRL** 6 Bc25
**Nadarzyn PL** 87 Jb37
**Naddvik N** 62 Da37
**Nådendal = Naantali FIN** 67 Jb39
**Nadvirna UA** 136 Ea16
**Nærbø N** 63 Ca45
**Næstved DK** 77 Eb57
**Näfels CH** 95 Cc54
**Náfpaktos GR** 128 Bb85
**Náfplio GR** 129 Bd88
**Nagele NL** 82 Bb35
**Nagold D** 95 Cc49
**Nagor'e RUS** 137 Ed09
**Nagoszewo PL** 87 Jd35
**Nago-Torbole I** 102 Dc58
**Nagu FIN** 67 Jb40
**Nagyalásony H** 98 Gd54
**Nagyatád H** 104 Gd57
**Nagybaracska H** 105 Hd58
**Nagyberki H** 105 Hb57
**Nagycenk H** 97 Gc53
**Nagydobos H** 99 Kb50
**Nagydorog H** 105 Hc56
**Nagyigmánd H** 98 Hb52
**Nagykamarás H** 116 Bd58
**Nagykáta H** 98 Ja53
**Nagykőrös H** 98 Ja54
**Nagylengyel H** 97 Gc55
**Nagylóc H** 98 Ja51
**Nagymányok H** 105 Hc57
**Nagymaros H** 98 Hc52
**Nagyrábé H** 99 Jd53
**Nagyrécse H** 104 Gd56
**Nagyszénás H** 99 Jc55
**Nagyvázsony H** 98 Ha55
**Nahe D** 83 Dc32
**Nahkiaisoja FIN** 54 Jc20
**Nahwinden D** 90 Dd42
**Naila D** 90 Ea43
**Nailly F** 24 Hb39
**Nailsea GB** 14 Eb28
**Nailstone GB** 13 Fa24
**Nailsworth GB** 15 Ec27
**Nairn GB** 9 Ea07
**Naizin F** 22 Eb39
**Najac F** 27 Gd52
**Nájera E** 32 Ea58
**Nakielno PL** 85 Gb34
**Näkkälä FIN** 50 Ja12
**Nakkila FIN** 67 Jb36
**Nakło nad Notecią PL** 86 Gd34
**Nakskov DK** 77 Ea58
**Nal'čik RUS** 137 Ga17
**Nälden S** 57 Fb30
**Nałęczów PL** 93 Ka40
**Naleda E** 31 Bc55
**Nambroca E** 38 Db66
**Namen = Namur B** 21 Ja31
**Náměšť nad Oslavou CZ** 97 Gb47
**Námestovo SK** 92 Hd46
**Nämpnäs FIN** 59 Hd32
**Namsos N** 57 Ec26
**Namsskogan N** 57 Fa25
**Namur B** 21 Ja31
**Namysłów PL** 92 Gd41
**Nançay F** 24 Gd42
**Nancray F** 25 Jd41
**Nancy F** 21 Jd37
**Nandlstadt D** 96 Ea49
**Nangis F** 24 Hb38
**Nannerch GB** 12 Eb22
**Nans-les-Pins F** 29 Jd54
**Nans-sous-Sainte-Anne F** 25 Jd42
**Nant F** 28 Hc53
**Nant-ddu GB** 14 Ea27
**Nanterre F** 20 Gd37
**Nantes F** 23 Ed42
**Nanteuil-en-Vallée F** 23 Fd46
**Nanteuil-la-Forêt F** 20 Hc36
**Nantgaredig GB** 14 Dd26
**Nantiat F** 24 Gb46
**Nantua F** 25 Jc45
**Nantwich GB** 13 Ec23
**Nantyffyllon GB** 14 Ea27
**Nantyglo GB** 14 Eb27
**Nant-y-moel GB** 14 Ea27
**Naours F** 20 Gd33
**Náousa GR** 133 Db90
**Náoussa GR** 125 Bc77
**Napajedla CZ** 98 Gd47
**Napiwoda PL** 86 Ja33
**Napkor H** 99 Ka51
**Napoli I** 112 Fb75
**Napton GB** 15 Fa25
**Narač BY** 136 Ea12
**Narberth GB** 14 Dc27
**Narbonne F** 35 Hb55
**Narbonne-Plage F** 35 Hb55
**Narcao I** 107 Bd80
**Narcy F** 24 Hb42
**Nardevitz D** 84 Fa29
**Nardò I** 113 Hb77
**Narečenski bani BG** 126 Db74
**Narewka PL** 87 Kc34
**Narjordet N** 65 Eb33
**Narkaus FIN** 55 Ka19
**Narni I** 109 Eb69
**Naro I** 114 Ed86
**Narodowy PL** 91 Gb43
**Naro-Fominsk RUS** 137 Ed10
**Narovlja BY** 136 Eb13
**Närpes FIN** 67 Hd33
**Närpiö FIN** 67 Hd33
**Narros del Castillo E** 37 Cd63
**Narta AL** 124 Aa77
**Nartkala RUS** 137 Ga17
**Narty PL** 87 Jb32
**Naruska FIN** 51 Kd16
**Narva EST** 69 Lc41
**Narva-Jõesuu EST** 69 Lc41
**Narvik N** 48 Gb13
**Naryškino RUS** 137 Ed12
**Näsåker S** 58 Gb30
**Na Sceirí IRL** 5 Da20
**Naseby GB** 15 Fb25
**Näset S** 66 Fc37
**Nasielsk PL** 87 Jb36
**Naso I** 115 Fc84
**Nassau D** 88 Ca43
**Nassenfels D** 96 Dd48
**Nassenheide D** 84 Ed35
**Nässjö S** 72 Fc49
**Nässvallen S** 65 Fb33
**Nastätten D** 89 Cb43
**Nastazin PL** 85 Fd33
**Nästi FIN** 67 Ja38
**Nastola FIN** 68 Kc37
**Nasuty PL** 87 Jd30
**Näsviken S** 58 Fd28
**Näsviken S** 66 Gb35
**Nattavaara by S** 54 Hc18
**Nattheim D** 95 Db49
**Nättraby S** 78 Fd54
**Naucelle F** 27 Ha52
**Nauen D** 84 Ec36
**Nauheim D** 89 Cc44
**Naul IRL** 5 Cd20
**Naumburg D** 89 Cd40
**Naumburg D** 90 Ea41
**Naumovskij RUS** 137 Fd15
**Naundorf D** 90 Ec40
**Naunhof D** 90 Ec40
**Naustbukt N** 49 Gc09
**Naustdal N** 62 Cb35
**Nautsund N** 62 Ca36
**Nauvo FIN** 67 Jb40
**Nava E** 31 Cc54
**Navacepedilla de Corneja E** 37 Cc64
**Navacerrada E** 38 Db63
**Nava de Arévalo E** 37 Cd62
**Nava de la Asunción E** 38 Da62
**Nava de Roa E** 32 Db60
**Navahermosa E** 38 Da67
**Navahrudak BY** 136 Ea13
**Navalagamella E** 38 Db64
**Navalcarnero E** 38 Db65
**Navalcuervo E** 43 Cb71
**Navaleno E** 32 Ea60
**Navalmoral de la Mata E** 37 Cb66
**Navalón de Arriba E** 39 Fa69
**Navalonguilla E** 37 Cb64
**Navaluenga E** 37 Cd64
**Navalvillar de Pela E** 37 Cb68
**Navan IRL** 5 Cd20
**Navapolack BY** 136 Eb11
**Navarcles E** 35 Gd60
**Navarrenx F** 33 Fb55
**Navarrés E** 39 Fb69
**Navarrete E** 32 Eb58
**Navarrevisca E** 37 Cd64
**Navàs E** 35 Gd60
**Navas de Estena E** 38 Da67
**Navas de Jorquera E** 39 Ec68
**Navas del Madroño E** 37 Bd66
**Navas del Rey E** 38 Da64
**Navas de Oro E** 38 Da62
**Navas de San Antonio E** 38 Da63
**Navasëlki BY** 136 Eb13
**Navašino RUS** 137 Fb10
**Navata E** 35 Hb58
**Navatrasierra E** 37 Cc67
**Nave I** 101 Da59
**Navelli I** 109 Ed70
**Navenby GB** 16 Fc23
**Näveråsen FIN** 59 Hd32
**Navia E** 31 Ca53
**Navit N** 49 Hc09
**Navlja RUS** 137 Ed12
**Navlus N** 57 Ed27
**Navoloki RUS** 137 Fa09
**Nawiady PL** 87 Jc32
**Nawojowa PL** 93 Jc46
**Na Xamena E** 40 Gc69
**Náxos GR** 133 Db90
**Nay F** 33 Fc56
**Nayland GB** 16 Ga26
**Nazaré P** 36 Ab66
**Nazilli TR** 131 Fb88
**Néa Artáki GR** 129 Cb85
**Néa Fókea GR** 125 Cb79
**Nea Iraklitsa GR** 126 Da77
**Néa Kalikrátia GR** 125 Cb79
**Nealstown IRL** 7 Cb22
**Neap GB** 9 Fb04
**Neapel = Napoli I** 112 Fb75
**Neápoli GR** 133 Db96
**Néa Potídea GR** 125 Cb79
**Néa Stíra GR** 129 Cd86
**Neath GB** 14 Dd27
**Nebra D** 90 Ea40
**Neckarbischofsheim D** 89 Cc46
**Neckargemünd D** 89 Cc46
**Neckarsteinach D** 89 Cc46
**Neckarsulm D** 95 Cd47
**Neckartailfingen D** 95 Cd49
**Neckarzimmern D** 89 Cd46
**Neckenmarkt A** 97 Gb53
**Nedansjö S** 66 Gb33
**Neded SK** 98 Ha51
**Nedervetil FIN** 60 Jc28
**Nederweert NL** 88 Bb39
**Nedre Bäck S** 59 Hd26
**Nedreberg N** 65 Eb38
**Nedre Flåsjön S** 54 Hd21
**Nedrenes N** 50 Jc09
**Nedre Saxnäs S** 53 Gb23
**Nedre Vojakkala S** 54 Jc21
**Nedryhajliv UA** 137 Ed14
**Nędza PL** 92 Hb44
**Neede NL** 82 Bd37
**Needham Market GB** 16 Ga26
**Neerijnen NL** 82 Ba37
**Neerpelt B** 88 Ba39
**Nefyn GB** 12 Dc23
**Négrondes F** 27 Ga48
**Nehaevskij RUS** 137 Fc13
**Neheim D** 89 Cb39
**Nehrybka PL** 93 Kb45
**Neiden N** 51 Kc08
**Neitaskaite S** 54 Hd19
**Nejdek CZ** 90 Ec43
**Nekrasovskoe RUS** 137 Fa09
**Nelidovo RUS** 136 Ec10
**Nellimö FIN** 51 Kb11
**Nelson GB** 13 Ed20
**Nelson GB** 14 Ea27
**Neman RUS** 136 Dc12
**Nembro E** 31 Cc54
**Nembro I** 101 Cd58
**Nemecká SK** 98 Hd48
**Nemesnádudvar H** 105 Hd57
**Németkér H** 98 Hc55
**Nemi I** 109 Eb72
**Nemours F** 24 Ha39
**Nemyriv UA** 136 Dd15
**Nemyriv UA** 136 Eb15
**Nenagh IRL** 6 Ca22
**Nentershausen D** 89 Cb42
**Nentershausen D** 89 Db41
**Nenthead GB** 13 Ec17
**Nenzing A** 95 Cd54
**Néos Marmarás GR** 129 Cc80
**Nepomuk CZ** 90 Fa46
**Neptun RO** 123 Fc68
**Nérac F** 26 Fd52
**Neratovice CZ** 91 Fb44
**Nerchau D** 90 Ec40
**Nerehta RUS** 137 Fa09
**Neresheim D** 95 Db48
**Nereta LV** 81 Kd53
**Nereto I** 109 Fa68
**Neringa-Nida LT** 80 Jb56
**Neringa-Pervalka LT** 80 Jb56
**Nerja E** 44 Db76
**Nerkoo FIN** 68 Jc33
**Nerkoonniemi FIN** 60 Kd28
**Nerl' RUS** 137 Ed09
**Nersingen D** 95 Db49
**Nerva E** 43 Bc72
**Nervesa della Battaglia I** 102 Ea58
**Nervi I** 101 Cb63
**Nes N** 48 Fd14
**Nes NL** 82 Bc32
**Nesberg N** 48 Fd15
**Nesbyen N** 64 Dc39
**Nesebăr BG** 127 Fa72
**Neset N** 46 Hb07
**Nesjahverfi IS** 3 Cb07
**Neskaupstaður IS** 3 Cd04
**Nesna N** 52 Fa21
**Nesscliff GB** 12 Eb24
**Neßmersiel D** 83 Cb32
**Nesterov RUS** 136 Dd12
**Neston GB** 12 Eb22
**Nesttun N** 62 Ca39
**Nesvady SK** 98 Hb51
**Netherfield GB** 16 Fd30
**Nether Langwith GB** 13 Fa22
**Netherley GB** 9 Ed09
**Netherton GB** 11 Ed15
**Netherwitten GB** 11 Ed15
**Netolice CZ** 97 Fb48
**Netphen D** 89 Cb41
**Nettancourt F** 21 Ja36
**Nettersheim D** 88 Bc42
**Nettetal D** 88 Bc39
**Nettlebed GB** 15 Fb28
**Nettleton GB** 13 Fc21
**Nettuno I** 109 Eb73
**Neuanspach D** 89 Cc43
**Neuberg an der Mürz A** 97 Fd52
**Neubeuern D** 96 Eb52
**Neubrandenburg D** 84 Ed33
**Neubruck A** 97 Fd51
**Neubukow D** 84 Ea31
**Neuburg D** 96 Ed50
**Neuburg an der Donau D** 96 Dd49
**Neuchâtel CH** 94 Bc54
**Neuchâtel-Hardelot F** 20 Gc31
**Neu Darchau D** 84 Dd34
**Neudenau D** 89 Cd46
**Neudietendorf D** 90 Dd41
**Neudorf D** 90 Ec43
**Neu-Eichenberg D** 89 Db40
**Neuenburg D** 94 Bd51
**Neuendettelsau D** 95 Dc47
**Neuendorf D** 83 Cc33
**Neuendorf D** 84 Fa36
**Neuenhagen D** 84 Fa36
**Neuenhaus D** 82 Ca35
**Neuenkirch CH** 94 Ca54
**Neuenkirchen D** 82 Ca36
**Neuenkirchen D** 83 Cb36
**Neuenkirchen D** 83 Cd32
**Neuenkirchen D** 83 Db34
**Neuenkirchen D** 84 Ed31
**Neuenkirchen-Vöhrden D** 83 Cc36
**Neuenrade D** 89 Cb40
**Neuenstadt D** 95 Cd47
**Neuenstein D** 89 Da41
**Neuenweg D** 94 Ca51
**Neuerburg D** 88 Bb43
**Neufahrn D** 96 Ea50
**Neufahrn D** 96 Eb49
**Neuf-Brisach F** 94 Bd50
**Neufchâteau F** 25 Jc38
**Neufchâtel-en-Bray F** 20 Gb34
**Neufchâtel-en-Saosnois F** 23 Fd38
**Neuffen D** 95 Cd49
**Neufra D** 95 Cd50
**Neuhardenberg D** 85 Fb36
**Neuhaus A** 97 Fd52
**Neuhaus D** 90 Ea46
**Neuhaus D** 96 Ed50
**Neuhaus am Rennweg D** 90 Dd43
**Neuhausen CH** 95 Cb52
**Neuhausen D** 90 Ed42
**Neuhausen D** 91 Fb39
**Neuhausen D** 95 Cc48
**Neuhausen ob Eck D** 95 Cc51
**Neuhaus-Schierschnitz D** 90 Dd43
**Neuhof D** 89 Da43
**Neuillé-Pont-Pierre F** 23 Ga41
**Neuilly-Saint-Front F** 20 Hb36
**Neu-Isenburg D** 89 Cc44
**Neukamperfehn D** 83 Cb33
**Neukieritzsch D** 90 Eb41
**Neukirchen A** 96 Ec51
**Neukirchen D** 90 Ec42
**Neukirchen D** 96 Ec47
**Neukirchen-Balbini D** 96 Eb47
**Neukirchen-Vluyn D** 88 Bc39
**Neukirchen-Wyhra D** 90 Ec41
**Neukloster D** 84 Ea32
**Neu Kosenow D** 84 Fa32
**Neulengbach A** 97 Ga51
**Neum BIH** 110 Ha68
**Neumagen-Dhron D** 88 Bd44
**Neumark D** 90 Eb42
**Neumarkt A** 96 Fa50
**Neumarkt D** 96 Dd47
**Neumarkt I** 102 Dd57
**Neumarkt am Wallersee A** 96 Ed51
**Neumarkt an der Ybbs A** 97 Fc51
**Neumarkt in Steiermark A** 97 Fb54
**Neumarkt-Sankt Veit D** 96 Eb50
**Neumünster D** 83 Db31
**Neunburg vorm Wald D** 96 Eb47
**Neundorf D** 90 Ea38
**Neunkirch CH** 95 Cb52
**Neunkirchen A** 97 Gb52
**Neunkirchen D** 88 Bd46
**Neunkirchen D** 89 Cb41
**Neunkirchen D** 90 Dd46
**Neunkirchen-Seelscheid D** 88 Ca41
**Neuötting D** 96 Ec50
**Neupetershain D** 91 Fb39
**Neuranft D** 85 Fb35
**Neurázy CZ** 96 Ed47
**Neureichenau D** 96 Fa49
**Neurenberg = Nürnberg D** 90 Dd46
**Neuried D** 94 Ca49
**Neuruppin D** 84 Ec35
**Neusach A** 96 Ed55
**Neusäß D** 95 Dc50
**Neusiedl am See A** 97 Gc51
**Neusitz D** 89 Db46
**Neuss D** 88 Bd40
**Neustadt D** 83 Da36
**Neustadt D** 84 Dd31
**Neustadt D** 84 Ec35
**Neustadt D** 91 Fb41
**Neustadt, Titisee- D** 94 Ca51
**Neustadt/ Donau D** 96 Ea48
**Neustadt am Kulm D** 90 Ea45
**Neustadt am Main D** 89 Da44
**Neustadt an der Aisch D** 89 Dc46
**Neustadt an der Orla D** 90 Ea42
**Neustadt an der Waldnaab D** 90 Eb45
**Neustadt an der Weinstraße D** 89 Cb46
**Neustadt bei Coburg D** 90 Dd43
**Neustadt-Glewe D** 84 Ea33
**Neustadt (Hessen) D** 89 Cd41
**Neustadt (Wied) D** 88 Ca42
**Neustift im Stubaital A** 96 Dd54
**Neustrelitz D** 84 Ed33
**Neutraubling D** 96 Eb48
**Neu-Ulm D** 95 Da50
**Neuves-Maisons F** 21 Jd37
**Neuvic F** 26 Fd49
**Neuvic F** 27 Gd48
**Neuvic-Entier F** 27 Gc47
**Neuville F** 27 Gc49
**Neuville-aux-Bois F** 24 Gd39
**Neuville-de-Poitou F** 23 Fd44
**Neuville-les-Decize F** 24 Hb43
**Neuville-sur-Saône F** 25 Jb46
**Neuvy-Bouin F** 23 Fb44
**Neuvy-le-Roi F** 23 Ga41
**Neuvy-Saint-Sépulcre F** 24 Gc44
**Neuvy-sur-Barangeon F** 24 Gd42
**Neuvy-sur-Loire F** 24 Ha41
**Neuwied D** 88 Ca42
**Neuwiller-lès-Saverne F** 94 Bd48
**Neu Wulmstorf D** 83 Db33
**Neuzelle D** 91 Fc38
**Neu Zittau, Gosen- D** 84 Fa37
**Névache F** 29 Kb49
**Neveklov CZ** 91 Fb45
**Nevel' RUS** 136 Eb11
**Neverfjord N** 46 Ja06
**Nevernes N** 52 Fc20
**Nevers F** 24 Hc43
**Neviano I** 113 Hc77
**Nevinnomyssk RUS** 137 Fd16
**New Abbey GB** 11 Ea16
**New Aberdour GB** 9 Ed07
**New Alresford GB** 15 Fa29
**Newark-on-Trent GB** 13 Fb23
**Newbald GB** 13 Fb20
**Newbiggin GB** 13 Ed17
**Newbiggin-by-the-Sea GB** 11 Fa16
**Newbliss IRL** 5 Cc18
**Newborough GB** 12 Dd22
**Newbridge IRL** 4 Bd20
**Newbridge IRL** 7 Cc22
**Newbridge-on-Wye GB** 14 Ea25
**New Buckenham GB** 16 Ga25
**Newburgh GB** 9 Ed08
**Newburgh GB** 11 Eb12
**Newburn GB** 11 Ed16
**Newbury GB** 15 Fa28
**Newby Bridge GB** 12 Eb19
**Newcastle GB** 5 Da18
**Newcastle GB** 14 Eb25
**Newcastle IRL** 6 Ca24
**Newcastle IRL** 7 Cd21
**Newcastle IRL** 7 Da22
**Newcastle Emlyn GB** 14 Dc26
**New Castleton GB** 11 Ec15
**Newcastle-under-Lyme GB** 13 Ec23
**Newcastle upon Tyne GB** 11 Fa16
**Newcastle West IRL** 6 Bc24
**Newchurch GB** 14 Dc26
**New Cumnock GB** 10 Dd15
**New Deer GB** 9 Ed08
**Newent GB** 15 Ec26
**Newgale GB** 14 Db26
**New Galloway GB** 10 Dd16
**Newham GB** 11 Fa14
**Newhaven GB** 16 Fd30
**New Holland GB** 13 Fc21
**Newick GB** 16 Fd30
**New Inn IRL** 5 Cc19
**Newinn IRL** 6 Ca24
**New Luce GB** 10 Dc16
**Newmachar GB** 9 Ed09
**Newmains GB** 11 Ea13
**New Malden GB** 16 Fc28
**Newmarket GB** 8 Da05
**Newmarket GB** 16 Fd25
**Newmarket IRL** 6 Bc24
**Newmarket on Fergus IRL** 6 Bc23
**New Mills GB** 12 Ea24
**New Mills GB** 13 Ed22
**New Milton GB** 15 Ed30
**Newnham Bridge GB** 15 Ec25
**New Pitsligo GB** 9 Ed07
**Newport GB** 13 Ec24
**Newport GB** 14 Dc26
**Newport GB** 14 Eb28
**Newport GB** 15 Fa31
**Newport IRL** 4 Bc19
**Newport IRL** 6 Bd23
**Newport Pagnell GB** 15 Fb26
**Newport Trench GB** 5 Cd17
**New Quay GB** 14 Dc25
**Newquay GB** 14 Db31
**New Romney GB** 16 Ga30
**New Ross IRL** 7 Cc24
**New Rossington GB** 13 Fb21
**Newry GB** 5 Cd18
**Newton Abbot GB** 14 Ea31
**Newton-Aycliffe GB** 13 Fa17
**Newtonhill GB** 9 Ed09
**Newton-le-Willows GB** 13 Ec21
**Newtonmore GB** 9 Ea09
**Newton-on-Trent GB** 13 Fb22
**Newton Poppleford GB** 14 Ea30
**Newton Stewart GB** 10 Dd16
**Newtown GB** 12 Ea24
**Newtown GB** 15 Ec26
**Newtown IRL** 6 Ca21
**Newtown IRL** 6 Bc22
**Newtown IRL** 6 Ca22
**Newtown IRL** 6 Bd24
**Newtown IRL** 6 Bd24
**Newtown IRL** 7 Cc23
**Newtownabbey GB** 5 Da17
**Newtownards GB** 5 Db17
**Newtownbreda GB** 5 Da17
**Newtownbutler GB** 5 Cc18
**Newtown Cunningham IRL** 5 Cc15
**Newtown Forbes IRL** 4 Cb19
**Newtownhamilton GB** 5 Cd18
**Newtown Saint Boswells GB** 11 Ec14
**Newtown Sandes IRL** 6 Bb23
**Newtownshandrum IRL** 6 Bc24
**Newtownstewart GB** 5 Cc16
**New Tredegar GB** 14 Eb27
**New Twopothouse IRL** 6 Bd25
**Nibe DK** 76 Dc51
**Nicastro I** 113 Gc81
**Niccone I** 108 Ea67
**Nice F** 29 Kd53
**Nickelsdorf A** 98 Gd51
**Nicknoret S** 53 Ha24
**Nicosia I** 115 Fb85
**Nicotera I** 115 Gb82
**Nidda D** 89 Cd43
**Niddatal D** 89 Cc43
**Nidderau D** 89 Cc43
**Nideggen D** 88 Bc41
**Nídri GR** 128 Ac83
**Nidzica PL** 86 Ja33
**Niebieszczany PL** 93 Ka45
**Niebüll D** 76 Da58
**Niechcice PL** 92 Hd40
**Niechorze PL** 85 Fc31
**Niedalino PL** 85 Ga31
**Niederaichbach D** 96 Eb49
**Niederaula D** 89 Da42
**Niederbronn-les-Bains F** 94 Ca47
**Niedereschach D** 95 Cb50
**Niederfischbach D** 89 Cb41
**Niederfüllbach D** 90 Dd44
**Niederkrüchten D** 88 Bc40
**Niedermurach D** 90 Eb46
**Niederndodeleben D** 84 Ea37
**Niedernhall D** 95 Da47
**Niederoderwitz D** 91 Fc41
**Nieder-Olm D** 89 Cb44
**Niedersachswerfen D** 89 Dc39
**Nieder-Seifersdorf D** 91 Fc41
**Niederstetten D** 89 Da46
**Niederstotzingen D** 95 Db49
**Niedersulz A** 97 Gc50
**Niederwerrn D** 89 Db44
**Niederwiesa D** 90 Ed42
**Niederwinkling D** 96 Ec48
**Niederzier D** 88 Bc41
**Niedoradz PL** 91 Ga38
**Niedorp NL** 82 Ba34
**Niedrzew PL** 86 Hc37
**Niedźwiada PL** 93 Kb39
**Niedźwiedź PL** 85 Fd37
**Niedźwiedź PL** 86 Hc34
**Niegosławice PL** 91 Ga39
**Niegowonice PL** 92 Hd43
**Nieheim D** 89 Cd38
**Niemberg D** 90 Eb39
**Niemcza PL** 91 Gc42
**Niemenkylä FIN** 60 Ka28
**Niemenkylä FIN** 67 Jb35
**Niemetal D** 89 Da39
**Niemica PL** 85 Fc32
**Niemijärvi FIN** 61 Mb29
**Niemikylä FIN** 61 Lb29
**Niemis S** 54 Jb20
**Niemiskylä FIN** 60 Jd32
**Niemodlin PL** 92 Gd42
**Niemojki PL** 87 Ka36
**Nienburg D** 83 Da35
**Nienburg D** 90 Ea38
**Nienhagen D** 83 Db36
**Nienstädt D** 83 Da37
**Niepars D** 84 Ed30
**Niepołomice PL** 92 Ja44
**Nieporęt PL** 87 Jb36
**Nierstein D** 89 Cb44
**Niesky D** 91 Fc40
**Niestetal D** 89 Da40
**Nieszawa PL** 86 Hb35
**Nieuil-l'Espoir F** 23 Fd45
**Nieul-le-Dolent F** 23 Ed44
**Nieuw-Amsterdam NL** 82 Ca35
**Nieuwegein NL** 82 Ba36
**Nieuwekerk aan de IJssel NL** 17 Hd26
**Nieuwendijk NL** 82 Ba37
**Nieuwe Pekela NL** 82 Ca34
**Nieuweschans NL** 82 Ca33
**Nieuwkerke B** 17 Ha30
**Nieuwkoop NL** 17 Hd25
**Nieuwleusen NL** 82 Bc35
**Nieuw Milligen NL** 82 Bb36
**Nieuwolda NL** 82 Ca33
**Nieuwpoort B** 17 Ha29
**Nieuwpoort-Bad B** 17 Ha29
**Nieves (Capela) E** 30 Bb53
**Niewęgłosz PL** 93 Kb38
**Niezabyszewo PL** 86 Gd31
**Nigrán E** 30 Ac58
**Niinilahti FIN** 60 Kb30
**Niinilahti FIN** 61 Lc28
**Niinimäki FIN** 61 Lb31
**Niininkoski FIN** 68 Kc37
**Níjar E** 44 Eb76
**Nij Beets NL** 82 Bc33
**Nijkerk NL** 82 Bb36
**Nijmegen NL** 82 Bb37
**Nijverdal NL** 82 Bd36
**Nikítas GR** 125 Cc79
**Nikkala S** 54 Jc21
**Nikkaluokta S** 49 Gd15
**Nikkaroinen FIN** 68 Kc35
**Nikkeby N** 49 Hb08
**Nikolaevka RUS** 137 Fd10
**Nikolaevsk RUS** 137 Fd13
**Nikol'sk RUS** 137 Fd10
**Nikopol' UA** 137 Fa16
**Nikópoli GR** 128 Ad82
**Nikosia = Lefkosia CY** 135 Ca95
**Nikšić MNE** 111 Hd68
**Nilivaara S** 54 Hc17
**Nilsiä FIN** 61 La29
**Nîmes F** 28 Ja53
**Nimféo GR** 124 Bb77
**Nin HR** 104 Fd64
**Ninebanks GB** 13 Ec17
**Ninfield GB** 16 Fd30
**Niort F** 23 Fb45
**Nipen N** 48 Ga13
**Nipuli FIN** 68 Kd35
**Niš SRB** 120 Bd69
**Nisa P** 36 Ba66
**Niscemi I** 115 Fb87
**Niška Banja SRB** 120 Bd69
**Niskanperä FIN** 54 Jd19
**Nisko PL** 93 Ka42
**Nispen NL** 17 Hd28
**Nistelrode NL** 88 Bb38
**Niton GB** 15 Fa31
**Nitra SK** 98 Hb50
**Nittel D** 88 Bc45
**Nittenau D** 96 Eb47
**Nittendorf D** 96 Ea48
**Niukkala FIN** 69 Ld33
**Niva FIN** 61 Lb25
**Nivala FIN** 60 Ka27
**Nivelles B** 21 Hd31
**Niwica PL** 91 Fc39
**Niziny PL** 93 Jc42
**Nižná SK** 98 Hd47
**Nižna Polianka SK** 93 Jd46
**Nižnij Novgorod RUS** 137 Fb09
**Nizy-le-Comte F** 20 Hc34
**Nižyn UA** 136 Ec14
**Nizza Monferrato I** 100 Ca61
**Nizza = Nice F** 29 Kd53
**Njakaure S** 53 Hb21
**Njallavárri S** 54 Hc17
**Njarðvík IS** 2 Ac07
**Njasviž BY** 136 Ea13
**Njellim FIN** 51 Kb11
**Njuorggam FIN** 47 Ka07
**Njurundabommen S** 66 Gc34
**Njutånger S** 66 Gb36
**Noailles F** 20 Gd35
**Noailly F** 25 Hd45
**Noale I** 102 Ea59
**Noasca I** 100 Bc59
**Nobber IRL** 5 Cd20
**Nöbdenitz D** 90 Eb42
**Nobitz D** 90 Ec41
**Nocé F** 23 Ga38
**Nocedo de Curueño E** 31 Cc56
**Nocera Inferiore I** 112 Fb75
**Nocera Umbra I** 109 Eb67
**Noceto I** 101 Da61
**Noci I** 113 Gd75
**Nœux-les-Mines F** 20 Ha31
**Noez E** 38 Da66
**Nogales E** 43 Bc70
**Nogara I** 102 Dc60
**Nogarejas E** 31 Ca58
**Nogaro F** 26 Fc54
**Nogawczyce PL** 92 Hb43
**Nogent F** 25 Jb39
**Nogent-le-Rotrou F** 23 Ga38
**Nogent-sur-Marne F** 20 Gd37
**Nogent-sur-Seine F** 24 Hb38
**Nogent-sur-Vernisson F** 24 Ha40
**Nogheredo I** 103 Eb58
**Noginsk RUS** 137 Fa10
**Nógrádmegyer H** 98 Ja51
**Nogueira de Ramuín E** 30 Bb57
**Nohant-en-Graçay F** 24 Gc42
**Nohant-Vic F** 24 Gd44
**Nohèdes F** 35 Ha57
**Nohfelden D** 88 Bd45
**Nohra D** 89 Dc40
**Noia E** 30 Ac55
**Noicattaro I** 113 Gd74
**Noidanpola FIN** 50 Ja14
**Nois E** 31 Bc53
**Nokia FIN** 68 Jd36
**Nokkamäki FIN** 61 La28
**Nola I** 112 Fb75
**Nolay F** 25 Ja43
**Noli I** 100 Ca63
**Nolimo FIN** 55 Kc18
**Nomansland GB** 14 Ea30
**Nomeny F** 21 Jd36
**Nomexy F** 25 Jd38
**Nomparedes E** 32 Eb61
**Nonant-le-Pin F** 19 Fd37
**Nonantola I** 102 Dc62
**Nonnweiler D** 88 Bd45
**Noordbeemster NL** 82 Ba35
**Noordwijk aan Zee NL** 17 Hd25
**Noordwijkerhout NL** 17 Hd25
**Noormarkku FIN** 67 Ja35
**Nopala FIN** 69 Lb37
**Nopankylä FIN** 59 Ja32
**Noppikoski S** 66 Fc36
**Nor S** 58 Fd32
**Nora S** 66 Gb33
**Nora S** 72 Fc43
**Nørager DK** 76 Db52
**Norberg S** 66 Ga41
**Norcia I** 109 Ec68
**Nordanåker S** 58 Ga30
**Nordanås S** 53 Gd22
**Nordanås S** 58 Gd27
**Nordankäl S** 58 Ga29
**Nordansjö S** 58 Ga25
**Nordausques F** 16 Gc30
**Nordborg DK** 76 Db57
**Nordby N** 65 Eb37
**Norddal N** 62 Cb35
**Norddorf D** 76 Cd58
**Nordelph GB** 16 Fd24
**Norden D** 82 Ca32
**Nordenham D** 83 Cd32
**Norderåsen S** 58 Fc30
**Norderney D** 82 Ca31
**Norderstedt D** 83 Db32
**Nordfjordbotn N** 49 Gd11
**Nordfjordeid N** 62 Cc34
**Nord-Flatanger N** 57 Eb26
**Nordfold N** 48 Fd16
**Nordhamna N** 46 Ja05

# Nordhausen – Pasian di Prato

Nordhausen D 89 Dc39
Nordheim vor der Rhön D 89 Db43
Nordholz D 83 Cd32
Nordhorn D 82 Ca36
Nordingrå S 58 Gd31
Nordkirchen D 88 Ca38
Nordkjosbotn N 49 Gd11
Nordli N 52 Fb23
Nördlingen D 95 Db48
Nordmaling S 59 Ha29
Nordmannset N 46 Jb06
Nordmannvik N 49 Ha09
Nordmela N 48 Fd11
Nordnes N 52 Fc18
Nordøyvågen N 52 Ed21
Nord-Sel N 56 Fa35
Nordsjö S 58 Gd26
Nordskjorn N 57 Ea27
Nordstemmen D 83 Db37
Nordstrand D 83 Da29
Nordstrand N 56 Cc32
Nord-Værnes N 52 Fa19 Fc61
Nordvågen N 47 Jc04
Nordvika N 56 Db29
Nordwalde D 82 Ca37
Nore S 66 Ga35
Noreña E 31 Cc54
Norg NL 82 Bd33
Norgravsjö S 58 Gd28
Norham GB 11 Ed14
Norheimsund N 62 Cb39
Norma I 109 Gc72
Normandy GB 15 Fb29
Normanton GB 13 Fa21
Normée F 21 Hd37
Nornäs S 65 Fa36
Norrahult S 78 Fd51
Norra Finnåkoga S 65 Ed38
Norråker S 58 Gb25
Norra Skärvången S 57 Fb29
Norra Stensund S 53 Gb23
Norra Sunderbyn S 54 Hd22
Norra Umstrand S 53 Ga24
Norrbo S 66 Gb35
Norrby S 59 Hb26
Norrbyberg S 58 Gd27
Nørre Alslev DK 77 Eb58
Nørre Havrvig DK 76 Da54
Nørre Lyngby DK 70 Dc50
Nørre Vorupør DK 76 Cd51
Norrfjärden S 54 Ha23
Norrflärke S 59 Ha30
Norrnäs S 58 Gd24
Norrsjön S 58 Fd26
Norrtälje S 73 Haa2
Norrvik S 58 Gc26
Norsjö S 59 Ha25
Norsjövallen S 59 Ha25
Norskbukta N 47 Kc07
Nörten-Hardenberg D 89 Db39
Northallerton GB 13 Fa18
Northam GB 14 Dc29
Northampton GB 15 Fb25
North Berwick GB 11 Ec13
Northchapel GB 15 Fb29
North Charlton GB 11 Fa14
North Dalton GB 13 Fb20
Northeim D 89 Db39
North Ferriby GB 13 Fc20
North Ferriby GB 13 Fc21
North Grimston GB 13 Fb19
Northiam GB 16 Ga30
North Kilworth GB 15 Fa25
Northleach GB 15 Ed27
North Molton GB 14 Dc29
North Petherton GB 14 Eb29
North Somercotes GB 13 Fd21
North Tawton GB 14 Dd30
North Thoresby GB 13 Fc21
North Tidworth GB 15 Fa25
Northton GB 8 Cd06
Northwall GB 9 Ed02
North Walsham GB 16 Gd23
North Weald Bassett GB 16 Fd27
Northwich GB 13 Ec22
Northwood GB 12 Eb23
North Wootton GB 16 Fd24
Norton GB 13 Fb19
Nortorf D 83 Db30
North Creake GB 16 Ga23
Nortrup D 83 Cb35
Norum N 62 Ad33
Norvalahti FIN 54 Jd18
Nörvenich D 88 Bc41
Norwich GB 16 Gba4
Nosivka UA 136 Ec14
Ness N 48 Fd11
Nossa Senhora da Graça do Divor P 36 Ad69
Nossa Senhora das Neves P 42 Ad71
Nossen D 90 Ed41
Noss Mayo GB 14 Dd32
Noto I 115 Fd48
Notodden N 70 Dc42
Notre-Dame-de-Gravenchon F 19 Ga35
Notre Dame du Laus F 29 Ka50
Nottage GB 14 Dd28
Nottingham GB 13 Fa23
Nottuln D 82 Ca37
Nouaillé-Maupertuis F 23 Fd45
Nouan-le-Fuzelier F 24 Gd41
Nouans-les-Fontaines F 24 Gd42
Nouart F 21 Ja34
Nouvion F 20 Gc32
Nouzonville F 21 Ja34
Nova Baña SK 98 Hc50
Nová Bystřice CZ 97 Gd48
Nová Dubnica SK 98 Hd48
Novafeltria I 108 Ea65
Nova Gorica SLO 103 Fd38
Nova Kachovka UA 137 Fa16
Nováky SK 98 Hd48
Novalaise F 29 Jd47
Novalja HR 103 Fc31
Novalukoml' BY 136 Eb12
Nová Paka CZ 91 Fd43
Novara d'Sicilia I 115 Fd84
Novara di Sicilia I 115 Fd84
Novate Mezzola I 101 Cd42
Nove I 102 Dc30
Nová Řiše CZ 91 Ga47
Novaya Sil'ga CZ 77 Gd77
Novate Mezzola I 101 Cd42
Nové I 102 Dc30
Nové Heřmínovy CZ 92 Gd44
Nové Hrady CZ 91 Gd45
Nové Hrady CZ 97 Fc50
Novelda E 45 Fb71
Novellara I 102 Db61
Nové Mesto nad Metují CZ 91 Gb43
Nové Mesto nad Vahom SK 98 Hd48
Nové Město na Moravě CZ 91 Gb46

Nové Město pod Smrkem CZ 91 Fd42
Noventa Vicentino I 102 Dd60
Nové F 28 Jb53
Nové Sady SK 98 Ha50
Nové Veseli CZ 91 Gb46
Nové Zámky SK 98 Hb51
Novgorod UA 137 Ed15
Novhorod-Sivers'kyj UA 137 Ed16
Novi Bilokorovyči UA 136 Ec14
Novigrad HR 103 Fd31
Novigrad HR 104 Ga64
Novik N 57 Eb28
Novi Ligure I 101 Cb61
Novion-Porcien F 21 Hd34
Novi Pazar SRB 120 Bab69
Novi Sad SRB 120 Ad62
Novi Sanžáry UA 137 Fb15
Novi Vinodolski HR 103 Fc61
Novoaleksandrovsk RUS 137 Fd16
Novoannínskij RUS 137 Fc13
Novoarchanhel's'k UA 136 Ec15
Novoazovs'k UA 137 Fc16
Novočerkassk RUS 137 Fc15
Novocimljanskaja RUS 137 Fd14
Novofedorivka UA 137 Ed17
Novohrad-Volyns'kyj UA 136 Eb14
Novokašpirskij RUS 137 Ga10
Novokubansk RUS 137 Fd16
Novokujbyševsk RUS 137 Fd16
Novo Mesto SLO 104 Fd59
Novomičurinsk RUS 137 Fa11
Novocimljanskaja RUS 137 Fd14
Novomihajlovskij RUS 137 Fc17
Novomoskovsk RUS 137 Fc15
Novomoskovs'k UA 137 Fa15
Novomykolajivka UA 137 Fa15
Novomykolajivka UA 137 Fa15
Novomyrhorod UA 137 Ed15
Novonikolaevskij RUS 137 Fc13
Novooleksijivka UA 137 Fa17
Novopokrovskaja RUS 137 Ga17
Novopokrovka UA 137 Fa15
Novopokrovskaja RUS 137 Fd16
Novopskov UA 137 Fb14
Novorossijsk RUS 137 Fc17
Novoržev RUS 136 Eb10
Novošahtinsk RUS 137 Fc15
Novoselivs'ke UA 137 Fa17
Novosokol'niki RUS 136 Eb10
Novotroickoe RUS 137 Fc10
Novotrojic'ke UA 137 Fa17
Novotulka RUS 137 Ga12
Novoukrajinka UA 137 Ed16
Novoul'janovsk RUS 137 Fd38
Novouzensk RUS 137 Ga12
Novovolyns'k ua 136 Dd15
Nový Bor CZ 91 Fd42
Nový Bydžov CZ 91 Fd43
Nový Buh UA 137 Ed16
Nový Jičín CZ 92 Ha45
Nowa Brzeźnica PL 92 Hd41
Nowa Deba PL 93 Jd43
Nowa Huta PL 92 Ja44
Nowa Rozedranka PL 87 Kb32
Nowa Ruda PL 91 Gb43
Nowa Sarzyna PL 93 Ka43
Nowa Sól PL 91 Ga39
Nowa Somianka PL 87 Jc36
Nowa Wieś PL 87 Jc34
Nowa Wieś Lęborska PL 86 Gd29
Nowa Wieś Wielka PL 86 Ha35
Nowe Berezowo PL 87 Kc34
Nowe Dwór PL 86 Hd30
Nowe Laski PL 85 Gd33
Nowe Miasto Lubawskie PL 86 Hd33
Nowe Miasto nad Pilicą PL 93 Jb39
Nowe Warpno PL 85 Fb32
Nowinka PL 87 Ka31
Nowodwór PL 93 Ka38
Nowogard PL 85 Fd33
Nowogard Bobrzański PL 91 Fd39
Nowogrodziec PL 91 Fd41
Nowo Miasto nad Wartą PL 92 Gd38
Nowe Dwór PL 87 Kb31
Nowy Dwór Gdański PL 86 Hc30
Nowy Dwór Mazowiecki PL 87 Jb36
Nowy Gaj PL 86 Hc37
Nowy Korczyn PL 93 Jd43
Nowy Orzechów PL 86 Kb39
Nowy Sącz PL 93 Jd45
Nowy Targ PL 92 Ja46
Nowy Wiśnicz PL 93 Jb44
Noyant F 23 Fd41
Noyelles-sur-Mer F 20 Gc32
Noyers F 25 Hd40
Noyers-Saint-Martin F 20 Gd34
Nozdrzec PL 93 Ka45
Nudersdorf D 90 Ec38
Nüdlingen D 89 Db44
Nudol' RUS 137 Fa10
Nueil-les-Aubiers F 23 Fb43
Nuenen NL 88 Bb38
Nueva Andalucia E 43 Cb76
Nuevalos E 33 Bd57
Nueva Carteya E 43 Cd73
Nueva Jarilla E 43 Bd77
Nueva Andalucia E 43 Db65
Nuevo Baztán E 38 Dd64
Nuijamaa FIN 69 La33
Nuisement-sur-Coôle F 21 Hd36
Nuits F 25 Hd40
Nuits-Saint-Georges F 25 Hd41
Nukari FIN 63 Kb38
Nukkumajoki FIN 51 Ka11
Nules E 39 Fc66

Numansdorp NL 17 Hd27
Nümbrecht D 88 Ca41
Nummela FIN 62 Ka39
Nummenkylä FIN 63 Jd38
Nummi-Pusula FIN 62 Kb39
Nummikoski FIN 67 Jb33
Nünchritz D 90 Ed40
Nuneaton GB 13 Fa24
Nunney GB 15 Ec29
Nunspeet NL 82 Bb36
Nunton GB 15 Ed29
Nuojua FIN 60 Kc23
Nuorgam FIN 47 Ka07
Nuoro I 107 Cb78
Núpsstaður IS 3 Bd06
Nurachi I 107 Bd77
Nuraminis I 107 Ca79
Nurallao I 107 Ca78
Nurmaa FIN 68 Kd35
Nurmes FIN 61 La27
Nurmijärvi FIN 61 Lc27
Nurmo FIN 59 Jb31
Nurmijärvi FIN 60 Dd46
Nurney IRL 7 Cc22
Nurrasuanto S 50 Hd16
Nürtingen D 95 Cd49
Nurzec PL 87 Kb35
Nurzec-Stacja PL 87 Kb36
Nusfjord N 48 Fa15
Nusnäs S 66 Fc38
Nusplingen D 95 Cc50
Nuthetal D 84 Ec37
Nutley GB 16 Fd29
Nuutajärvi FIN 68 Jd37
Nuutila FIN 60 Kb25
Nuuttilanmäki FIN 69 La33
Nuvvos FIN 50 Jc08
Nyåker S 58 Gb30
Nyåker S 59 Ha28
Nyberg S 59 Ha25
Nybergsund N 65 Ec37
Nyborg DK 77 Dd57
Nyborg S 54 Jb21
Nybro S 78 Ga52
Nybyn S 54 Hc23
Nyergesujfalu H 98 Hc52
Nygård N 48 Gb13
Nygård N 49 Gc11
Nyíddalur IS 3 Bc06
Nyíregyháza H 99 Ka51
Nyírmada H 99 Kb50
Nyírmeggyes H 99 Kb51
Nyírtura H 99 Ka51
Nykarleby FIN 59 Ja29
Nykøbing Falster DK 77 Eb59
Nykøbing M DK 76 Da51
Nyköping S 72 Gb45
Nykroppa S 72 Fd42
Nyksund N 48 Fc12
Nyland S 72 Gd44
Nyland S 58 Gc31
Nyland S 59 Ha29
Nylderen S 53 Gc22
Nyliden S 58 Gd29
Nyiraskoski CZ 91 Fc44
Nynäshamn S 73 Gd45
Nyneset N 57 Ed26
Nyon CH 94 Ba55
Nyons F 29 Jc51
Nyfany CZ 90 Fa36
Nyrola FIN 60 Kb32
Nysa PL 92 Ha43
Nysäter S 65 Fa33
Nysele S 59 Ha27
Nystad = Uusikaupunki FIN 67 Ja38
Nysted DK 77 Eb59
Nystrand S 54 Hc22
Nystu Trønnes N 65 Eb36
Nytorp S 54 Hd17
Nyvall S 53 Ha23
Nyžni Sirohozy UA 137 Fa16
Nyžni Torhaji UA 137 Fa16
Nyžn'ohirs'kyj UA 137 Fa17

## O

Oaivos N 50 Hd11
Oakford GB 14 Dd30
Oakham GB 13 Fb24
Oakington GB 16 Fd25
Oakley GB 15 Fb27
Oakley GB 15 Fa29
Oban GB 10 Db11
O Barco E 31 Bd57
Obdach A 97 Fc54
Obedacht PL 87 Kb30
Obeira UA 137 Ed16
Oberammergau D 95 Dc52
Oberasbach D 89 Dc46
Oberau A 96 Ea53
Oberaudorf D 96 Ed52
Oberaula D 89 Da41
Oberbipp CH 94 Bd53
Oberdrauburg A 96 Ec55
Oberei OH 94 Bd54
Obereisenheim D 89 Db44
Obergrafendorf A 97 Fd51
Obergünzburg D 95 Db52
Obergurgl A 95 Dc55
Oberhaching D 96 Dd52
Oberhaid D 89 Dc45
Oberhaslach D 83 Da30
Oberhausen D 88 Bd38
Oberhof D 94 Cb49
Oberkappel A 96 Fa49
Oberkirchen D 94 Cc49
Oberkochen D 95 Db48
Oberkotzau D 90 Ea44
Oberlungwitz D 90 Ec42
Obermaßfeld-Grimmenthal D 89 Dc43
Obermoschel D 94 Ca45
Obernberg am Inn A 96 Fa50
Obernberg am Brenner A 96 Dd54
Oberndorf am Neckar D 95 Cc50
Oberndorf bei Salzburg A 96 Ed51
Obernheim-Kirchenarnbach D 94 Ca46
Obernzenn D 89 Db46
Oberpframmern D 96 Ea51
Ober-Ramstadt D 89 Cc45
Oberriet CH 95 Cd53
Oberrot D 95 Cd47
Oberschleißheim D 96 Dd50
Oberschöna D 90 Ed42
Obersontheim D 95 Da47
Oberstaufen D 95 Da52
Oberstdorf D 95 Db53
Obersteigen F 94 Bd48
Obersteinbach F 94 Cb47
Oberteuringen D 95 Cd51
Oberthulba D 89 Db44
Oberursel D 89 Cc44

Oberviechtach D 90 Eb40
Oberwald CH 94 Cb55
Oberwart A 97 Gb54
Oberweißbach D 90 Dd42
Oberwesel D 88 Ca43
Oberweser D 89 Da39
Oberwiesenthal D 90 Ec43
Oberzeiring A 97 Fb54
Oiching D 96 Dd50
Oid GB 15 Fd25
Oldcastle IRL 5 Cc20
Old Deer GB 9 Ed08
Olderfjord N 46 Jb06
Oldeboorn NL 82 Bb34
Olderzee NL 82 Bc34
Oldeholtpade NL 82 Bb35
Oldekerk NL 82 Bd33
Oldemarkt NL 82 Bb35
Olden S 57 Fa29
Oldenburg D 83 Cc34
Oldenburg in Holstein D 83 Dc30
Oldenswort D 83 Da30
Oldenzaal NL 82 Bd36
Oldervik N 49 Ha09
Olderdalen N 49 Ha09
Olderneset N 47 Ka07
Oldham GB 13 Ed22
Oldhamstocks GB 11 Ec13
Old Head IRL 6 Bc26
Oldisleben D 90 Dd40
Old Lake GB 16 Fd22
Oldmeldrum GB 9 Ed08
Old Radnor GB 14 Ea26
Oldřichov CZ 92 Hb46
Oldřichovice CZ 92 Hb46
Oldsdurg GB 15 Ec28
Oldsum D 83 Db30
Oldways End GB 14 Ea29
Olecko PL 87 Ka30
Oledy PL 87 Ka35
Oleggio I 101 Cb59
Olekandrija UA 137 Ed15
Oleksandrivka UA 137 Ed15
Oleksandrivka UA 137 Ed15
Oleksandrivka UA 137 Fb13
Oleksandrivka UA 137 Fb15
Olelas E 30 Ba58
Olenino RUS 136 Ec10
Olenivka UA 137 Ed17
Oleśná CZ 92 Fa45
Oleśnica PL 92 Gd40
Oleśnica CZ 91 Gd46
Olesno PL 93 Jc43
Oleszyce PL 93 Kc43
Olevs'k UA 136 Eb14
Olen B 88 Ca38
Olhalvo P 36 Ad67
Ølhammeren N 57 Ec26
Olhão P 42 Ad74
Olhava FIN 54 Jd22
Olhava FIN 54 Jd22
O'hi RUS 137 Fb11
Ol'hovatka RUS 137 Fb13
Olia FIN 59 Jd30
Olimbia GR 128 Ba87
Olimbiáda GR 125 Cc78
Oliva E 45 Fc70
Oliva de la Frontera E 43 Bc71
Oliva de Mérida E 43 Bd70
Olivar F 28 Jd47
Olivares de Júcar E 38 Dc66
Oliveira de Azeméis P 36 Ad62
Oliveira de Barreiros P 36 Ba63
Oliveira do Bairro P 36 Ad63
Oliveira do Hospital P 36 Ba64
Olivenza E 36 Bb69
Olivet F 24 Gc40
Olivone CH 101 Cc56
Olkamangi S 54 Jb18
Olkiluoto FIN 60 Jb32
Olkkola FIN 60 Jd37
Olkusz PL 92 Hd44
Ollaberry GB 9 Fb04
Ollala FIN 60 Ja26
Ollerton GB 13 Fb22
Olletta E 33 Ed57
Olliergues F 28 Hc47
Ollikkala FIN 69 Lb35
Ollilia FIN 69 La35
Ollioules F 29 Jd55
Öllölä FIN 61 Ma31
Olloniego E 31 Cc55
Olmeda de la Cuesta E 38 Dc66
Olmeda del Rey E 38 Dc67
Olmedilla de Alarcón E 38 Dc67
Olmedo E 32 Da61
Olmeto F 112 Ca71
Olmi-Capella I 106 Cb69
Olmillos de Sasamón E 32 Db58
Olmo di Brembo I 101 Cd43
Olmos P 31 Bd60
Olmütz = Olomouc CZ 92 Gd46
Olney GB 15 Fb26
Olofok PL 92 Hd39
Olofström N 78 Fc54
Olomouc CZ 92 Gd46
Olonne-sur-Mer F 22 Ed44
Oloron-Sainte-Marie F 33 Fb55
Olot E 35 Ha59
Olovo BIH 105 Hd64
Olpe D 89 Cb39
Olpe D 89 Cb40
Ol'ša RUS 136 Ec11
Olszanica PL 93 Kb46
Olszana PL 87 Ka32
Olsztyn PL 86 Hd42
Olsztyn PL 92 Ja46
Olsztynek PL 86 Ja32
Olszyn PL 87 Kc31
Olten CH 94 Ca53
Oltre il Colle I 101 Cd43
Olvan E 35 Gd59
Olveda E 30 Bb56
Olveira E 30 Ac55
Olvera E 43 Cb75
Omagh GB 5 Cc17
Ómassa H 99 Jd50
Omeath IRL 5 Cd19
Omegna I 101 Cb58
Meñaca E 32 Eb60
Omiš HR 103 Fb61
Omišalj HR 103 Fc61
Ommen NL 82 Bc36
Ommundsaln N 57 Ed30
Onano I 108 Dd69
Onani I 107 Cb77
Onarheim N 62 Ca40
Oñate E 32 Ea56
Onda E 39 Fc66
Ondara E 45 Fc70
Ondarroa E 32 Ea55
Onesse-et-Laharie F 26 Fa53
Onet-le-Château F 27 Ha51
Onich GB 10 Dc10
Onifai I 107 Cb76
Onifari I 107 Cb78
Onkamo FIN 55 Kd17
Onkamo RUS 136 Ec10
Onkemäki FIN 68 Jd38
Onno I 101 Cc43
Onstwedde NL 82 Ca34

Olague E 33 Ed56
Olang I 96 Ea55
Oława PL 92 Gd41
Olbernhau D 90 Ed42
Olbia I 107 Cb74
Ølbięcin PL 93 Ka41
Olbramovice CZ 91 Fc46
Olbramovice CZ 97 Gd48
Olching D 96 Dd50
Old GB 15 Fb25
Ølberg N 62 Bd43
Obonin RUS 137 Ed11
Obornjak D 82 Bc33
Oborniki PL 85 Gc36
Oborniki Śląskie PL 91 Gc40
Ob'mov CZ 91 Fb46
Obra PL 91 Ga38
Obrigheim D 89 Cd46
Obrnice CZ 90 Fa36
Obrzycko PL 85 Gb36
Obśistvi CZ 91 Fb44
Øby DK 76 Cd53
Óbidos E 36 Ac61
Ocaña E 38 Dc66
Ocana F 106 Ca71
O Canizo E 31 Bc58
Óceretvate UA 137 Fa16
Ocharán E 32 Dd55
Ochiltree GB 10 Dd14
Ochla PL 91 Fd38
Ochsenfurt D 89 Db46
Ochtendung D 88 Ca42
Ochtrup D 82 Ca36
Ochtyrka UA 137 Ed14
Ockelbo S 66 Gb38
Ockholm D 83 Da29
Ockley GB 15 Fc29
Ocksjön S 58 Fd32
Ocna Sibiului RO 117 Db61
Octeville-sur-Mer F 19 Fd34
Öd S 58 Fc31
Odda DK 76 Dc54
Odeceixe P 42 Ab73
Odelzhausen D 96 Dd50
Odemira P 42 Ab72
Ódenäs S 72 Gc44
Odense DK 76 Dc56
Oderberg D 85 Fb35
Oderzo I 103 Eb59
Odesa UA 136 Ec17
Odiham GB 15 Fb28
Odincovo RUS 137 Fa10
Odnes N 64 Dd38
Ódorheiu Secuiesc RO 117 Db61
Odos F 26 Fd55
Odrowąż PL 93 Jb40
Oebisfelde D 84 Dd36
Oederquart D 83 Da32
Oeffelt NL 88 Bb38
Oegstgeest NL 17 Hd25
Oehna D 90 Dd40
Oelde D 89 Cc38
Oelsnitz D 90 Eb43
Oelsnitz D 90 Ec42
Oerlinghausen D 89 Cd38
Oestrich-Winkel D 89 Cd44
Oettingen D 95 Dc48
Ofena I 109 Fa70
Offenau D 89 Cd47
Offenbach D 89 Cd44
Offenbach an der Queich D 95 Cb47
Offenburg D 94 Ca48
Offerdal S 57 Fb30
Offida I 109 Ed68
Offingen D 95 Db49
Ofterdingen D 95 Cc49
Ogardy PL 85 Fd35
Ogbourne Saint George GB 15 Ed28
Ogéviller F 25 Jd37
Ogliastro Cilento I 112 Fc76
Ogliastro Marina I 112 Fc76
Ogmore-by-Sea GB 14 Ea28
Ognjanovo BG 125 Cd75
Ogonnelloe IRL 6 Bd22
Ogrodek PL 87 Jc33
Ogrodniczki PL 87 Kb33
Ogrosen D 90 Fa39
O Grove E 30 Ac56
Ogulin HR 103 Fd60
Ohistadt D 96 Dd52
Ohrdruf D 90 Dc42
Ohrid MK 124 Ba75
Ohta RUS 69 Mb30
Ohtanajärvi S 54 Jb18
Ohtola FIN 68 Jd33
Ohtsejohka FIN 47 Jd07
Oijärvi FIN 55 Ka21
Oilean Ciarraí IRL 6 Bb24
Oilgate IRL 7 Cc24
Oimbra E 30 Bb59
Oinaala FIN 68 Ka33
Oineskoski FIN 68 Kb32
Oingt F 25 Ja46
Oinasjärvi FIN 60 Kd37
Oinasjärvi FIN 62 Ka39
Oion E 33 Eb57
Ois E 30 Ba54
Oisemont F 20 Gc33
Oisterwijk NL 88 Ba38
Oja FIN 59 Ja29
Öja FIN 73 Jd84
Ojakkala FIN 54 Jd24
Ôjan S 57 Ea32
Öje S 58 Gd60
Ojebyn S 59 Hc25
Øjersby S 54 Hc22
Ojos Negros E 39 Gd63
Øjrzanów PL 87 Jd36
Ojvasselen S 65 Fa35
Okáka FIN 60 Jd37
Okány H 99 Ka54
Oken S 58 Gb30
Okkenhaug N 57 Ec29
Oksajärvi S 50 Hd15
Øksakoski FIN 60 Kb24
Øksfjord N 46 Hd06
Øksfjordbotn N 46 Hd07
Oksval N 56 Bd59
Øksvoll N 57 Ea28
Øktsmyr RUS 137 Fa16
Okučani HR 103 Hc61
Okulice PL 93 Jc40
Okulovka RUS 136 Ec09
Oksa FIN 69 Ld33
Okúnev H 99 Kd17
Õra SY 136 Eb12
Ólafsfjördur IS 3 Bc02
Ólafsvík IS 2 Ab05

Olsomarso I 113 Gb78
Orta N 64 Cc33
Orta Nova I 110 Ga73
Orta San Giulio I 101 Cb58
Orte I 108 Ea69
Ortenberg D 89 Cd43
Ortenburg D 96 Ec49
Orthez F 26 Fb54
Ortigosa E 38 Ea58
Ortigosa de Rioalmar E 32 Ac65
Ortigueira E 30 Bb53
Orton GB 13 Ec18
Ortrand D 90 Fa40
Ortueri I 107 Ca77
Ortwig D 85 Fb36
Orune I 107 Cb76
Orvalut E 23 Ed42
Orvelte NL 82 Bd34
Orvieto I 108 Ea69
Orvin GB 15 Hc25
Orwell GB 16 Fc26
Orzechowo D 90 Fa41
Orzesze PL 92 Hd44
Orzinuovi I 101 Cd59
Orzivu UA 136 Ea14
Orzyca UA 137 Ed15
Orzysz PL 87 Jc32
Os N 48 Fc16
Os N 65 Ca40
Os N 65 Eb33
Osa de la Vega E 38 Ea67
Osby S 78 Fb53
Oscaig GB 8 Db08
Oschatz D 90 Ed40
Oschersleben D 90 Dd38
Osečná CZ 91 Fc42
Osek CZ 90 Fa36
Osen D 84 Db36
Osen N 57 Eb26
Øsenskog N 65 Eb37
Øsevollen S 58 Gb30
Oskarshamn S 78 Ga52
Oskarström S 77 Ed52
Oskowo PL 86 Gd30
Osli H 98 Gd52
Oslo N 65 Ea41
Oslomare I 100 Gc60
Osmington GB 15 Ec31
Os'mino RUS 136 Ea09
Ösmo S 73 Gd45
Osnabrück D 83 Cc36
Ośno Lubuskie PL 85 Fc36
Osny F 20 Gc36
Osoblaha CZ 92 Ha44
Osoppo I 103 Ec57
Osor E 35 Hb59
Osoyoen N 57 Ea32
Ospitaletto I 101 Da59
Osor E 35 Fa55
Ossett GB 13 Fa21
Ossa de Montiel E 38 Ea69
Osse-en-Aspe F 33 Fb55
Osset RUS 137 Fd39
Ossiach A 97 Fb56
Ostabat GB 13 Fa18
Ôstanbo S 66 Gd37
Ostanbäck S 59 Ha29
Østansjö S 53 Gd21
Ostaskov RUS 136 Ec10
Ostavall S 58 Gb30
Ostbevern D 83 Cb37
Østby N 57 Ec31
Osten D 83 Da32
Ostende = Oostende B 17 Ha29
Osterburg D 84 Ea35
Osterburken D 89 Cd46
Osterbymo S 72 Ga45
Osterbruck GB 9 Ec06
Östercappeln D 83 Cc36
Österfärnebo S 66 Gb40
Österfeld D 90 Ea41
Osterhofen D 96 Ec49
Osterholz-Scharmbeck D 83 Cd33
Øster Hurup DK 77 Dd52
Østerlars DK 78 Fd58
Ostermiething A 96 Ec51
Osterøde D 89 Db39
Osteröd S 72 Fd42
Osterode am Harz D 89 Db39
Østersund FIN 68 Kb30
Österwieck D 89 Dc38
Østervåla S 66 Gd40
Østerwieck D 89 Dc38
Østerwik D 89 Cd47
Østfildern D 95 Cd48
Osthammar S 66 Gd40
Ostheim vor der Rhön D 89 Db43
Osthofen D 89 Cc45
Ostiano I 101 Da60
Ostiglia I 102 Dc61
Östloning S 58 Gb32
Ostra I 109 Ed66
Ostrach D 95 Cd51
Ostrava CZ 92 Hb45
Østre Bredek IRL 4 Bb19
Ostrhauderfehn D 83 Cb33
Ostritz D 91 Fb41
Ostróda PL 86 Hd32
Ostroh UA 136 Ea15
Ostrołeka PL 87 Jc34
Ostros MNE 119 Jb71
Ostrov CZ 90 Ec44
Ostrov RUS 136 Ea10
Ostrov UA 137 Ed17
Ostrov CZ 91 Fd42
Ostrovce CZ 91 Ga42
Ostrovnoje RUS 137 Fd17
Ostrów PL 93 Jd45
Ostrowiec PL 85 Fc32
Ostrowite PL 86 Hc36
Ostrów Mazowiecka PL 87 Jd35
Ostrowo PL 86 Hc34
Ostrów Wielkopolski PL 92 Gd39
Ostrowy Tuszowskie PL 93 Jd43
Ostrožac BIH 103 Ga61
Ostrožac BIH 105 Hd65
Ostrožská Nová Ves CZ 92 Gd48
Ostseebad Kühlungsborn D 84 Eb31
Ostuni I 113 Hb75
Osturňa SK 92 Jb46
Osvik S 59 Hc25
Oświęcim PL 92 Hd44
Oszkó H 98 Gc54
Oszmianka-Nowa PL 87 Ka35
Otaci MD 117 Db55
Otalampi FIN 62 Ka39
Otanmäki FIN 60 Kc25
Otava FIN 68 Kd34
Oteiza E 33 Ec57
Oteo E 32 Dd56
Otepää EST 75 Lb46
Oteren N 49 Ha11
Otfinów PL 93 Jc43
Otford GB 16 Fd28
Othery GB 14 Eb29
Otley GB 16 Gb26
Otočzyn PL 86 Hb35
Otofwiec PL 86 Hd35
Otmuchów PL 92 Gd43
Otnes N 65 Eb35
Otradnaja RUS 137 Fd17
Otradnyj RUS 137 Ga09
Otrokovice CZ 98 Gd48
Otta I 107 Ca76
Ottana I 107 Cb77
Ottanway I 96 Fa51
Ottenby S 78 Ga53
Ottendorf-Okrilla D 90 Fa41
Ottenhöfen D 95 Fb50
Ottensheim A 97 Fb50
Otter Ferry GB 10 Dc12
Otterfing D 96 Ea51
Otterlo NL 82 Bb36
Otterndorf D 83 Cd31
Ottersweier D 95 Cb48
Otterswick GB 9 Fb04
Ottery Saint Mary GB 14 Ea30
Ottnang A 96 Fa51
Ottobeuren D 95 Db51
Ottobrunn D 96 Ea51
Ottone I 101 Cc62
Ottrau D 89 Da41
Ottweiler D 88 Bd46
Otvice CZ 90 Ed43
Otwock PL 87 Jd37
Otxandio E 32 Eb56
Ouanne F 24 Hd40
Oud-Beijerland NL 17 Hd27
Ouddorp NL 17 Hc26
Oude Pekela NL 82 Ca34
Oudenaarde B 17 Hb30
Oudenbosch NL 17 Hd27
Oudeschoot NL 82 Bb34
Oude-Tonge NL 82 Bb36
Oudewater NL 82 Ba36
Oud Gastel NL 17 Hd27
Oudleusen NL 82 Bc35
Oughterard IRL 4 Bc20
Ougney F 25 Jc42
Ouguela P 36 Bb68
Ouistreham F 19 Fc35
Oulainen FIN 60 Jd25
Oulanka FIN 55 Kd18
Oulart IRL 7 Cc24
Oulins F 20 Gc36
Oulu FIN 54 Ka23
Oulunsalo FIN 54 Ka24
Ouranoúpoli GR 125 Cd79
Oureil E 30 Bb53
Ourense E 30 Bb57
Ouroux-en-Morvan F 25 Hd42
Ouroux-sur-Saône F 25 Jc43
Ourville-en-Caux F 19 Ga34
Oust F 34 Gb56
Outeiro da Cabeça P 36 Aa67
Outeiro de Rei E 30 Bb55
Outines F 21 Ja37
Outokumpu FIN 61 Lc30
Outomuro (Cartelle) E 30 Bb57
Outreau F 20 Gb31
Ouzouer-le-Marché F 24 Gc40
Ovada I 100 Ca62
Ovanmo S 58 Ga29
Ovansjö S 66 Gd22
Ovar P 36 Ac62
Ovelgönne D 83 Cc33
Øverås N 58 Gb30
Øveråt D 88 Ca41
Øverbygd N 49 Gd11
Overdinkel NL 82 Ca36
Overgård S 53 Ga21
Øvergård N 64 Dd33
Overhalla N 57 Ec26
Overhogdal S 58 Fd31
Øverjeppo FIN 59 Jb29
Øverkalix S 54 Jb20
Overkil NL 88 Bb38
Overmark FIN 59 Ja32
Øvermo S 64 Dd38
Øvermoriärv S 54 Jb19
Øvermyrarv S 54 Jb19
Øverpelt B 88 Bb39
Øverris B 88 Bb39
Øverton GB 13 Ec23
Øverton GB 15 Fa28
Øvervågd N 49 Ha11
Øvergåsrd N 64 Dd33
Øvergård N 49 Ha11
Overrede N 65 Ec37
Øvervad N 49 Ha11
Overum S 72 Ga46
Ovindoli I 109 Fa70
Oviedo E 31 Cc54
Øvitsböle FIN 68 Kd38
Øvra S 59 Gd28
Øvra S 59 Gd28
Øvre Årdal N 63 Da37
Øvre Rendal N 65 Eb36
Øvre Soppero S 50 Ha15
Øvre Vang N 65 Eb38
Øwik S 53 Gd21
Øxelösund S 72 Gb46
Oxford GB 15 Fa27
Oxhill GB 15 Fa26
Øxna N 57 Ed26
Oyber S 52 Fd15
Oye-et-Pallet F 25 Ka43
Øye-Plage F 20 Gc30
Øyem N 52 Fc21
Oyonnax F 25 Jc45
Øyslebø N 62 Cb47
Oyten D 83 Cd34
Ozalj HR 104 Ga60
Oża dos Rios E 30 Ba54
Ozeblio PL 87 Kb32
Ózd H 99 Jd50
Ozerki RUS 137 Fd10
Ozery RUS 137 Fa11
Ozieri I 107 Ca76
Ozimek PL 92 Ha42
Ozorków PL 92 Hc38
Ozzano Monferrato I 101 Ca61

## P

Paajalankylä FIN 69 La34
Pääjärvi FIN 60 Ka31
Paakkola FIN 54 Jc20
Paal B 88 Ba39
Paanala FIN 60 Kc32
Paaslahti FIN 60 Kd28
Pabianice PL 92 Hc39
Pabiržė LT 81 Kc54
Pabradė LT 81 Kd56
Paceco CZ 91 Fc46
Pacsa H 98 Gd55
Pacyna PL 86 Hd37
Paczków PL 91 Gc43
Padankoski FIN 68 Kb36
Pádaste EST 74 Jd45
Paddeby N 47 Kc06
Padinska Skela SRB 120 Bb62
Padina MNE 120 Ad60
Padinska Skela SRB 120 Bb62
Paderborn D 89 Cd38
Padern F 35 Ha56
Padėsė EST 74 Ka43
Padova I Padova I 102 Ea60
Padul E 44 Db75
Padula I 112 Ga76
Paduli I 112 Fc74
Padure LV 80 Jc51
Padworth GB 15 Fa28
Paesana I 100 Bc61
Paese I 102 Ea59
Pag HR 103 Fc63
Pagani I 112 Fd75
Pago E 44 Dc76
Paguera E 41 Ha67
Pagny-sur-Meuse F 21 Jc37
Pagny-sur-Moselle F 21 Jc36
Pago E 44 Dc76
Paguera E 41 Ha67
Paharova S 54 Hd18
Pahila FIN 60 Kc29
Pahkakangas FIN 60 Kc30
Pahkala FIN 60 Jc27
Pahkamäki FIN 60 Kc29
Pahranitchny BY 136 Dd13
Paignton GB 14 Ea31
Paimbœuf F 22 Ed42
Paimio FIN 68 Jd38
Paimpol F 18 Ed37
Paimpont F 23 Ed39
Painswick GB 15 Ec27
Paisley GB 10 Dd13
Paittasjärvi S 50 Hd13
Pajala S 50 Hd16
Pajarón E 38 Dc66
Pajęczno PL 92 Hc40
Pajujärvi FIN 60 Kd28
Pajukoski FIN 61 Lb28
Pajula FIN 68 Jd37
Pajulankylä FIN 69 Ld32
Pajupuro FIN 60 Kb29
Paka FIN 63 Kb37
Pakankylä FIN 68 Jd38
Pakila FIN 63 Kb38
Pakosze PL 86 Hd30
Pakość PL 86 Hb36
Paks H 98 Hc55
Palacios del Sil E 31 Ca56
Palaciosrubios E 37 Cc62
Palafrugell E 35 Hd59
Palagiano I 111 Gd76
Palagonia I 115 Fd48
Palaia I 102 Db65
Palaichori CY 135 Bc96
Palaios E 31 Cb57
Palaiseau F 20 Gd37
Palamás GR 129 Bc82
Palamós E 35 Hd59
Palana LT 80 Ja54
Palanga LT 80 Ja54
Palas de Rei E 30 Bb55
Palast-Iguereta GB 13 Fd22
Palau I 107 Cb74
Palazuelos de la Sierra E 32 Dd58
Palazzo Acreide I 115 Fc87
Palazzolo sull 'Oglio I 101 Cd59
Palazzo San Gervasio I 113 Gb75
Paldiski EST 74 Jd42
Palekastro GR 133 Da96
Paleochora GR 132 Ca95
Palencia E 32 Da59
Palenciana E 43 Cd74
Palenzuela E 32 Db59
Paléokastritsa GR 124 Ac79
Paleokastro GR 123 Cb80
Paleopoli GR 126 Da79
Palermo I 114 Ec84
Páleros GR 128 Ad82
Palestrina I 109 Eb72
Palguta LT 80 Ja54
Palharesa samevište S 53 Gb19
Paliano I 109 Eb72
Palić SRB 120 Ba59
Palianec I 32 Ea56
Palinuro I 112 Fd77
Paliouri GR 129 Ca80
Palizzi I 115 Gc96
Palizzi Marina I 115 Gc96
Paljakka FIN 55 Kd19
Paljakka FIN 60 Kd26
Paljavaara FIN 69 Mb31
Pälkäne FIN 68 Ka36
Pälkjärvi FIN 61 Ld31
Palkovice CZ 92 Hb46
Pålkem S 54 Hd18
Pallagorio I 111 Gc80
Pallaresa samevište S 53 Gb19
Pallarés E 43 Bd72
Pallastunturi FIN 50 Ja13
Pallerols del Cantó E 34 Gb58
Palling D 96 Ec51
Pallisieux F 19 Gb36
Palluau F 22 Ed43
Palluau-sur-Indre F 24 Gb43
Palma E 41 Hb67
Palma Campania I 112 Fb75
Palma de Mallorca E 41 Hb67
Palma del Río E 43 Cb73
Palmadula I 106 Bd73
Palmanova I 103 Ec59
Palmela P 36 Ac69
Palmanyola E 41 Hb67
Palmi I 113 Gb83
Palo del Colle I 113 Gd74
Palo del Colle I 113 Gd74
Palojoensuu FIN 50 Ja13
Palojärvi FIN 50 Jb12
Palokangas FIN 60 Kd28
Palokastër AL 128 Ac79
Palomas E 43 Bd70
Palombara Sabina I 109 Eb71
Palomera E 38 Dc66
Palombaio I 113 Gc74
Palos de la Frontera E 43 Bc74
Palota I 109 Fa70
Palovaara FIN 55 Kd20

Palovaara FIN 61 Ma29
Palsina FIN 68 Ka34
Pålsträsk S 54 Hc22
Paltamo FIN 60 Kd25
Paltanen FIN 60 Kd32
Paltusmäki FIN 60 Kc29
Paluzza I 97 Ed56
Pámfila GR 127 Db79
Pamhagen A 98 Gb53
Pamiątkowo PL 85 Gb36
Pamiers F 34 Gc56
Pampaneira E 44 Db75
Pamparato I 100 Bd63
Pamplona E 33 Ed57
Pamporovo BG 125 Da77
Pamukkale TR 131 Fd88
Pana FIN 61 Ma29
Panagia GR 126 Da72
Panagiurište BG 126 Da72
Panagsueira P 42 Ac71
Panazol F 27 Gb47
Pandino I 101 Cd60
Pandrup DK 70 Dc50
Pandy GB 12 Eb27
Panelia FIN 67 Ja37
Panévėžys LT 80 Kc54
Pangbourne GB 15 Fa28
Panicale I 108 Ea68
Paničkovo RUS 137 Fd17
Panicale I 108 Ea68
Panikva BY 136 Dc12
Panika GR 125 Cc79
Panissières F 28 Ja47
Paniza E 39 Fa62
Pankajärvi FIN 61 Ld28
Pankasz H 97 Gb55
Panker D 84 Dd30
Pannarano I 98 Hd53
Pano Panagia CY 135 Bc96
Pánormos GR 130 Db80
Pánormos GR 134 Eb90
Pantaleone E 43 Cd77
Pantano de Puentes E 45 Ec73
Pantelleria I 114 Eb76
Panticosa E 33 Fc57
Pant Mawr GB 14 Ea26
Pantão I 32 Ea56
Pantijärvi FIN 61 La28
Pankasz H 97 Gb55
Panttila FIN 59 Ja32
Pantymenyn GB 14 Dc26
Paola I 113 Gb80
Pápa H 98 Gd53
Papasidero I 113 Gb78
Papenburg D 83 Cb34
Päpigo GR 124 Ad79
Papinniemi FIN 61 Ld31
Papowo Biskupie PL 86 Hb34
Pappenheim D 95 Dc48
Páhka Amnos GR 133 Dc96
Paprotnia PL 86 Ja37
Papworth Everard GB 16 Fc25
Par GB 14 Db31
Parabita I 113 Hc77
Paracuellos E 39 Gc63
Paracuellos de Jiloca E 39 Ec62
Paracuellos de Jiloca E 39 Ec62
Párad H 99 Jd51
Paradas E 43 Cb74
Paradela E 30 Bb55
Paradela P 36 Ba62
Paradinas de San Juan E 37 Cc62
Paradinas de San Juan E 37 Cc62
Paragouda GR 129 Bc85
Parainen FIN 67 Jd40
Parakalamos GR 124 Ad79
Parakka S 50 Hc15
Paralakrel FIN 54 Jc20
Paralia GR 128 Ba83
Paralia GR 129 Bc84
Paralía Akrátas GR 129 Bc85
Paralía Tiroú GR 132 Bd89
Paralía Ástros GR 129 Bd88
Paralío Irion GR 129 Bc87
Paramithiá GR 128 Ac81
Páramo E 31 Cb55
Páramo del Sil E 31 Ca56
Paramos E 30 Ba55
Paray-le-Monial F 25 Hd44
Parchim D 84 Eb33
Parcé-sur-Sarthe F 23 Fc40
Parchim D 84 Eb33
Parczew PL 93 Kb38
Pardé E 31 Cc56
Pardubice CZ 91 Ga44
Paredes de Nava E 32 Da58
Pareja E 38 Dd64
Parekis samevište S 53 Gb19
Parenza E 31 Cc56
Parentis-en-Born F 26 Fa52
Parets del Vallès E 35 Ha60
Parikkala FIN 69 Ld33
Paris F 20 Gd37
Parisot F 27 Gd52
Park GB 5 Cc16
Parknadi S 53 Gd19
Parlamentí GR 129 Bd85
Parla E 38 Db65
Parlier-l'Evèque F 23 Fd40
Parndorf A 98 Gc51
Pärnu EST 74 Jd45
Pärnu-Jaagupi EST 74 Jd44
Parola FIN 68 Ka37
Parpan CH 94 Cd55
Parsberg D 95 Dd47
Parsów PL 85 Fd33
Partakko FIN 51 Kb10
Partanna I 114 Eb85
Partanna-Mondello I 114 Ec83
Partenkirchen, Garmisch- D 95 Dc53
Parterre GR 127 Db80
Partille S 72 Fd48
Partinico I 114 Ec84
Partinitsa SK 98 Hd49
Partry IRL 4 Bc19
Parwich GB 13 Ed23
Parzęczew PL 92 Hc38
Parzymiechy PL 92 Hc41
Pasaje de la Frontera E 33 Ec55
Pasaron de la Vera E 37 Cb65
Pas-de-Jeu F 23 Fc43
Pasewalk D 85 Fc33
Pasian di Prato I 103 Ec58

Paškovskij – Psebaj


Paškovskij RUS 137 Fc17
Pasłek PL 86 Hd31
Passage East IRL 7 Cc25
Passail A 97 Fd54
Passais F 23 Fb38
Passariano I 103 Ec58
Passau D 96 Ed49
Passekårsa S 49 Ha15
Passow D 84 Eb33
Pastavy BY 136 Ea12
Pastetten D 96 Ea50
Paštiky CZ 90 Fa46
Pasto FIN 60 Jc32
Pastor E 30 Ba55
Pastoriza E 31 Bc54
Pastrana E 38 Ea64
Pastwiska PL 93 Jc40
Pasynki PL 87 Kb34
Pásztó H 98 Ja51
Pat H 104 Gd56
Patana FIN 60 Jc29
Patavesi FIN 68 Kb35
Patay F 24 Gc39
Pateley Bridge GB 13 Ed19
Pateniemi FIN 55 Ka23
Paterek PL 86 Gd34
Paterna E 39 Fb67
Paternion A 96 Ed55
Paternò I 115 Fc85
Paterswolde NL 82 Bd33
Patitiri GR 129 Cc83
Pátmos GR 134 Ea89
Patna GB 10 Dd15
Patolankylä FIN 67 Jb34
Patoniva FIN 50 Jd08
Pátra GR 128 Bb85
Patras = Pátra GR 128 Bb85
Pătrăuți RO 118 Eb55
Patreksfjörður IS 2 Aa03
Patrickswell IRL 6 Bd23
Patrikka FIN 61 Mb30
Patrington GB 13 Fc21
Patsola FIN 61 Ma31
Pattada I 107 Cb75
Pattensen D 83 Db37
Patti I 115 Fc84
Pattijoki FIN 60 Jd25
Pattishall GB 15 Fb26
Patù I 113 Hc78
Pau F 33 Fc55
Pauillac F 26 Fb49
Paulerspury GB 15 Fb26
Paulhac-en-Margeride F 28 Hc50
Paulhaguet F 28 Hc49
Paulhan F 28 Hc54
Paulinenaue D 84 Ec36
Paullo I 101 Cc59
Paüls E 40 Fd63
Pausa D 90 Eb43
Pauträsk S 58 Gc25
Pavezin F 28 Ja48
Pavia I 101 Cc60
Pavilly F 19 Ga34
Pāvilosta LV 79 Ja51
Pavlohrad UA 137 Fa15
Pavlov CZ 97 Fd47
Pavlovka RUS 137 Fd11
Pavlovo RUS 137 Fb09
Pavlovsk RUS 137 Fb13
Pavlovskaja RUS 137 Fc16
Pavlovskij Posad RUS 137 Fa10
Pavlovskoe RUS 137 Fb09
Pavlyš UA 137 Ed15
Pavullo nel Frignano I 102 Db63
Päwesein D 84 Ec36
Pawlett GB 14 Eb29
Pawlikowice PL 92 Hc39
Pawłow PL 92 Ha44
Pawłów PL 93 Kc40
Pawłowice PL 91 Gc39
Pawłowice PL 92 Hb45
Pawłowice PL 93 Jd39
Pawonków PL 92 Hb42
Payerne CH 94 Bc54
Paymogo E 42 Ba72
Payrac F 27 Gc50
Payzac F 27 Gb48
Pazardžik BG 126 Da73
Pazin HR 103 Fa60
Pazuengos E 32 Ea58
Pcim PL 92 Ja45
Peädsek FIN 51 Ka09
Peal de Becerro E 44 Db72
Peasedown Saint John GB 15 Ec28
Peasemore GB 15 Fa28
Peasenhall GB 16 Gb25
Péaule F 22 Ec41
Pebworth GB 15 Ed26
Peć KSV 120 Ad70
Peccioli I 108 Db66
Pécel H 98 Hd53
Pechina E 44 Ea76
Peckelsheim D 89 Cd39
Pečory RUS 136 Ea10
Pécs H 105 Hb57
Pedagaggi I 115 Fc87
Pederobba I 102 Ea58
Pedersöre FIN 59 Jb29
Pedersören kunta FIN 59 Jb29
Pedoulas CY 135 Bd96
Pedralba E 39 Fb67
Pedraza E 38 Dc62
Pedreguer E 45 Fc70
Pedreña E 32 Dc54
Pedrera E 43 Cc74
Pedro Bernardo E 37 Cd65
Pedrógão P 36 Ab65
Pedrógão Pequeno P 36 Ad65
Pedro Muñoz E 38 Dd68
Pedrosa del Principe E 32 Db58
Pedrosa de Tobalina E 32 Dd56
Peebles GB 11 Eb14
Peel GB 12 Dc19
Peenemünde D 84 Fa31
Peer B 88 Ba40
Peffingen D 88 Bc44
Pegau D 90 Eb41
Pegnitz D 90 Ea45
Pego E 45 Fc70
Peinchorran GB 8 Db08
Peine D 83 Dc37
Peipin F 29 Jd52
Peißen D 90 Ea39
Peißen D 90 Eb39
Peißenberg D 95 Dc52
Peiting D 95 Dc52
Peitz D 91 Fb38
Peize NL 82 Bd33
Pekkala FIN 51 Kb09
Pekkaperä FIN 60 Ka28
Pelacoy F 27 Gc51
Pelago I 108 Dd65
Pełczyce PL 85 Fd34
Pelhřimov CZ 97 Fd47
Pelisalmi FIN 68 Ka35
Pelkoseniemi FIN 51 Kb16
Pellafol F 29 Jd50
Pellaro I 115 Ga84
Pellegrino Parmense I 101 Cd62
Pellérd H 105 Hb58
Pellingen D 88 Bc45
Pello FIN 54 Jb18
Pello S 54 Jb18
Peltokangas FIN 60 Jd30
Peltomaa FIN 59 Ja31
Peltosalmi FIN 60 Kd28
Peltovuoma FIN 50 Jb13
Pełty PL 86 Ja30
Pélussin F 28 Ja48
Pembroke GB 14 Db27
Pembroke Dock GB 14 Db27
Pembury GB 16 Fd29
Pemfling D 96 Ec47
Penacova P 36 Ad64
Peñafiel E 32 Db60
Peñaflor E 43 Cb73
Peñafuente E 31 Bd55
Peñalén E 39 Ec64
Penalva do Castelo P 36 Ba63
Penänö FIN 55 Kc20
Peñaranda de Bracamonte E 37 Cc62
Peñaranda de Duero E 32 Dc60
Peñarroya de Tastavins E 40 Fd63
Peñarroya-Pueblonuevo E 43 Cc71
Penarth GB 14 Eb28
Peñas de San Pedro E 45 Ec70
Peñausende E 31 Cb61
Penc H 98 Hd52
Pencaitland GB 11 Ec13
Penderyn GB 14 Ea27
Pendilla E 31 Cc55
Pendine GB 14 Dc27
Penészlek H 99 Kb52
Penge GB 16 Fc28
Pengsjö S 59 Hb28
Penha Garcia P 37 Bc65
Penhors F 22 Db39
Peniche P 36 Aa66
Penicuik GB 11 Eb13
Penig D 90 Ec41
Penilhos P 42 Ad72
Peñíscola E 40 Fd65
Penkridge GB 13 Ed24
Penmachno GB 12 Ea23
Penmaenmawr GB 12 Dd22
Penmarc'h F 22 Dc40
Pennant GB 12 Ea24
Pennapiedimonte I 109 Fa71
Penne F 27 Gc53
Penne I 109 Fa70
Penne-d'Agenais F 27 Ga52
Pennerley GB 12 Eb24
Pennyghael GB 10 Da11
Peno RUS 136 Ec10
Penol F 28 Jb48
Penrhyn Bay GB 12 Ea22
Penrith GB 13 Ec17
Penruddock GB 12 Eb17
Penryn GB 14 Db32
Pensala FIN 59 Jb30
Pensilva GB 14 Dc31
Penta di Casinca F 106 Cc69
Pentinkylä FIN 69 Lb37
Pentling D 96 Ea48
Pentraeth GB 12 Dd22
Pentrefoelas GB 12 Ea23
Pentyrch GB 14 Ea28
Penvins F 22 Eb41
Penybont GB 14 Ea25
Penygroes GB 12 Dd22
Penysarn GB 12 Dd21
Penza RUS 137 Fc11
Penzance GB 14 Da32
Penzberg D 96 Dd52
Penzing D 95 Dc51
Penzlin D 84 Ed33
Pér H 98 Ha52
Perach D 96 Ec50
Perahóri GR 128 Ac84
Peräkylä FIN 59 Ja32
Peräkylä FIN 69 Lb36
Perälä FIN 55 Kc19
Peralada E 35 Hb58
Peralejos de las Truchas E 39 Ec64
Peralta de la Sal E 34 Fd59
Peranka FIN 55 La21
Peränkylä FIN 67 Ja36
Peräseinäjoki FIN 60 Jc32
Perast MNE 111 Hd69
Perävaara S 54 Jb19
Perchtoldsdorf A 97 Gb51
Perdasdefogu I 107 Cb78
Perdaxius I 107 Bd80
Perdoche E 43 Cd71
Peréa GR 125 Ca78
Perečyn UA 136 Dd16
Perehins'ke UA 136 Ea16
Pereira E 30 Ad55
Perejaslav-Chmel'nyc'kyj UA 136 Ec14
Perekopka RUS 137 Fd13
Perelešinskij RUS 137 Fb12
Pereruela E 31 Cb61
Pereščepyne UA 137 Fa15
Pereslavl'-Zalesskij RUS 137 Fa09
Pereszne H 97 Gc53
Peret F 28 Hc54
Perg A 97 Fc50
Pergine Valsugana I 102 Dc57
Pergola I 109 Ec66
Perheniemi FIN 68 Kd37
Perho FIN 60 Jd30
Peri I 102 Dc59
Periam RO 116 Bc59
Periana E 44 Da75
Périgné F 23 Fc46
Périgueux F 27 Ga49
Pērkone LV 79 Ja53
Perl D 88 Bb45
Perlé L 21 Jc33
Perleberg D 84 Eb34
Pernå FIN 68 Kd38
Pernaa FIN 59 Jb30
Pernaja FIN 68 Kd38
Pernarec CZ 90 Ed45
Pernek SK 98 Gd50
Pernes P 36 Ac67
Pernes-les-Fontaines F 29 Jc52
Perniö FIN 68 Jc40
Pernitz A 97 Ga52
Peroguarda P 42 Ad71
Péronne F 20 Ha33
Pêro Pinheiro P 36 Aa68
Perosa Argentina I 100 Bb60
Perpignan F 35 Hb57
Perranporth GB 14 Db31
Perrecy-les-Forges F 25 Hd44
Perrero I 100 Bb60
Perrone I 113 Gd76
Perros-Guirec F 18 Ea37
Persan F 20 Gd36
Pershagen S 72 Gc44
Persön S 54 Hd22
Perstorp S 77 Fa54
Perth GB 11 Eb11
Perthes F 21 Hd34
Perthes F 24 Ha38
Pertoúli GR 128 Ba81
Perttaus FIN 54 Jd17
Pertunmaa FIN 68 Kd35
Pertusa E 33 Fc59
Peruc CZ 90 Fa43
Perugia I 108 Ea67
Perunkajärvi FIN 55 Ka18
Pervijze B 17 Ha29
Pervomajsk RUS 137 Fc10
Pervomajs'k UA 136 Ec16
Pervomajskij RUS 137 Fb11
Pervomajskoe RUS 137 Ga11
Pervomajs'kyj UA 137 Fa14
Perzów PL 92 Ha40
Pesadas de Burgos E 32 Dc57
Pesaro I 109 Ec65
Pesčanokopskoe RUS 137 Fd16
Pescara I 109 Fb70
Pescasseroli I 109 Fa72
Peschici I 110 Gb71
Peschiera Borromeo I 101 Cc59
Peschiera del Garda I 102 Db59
Pescia I 108 Db65
Pescina I 109 Ed71
Pescolanciano I 109 Fb72
Peso P 42 Ba71
Pesqueira E 30 Ac56
Pessac F 26 Fb50
Pestovo RUS 136 Ec09
Pestravka RUS 137 Ga10
Petäiskylä FIN 61 Lb27
Petäjäkangas FIN 55 Kb22
Petäjäkylä FIN 60 Kb29
Petäjämäki FIN 60 Ka25
Petäjäskoski FIN 60 Jd26
Petäjävesi FIN 68 Kb33
Petalax FIN 59 Hd31
Petalidi GR 132 Bb89
Pétange L 21 Jc34
Petäys FIN 61 La28
Peterborough GB 16 Fc24
Peterchurch GB 14 Eb26
Peterculter GB 9 Ed09
Peterhead GB 9 Fa08
Peterlee GB 13 Fa17
Petersaurach D 95 Dc47
Petersberg D 89 Da42
Petersdorf D 95 Dc49
Petersfield GB 15 Fb30
Petershagen D 83 Cd36
Petershagen-Vogelsdorf D 84 Fa36
Petershausen D 96 Dd50
Peterstone Wentlooge GB 14 Eb28
Peterstow GB 15 Ec26
Peterswell IRL 6 Bd21
Pétfürdő H 98 Hb54
Petiknäs S 59 Hb25
Petilia Policastro I 113 Gd80
Petin E 31 Bc57
Petit-Palais-et-Cornemps F 26 Fc50
Petra E 41 Hc67
Petra GR 130 Ea83
Petralia Soprana I 114 Fa85
Petralia Sottana I 114 Fa85
Petrálona GR 125 Cb79
Petrer E 45 Fb71
Petrinja HR 104 Gb60
Petrivka UA 136 Ec14
Pétrola E 45 Ed70
Petromäki FIN 61 La31
Petropavlivka UA 137 Fa15
Petropavlovka RUS 137 Fc13
Petrosino I 114 Ea85
Petrovaara FIN 61 Lb29
Petrovaradin SRB 120 Ad62
Petrova Ves SK 98 Gd49
Petrovce SK 98 Ja50
Petrovičky CZ 96 Ed47
Petrovo RUS 136 Ec09
Petrovsk RUS 137 Fd11
Petrovskoe RUS 137 Fa09
Petrovskoe RUS 137 Fb12
Petrykav BY 136 Eb13
Petrykozy PL 92 Ja40
Pettaugh GB 16 Gb26
Pettendorf D 96 Ea48
Pettigoe GB 4 Cb17
Petting D 96 Ec52
Pettorano sul Gizio I 109 Fa71
Pettstadt D 89 Dc45
Petuški RUS 137 Fa10
Petworth GB 15 Fb30
Peuerbach A 96 Fa50
Peurajärvi FIN 55 Ka20
Peurasuvanto FIN 51 Ka14
Peure FIN 54 Jd20
Pevensey GB 16 Fd30
Peveragno I 100 Bc63
Pewsey GB 15 Ed28
Peyrat-de-Bellac F 24 Gb46
Peyrat-la-Nonière F 24 Gd46
Peyrat-le-Château F 27 Gc47
Peyrehorade F 26 Fa54
Peyriac-Minervois F 35 Ha55
Peyruis F 29 Jd52
Peyrusse-le-Roc F 27 Gd51
Pézenas F 28 Hc54
Pezens F 35 Gd55
Pezinok SK 98 Gd50
Pezou F 24 Gb40
Pezoúla GR 128 Bb82
Pezuela de las Torres E 38 Dd64
Pézy F 24 Gc38
Pfaffenhausen D 95 Db51
Pfaffenhofen D 95 Db50
Pfaffenhofen an der Ilm D 96 Dd49
Pfäffikon CH 95 Cc53
Pfaffing D 96 Ea51
Pfalzgrafenweiler D 95 Cb49
Pfarrkirchen D 96 Ec50
Pfarrweisach D 89 Dc44
Pfatter D 96 Eb48
Pfeffenhausen D 96 Ea49
Pfinztal D 95 Cc47
Pflersch I 96 Dd55
Pfofeld D 95 Dc47
Pförring D 96 Ea48
Pforzheim D 95 Cc48
Pfreimd D 90 Eb46
Pfronten D 95 Db52
Pfullendorf D 95 Cd51
Pfullingen D 95 Cd49
Pfunders I 96 Ea55
Pfunds A 95 Db54
Pfungstadt D 89 Cc45
Philippsburg D 95 Cb47
Piaam NL 82 Bb33
Piacenza I 101 Cd61
Piamprato I 100 Bc58
Piana degli Albanesi I 114 Ec84
Piancavallo I 103 Eb57
Pianche I 100 Bb62
Pianella I 108 Dc66
Pianella I 109 Fa70
Pianello Val Tidone I 101 Cc61
Piani Resinelli I 101 Cc58
Piano d'Arci I 115 Fc86
Pianoro I 102 Dc63
Piansano I 108 Dd69
Piaseczno PL 85 Fd34
Piaseczno PL 87 Jb37
Piasek PL 85 Fb35
Piaski PL 86 Hc30
Piaski PL 91 Gc38
Piaski PL 93 Kb40
Piastów PL 87 Jb37
Piastre I 102 Db64
Piau-Engaly F 34 Fd57
Piazza al Serchio I 101 Da64
Piazza Armerina I 115 Fb86
Piazzatorre I 101 Cd57
Piazzola sul Brenta I 102 Dd59
Pičaevo RUS 137 Fb11
Picarreau F 25 Jc43
Piccione I 109 Eb67
Piccovagia F 106 Cb72
Picerno I 112 Ga75
Pickering GB 13 Fb19
Pickwillow GB 16 Fd25
Picoto P 30 Ad61
Piece PL 86 Ha32
Piechcin PL 86 Ha35
Piechowice PL 91 Fd42
Pieczonki PL 87 Jd30
Piedicavallo I 100 Bd58
Piedimonte Etnea I 115 Fd85
Piedimulera I 100 Ca57
Piedipaterno I 109 Ec68
Piedrafita de Babia E 31 Cb56
Piedrahita E 37 Cc64
Piedrahita de Castro E 31 Cb60
Piedras Blancas E 31 Cb54
Piekary Śląskie PL 92 Hc43
Piekielnik PL 92 Ja46
Pieksämäki FIN 60 Kd32
Pielavesi FIN 60 Kc29
Pielgrzymka PL 91 Ga41
Pieniężno PL 86 Hd30
Pieńsk PL 91 Fc40
Pienza I 108 Dd67
Piera E 34 Gc61
Pierkunowo PL 87 Jc30
Piérnigas E 32 Dd57
Pierowall GB 9 Ec02
Pierre-Buffière F 27 Gb47
Pierrefitte-Nestales F 33 Fc56
Pierrefitte-sur-Aire F 21 Jb36
Pierrefontaine-les-Varans F 25 Ka41
Pierrefontaines F 25 Jb40
Pierrelatte F 28 Jb51
Pierremont F 20 Gd32
Pierre-Perthuis F 24 Hc41
Pierrepont-sur-Avre F 20 Gd34
Pierzchnica PL 93 Jb42
Pieskowo PL 86 Ja30
Piešt'any SK 98 Ha49
Pieszyce PL 91 Gb42
Pietarsaari FIN 59 Jb28
Pieterburen NL 82 Bd32
Pietragalla I 112 Ga75
Pietraia I 108 Ea68
Pietralba F 106 Cb69
Pietra Ligure I 100 Ca63
Pietralunga I 109 Eb66
Pietrapertosa I 113 Gb76
Pietraperzia I 114 Fa86
Pietraporzio I 100 Bb62
Pietraroja I 109 Fb73
Pietrasanta I 101 Da64
Pietrasecca I 109 Ec71
Pietraserena F 106 Cb70
Pietrastornina I 112 Fc74
Pietrelcina I 112 Fc74
Pietrowice Wielkopolski PL 92 Ha44
Pietrzwałd PL 86 Hd32
Pieve del Cairo I 101 Cb60
Pieve di Cadore I 103 Eb56
Pieve di Cento I 102 Dc62
Pieve di Ledro I 102 Db58
Pieve di Soligo I 102 Ea58
Pievepelago I 102 Db64
Pieve San Stefano I 108 Ea65
Pieve Torina I 109 Ec68
Pigí GR 133 Db96
Pigna I 100 Bc64
Pignataro Maggiore I 112 Fa74
Pigniu CH 95 Cc55
Pihkainmäki FIN 60 Kd30
Pihkalanranta FIN 60 Kb26
Pihlajalahti FIN 68 Kb34
Pihlajalahti FIN 68 Jd34
Pihlajaveden asema FIN 60 Ka32
Pihtipudas FIN 60 Kb29
Piilijärvi S 49 Hc16
Piilijoki FIN 67 Jb36
Piilo FIN 61 Ma28
Piippola FIN 60 Kb26
Piispala FIN 60 Ka30
Pijnacker NL 17 Hd26
Pike IRL 6 Ca22
Pike of Rush Hall IRL 7 Cb22
Pikkarala FIN 55 Ka24
Pikku-Kulus FIN 55 Ka19
Piła I 100 Bc58
Piła PL 85 Gb34
Pilajamäki FIN 60 Kc28
Pilar de la Mola, el E 40 Gc70
Pilas E 43 Bd74
Pilawa PL 87 Jc37
Pile PL 85 Gb33
Pilgersdorf A 97 Gb53
Pilgrims Hatch GB 16 Fd27
Pilgrimstad S 58 Fc31
Pilica PL 92 Hd43
Pilisvörösvár H 98 Hc52
Pillerton Priors GB 15 Fa26
Pillon F 21 Jb34
Pilning GB 15 Ec28
Pilos GR 132 Ba89
Pilsach D 96 Dd47
Pilsen = Plzeň CZ 90 Ed45
Pilsting D 96 Ec49
Pilträsk S 53 Hb22
Pilzno PL 93 Jd44
Pina de Ebro E 33 Fb61
Piñar E 44 Dc74
Pincehely H 98 Hb55
Pinchbeck GB 16 Fc24
Pińczów PL 93 Jb42
Pineda de la Sierra E 32 Dd58
Pineda de Mar E 35 Hb60
Pinedo E 39 Fc68
Piñeira E 30 Bb57
Piñeiro E 30 Ad57
Pinela P 31 Bd60
Pinelo P 31 Bd60
Pinerolo I 100 Bc61
Pineto I 109 Fa69
Pingeyri IS 2 Ab02
Pinhão P 30 Bb61
Pinheiro P 30 Ad61
Pinheiro P 36 Ab69
Pinhel P 37 Bc62
Pinilla de Toro E 31 Cc60
Pinkafeld A 97 Gb53
Pinkamindszent H 97 Gb54
Pinmore Mains GB 10 Dc15
Pinneberg D 83 Db32
Pinnow D 91 Fb38
Pino E 32 Dd57
Pino F 106 Cc68
Pino Lago Maggiore I 101 Cb57
Piñor E 30 Ba57
Pinoso E 45 Fa71
Pinos-Puente E 44 Db74
Pino Torinese I 100 Bd60
Pinsk BY 136 Ea14
Pinsoro E 33 Ed59
Pinsot F 29 Jd48
Pintamo FIN 55 Kc22
Pinto E 38 Dc65
Pinwherry GB 10 Dc15
Pinzolo I 102 Db57
Pinzón E 43 Bd74
Piobbico I 109 Eb66
Piolenc F 28 Jb52
Pioltello I 101 Cc59
Piombino I 108 Da68
Pionki PL 93 Jc39
Pioppi I 112 Fd77
Pioppo I 114 Ec84
Pioraco I 109 Ec67
Piorna E 37 Cb65
Piors Hardwick GB 15 Fa26
Piorunkowice PL 92 Gd43
Piotrków Trybunalski PL 92 Hd40
Piotta CH 101 Cb56
Piove di Sacco I 102 Ea60
Piovene I 102 Dd59
Pipriac F 22 Ec40
Piran SLO 103 Ed59
Piräus = Pireás GR 129 Cb87
Pireás GR 129 Cb87
Pirgi GR 130 Dd86
Piriac-sur-Mer F 22 Eb42
Pirki BY 136 Ec14
Pirkkala FIN 68 Jd36
Pirmasens D 88 Ca46
Pirna D 90 Fa41
Pirnesperä FIN 60 Ka26
Pirnmill GB 10 Db14
Pirttijärvi FIN 67 Ja35
Pirttikoski FIN 55 Kb19
Pirttikoski FIN 68 Jd37
Pirttimäki FIN 60 Kc27
Pirttimäki FIN 61 La26
Pirttimäki FIN 61 Lb28
Pisa I 108 Da65
Pisany F 26 Fb47
Pisarzowice PL 91 Fd41
Pischeldorf A 103 Fb56
Pisciotta I 112 Fd77
Písek CZ 97 Fb47
Pishill GB 15 Fb28
Piskorzyna PL 91 Gb40
Pisogne I 101 Da58
Píso Livádi GR 133 Db90
Pisseloup F 25 Jc40
Pissignano I 109 Eb68
Pissodéri GR 124 Ba77
Pissos F 26 Fb52
Pissouri CY 135 Bd97
Pisticci I 113 Gc76
Pistoia I 102 Db64
Pisz PL 87 Jc32
Pitäjänmäki FIN 60 Kb28
Pitälvbron S 53 Ha21
Pitcape GB 9 Ec08
Piteå S 54 Hd23
Pitelino RUS 137 Fb10
Pitești RO 122 Dc64
Pithiviers F 24 Gd39
Pitigliano I 108 Dd69
Pitkämäki FIN 60 Kc27
Pitkäsenkylä FIN 60 Jc26
Pitlochry GB 11 Ea10
Pitmedden GB 9 Ed08
Pitscottie GB 11 Ec12
Pittentrail GB 9 Ea06
Pitvaros H 105 Jc56
Piúgos E 31 Bc55
Pivca SLO 103 Fb59
Piwniczna-Zdrój PL 93 Jc46
Pizarra E 43 Cd76
Pizzighettone I 101 Cd60
Pizzolato I 114 Ea85
Pizzoli I 109 Ec70
Pjatigorsk RUS 137 Ga17
P'jatychatky UA 137 Ed15
Pjelax FIN 67 Hd33
Plabennec F 22 Dc38
Plaimpied-Givaudins F 24 Ha43
Plaisance F 26 Fd54
Plaisance-du-Toulouse F 27 Gb54
Pláka GR 132 Bb89
Pláka GR 133 Cd91
Plakiás GR 133 Cc96
Plakovo BG 126 Dd71
Plan E 34 Fd57
Planá CZ 90 Ec45
Planá nad Lužnicí CZ 97 Fc47
Plancher-les-Mines F 25 Ka40
Plancoët F 22 Ec38
Plankstadt D 89 Cc46
Planty F 24 Hc38
Plasencia E 37 Ca65
Platamona Lido I 107 Bd74
Platamónas GR 129 Bd80
Plataniá GR 129 Cb83
Platania I 113 Gb81
Plate D 84 Ea33
Plateau-d'Assy F 100 Bb57
Plati I 115 Gb83
Platischis I 103 Ed57
Platís Gialós GR 133 Db89
Platís Gialós GR 133 Da90
Platja d'Aro E 35 He60
Platja d'en Bossa E 40 Gc69
Plátsa GR 132 Bb90
Plattling D 96 Ec49
Plau D 84 Eb33
Plauen D 90 Eb43
Plav MNE 111 Jc69
Plaveč SK 99 Jc47
Plavsk RUS 137 Fa11
Playa Serena E 44 Ea76
Playing Place GB 14 Db32
Płazów PL 93 Kc43
Pleaux F 27 Gd49
Pleinfeld D 95 Dc47
Pleiskirchen D 96 Eb50
Plélan-le-Grand F 22 Ec39
Pléneuf-Val-André F 22 Eb38
Plentzia E 32 Ea55
Plérin F 22 Eb38
Pleščanicy BY 136 Ea12
Plešivec SK 99 Jb49
Pleslin-Trigavou F 22 Ec38
Pleśna PL 93 Jc44
Plessé F 23 Ed41
Pleszew PL 92 Ha38
Plettenberg D 89 Cb40
Pleurs F 20 Hc37
Pleven BG 121 Db69
Pliego E 45 Ed72
Pliešovce SK 98 Hd50
Pliezhausen D 95 Cd49
Pliska BG 123 Ed70
Plitra GR 132 Bd90
Plittersdorf D 95 Cb48
Pljevlja MNE 111 Ja66
Pljussa RUS 136 Ea09
Ploče HR 110 Ha68
Plochingen D 95 Cd48
Płociczno PL 87 Ka30
Płock PL 86 Hd36
Ploemeur F 22 Dd40
Ploërdut F 22 Ea39
Ploërmel F 22 Ec40
Plœuc-sur-Lié F 22 Eb38
Plomári GR 130 Ea84
Plombières-les-Bains F 25 Ka39
Plomion F 20 Hc33
Plön D 83 Dc31
Plonévez-Porzay F 22 Dc39
Płońsk PL 86 Ja35
Płoskinia PL 86 Hd30
Ploskoš' RUS 136 Eb10
Plößberg D 90 Eb45
Plothen D 90 Ea42
Płotno PL 85 Fd34
Płoty PL 85 Fd32
Ploubalay F 22 Ec38
Ploudalmézeau F 18 Db37
Plouégat-Moysan F 18 Dd37
Plouezoch F 18 Dd37
Plougastel-Daoulas F 22 Dc38
Plougonvelin F 22 Db38
Plouguenast F 22 Eb39
Plouguerneau F 18 Db37
Plouguernevel F 22 Ea39
Plouha F 18 Eb37
Plouharnel F 22 Ea41
Ploumanach F 18 Dd37
Plounéour-Menez F 22 Dd38
Plounéventer F 22 Dc38
Plounévez-du-Faou F 22 Dd39
Plounévez-Quintin F 22 Ea38
Plourac'h F 22 Dd38
Plouvorn F 18 Dc37
Plouzané F 22 Db38
Plovdiv BG 126 Db73
Płowce PL 86 Hb36
Plumbridge GB 5 Cc16
Plumieux F 22 Eb39
Plumpton GB 13 Ec17
Plungė LT 80 Jc54
Pluty PL 87 Ka33
Plutycze PL 87 Kb34
Płużnica PL 86 Hb33
Plymouth GB 14 Dc31
Plympton GB 14 Dd31
Plzeň CZ 90 Ed45
Pniewo PL 85 Fb34
Pniewo PL 85 Fd32
Pniewo PL 87 Jc35
Pniewo-Czeruchy PL 86 Ja34
Pniewy PL 93 Jb38
Pobes E 32 Ea57
Pobikry PL 87 Ka35
Población de Cerrato E 32 Da60
Pobladura de la Sierra E 31 Ca57
Pobladura de Pelayo García E 31 Cc58
Poboleda E 34 Ga62
Pobórka PL 85 Gc34
Počátky CZ 97 Fd47
Poceirão P 36 Ab69
Počep RUS 137 Ed12
Pöchlarn A 97 Fd51
Počinok RUS 136 Ec12
Počitelj BIH 110 Ha67
Pockar FIN 68 Kd38
Pockau D 90 Ed42
Pöcking D 96 Dd51
Pocking D 96 Ed50
Pocklington GB 13 Fb20
Pöckstein Zwischenwässern A 97 Fb55
Poços P 42 Ad72
Podanin PL 85 Gc35
Podbereze'e RUS 136 Eb09
Podbereze'e RUS 136 Eb10
Podbořany CZ 90 Ed44
Podborov'e RUS 136 Ea10
Poddor'e RUS 136 Eb10
Poděbrady CZ 91 Fd44
Podedwórze PL 93 Kc38
Podersdorf am See A 97 Gc52
Podgorenskij RUS 137 Fb13
Podgorica MNE 111 Ja69
Podgórze PL 87 Jd34
Podil UA 137 Ed14
Podivín CZ 97 Gc48
Podkowa Leśna PL 87 Jb37
Podlesnoje RUS 137 Fd11
Podolínec SK 99 Jb47
Podol'sk RUS 137 Ed10
Podsnežnoe RUS 137 Fd11
Poffabro I 103 Ec57
Pogar RUS 137 Ed13
Poggendorf D 84 Ed31
Poggiardo I 113 Hc77
Poggibonsi I 108 Dc66
Poggio Mirteto I 109 Eb70
Poggio Rusco I 102 Dc61
Pöggstal A 97 Fd50
Pogódki PL 86 Ha31
Pogorzelice PL 86 Gd30
Pogubie-Średnie PL 87 Jc32
Pohjajoki FIN 60 Kd25
Pohja-Lankila FIN 69 Lc34
Pohjavaara FIN 61 La25
Pohjois-li FIN 55 Ka22
Pohjosjärvi FIN 68 Ka33
Pöhl D 90 Eb43
Pohlheim D 89 Cc42
Pohořelice CZ 97 Gb48
Pohrebyšče UA 136 Eb15
Pohtola FIN 68 Jd35
Poienile Izei RO 117 Db55
Poikajärvi FIN 54 Jd18
Poillé-sur-Vègre F 23 Fc40
Poisson F 25 Hd45
Poissy F 20 Gd36
Poisvilliers F 24 Gb38
Poitiers F 23 Fd44
Poix-de-Picardie F 20 Gc34
Poix-Terron F 21 Ja34
Pokka FIN 50 Jd13
Pokrov RUS 137 Fa10
Pokrovskaja Arčada RUS 137 Fc11
Pokrovs'ke UA 137 Fa15
Pokrovs'ke UA 137 Fb14
Polack BY 136 Eb11
Pola de Allande E 31 Ca54
Pola de Laviana E 31 Cc55
Pola de Lena E 31 Cb55
Pola de Siero E 31 Cc54
Polaincourt-et-Clairfontaine F 25 Jd39
Polanica-Zdrój PL 91 Gb43
Połaniec PL 93 Jc43
Polanów PL 85 Gb31
Polbathic GB 14 Dc31
Polcirkeln S 54 Hc19
Połczyn-Zdrój PL 85 Ga32
Polebrook GB 16 Fc25
Połęcko PL 85 Fc37
Polegate GB 16 Fd30
Polessk RUS 136 Dc12
Polia I 115 Gc82
Police PL 85 Fc33
Police nad Metují CZ 91 Gb43
Polička CZ 91 Gb46
Policoro I 113 Gc77
Polígiros GR 125 Cb79
Polignac F 28 Hd49
Polignano a Mare I 113 Gd74
Poligny F 25 Jc43
Polihnitos GR 130 Ea83
Polirinía GR 132 Ca95
Polis CY 135 Bc96
Polis'ke UA 136 Eb14
Politiká GR 129 Cb84
Polizzi Generosa I 114 Fa85
Pölja FIN 60 Kd29
Pöljänmylly FIN 61 La29
Poljustrovo RUS 69 Mb39
Polkowice PL 91 Ga40
Polla I 112 Fd76
Pollachar GB 8 Cc08
Pölläkkä FIN 61 Lc32
Pollatomish IRL 4 Bb17
Pöllau A 97 Ga54
Polle D 89 Da38
Pollen N 49 Ha10
Pollença E 41 Hc66
Pollica I 112 Fc77
Polling D 95 Dc52
Polloch GB 10 Db10
Pollos E 31 Cd61
Polná CZ 91 Ga46
Polná na Šumavě CZ 97 Fb49
Polne PL 85 Gb32
Polnica PL 86 Gd32
Pologoe Zajmišče RUS 137 Ga13
Polohy UA 137 Fb16
Połomia PL 93 Ka44
Polomka SK 98 Ja48
Polonne UA 136 Eb15
Polope E 45 Ec70
Polopos E 44 Eb75
Polperro GB 14 Dc32
Polska Cerkiew PL 92 Ha44
Poltár SK 98 Ja50
Poltava UA 137 Ed14
Põltsamaa EST 75 Kd44
Põlva EST 75 Lb46
Polvenkylä FIN 59 Ja32
Polverigi I 109 Ed66
Polvijärvi FIN 61 Lc30
Półwieś PL 86 Hb32
Polzeath GB 14 Db31
Pomarance I 108 Db67
Pomarão P 42 Ba73
Pomar de Cinca E 34 Fd60
Pomarez F 26 Fb54
Pomarkku FIN 67 Ja35
Pombal P 36 Ac65
Pomeroy GB 5 Cc17
Pomezia I 109 Eb72
Pomiechówek PL 87 Jb36
Pommelsbrunn D 90 Ea46
Pomorie BG 127 Fa72
Pomorska Wieś PL 86 Hc30
Pomos CY 135 Bc95
Pomoy F 25 Jd40
Pompei I 112 Fb75
Pompeji = Pompei I 112 Fb75
Pompey F 21 Jd36
Pompignan F 28 Hb53
Poncé-sur-le-Loir F 23 Ga40
Ponferrada E 31 Ca57
Poniatowa PL 93 Ka40
Poniatowo PL 86 Hd34
Poniec PL 91 Gc39
Poniky SK 98 Hd49
Ponjos E 31 Cb56
Pons F 26 Fb48
Ponsa FIN 68 Ka35
Ponsacco I 108 Db65
Ponsworthy GB 14 Dd31
Pont I 100 Bc59
Pont-à-Bucy F 20 Hb34
Pontailler-sur-Saône F 25 Jc41
Pont-à-Mousson F 21 Jc36
Pontão P 36 Ad65
Pontardawe GB 14 Dd27
Pontardulais GB 14 Dd27
Pontarion F 24 Gc46
Pontarlier F 25 Ka43
Pontarsais GB 14 Dd26
Pontassieve I 108 Dc65
Pont-Audemer F 19 Fd35
Pontaumur F 24 Ha46
Pont-Authou F 19 Ga35
Pontavert F 20 Hc35
Pontcharra-sur-Tudine F 25 Ja46
Pontcharraud F 27 Gd47
Pontchartrain F 20 Gc37
Pontchâteau F 22 Ec41
Pont-d'Ain F 25 Jc46
Pont-de-Chéruy F 28 Jb47
Pont-de-Dore F 28 Hc47
Pont-de-la-Chaux F 25 Jd44
Pont-de-l'Arche F 20 Gb35
Pont-de-l'Isère F 28 Jb49
Pont-de-Pany F 25 Ja42
Pont-de-Poitte F 25 Jc44
Pont-de-Rhodes F 27 Gc51
Pont-de-Salars F 27 Ha52
Pont-de-Veyle F 25 Jb45
Ponte alla Chiassa I 108 Dd66
Ponteareas E 30 Ad58
Pontebba I 103 Ed56
Ponte Caffaro I 102 Db58
Pontecagnano I 112 Fc75
Ponte-Caldelas E 30 Ad57
Pontecorvo I 109 Ed73
Pontecurone I 101 Cb61
Ponte da Barca P 30 Ad59
Pontedecimo I 101 Cb62
Ponte de Lima P 30 Ad59
Ponte dell'Olio I 101 Cd61
Pontedera I 108 Db65
Ponte de Sor P 36 Ad67
Pontedeume E 30 Ba54
Ponte di Piave I 103 Eb59
Pontefract GB 13 Fa21
Pontelagoscuro I 102 Dd61
Pontelandolfo I 109 Fc73
Ponte nelle Alpi I 103 Eb57
Pont-en-Royans F 29 Jc49
Pontenure I 101 Cd61
Pontenx-les-Forges F 26 Fa52
Ponterwyd GB 14 Dd25
Ponte San Pietro I 101 Cd58
Pontesbury GB 12 Eb24
Pontestura I 100 Ca60
Ponte Tresa I 101 Cb57
Pontevedra E 30 Ad57
Pontevico I 101 Da60
Pont-Farcy F 19 Fa36
Pontgibaud F 27 Ha47
Ponthierry F 24 Ha38
Pontigny F 19 Fc36
Pontigny F 24 Hc40
Pontijou F 24 Gb40
Pontivy F 22 Ea39
Pont-l'Abbé F 19 Fa35
Pont-l'Abbé F 22 Dc40
Pont-l'Abbé-d'Arnoult F 26 Fb47
Pont-la-Ville F 25 Ja39
Pont-l'Évêque F 19 Fd35
Pont-Losquet F 18 Ea37
Pontoise F 20 Gd36
Pontones E 44 Ea72
Pontonx-sur-l'Adour F 26 Fa54
Pontoon IRL 4 Bc18
Pontorson F 23 Ed38
Pontremoli I 101 Cd63
Pont-Rémy F 20 Gc33
Pontrhydfendigaid GB 14 Dd25
Pontrhydygroes GB 14 Dd25
Pontrieux F 18 Ea37
Pontrilas GB 14 Eb26
Pont-Sainte-Maxence F 20 Ha35
Pont-Saint-Esprit F 28 Jb52
Pont-Saint-Martin F 23 Ed42
Pont-Scorff F 22 Ea40
Pont-sur-Yonne F 24 Hb38
Pontyberem GB 14 Dd27
Pontyclun GB 14 Ea28
Pontypool GB 14 Eb27
Pontypridd GB 14 Ea27
Ponzone I 100 Ca58
Ponzone I 100 Ca62
Poola FIN 59 Ja31
Poole GB 15 Ed31
Poolewe GB 8 Dc07
Pooley Bridge GB 13 Ec17
Poperinge B 17 Ha30
Popioły PL 87 Jd30
Popławy PL 87 Jb35
Popoli I 109 Fa70
Popów PL 92 Hd38
Popowo PL 86 Gd30
Popowo Kościelne PL 85 Gc36
Poppel B 88 Ba39
Poppenhausen D 89 Da43
Poppenhausen D 89 Db44
Poppi I 108 Dd65
Poprad SK 99 Jb47
Poraj PL 92 Hc42
Porajów PL 91 Fc42
Poranen FIN 60 Jd30
Porazava BY 136 Dd13
Pörböly H 105 Hc57
Porcsalma H 99 Kc51
Porcuna E 44 Da72
Pordenone I 103 Eb58
Poreč HR 103 Ed60
Porhov RUS 136 Eb10
Pori FIN 67 Ja36
Porjus S 53 Ha18
Porkanranta FIN 60 Ka25
Porkkakylät FIN 68 Ka33
Porkkala FIN 60 Kb27
Þorlákshöfn IS 2 Ad08
Porlock GB 14 Ea29
Pornello I 108 Ea68
Pornic F 22 Ec42
Pornichet F 22 Ec42
Póros GR 128 Ac85
Póros GR 129 Cb88
Porosalmi FIN 61 Lb32
Porovesi FIN 60 Kd28
Porquerolles F 29 Ka55
Porras FIN 68 Jd38
Porrentruy CH 94 Bc52
Porreres E 41 Hc67
Porretta Terme I 102 Db64
Porriño E 30 Ad58
Porrogszentkirály H 104 Gd57
Porsgrunn N 70 Dc44
Þórshöfn IS 3 Cb02
Porsi S 53 Hb19
Port IRL 4 Bd16
Port N 50 Jc08
Portacloy IRL 4 Bb17
Portadown GB 5 Cd18
Portaferry GB 5 Db18
Portalegre P 36 Bb67
Portalrubio E 39 Fa63
Portals Vells E 41 Ha67
Port Appin GB 10 Dc11
Portarlington IRL 7 Cc22
Port Askaig GB 10 Da13
Portavadie GB 10 Dc13
Porta Westfalica D 83 Cd37
Portbail F 19 Ed35
Port-Barcarès F 35 Hb57
Portbradden GB 5 Cd15
Portbron S 52 Fc22
Port Charlotte GB 10 Da13
Port-Cros F 29 Kb55
Port d'Addaia E 41 Ja65
Port d'Agrès F 27 Gd51
Port d'Andratx E 41 Ha67
Port d'Atelier-Amance F 25 Jd40
Port-de-Bouc F 28 Jb54
Port-de-Miramar F 29 Ka55
Port de Pollença E 41 Hc66
Port-des-Barques F 23 Fa46
Port des Callonges F 26 Fb49
Port de Sóller E 41 Hb66
Port d'es Torrent E 40 Gb69
Port Durlainne IRL 4 Bc17
Portegrandi I 103 Eb59
Portela P 42 Ad73
Portela de Santa Eulália P 30 Ba60
Portell de Morella E 39 Fc64
Port-en-Bessin F 19 Fb35
Portencross GB 10 Dc14
Port Erin GB 12 Dc19
Port-Eynon GB 14 Dd28
Port George GB 9 Ea07
Port Glasgow GB 10 Dd13
Portglenone GB 5 Cd16
Porth GB 14 Ea27
Porthcawl GB 14 Dd28
Porthleven GB 14 Da32
Porthmadog GB 12 Dd23
Porthoustock GB 14 Db32
Porticcio F 106 Ca71
Portici I 112 Fb75
Portiglione I 108 Dd68
Portilla de la Reina E 32 Da56
Portillo E 32 Da61
Portimão P 42 Ab74
Portinniska FIN 55 Kc18
Port Isaac GB 14 Db31
Portishead GB 14 Eb28
Port-Joinville F 22 Ec44
Portknockie GB 9 Ec07
Port Láirge IRL 7 Cb25
Port Lamont GB 10 Dc13
Port Laoise IRL 7 Cb22
Port-Leucate F 35 Hb56
Portloe GB 14 Db32
Port-Louis F 22 Ea40
Portmagee IRL 6 Ad25
Portmahomack GB 9 Ea07
Port-Manec'h F 22 Dd40
Portmarnock IRL 7 Cd21
Port Maubert F 26 Fb48
Port-Mort F 20 Gb36
Portmossen FIN 59 Hd32
Portmuck GB 5 Db16
Portnacroish GB 10 Dc11
Portnaguran GB 8 Db05
Portnahaven GB 10 Da13
Port Nan Long GB 8 Cd07
Port-Navalo F 22 Ea41
Portnoo IRL 4 Ca16
Porto F 106 Ca70
Porto P 30 Ac61
Porto Alabe I 107 Bd76
Porto Azzurro I 108 Da68
Porto Cesareo I 113 Hb77
Porto Cristo E 41 Hc67
Porto da Balsa P 36 Ba64
Porto de Mós P 36 Ab66
Porto do Son E 30 Ac56
Porto Empedocle I 114 Ed86
Portoferraio I 108 Da68
Portofino I 101 Cc63
Port of Menteith GB 10 Dd12
Port of Ness GB 8 Db04
Porto Germenó GR 129 Ca86
Portogruaro I 103 Ec59
Portohéli GR 129 Ca88
Pórto Koufós GR 129 Cc80
Porto Levante I 103 Eb61
Portomaggiore I 102 Dd62
Portomarín E 30 Bb56
Porto Maurizio I 100 Bd64
Port Omna IRL 6 Ca22
Portomouro E 30 Ad55
Porton GB 15 Ed29
Portonovo E 30 Ac57
Portonovo I 109 Ed66
Porto Palermo AL 124 Ab78
Porto Pollo F 106 Ca71
Porto Potenza Picena I 109 Ed67
Porto Pozzo I 107 Cb73
Porto Recanati I 109 Ed66
Portorož SLO 103 Ed60
Porto San Elpidio I 109 Fa67
Porto San Giorgio I 109 Fa67
Porto Santo Stefano I 108 Db69
Porto Tolle I 103 Eb61
Porto Torres I 107 Bd74
Porto-Vecchio F 106 Cb72
Portpatrick GB 10 Dc16
Portreath GB 14 Da32
Portree GB 8 Da08
Portroe IRL 6 Bd22
Portrush GB 5 Cd15
Port-Sainte-Marie F 26 Fd52
Port-Saint-Louis-du-Rhône F 28 Jb54
Portsall F 18 Db37
Portsalon IRL 4 Cb15
Pörtschach am Wörthersee A 103 Fb56
Portslade-by-Sea GB 16 Fc30
Portsmouth GB 15 Fa30
Portsoy GB 9 Ec07
Portstewart GB 5 Cd15
Port Talbot GB 14 Dd27
Portugalete E 32 Ea55
Portumna IRL 6 Ca22
Porturlin IRL 4 Bc17
Port-Vendres F 35 Hb57
Port William GB 10 Dd17
Porvola FIN 68 Ka34
Porvoo FIN 68 Kc39
Porzádez E 31 Cd61
Porzuna E 38 Da68
Posada E 32 Da54
Posada (Llanera) E 31 Cb54
Poschiavo CH 102 Da56
Posen = Poznań PL 85 Gc37
Posesse F 21 Ja36
Posio FIN 55 Kd19
Positano I 112 Fb75
Posseck D 90 Eb43
Possendorf D 90 Fa41
Possens CH 94 Bb55
Pößneck D 90 Ea42
Posta Demani I 110 Ga73
Postau D 96 Eb49
Postbauer-Heng D 96 Dd47
Postel B 88 Ba39
Posterholt NL 88 Bb40
Postojna SLO 103 Fb59
Postomino PL 85 Gb30
Postřelmov CZ 91 Gc45
Poświętne PL 87 Ka34
Potenza I 112 Ga75
Potenza Picena I 109 Ed67
Potes E 32 Da55
Potku FIN 55 Kc24
Potlogi RO 122 Dd65
Potok Złoty PL 92 Hd42
Potsdam D 84 Ed37
Pottenstein D 90 Dd45
Potters Bar GB 16 Fc27
Pöttmes D 95 Dc49
Potton GB 16 Fc26
Pouan-les-Vallées F 25 Hd38
Poudenas F 26 Fd53
Pougny F 24 Hb41
Pougy F 25 Hd38
Pouilly-sur-Saône F 25 Jb42
Poujols F 28 Hc53
Poulaines F 24 Gc42
Pouldreuzic F 22 Dc39
Poulton-le-Frylde GB 12 Eb20
Pourrières F 29 Jd54
Pourunperä FIN 68 Jd33
Pousada E 30 Ba54
Poussu FIN 55 La20
Pouzauges F 23 Fb44
Pouzilhac F 28 Jb52
Považská Bystrica SK 98 Hb47
Póvoa das Quartas P 36 Ba64
Póvoa de Varzim P 30 Ac60
Póvoa e Meadas P 36 Ba66
Powardennan Lodge GB 10 Dd12
Powburn GB 11 Ed15
Power's Cross IRL 6 Bd22
Powodów PL 92 Hc38
Powroźnik PL 93 Jc46
Poyales del Hoyo E 37 Cc65
Poynton GB 13 Ed22
Poyntz Pass GB 5 Cd18
Poyols F 29 Jc50
Poysdorf A 97 Gc49
Pöytyä FIN 68 Jc38
Pozdeň CZ 90 Fa44
Pozdišovce SK 99 Ka48
Poznań PL 85 Gc37
Pozo Alcón E 44 Dd73
Pozoblanco E 43 Cd71
Pozo-Cañada E 45 Ec70
Pozohondo E 45 Ec70
Pozondón E 39 Ed64
Pozořice CZ 97 Gc47
Pożrzadło Wielkie PL 85 Ga33
Pozuelo E 44 Eb70
Pozuelo de Alarcón E 38 Db64
Pozuelo de Zarzón E 37 Bd65
Pozza di Fassa I 102 Dd56
Pozzallo I 115 Fc88
Pozzomaggiore I 107 Bd76
Pozzuoli I 112 Fa75
Pozzuolo I 108 Dd67
Prag = Praha CZ 91 Fb44
Prabuty PL 86 Hc32
Prachatice CZ 96 Fa48
Prackenbach D 96 Ec48
Prada E 31 Bd57
Prádanos de Ojeda E 32 Db57
Pradelles F 28 Hd50
Pradelles-Cabardès F 35 Ha55
Prades E 34 Gb62
Prado E 30 Ba56
Prado E 31 Cd54
Prado P 30 Ad59
Pradoluengo E 32 Dd58
Præstø DK 77 Eb57
Prag = Praha CZ 91 Fb44
Praha CZ 91 Fb44
Praia da Areia Branca P 36 Aa67
Praia da Rocha P 42 Ab74
Praia da Vieira P 36 Ab65
Praia de Esmoriz P 30 Ac61
Praia de Mira P 36 Ac63
Praia de Ofir P 30 Ac60
Praia de Quiaios P 36 Ab64
Praiano I 112 Fb76
Prakovce SK 99 Jc48
Pralognan F 29 Kb47
Pralormo I 100 Bd61
Prámanda GR 128 Ba81
Prameny CZ 90 Ec44
Pramet A 96 Ed51
Pramort D 84 Ed30
Pramouton F 29 Kb50
Praslay F 25 Jb40
Praszka PL 92 Hb41
Prat F 34 Gb56
Prata Sannita I 109 Fa73
Prat-de-Chest F 35 Hb55
Pratella I 109 Fa73
Prato I 108 Dc65
Prato all'Isarco I 102 Dd56
Prato di Resia I 103 Ed57
Pratola Peligna I 109 Fa71
Pratorotondo I 100 Bb62
Prats-de-Mollo-la-Preste F 35 Ha58
Pratteln CH 94 Bd52
Pravdinsk RUS 136 Dc12
Pravia E 31 Cb54
Praze-an-Beeble GB 14 Da32
Préaux F 20 Gb35
Přebuz CZ 90 Ec43
Préchac F 26 Fc52
Prečistoe RUS 136 Ec11
Précy-sous-Thil F 25 Hd41
Précy-sur-Oise F 20 Gd35
Predappio I 102 Ea64
Predazzo I 102 Dd57
Preding A 97 Fd55
Predlitz A 96 Fa54
Predosa I 101 Cb61
Prees GB 13 Ec23
Preetz D 83 Dc30
Préfailles F 22 Ec42
Prefontaines F 24 Ha39
Pregarten A 97 Fb50
Preitenegg A 97 Fc55
Přelouč CZ 91 Fd45
Prémery F 24 Hb42
Premià de Mar E 35 Ha61
Premnitz D 84 Eb36
Prenčov SK 98 Hc50
Prendwick GB 11 Ed15
Prenzlau D 84 Fa34
Přerov CZ 92 Gd46
Prerow D 84 Ec30
Pré-Saint-Didier I 100 Bb58
Prescot GB 12 Eb21
Preseľany SK 98 Hb50
Presencio E 32 Dc58
Presicce I 113 Hc78
Prešov SK 99 Jd47
Pressac F 23 Ga46
Pressath D 90 Ea45
Preßburg = Bratislava SK 98 Gd51
Presseck D 90 Ea44
Pressgutz A 97 Ga54
Pressig D 90 Dd43
Prestatyn GB 12 Ea22
Prestbakken N 49 Gc12
Presteigne GB 14 Eb25
Prestelvbakken N 47 Jd06
Přeštice CZ 90 Ed46
Preston GB 13 Ec20
Preston GB 15 Ec31
Preston GB 16 Gb29
Preston Capes GB 15 Fa26
Prestwick GB 10 Dd14
Prestwood GB 15 Fb27
Prettin D 90 Ec39
Pretzfeld D 90 Dd45
Preuilly-sur-Claise F 23 Ga43
Preußisch Oldendorf D 83 Cc36
Prevalje SLO 103 Fc56
Prévenchères F 28 Hd51
Préveza GR 128 Ac82
Prey F 20 Gb36
Priaranza del Bierzo E 31 Bd57
Příbor CZ 92 Ha46
Příbram CZ 90 Fa46
Pribylina SK 98 Ja47
Přibyslav CZ 91 Ga46
Prichsenstadt D 89 Db45
Priego E 38 Eb64
Priego de Córdoba E 44 Da74
Prien D 96 Eb52
Prievidza SK 98 Hc48
Prijutnoe RUS 137 Ga15
Prilep MK 124 Bb75
Prima Porta I 109 Eb71
Přimda CZ 90 Ec46
Primolano I 102 Dd58
Primorsk RUS 136 Dc12
Primorsk RUS 137 Fd13
Primorsko-Ahtarsk RUS 137 Fc16
Primošten HR 110 Ga66
Primstal D 88 Bd45
Princetown GB 14 Dd31
Principina a Mare I 108 Db69
Prioiro E 30 Ba53
Priolo Gargallo I 115 Fd87
Prioro E 31 Cd56
Prisdorf D 83 Db32
Pritzier D 84 Dd33
Pritzwalk D 84 Eb34
Privas F 28 Ja50
Priverno I 109 Ec73
Privlaka HR 104 Fd64
Privolžsk RUS 137 Fa09
Prizzi I 114 Ec85
Prjamicyno RUS 137 Fa13
Probsteierhagen D 83 Dc30
Probus GB 14 Db32
Procchio I 108 Da68
Proença-a-Nova P 36 Ba65
Profitis Ilías GR 133 Da96
Prohor Pčinski SRB 125 Bd72
Proletarij RUS 136 Eb09
Proletarsk RUS 137 Fd15
Pronin RUS 137 Fc14
Pronsfeld D 88 Bc43
Pronstorf D 83 Dc31
Propriano F 106 Ca71
Prösen D 90 Fa40
Prosperous IRL 7 Cc21
Prostějov CZ 91 Gc46
Prostki PL 87 Ka32
Prószków PL 92 Ha43
Proszowice PL 93 Jb44
Protivanov CZ 91 Gc46
Protivín CZ 97 Fb47
Prötzel D 84 Fa36
Proussós GR 128 Bb83
Provenchères F 94 Bc49
Provins F 24 Hb38
Pruchnik PL 93 Kb44
Prudentov RUS 137 Ga13
Prudhoe GB 11 Ed16
Prudnik PL 92 Gd43
Prudziszki PL 87 Ka30
Prüm D 88 Bc43
Pruna E 43 Cb75
Prunelli di Fiumorbo F 106 Cb70
Prunete F 106 Cc70
Prusac BIH 104 Ha64
Pruśce PL 85 Gc35
Pruszcz PL 86 Ha33
Pruszcz Gdański PL 86 Hb30
Pruszków PL 87 Jb37
Pružany BY 136 Dd13
Pružina SK 98 Hb48
Pryazovs'ke UA 137 Fa16
Pryłęk PL 93 Jd43
Pryluky UA 137 Ed14
Prymors'k UA 137 Fb16
Przasnysz PL 87 Jb34
Przecław PL 85 Fb33
Przeczów PL 92 Gd41
Przedbórz PL 92 Ja41
Przedświt PL 87 Jc35
Przegędza PL 92 Hb44
Przelewice PL 85 Fc34
Przemyśl PL 93 Kb44
Przerzeczyn-Zdrój PL 91 Gc42
Przewłoka PL 85 Gc29
Przewłoka PL 93 Kb38
Przeworsk PL 93 Kb44
Przezmark PL 86 Hc31
Przodkowo PL 86 Ha30
Przybiernów PL 85 Fc32
Przybychowo PL 85 Gb35
Przybysławice PL 93 Ka39
Przyjezierze PL 86 Ha36
Przylep PL 91 Fd38
Przyłubie PL 86 Ha34
Przyrów PL 92 Hd42
Przystawka PL 87 Kb32
Przysucha PL 93 Jb40
Przyszów PL 93 Ka42
Przytyk PL 93 Jb39
Przywidz PL 86 Ha30
Przywóz PL 92 Hb41
Psahná GR 129 Cb84
Psará GR 130 Dc85
Psarádes GR 124 Ba76
Psáthi GR 133 Db91
Psebaj RUS 137 Fd17

Pskov RUS 136 Ea10
Pszczew PL 85 Ga36
Pszczółki PL 90 Hb31
Pszczyna PL 92 Hd44
Pszów PL 92 Hb44
Ptuj SLO 104 Ga57
Ptujska Gora SLO 104 Ga57
Pučež RUS 137 Fb09
Puchaly Stare PL 87 Kb35
Puchberg am Schneeberg A 97 Ga52
Puchheim A 96 Fa51
Puchheim D 96 Dc51
Púchov SK 98 Hd47
Puck PL 86 Ha29
Puckakaun IRL 6 Ca22
Pucol E 39 Fc67
Pudas FIN 51 Ka14
Pudasjärvi FIN 55 Kc22
Puddletown GB 15 Ec30
Puderbach D 88 Ca42
Puebla de Alborton E 33 Fa61
Puebla de Alcocer E 37 Cc69
Puebla de Almenara E 38 Ea66
Puebla de Don Fadrique E 44 Ea72
Puebla de Don Rodrigo E 37 Cd68
Puebla de la Calzada E 37 Bc69
Puebla de la Sierra E 38 Dc62
Puebla de Lillo E 31 Cd56
Puebla del Maestre E 43 Ca71
Puebla del Prior E 43 Bd70
Puebla de Obando E 37 Bc68
Puebla de San Miguel E 39 Fa66
Puebla de Trives E 31 Bc57
Puente de los Fierros E 31 Cc55
Puente de Montañana E 34 Ga59
Puente de Sanabria E 31 Bd58
Puente de San Martín E 31 Cb54
Puentedeey E 32 Dc56
Puente-Genil E 43 Cd74
Puente la Reina E 33 Ec57
Puentelarra E 32 Ea57
Puentenansa (Rionansa) E 32 Db55
Puente Pumar E 32 Db55
Puente Viesgo E 32 Dc55
Puerto de Conil E 43 Bd77
Puerto de San Vicente E 37 Cc67
Puertollano E 44 Da70
Puerto Lumbreras E 45 Ec74
Puertomingalvo E 39 Fb65
Puerto Real E 43 Bd76
Puerto Seguro E 37 Bd62
Puerto Serrano E 43 Cb75
Pueyo de Fañanás E 34 Fc59
Pugačev RUS 137 Ga11
Puget-Théniers F 29 Kc52
Puget-Ville F 29 Ka54
Puianello I 102 Db62
Puigcerdà E 35 Gd58
Puisserguier F 35 Hb55
Pukaro FIN 68 Kd38
Pukkila FIN 68 Kc38
Pula HR 103 Fa62
Puławy PL 93 Jd39
Pulborough GB 16 Fc30
Pulgar E 38 Da67
Pulham Market GB 16 Gb25
Pulheim D 88 Bd40
Pulkkila FIN 55 Kd23
Pulkkila FIN 68 Kb40
Pullenried D 90 Eb46
Pulpi E 45 Ec74
Pulsano I 113 Ha76
Pulsen D 90 Ed40
Pulsnitz D 90 Fa41
Pułtusk PL 87 Jb35
Pumsaint GB 14 Dd26
Pungesetrene N 64 Dd35
Punkaharju FIN 69 Ld33
Punsk PL 87 Kb30
Punta Križa HR 103 Fb62
Punta Marina I 102 Ea64
Punta Umbría E 42 Bd74
Puolakkavaara FIN 51 Ka15
Puolanka FIN 55 Kd23
Puolitkasvaara S 49 Hc16
Puottaure S 53 Hb20
Purchena E 44 Ea74
Purda PL 86 Ja32
Purdoški RUS 137 Fc10
Puriton GB 14 Eb29
Purkersdorf A 97 Gb51
Purmerend NL 82 Ba35
Purmojärvi FIN 68 Hb31
Purnuvaara FIN 55 Kd20
Purola Svartbäck FIN 69 La38
Puromäki FIN 61 Lc31
Puronkylä FIN 68 Kb33
Puroranta FIN 60 Kd25
Purtse EST 75 Lb42
Pusaankylä FIN 60 Jd32
Puškino RUS 137 Fa09
Puškinskie Gory RUS 136 Ea10
Püspökladány H 99 Jd53
Pussay F 24 Gc38
Pustelnik PL 87 Jc36
Pustevny CZ 92 Hc44
Pustoška RUS 136 Eb11
Pustynia FIN 93 Jd44
Puszcza Mariańska PL 92 Ja38
Puszczykowo PL 85 Gc36
Pusztakovácsi H 104 Ha56
Pusztaszabolcs H 104 Hc55
Putaja FIN 67 Jb36
Putanges F 19 Fc37
Putbus D 84 Fa30
Putignano I 113 Gd75
Putkitaholti FIN 68 Kc34
Putten NL 82 Bb36
Puttgarden D 84 Dd30
Puttelange D 88 Bc46
Putula FIN 68 Kb37
Putyvl' UA 137 Ed12
Puukari FIN 61 Ld24
Puumala FIN 69 Lb34
Puumala FIN 69 Lb34
Puutikkala III 68 Kb37
Puuttenperä FIN 54 Jd21
Puy-Guillaume F 24 Hc46
Puylaroque F 27 Gc52
Puylaurens F 27 Gd53
Puy-l'Évêque F 27 Gd51
Puymirol F 27 Ga51
Puyôo F 26 Fa55
Puy-Saint-Vincent F 29 Ka49
Pužació RUS 137 Fa13
Pwllheli GB 12 Dc23
Pyecombe GB 16 Fc30
Pyhäjärvi FIN 51 Jd11
Pyhäjärvi FIN 51 Kb16
Pyhäjärvi FIN 60 Kb28
Pyhäjärvi FIN 60 Kc31

Pyhältö FIN 69 La37
Pyhämaa FIN 67 Ja38
Pyhänkoski FIN 60 Jd23
Pyhänsivu FIN 55 Kb24
Pyhäntä FIN 60 Kb26
Pyhävibaer IS 2 Ba08
Pyle GB 14 Ea28
Pyle GR 128 Bb81
Pylkönmäki FIN 60 Ka31
Pylväinälä FIN 60 Kb33
Pylväsperä FIN 60 Jd27
Pyntäinen FIN 67 Ja36
Pyöree FIN 60 Kd27
Pyrbaum D 96 Dd47
Pyrénées 2000 F 35 Gd58
Pyrill IS 2 Ad06
Pyrzowice PL 92 Hc43
Pyrzyce PL 85 Fd34
Pyšély CZ 92 Hd43
Pystyoja FIN 50 Jc13
Pytalovo (Abrene) RUS 136 Ea10
Pytkynharju FIN 55 Kc21
Pyttis FIN 68 Kd38
Pyydysmäki FIN 67 Ja33
Pyykkölänvaara FIN 55 La24

## Q

Qormi M 115 Gb89
Quaglietta I 112 Fd75
Quainton GB 15 Fb27
Quakenbrück D 83 Cc35
Quarff GB 9 Fb05
Quarré-les-Tombes F 25 Hd41
Quarteira P 42 Ac74
Quarto d'Altino I 103 Eb59
Quartu San Elena I 107 Ca79
Quattro Venti, i I 109 Fb73
Quebradas P 36 Ab67
Quédillac F 22 Ec39
Quedlinburg D 90 Dd38
Queidersbach D 88 Ca46
Quelaines F 23 Fb40
Quemada E 32 Dc60
Quengstedt D 90 Ea39
Queralbs E 35 Gb59
Querceta I 101 Da64
Quercianella I 108 Da66
Querfurt D 90 Ea40
Querol E 34 Gc61
Querol IRL 6 Bb23
Quesada E 44 Dd73
Questembert F 22 Eb41
Quettetot F 19 Ed35
Queudes F 20 Hc37
Quiaios P 36 Ac64
Quiberon F 22 Ea41
Quickborn D 83 Db42
Quiddelbach D 88 Bd43
Quigley's Point IRL 5 Cc15
Quillan F 35 Gd56
Quilty IRL 6 Bb22
Quimper F 22 Dc39
Quimperlé F 22 Dd40
Quin IRL 6 Bc22
Quindós E 31 Bd56
Quinéville F 19 Fa35
Quinson F 29 Ka53
Quintana de la Serena E 37 Cc69
Quintana de la Orden E 38 Dd67
Quintana Redonda E 32 Ea60
Quintanilla de Arriba E 32 Db60
Quintanilla de Flórez E 31 Cb58
Quintanilla de Onésimo E 32 Db60
Quintanilla San García E 32 Dd57
Quintanilla-Sobresierra E 32 Dc57
Quintela E 31 Bd56
Quintes E 31 Cc54
Quinto E 33 Fa61
Quinzano d'Oglio I 101 Da60
Quiroga E 31 Bc57
Quirra I 107 Cb79
Quismondo E 38 Da65
Quistello I 102 Dc61
Qundle GB F 25

## R

Raab A 96 Fa51
Raabs an der Thaya A 97 Fd48
Raahe FIN 60 Jd25
Raajärvi FIN 55 Kb18
Raalte NL 82 Bc36
Raanujärvi FIN 50 Jb17
Rääkkylä FIN 61 Ld31
Raamsdonk NL 82 Ba38
Raananen IS 2 Ba08
Raattama FIN 29 Kb55
Rambervillers F 25 Ka38
Rambo S 59 Fd27
Rambouillet F 20 Gc37
Rameški RUS 137 Ed09
Ramnos GH 95 Cb52
Ramsbottom GB 13 Ec21
Ramsberg S 52 Fd28
Ramsburg S 52 Fd28
Ramsei CH 94 Bd54
Ramsele S 58 Ga29
Ramsey GB 12 Dd18
Ramsey GB 16 Fc25
Ramsey GB 16 Fc26
Ramsey GB 16 Fb26
Ramsey Saint Mary's GB 16 Fc25
Ramsgate GB 16 Gb28
Ramsjö S 66 Fd34
Ramsjö S 66 Fd34
Ramstein-Miesenbach D 88 Ca46
Ramsthal D 89 Db44
Ramsund N 48 Ga13
Ramsvika N 58 Ec32
Ramvik S 58 Gc32
Ranan F 24 Gd46
Ranco F 24 Gd46
Randalstown GB 5 Da16
Randan F 28 Hb47
Randazzo I 115 Fc84
Randbygd N 62 Cc34
Randegg A 97 Fc51
Randers DK 76 Dc53
Randersacker D 89 Db45
Rânea S 54 Hd21
Rânes F 19 Fc37
Rangendingen D 95 Cc49
Ranis D 90 Ea42
Rannoch PL 93 Ka43
Rannankangas FIN 60 Ka25
Rannanmäki FIN 67 Jb37
Rännö S 66 Gb33
Rannoch Station GB 9 Dd10
Ranrupt F 94 Bd49
Ransbach-Baumbach D 88 Ca42
Ransta S 52 Ga28
Rantasalmi FIN 61 Lb32
Rante S 80 Bb57
Rantsila FIN 60 Kb24
Rantum D 76 Cd52
Ranty PL 87 Jd31
Rao E 31 Bd55
Raon-l'Étape F 25 Ka38
Rapallo I 101 Cc63
Rapice PL 91 Gd38
Rapness GB 9 Ec02
Rapolano Terme I 108 Dd67
Rapotín CZ 91 Gd44
Rappin D 84 Fa30
Rapsani GR 129 Ca81
Rapla EST 75 La43
Raša HR 103 Fa61
Rasal E 33 Fa58

Râsca RO 118 Eb56
Rascafría E 38 Db63
Rashairlin GB 5 Cc18
Rashedoge IRL 4 Cb16
Rasimäki FIN 61 Ld29
Rasimäki FIN 61 Lb29
Rasines E 32 Dd55
Rasinkylä FIN 55 Kd24
Rasivaara FIN 61 Ma30
Rasivaara FIN 61 Ld31
Rašjo S 66 Fd33
Râşnov RO 122 Dd62
Rasskazovo RUS 137 Fc12
Rastatt D 95 Cb48
Rastede D 83 Cc33
Rastenberg D 90 Ea41
Rastenfeld A 97 Fd49
Rasti FIN 50 Jc15
Râstrand S 53 Gc24
Rasueros E 37 Cd62
Raszków PL 85 Gd38
Raszyn PL 87 Jb37
Ratan S 59 He28
Ratby GB 13 Fa24
Ratekau D 84 Dd31
Rathangan IRL 7 Cc21
Ráth Caola IRL 6 Bc23
Rathcoole IRL 7 Cc21
Rathcormack IRL 6 Bd25
Rathcroghan IRL 4 Ca19
Rathdangan IRL 7 Cc22
Rathdowney IRL 7 Cc23
Rathdrum IRL 7 Cd23
Rathen GB 9 Ed08
Rathenow D 84 Eb36
Rathfriland GB 5 Da18
Rathlyane IRL 7 Cc24
Rathkeale IRL 6 Bc23
Rathkeevin IRL 6 Bd24
Rathlackan IRL 4 Bc17
Rath Luirc IRL 6 Bc23
Rathnew IRL 7 Cd22
Rathowen IRL 4 Cb20
Rathsweiler D 88 Ca45
Rathvilla IRL 7 Cc21
Rathvilly IRL 7 Cc23
Ratibořice CZ 91 Ga43
Ratingen D 88 Bd39
Ratipeřá FIN 60 Ka25
Ratiškovice CZ 98 Gd48
Ratne UA 136 Ea25
Ratoath IRL 7 Cd21
Ráttelsdorf D 89 Dc44
Ratten A 97 Gb54
Rattiscell D 96 Ec48
Rattlesden GB 16 Ga26
Rattosjärvi FIN 54 Jc18
Rattray GB 9 Ec11
Rättsel S 53 Ha22
Ratzeburg D 84 Dd32
Rätzlingen D 84 Dd36
Raubling D 96 Ea52
Raucourt-et-Flaba F 21 Ja34
Raudeberg N 62 Ca35
Raudlitt LT 80 Ka57
Raudlar D 80 Ka56
Raudorfth IS 3 Ca01
Raufoss N 65 Ea39
Rauhala FIN 50 Jc15
Rauhanlahti FIN 61 Lb31
Raulhac F 28 Ha50
Rauma FIN 67 Ja38
Raumland D 89 Cc41
Raumünzach D 95 Cb49
Raunds GB 16 Fc25
Rauris A 96 Fa53
Rauschenberg D 89 Cc41
Rautajärvi FIN 68 Ka35
Rautalampi FIN 60 Kd31
Rautas S 49 Ha15
Rautavaara FIN 61 Lc24
Rautila FIN 60 Jd27
Rautjärvi FIN 69 Lc35
Rautjärvi FIN 69 Ld33
Rauvanniemi FIN 61 Ld32
Rauville FIN 50 Jb16
Rauwiller F 94 Bd48
Ravanusa I 114 Fa86
Rava Rus'ka UA 136 Dd15
Ravells I 102 Fb75
Ravenglass GB 12 Ea18
Ravenna I 102 Ea63
Ravensburg D 95 Cd52
Ravenscar GB 13 Fc18
Ravenstein D 89 Da47
Ravenstonedale GB 13 Ec17
Rawdon NL 17 Hd27
Rawa Mazowiecka PL 92 Ja38
Rawicz PL 91 Gc39
Ravtenstall GB 13 Ec20
Ray IRL 4 Cb15
Rayenstonedale GB 13
Ec18
Rayleigh GB 16 Ga28
Rayrinki FIN 60 Jc29
Razgrad BG 122 Eb69
Razimet F 26 Fd52
Reading GB 15 Fb28
Reaghstown IRL 5 Cd19
Réalcamp F 20 Gb33
Réalmont F 27 Gd53
Réaumur F 24 Fc42
Reanascreena IRL 6 Bb25
Rear Cross IRL 6 Bc23
Reay GB 9 Eb04
Rebate E 45 Fa72
Rébénacq F 33 Fb56
Rebordelo P 31 Bc59
Recanati I 109 Ed66
Recco I 101 Cc63
Recess IRL 4 Bb20
Recey-sur-Ource F 25 Ja40
Rechenberg-Bienenmühle D 90 Ed42
Rechnitz A 97 Gb54
Rechytsa BY 137 Ed13
Recke D 83 Cb36
Reckingen CH 100 Ca56
Recke D 17 Hc27
Recz PL 85 Fd36
Reda PL 86 Ha29

Regen D 96 Ed48
Regensburg D 96 Eb48
Regenstauf D 96 Ea47
Reggio di Calabria I 115 Ga84
Reggio nell'Emilia I 102
Reggiolo I 102 Db61
Regis-Breitingen D 90 Eb41
Registozsau D 90 Ed39
Regonkylä FIN 59 Jb32
Reguengo P 22  Eb40
Reguiméil de la Sierra E 32 Ea59
Rehau D 90 Eb44
Rehburg-Loccum D 83 Da36
Rehfelde D 84 Fa36
Reichelsheim D 88 Cd44
Rehna D 83 Dd32
Rehula FIN 69 Lb35
Reichelsheim D 88 Cd44
Reichenau CH 95 Cd52
Reichenbach CH 94 Bd55
Reichenbach D 90 Eb42
Reichenbach D 91 Fc41
Reichenbach D 85 Fb36
Reichenberg D 89 Da45
Reichenberg = Liberec CZ 91 Fc42
Reichenschwand D 90 Dd46
Reichersberg A 96 Ed50
Reichertshausen D 96 Dc49
Reichshof D 89 Cb41
Reichshoffen F 94 Ca47
Reichenau an der Rax A 97 Ga52
Reigada E 31 Ca54
Reigate GB 16 Fc29
Reignac-sur-Indre F 23 Ga45
Reila FIN 67 Ja38
Reims F 20 Hc35
Reina E 43 Ca71
Reinach CH 94 Bd52
Reinach CH 94 Ca54
Reinbek D 83 Dc33
Reine N 48 Fa15
Reinfeld D 83 Dc32
Reinhardshagen D 89 Da38
Reinheim D 89 Cc45
Reinsdorf D 90 Ec38
Reinsfeld D 88 Bc44
Reinstorf D 83 Dc34
Reipä N 52 Fb18
Reisbach D 96 Ec49
Reiskirchen D 89 Cc42
Reiss GB 9 Ec04
Reitano I 115 Fb84
Reite N 48 Gb12
Reit im Winkl D 96 Eb52
Rejowiec Fabryczny PL 93 Kc42
Rekeland N 64 Cc38
Rekijoki FIN 67 Jc39
Reken D 88 Ca38
Rekovac SRB 134 Cb68
Remagen D 88 Bd42
Rémalard F 23 Ga38
Remich L 21 Jd34
Rémilly F 24 Hc43
Remiremont F 25 Ka39
Remmarn S 58 Gd28
Remnes N 52 Fa21
Remoncourt F 25 Jd38
Remontnoe RUS 137 Ga15
Remouilins F 26 Ja53
Rempstone GB 13 Fa24
Remscheid D 88 Ca40
Remseck D 89 Cd47
Remshalden D 95 Cd48
Remungol F 22 Ea40
Remuzat F 29 Jc51
Rémy F 20 Ha34
Renaison F 25 Hd46
Renazé F 23 Fa40
Renchen D 94 Cc49
Renède de Valderaduey E 31 Cd57
Renesse NL 17 Hd27
Renieblas E 32 Ea60
Renko FIN 68 Kc38
Renkum NL 82 Bc37
Rennebu N 63 Dc30
Rennerod D 88 Cd42
Rennertshofen D 95 Dd48
Rennes F 23 Ed39
Renningen D 95 Cc48
Reńska Wieś PL 92 Ha43
Rensvik N 63 Dc30
Renvilen S 53 Gd22
Renvyle IRL 4 Ba20
Renzendorf D 89 Db42
Reocol E 44 Eb70
Rep'evka RUS 137 Fb13
Repki PL 87 Ka36
Reposaari FIN 67 Ja35
Resana I 102 Ea59
Reschen I 95 Db55
Resmo S 78 Gc56
Resolven GB 14 Ea27
Respenda de la Peña E 32 Da56
Resse D 83 Da36
Restumfang I 114 Fd85
Reszel PL 87 Jb31
Retamosa E 37 Cc66
Retford GB 13 Fb22
Réthimno GR 130 Cb95
Rethondes F 20 Ha35
Retie B 88 Ba39
Retiers F 23 Fa40
Rettenbach D 96 Ec49
Rettenberg D 95 Db52
Rette PL 92 Hc41
Reugny F 23 Ga43
Reuilly F 24 Gd43
Reus E 34 Gb62
Reusel NL 88 Ba39
Reut D 96 Ec50
Reuterstadt Stavenhagen D 84 Ed34
Reutlingen D 95 Cc49
Reuth D 90 Eb42
Reutte A 95 Db53
Reuver NL 88 Bc40
Revel F 27 Gd54
Revello I 100 Bd62
Revenga E 38 Bc63
Revilla de Collazos E 32 Da57

Regen D 96 Ed48
Revin F 21 Hd33
Revsund S 58 Fc32
Reykholar IS 2 Ac04
Reykholt IS 2 Ad06
Reykhólar IS 3 Ca03
Reykjanes IS 2 Ac02
Reykjavík IS 2 Ac07
Rezé F 23 Ed42
Rézekne LV 81 Ld51
Rezzato I 100 Db64
Rezzo I 100 Bd64
Rhade D 83 Da33
Rhade D 88 Bd44
Rhandirmwyn GB 14 Dd26
Rhauderfehn D 83 Cb33
Rhaunen D 88 Bd44
Rhayader GB 14 Ea26
Rheda-Wiedenbrück D 89 Cc38
Rhede D 88 Bd38
Rheden NL 82 Bc37
Rheinau D 94 Ca48
Rheine D 83 Cb37
Rheinbrohl D 88 Ca42
Rheinberg D 88 Bc39
Rheine D 82 Ca36
Rheinfelden CH 94 Ca52
Rheinhausen D 94 Ca52
Rheinsberg D 84 Ed34
Rhinau F 94 Ca48
Rhode IRL 7 Cc21
Rhonda GB 14 Ea27
Rhoose GB 14 Ea28
Rhos GB 14 Dd27
Rhossili GB 14 Dc27
Rhu GB 10 Dc12
Rhubodach GB 10 Dc13
Rhumspringe D 89 Dc39
Rhyl GB 12 Ea22
Rhymney GB 14 Ea27
Rhynie GB 9 Ec08
Riaño E 31 Cd56
Rians F 29 Jd54
Rianxo E 30 Ac54
Riaza E 38 Dc62
Ribadavia E 30 Ba57
Ribadelago E 31 Bc58
Ribadeo E 31 Bd53
Ribadesella E 31 Cd54
Ribaforada E 33 Ec59
Ribarica BG 126 Da71
Ribarska Banja SRB 134 Cb68
Ribe DK 76 Da56
Ribeauville F 94 Bd48
Ribécourt-Dreslincourt F 20 Ha34
Ribera I 114 Eb86
Ribera del Fresno E 43 Bd70
Ribera del Turia E 39 Fb67
Ribnica BG 126 Da71
Ribnitz-Damgarten D 84 Eb31
Ríčany CZ 91 Fc45
Riccall GB 13 Fb20
Riccione I 102 Eb65
Richebourg F 20 Ha34
Richmond GB 13 Fa18
Richmond GB 16 Fc28
Richtenberg D 84 Ed31
Richterswil CH 95 Cc53
Rickeå S 59 Hc27
Rickenbach D 94 Ca52
Ricla E 33 Ec61
Ridala EST 74 Kb44
Riddes CH 100 Bc56
Ridderkerk NL 17 Hd26
Riddes CH 100 Bc56
Ried im Innkreis A 96 Ed51
Riedlingen D 95 Cd50
Riega del Camino E 31 Cb59
Rieneck D 89 Db44
Riesa D 90 Ed40
Riesi I 114 Fa86
Rietberg D 89 Cc38
Rietschen D 91 Fc40
Rieumes F 35 Gc54
Rieux F 35 Gc55
Riez F 29 Jd53
Rigolato I 103 Ed56
Riihimäki FIN 68 Kb38
Riihiniemi FIN 67 Jd35

Rimini I 103 Eb64
Rimmi FIN 59 Jb28
Rimpar D 89 Da45
Rimplänniemi FIN 60 Kd25
Rinchnach D 96 Ed48
Rincón de la Victoria E 44 Da76
Rinchbridge IRL 7 Cc21
Rindbøn N 48 Fd14
Rinella I 115 Fc82
Ringaskiddy IRL 6 Bc26
Ringebu N 64 Dd36
Ringford GB 11 Dd18
Ringgau D 89 Db41
Ringkøbing DK 76 Cc54
Ringleben D 90 Dd40
Ringsås S 65 Fa37
Ringsend GB 5 Cd16
Ringsted DK 77 Eb56
Ringwood GB 15 Ed30
Rinkilä FIN 69 Lc33
Rinlo E 31 Bd53
Rinøya N 48 Fd14
Rödänäs S 59 Hd27
Rodbergshamn N 49 Gc10
Rødbyhavn DK 77 Ea59
Rosalejo E 37 Cb65
Rosans F 29 Jc51
Rosapenna IRL 4 Ca15
Rosarito E 37 Cb65
Rosarno I 115 Gb82
Rovanieni FIN 54 Jd19
Rovapää FIN 50 Jc15
Rovato I 101 Da59
Roverbella I 102 Db60
Rovereto I 102 Dc59
Rövershagen D 84 Eb31
Rovetta I 101 Da58
Rovigo I 102 Dd61
Roznosov CZ 97 Gc47
Roznov pod Radhoštěm CZ 92 Hb46

Rundfloen – Santa Croce di Magliano


Rundfloen N 65 Ed38
Rundvik S 59 Ha29
Runemo S 66 Ga37
Rungsted DK 77 Ec55
Runnabackan IRL 4 Ca20
Runowo PL 86 Ja30
Runtaleave GB 11 Eb10
Ruokee FIN 69 Ld33
Ruokojärvi FIN 54 Jc17
Ruokojärvi FIN 69 Lc33
Ruokojärvi S 54 Ja19
Ruokokoski FIN 61 La32
Ruokola FIN 69 Lc36
Ruokolahti FIN 69 Lc35
Ruokotaipale FIN 69 Lb35
Ruoms F 28 Ja51
Ruorasmäki FIN 68 Kd34
Ruosniemi FIN 67 Ja36
Ruoti I 112 Ga75
Ruotsinpyhtää FIN 68 Kd38
Ruovesi FIN 68 Jd34
Rupea RO 118 Dd61
Ruppichteroth D 88 Ca41
Ruppovaara FIN 61 Ma32
Ruše SLO 104 Fd56
Rusele S 58 Gc25
Rush IRL 7 Da21
Rushden GB 15 Fb25
Ruské SK 99 Kb47
Ruskington GB 16 Fc23
Rusksand S 58 Gb29
Rusksele S 58 Gd25
Rusktriäsk S 58 Gd25
Rusovce SK 98 Gd51
Rüsselsheim D 89 Cc44
Russkij Kameškir RUS 137 Fd11
Rust A 97 Gc52
Rustefjelbma N 47 Ka06
Ruszów PL 91 Fd40
Rutakoski FIN 60 Kc32
Rutava FIN 68 Jc37
Rute E 44 Da74
Rüthen D 89 Cc39
Rutherglen GB 10 Dd13
Ruthin GB 12 Eb22
Rüthnick D 84 Ed35
Ruthwell GB 11 Eb16
Rüti CH 95 Cc53
Rutigliano I 113 Gd74
Rutledal N 62 Ca37
Rutten NL 82 Bb34
Rutvik S 54 Hd22
Rutwica PL 85 Gb34
Ruuhijärvi FIN 54 Jc18
Ruuhijärvi FIN 68 Kc36
Ruuhimäki FIN 68 Kc33
Ruukki FIN 60 Jd25
Ruurlo NL 82 Bd37
Ruuskankylä FIN 60 Ka27
Ruutana FIN 60 Kc28
Ruutana FIN 68 Jd35
Ruvo di Puglia I 113 Gc74
Ruynes-en-Margeride F 28 Hb49
Ruza RUS 137 Ed10
Ruzaevka RUS 137 Fc10
Ružany BY 136 Ea13
Ružomberok SK 98 Hd47
Rybany SK 98 Hb49
Rybczewice PL 93 Kb40
Rybinsk RUS 137 Ed09
Rybnica Leśna PL 91 Gb42
Rybnik PL 92 Hb44
Rybno PL 86 Hd33
Rybno PL 87 Jb32
Rybnoe RUS 137 Fa11
Ryboły PL 87 Kb34
Rybotycze PL 93 Kb45
Rychłocice PL 92 Hc40
Rychnov nad Kněžnou CZ 91 Gb44
Rychnów PL 92 Ha41
Rychnowy PL 86 Gd32
Ryczów PL 92 Hd44
Ryde GB 15 Fa30
Rydułtowy PL 92 Hb44
Rydzewo PL 87 Ka32
Rydzyna PL 91 Gb39
Rye GB 16 Ga30
Ryhälänmäki FIN 60 Kd27
Ryki PL 93 Jd38
Ryl'sk RUS 137 Ed13
Rymanów PL 93 Ka45
Rýmařov CZ 92 Gd45
Rymättylä FIN 67 Jb39
Ryn PL 87 Jc31
Rynarcice PL 91 Gb40
Rynie PL 87 Ka30
Rynkänpuoli FIN 55 Kb20
Ryńsk PL 86 Hb34
Ryönä FIN 61 La30
Rypefjord N 46 Hd06
Rypin PL 86 Hc34
Rysjedalsvika N 62 Ca36
Rytilahti FIN 55 Kc18
Ryttylä FIN 68 Kb37
Rzeczyca PL 92 Ja39
Rzęgnowo PL 87 Jb34
Rzemień PL 93 Jd43
Rzepedź PL 93 Ka46
Rzepin PL 85 Fc37
Rzerzęczyce PL 92 Hd41
Rzeszów PL 93 Ka44
Ržev RUS 136 Ec10
Rzewnie PL 87 Jc35
Rzucewo PL 86 Ha29
Rzuców PL 93 Jb40
Ržyščiv UA 136 Ec15


## S


Saá E 31 Bc56
Sääksjärvi FIN 67 Jb36
Saal D 84 Ec30
Saalahti FIN 68 Kb34
Saal an der Donau D 96 Ea48
Saal an der Saale D 89 Db43
Saalbach A 96 Eb53
Saalburg-Ebersdorf D 90 Ea43
Saalfeld D 90 Dd42
Saalfelden am Steinernen Meer A 96 Ec53
Saalow D 84 Ed37
Saanen CH 94 Bc55
Säänjärvi FIN 69 Lb36
Saaramaa FIN 69 La37
Saarbrücken D 88 Bd46
Saarburg D 88 Bc45
Sääre EST 74 Jc48
Saarela FIN 60 Kc29
Saaresmäki FIN 60 Kc26
Saari FIN 69 Ld33
Saarijärvi FIN 60 Kb31
Saarikas FIN 60 Kc31
Saarikoski FIN 49 Hb12
Saarikylä FIN 55 Lc22
Saarinen FIN 60 Kd25
Saariselkä FIN 51 Ka12
Saarivaara FIN 55 Lb24
Saarlouis D 88 Bc46
Saarwellingen D 88 Bc46
Saas Almagell CH 100 Bd57
Saas Fee CH 100 Bd57
Sääskiniemi FIN 61 La28
Sabadell E 35 Gd61
Sabarat F 34 Gc56
Sabaudia I 109 Ec73
Sabbioneta I 102 Db61
Sab Gregório P 30 Ba58
Sabile LV 74 Jd50
Sabinov SK 99 Jc47
Sabiote E 44 Dc72
Sables-d'Or-les-Pins F 18 Ec37
Sablé-sur-Sarthe F 23 Fc40
Säbrå S 58 Gc32
Sabres F 26 Fb52
Sabrosa P 30 Bb61
Säbyggeby S 66 Gb38
sa Cabaneta E 41 Hb67
sa Calobra E 41 Hb66
Săcăşeni RO 117 Cc55
Sacavém P 36 Aa68
Sacecorbo E 38 Eb63
Sacedón E 38 Ea64
Sachsen D 95 Dc47
Sachsenbrunn D 90 Dd43
Sachsenburg A 96 Ed55
Sachsenhagen D 83 Da36
Sachsenheim D 95 Cd48
Sacile I 103 Eb58
Šack BY 136 Ea13
Šack RUS 137 Fb11
Šac'k UA 136 Dd14
Sacquenay F 25 Jb41
Sacramenia E 32 Db61
Sádaba E 33 Ed58
Sadelkow D 84 Fa33
Sadjem S 54 Hc18
Sadki PL 86 Gd34
Sadlinki PL 86 Hb32
Sadłowo PL 86 Hc34
Sadovoe RUS 137 Ga14
Sadów PL 92 Hc42
Sadowne PL 87 Jd35
Sädvaluspen S 53 Ga20
Sady PL 93 Jb39
Sæby DK 71 Dd50
Saelices E 38 Ea66
Saelices de Mayorga E 31 Cd58
Saerbeck D 83 Cb37
Sætra N 48 Gb10
Sætre N 65 Ec38
Saeul L 21 Jc33
Safara P 42 Bb71
Säffle S 71 Ed44
Saffré F 23 Ed41
Saffron Walden GB 16 Fd26
Safonovo RUS 136 Ec11
Sagfjorden N 48 Fd16
Sagmoen N 53 Ga18
Sagone F 106 Ca70
Sagres P 42 Aa74
Sagunt E 39 Fc67
Sagunto E 39 Fc67
Sahagún E 31 Cd58
Sahalahti FIN 68 Ka35
Sahankylä FIN 67 Jb33
Sahechores E 31 Cd57
Sahloinen FIN 68 Kb33
Šahty RUS 137 Fc15
Šahy SK 98 Hc51
Saignelégiers CH 94 Bc53
Saignes F 27 Ha48
Saignon F 29 Jc53
Saija FIN 51 Kd16
Säijä FIN 68 Jd36
Saikari FIN 60 Kd30
Saillans F 29 Jc50
Sains-en-Amiénois F 20 Gd33
Saint Abbs GB 11 Ed13
Saint-Affrique F 28 Hb53
Saint-Agil F 23 Ga39
Saint Agnes GB 14 Da31
Saint-Agrève F 28 Ja49
Saint-Aignan F 24 Gb42
Saint Alban F 22 Eb38
Saint Albans GB 16 Fc27
Saint-Alban-sur-Limagnole F 28 Hc50
Saint-Amand-en-Puisaye F 24 Hb41
Saint-Amand-les-Eaux F 20 Hb31
Saint-Amand-Montrond F 24 Ha44
Saint-Amans-de-Mounis F 28 Hb54
Saint-Amans-des-Cots F 27 Ha50
Saint-Amans-Soult F 27 Ha54
Saint-Amant-Tallende F 28 Hb47
Saint-Ambroix F 28 Ja52
Saint-Amé F 25 Ka39
Saint-André-de-Corcy F 25 Jb46
Saint-André-de-Cubzac F 26 Fb50
Saint-André-de-l'Eure F 20 Gb37
Saint-André-de-Sangonis F 28 Hc54
Saint Andrews GB 11 Ec12
Saint-Angeau F 26 Fd47
Saint Ann's GB 11 Eb15
Saint-Anne GBA 18 Ec34
Saint-Anthème F 28 Hd47
Saint-Antonin-Noble-Val F 27 Gc52
Saint-Août F 24 Gd44
Saint-Apollinaire F 25 Jb41
Saint-Arnoult-des-Bois F 24 Gb38
Saint Arvans GB 14 Eb27
Saint Asaph GB 12 Ea22
Saint-Astier F 27 Ga49
Saint Athan GB 14 Ea28
Saint-Auban-sur-l'Ouvèze F 29 Jc51
Saint Aubin CH 94 Bb54
Saint-Aubin F 26 Fb54
Saint-Aubin-des-Châteaux F 23 Ed40
Saint-Aubin-des-Coudrais F 23 Ga39
Saint-Aubin-du-Cormier F 23 Fa39
Saint-Aubin-lès-Elbeuf F 19 Ga35
Saint-Aubin-sur-Aire F 21 Jb37
Saint-Aubin-sur-Mer F 19 Fc35
Saint-Augustin F 27 Gc48
Saint-Aulaye F 26 Fd49
Saint Austell GB 14 Db31
Saint-Avit F 24 Ha46
Saint-Avold F 21 Ka35
Saint-Aygulf F 29 Kb54
Saint-Barthélemy-d'Anjou F 23 Fb41
Saint-Barthélemy-le-Plain F 28 Jb49
Saint-Bauzille-de-Montmel F 28 Hd53
Saint-Bauzille-de-Putois F 28 Hd53
Saint-Beat F 34 Ga56
Saint-Beauzély F 28 Hb52
Saint Bees GB 12 Ea18
Saint-Benin-d'Azy F 24 Hb43
Saint-Bernard F 29 Jd48
Saint-Blaise-la-Roche F 94 Bb49
Saint-Blimont F 20 Gc32
Saint-Blin F 25 Jb38
Saint Boswells GB 11 Ec14
Saint-Brelade GBJ 18 Ec36
Saint-Brévin-les-Pins F 22 Ec42
Saint Briavels GB 15 Ec27
Saint Brides GB 14 Db27
Saint-Brieuc F 22 Eb38
Saint-Bris-le-Vineux F 24 Hc40
Saint Buryan GB 14 Da32
Saint-Calais F 23 Ga40
Saint-Cannat F 29 Jc54
Saint-Caprais F 24 Gd43
Saint-Capraise-de-Lalinde F 27 Ga50
Saint-Cast-le-Guildo F 18 Ec37
Saint Catherines GB 10 Dc12
Saint-Céré F 27 Gd50
Saint-Cernin-de-l'Herm F 27 Gb51
Saint-Chamas F 29 Jc54
Saint-Chamond F 28 Ja48
Saint-Christol-lès-Alès F 28 Hd52
Saint-Christophe-de-Double F 26 Fc49
Saint-Christophe-du-Ligneron F 23 Ed43
Saint-Christophe-en-Oisans F 29 Ka49
Saint-Ciers-Champagne F 26 Fc48
Saint-Ciers-du-Taillon F 26 Fb49
Saint-Cirgues-de-Jordanne F 27 Ha49
Saint-Cirgues-en-Montagne F 28 Hd50
Saint-Clar F 27 Ga53
Saint-Claude F 25 Jd44
Saint-Claud-sur-le-Son F 26 Fd47
Saint Clears GB 14 Dc27
Saint-Clement F 24 Hb39
Saint-Clément F 27 Gc48
Saint-Clément-des-Baleines F 23 Ed45
Saint-Colombier F 22 Eb41
Saint Columb Major GB 14 Db31
Saint Combs GB 9 Ed07
Saint-Cosme-en-Vairais F 23 Fd39
Saint-Cyprien F 27 Gb50
Saint-Cyprien F 28 Hd47
Saint-Cyprien F 35 Hb57
Saint Cyrus GB 11 Ed10
Saint-Dalmas-le-Selvage F 29 Kb51
Saint David's GB 14 Db26
Saint-Denis F 20 Gd36
Saint-Denis-de-Gastines F 23 Fb38
Saint-Denis-de-l'Hotel F 24 Gd40
Saint-Denis-de-Pile F 26 Fc50
Saint-Denis-d'Oléron F 23 Ed46
Saint Dennis GB 14 Db31
Saint-Désiré F 24 Ha44
Saint-Dié-des-Vosges F 25 Ka38
Saint-Dizier F 21 Ja37
Saint-Dizier-Leyrenne F 24 Gc46
Saint-Dolay F 22 Ec41
Saint-Domineuc F 23 Ed38
Saint-Doulchard F 24 Gd42
Sainte-Cécile-d'Andorge F 28 Hd52
Sainte-Cécile-les-Vignes F 28 Jb52
Sainte-Colombe F 19 Ga36
Sainte-Colombe F 24 Hb42
Sainte Croix CH 94 Bb54
Sainte-Croix-du-Mont F 26 Fc51
Sainte-Croix-en-Plaine F 94 Bd50
Sainte-Eulalie F 28 Hd50
Sainte-Eulalie-d'Olt F 28 Hb51
Sainte-Eulalie-en-Royans F 29 Jc49
Sainte-Féréole F 27 Gc49
Sainte-Foy-Tarentaise F 29 Kb47
Sainte-Gauburge-Sainte-Colombe F 19 Fd37
Sainte-Geneviève-des-Bois F 20 Gd37
Sainte-Geneviève-des-Bois F 24 Ha40
Sainte-Geneviève-sur-Argence F 27 Ha50
Sainte-Hélène F 26 Fb50
Sainte-Jalle F 29 Jc51
Sainte-Livrade-sur-Lot F 27 Ga52
Saint-Elix-Theux F 34 Fd55
Saint-Eloy-les-Mines F 24 Ha45
Sainte-Lucie-de-Tallano F 106 Cb71
Sainte-Maure F 28 Hb50
Sainte-Marie-aux-Mines F 94 Bd50
Sainte-Marie-de-Ré F 23 Fa46
Sainte-Maxime F 29 Kb54
Sainte-Menehould F 21 Ja36
Saint-Émilion F 26 Fc50
Sainteny F 19 Fa35
Saintes F 26 Fb47
Sainte-Savine F 25 Hd38
Sainte-Sigolene F 28 Ja48
Saint-Estèphe F 26 Fb49
Saint-Estève F 29 Jc52
Saint-Estève F 35 Hb57
Sainte-Suzanne F 23 Fc39
Saint-Etienne F 28 Ja48
Saint-Étienne-de-Cuines F 29 Ka48
Saint-Étienne-de-Montluc F 22 Ed42
Saint-Étienne-de-Saint-Geoirs F 29 Jc48
Saint-Étienne-des-Sorts F 28 Jb52
Saint-Étienne-de-Tinée F 29 Kc51
Saint-Étienne-du-Rouvray F 20 Gb35
Saint-Étienne-en-Dévoluy F 29 Jd50
Saint-Étienne-Estréchoux F 28 Hb54
Saint-Étienne-les-Orgues F 29 Jd52
Saint-Félix-de-Sorgues F 28 Hb53
Saint-Félix-de-Villadeix F 27 Ga50
Saint Fergus GB 9 Fa08
Saintfield GB 5 Da18
Saint Fillans GB 11 Ea11
Saint-Firmin F 29 Ka50
Saint-Florent F 106 Cb68
Saint-Florentin F 24 Hc39
Saint-Florent-le-Vieil F 23 Fa42
Saint-Florent-sur-Cher F 24 Gd43
Saint-Flour F 28 Hb49
Saint-Folquin F 17 Gd30
Saint-Fraigne F 23 Fc46
Saint-Galmier F 28 Ja47
Saint-Gaudens F 34 Ga56
Saint-Gaultier F 24 Gb44
Saint-Genest-Malifaux F 28 Ja48
Saint-Geniès-des-Mourgues F 28 Hd54
Saint-Geniez-d'Olt F 28 Hb51
Saint-Genis-Laval F 28 Jb47
Saint-Genis-Pouilly F 25 Jd45
Saint Gennys GB 14 Dc30
Saint-Georges-d'Aurac F 28 Hc49
Saint-Georges-de-Commiers F 29 Jd49
Saint-Georges-de-Noisne F 23 Fc45
Saint-Georges-en-Couzan F 28 Hd47
Saint-Gérand F 22 Eb39
Saint-Germain-de-Confolens F 23 Ga46
Saint-Germain-de-Coulamer F 23 Fc39
Saint-Germain-de-Tallevende F 19 Fb37
Saint-Germain-du-Bois F 25 Jb43
Saint-Germain-du-Plain F 25 Jb43
Saint-Germain-en-Laye F 20 Gd37
Saint-Germain-Laval F 25 Hd46
Saint-Germain-Lembron F 28 Hb48
Saint-Germain-les-Arlay F 25 Jc43
Saint-Germain-l'Herm F 28 Hc48
Saint-Germer-de-Fly F 20 Gc35
Saint-Gervais-la-Forêt F 24 Gb41
Saint-Gervais-les-Bains F 100 Bb57
Saint-Gervais-les-Trois-Clochers F 23 Fd43
Saint-Géry F 26 Fd50
Saint-Gildas-des-Bois F 22 Ec41
Saint-Gilles F 19 Fa36
Saint-Gilles F 23 Ed39
Saint-Gilles F 23 Fd42
Saint-Gilles F 28 Ja54
Saint-Gilles-Croix-de-Vie F 22 Ec44
Saint-Gilles-Pligeaux F 22 Ea38
Saint-Gingolph F 100 Bb56
Saint-Girons F 34 Gb56
Saint-Girons-en-Marensin F 26 Fa53
Saint-Girons-Plage F 26 Ed53
Saint-Gobain F 20 Hb34
Saint-Gondon F 24 Ha40
Saint-Gondran F 23 Ed39
Saint-Gonnery F 22 Eb39
Saint-Guénolé F 22 Dc40
Saint-Haon-le-Châtel F 25 Hd46
Saint Harmon GB 14 Ea25
Saint Helens GB 13 Ec21
Saint-Helier GBJ 18 Ec36
Saint-Hilaire F 35 Ha56
Saint-Hilaire-de-Riez F 22 Ec44
Saint-Hilaire-de-Villefranche F 26 Fb47
Saint-Hilaire-du-Harcouët F 23 Fa38
Saint-Hilaire-la-Pallud F 23 Fb45
Saint-Hilaire-Petitville F 19 Fa35
Saint-Honoré-les-Bains F 24 Hc43
Saint-Hubert B 21 Jb32
Saint-Hubert F 23 Fd40
Saint Imier CH 94 Bc53
Saint Ives GB 14 Da32
Saint Ives GB 16 Fc25
Saint-Jacut-de-la-Mer F 22 Ec38
Saint-James F 23 Fa38
Saint-Jean-d'Angely F 23 Fc46
Saint-Jean-d'Angle F 26 Fa47
Saint-Jean-d'Avelanne F 29 Jd47
Saint-Jean-de-Barrou F 35 Hb56
Saint-Jean-de-Durfort F 29 Jc52
Saint-Jean-de-Luz F 33 Ed55
Saint-Jean-de-Maurienne F 29 Ka48
Saint-Jean-de-Monts F 22 Ec43
Saint-Jean-de-Niost F 25 Jc46
Saint-Jean-de-Sauves F 23 Fd44
Saint-Jean-de-Verges F 34 Gc56
Saint-Jean-du-Doigt F 18 Dd37
Saint-Jean-en-Royans F 29 Jc49
Saint-Jean-la-Rivière F 29 Kc52
Saint-Jean-le-Blanc F 24 Gc40
Saint-Jean-Pied-de-Port F 33 Fa56
Saint-Jean-Saint-Maurice-sur-Loire F 25 Hd46
Saint-Jean-sur-Reyssouze F 25 Jb44
Saint-Jeoire F 25 Ka45
Saint John GBJ 18 Ec35
Saint John's Chapel GB 13 Ed17
Saint John's GB 12 Dc19
Saint-Jouin-de-Marnes F 23 Fc43
Saint-Juan F 25 Ka41
Saint-Julien F 27 Gd53
Saint-Julien F 29 Ka50
Saint-Julien-de-Jonzy F 25 Hd45
Saint-Julien-de-Vouvantes F 23 Fa41
Saint-Julien-du-Sault F 24 Hb39
Saint-Julien-en-Born F 26 Fa53
Saint-Julien-en-Genevois F 25 Jd45
Saint-Julien-l'Ars F 23 Ga44
Saint-Julien-le-Faucon F 19 Fd36
Saint-Julien-sur-Cher F 24 Gc42
Saint-Junien F 27 Ga47
Saint-Junien-la-Bregère F 24 Gc46
Saint-Junien-la-Bregère F 27 Gc47
Saint-Just F 24 Ha43
Saint-Just GB 14 Cd32
Saint-Just-Ibarre F 33 Fa55
Saint-Justin F 26 Fc53
Saint-Just-Saint-Rambert F 28 Ja48
Saint-Juvin F 21 Ja35
Saint-Lambert-du-Lattay F 23 Fb42
Saint-Laurent F 24 Gd46
Saint-Laurent F 29 Kb51
Saint-Laurent-d'Aigouze F 28 Ja54
Saint-Laurent-de-Chamousset F 28 Ja47
Saint-Laurent-de-la-Salanque F 35 Hb57
Saint-Laurent-du-Pont F 29 Jd48
Saint-Laurent-Nouan F 24 Gc40
Saint-Laurent-sur-Sèvre F 23 Fb43
Saint-Léger-des-Vignes F 24 Hc43
Saint-Léger-sous-Beuvray F 25 Hd43
Saint-Léger-sur-Dheune F 25 Ja43
Saint-Léon F 34 Gc55
Saint-Léonard-de-Noblat F 27 Gc47
Saint-Leu-d'Esserent F 20 Gd35
Saint-Lizier F 34 Gb56
Saint-Lô F 19 Fa36
Saint-Loup-de-Naud F 24 Hb38
Saint-Loup-sur-Semouse F 25 Jd39
Saint-Lunaire F 18 Ec37
Saint-Lyé F 24 Gc39
Saint-Lyphard F 22 Ec42
Saint-Magne F 26 Fb51
Saint-Maime F 29 Jd53
Saint-Maixent-l'École F 23 Fc45
Saint-Malo F 18 Ec37
Saint-Marc F 22 Ec42
Saint-Marcel-de-Careiret F 28 Ja52
Saint-Marcel-lès-Valence F 28 Jb49
Saint-Marcellin F 29 Jc48
Saint-Mards-en-Othe F 24 Hc39
Saint Margaret's Hope GB 9 Ec03
Saint Margaret's at Cliffe GB 16 Gb29
Saint-Mars-d'Outille F 23 Fd40
Saint-Martin F 19 Fb36
Saint-Martin F 22 Ec40
Saint-Martin F 94 Bd49
Saint-Martin-d'Ardeche F 28 Ja51
Saint-Martin-de-Boscherville F 19 Ga35
Saint-Martin-de-Crau F 28 Jb54
Saint-Martin-de-la-Lieue F 19 Fd36
Saint-Martin-de-Landelles F 23 Fa38
Saint-Martin-d'Entraunes F 29 Kb52
Saint-Martin-de-Queyrières F 29 Kb49
Saint-Martin-de-Ré F 23 Fa45
Saint-Martin-de-Salencey F 25 Ja44
Saint-Martin-de-Seignanx F 26 Ed54
Saint-Martin-d'Estréaux F 24 Hc45
Saint-Martin-de-Valmas F 28 Ja49
Saint-Martin-d'Oney F 26 Fb53
Saint-Martin-du-Fouilloux F 23 Fc44
Saint-Martin-en-Bresse F 25 Jb43
Saint-Martin-en-Campagne F 20 Gb33
Saint-Martin-en-Haut F 28 Ja47
Saint-Martin-en-Vercors F 29 Jc49
Saint-Martin-la-Plaine F 28 Ja47
Saint-Martin-l'Ars F 23 Ga45
Saint-Martin-sur-Armançon F 25 Hd40
Saint-Martin-Valmeroux F 27 Ha49
Saint Mary's GB 9 Ec03
Saint Mary's Bay GB 16 Ga30
Saint-Mathieu F 27 Ga47
Saint-Mathieu-de-Tréviers F 28 Hd53
Saint-Mathurin-sur-Loire F 23 Fc42
Saint-Maur F 20 Gd37
Saint-Maurice F 28 Hb53
Saint-Maurice-de-Cazevieille F 28 Ja52
Saint-Maurice-en-Trieves F 29 Jd50
Saint-Maurice-lès-Charencey F 19 Ga37
Saint-Maurice-lès-Châteauneuf F 25 Hd45
Saint-Maurice-sous-les-Côtes F 21 Jb36
Saint-Maurice-sur-Moselle F 25 Ka39
Saint Mawes GB 14 Db32
Saint-Maximin-la-Sainte-Baume F 29 Jd54
Saint-Médard-de-Gurçon F 26 Fd50
Saint-Médard F 27 Gb51
Saint-Médard-de-Guizières F 26 Fc49
Saint-Médard-en-Jalles F 26 Fb50
Saint-Méen-le-Grand F 22 Ec39
Saint-Meloir-des-Ondes F 23 Ed38
Saint-Michel-de-Double F 26 Fd49
Saint-Michel-de-Lanès F 34 Gc55
Saint-Michel-en-Greve F 18 Dd37
Saint-Michel-l'Observatoire F 29 Jd53
Saint-Mihiel F 21 Jb36
Saint Minver GB 14 Db31
Saint-Nazaire F 22 Ec42
Saint-Nectaire F 28 Hb47
Saint Neots GB 16 Fc25
Saint Nicholas GB 14 Db26
Saint-Nicolas-de-la-Grave F 27 Gb53
Saint-Nicolas-de-Port F 21 Jd37
Saint-Nicolas-des-Eaux F 22 Ea40
Saint-Nizier-du-Moucherotte F 29 Jd48
Saint-Omer F 17 Gd30
Saint Osyth GB 16 Ga27
Saint-Ouen-lès-Parey F 25 Jc38
Saint-Pair-sur-Mer F 19 Ed37
Saint-Palais-sur-Mer F 26 Fa47
Saint-Pal-de-Senouire F 28 Hc48
Saint-Pancrace F 27 Ga48
Saint-Pardoux-la-Riviere F 27 Ga48
Saint-Parres-lès-Vaudes F 25 Hd39
Saint-Paterne-Racan F 23 Fd41
Saint-Paul F 29 Kc53
Saint-Paul-de-Fenouillet F 35 Ha57
Saint-Paul-de-Varax F 25 Jb45
Saint-Paul-et-Valmalle F 28 Hd54
Saint-Paulien F 28 Hd49
Saint-Paul-le-Jeune F 28 Hd51
Saint-Paul-lès-Dax F 26 Fa54
Saint-Paul-sur-Ubaye F 29 Kb50
Saint-Pée-sur-Nivelle F 33 Ed55
Saint-Péran F 22 Ec39
Saint-Péravy-la-Colombe F 24 Gc40
Saint-Péray F 28 Jb49
Saint-Père F 24 Hc41
Saint-Peter-Port GBG 18 Eb35
Saint-Philbert-de-Grand-Lieu F 23 Ed43
Saint-Pierre-d'Albigny F 29 Ka47
Saint-Pierre-de-Bétirac F 27 Ha53
Saint-Pierre-de-la-Fage F 28 Hc53
Saint-Pierre-de-Maille F 23 Ga44
Saint-Pierre-d'Entremont F 19 Fb37
Saint-Pierre-des-Nids F 23 Fc38
Saint-Pierre-du-Chemin F 23 Fb44
Saint-Pierre-du-Mont F 19 Fa35
Saint-Pierre-la-Bourlhonne F 28 Hc47
Saint-Pierre-la-Cour F 23 Fa39
Saint-Pierre-Montlimart F 23 Fa42
Saint-Pierre-sur-Mer F 35 Hc55
Saint-Pierreville F 28 Ja50
Saint-Pois F 19 Fa37
Saint-Pol-de-Léon F 18 Dc37
Saint-Pol-sur-Mer F 17 Gd29
Saint-Pol-sur-Ternoise F 20 Gd32
Saint-Pompain F 23 Fb45
Saint-Porquier F 27 Gb53
Saint-Pouange F 25 Hd39
Saint-Pourçain-sur-Sioule F 24 Hb45
Saint-Priest F 28 Jb47
Saint-Privat F 27 Gd49
Saint-Privat-d'Allier F 28 Hc49
Saint-Privat-des-Vieux F 28 Hd52
Saint-Prouant F 23 Fa44
Saint-Puy F 26 Fd53
Saint-Quai F 18 Ea37
Saint-Quentin F 20 Hb33
Saint-Quentin-des-Isles F 19 Ga36
Saint-Quentin-les-Anges F 23 Fb40
Saint-Quentin-sur-Isère F 29 Jc48
Saint-Rabier F 27 Gb49
Saint-Rambert-d'Albon F 28 Jb48
Saint-Raphaël F 29 Kb54
Saint-Rémy-de-Provence F 28 Jb53
Saint-Rémy-sur-Durolle F 24 Hc46
Saint-Renan F 22 Db38
Saint-Romain-de-Colbosc F 19 Fd34
Saint-Romain-sur-Cher F 24 Gb42
Saint-Roman F 29 Jc50
Saint-Saëns F 20 Gb34
Saint-Sampson GBG 18 Ec35
Saint-Samson-la-Poterie F 20 Gc34
Saint-Saturnin F 28 Hb47
Saint-Saturnin-d'Apt F 29 Jc53
Saint-Saturnin-de-Lenne F 28 Hb51
Saint-Saulge F 24 Hc42
Saint-Saury F 27 Gd50
Saint-Sauvant F 26 Fb47
Saint-Sauveur-d'Aunis F 23 Fb46
Saint-Sauveur-de-Montagut F 28 Ja50
Saint-Sauveur-de-Peyre F 28 Hc50
Saint-Savin F 23 Ga44
Saint-Savin F 26 Fb49
Saint-Seine-l'Abbaye F 25 Ja41
Saint-Senier-sous-Avranches F 19 Fa37
Saint-Sernin-sur-Rance F 27 Ha53
Saint-Servan F 18 Ec37
Saint-Sever F 26 Fb54
Saint-Sorlin-d'Arves F 29 Ka48
Saint-Sornin-Leulac F 24 Gb45
Saint-Sulpice-les-Champs F 24 Gd46
Saint-Sulpice-les-Feuilles F 24 Gb45
Saint-Sylvestre-sur-Lot F 27 Ga51
Saint-Symphorien F 25 Hd46
Saint-Symphorien-de-Mahun F 28 Ja49
Saint Teath GB 14 Db31
Saint-Thibault F 25 Ja41
Saint-Thiébault F 25 Jc38
Saint-Tropez F 29 Kb54
Saint Tudy GB 14 Db31
Saint-Tugen F 22 Db39
Saint Ursanne CH 94 Bc52
Saint-Vaast-la-Hougue F 19 Fa34
Saint-Vallier F 25 Ja44
Saint-Vallier F 28 Jb49
Saint-Victor F 24 Ha45
Saint-Victor F 27 Ga52
Saint-Vincent F 29 Jd52
Saint-Vincent I 100 Bd58
Saint-Vincent F 29 Ka52
Saint-Vincent-de-Tyrosse F 26 Fa54
Saint-Vincent-les-Forts F 29 Ka51
Saint-Voir F 24 Hc45
Saint-Vulbas F 25 Jc46
Saint Weonards GB 14 Eb26
Saint-Xandre F 23 Fa45
Saint-Yan F 25 Hd45
Saint-Yrieix-la-Perche F 27 Gb48
Saint-Yrieix-le-Déjalat F 27 Gd48
Saint-Yzans-de-Médoc F 26 Fb48
Saissac F 35 Gd55
Saiva sameviste S 53 Gd17
Säivis S 54 Jb21
Saivomuotka S 50 Ja14
Saja E 32 Db55
Sajaniemi FIN 68 Ka38
Sajólád H 99 Jc51
Sajószámos H 99 Jc50
Sajószentpéter H 99 Jc50
Sakaravaara FIN 55 La23
Säkkilä FIN 55 La19
Sakkoperä FIN 60 Jd26
Sakmara RUS 137 Fb10
Sakshaug N 57 Eb28
Saksild DK 76 Dc54
Saksnes N 56 Db31
Saky UA 137 Fa17
Sala S 66 Gb41
Šaľa SK 98 Ha51
Salacgiva LV 74 Kb48
Sala Consilina I 112 Ga76
Salahmi FIN 60 Kc27
Salamanca E 37 Cb62
Salamina GR 129 Cb86
Salandra I 113 Gb76
Salantai LT 80 Jb54
Salara I 102 Dd61
Salas E 31 Ca54
Salas Altas E 34 Fd59
Salas de Bureba E 32 Dd57
Salaspils LV 80 Kc51
Salaunes F 26 Fb50
Salavaux CH 94 Bc54
Salbris F 24 Gd41
Salcombe GB 14 Dd32
Saldaña E 32 Da57
Sale GB 13 Ec21
Saleen IRL 6 Bd26
Salem D 95 Cd51
Salemi I 114 Eb85
Salen GB 10 Db10
Salen GB 10 Db11
Salerno I 112 Fc75
Salers F 27 Ha49
Salford GB 13 Ec21
Salgótarján H 98 Ja51
Salgueiras E 30 Ad54
Salgueiro do Campo P 36 Ba65
Sali HR 110 Fd65
Salica I 113 Gd81
Salice Salentino I 113 Hb76
Salice Terme I 101 Cb61
Saliente Alto E 44 Eb74
Salientes E 31 Ca56
Salies-de-Béarn F 33 Fa55
Saligny-sur-Roudon F 24 Hc44
Salihli TR 131 Fa86
Salihorsk BY 136 Ea13
Salinas E 45 Fa71
Salinas de Pinilla E 44 Ea70
Salinas de Pisuerga E 32 Db56
Sälinkää FIN 68 Kb38
Salins-les-Bains F 25 Jd43
Salir P 42 Ac74
Salisbury GB 15 Ed29
Salla FIN 55 Kd17
Sallanches F 25 Ka46
Sallent E 35 Gd60
Salles F 26 Fa51
Salles-Curan F 28 Hb52
Salletjokka N 46 Jb06
Sällsjö S 57 Fa30
Salmantón E 32 Ea56
Salmenniemi FIN 60 Ka31
Salmerón E 38 Eb64
Salmi FIN 68 Jc36
Salminen FIN 60 Kd31
Salmis S 54 Jc21
Salmivaara FIN 55 Kc17
Salmoral E 37 Cc63
Salmünster, Bad Soden- D 89 Cd43
Salò I 102 Db59
Salobre E 44 Ea70
Salobreña E 44 Db76
Saloinen FIN 68 Kb37
Salokylä FIN 61 Ld31
Salomäki FIN 55 La21
Salo-Mehikkälä FIN 69 Lb37
Salon-de-Provence F 29 Jc54
Salonkylä FIN 60 Jc28
Salorino E 37 Bc67
Salou E 34 Gb62
Salouf CH 95 Cd55
Salses-le-Château F 35 Hb56
Sal'sk RUS 137 Fd15
Salsomaggiore Terme I 101 Cd61
Saltash GB 14 Dc31
Saltburn-by-the-Sea GB 13 Fb18
Saltcoats GB 10 Dc14
Saltfleet GB 13 Fd21
Salto P 30 Ba59
Salton GB 13 Fb19
Saltsjöbaden S 73 Gd44
Saltvik N 50 Hd08
Saltvik S 66 Gb36
Saltvika N 48 Gb14
Salubolle S 59 Ha29
Salussola I 100 Ca59
Saluzzo I 100 Bc61
Salvatierra de Escá E 33 Fa57
Salviac F 27 Gb51
Šalyhyne UA 137 Ed13
Salzbergen D 82 Ca36
Salzburg A 96 Ec52
Salzgitter D 83 Dc37
Salzhausen D 83 Dc34
Salzhemmendorf D 83 Da37
Salzkotten D 89 Cc38
Salzwedel D 84 Dd35
Samachvalavičy BY 136 Ea12
Sama de Langreo = Langreo E 31 Cc55
Samara RUS 137 Ga10
Samassi I 107 Ca79
Sambade P 31 Bc60
Sambiase I 113 Gb81
Sambin F 24 Gb41
Sambir UA 136 Dd15
Sambor UA 136 Dd15
Samborzec PL 93 Jd42
Sambuca di Sicilia I 114 Ec85
Sambuci I 109 Ec71
Samedan CH 101 Cc57
Sames E 31 Cd55
Sámi GR 128 Ac85
Sammakkola FIN 61 La27
Sammakkovaara FIN 61 Lc29
Sammichele di Bari I 113 Gd75
Samnaun CH 95 Db54
Samobor HR 104 Ga59
Samoëns F 100 Bb57
Samoilovka RUS 137 Fd13
Samolubie PL 86 Ja30
Samos GR 130 Eb88
Samper E 34 Fd58
Sampeyre I 100 Bb62
Sampława PL 86 Hd33
Sampu FIN 67 Jb37
Samsun TR 137 Fa18
Samswegen D 84 Dd38
San Adrián E 33 Ec58
Sanaigmore GB 10 Da13
San Andrés del Rabanedo E 31 Cc57
San Andrés de San Pedro E 32 Eb59
San Antoniño (Barro) E 30 Ad56
San Antonio del Fontanar E 43 Cb74
Sanary-sur-Mer F 29 Jd55
San Augustín de Guadalix E 38 Dc63
San Bartolomé de las Abiertas E 37 Cd66
San Bartolomé de la Torre E 42 Bb73
San Bartolomeo in Galdo I 109 Fc73
San Benedetto dei Marsi I 109 Ed71
San Benedetto del Tronto I 109 Fa68
San Benedetto in Alpe I 102 Dd64
San Benito E 43 Cd70
San Bernardino CH 101 Cc56
San Biagio di Callalta I 103 Eb59
San Biagio Platani I 114 Ed86
San Biase I 112 Fd77
San Blas E 39 Fa65
San Bonifacio I 102 Dc60
San Calixto E 43 Cb72
San Candido I 96 Eb55
San Carlos del Valle E 38 Dd69
San Casciano in Val di Pesa I 108 Dc65
San Cassiano I 102 Ea56
San Cataldo I 114 Fa86
San Cebrián de Campos E 32 Da58
Sancergues F 24 Ha42
Sancerre F 24 Ha42
San Cesario di Lecce I 113 Hc76
Sancey-le-Grand F 25 Ka41
San Chirico Nuovo I 113 Gb75
Sanchón de la Ribera E 37 Ca62
San Clemente E 38 Eb68
San Clemente E 44 Ea73
San Colombano al Lambro I 101 Cc60
San Costantino Albanese I 113 Gb77
San Costanzo I 109 Ec65
San Cristóbal de Entreviñas E 31 Cc59
San Cristóbal de la Vega E 38 Da62
San Cristobo E 31 Bc58
Sancy F 20 Ha36
San Damiano d'Asti I 100 Bd61
Sandane N 62 Cc35
San Daniele di Friuli I 103 Ec57
San Daniele Po I 101 Da61
Sandanski BG 125 Cb75
Sandarne S 66 Gb37
Sandata RUS 137 Fd16
Sandbach GB 13 Ec22
Sandbukt N 49 Hb08
Sande D 83 Cc32
Sande P 30 Ad60
Sandefjord N 71 Dd44
San Demetrio Corone I 113 Gc79
San Demetrio ne' Vestini I 109 Ed70
Sanden N 48 Fc13
Sandersleben D 90 Ea39
Sandfors S 59 Hc25
Sandgarth GB 9 Ec03
Sandgerði IS 2 Ab07
Sandhausen D 89 Cc46
Sandhead GB 10 Dc17
Sandholmen N 47 Ka04
Sandiás E 30 Bb58
Sandillon F 24 Gd40
Sandim P 31 Bc59
Sandin E 31 Ca59
Sand in Taufers I 96 Ea55
Sandl A 97 Fc49
Sandland N 46 Hb07
Sandnes N 57 Fa26
Sandnes N 63 Ca44
Sandness GB 9 Fa04
Sandnessjøen N 52 Ed21
Sando E 37 Ca62
San Domenico I 100 Ca56
Sandomierz PL 93 Jd42
San Donaci I 113 Hb76
San Donà di Piave I 103 Eb59
Sandovo RUS 137 Ed09
Sandown GB 15 Fa31
Sandøysund N 71 Dd44
Sandplace GB 14 Dc31
Sandrigo I 102 Dd59
Šandrivka UA 137 Fa15
Sandset N 48 Fc12
Sandsjö S 58 Gc26
Sandsjönäs S 53 Gc24
Sandslån S 58 Gc31
Sandstad N 56 Dc29
Sandstedt D 83 Cd33
Sandstrand N 48 Ga13
Sandträsk S 54 Hc21
Sandvig DK 78 Fc57
Sandvik N 49 Gc11
Sandvik N 62 Cb33
Sandvik N 65 Ec37
Sandvika N 49 Ha10
Sandvika N 57 Ed29
Sandviken S 58 Gc31
Sandviken S 66 Gb39
Sandwell GB 15 Ed25
Sandwich GB 16 Gb29
Sandwick GB 9 Fb05
Sandy GB 16 Fc26
Sandygate GB 12 Dd18
Sandyhills GB 11 Ea16
Sanem L 21 Jc34
San Esteban de Gorma E 32 Dd61
San Esteban del Molar E 31 Cc59
San Esteban de los Buitres E 31 Bd54
San Fele I 112 Ga75
San Felices de los Gallegos E 37 Bd62
San Felice sul Panaro I 102 Dc62
San Felipe E 30 Ba53
San Félix de las Lavanderas E 31 Cb57
San Feliz de Torío E 31 Cc57
San Ferdinando I 115 Gb83
San Ferdinando di Puglia I 110 Gb73
San Fernando E 43 Bd77
San Fernando de Henares E 38 Dc64
San Francisco de Olivenza E 36 Bb69
San Fratello I 115 Fb84
Sånga S 58 Gc31
Sangaste EST 75 La47
San Gavino Monreale I 107 Bd78
San Gemini I 109 Eb69
Sangerhausen D 90 Dd40
San Germano Vercellese I 100 Ca59
San Gimignano I 108 Db66
San Ginesio I 109 Ed67
San Giorgio I 113 Gd74
San Giorgio a Cremano I 112 Fb75
San Giorgio del Sannio I 112 Fc74
San Giorgio di Livenza I 103 Ec59
San Giorgio di Nogaro I 103 Ec58
San Giorgio Ionico I 113 Ha76
San Giovanni I 109 Ed69
San Giovanni Bianco I 101 Cd58
San Giovanni d'Asso I 108 Dd67
San Giovanni Incarico I 109 Ed73
San Giovanni in Croce I 101 Da61
San Giovanni in Fiore I 113 Gc80
San Giovanni in Persiceto I 102 Dc62
San Giovanni Lupatoto I 102 Dc60
San Giovanni Reatino I 109 Eb70
San Giovanni Rotondo I 110 Ga72
San Giovanni Suergiu I 107 Bd80
San Giovanni Valdarno I 108 Dd66
Sangis S 54 Jb21
San Giuliano Terme I 108 Da65
San Giuseppe I 112 Fb75
San Giuseppe Jato I 114 Ec84
Sangonera La Verde E 45 Ed73
San Gregorio Magno I 112 Fd75
Sangüesa E 33 Fa57
Sanguinet F 26 Fa51
Sani GR 129 Cb80
San Ildefonso o La Granja E 38 Db63
San Javier E 45 Fa73
San Jerónimo E 43 Cc72
San José de la Rábita E 44 Da74
San Juan de la Nava E 37 Cd64
San Juan del Puerto E 42 Bb74
San Juan de Nieva E 31 Cb54
Sankola FIN 68 Kb36
Sankt Aegidi A 96 Fa50
Sankt Andrä A 97 Fc55
Sankt Andreasberg D 89 Dc39
Sankt Anton am Arlberg A 95 Db54
Sankt Antönien CH 95 Da54
Sankt Blasien D 94 Ca51
Sankt Egidien D 90 Ec42
Sankt Gallen A 97 Fc52
Sankt Gallen CH 95 Cd53
Sankt Georgen an der Gusen A 97 Fb50
Sankt Georgen an der Stiefing A 97 Ga55
Sankt Georgen im Schwarzwald D 95 Cb50
Sankt Georgen ob Judenburg A 97 Fb54
Sankt Gertraud I 102 Dc56
Sankt Gilgen A 96 Ed52
Sankt Goar D 88 Ca43
Sankt Goarshausen D 88 Ca43
Sankt Ingbert D 88 Bd46
Sankt Jakob bei Mixnitz A 97 Fd53
Sankt Jakob im Lesachtal A 103 Ec56
Sankt Jakob in Defereggen A 96 Eb55
Sankt Johann A 96 Eb53
Sankt Johann D 95 Cd49
Sankt Johann im Pongau A 96 Ed53
Sankt Johann im Saggautal A 104 Fd56
Sankt Leonhard A 97 Fc55
Sankt Leonhard A 103 Fc56
Sankt Leonhard am Forst A 97 Fd51
Sankt Leon-Rot D 89 Cc46
Sankt Lorenzen I 96 Ea55
Sankt Lorenzen im Lesachtal A 96 Ec55
Sankt Lorenzen im Paltental A 97 Fb53
Sankt Marein im Mürztal A 97 Fd53
Sankt Margareten im Rosental A 103 Fb56
Sankt Märgen D 94 Ca51
Sankt Margrethen CH 95 Cd53
Sankt Martin A 96 Ed50
Sankt Martin CH 95 Cc55
Sankt Martin am Grimming A 96 Fa53
Sankt Martin am Tenn A 96 Ed53
Sankt Martin in Passeier I 95 Dc55
Sankt Michael A 96 Fa54
Sankt Michaelisdonn D 83 Da31
Sankt Moritz CH 101 Cd56
Sankt Niklaus CH 100 Bd57
Sankt Nikolai im Sölktal A 96 Fa54
Sankt Oswald A 96 Fa55
Sankt Oswald A 97 Fd55
Sankt Oswald-Riedlhütte D 96 Ed48
Sankt Paul im Lavanttal A 103 Fc56
Sankt-Peterburg RUS 69 Mb39
Sankt Peter-Ording D 83 Cd30
Sankt Pölten A 97 Ga51
Sankt Stefan A 97 Fc55
Sankt Stefan an der Gail A 103 Ed56
Sankt Valentin A 97 Fb51
Sankt Veit an der Glan A 97 Fb55
Sankt Veit im Defereggen A 96 Eb55
Sankt Wendel D 88 Bd46
Sankt Willibald A 96 Fa50
Sankt Wolfgang im Salzkammergut A 96 Ed52
San Lazzaro di Savena I 102 Dc63
San Leo I 108 Ea65
San Leone I 114 Ed86
San Lorenzo a Merse I 108 Dc67
San Lorenzo de El Escorial E 38 Db64
San Lorenzo in Campo I 109 Ec66
San Luca I 115 Gb84
Sanlúcar de Barrameda E 43 Bc75
Sanlúcar la Mayor E 43 Bd74
San Lugano I 102 Dd57
San Lupo I 109 Fc73
Sanluri I 107 Ca78
San Mamed E 30 Bb58
San Mamés de Campos E 32 Da58
San Marcello Pistoiese I 102 Db64
San Marco Argentano I 113 Gb79
San Marco dei Cavoti I 109 Fc73
San Marco in Lamis I 110 Ga72
San Marino RSM 109 Eb65
San Martín de Boniches E 39 Ed66
San Martín de la Vega E 38 Dc65
San Martín de Luiña E 31 Cb54
San Martín de Valdeiglesias E 38 Da64
San Martino di Campagna I 103 Eb58
San Martino di Castrozza I 102 Ea57
San Martino di Lota F 106 Cc68
San Martino in Pensilis I 109 Fc71
San Mateo de Gállego E 33 Fb60
San Mauro Forte I 113 Gb76
San Michele all'Adige I 102 Dc57
San Michele dei Mucchietti I 102 Db63
San Michele di Ganzaria I 115 Fb86
San Michele in Teverina I 108 Ea69
San Michele Salentino I 113 Ha75
San Miguel E 31 Bc58
San Miguel E 32 Dc56
San Miguel de las Dueñas E 31 Ca57
San Millán E 32 Dd56
San Miniato I 108 Db65
Sannicandro di Bari I 113 Gd74
San Nicandro Garganico I 110 Ga72
San Nicola di Tremiti I 110 Fd71
Sânnicolau Mare RO 116 Bb59
San Nicolò d'Arcidano I 107 Bd78
San Nicolò Gerrei I 107 Cb79
Sanok PL 93 Ka45
San Pablo de Buceite E 43 Cb77
San Pablo de los Montes E 38 Da67
San Pancrazio Salentino I 113 Hb76
San Pataleón de Losa E 32 Dd56
San Pawl il Bahar M 115 Fb88
San Pedro E 32 Dd55
San Pedro E 44 Eb70
San Pedro Cansoles E 31 Cd56
San Pedro de Alcántara E 43 Cc77
San Pedro del Arroyo E 37 Cd63
San Pedro del Pinatar E 45 Fb73
San Pedro del Valle E 37 Cb62
San Pedro Manrique E 32 Eb59
San Pedro Palmiches E 38 Eb64
San Pelaio E 32 Ea54
San Pellegrino I 102 Dc64
San Pellegrino in Alpe I 101 Da64
San Pellegrino Terme I 101 Cd58
San Piero in Bagno I 108 Ea65
San Piero Patti I 115 Fc84
San Pietro in Casale I 102 Dd62
San Pietro Infine I 109 Fa73
San Pietro Vernòtico I 113 Hb76
Sanquhar GB 11 Ea15
San Remo I 100 Bc64
San Román E 31 Cc58
San Román de la Cuba E 31 Cd58
San Romolo I 100 Bc64
San Roque E 32 Da54
San Roque E 43 Cb78
San Roque (Coristanco) E 30 Ad54
San Roque (Padrenda) E 30 Ba58
San Roque Torre Guadiaro E 43 Cb77
San Salvatore Monferrato I 100 Ca61
San Salvo I 109 Fc71
San Salvo Marina I 109 Fc71
San Sebastian de Garabandal E 32 Db55
San Sebastián de los Reyes E 38 Dc64
San Sebastián = Donostia E 33 Ec55
Sansepolcro I 108 Ea66
San Severino Lucano I 113 Gb77
San Severino Marche I 109 Ec67
San Severo I 110 Fd72
San Silvestre de Guzmán E 42 Ba73
Sanski Most BIH 104 Gc62
Sansol E 32 Eb57
San Sosti I 113 Gb79
Santa Agata de' Goti I 112 Fb74
Santa Agata del Bianco I 115 Gb84
Santa Agata di Militello I 115 Fb84
Santa Agata di Puglia I 112 Fd74
Santa Amalia E 37 Ca68
Santa Bárbara E 39 Ed68
Santa Bárbara P 42 Ab73
Santa Bárbara E 40 Ga63
Santa Bárbara de Casa E 42 Bb72
Santa Bárbara de Nexe P 42 Ad74
Santa Brigida E 44 Da72
Santacara E 33 Ed58
Santa Catarina da Fonte do Bispo P 42 Ad74
Santa Catarina Villarmosa I 114 Fa85
Santa Caterina I 113 Hb77
Santa Caterina Valfurva I 102 Db56
Santa Cecilia de Alcor E 32 Da59
Santa Clara-a-Velha P 42 Ab73
Santa Coloma de Queralt E 34 Gc61
Santa Colomba de Somoza E 31 Ca57
Santa Comba E 30 Ad55
Santa Cristina Gela I 114 Ec84
Santa Croce Camerina I 115 Fb88
Santa Croce del Sannio I 109 Fc73
Santa Croce di Lago I 103 Eb58
Santa Croce di Magliano I 109 Fc72

Szudziałowo – Ujazd


Szudziałowo PL 87 Kc33
Szulborze Wielkie PL 87 Jd35
Szulmierz PL 86 Ja34
Szulok H 104 Ha58
Szydlak PL 86 Hd32
Szydłów PL 93 Jc42
Szydłowiec PL 93 Jb40
Szydłowo PL 85 Gb34
Szymbark PL 86 Hc32
Szymki PL 87 Kc34
Szymonka PL 87 Jc31

## T

Taasia FIN 68 Kd37
Taattola FIN 61 La26
Tabágon E 30 Ac58
Tabanera de Cerrato E 32 Db59
Tabanera la Luenga E 38 Db62
Tabaqueros E 39 Ed68
Tábara E 31 Cb59
Tabarz D 89 Dc41
Tabaza E 31 Cc54
Tabernas E 44 Ea75
Taboada E 30 Bb56
Tabód H 105 Hc56
Tábor CZ 97 Fc47
Tabuyo de Monte E 31 Ca58
Täby S 73 Gd43
Taceno I 101 Cc57
Tacherting D 96 Eb51
Tachov CZ 90 Ec45
Tacinskij RUS 137 Fc14
Tadcaster GB 13 Fa20
Tadmarton GB 15 Fa26
Taevaskoja EST 75 Lb46
Tafalla E 33 Ed58
Täfteå S 59 Hc28
Tagaj RUS 137 Fd10
Taganrog RUS 137 Fc15
Taggia I 100 Bd64
Taghmon IRL 7 Cc25
Tagliacozzo I 109 Ec71
Taglio di Po I 102 Ea61
Tagoat IRL 7 Cd25
Tahilla IRL 6 Ba25
Tahivilla E 43 Ca78
Tahta RUS 137 Fd16
Tähtelä FIN 51 Ka16
Tain GB 9 Ea07
Taingy F 24 Hb41
Tainiemi FIN 55 Ka21
Tain-l'Hermitage F 28 Jb49
Taipale FIN 54 Jd22
Taipale FIN 60 Kc29
Taipale FIN 60 Ka31
Taipale FIN 68 Kd33
Taipalsaari FIN 69 Lb35
Taiskirchen im Innkreis A 96 Ed50
Taivalkoski FIN 55 Kd21
Taivalkunta FIN 68 Jc36
Taizé F 23 Fc43
Taizon F 23 Fc43
Takamaa FIN 68 Jd35
Takeley GB 16 Fd27
Takkulankulma FIN 67 Jb38
Taklax FIN 59 Hd32
Talačyn BY 136 Eb12
Talairan F 35 Ha56
Talais F 26 Fa48
Talamanca E 35 Gd60
Talamillo del Tozo E 32 Db57
Talamone I 108 Dc69
Talarrubias E 37 Cc68
Talasjoki FIN 60 Kd27
Talavera de la Reina E 37 Cd66
Talavera la Real E 37 Bc69
Talayuela E 37 Cb65
Talayuelas E 39 Ed66
Talcy F 24 Gb40
Taldom RUS 137 Ed10
Talefe P 36 Aa67
Talgarreg GB 14 Dd26
Talgarth GB 14 Ea26
Táliga E 42 Bb70
Talisker GB 8 Da08
Tálknafjörður IS 2 Ab03
Talladale GB 8 Dc07
Tallaght IRL 7 Cd21
Tállara E 30 Ac56
Tallard F 29 Ka51
Tallåsen S 66 Ga35
Tallberg S 59 Ha28
Tällberg S 66 Fc38
Talley GB 14 Dd26
Tallinn EST 74 Kb42
Talljärv S 54 Hd20
Tallowbridge IRL 6 Ca25
Tallsjö S 58 Gc27
Talluskylä FIN 60 Kd30
Tallvik S 54 Ja20
Tállya H 99 Jd50
Talmas F 20 Gd33
Talmay F 25 Jc41
Talmine GB 9 Ea04
Talmont-Saint-Hilaire F 23 Ed45
Talmont-sur-Gironde F 26 Fb48
Tal'ne UA 136 Ec15
Talovaja RUS 137 Fb13
Talsarnau GB 12 Dd23
Talsi LV 74 Jd50
Talviainen FIN 68 Ka34
Talvik N 50 Hd08
Tal-y-bont GB 12 Dd24
Tal-y-cafn GB 12 Ea22
Tamala RUS 137 Fc11
Tamallancos E 30 Bb57
Tamarit E 34 Gc62
Tamarite de Litera E 34 Fd60
Tamariz de Campos E 31 Cd59
Tambach-Dietharz D 89 Dc42
Tambov RUS 137 Fb12
Tåme S 54 Hc24
Tamlaght GB 4 Cb18
Tammela FIN 68 Jd38
Tammenlahti FIN 69 Lc33
Tammijärvi FIN 68 Kc34
Tammisaari FIN 68 Jd40
Tamnay-en-Bazois F 24 Hc42
Tamnes N 57 Ec32
Tamniès F 27 Gb50
Támoga E 30 Bb54
Tampere FIN 68 Jd35
Tamsweg A 96 Fa54
Tamurejo E 37 Cc69
Tamworth GB 13 Ed24
Tana bru N 47 Ka06
Tanakajd H 97 Gc54
Tandern D 96 Dd50
Tandragee GB 5 Cd18
Tandsbyn S 58 Fc31
Tang IRL 4 Cb20
Tanganheira P 42 Ab71
Tangaveane IRL 4 Ca16
Tångböle S 57 Ed30
Tangen N 56 Cd31
Tangen N 57 Fb27
Tangerhütte D 84 Ea36
Tangermünde D 84 Eb36
Tangstedt D 83 Db32
Tanhua FIN 51 Kb15
Tani FIN 69 Lb36
Tankavaara FIN 51 Ka13
Tann D 96 Ec50
Tanna D 90 Ea43
Tannadice GB 11 Ec10
Tännäs S 65 Ed33
Tannay F 21 Ja34
Tannay F 24 Hc41
Tänndalen S 65 Ed33
Tanne D 89 Dc39
Tanowo PL 85 Fb33
Tantonville F 21 Jd37
Tanum N 64 Dd41
Tanum S 71 Eb45
Tanumshede S 71 Eb45
Tanus F 27 Ha52
Tan-y-llyn GB 12 Dd24
Tan-y-pistyll GB 12 Ea23
Taormina I 115 Fd85
Tapfheim D 95 Dc49
Tapia de Casariego E 31 Bd53
Tápiógyörgye H 98 Ja53
Tápiószentmárton H 98 Ja53
Tapojärvi FIN 50 Ja16
Tappeluft N 49 Hc08
Taragona E 30 Ad56
Taraguilla E 43 Cb78
Tarancón E 38 Dd66
Taranto I 113 Ha76
Tárány H 98 Ha53
Tarany H 104 Gd57
Tarare F 25 Ja46
Tarašča UA 136 Ec15
Tarascon F 28 Jb53
Tarassac F 28 Hb54
Tarazona E 33 Ec60
Tarazona de Guareña E 37 Cc62
Tarazona de la Mancha E 39 Ec68
Tarbert GB 8 Da06
Tarbert GB 10 Db13
Tarbert IRL 6 Bb23
Tarbes F 34 Fd55
Tarbolton GB 10 Dd14
Tarcento I 103 Ed57
Tarczyn PL 93 Jb38
Tardajos E 32 Dc58
Tardelcuende E 32 Ea61
Tardets-Sorholus F 33 Fa56
Tardienta E 33 Fb59
Tärendö S 54 Hd17
Tarente = Taranto I 113 Ha76
Tarent = Taranto I 113 Ha76
Targon F 26 Fc50
Târgovişte RO 122 Dd64
Târgu Frumos RO 119 Ed57
Târgu Jiu RO 121 Cd63
Târgu Mureş RO 118 Dc59
Târgu-Neamț RO 118 Ec57
Tarhos H 99 Jd55
Tarifa E 43 Ca78
Tarland GB 9 Ec09
Tarleton GB 12 Eb21
Tarmon IRL 4 Ca18
Tärnaby S 52 Fd22
Tarnalelesz H 99 Jb51
Tarnaörs H 99 Jb52
Tarnawatka PL 93 Kc42
Tarnobrzeg PL 93 Jd42
Tarnogród PL 93 Kb43
Tárnok H 98 Hc53
Tarnów PL 93 Jc44
Tarnowiec PL 93 Jd45
Tarnówka PL 85 Gc33
Tarnowo-Podgórne PL 85 Gb36
Tarnowska Wola PL 93 Jd42
Tarnowskie Góry PL 92 Hc43
Tarp D 83 Db29
Tarporley GB 13 Ec22
Tarquinia I 108 Dd70
Tarragona E 34 Gb62
Tàrrega E 34 Gb60
Tarsdorf A 96 Ec51
Tarsogno I 101 Cd63
Tartigny F 20 Gd34
Tartonne F 29 Ka52
Tarttila FIN 68 Jd36
Tartu EST 75 Lb45
Tarusa RUS 137 Ed11
Tarvaala FIN 60 Kb31
Tarvin GB 12 Eb22
Tarvisio I 103 Ed56
Tasapää FIN 61 Ld32
Tass H 98 Hd54
Tata H 98 Hb52
Tatabánya H 98 Hb52
Tatanovo RUS 137 Fb11
Tatarbunary UA 136 Ec17
Tatiščevo RUS 137 Fd12
Tatranská Lomnica SK 99 Jb47
Tattershall GB 16 Fc23
Taubenheim D 90 Ed41
Tauberbischofsheim D 89 Da45
Taucha D 90 Ec40
Taufkirchen (Vils) D 96 Eb50
Taulignan F 28 Jb51
Taunton GB 14 Eb29
Taunusstein D 89 Cb43
Tauplitz A 96 Fa53
Tauragė LT 80 Jd56
Taurianova I 115 Gb83
Taurisano I 113 Hc78
Taús E 34 Gb58
Taussat F 26 Fa50
Tauste E 33 Fa60
Tauves F 27 Ha47
Tavannes CH 94 Bc53
Tavaux F 25 Jc42
Tavelsjö S 59 Hb28
Tavernes F 29 Ka54
Tavernes de la Valldigna E 39 Fc69
Tavernola Bergamasca I 101 Da58
Taverny F 20 Gd36
Taviano I 113 Hc77
Tavíkovice CZ 97 Ga48
Tavira P 42 Ad74
Tavistock GB 14 Dd31
Täxan S 58 Fd29
Taynloan GB 10 Db14
Tayport GB 11 Ec11
Tazona E 45 Ec71
Tczew PL 86 Hb31
Teaca RO 118 Dc58
Teano I 112 Fa74
Teba E 43 Cc75
Tebay GB 13 Ec18
Teberda RUS 137 Ga17
Techirghiol RO 123 Fc68
Tecklenburg D 83 Cb37
Tedburn Saint Mary GB 14 Dd30
Teddington GB 15 Ed26
Teeranea IRL 6 Bb21
Teerivaara FIN 55 Kb19
Teernakil IRL 4 Bb20
Tegau D 90 Ea42
Tegelen NL 88 Bc39
Tegelträsk S 58 Gc28
Tegernau D 94 Ca51
Tegernsee D 96 Ea52
Teggiano I 112 Ga76
Teglio I 101 Da57
Tegsnäset S 59 Ha27
Tehi FIN 68 Kb35
Teichel D 90 Dd42
Teichwolframsdorf D 90 Eb42
Teignmouth GB 14 Ea31
Teijo FIN 68 Jc40
Teillet-Argently F 24 Ha45
Teistungen D 89 Db39
Teixeiro (Curtis) E 30 Bb55
Tejadillos E 39 Ed65
Tejeda y Segoyuela E 37 Ca63
Tejkovo RUS 137 Fa09
Tekirdağ TR 127 Ed78
Tekirova TR 135 Cc92
Telaščica (Mir) HR 110 Fd65
Telataipale FIN 69 Lc34
Telč CZ 97 Fd47
Telese Terme I 112 Fb74
Telford GB 13 Ec24
Telfs A 95 Dc53
Telgte D 83 Cb37
Telkibánya H 99 Jd49
Tellancourt F 21 Jb34
Tellaro I 101 Cd64
Tel'manove UA 137 Fb15
Telšiai LT 80 Jc54
Telti I 107 Cb74
Teltow D 84 Ed37
Tembleque E 38 Dc67
Temletouhy IRL 6 Ca23
Temmes FIN 60 Ka25
Tempio Pausania I 107 Cb74
Templederry IRL 6 Ca23
Templeglentan IRL 6 Bc24
Templemore IRL 6 Ca23
Templenoe IRL 6 Ba25
Templepatrick GB 5 Da17
Temple Sowerby GB 13 Ec17
Templetown IRL 7 Cc25
Templewo PL 85 Fd36
Templin D 84 Fa34
Tempo GB 4 Cb18
Temrjuk RUS 137 Fb17
Temu I 102 Db57
Tenala FIN 68 Jd40
Ten Boer NL 82 Bd33
Tenbury Wells GB 15 Ec25
Tenby GB 14 Dc27
Tencin F 29 Jd48
Tengen D 95 Cb51
Tenhola FIN 68 Jd40
Teningen D 94 Ca50
Tennänget S 65 Fa38
Tennenbronn D 95 Cb50
Tennevoll N 49 Gc12
Tennie F 23 Fc39
Tennilä FIN 55 Ka19
Tennilä FIN 68 Kb37
Tennilä FIN 68 Kc37
Tentellatge E 34 Gc59
Tenterden GB 16 Ga29
Teofipol' UA 136 Ea15
Teolo I 102 Dd60
Teplá CZ 90 Ec45
Teplice CZ 90 Fa42
Teplička nad Váhom SK 98 Hc47
Teploe RUS 137 Fa11
Teplý Vrch SK 99 Jb49
Terälahti FIN 68 Jd35
Teramo I 109 Ed69
Ter Apel NL 82 Ca34
Terbuny RUS 137 Fa12
Terebovlja UA 136 Ea15
Teren'ga RUS 137 Fd10
Teresa E 39 Fb66
Teresa de Cofrentes E 39 Fa69
Terešov CZ 90 Fa45
Terespol PL 86 Ha33
Terespol PL 87 Kc37
Terezín CZ 91 Fb43
Tergnier F 20 Hb34
Tergu I 107 Ca74
Ter Hole NL 17 Hc28
Terlizzi I 113 Gc74
Termachivka UA 136 Eb14
Termal TR 127 Fd79
Termas de Monfortinho P 37 Bc65
Terme di Caldana I 108 Da67
Terme di Lurisia I 100 Bc63
Terme di Miradolo I 101 Cc60
Terme di Salvarola I 102 Db63
Terme di Valdieri I 100 Bb63
Termes-d'Armagnac F 26 Fc54
Termignon F 29 Kb48
Terminiers F 24 Gc39
Termini Imerese I 114 Ed84
Terminillo I 109 Ec70
Termoli I 109 Fc71
Termonbarry IRL 4 Ca20
Termonfeckin IRL 5 Cd20
Termunten NL 82 Ca33
Terneuzen NL 17 Hc28
Terni I 109 Eb69
Ternitz A 97 Ga52
Ternopil' UA 136 Ea15
Terracina I 109 Ec73
Terranova da Sibari I 113 Gc79
Terranova di Pollino I 113 Gb78
Terras de Bouro P 30 Ad59
Terrasini I 114 Ec84
Terrassa E 35 Gd61
Terrasson-Lavilledieu F 27 Gb49
Terravecchia I 113 Gd79
Terrazos E 32 Dd57
Terreiro das Bruxas P 37 Bc64
Terriente E 39 Ed65
Terrrinches E 44 Dd70
Terskanperä FIN 60 Kb26
Tertíveri I 110 Fd73
Teruel E 39 Fa65
Tervajoki FIN 59 Ja31
Tervakoski FIN 68 Ka37
Tervo FIN 60 Kc30
Tervola FIN 54 Jc20
Terwolde NL 82 Bc36
Teslić BIH 104 Ha62
Tespe D 83 Dc33
Tessenderlo B 88 Ba40
Tesseosen N 64 Dc35
Tessjö FIN 68 Kd38
Tesson F 26 Fb47
Tetbury GB 15 Ec27
Teterow D 84 Ec32
Teteven BG 126 Da71
Tetford GB 13 Fc22
Tetijiv UA 136 Ec15
Tettau D 90 Dd43
Tettau D 90 Fa40
Tettnang D 95 Cd52
Teublitz D 96 Eb47
Teuchern D 90 Eb41
Teufen CH 95 Cd53
Teugn D 96 Ea48
Teulada E 45 Fd70
Teunz D 90 Eb46
Teupitz D 84 Fa37
Teurajärvi S 54 Ja18
Teuro FIN 68 Jd37
Teutschenthal D 90 Ea40
Teuva FIN 59 Ja32
Tevrin IRL 5 Cc20
Tewkesbury GB 15 Ec26
Thale D 90 Dd39
Thaleischweiler-Fröschen D 88 Ca46
Thalheim D 90 Ec42
Thalkirch CH 95 Cc55
Thallwitz D 90 Ec40
Thalmässing D 96 Dd47
Thalwil CH 95 Cb53
Thame GB 15 Fb27
Thamsbrück D 89 Dc41
Thann F 94 Bc51
Thannenkirch F 94 Bd50
Thannhausen D 95 Db50
Thaon-les-Vosges F 25 Jd38
't Harde NL 82 Bc35
Tharsis E 42 Bb73
Thássos GR 126 Db78
Thatcham GB 15 Fa28
Thaxted GB 16 Fd26
Thayngen CH 95 Cc52
Theberton GB 16 Gb25
The Butts IRL 7 Cc23
Thedinghausen D 83 Da34
The Five Roads IRL 7 Cd21
The Hand Cross Roads IRL 6 Bc22
The Harrow IRL 7 Cd24
Theillay F 24 Gd42
Theißen D 90 Eb41
Thelbridge GB 14 Dd30
The Leap IRL 7 Cc24
The Loup GB 5 Cd17
Themar D 89 Dc43
The Mumbles GB 14 Dd27
Thénezay F 23 Fc44
Thenon F 27 Gb49
The Pike IRL 6 Ca25
The Pole of Law GB 9 Ec07
Theresienstadt = Terezín CZ 91 Fb43
Thérma GR 130 Ea88
Thermo GR 128 Bb84
The Rower IRL 7 Cc24
The Sheddings GB 5 Da16
The Six Towns GB 5 Cd16
Thespiés GR 129 Ca85
Thessaloníki GR 125 Ca78
The Stocks GB 16 Ga30
The Temple GB 5 Da17
Thetford GB 16 Ga25
Thevet-Saint-Julien F 24 Gd44
Thèze F 33 Fc55
Thiaucourt-Regniéville F 21 Jc36
Thiéblemont-Farémont F 21 Ja37
Thiel-sur-Acolin F 24 Hc44
Thiene I 102 Dd59
Thierhaupten D 95 Dc49
Thierrens CH 94 Bb55
Thiers F 24 Hc46
Thiersheim D 90 Eb44
Thiery F 29 Kc52
Thiesi I 107 Ca75
Thionville F 21 Jd34
Thíra GR 133 Db92
Thirsk GB 13 Fa19
Thísbi GR 129 Ca85
Thisted DK 76 Da51
Thíva GR 129 Ca85
Thivars F 24 Gb38
Thixendale GB 13 Fb19
Thoard F 29 Ka52
Thoirette F 25 Jc45
Tholária GR 133 Dd90
Tholey D 88 Bd45
Thollon-les-Mémises F 100 Bb56
Thomas Street IRL 4 Ca20
Thomastown IRL 7 Cb24
Thomm D 88 Bc44
Thompson GB 16 Ga24
Thonelle F 21 Jb34
Thônes F 25 Ka46
Thonon-les-Bains F 25 Ka44
Thorame-Basse F 29 Kb52
Thorenc F 29 Kb53
Thorens-Glières F 25 Ka46
Thorigné-sur-Dué F 23 Ga39
Thorikó GR 129 Cc87
Thörl A 97 Fd53
Thorn NL 88 Bb40
Thorn = Toruń PL 86 Hb34
Thornbury GB 15 Ec27
Thornby GB 15 Fb25
Thorne GB 13 Fb21
Thorney GB 16 Fc24
Thornfalcon GB 14 Eb29
Thornham GB 16 Ga23
Thornhill GB 11 Ea15
Thornhill GB 14 Ea28
't Horntje NL 82 Ba33
Thornton GB 12 Eb20
Thornton Curtis GB 13 Fc21
Thorpe-le-Soken GB 16 Gb27
Thorpe Market GB 16 Gb23
Thorpeness GB 16 Gb26
Thors F 25 Ja38
Thouarcé F 23 Fb42
Thouars F 23 Fc43
Thourie F 23 Ed40
Thourotte F 20 Ha34
Thrapston GB 16 Fc25
Three Cocks GB 14 Eb26
Threlkeld GB 12 Eb17
Thresfield GB 13 Ed19
Thropton GB 11 Ed15
Thrumster GB 9 Ec05
Thuir F 35 Hb57
Thun CH 94 Bd55
Thüngen D 89 Da44
Thurcroft GB 13 Fa22
Thuré F 23 Fd43
Thüringen A 95 Da54
Thürkow D 84 Ec32
Thurles IRL 6 Ca23
Thurlow GB 16 Fd26
Thurmaston GB 13 Fb24
Thurnau D 90 Dd44
Thursby GB 12 Eb17
Thurso GB 9 Eb04
Thurstonfield GB 11 Eb16
Thury F 25 Ja42
Thusis CH 95 Cd55
Thyrnau D 96 Ed49
Tibava SK 99 Kb48
Tibberton GB 13 Ec24
Tibi E 45 Fb71
Tibro S 72 Fb46
Tidaholm S 72 Fb47
Tideswell GB 13 Ed22
Tiduff IRL 6 Ba24
Tiefenbach D 90 Ec46
Tiefenbach D 96 Ed49
Tiefenbronn D 95 Cc48
Tiefencastel CH 95 Cd55
Tiefensee D 84 Fa36
Tiel NL 82 Bb37
Tielmes E 38 Dd65
Tielt B 17 Hb29
Tiemassaari FIN 61 Lb32
Tienen B 17 Ja30
Tiercé F 23 Fc41
Tierga E 33 Ed61
Tierp S 66 Gc40
Tieva FIN 50 Jd14
Tievaperä FIN 50 Jb16
Tievemore IRL 4 Cb17
Tiffauges F 23 Fa43
Tigerton GB 11 Ec10
Tigharry GB 8 Cc07
Tigy F 24 Gd40
Tihoreck RUS 137 Fc16
Tihusniemi FIN 61 La32
Tiimola FIN 69 Lb34
Tiironkylä FIN 60 Ka30
Tikkakoski FIN 60 Kb32
Tikkala FIN 68 Kb33
Tilburg NL 88 Ba38
Tilbury GB 16 Fd28
Til-Châtel F 25 Jb41
Tillberga S 72 Gb42
Tilleda D 90 Dd40
Tillicoultry GB 11 Ea12
Tilsaperä FIN 68 Kb33
Tilshead GB 15 Ed29
Tilstock GB 13 Ec23
Tim RUS 137 Fa13
Timahoe IRL 7 Cb22
Timaševsk RUS 137 Fc16
Timbáki GR 133 Cd96
Timberscombe GB 14 Ea29
Timişoara RO 116 Bd60
Timmendorfer Strand D 84 Dd31
Timmenrode D 90 Dd38
Timoleague IRL 6 Bc26
Timpinvaara FIN 55 Lb21
Timrå S 66 Gc33
Timsbury GB 15 Fa29
Tinahely IRL 7 Cd23
Tinajas E 38 Ea65
Tinca RO 117 Ca57
Tinden N 56 Dd29
Tineo E 31 Ca54
Tingsryd S 78 Fc53
Tingstäde S 73 Ha49
Tingvoll N 56 Db31
Tinieblas E 32 Dd59
Tínos GR 130 Db88
Tinqueux F 20 Hc35
Tintagel GB 14 Db30
Tinténiac F 23 Ed38
Tintern Parva GB 14 Eb27
Tiobraid Árann IRL 6 Ca24
Tione di Trento I 102 Db58
Tipperary IRL 6 Ca24
Tiptree GB 16 Ga27
Tiranë AL 124 Ab74
Tirano I 101 Da57
Tiraspol MD 119 Ga58
Tire TR 131 Ed87
Tirig E 40 Fd64
Tirley GB 15 Ec26
Tirnaneill IRL 5 Cc18
Tírnavos GR 129 Bd80
Tirós GR 132 Bd89
Tirrenia I 108 Da65
Tirschenreuth D 90 Eb45
Tiscar Don Pedro E 44 Dd73
Tišnov CZ 97 Gb47
Tisovec SK 98 Ja49
Tisvildeleje DK 77 Eb54
Tiszaalpár H 99 Jb55
Tiszabecs H 99 Kc50
Tiszabura H 99 Jc53
Tiszacsege H 99 Jd52
Tiszadada H 99 Jd51
Tiszaeszlár H 99 Jd51
Tiszaföldvár H 99 Jb54
Tiszafüred H 99 Jc52
Tiszajenő H 99 Jb54
Tiszakécske H 99 Jb54
Tiszalúc H 99 Jd51
Tiszanána H 99 Jc52
Tiszatelek H 99 Ka50
Tiszaújváros H 99 Jd51
Tiszavasvári H 99 Jd51
Titisee-Neustadt D 94 Ca51
Titran N 56 Db29
Tittling D 96 Ed49
Tittmoning D 96 Ec51
Tiuccia F 106 Ca70
Tivat MNE 111 Hd69
Tivenys E 40 Ga63
Tiverton GB 14 Ea30
Tivoli I 109 Eb71
Tizzano F 106 Ca72
Tizzano Val Parma I 101 Da62
Tjačiv UA 136 Dd16
Tjärn S 58 Gc28
Tjäruträsk S 54 Ja20
Tjautjas S 53 Hb17
Tjeldstø N 62 Bd38
Tjeldsundbrua N 48 Ga13
Tjentište BIH 111 Hc66
Tjöck FIN 67 Hd33
Tjønnvik N 57 Fa25
Tjøtta N 52 Ed22
Tjulträsk S 53 Ga21
Tjuvskjær N 48 Gb12
Tlučná CZ 90 Ed45
Tlumačov CZ 98 Gd47
Tłuszcz PL 87 Jc36
Toano I 102 Db63
Tobar an Choire IRL 4 Bd18
Tobarra E 45 Ec70
Tobercurry IRL 4 Bd18
Toberdoney GB 5 Cd15
Tobermore GB 5 Cd16
Tobermory GB 10 Da10
Toberonochy GB 10 Db12
Toberscanavan IRL 4 Ca18
Toblach I 96 Eb55
Tobson GB 8 Da05
Tocha P 36 Ac63
Tocina E 43 Ca73
Todal N 56 Dc30
Toddington GB 15 Fb26
Todendorf D 83 Dc30
Todendorf D 84 Dd30
Todenham GB 15 Ed26
Todi I 108 Ea68
Todmorden GB 13 Ed20
Todtnau D 94 Ca51
Todzia PL 87 Jc33
Toft GB 9 Fb04
Tofta S 73 Gd49
Tofte N 52 Ed23
Tofte N 64 Dc34
Toftevåg N 62 Bd39
Togher IRL 5 Cd20
Togher IRL 6 Bb26
Töging D 96 Eb50
Tohmajärvi FIN 61 Ma31
Tohmo FIN 55 Kb17
Tohni FIN 60 Jc31
Toholampi FIN 60 Jd28
Toijala FIN 68 Jd36
Toirano I 100 Bd63
Toivakka FIN 68 Kc33
Toiviaiskylä FIN 60 Kc28
Toivola FIN 61 Lb26
Toivola FIN 68 Kd35
Tokaj H 99 Jd50
Tokarevka RUS 137 Fb12
Tokarnia PL 93 Jb42
Tokmak UA 137 Fa16
Tokod H 98 Hc52
Tölby FIN 59 Ja31
Tolcsva H 99 Jd50
Toledo E 38 Db66
Tolentino I 109 Ec67
Tolfa I 108 Dd70
Tolga N 65 Eb33
Tolinas E 31 Cb55
Tolivia E 31 Cc55
Tol'jatti RUS 137 Ga10
Tolk D 83 Db29
Tolkmicko PL 86 Hc30
Tollarp S 78 Fb55
Tolle I 103 Eb61
Tollesbury GB 16 Ga27
Töllinperä FIN 60 Ka27
Tollo I 109 Fb70
Tolmezzo I 103 Ec56
Tolmin SLO 103 Fa57
Toló GR 129 Bd88
Tolonen FIN 51 Ka12
Tolosa E 33 Ec55
Tolox E 43 Cc76
Tolsta GB 8 Db05
Tolve I 113 Gb75
Tomakivka UA 137 Fa16
Tömäperä FIN 60 Jd26
Tomar P 36 Ac66
Tomarovka RUS 137 Fa14
Tomášovce SK 98 Ja50
Tomašpil' UA 136 Eb16
Tomaszowice PL 93 Ka40
Tomaszów Lubelski PL 93 Kc42
Tomaszów Mazowiecki PL 92 Ja39
Tomatin GB 9 Ea08
Tombebœuf F 26 Fd51
Tomcrasky GB 8 Dd09
Tomelilla S 78 Fb56
Tomelloso E 38 Dd68
Tomich GB 8 Dd08
Tomintoul GB 9 Eb08
Tomiszowice PL 92 Hd42
Tømmerneset N 48 Fd15
Tømmervåg N 56 Db30
Tommola FIN 69 La35
Tømra N 57 Eb30
Tomrefjord N 56 Cd32
Tonbridge GB 16 Fd29
Tondela P 36 Ad63
Tønder DK 76 Da58
Tondu GB 14 Ea28
Tonezza I 102 Dd58
Tongeren B 21 Jb30
Tongue GB 9 Ea04
Tönisvorst D 88 Bc39
Tønjum N 62 Cd37
Tonna GB 14 Dd27
Tonnay-Boutonne F 23 Fb46
Tonneins F 26 Fd52
Tonnerre F 25 Hd40
Tonnes N 52 Fa20
Tönning D 83 Da30
Tono I 115 Fd83
Tønsberg N 71 Dd44
Tønsnes N 49 Gd09
Toome GB 5 Cd16
Toomyvara IRL 6 Ca22
Topas E 31 Cb61
Topcliffe GB 13 Fa19
Topczewo PL 87 Kb34
Töpen D 90 Ea43
Topolcafő H 98 Ha54
Topoľčany SK 98 Hb49
Topoľčianky SK 98 Hb50
Topólka PL 86 Hb36
Topolšica SLO 103 Fc57
Toponár H 104 Ha56
Toral E 31 Cb58
Torba TR 134 Ec90
Torbalı TR 131 Ec87
Torbay GB 14 Ea31
Torcé-en Vallée F 23 Fd39
Torcross GB 14 Dd32
Torcy F 20 Ha37
Tordehumos E 31 Cd59
Tordera E 35 Hb60
Tordesillas E 31 Cd61
Tordómar E 32 Dc59
Tore GB 9 Ea07
Töre S 54 Ja21
Töreboda S 72 Fb46
Torella del Sannio I 109 Fb72
Torelló E 35 Ha59
Toreno E 31 Ca56
Torfou F 23 Fa43
Torgau D 90 Ed39
Torgelow D 85 Fb33
Torhout B 17 Ha29
Torigni-sur-Vire F 19 Fb36
Torija E 38 Dd63
Torino I 100 Bc60
Toritto I 113 Gc74
Törmäkylä FIN 60 Kc25
Törmänmäki FIN 55 Kd24
Tornal'a SK 99 Jb49
Tornanádska H 99 Jc49
Tornavacas E 37 Cb64
Tornehamn S 49 Gc13
Tornesch D 83 Db32
Tornio FIN 54 Jc21
Toro E 31 Cc60
Törökbalint H 98 Hc53
Törökkoppány H 105 Hb56
Törökszentmiklós H 99 Jc54
Toróni GR 129 Cc80
Toropec RUS 136 Eb10
Torpao N 64 Dd38
Torphins GB 9 Ec09
Torpoint GB 14 Dc31
Torpshammar S 66 Ga33
Torquay GB 14 Ea31
Torquemada E 32 Db59
Torralba E 38 Eb65
Torralba de Aragón E 33 Fb60
Torralba de Calatrava E 38 Db69
Torralba del Moral E 38 Eb62
Torrão P 42 Ac70
Torrão do Lameiro P 36 Ac62
Torrböle S 59 Hb29
Torre F 106 Cb72
Torre P 30 Ac59
Torre P 42 Ab70
Torre a Mare I 113 Gd74
Torre Annunziata I 112 Fb75
Torrebarrio E 31 Cb55
Torreblacos E 32 Ea60
Torreblanca E 40 Fd65
Torreblanca de los Caños E 43 Ca74
Torre Cardela E 44 Dc74
Torrecilla E 44 Da72
Torrecilla de la Jara E 37 Cd66
Torrecilla de Valmadrid E 33 Fa61
Torrecilla en Cameros E 32 Ea58
Torre de Juan Abad E 44 Dd70
Torre de la Higuera E 43 Bc75
Torre del Campo E 44 Db73
Torre del Greco I 112 Fb75
Torre del Lago Puccini I 108 Da65
Torre dell'Impiso I 114 Eb84
Torre dell'Orso I 113 Hc77
Torre del Mar E 44 Da76
Torredembarra E 34 Gc62
Torre de Moncorvo P 31 Bc61
Torre d'en Doménec E 40 Fd65
Torredonjimeno E 44 Db73
Torre Faro I 115 Ga83
Torregrossa E 34 Ga61
Torrejoncillo E 37 Bd65
Torrejón de Ardoz E 38 Dc64
Torrelaguna E 38 Dc63
Torrelavega E 32 Db55
Torremaggiore I 110 Fd72
Torremayor E 37 Bd69
Torremazanas E 45 Fb70
Torre Melissa I 113 Gd80
Torremocha E 37 Ca67
Torremolinos E 43 Cd76
Torrent E 39 Fb68
Torre Orsaia I 112 Fd77
Torre-Pacheco E 45 Fa73
Torre Pellice I 100 Bc61
Torreperogil E 44 Dc72
Torre Ruffa I 115 Ga82
Torresandino E 32 Db60
Torre San Gennaro I 113 Hc76
Torre Santa Susanna I 113 Hb76
Torres de Albánchez E 44 Ea71
Torres de Berrellén E 33 Fa60
Torres de la Alameda E 38 Dd64
Torres de Segre E 34 Ga61
Torres Novas P 36 Ac66
Torres-Torres E 39 Fc67
Torres Vedras P 36 Aa67
Torretta I 102 Dc61
Torretta I 108 Da66
Torrevieja E 45 Fb72
Torricela I 113 Ha76
Torricella Peligna I 109 Fb71
Torrico E 37 Cc66
Torri del Benaco I 102 Db59
Torridon GB 8 Dc07
Torriglia I 101 Cc62
Torrijo del Campo E 39 Ed63
Torrijos E 38 Da66
Torrin GB 8 Db08
Torro FIN 68 Jd38
Torroella de Fluvià E 35 Hb59
Torrubia del Campo E 38 Dd66
Torsåker S 58 Gc31
Torsby S 65 Ed41
Torsetnes N 56 Dc30
Torsfjärden S 58 Fc27
Torshälla S 72 Gb43
Torsken N 48 Gb10
Torthorwald GB 11 Ea16
Tórtola E 38 Eb66
Tórtola de Heneras E 38 Dd63
Tortolì I 107 Cc77
Tortona I 101 Cb61
Tortorella I 112 Ga77
Tortorici I 115 Fc84
Tortosa E 40 Ga63
Tortosendo P 36 Bb64
Tortuera E 39 Ec63
Toruń PL 86 Hb34
Torvela FIN 60 Kd25
Torver GB 12 Eb18
Tørvik N 56 Dd28
Torvik N 56 Db31
Tørvikbygd N 62 Cb39
Torvizcón E 44 Dc76
Torvsjö S 58 Gb27
Toržok RUS 136 Ec10
Torzym PL 85 Fc37
Tosaunet N 52 Ed24
Toscaig GB 8 Db08
Toscolano-Maderno I 102 Db59
Tösens A 95 Db54
Tossa S 54 Jb20
Tossa de Mar E 35 Hb60
Tossåsen S 57 Fb32
Tostedt D 83 Db33
Totana E 45 Ed73
Totenviken N 65 Ea39
Totland GB 15 Fa31
Totnes GB 14 Dd31
Tottenham GB 16 Fc28
Totton GB 15 Fa30
Toudon F 29 Kc52
Touët-sur-Var F 29 Kc52
Toul F 21 Jc37
Toulat FIN 60 Kc30
Toulon F 29 Ka55
Toulouse F 27 Gc54
Toulx Sainte-Croix F 24 Gd45
Tourcoing F 17 Ha30
Tourigo P 36 Ad63
Tourlaville F 19 Ed34
Tourmakeady IRL 4 Bc19
Tournai B 20 Hb31
Tournan-en-Brie F 20 Ha37
Tournay F 34 Fd56
Tournecoupe F 27 Ga53
Tournehem-sur-la-Hem F 16 Gc30
Tournon-d'Agenais F 27 Gb51
Tournon-sur-Rhône F 28 Jb49
Tournus F 25 Jb44
Tourny F 20 Gc36
Tourouvre F 23 Ga38
Tours F 23 Ga42
Tours-en-Vimeu F 20 Gc33
Tourteron F 21 Ja34
Tourtour F 29 Ka53
Tourves F 29 Ka54
Tourville-sur-Sienne F 19 Ed36
Touzac F 27 Gb51
Toužim CZ 90 Ec44
Tovačov CZ 92 Gd46
Tovarkovskij RUS 137 Fa11
Towcester GB 15 Fb26
Tow Law GB 13 Ed17
Town Yetholm GB 11 Ed14
Töysä FIN 60 Jd32
Töysänperä FIN 60 Ka32
Trabada E 31 Bc54
Trabazos E 31 Ca59
Traben-Trarbach D 88 Bd44
Trabia I 114 Ed84
Trabitz D 90 Ea45
Tradate I 101 Cb58
Træna N 52 Ed20
Trafask IRL 6 Ba26
Tragacete E 39 Ec65
Traghetto I 102 Dd62
Tragöss-Oberort A 97 Fc53
Traiguera E 40 Fd64
Traînel F 24 Hb38
Trainou F 24 Gd40
Traisen A 97 Ga51
Traismauer A 97 Ga50
Traitsching D 96 Ec47
Trakai LT 81 La58
Trakiszki PL 87 Kb30
Tralee IRL 6 Bb24
Trá Lí IRL 6 Bb24
Tramayes F 25 Ja45
Trá Mhór IRL 7 Cb25
Tramore IRL 7 Cb25
Tramutola I 112 Ga77
Tranås S 72 Fc48
Trancault F 24 Hc38
Trancoso P 36 Bb62
Trandal N 64 Cc33
Tranekær DK 77 Dd58
Tranent GB 11 Ec13
Trängslet S 65 Fa37
Trångsviken S 57 Fb30
Trani I 110 Gc73
Trannes F 25 Ja38
Transtrand S 65 Fa38
Trapani I 114 Ea84
Trapp GB 14 Dd27
Trappenkamp D 83 Dc31
Trappes F 20 Gc37
Trappeto I 114 Eb84
Trappstadt D 89 Dc43
Trasacco I 109 Ed71
Trascastro E 30 Ba56
Trasmonte E 30 Bb55
Traun A 97 Fb51
Traunkirchen A 96 Fa52
Traunreut D 96 Eb51
Traunstein D 96 Ec52
Trautskirchen D 89 Dc46
Travemünde D 84 Dd31
Traviesas E 30 Ba54
Travnik BIH 104 Ha64
Travo F 106 Cb71
Trawsfynydd GB 12 Dd23
Trbovlje SLO 103 Fc57
Trean IRL 4 Bc20
Trearddur Bay GB 12 Dc22
Trébago E 33 Ec60
Tréban F 24 Hb45
Trebbin D 84 Ed37
Třebechovice pod Orebem CZ 91 Ga44
Trebel D 84 Ea34
Trèbes F 35 Ha55
Třebíč CZ 97 Ga47
Trebinje BIH 111 Hc69
Trebisacce I 113 Gc78
Trebisov SK 99 Ka48
Trebnje SLO 103 Fc58
Třebohostice CZ 96 Fa47
Třeboň CZ 97 Fc48
Třebovice CZ 91 Gb45
Trebur D 89 Cc44
Treburley GB 14 Dc31
Trecastagni I 115 Fd85
Trecastle GB 14 Ea26
Trecate I 101 Cb59
Trecwn GB 14 Db26
Tredegar GB 14 Ea27
Trédion F 22 Eb40
Treehoo IRL 5 Cc19
Treen GB 14 Da32
Trefeglwys GB 12 Ea24
Treffen A 103 Fa56
Treffort-Cuisat F 25 Jc45
Treffurt D 89 Db41
Trefnant GB 12 Ea22
Tre Fontane I 114 Eb85
Trefor GB 12 Dd22
Trefriw GB 12 Ea22
Tregaron GB 14 Dd25
Trégastel-Plage F 18 Dd37
Trégomeur F 22 Eb38
Tregony GB 14 Db32
Trégourez F 22 Dd39
Tréguier F 18 Ea37
Trehörningsjö S 59 Ha29
Treia D 83 Da29
Treia I 109 Ed67
Treignat F 24 Gd45
Treigny F 24 Hb41
Treillières F 23 Ed42
Trekilen S 58 Fc30
Trelawnyd GB 12 Ea22
Trélazé F 23 Fc41
Trelech GB 14 Dc26
Treleth GB 12 Eb19
Trelleborg S 77 Ed57
Trelleck GB 14 Eb27
Trélon F 20 Hc32
Tremblois-lès-Rocroi F 21 Hd33
Tremelo B 17 Hd29
Třemešná CZ 92 Gd44
Tremezzo I 101 Cc57
Tremosine I 102 Db58
Třemošnice CZ 91 Fd45
Tremp E 34 Ga59
Trenance GB 14 Db31
Trenčín SK 98 Ha48
Trendelburg D 89 Da39
Trengereiddal N 62 Ca39
Trento I 102 Dc58
Trentola I 112 Fa74
Tréogan F 22 Dd39
Tréon F 20 Gb37
Treorchy GB 14 Ea27
Trept F 29 Jc47
Trepuzzi I 113 Hc76
Trerulefoot GB 14 Dc31
Třešť CZ 97 Fd47
Trescares E 32 Da55
Trescore Balneario I 101 Cd59
Trescore Cremasco I 101 Cd59
Tresfjord N 56 Cd32
Tresigallo I 102 Ea62
Tressait GB 11 Ea10
Tresson F 23 Ga40
Treuchtlingen D 95 Dc48
Treuen D 90 Eb43
Treuenbrietzen D 90 Ec38
Trevélez E 44 Dc75
Trevi I 109 Eb68
Treviglio I 101 Cd59
Trevignano Romano I 108 Ea70
Treviso I 102 Ea59
Trevor GB 12 Dc23
Trewithian GB 14 Db32
Trezzano sul Naviglio I 101 Cc59
Triaize F 23 Fa45
Triangelen N 51 Kc09
Triberg D 95 Cb50
Tribsees D 84 Ec31
Tricarico I 113 Gb76
Tricase I 113 Hc78
Tricase Porto I 113 Hc78
Tricesimo I 103 Ed57
Triebel D 90 Eb43
Trieben A 97 Fb53
Triebes D 90 Eb42
Triei I 107 Cc77
Triengen CH 94 Ca53
Trier D 88 Bc44
Trieste I 103 Fa59
Triest = Trieste I 103 Fa59
Triftern D 96 Ec50
Trignac F 22 Ec42
Trigrad BG 126 Da75
Triguères F 24 Hb40
Trijueque E 38 Dd63
Tríkala GR 128 Bb81
Trikéri GR 129 Ca83
Trikomo CY 135 Cc95
Trim IRL 5 Cc20
Trimsaran GB 14 Dd27
Trinay F 24 Gc39
Třinec CZ 92 Hb45
Tring GB 15 Fb27
Trinità I 100 Bc63
Trinitapoli I 110 Gb73
Trinity GBJ 18 Ec35
Trino I 100 Ca60
Trípoli GR 129 Bc88
Triptis D 90 Ea42
Trispen GB 14 Db31
Tři Studně CZ 91 Ga46
Trittau D 83 Dc32
Trittenheim D 88 Bd44
Trivento I 109 Fb72
Trivignano Udinese I 103 Ed58
Trizac F 27 Ha48
Trjavna BG 126 Dd71
Trnava SK 98 Ha50
Troarn F 19 Fc36
Tröbitz D 90 Ed39
Trobo E 30 Bb54
Tročany SK 99 Jd47
Trochry GB 11 Ea11
Trochtelfingen D 95 Cd50
Trödje S 66 Gc38
Troedyrhiw GB 14 Ea27
Troekurovo RUS 137 Fb11
Trofaiach A 97 Fc53
Trofors N 52 Fa23
Trogir HR 110 Gb66
Tröglitz D 90 Eb41
Troia I 110 Fd73
Tróia P 36 Ab69
Troickaja RUS 137 Fc17
Troina I 115 Fb85
Troisdorf D 88 Bd41
Troistorrents CH 100 Bb56
Troisvierges L 21 Jc32
Trolla N 57 Ea29
Trollhättan S 71 Ec47
Tromsdal N 57 Ec29
Tromsdalen N 49 Gd09
Tromsø N 49 Gd09
Tromvik N 49 Gc09
Trondheim N 57 Ea30
Trönninge S 77 Ec51
Tronvik N 57 Eb29
Troodos CY 135 Bd96
Troon GB 10 Dd14
Troøyen N 57 Ea31
Tropea I 115 Ga82
Tröpolach A 103 Ed56
Tropy Sztumskie PL 86 Hc31
Trory GB 4 Cb17
Trosa S 72 Gc45
Trosna RUS 137 Ed12
Trossingen D 95 Cb50
Trostan' RUS 136 Ec13
Tröstau D 90 Ea44
Trostberg D 96 Eb51
Trostjanec' UA 137 Ed14
Trostjanskij RUS 137 Fc13
Troszczyno PL 85 Fd32
Trouans F 21 Hd37
Troubky CZ 92 Gd46
Troutbeck GB 12 Eb18
Trouville-sur-Mer F 19 Fd35
Trowbridge GB 15 Ec28
Troyes F 25 Hd38
Trpanj HR 110 Gd68
Trstice SK 98 Ha51
Trubčevsk RUS 137 Ed13
Trubetčino RUS 137 Fb12
Truchas E 31 Ca58
Trujillo E 37 Ca67
Trulben D 94 Ca47
Trupel PL 86 Hc32
Truro GB 14 Db32
Trusetal D 89 Dc42
Truskolasy PL 92 Hc42
Trutnov CZ 91 Ga43
Trutnowy PL 86 Hb30
Tryggestad N 62 Cd34
Trygort PL 87 Jc30
Trysil N 65 Ec37
Tryszczyn PL 86 Ha34
Trzcianka PL 85 Gb34
Trzcianka PL 87 Jc35
Trzcianka PL 87 Kb32
Trzcianne PL 87 Ka33
Trzcinica PL 92 Ha41
Trzcinna PL 85 Fc35
Trzcinno PL 85 Gc31
Trzcińsko-Zdrój PL 85 Fc35
Trzebce PL 92 Hd41
Trzebiatów PL 85 Fd31
Trzebiel PL 91 Fc39
Trzebień PL 91 Fd40
Trzebieszów PL 87 Ka37
Trzebinia PL 92 Hd44
Trzebnica PL 91 Gc40
Trzebnice PL 91 Ga40
Trzemeszno PL 86 Gd36
Trzemżal PL 86 Ha36
Trzepnica PL 92 Hd40
Trześcianka PL 87 Kc34
Trzęsów PL 91 Gb39
Tržič SLO 103 Fb57
Tsaritsáni GR 129 Bc80
Tschenstochau = Częstochowa PL 92 Hc42
Tschiertschen CH 95 Cd55
Tschierv CH 102 Db56
Tševetjävri FIN 51 Kb08
Tsilivi GR 128 Ac86
Tsjernobyl UA 136 Ec14
Tsz-lakótelep H 98 Hd55
Tuaim IRL 4 Bd20
Tuam IRL 4 Bd20
Tuapse RUS 137 Fc17
Tuar Mhic Éadaigh IRL 4 Bc19
Tubbergen NL 82 Bd36
Tubilleja E 32 Dc56
Tübingen D 95 Cc49
Tuchan F 35 Ha56
Tuchola PL 86 Gd33
Tuchów PL 93 Jc44
Tučovo RUS 137 Ed10
Tuczki PL 86 Hd33
Tuczno PL 85 Ga34
Tuddenham GB 16 Fd25
Tudela E 33 Ed59
Tudela de Duero E 32 Da60
Tudweiliog GB 12 Dc23
Tuéjar E 39 Fa67
Tufjord N 46 Jb04
Tugford GB 15 Ec25
Tuggensele S 58 Gd26
Tuhkakylä FIN 61 La26
Tui E 30 Ad58
Tuiskula FIN 59 Jb32
Tūja LV 74 Kb49
Tukums LV 80 Ka51
Tula I 107 Ca75
Tula RUS 137 Fa11
Tulach Mhór IRL 7 Cb21
Tulcea RO 123 Fc64
Tul'čyn UA 136 Eb16
Tuliszków PL 92 Ha38
Tulla IRL 6 Bc22
Tullaghanstown IRL 5 Cc20
Tullamore IRL 7 Cb21
Tulle F 27 Gc49
Tulleråsen S 57 Fb30
Tulln A 97 Ga50
Tullow IRL 7 Cc23
Tully GB 4 Cb17
Tullyamalra IRL 5 Cc19
Tułowice PL 86 Ja36
Tulppio FIN 51 Kd14
Tulsk IRL 4 Ca19
Tum PL 92 Hc38
Tuma RUS 137 Fb10
Tumba S 73 Gd44
Tumbo E 31 Bc54
Tumbo S 72 Ga43
Tummel Bridge GB 11 Ea10
Tuna S 66 Gb33
Tunadal S 66 Gc33
Tungaseter N 64 Da33
Tuningen D 95 Cb51
Tunkkari FIN 60 Jc29
Tunnsjørørvika N 57 Fa25
Tunstall GB 13 Ec19
Tunstall GB 13 Fc21
Tunstall GB 16 Gb26
Tuntenhausen D 96 Ea51
Tunturikeskus Kiilopää FIN 51 Kb12
Tuolluvaara S 49 Hb15
Tuomela FIN 55 Ka18
Tuomikylä FIN 59 Jb31
Tuomioja FIN 60 Jd25
Tuomiperä FIN 60 Jd27
Tuomiperä FIN 60 Ka28
Tuopanjoki FIN 61 Lc29
Tuoro sul Trasimeno I 108 Ea67
Tupos FIN 55 Ka24
Tur PL 86 Gd34
Turaida LV 74 Kc49
Turajärvi FIN 67 Ja37
Turbenthal CH 95 Cc53
Turbigo I 101 Cb59
Turckheim F 94 Bd50
Turda RO 117 Da59
Turek PL 92 Hb38
Turenne F 27 Gc49
Turgutreis TR 134 Ec90
Turhala FIN 60 Kc27
Turi I 113 Gd75
Turijs'k UA 136 Ea14
Turin = Torino I 100 Bc60
Turís E 39 Fb68
Turiščevo RUS 137 Ed12
Türje H 98 Gd55
Turka UA 136 Dd16
Türkbükü TR 134 Ec90
Türkeli TR 127 Ed79
Túrkeve H 99 Jc54
Türkheim D 95 Dc51
Turkkale FIN 68 Jc38
Turksad RUS 137 Ga16
Turku FIN 67 Jb39
Tur Langton GB 13 Fb24
Turloughmore IRL 6 Bd21
Turmiel E 39 Ec63
Turnberry GB 10 Dc15
Turnditch GB 13 Fa23
Turnhout B 88 Ad39
Türnitz A 97 Fd52
Turnov CZ 91 Fd43
Turośń Kościelna PL 87 Kb34
Turów PL 93 Kb38
Turquel P 36 Ab66
Turriff GB 9 Ed08
Tursi I 113 Gc77
Turtagrø N 62 Da36
Turtola FIN 54 Jb18
Turunç TR 134 Ba91
Turza Wielka PL 86 Hd33
Tus E 44 Ea71
Tusa I 114 Fa84
Tuscania I 108 Dd70
Tushielaw GB 11 Eb15
Tustervatnet N 52 Fb22
Tuszów Narodowy PL 93 Jd43
Tuszyn PL 92 Hd39
Tutaev RUS 137 Fa09
Tutbury GB 13 Ed23
Tuttlingen D 95 Cc51
Tutzing D 96 Dd51
Tuukkala FIN 69 La34
Tuuliharju FIN 50 Jc16
Tuulimäki FIN 61 La25
Tuulos FIN 68 Kb36
Tuupovaara FIN 61 Ma30
Tuuri FIN 60 Jc32
Tuusjärvi FIN 61 Lb30
Tuuski FIN 68 Kd38
Tuusniemi FIN 61 Lb30
Tuxford GB 13 Fb22
Tuzla BIH 105 Hc62
Tuzly UA 136 Ec17
Tvååker S 77 Ec51
Tväråbäck S 59 Hb28
Tvärålund S 59 Hb27
Tvärån S 54 Hc22
Tväråträsk S 53 Gc24
Tvedestrand N 70 Db45
Tver' RUS 137 Ed10
Tverråmoen N 52 Fd17
Tverrelv N 48 Gb11
Tverrvika N 52 Fc18
Tvinde N 62 Cc38
Twann CH 94 Bc53
Twarda PL 92 Ja39
Twardogóra PL 92 Gd40
Twatt GB 9 Eb02
Tweedsmuir GB 11 Eb14
Twello NL 82 Bc36
Twist D 82 Ca35
Twistetal D 89 Cd40
Twistringen D 83 Cd35
Two Bridges GB 14 Dd31
Twomileborris IRL 6 Ca23
Tworóg PL 92 Hb43
Twycross GB 13 Fa24
Twyford GB 13 Fb24
Twyford GB 15 Fb28
Twyford GB 15 Fa30
Twynholm GB 10 Dd16
Twynllanan GB 14 Dd26
Tychowo PL 85 Gb32
Tychy PL 92 Hc44
Tyczyń PL 93 Ka44
Tykocin PL 87 Ka33
Tykolä FIN 68 Ka36
Tylawa PL 93 Jd46
Tylkowo PL 87 Jb32
Tylldalen N 65 Ea34
Tylösand S 77 Ed52
Tymbark PL 93 Jb45
Tyndrum GB 10 Dd11
Tynemouth GB 11 Fa16
Tyngáki GR 134 Ec91
Týniště nad Orlicí CZ 91 Ga44
Týn nad Vltavou CZ 97 Fb47
Tynset N 65 Ea33
Typpö FIN 60 Jc27
Tyrämäki FIN 55 La21
Tyresö S 73 Gd44
Tyriä FIN 69 Ld34
Tyringe S 77 Fa54
Tyrnävä FIN 55 Ka24
Tyrnień PL 85 Ga31
Tyrnyauz RUS 137 Ga17
Tyrrellspass IRL 7 Cb21
Tyškivka UA 136 Ec16
Tyśmienica PL 93 Kb39
Tyssedal N 63 Cc40
Tyszki-Nadbory PL 87 Jd34
Tytuvėnai LT 80 Ka55
Tyukod H 99 Kc51
Tywyn GB 12 Dd24
't Zandt NL 82 Ca33
Tzasténi GR 129 Ca83
Tzummarum NL 82 Bb33

## U

Uachtar Ard IRL 4 Bc20
Übach-Palenberg D 88 Bb40
Ubbergen NL 82 Bb37
Úbeda E 44 Dc72
Übelbach-Markt A 97 Fd54
Überherrn D 88 Bc46
Überkingen, Bad D 95 Da49
Überlingen D 95 Cc52
Übersee D 96 Eb52
Ubieszyn PL 93 Kb43
Ubrique E 43 Cb76
Ubstadt-Weiher D 95 Cc47
Uceira E 30 Bb53
Ucero E 32 Dd60
Uchacq-et-Parentis F 26 Fb53
Uchte D 83 Cd36
Üchtelhausen D 89 Db44
Uckange F 21 Jd35
Uckfield GB 16 Fd30
Udačnoe RUS 137 Ga14
Udalla E 32 Dd55
Uddevalla S 71 Ec47
Uden NL 88 Bb38
Udenhout NL 88 Ba38
Udine I 103 Ed58
Udomlja RUS 136 Ec09
Udrycze PL 93 Kc41
Udtja S 53 Gd20
Udvar H 105 Hc58
Ueckermünde D 85 Fb32
Uelsen D 82 Ca35
Uelzen D 83 Dc34
Uetersen D 83 Db32
Uettingen D 89 Da45
Uetze D 83 Dc36
Uffenheim D 89 Db46
Uffington GB 15 Fa28
Uftrungen D 90 Dd39
Ugaran E 32 Eb55
Ugento I 113 Hc78
Uggdal N 63 Ca40
Uggerslev DK 76 Dc56
Ugglarp S 77 Ec52
Ugíjar E 44 Dd76
Ugine F 25 Ka46
Uglič RUS 137 Ed09
Ugra RUS 137 Ed11
Uherce Mineralne PL 93 Kb46
Uherské Hradiště CZ 98 Gd48
Uherský Brod CZ 98 Ha48
Uherský Ostroh CZ 98 Gd48
Uhingen D 95 Cd49
Uhldingen D 95 Cd52
Uhlířské Janovice CZ 91 Fc45
Uhlstädt-Kirchhasel D 90 Ea42
Uhniv UA 136 Dd15
Uhorské SK 98 Ja49
Uig GB 8 Da07
Uimaharju FIN 61 Ld29
Uimaniemi FIN 50 Jd16
Uimaniemi FIN 68 Kd34
Uitgeest NL 82 Ba35
Uithoorn NL 17 Hd25
Uithuizen NL 82 Bd32
Ujazd PL 91 Gb41

Vónitsa GR 128 Ad82
Voorburg NL 17 Hd26
Voorthuizen NL 82 Bb36
Vopnafjörður IS 3 Cc03
Vöra FIN 59 Ja30
Voray-sur-l'Ognon F 25 Jd41
Vorden NL 82 Bc37
Vorderstoder A 97 Fb50
Vordingborg DK 77 Eb58
Vordorf D 83 Dc57
Voreppe F 29 Jd48
Vorey F 28 Hd49
Vóri GR 133 Cd96
Vormsele S 58 Gd25
Voronež RO 118 Eb56
Voronet RUS 137 Fb13
Vorožba UA 137 Ed13
Vorra D 90 Dd46
Vorterayskogen A 49 Ha08
Võru EST 75 Lb47
Voshod RUS 137 Ga14
Voskopojë AL 124 Ad77
Voskresenskoe RUS 137 Ed09
Voss N 62 Cc38
Votice CZ 91 Fc46
Voue F 25 Hd38
Vougécourt F 25 Jd39
Vougel F 25 Jb42
Vouhé F 23 Fd44
Vouliagméni GR 129 Cb87
Voumajärvi S 54 Jb20
Vourgaréli GR 128 Ba81
Vournikas F 119 68 Jc34
Vourvouroú GR 125 Cc79
Voutenay-sur-Cure F 24 Hc41
Vouvant F 23 Fd44
Vouzailles F 23 Fd44
Vouzela P 36 Ba62
Vouzeron F 24 Gd42
Vouziers F 21 Ja35
Vovčans'k UA 137 Fa14
Voves F 24 Gc39
Vóyri FIN 59 Ja30
Voznesens'k UA 137 Ed16
Voznesenskoe RUS 137 Fb10
Vracov CZ 98 Gd48
Vrådal N 63 Da43
Vradijivka UA 136 Ec16
Vráhos GR 128 Ac82
Vrana HR 110 Ga65
Vrangiana GR 128 Ba82
Vranov nad Top'ou SK 99 Ka48
Vranovská ves CZ 97 Ga48
Vratimov CZ 92 Hd45
Vravróna GR 129 Cc87
Vrbno pod Pradědem CZ 92 Gd44
Vrchlabí CZ 91 Fd43
Vrdy CZ 91 Fd45
Vreden D 82 Bd37
Vreta kloster S 72 Fd46
Vrhnika SLO 103 Fb58
Vries NL 82 Bd36
Vriezenveen NL 82 Bd36
Vrigne-au-Bois F 21 Ja33
Vrnjačka Banja SRB 120 Bb67
Vron F 20 Gc32
Vrondádos GR 130 Dd86
Vroomshoop NL 82 Bd35
Vroutek CZ 90 Ed44
Vrútky SK 98 Hd47
Všeruby CZ 96 Ec47
Všestary CZ 91 Gd44
Všetaty CZ 71 Fc44
Vsetín CZ 98 Ha47
Vught NL 88 Bc39
Vuillafons F 25 Jd42
Vukosanka FIN 61 Lb25
Vukovar HR 105 Hd60
Vulaines-sur-Seine F 24 Ha38
Vulcano Porto I 115 Fc83
Vuobmaved FIN 50 Jc10
Vuolijoki FIN 60 Kc26
Vuolledalen N 50 Ja09
Vuolerim R 53 Hb20
Vuonamo FIN 60 Kc29
Vuonos FIN 61 Lc34
Vuontisjärvi FIN 50 Jb13
Vuoreslahti FIN 60 Kd30
Vuorilahti FIN 60 Kb30
Vuoriniemi FIN 69 Ld34
Vuoskojaure sameviste S 49 Ha13
Vuostimojärvi FIN 55 Kb17
Vuotsa FIN 61 Ma29
Vuotso FIN 51 Ka13
Vuottolahti FIN 60 Kc26
Vuovdakuoihka FIN 50 Jc09
Vybor RUS 136 Ea10
Vyčapy Opatovce SK 98 Hb50
Východná SK 98 Ja47
Vygoniči RUS 137 Fb10
Vyhne SK 98 Hc51
Vy-lès-Lure F 25 Ka42
Vynnyky UA 136 Ec15
Vypolzovo RUS 136 Ec09
Vyšhorod UA 136 Ec14
Vyškov CZ 97 Gc47
Vyskytná CZ 91 Fd46
Vyšij Voloček RUS 136 Ec09
Vysoká SK 92 Hb46
Vysokovsk RUS 136 Ec10
Vyžnycja UA 136 Ea16

Waabs D 83 Dc29
Waakirchen D 96 Ea52
Waal D 95 Cd51
Waalre NL 88 Ba39
Waalwijk NL 88 Ba38
Waarn D 89 Da40
Wabrzezno PL 86 Hb33
Wachenheim D 89 Cb46
Wachock PL 93 Jc41
Wachtberg D 88 Ca42
Wachtendonk D 88 Bc39
Wächtersbach D 96 Cd41
Waddesdon GB 15 Fb27
Waddington GB 13 Fb22
Waddington IRL 7 Cc25
Wadebridge GB 14 Db31
Wadensvill D4 95 Cb53
Wadern D 89 Bd46
Wadhurst GB 16 Fd27
Wadowice PL 92 Hd45
Wagenfeld D 83 Cd36
Wageningen NL 82 Bb37
Waghäusel D 95 Cc47
Wagna A 97 Fd55
Wągrowiec PL 85 Gd35
Wahlstedt D 83 Dc31
Wahrenberg D 84 Ea35
Waiblingen D 95 Cd48
Waibstadt D 95 Cc46
Waidhaus D 96 Eb46
Waidhofen an der Thaya A 97 Fd49
Waidhofen an der Ybbs A 97 Fc51
Wainfleet All Saints GB 16 Fd23

Wainhouse Corner GB 14 Dc30
Waizenkirchen A 96 Fa50
Wakefield GB 13 Fa21
Walberswick GB 16 Gc25
Wałbrzych PL 91 Gb42
Walchen A 96 Ed34
Walchum D 82 Ca34
Walchwil CH 95 Cc54
Walcz PL 85 Gb34
Wald A 96 Ed54
Wald A 97 Fc53
Wald CH 95 Cc53
Waldaschaff D 89 Cd44
Waldbach A 97 Gd53
Waldbröl D 88 Ca41
Waldbronn D 95 Cd48
Waldbrunn D 89 Cd46
Waldbrunn (Westerwald) D 89 Cb42
Walddrehna D 90 Fa39
Waldeck D 89 Cb41
Waldenbuch D 95 Cd48
Waldenburg D 90 Ec42
Waldenburg D 95 Da47
Waldenburg D 90 Ed50
Walderbach D 96 Eb47
Walderton GB 15 Fb30
Waldfeucht D 88 Bb40
Waldfischbach-Burgalben D 88 Ca46
Waldheim D 90 Ed41
Waldkappel D 89 Da41
Waldkirch CH 95 Cd53
Waldkirch D 94 Ca50
Waldkirchen D 90 Ed42
Waldkirchen D 96 Fa49
Waldkraiburg D 96 Eb50
Waldmohr D 88 Bd46
Waldmünchen D 96 Ec47
Waldneukirchen A 97 Fb51
Waldringfield GB 16 Gb26
Waldsassen D 90 Eb46
Waldsee, Bad D 95 Da51
Waldshut-Tiengen D 94 Ca52
Waldsolms D 89 Cc43
Walenstadt CH 95 Cd54
Wales GB 13 Fa22
Walferdange L 21 Jc33
Walgherton GB 13 Ec20
Walichnowy PL 92 Hb40
Walkerburn GB 11 Eb14
Walkern GB 16 Fc27
Wallasey GB 12 Ed21
Waldorf D 89 Cc46
Walldürn D 89 Cd46
Wallenfels D 90 Ea42
Wallenhorst D 83 Cb36
Wallern im Burgenland A 97 Gc52
Wallers F 20 Hb32
Wallersdorf D 96 Ec49
Wallgau D 96 Dd53
Wallingford GB 15 Fa28
Wallmoden D 89 Dc38
Walls GB 9 Fa05
Wallwitz D 90 Eb39
Walpertskirchen D 96 Eb50
Walpole Saint Andrew GB 16 Fd24
Walsall GB 13 Ed24
Walsrode D 83 Dc35
Waltenhofen D 95 Db52
Waltershausen D 89 Dc41
Waltham GB 13 Fc21
Waltham-on-the-Wolds GB 15 Fb24
Walton East GB 14 Db23
Walton-on-the-Naze GB 16 Gc27
Waltrop D 88 Ca38
Waly F 21 Jb36

Wamba E 31 Cd60
Wanborough GB 15 Ed28
Wandlitz D 84 Ed35
Wanfried D 89 Da40
Wangen CH 94 Bd53
Wangenbourg F 94 Bd48
Wangen im Allgäu D 95 Da52
Wangerland D 83 Cc32
Wangerooge D 83 Cc31
Wanlockhead GB 11 Ea15
Wanna D 83 Cd32
Wanssum NL 88 Bc38
Wantage GB 15 Fa28
Wanzleben D 90 Ea38
Wapenveld NL 82 Bc35
Warboys GB 15 Fb25
Warburg D 89 Cd39
Warcq F 21 Ja35
Wardenburg D 83 Cc34
Wardhouse GB 16 Fc27
Waregem B 17 Hb30
Wareham GB 15 Ec31
Waren D 84 Ec33
Warendorf D 83 Cd37
Warffum NL 82 Bd34
Warga NL 82 Bc34
Warin D 84 Ea32
Warka PL 93 Jc38
Warley GB 15 Ed25
Warlingham GB 16 Fc28
Warlubie PL 86 Hb33
Warmenhuizen NL 82 Ba35
Warminster GB 15 Ec29
Warmwell GB 15 Ec31
Warnemünde D 84 Eb30
Warnford GB 15 Fa30
Warngau D 96 Ea52
Warnikajmy PL 87 Jd32
Warnołęka PL 85 Fb32
Warrenpoint IRL 5 Cd19
Warrington GB 13 Ec21
Warschau = Warszawa PL 87 Jb37
Warslow GB 13 Ed22
Warsop GB 13 Fa22
Warszawa PL 87 Jb37
Warszkowo PL 86 Gd32
Wart, Altensteig- D 95 Cd49
Warta PL 92 Hb40
Wartenberg D 89 Da42
Wartenberg D 96 Ea50
Warth A 95 Da54
Warthausen D 95 Da50
Wartin D 85 Fa34
Warton GB 11 Ed15
Warwick GB 15 Fa25
Wasbister GB 9 Eb06
Wasbüttel D 83 Dd36
Washaway GB 14 Db31
Washington GB 13 Fa17
Wasigny F 21 Hd34
Wasniów PL 93 Jc41
Wasilków PL 87 Kb33
Waskemeer NL 82 Bd33
Waśniów PL 93 Jc41
Wasosz PL 87 Jd32
Waspik NL 88 Ba38
Wassen CH 95 Cb55
Wassenaar NL 17 Hd25
Wassenberg B 84 Bc40
Wasserauen CH 95 Cd54

Wasserburg D 96 Eb51
Wasserburg am Bodensee D 95 Cd52
Wasserlosen D 89 Dd44
Wassermungenau D 95 Dc47
Wassertrüdingen D 95 Dc48
Wassigny F 20 Hb33
Wassy F 25 Ja39
Watchet GB 14 Eb29
Watchfield GB 14 Eb29
Waterford IRL 7 Cc25
Watergrasshill IRL 6 Bd25
Waterhouses GB 13 Ed22
Wateringbury GB 16 Fd29
Waterloo B 17 Hd30
Waterlooville GB 15 Fa30
Waterrow GB 14 Ea29
Waterville IRL 6 Ac26
Waterworks GB 5 Cd17
Watford GB 16 Fc27
Wathlingen D 83 Db36
Watlington D 15 Fb27
Watten GB 9 Ec04
Wattens A 96 Dd53
Wattle Bridge GB 5 Cc18
Watton GB 16 Ga24
Wattrelos F 17 Hb30
Wattwil CH 95 Cd54
Wavendon GB 16 Fb26
Waverton GB 13 Ec22
Wawern D 89 Bc45
Wawrów PL 85 Fb35
Wawrzeńczyce PL 93 Jb44
Waxweiler D 88 Bc43
Wdzydze PL 86 Ha31
Weasenham Saint Peter GB 16 Ga24
Weaverham GB 13 Ec22
Weaverthorpe GB 13 Fb19
Weeping Cross GB 13 Ed24
Weerselo NL 82 Bd36
Weert NL 88 Bb39
Weesp NL 82 Bb36
Weeting GB 16 Ga25
Weeze D 88 Bc39
Wefensleben D 84 Dd37
Wegberg D 88 Bc40
Wegeleben D 90 Dd38
Wegierska Górka PL 92 Hc46
Wegleszyn PL 93 Jb42
Weglosen CH 95 Cc54
Węgorzewo PL 87 Jd33
Węgorzyno PL 85 Fd33
Wegra PL 87 Jd36
Wegrów PL 87 Jd36
Węgrzce PL 93 Jb44
Wegscheid D 96 Fa49
Wehe- NL 82 Bd32
Wehretal D 89 Db40
Wehnrand D 84 Fa31
Weida D 90 Eb42
Weiden D 90 Eb46
Weidenberg D 90 Ea45
Weidenstetten D 95 Da49
Weidhausen D 89 Dd46
Weidhausen D 96 Eb49
Weikersheim D 89 Da46
Weil am Rhein D 94 Bd52
Weilbach D 89 Cd45
Weilburg D 89 Cb42
Weil der Stadt D 95 Cc48
Weiler D 95 Da52
Weilerbach D 88 Ca46
Weilersbach D 88 Ca46
Weilerswist D 88 Bd41
Weilheim D 95 Cd49
Weilheim i.OB D 96 Dd52
Weilmünster D 89 Cc43
Weilrod D 89 Cc43
Weimar D 90 Ea42
Weimar D 90 Fa41
Weinbohla D 90 Fa41
Weine D 89 Cc40
Weinfelden CH 95 Cd53
Weinsberg D 95 Cd47
Weinstadt D 95 Cd48
Weiskirchen D 88 Bc45
Weismain D 90 Dd44
Weissach D 95 Cc48
Weißandt-Gölzau D 90 Eb39
Weißbach bei Lofer A 96 Ec53
Weißenbach an der Triesting A 97 Ga51
Weißenborn-Lüderode D 89 Dc39
Weißenbrunn D 90 Dd44
Weißenburg D 95 Dc48
Weißenfels D 90 Eb41
Weißenhorn D 95 Db50
Weißenkirchen in der Wachau A 97 Fd50
Weißensee D 90 Dd40
Weißenstadt D 90 Ea44
Weißkeißel D 91 Fd40
Weißkirchen A 97 Fc54
Weisskirchen D 91 Fd40
Weißwasser D 91 Fd40
Weiswampach L 21 Jc32
Weitefeld D 89 Cb42
Weiten A 97 Fd50
Weiterstadt D 89 Cc44
Weitnau D 95 Da52
Weitra A 97 Fc49
Weitramsdorf D 89 Dd44
Weiz A 97 Ga54
Wejherowo PL 86 Ha30
Wekerom NL 82 Bb36
Welford GB 15 Fb25
Welkenraedt B 88 Ba41
Welland GB 15 Ec26
Welldorf D 89 Cd40
Wellin B 88 Ba42
Wellingborough GB 15 Fb25
Wellington GB 13 Ec24
Wellington GB 14 Ea30
Wellington GB 14 Eb26
Wells GB 15 Ec29
Wells-next-the-Sea GB 16 Ga23
Welney GB 16 Fd24
Wels A 96 Fa51
Welschenrohr CH 94 Bd53
Welschnofen I 102 Dd56
Welshpool GB 13 Eb24
Welsleben D 90 Ea38
Welver D 89 Cb39
Welwyn GB 16 Fc27
Welwyn Garden City GB 16 Fc27

Wem D 13 Ec23
Wembley GB 16 Fc28
Wemyss Bay GB 10 Dc13
Wenden D 89 Cb41
Wendlingen D 95 Cd49
Wendover GB 15 Fb27
Wendtorf D 83 Dd29
Weng A 96 Fa50
Wengen CH 94 Ca55
Wenningsen D 83 Da37
Wenningstedt (Sylt) D 76 Da31
Wenns A 96 Dc54
Wentorf GB 13 Dc33
Wenvoe GB 14 Eb28
Wenzenbach D 96 Eb48
Weobley GB 14 Eb26
Werben D 84 Eb35
Werben D 91 Fb39
Werda D 90 Eb43
Werdau D 90 Ec42
Werder D 84 Ed37
Werdohl D 89 Cb40
Werfen A 96 Ed53
Werkendam NL 82 Ad37
Werl D 89 Cb39
Werlte D 83 Cb34
Wermelskirchen D 88 Ca40
Wermsdorf D 90 Ed40
Wernberg-Köblitz D 90 Eb46
Werne D 84 Fa36
Werneck D 89 Dd44
Wernigerode D 89 Dd38
Wernsdorf D 84 Fa37
Wertheim D 89 Cd45
Wertingen D 95 Dc49
Wervershoof D 82 Ba34
Werl N 17 Ha30
Wesel D 88 Bd38
Wesenberg D 84 Ed34
Wesola PL 87 Jc37
Wesołowo PL 87 Jb33
Wesselburen D 83 Da30
Weßling D 96 Dd51
Wessobrunn D 95 Dc51
West Bay GB 14 Eb30
West Bridgford GB 13 Fa23
West Bromwich GB 13 Ed25
Westbury GB 13 Eb24
Westbury GB 15 Ec29
West Calder GB 11 Ea13
West Clandon GB 15 Fb29
West Down GB 14 Dd29
Westende D 17 Hb29
Westerbork NL 82 Bd34
Westerburg D 89 Cb42
Westerdale GB 9 Eb05
Westerdale GB 13 Fb18
Westerfield- Vriezenvees- ewijk NL 82 Bd35
Westerhever D 83 Cd30
Westerholt D 83 Cb33
Westerkappeln D 83 Cb36
Wester-Koggenland NL 82 Ba35
Westerland (Sylt) D 76 Cd58
Westerlo B 88 Ad40
Westernbödefeld D 89 Cc40
Westerrönfeld D 83 Db30
Westerstede D 83 Cc33
Westerstetten D 95 Da49
Westfield GB 11 Ea13
Westgate on Sea GB 16 Gb28
West Haddon GB 15 Fb25
Westham GB 16 Fd30
West Harptree GB 15 Ec28
Westhausen D 95 Db48
Westhay GB 14 Eb29
Westhofen D 89 Cb45
West Ilsley GB 15 Fa28
West Kilbride GB 10 Dc14
West Kingsdown GB 16 Fd28
West Kirby GB 12 Eb21
West Lavington GB 15 Ed29
West Linton GB 11 Eb14
West Lulworth GB 15 Ec31
West Lutton GB 13 Fb19
Westlyng GB 14 Eb29
West Mersea GB 16 Ga27
Westmill GB 16 Fc26
West Moors GB 15 Ed30
Weston GB 15 Fa26
Weston Rhyn GB 12 Eb23
Weston-super-Mare GB 14 Eb28
Weston-under-Lizard GB 13 Ec24
Westonzoyland GB 14 Eb29
Westoverledingen D 83 Cb34
Westport IRL 4 Bc19
West Runton GB 16 Gb23
Westruther GB 11 Ec14
West Tanfield GB 13 Fa19
West-Terschelling NL 82 Bb32
West Town IRL 4 Ca15
Westward Ho! GB 14 Dd24
West Winch GB 16 Fd24
West Wittering GB 15 Fb30
Westwell GB 15 Fa29
Wetherby GB 13 Fa21
Wetheringsett GB 16 Gb25
Wethersfield GB 16 Fd26
Wetschen D 83 Cc35
Wettenberg D 89 Cc42
Wetter (Hessen) D 89 Cc41
Wetteren B 17 Hc30
Wettin D 90 Eb39
Wettringen D 82 Ca36
Wetzelstein D 96 Dd48
Wetwang GB 13 Fb19
Wetzlar D 89 Cc42
Wexford IRL 7 Cd25
Weybridge GB 16 Fc28
Weyer-Markt A 97 Fc52
Weyhausen D 83 Dc36
Weyhe D 83 Cd34
Weymouth GB 15 Ec31
Wezep NL 82 Bc35
Whaley Bridge GB 13 Ed22
Whalley GB 13 Ec20
Whaplode GB 16 Fc24
Whauphill GB 10 Dd17
Wheatley Hill GB 13 Fa17
Wheaton Aston GB 13 Ec24
Wheddon Cross GB 14 Ea29
Wherwell GB 15 Fa29
Whickham GB 11 Fa16
Whiddon Down GB 14 Dd31
Whipsnade GB 15 Fb27
Whitburn GB 11 Ea13
Whitby GB 13 Fb18
Whitchurch GB 13 Ec23
Whitchurch GB 15 Fa29
Whitchurch GB 14 Eb28
Whitecross GB 5 Cd18
Whitegate IRL 6 Bd26
Whitehall GB 9 Ec06
Whitehall IRL 7 Cc23
Whitehaven GB 11 Ed17
Whitehead GB 5 Da17
Whitehouse GB 9 Ec09
Whitekirk GB 11 Ec13
Whiteparish GB 15 Ed29
Whitewell-on-the-Hill GB 13 Fb19
Whitfield GB 13 Fa18
Whitfield GB 16 Gb29
Whithorn GB 10 Dd17
Whitland GB 14 Dc26
Whitley Bay GB 11 Fa16
Whitminster GB 15 Ec27
Whitsgrove GB 5 Cd18
Whitstable GB 16 Ga28
Whitstone GB 14 Dc30
Whittingham GB 11 Ed15
Whittington GB 12 Eb23

Whittlesey GB 16 Fc24
Whitton GB 13 Fb22
Whitwick GB 13 Fa24
Whygate GB 11 Ec16
Wiąg PL 86 Hb33
Wibtoft GB 15 Fa25
Wichian Buri GB 16 Gb28
Wichow D 84 Ec37
Wicina PL 91 Fd39
Wick GB 9 Ec05
Wick GB 15 Ec28
Wick GB 15 Ed30
Wickede D 89 Cb39
Wickham GB 15 Fa30
Wickham Market GB 16 Gb26
Wicklow IRL 7 Da22
Wickwar GB 15 Ec28
Widawa PL 92 Hc40
Widdern D 89 Cd46
Widdington GB 16 Fd26
Widemouth Bay GB 14 Dc30
Widford GB 16 Fd27
Widminy PL 87 Jd31
Widnau CH 95 Cd53
Widnes GB 13 Ec22
Wiechov PL 86 Gd33
Wieck D 84 Ec30
Wieda D 89 Dc39
Wiedenbrück, Rheda- D 89 Cc38
Wiednitz D 90 Fa40
Wiefelstede D 83 Cc33
Wiehe D 90 Ea40
Wiek D 84 Ed29
Wiejki PL 87 Kc33
Wiele D 84 Ed29
Wiele PL 86 Gd31
Wieleń Północny PL 85 Ga35
Wielgomłyny PL 92 Hd41
Wieliczka PL 92 Ja44
Wielki PL 87 Ka31
Wielka Łąka PL 86 Hd34
Wielki Łąck PL 86 Hd34
Wielki Przeździęk PL 87 Jb33
Wielopole Skrzyńskie PL 93 Jd44
Wieluń PL 92 Hd40
Wień AT 97 Gb51
Wiener Neustadt A 97 Gb52
Wienhausen D 83 Db36
Wiepke D 84 Ea36
Wierden NL 82 Bd36
Wieringerwerf NL 82 Ba34
Wierzbica PL 93 Kc39
Wierzbowo PL 87 Jd36
Wierzchlas PL 92 Hb40
Wierzchosławice PL 93 Jc44
Wiesau D 90 Eb45
Wiesbaden D 89 Cb44
Wiesberg A 97 Fd51
Wiesenburg D 84 Ed38
Wiesenfelden D 96 Ec48
Wiesenhaid D 89 Dd45
Wiesenthau D 89 Dd45
Wiesloch D 89 Cc46
Wiesmath A 97 Gb53
Wiesmoor D 83 Cb33
Wietmarschen D 82 Ca35
Wietze D 83 Db35
Wieuwerd NL 82 Bc33
Wigan GB 13 Ec21
Wiggen CH 94 Ca54
Wiggensbach D 95 Db52
Wigmore GB 13 Eb25
Wigston GB 15 Fa24
Wigton GB 11 Ed17
Wigtown GB 10 Dd16
Wijchen NL 82 Bc37
Wijewo PL 91 Gb38
Wijhe NL 82 Bc36
Wijk bij Duurstede NL 82 Bb37

Wiktorówko PL 85 Gc34
Wil CH 95 Cc53
Wilamowo PL 93 Jd37
Wilchta PL 87 Jd37
Wilcza PL 92 Hd44
Wilcza Wola PL 93 Ka43
Wilczyn PL 86 Ha36
Wilczyny PL 87 Jc30
Wildau D 84 Fa37
Wildeck D 89 Db40
Wildenberg D 96 Ea49
Wildenbruch D 84 Ed37
Wildenfels D 90 Ec42
Wildeshausen D 83 Cd34
Wildflecken D 89 Da43
Wilga PL 93 Jc38
Wilhelmsburg D 84 Ea35
Wilhelmsdorf D 95 Cd51
Wilhelmshaven D 83 Cc32
Wilhering A 97 Fb50
Wilkau-Haßlau D 90 Ec42
Wilkinstown IRL 5 Cd20
Wilków PL 93 Jd40
Wilkowo Polskie PL 91 Gb38
Willebadessen D 89 Cd39
Willemstad NL 17 Hd27
Willersley GB 14 Eb26
Willich D 88 Bc39
Willingen D 89 Cc40
Willingham GB 16 Fd25
Willingshausen D 89 Da41
Willington GB 16 Fb26
Willisau CH 94 Ca53
Williton GB 14 Ea29
Willmering GB 96 Ec47
Willoughby GB 13 Fc22
Willoughby GB 15 Fa24
Willroth D 89 Ca42
Wilmington GB 16 Fd30
Wilmington GB 16 Fd29
Wilmslow GB 13 Ed22
Wilsdruff D 90 Ed41
Wilster D 83 Da31
Wilton GB 15 Ed29
Wilts L 21 Jc32
Wimbledon GB 16 Fc28
Wimblington GB 16 Fd25
Wimborne Minster GB 15 Ed30
Wimereux F 20 Gc31
Wimmenau F 94 Bd47
Wincanton GB 15 Ec29
Winchcombe GB 15 Ed26
Winchelsea GB 16 Ga30
Winchester GB 15 Fa29
Wincrange L 21 Jc32
Windeck D 89 Ca41
Windermere GB 11 Ed18
Windesheim D 89 Cb45
Windischgarsten A 97 Fb52
Windmill IRL 7 Cc21
Windorf D 96 Fa49
Winford GB 14 Eb28

Wingate GB 13 Fa17
Wingen-sur-Moder F 94 Bd47
Wingerworth GB 13 Fa22
Wingst D 83 Da32
Winhöring D 96 Ec50
Winklarn D 96 Ec47
Winnard's Perch GB 14 Db31
Winnenden D 95 Cd48
Winnigstedt D 83 Dd37
Winningen D 90 Ea38
Winnweiler D 88 Ca45
Winschoten NL 82 Ca33
Winsen (Aller) D 83 Db35
Winsen (Luhe) D 83 Dd33
Winsford GB 13 Ec22
Winsham GB 14 Eb30
Winsko PL 91 Gb40
Winslow GB 15 Fb26
Winston GB 13 Fa18
Winsum NL 82 Bd33
Winsum NL 82 Bc34
Winterberg D 89 Cd40
Winterbourne Abbas GB 14 Fb30
Winterlingen D 95 Cc50
Winterswijk NL 82 Bd37
Winterthur CH 95 Cc52
Winterton GB 13 Fb21
Winterton-on-Sea GB 16 Gc24
Wintrich D 88 Bd44
Wintzenheim F 94 Bd50
Winwick GB 16 Fc25
Winzer D 96 Ec49
Wipperdorf D 89 Dc39
Wipperfürth D 88 Ca40
Wirksworth GB 13 Fa22
Wisbech GB 16 Fd24
Wisła PL 92 Hd41
Wisławice PL 93 Jd43
Wismar D 84 Ea31
Wiśniew PL 93 Kc39
Wiśniewo PL 87 Jb34
Wiśniowa PL 92 Hd41
Wissembourg F 94 Ca47
Wissen D 88 Ca41
Wissenkerke NL 17 Hb27
Wiston GB 11 Ea14
Wiston GB 14 Db23
Wiświerz D 83 Fb19
Witanków PL 85 Gb34
Witaszyce PL 92 Ha38
Witham GB 16 Ga27
Witheridge GB 14 Ea29
Withern GB 13 Fc22
Withernsea GB 13 Fd20
Withington GB 15 Fa21
Withnell GB 13 Ec20
Witkowo PL 86 Ha36
Witmarsum NL 82 Bb33
Witney GB 15 Fa27
Witnica PL 85 Fc36
Witosław PL 85 Gc34
Witoszyce PL 91 Gb39
Witowo PL 86 Hb36
Witry-lès-Reims F 21 Hd35
Wittelshofen D 95 Db47
Witten D 88 Ca39
Wittenberge D 84 Ea34
Wittenburg D 84 Dd33
Wittenhagen D 84 Ed31
Wittenheim F 94 Bd51
Wittibreut D 96 Ec50
Wittichenau D 91 Fb40
Wittighausen D 89 Da46
Wittingen D 83 Dc35
Wittislingen D 95 Db49
Wittlich D 88 Bd44
Wittmund D 83 Cb32
Wittstock/Dosse D 84 Ec34
Witzenhausen D 89 Db40
Witzhave D 83 Dc32
Wiveliscombe GB 14 Ea29
Wiwern NL 82 Bb33
Wijhe NL 82 Bc37
Wloclawek PL 86 Hb36
Włodawa PL 93 Kc38
Włodzimierzów PL 92 Ja40
Włoszczowa PL 92 Ja41
Wloszow PL 93 Jc43
Wocławek PL 86 Ja31
Wockowa PL 92 Ja40
Wojnowo PL 85 Gc34
Woking GB 15 Fb28
Wokingham GB 15 Fb28
Wołbórz PL 92 Ja40
Wolbrom PL 93 Jb43
Wołczyn PL 92 Hd41
Woldegk D 84 Fa33
Wolfach D 95 Cd50
Wolfegg D 95 Da51
Wolfen D 90 Eb40
Wolfenbüttel D 83 Dd37
Wolferode D 90 Ea40
Wolfhagen D 89 Cd40
Wolframs-Eschenbach D 95 Dc47
Wolfratshausen D 96 Dd52
Wolfsberg A 97 Fc55
Wolfsburg D 84 Dd36
Wolf's Castle GB 14 Db26
Wolfsegg D 96 Ea47
Wolfurt A 95 Da53
Wolgast D 84 Fa31
Wolhusen CH 94 Ca54
Wolin PL 85 Fc32
Wolkenstein D 90 Ed42
Wollaston GB 15 Fb25
Wollbackon PL 87 Jc30
Wollerau CH 95 Cc53
Wöllstadt D 89 Cc43
Wolmirstedt D 84 Ea37
Wolnzach D 96 Ea49
Wolow PL 91 Gb40
Wolpertshausen D 95 Da47
Wolsingham GB 11 Fa17
Wolsztyn PL 91 Gb38
Wolvega NL 82 Bc34
Wolverhampton GB 13 Ec24
Wolverley GB 15 Ec25
Wombourn GB 15 Ec25
Wommels NL 82 Bc33
Womrath D 89 Ca45
Womaldsee GB 13 Fa23
Wonersh GB 15 Fb29
Wonfurt D 89 Dd44
Wootton GB 13 Fb23
Worb CH 94 Bd54
Worbis, Leinefelde- D 89 Dc40
Worcester GB 15 Ec26
Wördern A 97 Gb50
Wörgl A 96 Ea53
Wörishofen, Bad D 95 Db51
Workington GB 12 Ea17
Worksop GB 13 Fa22
Workum NL 82 Bb33
Wörlitz D 90 Ec38
Wormeldange L 21 Jd34
Wormerveer NL 82 Ba35
Wormhout F 17 Ha30
Worms D 89 Cb45
Wörnharts A 97 Fc49
Wornsund D 89 Cc43
Wörth D 89 Cc45
Wörth am Main D 89 Cd45
Wörth an der Donau D 96 Eb48
Worthen GB 13 Eb24
Worthing GB 16 Fc30
Worton GB 15 Ed28
Woskowice Górne PL 92 Ha41
Wotton-under-Edge GB 15 Ec28
Woudenberg D 82 Bb36
Woudsend NL 82 Bb34
Wozławki PL 87 Jd32
Woźnawieś PL 87 Ka32
Wragby GB 13 Fb22
Wrangle GB 16 Fd22
Wręczyca Wielka PL 92 Hd42
Wredenhagen D 84 Ec34
Wrefton GB 13 Fb19
Wrentham GB 16 Gc25
Wrestedt D 83 Dc35
Wrexham GB 12 Eb23
Wriedel D 83 Dc34
Wriezen D 85 Fb36
Wrist D 83 Db31
Wrocław PL 91 Gc41
Wronki PL 85 Gb36
Wronki Wielkie PL 87 Jd30
Wrotnow PL 87 Jd36
Wroughton GB 15 Ed28
Wroxham GB 16 Gb24
Wrzesień PL 86 Ha36
Wrzesina PL 86 Hd32
Wrzosowo PL 85 Ga31
Wuikow PL 92 Hd42
Wülfrath D 88 Bd39
Wulfen D 83 Dc33
Wulften D 89 Dc38
Wulkau D 84 Eb35
Wünnenberg D 89 Cd39
Wünschendorf D 90 Eb42
Wunsiedel D 90 Eb44
Wunstorf D 83 Da36
Wuppertal D 88 Ca40
Würenlos CH 95 Cc53
Wurmannsquick D 96 Ec50
Wurmsham D 96 Ec50
Würselen D 88 Bb41
Wurzach, Bad D 95 Da51
Würzburg D 89 Da45
Wurzen D 90 Ec40
Wüstenbrand D 90 Ec42
Wusterhausen D 84 Ec36
Wüstermarke D 84 Ed39
Wüsting D 83 Cc34
Wydrza PL 93 Jd42
Wyk auf Föhr D 83 Cd29
Wykrot PL 87 Jc33
Wymondham GB 16 Ga24
Wysall GB 13 Fa23
Wysoka PL 91 Gc40
Wysoka PL 92 Hd43
Wysokie PL 93 Kb42
Wysokie Mazowieckie PL 87 Ka34
Wyszanów PL 92 Hc40
Wyszków PL 87 Jc35
Wyszogród PL 86 Ja38
Wyszomierz Wielki PL 87 Jd34
Wyvis Lodge GB 8 Dd07

Xàbia E 45 Fd70
Xanten D 88 Bc38
Xánthi GR 126 Db77
Xàtiva E 39 Fd70
Xendive E 30 Ba64
Xeraco E 39 Fc69
Xinzo de Limia E 30 Bb58
Xixona E 45 Fb71
Xunqueira de Ambia E 30 Bb58

Yalding GB 16 Fd29
Yalıçiftlik TR 134 Ed90
Yalıkavak TR 134 Ec90
Yalıköy TR 127 Fb76
Yalova TR 127 Fd79
Yarcombe GB 14 Ea30
Yátova E 39 Fb68
Yattendon GB 15 Fa28
Yaxham GB 16 Ga24
Ybbs an der Donau A 97 Fc51
Ychoux F 26 Fa52
Ydby DK 76 Cd52
Yeadon GB 13 Fa20
Yealmpton GB 14 Dd32
Yeavon CZ 91 Fd48
Yecla E 45 Fa70
Yelland GB 14 Dd29
Yelvertoft GB 15 Fa25
Yelverton GB 14 Dd31
Yenice TR 126 Ec80
Yenice TR 128 Ac80
Yeniköy TR 130 Dd86
Yeovil GB 15 Ec30
Yeovilton GB 15 Ec29
Yerseke NL 17 Hc28
Yesa E 33 Fa58
Yeşilova TR 128 Ba89
Yeşilyurt TR 130 Dd86
Yetminster GB 15 Ec30
Yetts o'Muckhart GB 11 Ea12
Ygos-Saint-Saturnin F 26 Fb53
Yığılca TR 127 Gb79
Ylä-Luosta FIN 61 Lb28
Ylihärmä FIN 59 Ja30
Yli-Ii FIN 55 Kd22
Yli-Kärppä FIN 55 Ka21

Ylikiiminki FIN 55 Kb23
Ylikylä FIN 60 Jd29
Ylikylä FIN 60 Jc31
Yli-Livo FIN 55 Kc23
Yli-Muonio FIN 59 Hd32
Yli-Nampa FIN 55 Ka18
Yli-Olhava FIN 55 Ka22
Ylipää FIN 60 Jc31
Ylipää FIN 60 Jc30
Ylipää FIN 60 Jc30
Yli-Paakkola FIN 54 Jd20
Ylistaro FIN 59 Ja31
Ylitornio FIN 54 Jb20
Yli-Tynkä FIN 60 Jc27
Yli-Utos FIN 55 Kc24
Yli-Valli FIN 59 Ja32
Yli-Vuotto FIN 55 Kc23
Yläjärvi FIN 50 Jb15
Ylöjärvi FIN 68 Jd35
 Yläsmäki FIN 55 Ka18
Ymonville F 24 Gc39
Ynyslas GB 13 Ea24
York GB 13 Fb20
Youghal IRL 6 Ca26
Yougreave GB 13 Ed22
Yoxford GB 16 Gc25
Yrttivaara S 54 Hc18
Ysjö S 58 Ga29
Yssel nl. 88 Bb37
Yssingeaux F 28 Hd49
Ystad S 77 Fa57
Ystrad-Aeron GB 14 Dd25
Ystradfellte GB 14 Dd27
Ystradowen GB 14 Ea28
Ytre Kärvik N 49 Gc09
Ytre Leirpollen N 47 Jc06
Ytre Sandvik N 46 Jb06
Ytterån S 57 Ga31
Ytterbräsk S 59 Fd34
Ytterjeppo FIN 59 Ja30
Yttertogda S 66 Fc34
Yttervik S 57 Ga29
Yttre Lansjärv S 54 Hd19
Yvetot F 19 Ga34
Yvignac F 22 Ec38
Yvoire F 25 Ka44
Yvré-le-Pôlin F 23 Fd40
Yxskaftkälen S 58 Fd29
Yzeron F 28 Ja47

Zaamslag NL 17 Hc28
Zaanstad NL 82 Ba35
Zabalocce BY 136 Ec13
Zabartowo PL 86 Gd33
Zabeltitz D 90 Fa41
Zaberfeld D 95 Cc47
Żabia Wola PL 87 Jb37
Żabin PL 87 Jc34
Żabinka BY 136 Dd14
Żąbki PL 87 Jc36
Żąbkowice Śląskie PL 91 Gc43
Zablocie PL 93 Kb46
Żabludów PL 87 Kb34
Żabno PL 93 Jc44
Żabno PL 93 Jb39
Zabor PL 91 Ga39
Zaborowice PL 91 Gb39
Żabów PL 85 Fc34
Żabreh CZ 91 Gc45
Zabrodzie PL 87 Jc31
Żabrze PL 92 Hc45
Zabrzeź PL 92 Hd43
Zachenberg D 96 Ec48
Żachów PL 92 Ja44
Zadar HR 104 Ga58
Zádiel SK 99 Jd48
Zadonsk RUS 137 Fb12
Zadvorzany PL 87 Ka33
Zafarraya E 44 Da75
Zafferana Etnea I 115 Fd85
Zafra E 43 Bd69
Żagań PL 91 Fd39
Żaganie PL 93 Jd45
Zagnansk PL 93 Jc41
Zagorje ob Savi SLO 103 Fc57
Zagórz PL 93 Kb46
Zagreb HR 104 Ga58
Zahara de la Sierra E 43 Cc76
Zahinos E 42 Bc70
Zahna D 90 Ec38
Záhony H 99 Kb49
Záhorská Ves SK 97 Ga51
Zahrádky CZ 91 Fb43
Zaidín E 34 Fd61
Zaječ'ar SRB 121 Cb67
Zaječar PL 93 Ja42
Zajączki PL 87 Ka36
Zajezierze PL 93 Ja38
Zając H 104 Gd56
Zakamennoe SK 92 Hd48
Zákány H 104 Gc57
Zakopane PL 92 Hd46
Zakroczym PL 87 Jb36
Zakrzew PL 93 Kb41
Zakrzew PL 93 Ja39
Zakrzówek Osada PL 93 Ka41
Żakupy CZ 91 Fc42
Zalaegerszeg H 104 Gc55
Zalakoros H 104 Gd56
Zalalövő H 97 Gb54
Zalamea de la Serena E 43 Cb70
Zalamillas E 31 Cc58
Zalaszabar H 104 Gd55
Zalaszentbalázs H 104 Gc56
Żałe PL 85 Gc34
Zalec SLO 104 Fc57
Żalec SLO 104 Fc57
Zaleszany PL 93 Ka42
Zaleszczyki UA 136 Ea16
Zalewo PL 86 Hd31
Zalishchyky UA 136 Ea16
Zaltbommel NL 82 Bb37
Żałużna UA 136 Ea15
Zamárdi H 104 Ha55
Żamberk CZ 91 Gc44
Zambrów PL 87 Ka34
Żamość PL 93 Kc42
Zandhoven B 17 Hc29
Zandvoort NL 82 Ba35
Zanglegg H 104 Gd56
Zaniemyśl PL 92 Ha37
Żannowice PL 92 Hd43
Żaorejos E 37 Cc63
Zaova RUS 136 Eb10
Zapłow PL 92 Hb39
Zapolje PL 92 Hb39
Zaporižžja UA 137 Fa15
Zapponeta I 110 Gb73
Zaprudnja RUS 137 Ed10
Zaragoza E 33 Fa61
Zarajsk RUS 137 Fa11
Zaratán E 31 Cd60
Zarautz E 33 Fa55
Zarby Kościelne PL 87 Ka34
Zarenthin D 84 Ed33
Zarichne RUS 137 Ed49
Zieuwent NL 82 Bd37
Zarga de Alange E 37 Bd69
Żarki PL 92 Hd42
Żarnovec SK 98 Hc47
Zary PL 91 Fd39
Zárazka E 32 Eb59
Zarza E 37 Bd69
Zarza de Tajo E 38 Dc65
Zarza la Mayor E 37 Bd66
Zarzadilla de Totana E 45 Fa72
Zarza la Mayor E 37 Bd66
Zarza E 32 Eb59
Zas E 30 Ad54
Żaškiv UA 136 Ec15
Zasów PL 93 Jd44
Zástávka CZ 97 Gb47
Zászków PL 87 Ka35
Zatec CZ 90 Ed44
Zatom Nowy PL 85 Fd35
Zator PL 92 Hd45
Zatory PL 87 Jc35
Zavetnoe RUS 137 Ga15
Zavidovo PL 92 Hd42
Zavich PL 93 Jd41
Zawady PL 92 Ja42
Zawadzkie PL 92 Hb42
Zawdiów PL 91 Fd41
Zawidz Kościelny PL 86 Hd35
Zawiercie PL 92 Hd43
Zawierki PL 87 Ka33
Zawoja PL 92 Hd45
Zawyki PL 87 Kb34
Żazrivá SK 98 Hd47
Zbàraž UA 136 Ea15
Zbąszyń PL 85 Ga38
Zbečno CZ 90 Fa44
Zbirow UA 136 Ea15
Zbože PL 86 Gd33
Zbraslavice CZ 91 Fd45
Zbrudzewo PL 85 Gc37
Zbýšov CZ 97 Gb47
Żd'ár CZ 91 Fc43
Żdania PL 93 Kb43
Żdar nad Sázavou CZ 91 Ga46
Żdice PL 85 Gb33
Żdice CZ 90 Fa44
Żdírec nad Doubravou CZ 91 Ga46
Żdunska Wola PL 92 Hc39
Żdunska Wola PL 92 Hc39
Żduny PL 86 Hd37
Żdżary PL 93 Jb39
Żebrak CZ 90 Fa44
Żebrowice PL 92 Ha37
Żęczyn UA 136 Ea15
Zdolbuniv UA 136 Eb15
Zdounky CZ 98 Gd48
Żeblevice PL 92 Ha37
Żebrak CZ 90 Fa44
Żabrze PL 92 Hc45
Żechlin D 84 Ec34
Żedam SK 98 Hd47
Zeddam NL 82 Bc37
Zeebrugge B 17 Ha29
Zeewolde NL 82 Bb36
Żegestów PL 93 Jc46
Żegocin PL 92 Hd44
Żegrze Pomorskie PL 85 Gc32
Zehdenick D 84 Ed35
Zehren D 90 Ed41
Zeil D 89 Dd44
Zeist NL 82 Bb36
Zeitlarn D 96 Eb48
Zeitlofs D 89 Da43
Zeitz D 90 Eb41
Żelazowa Wola PL 86 Ja37
Żelazów PL 93 Jd38
Zelená Poljana RUS 137 Fb11
Zelenodol'sk UA 137 Ed17
Zelenogorsk RUS 136 Ea08
Zelenograd RUS 137 Ed10
Zelenokumsk RUS 137 Ga16
Żeleznaja Dvina RUS 137 Eb19
Żeleznica PL 87 Ka37
Żeleznodorožnyj RUS 136 Ec15
Żeleznogorsk RUS 137 Ed13
Żeleznovodsk RUS 137 Ga16
Żelezná PL 93 Kb38
Zell D 89 Da48
Zell D 89 Bd45
Zell (Mosel) D 89 Ca45
Zell am Harmersbach D 94 Bd49
Zella-Mehlis D 89 Dc42
Zell am Moos A 96 Ed52
Zell am See A 96 Ec53
Zell am Ziller A 96 Ea54
Zellingen D 89 Da45
Zell-Pfarre A 103 Fb58
Zeltweg A 97 Fc54
Żelwągi PL 87 Jd32
Żemberovce SK 98 Hc50
Żembrze PL 87 Ka37
Zembry PL 93 Kb38
Zemné SK 98 Ha51
Zemplénagárd H 99 Kb49
Zennor GB 14 Da32
Zenon BIH 105 Hb64
Żerawa BG 126 Db73
Zeralda PL 92 Ha37
Zerbst D 90 Eb38
Żerdevka RUS 137 Fc12
Żerkow PL 92 Ha37
Żernez CH 95 Dc55
Żerków PL 92 Ha37
Zernien D 84 Dd34
Zernograd RUS 137 Fd15
Zevenaar NL 82 Bc37
Zevenbergen NL 17 Hd28
Zeulenroda D 90 Eb42
Zeuthen D 84 Fa37
Zeven D 83 Da33
Zevio I 102 Dc60
Zeya RUS 137 Fa14
Żeżmariai LT 123 Kc37
Zgierz PL 92 Hd39
Zgłobień PL 93 Ka44
Zgorzelec PL 91 Fd41
Zhdani PL 93 Kb43
Żiano H 98 Ja52
Żidlochovice CZ 97 Gb48
Ziębice PL 91 Gc43

Zięby PL 86 Ja30
Zielenice PL 91 Gb43
Zielenice PL 91 Gb43
Zielin PL 85 Gc30
Zielitz D 84 Ea37
Zielona Góra PL 91 Fd38
Zielonka PL 87 Jc36
Zieluń PL 86 Hd34
Zierenberg D 89 Cd40
Zierikzee NL 17 Hc27
Ziersdorf A 97 Ga49
Zieuwent NL 82 Bd37
Żihle CZ 90 Ed44
Zilina SK 98 Hc47
Zillis CH 95 Cd55
Zilshausen D 88 Ca43
Ziltendorf D 85 Fc37
Zimna Brzeźnica D PL 91 Ga39
Zimnice Wielkie PL 92 Ha43
Zimovniki RUS 137 Ga15
Zinasco Vecchio I 101 Cb60
Zingst D 84 Ec32
Zinkovy CZ 91 Fa45
Zinnowitz D 84 Fa31
Zirchow D 85 Fb32
Zirndorf D 89 Dd46
Zirovnice CZ 91 Fd46
Zisterdorf A 97 Gc49
Zierádorf A 97 Gd47
Żihle CZ 90 Ed44
Zilina SK 98 Hc47
Zlatná na Ostrove SK 98 Hb51
Zlaté Hory CZ 92 Gd43
Zlaté Klasy SK 98 Gd51
Zlaté Moravce SK 98 Hb50
Zlatná Idka SK 99 Jc48
Zliv CZ 96 Fb48
Złobek PL 93 Kb46
Złobin BY 136 Eb13
Złoczeniec PL 85 Ga33
Złoczew PL 92 Hd40
Złotniki Kujawskie PL 86 Ha35
Złotoria PL 86 Hb34
Złotoryja PL 91 Ga41
Złotów PL 85 Gc33
Żmerynka UA 136 Ea15
Zmievka RUS 137 Fa11
Żmigród PL 91 Gb40
Zmijiv UA 137 Fa14
Znamenskoe RUS 137 Ed12
Znam'janka UA 137 Ed15
Znojmo CZ 97 Gb48
Zoagli I 101 Cc63
Zöblitz D 90 Ed42
Zocca RUS 136 Eb12
Zohor SK 97 Gc50
Zolling D 96 Ea50
Zollino I 111 Hc77
Zolociv UA 136 Ea15
Zolotonoša UA 137 Ed15
Zomba H 105 Hc56
Zonhoven B 88 Bb40
Zonza F 106 Cb71
Zórawina PL 91 Gc42
Zörbig D 90 Eb39
Zorita de la Loma E 31 Cd58
Zorita de los Canes E 38 Ea65
Zorneding D 96 Ea51
Zory PL 92 Hb44
Zossen D 84 Ed37
Zottegem B 17 Hb30
Zoutleeuw B 17 Hd30
Żovkva UA 136 Dd15
Zovti Vody UA 137 Ed15
Żovtneve UA 137 Ed14
Zruč nad Sázavou CZ 91 Fd45
Zsámbok P 99 Jb52
Zschadraß D 90 Ec41
Zschocken D 90 Ec42
Zschopau D 90 Ed42
Zschortau D 90 Eb40
Zubcov RUS 136 Ec10
Zubia E 44 Db75
Zubieta E 33 Ec56
Zürich CH 95 Cc53
Zuromin PL 86 Hc34
Zürs A 95 Da54
Zuromin PL 86 Hd35
Zusmarshausen D 95 Db50
Zuydcoote F 17 Ha29
Zvenigorod RUS 137 Fd09
Zwolen PL 93 Ka40
Zvonax WIT 95 Cb52
Zvornik BIH 105 Hb64
Zwaagwesteinde NL 82 Bc33
Zwanenburg NL 17 Hd25
Zwaring A 97 Fd54
Zwartsluis NL 82 Bc35
Zwedru GB 15 Fd24
Zweibrücken D 88 Ca46
Zweeloo NL 82 Bd34
Zwei-simmen CH 94 Bc55
Zweibrücken D 88 Ca46
Zweisimmen CH 94 Bc55
Zwei-simmen CH 94 Bc55
Zwettl an der Rodl A 97 Fb50
Zwickau D 90 Ec42
Żwiefalten D 95 Cd50
Zwierzyniec PL 93 Kc43
Zwierzyń PL 85 Fd35
Zwiesel D 96 Ed48
Zwiesel D 96 Ed48
Zwoleń PL 93 Ka40
Zwolle NL 82 Bc35
Zwönitz D 90 Ec42
Zwota CZ 90 Eb43
Żychlin PL 86 Hd37
Żydačiv UA 136 Ea15
Zygi CY 135 Ca97
Zyrzyn PL 93 Ka40
Zyrowa PL 92 Ha43
Żytkavičy BY 136 Eb13
Żytno PL 92 Hd41
Żytomyr UA 136 Eb15
Żywiec PL 92 Hd45